Reading this book in the midst of my “much-doin
exhaustion, it was both a salve to my soul and a prop
patient attention to the riches of deep church – equally at home in the Celtic lectionary as the Catholic catechism and Lausanne movement commitments – Charles models triple listening to the word of God, the world of scholarship, and one another in our stories of everyday faith. Charles beautifully weaves together missional activity and mystical spirituality in an integrated theological reflection which performed an open-heart surgery that lay bare my own pretension. Charles humbly deconstructed his nearly five decades of radical mission with the poor, stumbling toward a way of being that could sustain and energize the whole church's calling as whole-life disciples who are contemplative in our doing and on mission in our meditating, all in pursuit of union with Christ for the life of the world.

Dave Benson, PhD
Director of Culture and Discipleship,
The London Institute for Contemporary Christianity

For evangelicals whose mission activism has become increasingly wearisome, this book is a must-read. Ringma makes a strong case from Scripture and church history that evangelical mission is not sustainable without grounding it in a robust spirituality of ascetic practices, identification with a suffering world and Christian hope. But the work does far more than present cogent arguments for a missional spirituality, it engages the reader existentially as the author shares from his own personal struggles. For me, this is the book's most attractive feature.

Simon Chan, PhD
Editor, *Asia Journal of Theology*
Formerly Earnest Lau Professor of Systematic Theology,
Trinity Theological College, Singapore

Charles Ringma says that this is no work of academic theology, and in a sense that is true. Yet it draws upon a wide range of theological voices of many backgrounds and that gives the book an intellectual solidity. However, it is more invitational than instructional, more exploratory than expository. Above all, it is a work born of personal struggle through a now long life, which gives the book something of the feel of spiritual autobiography, weaving together many threads of a life that has been not only long but remarkably varied.

The inspiration of this book is radically biblical but it also stresses the need to listen to and learn from the voices of the poor, often heard on the peripheries. Listening to the voice of God in Scripture and the voice of God in the poor becomes the ground of the contemplative vision which the book builds. Words like contemplation, mysticism and spirituality can be slippery. But Charles Ringma makes it clear that they all look to the *experience* of the real God which the world craves. People, especially the young, are looking not for words or concepts about God but for the experience of God, and unless Christians have this experience in depth they will leave the world dying of hunger. The church can go out to the world only if the church goes down into God.

These are life-giving insights at a time when a Church under pressure may be tempted to close ranks in a form of self-defence but when the church in fact has to imagine and enact new forms of mission. In this book, Charles Ringma, humbly and wisely, points the true way ahead.

Mark Coleridge, PhD
Metropolitan Archbishop of Brisbane, Australia

The word I kept returning to as I read Ringma's book is depth. This book leads us deeper into the life of the Triune God, deeper into the rich reservoir of biblical and theological witnesses, deeper into a life of solidarity and action with our poor, oppressed or suffering neighbour, and deeper into a life of care for, wonder of and attention to the creation beneath and above us. In a digital and secular age where we struggle to pay any prolonged attention to God or our neighbour, this book offers the fullness of mature thought and practice from someone who has embodied this integral vision he espouses for a present-day missional Christianity. Please read this book. I have no doubt it will help you to live more deeply in your own human vocation as a bearer of the divine image in a tattered world.

Tim Dickau, DMin
Associate, Center for Missional Leadership,
St. Andrew's Hall, Canada
Director, CityGate Vancouver, Canada

This is a book to read slowly and deeply. It is the fruit of Charles Ringma's lifetime ministry as a missioner, teacher and writer. With a combination of rich theology and biblical reflection he invites the reader to follow Christ to that place where contemplation and action combine to make believers not only bearers of the message but an embodiment of it.

William Dyrness, PhD
Senior Professor of Theology and Culture,
Fuller Theological Seminary, California, USA

For centuries the church has struggled to find a way to bring the competitive sisters, the "Mary" of contemplative spirituality and the "Martha" of active serving, into a warm embrace. In this book Charles Ringma, writing as both scholar and mentor, shows us how. The fruit of his lifetime of personally integrating intense missional activity with an ever-deepening spirituality, this is Ringma's magnum opus. It is a work that will be read, marked, discussed and taught for a generation to come.

Maxine Hancock, PhD
Professor Emerita, Interdisciplinary Studies & Spiritual Theology,
Regent College, Canada

This book is an outstanding and welcome contribution to the growing area of the study of missional spirituality. It critiques our misplaced Western activism and offers in its place missional life that flows from the life of God made available to us through participation in Christ by the Spirit, in deep ecclesial community where we are working with God, not for God.

Ross Hastings, PhD
Sangwoo Youtong Chee Professor of Theology,
Regent College, Canada

Theology tends to work in the separate silos of its academic disciplines but Franciscan Tertiary and theologian Charles Ringma argues here for the integration of mission and spirituality. This important and original work draws on a wide range of sources, biblical and historical (including Luther, Francis of Assisi, the Anabaptists and Liberation Theology), but above all the author reflects on his own life engaged in a range of ministry in cross-cultural missional contexts. Spirituality and radical activism are integrally related and this book encourages us all to enter more deeply into that point of connection, that both prayer and active ministry may more profoundly nourish each other.

Brother Christopher John, SSF
Minister General, First Order Brothers of the Society of St Francis

In the Midst of Much-Doing: Cultivating a Missional Spirituality provides rich and valuable resources for an integrative view of mission and spirituality. Drawing from various Christian themes and traditions, the book integrates theology, spirituality and mission in a thought-provoking manner. It challenges us to cultivate a missional spirituality that is wholistic and life-transforming.

Jean Lee
Abundant Grace Professor of Theological Studies,
China Graduate School of Theology

In the midst of a "much-doing" period, this book came into my hands. The questions proposed captured my attention. They not only named my concerns but invited me to a deeper reflection on the theme of mission and spirituality. This book is clearly the result of a long journey in Christian discipleship that seeks to integrate mind, heart and hands, drawing our attention to the neglected realities that hinder an integrated Christian life. It is not material to be read in one sitting; you will benefit most if you allow the text to lead you into times of prayer, contemplation and reflection. The breadth and depth of reflection in this book open new windows of understanding and invites us to new paths of transformation. This excellent work is an essential reference for all who seek a spiritual life that guides, sustains and strengthens Christian witness and service.

Ziel J.O. Machado
Honorary President, International Fellowship of Evangelical Students
Vice-Rector and Professor of Pastoral Theology,
Seminário Teológico Servo de Cristo, Brazil

This book is a comprehensive integration of the lifelong learnings of a social activist turned contemplative, a thoughtful synthesis of what the intellectual heirs of Greek dualism had rent asunder – wedding spirituality to service, prayer to praxis, mission to mysticism. Charles Ringma, drawing from church history and a plurality of spiritual traditions, as well as from his own personal journey across cultures, has woven these strands together into a narrative that compels attention describing what faith can look like when it is lived in its fullness and not broken up into pieces and stored into neat little boxes. Charles Ringma faced what the poet W. H. Auden has called "human unsuccess." It is a thing for rejoicing that someone who belongs to cultures with a "can-do" mentality emerges out of disillusionment with this gift, the sense that we are only servants waiting and watching for the inbreaking of the hand of God in our history.

Melba Padilla Maggay, PhD
President,
Institute for Studies in Asian Church and Culture

Worthy reading for anyone who is seriously interested in the integration of church, prayer, and mission; and who is deeply concerned to explore what a missional spirituality could look like. This is the author's careful reflection on biblical and historical themes on the church, prayer and mission. The book will contribute towards the formation of practical integration of church, prayer and mission.

Moses Yamo Masala
Anglican Bishop of Rorya, Tanzania

This magnificent book invites us to an integrated life of contemplative missional servanthood. Dr. Ringma offers us the fruits of a lifetime of scholarship, cross-cultural missionary experience and reflective wisdom that is truly breathtaking. He draws on the riches of our diverse Christian traditions and the experience of the church's missionary endeavours through the ages. For missionally engaged Christians living in a social climate that is decidedly antagonistic to Christian mission that proclaims Christ as Saviour and Lord, Dr. Ringma's invitation to and wisdom for a deeply centring and sustaining missional spirituality is just what is needed. From the perspective of the Majority World church too, we need exactly the sort of mission partners formed by the missional spirituality that this book seeks to cultivate.

Prabo Mihindukulasuriya, PhD
Adjunct Faculty, Colombo Theological Seminary, Sri Lanka
Postdoctoral Fellow in the History of Christianity, Regent College, Vancouver

Ringma's book is a tour de force, the fruit of much intellectual labour in the Spirit. It is a veritable theological feast, which welcomes to the table readers from across the Christian spectrum. Ringma brings together personal, biblical, theological, spiritual, missional and historical insights to craft a fully integrated, missional Christian spirituality. Dissolving dichotomies that have plagued the church for centuries, Ringma weaves together a colourful tapestry that integrates personal faith and corporate Christian identity, individual sin and structural evil, the work of evangelism and social transformation, contemplation and action, mysticism and the prophetic. This book is a sure guide that will help the church to become a more faithful and vibrant witness in the world.

Charles E. Moore

Pastor, Teacher, Networker, the Bruderhof Community
Contributing Editor, Plough Publishing

In the journey through *In the Midst of Much-Doing* the reader will walk with its author in a mediated experience to learn about "missional Christian spirituality." Charles Ringma presents in a wise, learned, compelling and yet approachable way the vast range of the rich traditions within Christian spirituality. The reader will find themselves with a fresh and expanded vision of God, the Church and the possibilities of realistically and practically nurturing a transforming faith in Jesus in the midst of the serious contemporary challenges for the community of believers. As a Latin American believer, I am convinced that the sections on the spirituality of liberation theology – for many an ignored aspect of this theology and its forefathers – will contribute to sustain, in a creative and hopeful way, the struggle for justice and peace in our world. I strongly recommend its reading and studying this book.

Josué Olmedo

IFES Logos & Cosmos Initiative in Latin America

Charles Ringma brings his astute theological mind, big heart for the lost, vast missional experience and quest for a sustainable missional spirituality together in this brilliant book. It knits together biblical, theological, spiritual, missional, philosophical and sociological resources economically, even aesthetically, in ways that energize and also refresh. It integrates the whole person and missional process – the head (theological formation), heart (spiritual restoration) and hand (missional action). Ringma's personal quest for a more sustainable, grace-based Spirit and hope-inspired imagination has come to fruition in this magnum opus. He writes with a hard-earned sense of realism about individual sin and structural evil, balanced passion for evangelism and social transformation, contemplation and action, mysticism and prophesy. It is a tour de force.

In an increasingly precarious global situation Ringma humbly but hopefully offers a way forward for formation of Christ-like "lovers in a dangerous time."

Gordon Preece, PhD
Executive Director,
Ethos Centre for Christianity and Society, Australia

In this book, Charles Ringma has provided a valuable gift for students, teachers and practitioners of Christian mission – the fruit of a lifetime of service and reflection. By gathering together a rich collection of biblical and theological conversation partners, Ringma encourages a healthy breadth to missional thinking, introducing readers to voices from a range of historical, geographical and theological contexts. In this book, Ringma also nurtures a healthy depth in missional practice, by drawing readers deeper into the heart of the mission of God and identifying spiritual resources to sustain the life of Christian discipleship.

Rev. Jonathan Ryan, PhD
Presbyterian Minister,
Presbyterian Church of Aotearoa New Zealand

This momentous volume sums up a lifetime of Charles Ringma's personal mission engagement, his teaching interculturally, and his extensive research theologically, historically, spiritually, philosophically and practically. Ringma notes that "a missional spirituality is a way of life in Christ through the Spirit that animates our love and service to others." (p26) But he also shows how our missional engagement animates our relationship with God and the deepening of our faith. It is a non-dualistic process and above all biblical. In this self-revelatory book Ringma speaks of his own discoveries, struggles and hopes. It is an invaluable resource for all who wonder how and why the link should be made. The definitive work on the subject! Even the extensive footnotes are worth the price of the book.

R. Paul Stevens, PhD
Professor Emeritus, Marketplace Theology and Leadership, Regent College, Canada
Chairman, Institute for Marketplace Transformation

In the Midst of Much-Doing

In the Midst of Much-Doing

Cultivating a Missional Spirituality

Charles R. Ringma

Published 2023 by Langham Global Library
An imprint of Langham Publishing
www.langhampublishing.org

Langham Publishing and its imprints are a ministry of Langham Partnership

Langham Partnership
PO Box 296, Carlisle, Cumbria, CA3 9WZ, UK
www.langham.org

ISBNs:
978-1-83973-243-0 Print
978-1-83973-844-9 ePub
978-1-83973-846-3 PDF

British Library Cataloguing-in-Publication Data
A catalogue record for this book is available from the British Library

ISBN: 978-1-83973-243-0

Cover & Book Design: projectluz.com

He is the great destroyer of our constructions,
and we are struck dumb by his work.

–Rainer Maria Rilke[1]

1. Snow, *The Poetry of Rilke*, 30 (my translation).

For

Mark and Cathy Delaney

and their sons,

Tom and Oscar.

In their decades of service to the poor in India, they have lived what others only momentarily think about.

Contents

Section IV: Particular Themes

Foreword

I am sometimes asked who I count as the greatest influence on my own spiritual life, and I usually answer with three people. None of them, I think, would have used the word "spirituality" much – it was not so much a concept or doctrine in their era, as a simple lived reality to which that word could now be applied.

The first would be my own father, Joe Wright (1901–1986). He was a man of passionate and active Christian faith, which was tested through early years in the Irish police force soon after the First World War, and then twenty years as a pioneer missionary in the Amazon rain forest among the indigenous tribes peoples – single at first and then later with my mother. He was a man of constant and wide-ranging prayer. In the Amazon jungle it was a matter of spiritual warfare that he described as "wrestling with God." For him, spirituality was simply living close to God and obeying the perceived will of God, at any cost. I remember, when I was a theological student at undergraduate and postgraduate levels, it kept me humble when I reflected, "Perhaps I know more *theology* now than my Dad, but I would never claim to *know God* better than Dad." On the day I heard the news of his death, my first thought was, "Who's going to pray for me now?" I suppose we never know what we owe to the example and prayers of godly parents. A spirituality to emulate, in my own case.

The second would be the minister of the Presbyterian church I grew up in through my teenage years in Belfast – the Rev. J. Glyn Owen (1919–2017). For ten years, every Sunday morning and evening, he preached through different books of the Bible in systematic exposition that admirably combined faithful, clear, text-centred teaching that fed the mind, with Welsh eloquence and passion that warmed the heart. I filled notebooks with notes of his sermons and simply drank at a weekly fountain of biblical teaching that both nurtured in me a deep love of the Bible and also gave me a foundational model of what effective biblical preaching ought to be like. I suppose those became two elements of spirituality for what the rest of my life has majored on.

The third would be the Rev. Dr. John R.W. Stott (1921–2011), whom I heard and read as a student in the 1960s, met in person in 1978 at the start of a friendship that eventuated in him inviting me in 2001 to take over the leadership of ministries he had founded, now combined in the Langham

Partnership. My teenage years under Glyn Owen gave me immediate relish for John Stott's exceptional clarity and power of biblical exposition, but in terms of his spirituality (again, not a term I recall him using much), it was the incredible self-discipline of his daily habit of Bible study and prayer that stands out. He rose early (usually around 5.00am until he allowed himself an extra hour of sleep in later years) for this practice. I shared a room with him for a few weeks of ministry in Latin America once and saw the bulging notebook he used, stuffed with names and letters from those he was praying for and their families. For decades John Stott was hugely active and stretched to the limit in his global ministry and mission, and it must have been this deep well of personal devotion that sustained him. That and his very intentional rootedness and accountability within the fellowship of his beloved All Souls Church, Langham Place, London.

John Stott's habitual devotional life began every day with this morning prayer to the Holy Trinity.

> Heavenly Father, I pray that this day I may live in your presence and please you more and more. Lord Jesus, I pray that this day I may take up my cross and follow you. Holy Spirit, I pray that this day you will fill me with yourself and cause your fruit to ripen in my life – Love, Joy, Peace, Patience, Kindness, Goodness, Faithfulness, Gentleness, and Self-control.

All one might say about "John Stott's spirituality" is that God answered that prayer, and it was in many ways the secret of the phenomenal "success" (if that's the right word) of his lifetime's ministry and its legacy. For it is the ripening of the fruit of the Spirit that enables Christ to be formed in us, so that our lives not only become more and more like Christ, but are shaped and equipped to serve like Christ in Christ's humility and for Christ's glory. And John Stott, many people would say, was the most Christlike person they ever knew – in all those respects.

Charles Ringma's book brings spirituality and mission together. I think my three mentors above did so too, though mostly in unselfconscious ways. But he is right to lament that much mission thinking, writing, strategizing, training and practice tends to overlook some of the basics of Christian discipleship and their deep biblical roots, so his book is a welcome corrective to that lack. Even the Lausanne Movement, for all its own roots in the missional theology of John Stott and the godly zeal of Billy Graham, can bear some criticism for insufficient attention to this vital dimension of sustainable mission.

As the main writer and editor of *The Cape Town Commitment* (from the Third Lausanne Congress in 2010), I readily raise my hand to acknowledge that it contains no specific section on "spirituality" as such in relation to mission. In at least two places, however, it does focus on the kind of spiritual qualities that, on the one hand, ought to be true of those engaged in mission and especially those in mission leadership, and on the other hand, can flow only from the work of the Holy Spirit himself as the source of all authentically Christian spirituality. Two quotations in conclusion respectively sharpen those points.

Christ-centred Leaders

> The rapid growth of the Church in so many places remains shallow and vulnerable, partly because of the lack of discipled leaders, and partly because so many use their positions for worldly power, arrogant status or personal enrichment. As a result, God's people suffer, Christ is dishonoured, and gospel mission is undermined. . . .
>
> Some leadership training programmes focus on packaged knowledge, techniques and skills to the neglect of godly character. By contrast, authentic Christian leaders must be like Christ in having a servant heart, humility, integrity, purity, lack of greed, prayerfulness, dependence on God's Spirit, and a deep love for people. Furthermore, some leadership training programmes lack specific training in the one key skill that Paul includes in his list of qualifications – ability to teach God's Word to God's people. Yet Bible teaching is the paramount means of disciple-making and the most serious deficiency in contemporary Church leaders.
>
> a) We long to see greatly intensified efforts in disciple-making, through the long-term work of teaching and nurturing new believers, so that those whom God calls and gives to the Church as leaders are qualified according to biblical criteria of maturity and servanthood.
>
> b) We renew our commitment to pray for our leaders. We long that God would multiply, protect and encourage leaders who are biblically faithful and obedient. We pray that God would rebuke, remove, or bring to repentance leaders who dishonour his name and discredit the gospel. And we pray that God would

raise up a new generation of discipled servant-leaders whose passion is above all else to know Christ and be like him.

c) Those of us who are in Christian leadership need to recognize our vulnerability and accept the gift of accountability within the body of Christ. We commend the practice of submitting to an accountability group.

d) We strongly encourage seminaries, and all those who deliver leadership training programmes, to focus more on spiritual and character formation, not only on imparting knowledge or grading performance, and we heartily rejoice in those that already do so.[1]

We Love God the Holy Spirit

We love the Holy Spirit within the unity of the Trinity, along with God the Father and God the Son. He is the missionary Spirit sent by the missionary Father and the missionary Son, breathing life and power into God's missionary Church. We love and pray for the presence of the Holy Spirit because without the witness of the Spirit to Christ, our own witness is futile. Without the convicting work of the Spirit, our preaching is in vain. Without the gifts, guidance and power of the Spirit, our mission is mere human effort. And without the fruit of the Spirit, our unattractive lives cannot reflect the beauty of the gospel.

a) In the Old Testament we see the Spirit of God active in creation, in works of liberation and justice, and in filling and empowering people for every kind of service. Spirit-filled prophets looked forward to the coming King and Servant, whose Person and work would be endowed with God's Spirit. Prophets also looked to the coming age that would be marked by the outpouring of God's Spirit, bringing new life, fresh

1. *The Cape Town Commitment* II.D.3

obedience, and prophetic gifting to all the people of God, young and old, men and women.[2]

b) At Pentecost God poured out his Holy Spirit as promised by the prophets and by Jesus. The sanctifying Spirit produces his fruit in the lives of believers, and the first fruit is always love. The Spirit fills the Church with his gifts, which we "eagerly desire" as the indispensable equipment for Christian service. The Spirit gives us power for mission and for the great variety of works of service. The Spirit enables us to proclaim and demonstrate the gospel, to discern the truth, to pray effectively and to prevail over the forces of darkness. The Spirit inspires and accompanies our worship. The Spirit strengthens and comforts disciples who are persecuted or on trial for their witness to Christ.[3]

c) Our engagement in mission, then, is pointless and fruitless without the presence, guidance and power of the Holy Spirit. This is true of mission in all its dimensions: evangelism, bearing witness to the truth, discipling, peace-making, social engagement, ethical transformation, caring for creation, overcoming evil powers, casting out demonic spirits, healing the sick, suffering and enduring under persecution. All we do in the name of Christ must be led and empowered by the Holy Spirit. The New Testament makes this clear in the life of the early Church and the teaching of the apostles. It is being demonstrated today in the fruitfulness and growth of Churches where Jesus's followers act confidently in the power of the Holy Spirit, with dependence and expectation. There is no true or whole gospel, and no authentic biblical mission, without the Person, work and power of the Holy Spirit. We pray for a greater awakening to this biblical truth,

2. Genesis 1:1–2; Psalm 104:27–30; Job 33:4; Exodus 35:30–36:1; Judges 3:10; 6:34; 13:25; Numbers 11:16–17, 29; Isaiah 63:11–14; 2 Peter 1:20–21; Micah 3:8; Nehemiah 9:20, 30; Zechariah 7:7–12; Isaiah 11:1–5; 42:1–7; 61:1–3; 32:15–18; Ezekiel 36:25–27; 37:1–14; Joel 2:28–32.

3. Acts 2; Galatians 5:22–23; 1 Peter 1:2; Ephesians 4:3–6, 11–12; Romans 12:3–8; 1 Corinthians 12:4–11; 14:1; John 20:21–22; 14:16–17, 25–26; 16:12–15; Romans 8:26–27; Ephesians 6:10–18; John 4:23–24; 1 Corinthians 12:3; 14:13–17; Matthew 10:17–20; Luke 21:15.

> and for its experience to be reality in all parts of the worldwide body of Christ.[4]

May it be so. Amen.
Chris Wright

4. *The Cape Town Commitment* I.5. Bible references in the footnotes above are part of the original text.

Preface

My interest in exploring "missional spirituality" – a spirituality that can guide, sustain, and empower our Christian witness and service in the world – was not shaped by many years in academia, though that context did give me the liberty to read and think more about this topic and to teach various courses that sought to address the pressing need for such a spirituality.

Rather, the genesis for this book was formed in the midst of my own unsustainable evangelical activism, which was further complicated by my somewhat compulsive personality.[1] My search for a more sustainable spirituality was also influenced by some unhealthy theological concepts that I inherited from my Reformed tradition – particularly its election anxiety[2] and paramount focus on personal piety, with little attention to nurturing liturgical and communal spiritual practices. My focus on personal activism was also unwittingly reinforced by naïve Western notions about our capacity to change the world because we presume that God is "on our side." When we take on a calling that is well beyond our capabilities and resources,[3] we may boldly set out to try to make things better in our society while treating God as an onlooker, a boss we are seeking to please, or someone who is there simply to cheer us on.[4]

I am drawing on my own story in the beginning of this book to highlight the fact that much of what we seek to *do* as Western Christians is marked by an activism that is not always gospel-inspired and Spirit-sustained.[5] We foolishly think that the coming of the kingdom of God somehow depends on us!

---

1. Henri Nouwen mentions how compulsion can readily lead to "more work" and refers to Thomas Merton's insight that such compulsion is driven by "the false self" (Nouwen, *The Way of the Heart*, 23, 22). Nouwen's biographer, Jurjen Beumer, comments that Nouwen was "an unbelievably restless man," who gradually realized that as he restlessly sought after God, and "God was even more intensely seeking for him" (Beumer, *Henri Nouwen*, 167).

2. Weber, *The Protestant Ethic.*

3. The desert father, Abba Silvanus, makes the statement: "Woe to the person whose reputation is greater than his work" (quoted in *Celtic Daily Prayer*, 426).

4. Karl Barth rightly points out the "co-responsibility of Christians and the church in shaping all areas of life," but we engage the world under "Christ's royal reign," not as independent and self-sustained witnesses. Quoted in Jehle, *Ever Against the Stream*, 103.

5. In *Popular Evangelicalism in American Culture*, Richard Kyle notes how "activism" (10) is a key characteristic of the evangelical movement, which has caused members to grow "dramatically" (3), but in this push, "they have sanctified large segments of American culture,

In these opening reflections, a number of things stand out. First, there is always more to do, and humanity's needs are endless – particularly when we are working with those who are marginalized and wounded.[6] Thus, sooner or later, we have to come to terms with our limitations and the ongoing brokenness of our lives and our world.

Second, mere activism depletes us. If our action in the world is going to be sustained, it needs to emerge from deeper motivations and be nourished by inner well-springs of life.[7] But such inner resources can be difficult to discover and maintain,[8] because we so easily get distracted in the midst of our much-doing.

Third, it is so easy to abandon prayer,[9] which may be our greatest temptation.[10] The overwhelming pull in our contemporary world is always towards externalization and achievement rather than towards reflection and contemplation. To complicate matters even further, we are experiencing an increasing crisis of faith and prayer in our age. At this point in history, we may not know what to believe about God's engagement with our prayers and may sometimes feel that God has abandoned us and left us to our own devices.[11]

Fourth, it is a huge challenge to live and serve well within the mystery of God's sovereignty, on the one hand, and our own human responsibility and vulnerability, on the other hand. We may struggle with God's seeming lack of action and power in situations of need.[12] Or we may be frustrated by the seemingly slack service within the church to the one whom we call "Lord."

Finally, spiritual, physical, or emotional burnout is a terrible condition, and recovery is very difficult. I speak from experience, having suffered a major physical breakdown in my early thirties while in the midst of working with troubled young people and those with addictions. It took me six months to

---

especially its consumerism and middle-class values," and have blatantly embraced "the cult of personality" (3).

6. Ringma and Dickau, *The Art of Healing Prayer.*

7. Graeme Garrett makes the observation that the Australian NT scholar and activist, Athol Gill, was "tough, thoughtful, compassionate, socially active, yet steeped in worship and prayer" (Neville, *Prophecy and Passion*, 4). This is a rare combination of core qualities, indeed!

8. Green, *Wells Run Dry.*

9. Segundo Galilea speaks of the challenge to "balance communal and private prayer without abandoning either of the two" (*The Way of Living Faith*, 107).

10. Hubert Van Zeller makes the point that "outward works of any kind" – "whether self-chosen or under the cover of obedience" – may "*if allowed to*" actually "lower the degree of union with God in prayer" (*Spirituality Recharted*, 40, author's emphasis).

11. Ellul, *Hope in Time of Abandonment.*

12. Fretheim, *Creation Untamed.*

recover from that breakdown, and ever since, I have grappled with these issues and sought a more sustaining and empowering missional spirituality.[13] This challenge remains with me now that I am in my early eighties. Thus, this is a book of a lifetime, tracing my ongoing challenge to hold together the need for community, spirituality, graduate teaching and formation, and theological and missional reflection in contexts of urban ministry in Australia and Canada, along with cross-cultural missional contexts in the Philippines and Myanmar.

This book, therefore, is much more the product of struggle than of calm reflection in a library. As a consequence, it has a certain "edge." The reflections and practices that are forged in the midst of our lives are not always calm and well-reasoned, but may well be messy and complicated. I trust that this book will carry a certain passion, even if that is not always regarded as academically "cool."[14]

Moreover, this book engages some underlying themes that run a bit counter to most missiology books, which emphasize knowability (what God *said*) and do-ability (what we should *do* to bring good news into the world). While what we *know* and *do* are important, these themes do not convey the whole story of our lives. We also have to consider our passions and motivations,[15] the mystery of God, the practices of silence and sabbath, the reality of waiting, and the seemingly unproductive – yet fruitful – nature of emptiness.[16]

Further, the thrust of this book is invitational rather than directional. My purpose is not to outline a particular "way" to approach mission, but to invite readers to ponder these themes and perhaps learn something outside of their tradition. While we need to be deeply rooted in our own ecclesial tradition so that we can place our feet somewhere, we also need to be open to learn from those who can see beyond the limits of our horizons. This requires a commitment to a more dialogical and dialectic approach.[17] By its very nature,

13. Most of my published devotionals on Dietrich Bonhoeffer, Henri Nouwen, Jacques Ellul, Thomas Merton, Mother Teresa, and Martin Luther King Jr. have come from the concern that activists need to become more prayerful – and those who pray need to become more deeply involved in the needs and issues of our time.

14. I believe that theology should be written in the mode of James Cone's *God of the Oppressed* rather than the clinical language of Louis Berkhof's *Systematic Theology*. See, in particular, the work of Killen and de Beer, *The Art of Theological Reflection*.

15. See chapter 8 ("Grand Design and Fragile Engagement"), which explores the themes of orthodoxy, orthopraxis, and orthopathy.

16. In a poem about the Elisabeth story in the Gospels, the Dutch poet Nel Benschop writes: "*ook in haar droogde de levensbron*" ("in her barrenness, the wellspring of life," *Wit Als Sneeuw*, 10).

17. Gadamer, *Truth and Method*.

mission needs an ecumenical spirit and spirituality, since the broader Christian tradition is far richer than our own church or denomination.

Additionally, while I have worked in formal missionary settings both locally and overseas, much of my missional engagement has also been informal. We are all God's missional people, and wherever we find ourselves, we are called to carry the seeds of God's kingdom, pray for and serve others, and bear witness to God's love for the world. Thus I make no fundamental distinction between formal and informal mission in my reflections. The unhealthy dualism that is prevalent within the contemporary church robs us of recognizing the informal good in which so many people are quietly engaged in their neighbourhoods, workplaces, recreational spaces, and other areas of social gathering. It is a great pity when these informal ministries remain unacknowledged by the church's leadership, for then they cannot be supported or encouraged by the broader faith-community. What the scattered community of faith does informally from Monday through Saturday is just as important as the formal service of the church to the world![18] Thus, I am writing this book for all Christians – public servants, those caring for family, farmers, community workers, among others, as well as pastors and missionaries.

There is also a rich and complex dynamic between these expansive themes, for *spirituality forms mission*, and *mission forms spirituality*. Our spirituality nurtures and animates our sense of mission, while our mission authenticates our spirituality by regarding others rather than seeking only to enhance ourselves. In fact, mission and spirituality are integral and form the unity we see in the person and work of Christ, who is both an activist and a contemplative.[19] Van Zeller articulates this as follows: the *active* apostle "speaks to people about God," and the *contemplative* apostle "speaks to God about people."[20] But establishing such a division of labour within the faith-community can be unhelpful, for *every* Christian is to be a person of both prayer and service.[21]

Lastly, I am writing this book in a particular way, using a *functional hermeneutical spiral* – where I deal with a theme or topic in a provisional way and then expand on it later in a more developed way. For example, in

18. Stevens, *The Other Six Days*.

19. See the discussion in chapter 4 ("Contemplation in a World of Action").

20. Van Zeller, *Spirituality Recharted*, 41.

21. Karl Barth constantly emphasizes this double movement. In relation to the church's witness to the state, Barth notes that the church is to be committed to "prayer for the bearers of authority in the state." But, at the same time, Barth stresses the "co-responsibility of Christians and the church in shaping all areas of life, including . . . the state" (quoted in Jehle, *Ever Against the Stream*, 108, 103).

chapter 2, I reference the writings of the Latin American practitioner, Segundo Galilea. Then later, in chapter 15, I provide a fuller account of Latin American missional spirituality and develop Galilea's themes more fully within this larger framework. Similarly, I reference the Anabaptist perspective of David Augsburger in chapter 2 and then expand on Anabaptist missional spirituality in chapter 13. And in chapter 3, I introduce some theological themes of a missional spirituality and then develop those themes more fully in chapters 6 and chapter 7. Moreover, after introducing the themes of contemplation and integral mission early in the book, I later revisit and expand on them.[22]

I am taking this approach in order to keep the bigger narrative of the book moving ahead rather than writing exhaustively about a particular topic when I first introduce it. Then I loop back from time to time to offer further elaboration. Moreover, all the themes are inter-related, and so I am trying to find an integrated and developmental way of arranging the book, which has been shaped by my personal life experience, my missional engagement, as well as biblical and theological reflection. Finally, I have not crafted the book to be read in one go, from beginning to end, as I am assuming that certain themes may interest some people, and others may not. Hence each chapter is somewhat self-contained.

22. The topical index will help the reader in seeing where particular topics are reiterated or enhanced.

Acknowledgements

Some heartfelt thanks are in order. First, my wife, Rita, and I are grateful for the privilege of working with many people in diverse contexts: amongst Indigenous communities in Western Australia; with Teen Challenge in Brisbane, Australia; among Servants to Asia's Urban Poor in Manila, Philippines; with our friends at Grandview Calvary Baptist Church in East Vancouver, Canada. Second, we are grateful for everyone who has supported us, prayed for us, and extended places of hospitality to us over the years.[1]

In each of these unique settings, we have been blessed by our fellow workers, and we continue to be thankful for their faithful companionship. We have also been deeply blessed by those whom we were seeking to serve, and over the years, we have become increasingly aware of the grace of "mission in reverse."[2] Mission is not only about giving, but also receiving – and blessed are those who receive from the very people whom they are seeking to serve!

I have also lived in intentional Christian community for much of my life, and all of my missional activity has been within a communitarian frame. This has involved working in team settings and with a communal intentionality, which has meant that our basic impulse has not been to save isolated souls, but to bring people into fuller restoration with God, self, and others.

While writing is a highly individual pursuit, much of my writing has also occurred in communal settings, including writers' retreats, where we have followed a monastic rhythm. Thus, I am grateful to the members in these retreats: Irene Alexander, Christopher Brown, Terry Gatfield, Athena Gorospe, Jill Manton, Tim McCowan, Ross McKenzie, Paul Mercer, and Sarah Nicholl.[3] We irreverently call this group the "holy" scribblers,[4] and their friendship and feedback have been invaluable.

1. For some of the places of hospitality see Ringma, *Hear the Ancient Wisdom*, x.

2. Anthony Gittens notes that "mission in reverse" is a move towards mutuality and calls for a readiness on the part of the missioner "to acknowledge the presence of God" in others, long before he or she extends ministry to them (*Bread for the Journey*, 12).

3. Two others were able to join us for a limited time: Neville Carr and John Steward.

4. https://holyscribblers.blogspot.com.

My sincere thanks to Pieter Kwant, my literary agent, who always seems to find a publisher for me, and to Irene Alexander and Karen Hollenbeck-Wuest, whose skilful editorial work has made this a much more readable book.

And finally, my grateful thanks to Mark Arnold from Langham Publishing and to Chris Wright for writing the foreword for this book.

Charles Ringma

Brisbane, Australia, 2023

Introduction

For some people, the topics of mission and spirituality may not seem to belong together.[1] From this perspective, spirituality is concerned with our inner life and is therefore purely personal, whereas mission is concerned with our corporate task of seeking to witness to and bless others. In our setting of late modernity, spirituality is "cool,"[2] whereas mission is more problematical[3] in light of colonial religious imposition or psychological manipulation throughout the history of the church.[4]

Westerners often think in either/or categories,[5] playing one thing against another, and so swing the pendulum too far in one direction. Sometimes we focus on personal renewal, while at other times we emphasize ecclesiastical change. Sometimes we are concerned with piety, and others with the quest for justice. Because we seem intent on separating things into neat little boxes, the task of integration remains problematical.[6] But if our spirituality remains in one box, it will become an irrelevant mysticism. And if Christian mission or service remains in another isolated box, it will become a beast of burden.

The diversity of perspectives within the Christian church poses another challenge. The theologian H. Richard Niebuhr has served us well by characterizing whole denominations and major church movements by the way they conceive their relationship to the world and the nature of their missional task, though some of his typologies are overdrawn.[7] In *Christ and Culture*, he

1. Jürgen Moltmann, however, makes the point that "all Christian action is embedded in a particular spirituality" (*Ethics of Hope*, 6).

2. Tacey, *The Spirituality Revolution.*

3. Cotterell, *Mission and Meaningless.* In the history of the church, what has been particularly difficult is when mission has been coercive.

4. The present critique of the nearly two decades of work in which we were engaged in caring for people with addiction issues was that we took advantage of vulnerable people by "forcing" them to become Christians. Yet how many of our critics were willing to have these disadvantaged people live with their families as they made their slow and perilous journey towards wholeness and well-being? Many of us need spiritual practices to aid us in our journey towards wholeness. Do we equally want to condemn the high-flying executive for going to yoga classes to sustain his pressured lifestyle?

5. See Kierkegaard, *Either/Or*, vols. 1 & 2.

6. Ringma, "Holistic Ministry and Mission."

7. Niebuhr, *Christ and Culture.*

identifies many different understandings regarding this task, ranging from a world-denying form of Christianity to a world-transforming vision.[8] Some push the transformational model even further and speak of a world-formative Christianity.[9] This diversity of perspectives highlights that there cannot be a single understanding of the mission of the church. Furthermore, there are also many diverse expressions of Christian spirituality, such as Anabaptist, Methodist, and evangelical spirituality, among many others. And within the Roman Catholic tradition alone, there are many different expressions of spirituality, including Benedictine, Franciscan, and Ignatian.[10]

To make matters even more complicated, the history of Christianity has been plagued by dualism. *Ontological dualism* holds that one dimension or aspect of the human person is superior to other dimensions. Instead of seeing a person as a "psychosomatic unity," in the words of John Polkinghorne, the human being becomes fractured by having a "superior" spirit or soul and an "inferior" body.[11] *Functional dualism* suggests that a particular way of life is superior to another way of life. The early church historian, Eusebius (d. 371), puts this most clearly: "the one [way of life] is above common human living; it admits not marriage, property, nor wealth but wholly separate from the customary life of man [sic] devotes itself to [the] service of God alone in heavenly love. The other life, more humble and more human, permits men [sic] to marry, have children, undertake office, command soldiers fighting in a good cause, attend to farming, trade, and other secondary interests."[12] This dualism has resulted in the view that a "consecrated life," which is expressed through chastity, poverty, and obedience, has an "*objective superiority*"[13] over other "more humble and more human" Christians. This view has elevated those living a contemplative life over those involved in apostolic service. For example, the medieval Christian mystic, Jan van Ruysbroeck (1293–1381), places "inward friends of God" who are called to the "hidden way of ghostly [spiritual] life" above "faithful servants" who are "called [to] the outward or active life."[14]

---

8. For an evangelical articulation of this model, see Samuel and Sugden, *Mission as Transformation*.

9. See Wolterstorff, *Until Justice and Peace Embrace*.

10. See Collins, *Exploring Christian Spirituality*.

11. Quoted in Grenz, *Theology for the Community of God*, 160.

12. See Ringma, *Whispers from the Edge of Eternity*, 95.

13. *Vita Consecrata*, 29.

14. Petry, "The Sparkling Stone," 302.

Despite Martin Luther's notion of the "priesthood of all believers," this dualism has been prevalent in both the Roman Catholic church and evangelicalism. Distinctions continue to be made between clergy and laity,[15] the missionary and the business person, and works of evangelism and social justice, peacemaking, or caring for the earth.[16]

Given all these diversities and dualisms, it is challenging to bring mission and spirituality together. While this book argues that they belong together, we need to do so in a way that brings about true integration. We can't simply paste them together by saying that our "spirituality" is how we fill up at a petrol or gas station, and our mission is how we drive our car to do works of service in the world. This suggests that the only purpose of our inner life is to fuel our outer life, which is inadequate, since our inner life is also about nurturing friendship with God, offering worship and thanks to God, and growing personally.[17]

Yet instead of becoming a life-giving stream for others, our inner lives often become a stagnant swamp. Thus, this book seeks to explore how our outer life can *deepen* our inner life. Surely serving a neighbour will lead us to pray, which will deepen our relationship with God through the Spirit. And surely our acts of bearing witness to God's love are as spiritual as our life of prayer.[18] We will explore these – and many other – integrational themes throughout this book, considering, for example, how contemplation can be both transcendent and incarnational.

But as we embark on this journey of exploration, we will need to set aside binary thinking (with its either/or categories) and embrace dialogical thinking (with its both/and categories) and a dialectical way of coming to understanding.[19] This integrative approach is well served by the trialectic[20]

---

15. See Stevens, *The Abolition of the Laity.*

16. Yet as Lesslie Newbigin argues, "Any talk of salvation apart from action for the liberation of the exploited is false" (*The Open Secret*, 97). And in the words of "The Wheaton Declaration" (1983), "We must therefore evangelize, respond to immediate human needs and press for social transformation" (quoted in Webber, *The Church in the World*, 256).

17. Bishop Kallistos Ware highlights that the grand theme of Scripture is "our union with God" through Christ's salvation, as "*from within*, as one of us," through the gift of the Holy Spirit (*The Orthodox Way*, 169, 100, 118). But he also emphasizes that we are saved "through the neighbour," meaning that we are to live with compassion for the other "through imaginative sympathy" (67, 151).

18. Dorothy Day notes that "the Works of Mercy are a wonderful stimulus to our growth in faith as well as love" (*Selected Writings*, 99).

19. See Gadamer, *Truth and Method*; Ringma, *Gadamer's Dialogical Hermeneutic.*

20. Anthony Kelly and Sandra Sewell use the term "trialectic" in *With Head, Heart and Hand* (22); Dave Andrews speaks of "triangulation" and the "trey-way" in *A Divine Society* (106–110).

paradigm of the *head* (theological formation), *heart* (spiritual formation), and *hand* (missional formation). If we only use our head, we have vision but no inner sustenance or praxis. If we only engage our heart, we have passion but no framework or practical outworking. And if we only use our hands, we have activity but lack direction or inner resources.[21]

This book is not seeking to outline a spirituality that will result in a missional outworking, as this would reduce spirituality to a utilitarian means to a certain end – and inevitably, spirituality would be absorbed by mission. Rather, we will explore what a fully integrated, missional Christian spirituality might look like. For example, how might a missional spirituality be birthed out of how we live in Christ through the Spirit through the whole of our lives? How might such a missional spirituality sustain us through the joys and challenges of serving our neighbours and bearing witness to God's love for the whole world?

In pursuing these matters, we will take an ecumenical approach, probing the biblical narratives and listening to Protestant, Roman Catholic, Anabaptist, and Eastern Orthodox voices. Though I regard myself as an ecumenical evangelical,[22] my approach will not be polemical, seeking to argue, for example, that an evangelical missional spirituality is superior to a Franciscan missional spirituality. Rather, I am interested in how we might learn from all these various traditions.

However, this book will not seek to reduce our differences, advocating a sort of "dumbing down"[23] in order to find our commonalities. Such an approach would not serve us well and is not advocated in inter-religious dialogue.[24] Instead, as noted in the preface, our approach will be dialectical and dialogical,[25] which will require us to listen deeply to the other – and perhaps to revise our own perspectives. No theological position should ever be afraid to risk its presuppositions and be genuinely open to other perspectives. This

21. See Kelly and Sewell, *With Head, Heart and Hand*, for their discussion of the integration of head, heart, and hand in the context of social work (23–24).

22. I do, however, recognise that the term "evangelical" is becoming increasingly diverse and problematical. Nevertheless, I retain this self-designation because I continue to believe that the biblical narratives give us a glimpse of God's purposes for humanity. I also believe in the redemptive and restorative activity of God in Christ through the Spirit. Moreover, I believe that the church as the pilgrim people of God should live in anticipation of the life to come in God's final kingdom while living as an embodiment of the gospel and as servants to the world. Of course, some evangelicals will say that this is not precise or good enough, so I ask you to be generous and give me the benefit of the doubt until the last page of this book!

23. See McLaren, *A Generous Orthodoxy.*

24. In *Transforming Mission*, David Bosch writes, "Dialogue means witnessing to our deepest convictions, while listening to those of our neighbors" (484).

25. See Buber, *I and Thou*; Levinas, *Basic Philosophical Writings.*

ecumenical "spirit" is the core motivation of Jesus's high priestly prayer: "that [we] may all be one."[26]

Our exploratory journey will unfold as follows. Section I (chapters 1–5) engages *integrational* themes. To begin, chapter 1 will clarify what we mean by "mission" and "spirituality" and outline some core ideas about how these two domains might be dynamically brought together, thereby setting the scene for the fuller discussions in the rest of the book. This chapter also explores the theme of integration and seeks to draw us out of our silos.

Chapter 2 articulates what we mean by "missional spirituality" by looking at the writings of Evelyn Underhill, Mother Teresa, Segundo Galilea, and David Augsburger. These models of missional spirituality illustrate various ways in which prayer and service, contemplation and action are woven together amidst the tapestry of life. In my discussion of Mother Teresa's model, I draw on writings by Karl Rahner and Karl Barth, particularly around the theme of the salvific work of Christ in redeeming all humanity. I am not suggesting that any of these authors have set out specifically to articulate a missional spirituality, but am drawing on their writings in order to construct various models of such a spirituality.

Chapter 3 engages the key theological themes that lie at the heart of a missional spirituality and give it shape, colour, and vibrancy.[27] In other words, any missional spirituality must be cruciform, Trinitarian, and rooted in the paschal mystery, and it must engage the practices of *communitas*[28] and radical hospitality. This chapter will also illustrate how missional spirituality is intrinsic to the whole tradition of Christianity and thus should not be regarded as a mere footnote in the theological drama. I see this as the book's most foundational chapter.

Chapters 4 and 5 further elaborate the integral relationship between contemplation and action, and mysticism and ministry. These chapters reveal how the themes of contemplation and mysticism are not "trendy" contemporary notions, but are deeply embedded in the church's long march through history, both in terms of its reflection and praxis. Moreover, these chapters also highlight the inner logic of this book in terms of its spiral methodology – where core themes are introduced early in the book and then elaborated later in the book in order to deepen the discussion. One of the central themes in these chapters

---

26. John 17:21.

27. Clifford Geertz describes this as a "thick description" in *The Interpretation of Cultures*.

28. *Communitas* is a Latin noun that can either refer to an unstructured community where everyone is equal or the very spirit of community.

is how the contemplation of God can lead us into a deeper reflection on the heart of the world, thereby revealing how the mystic may well be the most authentic and radical social revolutionary.

Section II (chapters 6–9) focuses on *biblical* themes.[29] In chapter 6, I draw on both the Old Testament (OT) and the New Testament (NT) to craft some of the major themes in a "biblical spirituality," which is both personal and communal and oriented towards God as well as towards the love and care of the neighbour. This chapter also highlights various spiritual disciplines in the biblical tradition while emphasising that *all* of life is a spiritual practice.

In chapter 7, I set out the heart and scope of integral mission – highlighting the wideness of God's love and concern for the world and the impact of that love in shaping faith-communities and orienting their mission to the world. The chapter bristles with biblical paradigms rather than isolated biblical texts, modelling a creative and relevant engagement with biblical themes rather than simply repeating fragments of biblical verses. My intention in this chapter is twofold. First, I want to demonstrate that missional themes in Scripture are neither incidental nor arbitrary, but are integral to the entire biblical narrative. Second, while a biblical paradigm carries thematic weight, it remains open to interpretive application. Thus, the prophetic, social justice themes of the OT and the communal themes of the NT have a normative significance as well as a creative application. To give an example of the implications of this insight, we might ask, "What does the OT prophetic tradition mean for the cultural captivity of the church in the West and the 'oppression' of the faith-community in Myanmar?"

Chapter 8 further demonstrates the theme of integration, using the aforementioned typology of head, heart, and hand to highlight the importance of orthodoxy, orthopathy, and orthopraxis in forming a missional spirituality that incorporates theology, spirituality, and missional strategies. At the same time, this chapter tackles the problems of idealism and triumphalism. Mission is a *vulnerable* endeavour that needs to be concerned with faithfulness rather than success and also needs to remain self-critical. Thus, an integrated missional spirituality will need to follow a cyclical pattern of action and reflection to allow space for evaluation and change.

---

29. It should be noted that this does not mean that biblical perspectives are lacking in the first section and that theological themes are absent in the second section. This book is about integration, and therefore biblical, theological, spiritual, practical, and personal reflective themes flavour the whole book – but some of these themes gain greater emphasis in particular parts of the book.

Chapter 9 reflects on God's heart for the poor and God's call for the church to share this concern, as conveyed throughout the biblical narrative. In every age, the church runs the risk of becoming elitist, ethnic, and tribal, caring for its own instead of being there for the "other," including the stranger and the enemy. When the church demonstrates love for the poor, it reflects the very heartbeat of God. Thus, the faith-community is called to serve the poor not only by extending charity, but also by radically identifying with the poor.

Section III (chapters 10–15) draws on themes to set out some *historical* traditions of the Christian church. To cultivate a missional spirituality, we need to re-engage the traditions of the church so that we can hear both Scripture and tradition afresh in light of our changing circumstances. Listening to the past, while engaging our present situation, with all its possibilities and problems, suggests a basic hermeneutic,[30] which calls us to careful contextualization and application. While this process of contextualization may sometimes compromise the normativity of Scripture, it will guard us from applying a rigid and irrelevant missional approach.

Chapters 10 and 11 highlight the missional spirituality of two formative Protestant voices: Martin Luther (1483–1546), the "godfather" of the Reformation, and Dietrich Bonhoeffer (1906–1945), whose vision of Christological "deputyship" on behalf of the world prompted him to become involved in the German resistance movement to Nazism, for which he was eventually executed. While neither theologian is considered a "missiologist," this very categorization makes an oft-neglected point, which is that by putting Christian scholars into boxes, we neglect to read them well,[31] for any scholar who is faithful to Scripture and the broader Christian tradition will engage biblical, theological, spiritual, and missional themes.[32] These chapters on Luther and Bonhoeffer illustrate how both scholars integrate all these themes.

Chapter 12 deals with the radical evangelical movement (the tradition in which I am somewhat situated), tracing both its main themes as well as its most frequent weakness, which posits activism over self-care and spiritual practices. For this movement to become sustainable, it needs to drink more deeply from the various fountains of the Christian spiritual tradition.

---

30. Thiselton, *The Two Horizons*.

31. We have already seen that both Barth and Rahner also set out well-developed missiological perspectives.

32. A good example of a theologian who covers all these themes is Donald Bloesch, *Essentials of Evangelical Theology*, vols. 1 & 2.

Chapter 13 highlights the missional spirituality of the Anabaptist movement to reveal the importance of remaining open to "outliers" in the church – those irritants who hang out on the edges of our major traditions and yet may actually be living much closer to its centre. The Anabaptists were the primary missionaries in Europe (not those in the Lutheran and Reformed traditions), and the contemporary church is beginning to recognize the importance of marginal perspectives, as they often reveal a more richly textured picture of the church's theology, spirituality, and praxis.

In chapter 14, I focus on Franciscan spirituality, which can be typified in a number of ways in light of its orientation towards the poor, its engagement with social justice issues, and its concern for creation care. I have focused on its passion for peacemaking and have located that in the broader discussion of the peace tradition within the Christian tradition.

Chapter 15 explores the development of liberation theology and spirituality in the Majority World, which poses an important challenge to Western evangelical thinking and practice. The central concern and praxis of liberation theology is the healing and restoration of the poor, and so it exemplifies a missional spirituality that is in concert with the broader tradition of the church.

Section IV (chapters 16–18) concludes the book by identifying a few *particular* themes that need to receive greater emphasis in missional spirituality. In chapter 16, I seek to rehabilitate the concept of asceticism within a more "normal" understanding of the Christian life. Though ascetic practice occurs frequently within various Christian spiritualities, it is often cast in extreme, dualistic terms. Thus, I explore how the very nature of the Christian life will be marked by a certain asceticism, and how any missional activity that involves relinquishment and sacrifice is an ascetic practice.

In chapter 17, I draw attention to the theme of suffering, which is part of the general Christian experience and often lies at the heart of missional realities. It is particularly important to emphasize the connection between mission and suffering amidst the prevalent consumer Christianity of twenty-first century Western culture, with its emphasis on self-enhancement and privilege. At the same time, we are not simply called to suffer *for* others, but to suffer *with* them – just as the God of the Scriptures suffers *for* us and *with* us.

Chapter 18 concludes this section by exploring a spirituality of hope, which is not only fundamental to our humanity, but is a major theme throughout the biblical narratives. A posture of hope orients us towards the future while situating us between the "yet" and "not-yet" nature of God's kingdom. When we live with hope for what might *yet* be in the purposes of God for our world, we can give ourselves to living, breathing, and birthing hope in all we seek to do. Any missional task is rooted in the hope of the God who is with us and who goes before us.

While there is an overall cohesion to this book in its articulation of God's restorative purposes for our world and how we are called to extend God's healing restoration to others, I have written each chapter to be self-standing. Thus, you do not need to read progressively through the book, but may want to dip into a particular chapter or section within a chapter. Depending on your life story and circumstances, you may be interested in the relationship between contemplation and action (chapter 4), or the missional spirituality of Dietrich Bonhoeffer (chapter 11), or Franciscan spirituality (chapter 13), or the spirituality of hope outlined by Jacques Ellul (chapter 18). Both the name and the subject indexes at the end of the book will help you navigate your way through these various themes.

I conclude this introduction with insights from the Anabaptist tradition. In a world of "nationalism, materialism, militarism, classism, [and] self-centredness," we are not called to "cultural missions" with its Western imperialism, nor to "spiritual mission" with its concerns only for a personal ticket to heaven, nor to "post-Christian mission" with its relativism, but to "messianic mission."[33] This "messianic mission," in following the suffering Christ into the world through the power of the life-giving Spirit, is to be "drawn into the passion of the triune God for the salvation of the world."[34] And this is the calling of the "whole messianic community," as we are empowered to live "a life transformed through reconciliation with God," in "surrender to God's will," and set "free to serve God and others."[35]

33. Shenk, "The Relevance of a Messianic Missiology for Mission Today," 31, 26–28.

34. Shenk, 17.

35. Shenk, 29–30.

Section I

Integrational Themes

1

Mission and Spirituality

Towards Wider Horizons

Introduction

In this opening chapter, I seek to provide some clarity regarding the ways in which we understand mission and Christian spirituality. I will then make the case that mission and spirituality not only belong together, but should be integrated as a *missional spirituality*. Though we need to be careful about using over-confident language when articulating the church's missional task, this chapter introduces the fundamental theme that runs through this book, which is that mission is not just a task but a *way of life*. The heartbeat of any missional spirituality is our relationship with Christ, which grounds and orients who we are and all that we do as Christ's followers so that Christ can be "birthed" within others, our faith-communities, and our world.

Personal Reflections

My experience has been rather topsy-turvy when it comes to the topics of mission and spirituality. Neither prayer nor service has been a picnic in the park for me, and I certainly had no idea where my initial faith commitment to Christ would eventually lead. I have often felt uncomfortable in the role of a "professional" missionary or pastor, as this seemed to separate me from the very people I was seeking to serve and was often laden with huge expectations, including all sorts of statistics that were meant to prove my "success."

Thus, I have found it much easier to take on the informal role of seeking to be a servant of Christ and a witness to his kingdom while working in an ordinary job. You may draw your own conclusions about what this says about me! In any case, both my spiritual journey and my experience of mission have been diverse – amazing, plodding, gut-wrenching, despairing, and hopeful. There have been the glimmers of insight, whispers of heavenly love, blessings of the Spirit, and plenty of darkness and difficulty. In the life of faith, we can never really say, "I am happy with how I lived it."[1] Rather, our movement through the Christian life moves not only from the darkness of sin into the light of Christ, but also from that life-giving light into the darkness of the great mystery of faith.[2]

Both the mountaintop and the desert are metaphors for the long journey of faith. Throughout my faith journey, I have often reflected on Meister Eckhart's challenge: "When you are in low condition, and feel forsaken, see if you are just as true to him [God] as when your sense of him is most vivid and if you act the same when you think all help and comfort [is] far removed as you do when God seems nearest."[3] I have not always responded well to this challenge and have, at times, thought of giving up. And yet, the life of faith hovers closest to the cold winds of doubt, as we see in Mother Teresa's long journey of the "dark night of the soul."[4]

I don't mean to sound negative or gloomy. In the early 1970s, we saw hundreds of young people come to faith in Christ, but we have also lived the other side of the story – working for years with deeply wounded young people, seeing little progress and plenty of failures. It is gutting and tragic when a deeply wounded person comes to faith, receives something of the healing grace of Christ, and further down the track ends up committing suicide. In our work with Servants to Asia's Urban Poor in Manila, we saw urban poor churches come into being, the founding of cooperatives, and the development of training programs for urban pastors[5] – along with the tragedy of many lives lost and a decade of service and community-building in slum communities burned to the ground or demolished by bulldozers in a single day.[6]

1. The Australian novelist, Alex Miller, has one of his characters express: "everyone of us betrays something" (*The Passage of Love*, 358).

2. See Walter Hilton's perspective in Ringma and Alexander, *Of Martyrs, Monks, and Mystics*, 192.

3. Blakney, *Meister Eckhart: A Modern Translation*, 34.

4. See *Mother Teresa: Come Be My Light*, a collection of her private, personal letters, which describe the darkness, despair, pain, loneliness, and "strange suffering" that lasted for some fifty years. See also David Scott, *The Love that Made Her Mother Teresa*.

5. Craig, *Servants Among the Poor*.

6. Duncan, *Costly Mission*.

In the life of prayer and contemplation, we experience both light and shadows; in our mission and ministry, we may be blessed to see signs of new life, but we also have to walk the long road where so little seems to happen. And whatever comes into being through the life-giving Spirit, may fade so quickly with the passage of time, as if the renewal never took place. As Max Weber observes, charisma soon leads to routinization.[7]

Missional Language

Missional literature is often theologically one-sided, setting out the biblical vision of the shalom of Yahweh and the kingdom of Christ without acknowledging God's strange, upside-down ways of working in the world,[8] our own failures and dependency on the empowering Spirit, the refractory nature of our world and the persistence of the fallen powers, as well as the mystery of working with the God who moves ahead of us – but does not necessarily work in the ways we might expect.

Thus, we need a much more careful reflection that does not rely on one-sided language, calling Christians to proclaim and incarnate the victory of Christ in the world without acknowledging the language of the cross, the reality of suffering, and the mysterious workings of the Spirit.[9] Such one-sided language so easily leads to unrealistic expectations. While we serve others in the hope of God's in-breaking kingdom, we are living in between Christ's first and second coming,[10] and so the nature of God's kingdom is both "present and not-yet fully present."[11] While missional language is framed by the biblical narratives and so may highlight God's victory in Christ's resurrection, it also needs to reflect the human predicament and our failures in discipleship and mission. Triumphalism in ministry does not reflect the paschal mystery of the powers of death and the great surprise of resurrection.

In our secular age, we no longer have the Western missional optimism of the participants of the 1910 Edinburgh World Missionary Conference, with its catch-cry, "the evangelization of the world in this generation."[12] Yet the

7. Weber, "The Sociology of Charismatic Authority," 245–64.

8. Kraybill, *The Upside-Down Kingdom*.

9. Simone Weil makes the simple but challenging point that we must "empty ourselves of . . . false divinity" (*Gravity and Grace*, 30).

10. Padilla, *Mission Between the Times*.

11. Ladd, *A Theology of the New Testament*, 68–69.

12. Bosch, *Transforming Mission*, 337–38.

language of our major missional documents[13] tends to express a confident "managerialism,"[14] exuding both certainty and power. These documents are intended to set out what we the people of God need to be and do in our world. While the language is clearly positive and sometimes idealistic, it is often "used as a shield against uncertainty,"[15] thereby hiding as much as it reveals. It speaks of the mission of the church in the purposes of God, but does not deal with the "way of the world," the problems within the faith-community, or the vulnerability of our missionary efforts. Nor does it express the heart-cry of our spiritual journey, our hunger for bread and wine as we seek to live a life of faith and service. Unfortunately, these documents seem to promote the idea that if we *know* our missional task, everything we need to sustain us will somehow flow out of that. But such head knowledge is hardly adequate, for we also have hands and hearts, and so our life of Christian service must be framed in the midst of life's daily realities.

The truth of our contemporary reality is that brokenness and injustice remain entrenched in our global world, which continues to reflect its own idolatrous waywardness. Moreover, as Christians, we continue to struggle to live as God's faithful people amidst the pervasive darkness of the world.[16]

Biblical Language

Rather than employing the confident language of certainty and power to describe our missional engagement in the world, the gospels and writings of St. Paul can help us articulate a more honest and sustainable vision of our call to serve Christ. While these biblical narratives are certain about God's core purposes in seeking to redeem, heal, and mend our broken lives and world, they also express the agony and difficulties of serving God's purposes in our particular time, employing language that is accessible, inspirational, and realistic.[17]

---

13. See *The Sixteen Documents of Vatican II*; *The Ecumenical Movement*; *New Directions in Mission and Evangelization*, vols. 1 and 2; and *Making Christ Known*.

14. Watson, *Death Sentence*, 2, 30.

15. Watson, 36.

16. Jürgen Moltmann makes the helpful suggestion that "hope lives from the anticipation of the positive and therefore sees itself as the negation of the negative" (*In the End – The Beginning*, 91–92). This means that in living in hope, we also need to face the dark side of failure.

17. Simone Weil, with her typical incisive language, reminds us that "grace . . . [needs] a void to receive it," that "humility is the refusal to exist outside [of] God," that "to pray is like a death," and that "it is better to accept the limit, to contemplate it, and savour all its bitterness" (*Gravity and Grace*, 7, 35, 19, 88). This language, which is fraught with pain, hope, and suffering,

For example, in the Gospel of John, Jesus makes a confident assertion about those whom the Father "has given" to him (10:29; 17:9). However, this declaration is more broadly framed within the conflict about Jesus's identity (John 8) and his priestly prayer for protection and the furtherance of his influence (John 17), along with his prayers for the mysterious Spirit to come (John 14, 16), the foretelling of his death and resurrection (John 18–20), and the agonizing question he poses to his disciples, "Do you also wish to go away?" (John 6:67). Throughout John's Gospel, Jesus describes his mission as that of a faithful son who "only does what he sees the Father doing" (John 5:19). Rather than employing triumphal language to describe his mission, he enters the fray of the world in utter vulnerability, carrying out the signs of the kingdom of God amidst the scorn and rebuke of the people of his day (John 7:30, 32; 9:16), with only some identified as believing in him (John 4:48–54; 7:31).

Paul's journey is hardly different. Confident of his own calling (Rom 1:1–6) and God's purposes in Christ as the New Adam (1 Cor 15:45), Paul is clear about his mission (Gal 1:16). Yet like Jesus, Paul's mission unfolds amidst the challenges and extremities of life, so that at one point he thinks, "we had received the sentence of death" (2 Cor 1:9). Paul also makes it clear that "None of the rulers of this age understood" the wisdom of God in Christ, "for if they had, they would not have crucified the Lord of glory" (1 Cor 2:8).

In both Jesus's and Paul's narratives, we see God's redemptive love for humanity, along with the great difficulty of the missional journey amidst human self-assertion and the contours of our idolatrous world, which subverts the desire for God with a desire for much-having.[18] The spurious idea that Christ walked the hard road so that we can walk the easy road in his service is a serious misreading of the entire biblical narrative. Rather, the hard way of Jesus in his day will need to be repeated in us within our own time.

Towards a Christo-Mysticism

If the mission of the people of God is simply a task, then it may be initiated with great enthusiasm, but then wane when the going gets tough, or there may be little fruit, or we may eventually burn out. Furthermore, if the mission of the faith-community is only the task of "professional" missioners, then the rest of us can wash our hands of this calling and live vicariously through

---

reflects the language of the biblical narratives much more than the "confident" language of our missional documents.

18. Bell, *The Economy of Desire.*

those who are engaged in this work by praying for them and offering meagre financial support.

But if the missional task is *integral* to what it means to be a follower of Jesus, then our witness and service is fundamental to our Christianity.[19] If we embrace Jesus as Saviour, then we embrace him as Lord; if he is our healer, then he is seeking to heal others through our prayers and service. When we come to faith in Christ, we are called into God's redemptive purposes for the world, and so we need to take on the "heart of Jesus" by becoming people of compassion. Basil Pennington suggests that "centering" prayer can help us enter into the heart of Jesus, which both restores us to our true selves and draws us into unity with God. Pennington notes that in Christ and through the Spirit, we can say "a complete 'yes' to the Father."[20] In this "yes," there is "no dichotomy between prayer and work. All work becomes prayer."[21]

Thus, Jesus's way in the world becomes our way, and his mission to the world becomes our mission. In the words of Jacques Ellul, "all conduct in the Christian life can be thought of only on the basis of the dialectical relationship between the two opposing factors of salvation by grace and works."[22] To explore this dialectical relationship further, we will listen to the voices of Karl Barth, Ilia Delio, and some of our ancient Christian forebears.

Karl Barth

Karl Barth speaks of the *vocatio interna* as the work of the Holy Spirit, which calls a person to have a special attachment to Christ by being in union with Christ.[23] This union involves Christ speaking, acting, and ruling in the Christian – and the Christian responding to Christ and existing for and with Christ.[24]

This brings us to a key point that Barth highlights, which is that we are not called to our mission (*vocatio externa)* simply because we have been saved by Christ. Thus, our mission is not merely a work of gratitude or an act of worship, but rather a work we do in communion and solidarity with Christ. In the words of Barth, the story of Christ – his life, death, and resurrection – is

19. Guder, *Missional Church.*

20. Pennington, *Centering Prayer*, 97.

21. Pennington, 105.

22. Ellul, *What I Believe*, 41. See also Ringma, *Resist the Powers with Jacques Ellul.*

23. Barth, *Church Dogmatics*, vol. 4, part 3.2, 530.

24. Barth, part 3.2, 547.

to be *repeated* in each individual Christian.[25] This reflects Paul's central idea, which is that Christ is the new Adam of a new humanity, and therefore Christ is a pattern for who we are to become and how we are to live. As the *icon* of the new humanity, Christ is both the prototype and the fulfilment of who we are to become through the Spirit.

To put this in other words, the missional task is not simply what we do *for* Christ in serving the world, but is a small repetition of the very life of Christ, unfolding itself in our lives through the Spirit as we seek to serve the world. Because we are *in Christ*, we engage in witness and service.[26] Thus our mission is an *overflow* and *expression* of our inner life in Christ.

Ilia Delio

This way of thinking about our life and mission has been clearly articulated by the Franciscan sister and scholar, Ilia Delio. Drawing on the writings of Bonaventure and St. Clare, Delio highlights the Christian vocation as "putting on Christ in one's life."[27] In this way, we express a "'mysticism of maternity,' that is, giving birth to Christ in our lives and in our world."[28] The metaphor of "birthing" is helpful, as it uses feminine language for understanding our task in the world, and it emphasizes what is coming into the world – the child. Thus, the focus is not on the church, but on what God, through the Spirit, brings into being!

This does not suggest that we are to become "carbon copies" of Christ. The notion of *imitatio Christi* is not a mere historical repetition of the life of Christ, but rather the unfolding of the life of Christ in us and through us by the work of the Spirit. This life is sustained by spiritual practices, the gift of contemplation, and deeds of love. Zachary Hayes helpfully observes, "We are to fill the Christ-form with the elements of our own personal life and thus embody something of the Word in ourselves in a distinctive and personal way."[29] This means that the

25. Barth, part 3.2, 486.

26. One of my concerns with the language of the "missional" church is not its call for the church to be a missional community, but that this language takes priority over other dimensions of what it means to be church – such as a worshipping and sacramental community – and that the church can easily be seen in primarily *programmatic* terms. The emphasis in my discussion here is to prioritise a Christological and pneumatological grounding of what it means to be God's missional people.

27. Delio, *Franciscan Prayer*, 149.

28. Delio, 13.

29. Quoted in Delio, *Franciscan Prayer*, 155.

pervasive presence of the indwelling Christ does not negate our personhood or individuality. Rather, as we each mirror Christ in our own unique way, within our distinctive faith-communities, we become another *incarnation* of "the body of Christ" in which Christ takes form.[30] This form comes to expression in our world by the power of the Spirit through the faith-community's deeds of love, service, and justice. Yet the church must continually be challenged to become more fully conformed to Christ, to live the life of faith with greater fidelity, and to overcome our stupidities and indifference.

Ancient Christian Forebears

Our ancient forebears understood this connection between spirituality and mission in the world, seeing our *in-Christ* relationship as constitutive for our personhood, our identity as Christ followers, and our mission in the world.

For example, the church father, Gregory of Nyssa (c. 330–395), describes the *imitatio Christi* as follows: "those who have equal zeal for the good must thoroughly imitate and follow the pioneer of our salvation, and must put into practice what he has shown them."[31] This is reiterated by St. Cyril of Alexandria (d. 444): "Christ is for us a pattern and beginning and image of the divine way of life, and he displayed clearly how and in what manner it is fitting for us to live."[32]

St. Columbanus (c. 540–615) highlights the importance of the indwelling Christ, exclaiming in one of his sermons: "Let Christ paint his image in us."[33] The English medieval mystic, Richard Rolle (c. 1295–1349), prays "that Christ may stable [in] us."[34] St. Francis (c. 1181–1226) establishes a clear link between the notion of indwelling and our service to the world in *Later Admonition and Exhortation*, writing that:

> We are spouses when the faithful soul is united by the Holy Spirit to our Lord Jesus Christ. We are brothers, moreover, when we do the will of His Father who is in heaven; *mothers* when we carry Him in our heart and body through love and a pure and sincere

30. Bonhoeffer, *Christ the Center*, 58.

31. Hardy, "Address on Religious Instruction," 315.

32. Quoted in Weinandy and Keating, *The Theology of St. Cyril of Alexandria*, 174.

33. Davies, "Sermons of Columbanus," 358.

34. Petry, "The Mending of Life," 230. See also Ringma, *Hear the Ancient Wisdom*.

> conscience; and give Him birth through holy activity, which must shine before others by example.[35]

This discussion clearly roots our mission in Christo-mysticism rather than a sense of calling or duty that is merely clothed in gratitude. Our in-Christ relationship is intrinsically linked with our calling to be the servants of Christ in the world. Thus, mission is not simply a task, but an abiding connection to the grace of dwelling in and with Christ through the whole of our lives.

Missional Christianity

While some may insist that our central mission is evangelism, David Bosch highlights the richness and complexity of contemporary mission, identifying thirteen complimentary emphases.[36] For the purposes of this discussion, I wish to emphasize that mission is intrinsic to being a Christian and that it is not about working *for* God but *with* God. Having been blessed by the missional God of the biblical story, we engage in serving the purposes of God in the world. In describing our mission as Christians, we need to avoid pompous language about how *we* are bringing God to the world, a particular people, or a neighbourhood. This overplays our role, suggesting that the whole task is ours, and we are bringing a "reluctant" God into the world. Moreover, it undermines the nature of God, who created the entire world, provided Christ for the world's redemption and healing, and remains actively at work through the Spirit to bring forth the new creation.

Thus, our missional calling is: *to join and cooperate with God's redemptive, healing, and transformative activity in bringing all things into the new creation.* Yet joining and cooperating with God is not an immediately simple or obvious task, for God is shrouded in mystery, is both present and absent, and is visible by faith and hidden in the present context of our social world.

To join God's redemptive activity through Christ is multi-dimensional, for it involves our conversion, justification, and the long journey of our sanctification as we dwell with the God who is within us by the Spirit. This process will involve our participation in a whole range of spiritual practices, our theological formation in the light of Scripture and the Living Word, Jesus Christ, and our following God into the world as part of a discerning, witnessing, and serving community of faith.

---

35. Quoted in Delio, *Franciscan Prayer*, 150.

36. Bosch, *Transforming Mission*, 368–510.

To join with God is both a gift and an act of faith, which calls for discernment as we seek to be attentive to the Spirit's work in our own lives and the movement of the Spirit in the body of Christ and the world. Sometimes this discernment will be easier than others, as when the church is characterized by vitality and renewal, but other times the church may be prosaic and, at its worst, manipulative and oppressive.[37] Joining with God in the life of the church under these circumstances is challenging and will involve much suffering and intercession. Dietrich Bonhoeffer reminds us that "we enter into that common life not as demanders but as thankful recipients,"[38] which is particularly difficult when the church seems to be in a "twilight" zone. These challenging situations call us to persevere in the desert[39] and to live as a prophetic witness to the church.[40]

As difficult as it is to discern how to join God amidst the ups and downs of the faith-community, it is even more difficult to discern the workings of God in our world. Does every new social movement bear the imprint of God? Do political liberation movements further the shalom of God? Will so-called Christian political leaders bear the common good better than those who profess no faith at all? Somewhat typically, Jacques Ellul responds to these questions by noting: "When a movement is carried out on behalf of freedom, it produces the worst slavery. If it is on behalf of justice, it gives rise to countless and endless injustices. I don't know of a single one which has accomplished, even in the slightest degree, what it set out to accomplish."[41]

In many ways, Ellul is right. Our post-colonial world is still full of oppression and conflict.[42] Our post-slavery world still has millions of slaves.[43] The so-called Arab Spring has hardly blossomed. And our democratic and consumeristic world is hardly the epitome of virtue and justice. Yet we can also point to some social progress. The structures of racial segregation in the US have come to an end. The Berlin Wall has collapsed. The old apartheid regime in South Africa is no more. But we also need to acknowledge that much more

37. Wookey, *When a Church Becomes a Cult.*
38. Bonhoeffer, *Life Together*, 28.
39. Lane, *The Solace of Fierce Landscapes.*
40. Ellul, *The Subversion of Christianity.*
41. Ellul, *Hope in Time of Abandonment*, 20.
42. Heaney, *Post-Colonial Theology.*
43. Batstone, *Not for Sale.*

needs to be done, for we continue to be so far from a world of "flourishing" for all.[44]

To make a broad generalization, the church cannot assume that every social movement is marked by the hand of God, nor can it assume that the Spirit of God does not work outside the church to move our world toward justice and the common good. Martin Luther King Jr. hopefully declared, "I am convinced that we shall overcome, because the arc of the universe is long, but it bends towards justice."[45] Yet he also realistically acknowledged the sad fact that "all too often the religious community has been the tail light instead of a head light."[46]

Clearly, the community of faith will need to affirm what is good in our world and resist and overcome what is evil. The most basic way that the church can overcome evil is through its ongoing conversion as it embodies the very change it wants to see in the world. As such, the church is to be a servant of the reign of God and a second "incarnation" of the way of Christ.

Christian Spirituality

Zygmunt Bauman notes the complex nature of spirituality in our late-modern world: "the postmodern mind is altogether less excited than its modern adversary by the prospect . . . of enclosing the world in a grid of neat categories and clear-cut divisions."[47] Rather than being locked into scientific and rational categories, the contemporary mind is open to different ways of knowing[48] and experiencing life.

While there are complex historical factors that have led to the questioning of a mono-scientific worldview, there is no unanimity regarding explanations for the contemporary interest in "spiritual" things. Bauman suggests "that the ineffable is as much an integral part of the human mode of being-in-the-world,"[49] as are other dimensions of our humanity. In theological language, this is an approximate way of saying that because humans are made in the image of God, we have an intuitive sense of transcendental realities.

44. Volf, *Flourishing.*

45. Quoted in Ringma, *Let My People Go*, 77.

46. Ringma, *Let My People Go*, 147.

47. Bauman, *Postmodernity and its Discontents*, 167.

48. For a discussion of different ways of knowing, see Alexander, *A Glimpse of the Kingdom in Academia*, 57–73.

49. Bauman, *Postmodernity*, 165.

David Tacey describes this contemporary interest in the spirit as "a counter-cultural revolution, a romantic rebellion against the rise of materialism, inhumanity, and economic rationalism."[50] In other words, it is a reactionary movement to the dominant ethos of late modernity, though it remains to be seen if it can dig deep enough to find long-term sustaining resources. Tacey acknowledges this, observing that the movement is "caught . . . between a secular system we have outgrown and a religious system we cannot fully embrace."[51]

Tacey's observations leave us with a rather vague notion of spirituality.[52] He acknowledges this, observing that "Spirituality has become diverse, plural, manifold, and seems to have countless forms of expression, many of which are highly individualistic and personal" and "intensely inward," involving the exploration of the "inner or true self."[53] Finally, he defines spirituality as "our relationship with the sacredness of life, nature, and the universe."[54] While this is generous and open-ended, such a diffuse spirituality provides little grounding and might keep the practitioner locked into the dominant postmodern values of our time. Moreover, the degree to which it is inner-directed rather than also outer-oriented, it will have little impact on the practitioner, let alone our world.

Christian spirituality, on the other hand, has a different tenor. Part of a long and rich tradition that is rooted in the biblical narratives and the lived realities of the people of God for more than two thousand years, Christian spirituality is deeply grounded in the person and work of Christ through the Holy Spirit.[55] Through the open, vital, relevant, and revitalizing work of the Holy Spirit throughout the long history of the faith-community, various "schools" of Christian spirituality have emerged: Augustinian, Franciscan, Cistercian, Reformation, Anabaptist, Wesleyan, among many others.[56]

---

50. Tacey, *The Spirituality Revolution*, 4.

51. Tacey, 3.

52. The Irish writer, John O'Donohue, is particularly concerned with this situation, for despite our contemporary interest in spirituality, we live "in an intense and visually aggressive age" in which we are constantly "drawn outward." He continues that there is at play a "powerfully calculating industry of modern dislocation, where that which is deep and lives in the silence within us is completely ignored." Thus, he calls for the deep practices of silence as practised by the desert fathers and mothers and the Celtic Spiritual tradition (*Anam Cara*, 108–9).

53. Tacey, *The Spirituality Revolution*, 38.

54. Tacey, 38.

55. For a helpful overview of the theology of the Spirit in the life of the church, see Karkkainen, *Pneumatology.*

56. See Sheldrake, *Spirituality and History* and Jones, et al, *The Study of Spirituality.*

The common thread in this long history is the core idea that *Christian spirituality is motivated and shaped by a life devoted to following Christ in the power of the Holy Spirit.*[57] This definition has several key distinctions. First, it has to do with the whole of one's life, not simply one's interiority. Second, it is centred in the person and work of Christ rather than any and every idea of the sacred. Third, it is empowered by the Spirit, not simply self-generated. Finally, it is devoted to following Christ (thus being like Christ and doing the "works" of Christ), not simply one's own self-enhancement or self-fulfilment.[58]

Moreover, Christian spirituality is not simply about "spirit," nor only about the "Holy Spirit." Rather, it about Christ *in and through* the Spirit. This has several important implications. First, if Christ were frozen in the past, then Christian spirituality would only be a historical remembrance. Second, if Christian spirituality is only about the Holy Spirit, then we might find ourselves in a morass of vague mysticism. Third, if Christian spirituality is shaped by the living Christ, who is present to us through the Spirit, then our conformity to the way of Christ is enabled by the empowering Holy Spirit. Thus, Christ is *not* frozen in the past, but is a formative reality in our daily lives, giving the Christian life a particular shape, ethos, and purpose.

Christian spirituality is not devoid of traditional spiritual practices (such as prayer, meditation, and reflection), nor is it devoid of inner enhancement; rather, all these things are directed in a particular way: to be and become more Christlike.

Much of this book will be concerned with unpacking these most basic introductory statements. In this task, we will address the great tragedy of the contemporary church: in its captivity to contemporary values, it has failed to inculcate this rich tradition within its members. Some denominations have focused on teaching members to attend church and to engage in its liturgical practices, while others have focused on the freedom of the Spirit. In either case, the contemporary church has failed to *form* members into Christ[59] through

---

57. For similar definitions, see Cunningham and Egan, *Christian Spirituality*, 22–28.

58. George Lane defines Christian spirituality as a person's "possession by God in Christ through the Holy Spirit," which will take on different forms, styles, and emphases as it is concretized in history (*Christian Spirituality: An Historical Sketch*, 2). In his discussion of various "schools" of Christian spirituality, Lane looks particularly at the spirituality of Eastern monasticism, the Benedictines, the Mendicants, and Ignatian spirituality. Of course, there is much more to this story, and there is much greater diversity.

59. St. Paul's agonizing cry was: "My dear children, for whom I am again in the pains of childbirth until Christ is formed in you" (Gal 4:19 NIV).

prayer, contemplation, witness, and service, and so it has largely become devoid of "spirit."

Missional Christian Spirituality

If Christian spirituality is connected with following Christ and comes out of a Christo-mysticism (the *in*-Christ relationship), we might wonder if the idea of a "missional Christian spirituality" is mere tautology. There are several reasons why this phrase is not redundant. First, the words, "Christian spirituality," include prayer and other meditative practices that we don't immediately connect with witness and service. Second, within the monastic tradition of Christian spirituality, many people think primarily of their life of prayer, contemplation, and liturgy rather than the importance of their daily work, hospitality, and other forms of service. Third, we tend to think of spirituality in dualistic terms, highlighting, for example, the importance of prayer over the work for justice. Fourth, many books on Christian spirituality fail to integrate Christian mission with spirituality, which reinforces the contemporary idea that spirituality is only about personal and inward disciplines.[60]

For these and other reasons, "missional Christian spirituality" is not repetitive, but corrects dualistic thinking and invites us to reflect on the ways that prayer and work are interrelated and service is a form of spirituality. More specifically, the very movement of mission – going out towards the other in love and service – is a particular way of being and calls for a sustaining spirituality. Thus, a missional Christian spirituality seeks to link and interpenetrate the call to love both God and neighbour (Matt 22:37–40), prayer with the work of justice (Isa 58:6–7), the inner and the outer journey (Mark 1:35–39), and contemplation and action (Pss 46:10; 51:10, 13).

At this point in our discussion, a key definition might be helpful: *a missional Christian spirituality is a way of life in Christ through the Spirit that animates our love and service to others.* This way of life is supported by the faith-community and spiritual practices, and it will involve embracing our migrant, itinerant status as Christ followers.[61] In other words, we have come

60. For example, *Christian Spirituality* by Lawrence Cunningham and Keith Egan fails to emphasize mission as part of spirituality. Their chapter, "Hearers and Doers of the Word," is woefully weak on the "doers" part (29–46).

61. For a far-ranging discussion of these matters, see Ringma et al., *God at the Borders.*

"home" through the grace of God in Christ, and we are also "sent out" by the impulse and movement of the Spirit.[62]

The rest of the book will unpack these introductory shorthand statements, but a few initial comments are appropriate. First, we are not talking about certain missional projects that we might engage during youthful enthusiasm and later leave behind, but a whole way of life. Second, we are talking about a missional spirituality that takes on the way – the *gestalt* – of Christ, and thus follows a distinctly cruciform pattern. Third, missional spirituality and its unfolding in the world through works of witness and service is guided and sustained by the Spirit rather than self-effort. Fourth, missional spirituality is communal, the work of the body of Christ rather than a solo effort by so-called "heroes" of faith. Fifth, missional spirituality incorporates the spiritual disciplines and a disciplined way of life. Thus, sabbath practices and self-care are part of our missional engagement. Sixth, missional spirituality is for the life of the world, not simply our own personal enhancement. But as we serve others and engage the powers of our age, we will be challenged and enriched. Finally, missional spirituality calls us to be sent, to move out of our comfort zones, to connect with and reach out to the other. We are "sojourners" rather than "homesteaders," orienting ourselves towards the tabernacle rather than the temple, focusing on the journey rather than our arrival. As Psalm 84 declares, "blessed" are those who embark on such a pilgrimage![63]

Some confirming voices can accompany us on this journey. Bradley Holt helpfully notes that spirituality is about "integrating one's life in the world with one's relationship with God" and goes on to say that "Christian spirituality includes more than an introspective search for psychological health; ideally it integrates relationships to God and creation with those to self and others."[64] But when Holt discusses "mission spirituality," he speaks exclusively about the modern mission movement from the West to the rest of the world and describes it as including "love for the people served; courage in facing the unknown; confidence in God's provision . . ."[65] Clearly, Bradley is referring to a spirituality for "professional" missionaries, but these markers are surely

62. This theme occurs elsewhere in Scripture: "Blessed are those who dwell in your house; they are ever praising you. Blessed are those whose strength is in you, who have set their hearts on pilgrimage" (Ps 84:4–5 NIV).

63. We note that while a tourist demands, a pilgrim receives. Pilgrimage is intrinsic to Christian spirituality. The migrant God invites all of us on the journey of faith and service. See Ringma et al., *God at the Borders*.

64. Holt, *Thirsty for God*, 3.

65. Holt, 95–96.

appropriate for all Christians. For example, while one needs courage to take one's wife and young family to unevangelized groups of people in Papua New Guinea, one also needs courage to serve and bear witness to God's love to a neighbour across the street. Though there are certainly different degrees of difficulty and challenge, we all need courage and commitment as we move from self towards "the other" in Christian service. Moreover, Bradley's description of mission and spirituality reflects an outdated view of global Christianity, for the movement is no longer from the "West to the rest" of the world, but is multi-directional, which includes moving from the Majority World to the Minority World (the West).[66]

Pope John Paul II moves in the same direction as Bradley in *Redemptoris Missio*, where he speaks about a "missionary spirituality," although his insights are much fuller. He describes such a missionary as a "contemplative in action," with a life "of complete docility to the Spirit," exhibiting "the gifts of fortitude and discernment," who is "marked by apostolic charity" and acts as a "'universal brother' bearing in himself the Church's spirit, her openness to and interest in all peoples and individuals."[67]

These words identify a certain *gestalt* in missional activity, a certain way of being that is carried out in a posture of humility and service through the power of the enabling Spirit. This way of being is open to the other and implies an ability to move beyond one's own "world" in order to enter the "world" of those one seeks to serve. Though this calling and the particulars of our service may differ in degree, it is important to emphasize that this calling is for *all* Christians. The laity are not exempt from growing in a missional spirituality that reaches out to another.

More fully orbed, for our discussion, however, is the paradigm developed by Carlo Martini, the cardinal-archbishop of Milan. In speaking about the dimensions of Christian spiritual practices, he highlights the importance of *lectio*, which is a slow and reflective way of reading Scripture; *consolatio*, which is the fruit of *lectio* and results in hope and courage in embracing the ways and purposes of God; *discretio*, which issues in making life choices regarding God's purpose for one's life; *deliberatio*, which has to do with the motivation and outworking of the will; and *actio*, which is the outworking of one's love in Christian witness and service.[68] All these practices are interactive, and one issues into the other. However, as we will see in chapter 2, Martini's paradigm

66. See Jenkins, *The Next Christendom*.

67. *Redemptoris Missio*, 144–51.

68. Quoted in Cunningham and Egan, *Christian Spirituality*, 39.

falls short, for he does not account for the way that *actio* loops back to *lectio.* In other words, prayer not only leads to service, but service also leads to prayer. Put in another way, prayer is a form of service, and service is a form of spirituality.

Yet Martini's paradigm is important, as it suggests that the movement of Christian service needs to arise from listening to Scripture, prayer, discernment, and obedience. Service is not simply about doing things, but doing them with particular motivations for a particular purpose. Put most simply, our service flows out of God's love for the whole world and the life of God that dwells within us.

Thomas Merton, who was both an activist and a Trappist monk, is a helpful companion, for his life demonstrates how an activist can also live as a monk. In the latter phase of Merton's life, he sought to overcome the idea that being a monk was a higher form of spiritual existence by integrating spiritual practices with his witness and service. First, he points out that "in manual labour we become helpers and co-operators with God the creator and administrator of the world – we become instruments of his divine providence – we help him change and renew the face of the earth."[69] Second, though the monk spends much of his day in liturgical and personal prayer, he nevertheless carries the concerns of the world to God. As Merton puts it, "far from being exempted from service in the battles of his age, the monk, as a soldier of Christ, is appointed to fight these battles on a spiritual, hidden front – in mystery – by prayer and self-sacrifice."[70] Finally, Merton offers a helpful definition of an integrated missional spirituality: "action is charity looking outward to other men [and women], and contemplation is charity drawn inward to its own divine source. Action is the stream and contemplation is the spring."[71]

Conclusion

This chapter has sought to bring some initial clarity to Christian spirituality and mission, which I describe as "missional Christian spirituality." But my reference to "wider horizons" in the title for this chapter acknowledges the importance of going beyond definitions, for we need narratives that can both *expand* our definitions and *ground* them in lived realities.

69. Merton, *The Monastic Journey*, 28. See also Ringma, *Seek the Silences*, 158.

70. Merton, 35. See also Ringma, *Seek the Silences*, 164.

71. Merton, *No Man is an Island*, 70. See also Ringma, *Seek the Silences*, 163.

As Christians, rather than turning our faces away from the problems and issues of our time, we are called to immerse ourselves in nurturing our families and friendships, building institutions, involving ourselves in society, and caring for creation. Thus, we are called to live a *world-formative spirituality.* As we "build" the human community, we seek to enhance the common good in anticipation[72] of the reign of God. At the same time, we are also called to "build" the community of faith so that it may flourish to the glory of God and in service to humanity. But this comprehensive building project is not ours alone, for we are not building the kingdom of God; rather, the kingdom of God is building us. Though we live in and serve the kingdom, the kingdom of God moves amongst us – and beyond us.

Moreover, we are not only called to resist the "worldliness" of the world and the powers of this age, but also to worship, pray, reflect, and meditate. Thus, we are called to live a *contemplative spirituality.* As we live with the God of revelation and mystery, we are invited into a relationship of intimacy and discernment so that we can engage the world around us with a renewed heart and open eyes.

The Irish Abbess, St. Bridget of Kildare (c. 450–523), poetically summarizes some of the dimensions of this chapter in the following liturgy:

> There is a friend's love
> in the gentle heart of the Saviour.
> For love of Him we offer friendship
> and welcome every guest.
> Lord, kindle in my heart
> a flame of love to my neighbour,
> to my enemies, my friends, my kindred all,
> from the lowliest thing that liveth
> to the name that is highest of all.[73]

---

72. I think we need to be most careful that we don't use the terminology of "building the kingdom." We don't "build" it, but are "caught up in the kingdom" and are thus carried along in kingdom impulses through the movement of the Spirit and our happy cooperation.

73. *Celtic Daily Prayer*, 146.

2

Towards a Missional Spirituality

Introduction

In likening the structure of this book to building a house, we might say that this chapter serves as the concrete slab for the foundation of the house. Or, to use the language of a painting, we might say that this chapter outlines the rough brushstrokes for the picture that is to come.

My task here has been to "mine" various authors whose writings reflect an implicit missional spirituality, including Evelyn Underhill, Mother Teresa, Segundo Galilea, and David Augsburger. While these choices may surprise you, I trust you will be happily surprised. I also bring into the conversation two of the greatest theologians of the twentieth century: the Roman Catholic, Karl Rahner, and the Protestant, Karl Barth. Together, they provide a depth perspective on two challenging questions: how do we understand the nature and scope of Christ's salvific work? and how do we "see" Christ in others?

Writing this chapter brought me a lot of joy, and I hope some of that joy will overflow to you.

Some Personal Reflections

Cultivating a life of integration and balance is a great challenge. Influenced by the times in which we live, our personal biography, spiritual giftedness, and the institutions or movements of which we are a part, all tend to pull us in certain, often one-sided, directions. When we move toward the centre of the church, we may find that we are not sufficiently open to the stranger. When our focus is on serving the marginalized, we may become overly critical of the church. When we concern ourselves with inward piety, we may become irrelevant to the world around us, which desperately needs God's healing. When we become consumed with our projects, we may easily neglect prayer. When we direct our passion towards justice issues, we may become nervous about witness and evangelism. The dysfunctionalities of our one-sidedness are endless.

As an evangelical with a dose of charismatic renewal and an orientation towards liberation theology,[1] my Christian life has focused on serving the needy and poor. This orientation towards the poor was my "second conversion," following my coming to personal faith in Jesus Christ as my saviour, healer, friend, and director. This second conversion occurred during my service amongst Indigenous communities in Western Australia, among whom I learned more about the life of faith than I ever contributed. Despite their pain, dislocation, and marginalization, their way of life was much more integrated and rooted in sharing, which challenged me to think outside my Western, middle-class values and ideas. Aboriginal ways of connecting to land and place were also beyond my frame of reference at that time, but I was a slow learner, and activism and fragmentation continued to dominate much of my way of life.

My breakdown in the midst of ministry during my thirties was a turning point. Over the course of many months on the slow road to recovery, I had to face some of my inner "demons" and compulsions. For the first time, I experienced a "dark night of the soul."[2] I would love to report that things changed significantly after that, and I became more prayerful and worshipful, but things did not change all that much. Soon, it was "business" as usual, and activism remained my dominant reality. Though we prayed, our focus was on how prayer served our ministry rather than also building a friendship with God.

But in a small way, a new journey had begun, for my experience of the "dark night of the soul" reminded me that God loves us for *who we are*, not for what we *do*. That "small way" over time was also reinforced by a number of ministry-related issues. First, in working with deeply troubled young people who were in the drug scene, we became more aware of our own needs and vulnerabilities. Second, we continued to be blessed by the wounded people we were seeking to serve, which reminded us that blessing and goodness do not simply come from "strong" people, but also from the "weak."[3] Finally, we were drawn to pray for those we were seeking to serve, particularly through the ministry of inner healing,[4] and this, in turn, made us even more aware of our own need for healing and renewal.

---

1. See Ringma, "Liberation Theologians Speak to Evangelicals," 7–53.
2. See Kavanagh, "Dark Night of the Soul," in *The Collected Works*.
3. See Nouwen, *The Wounded Healer*.
4. Scanlan, *Inner Healing*; MacNutt, *Healing*; Ringma and Dickau, *The Art of Healing Prayer*.

My point in offering these personal reflections is that ministry will burn us out if it is not sustained by inner resources and spiritual disciplines. Moreover, our ministry should, inevitably, draw us into deeper prayer, self-reflection, and transformation. These two observations reinforce the connection between mission and spirituality, which I will explore in this chapter. The authors we will consider serve as "models"[5] who can help us see the key contours of a missional spirituality. In exploring these authors, I am not at all suggesting that they set out to develop a missional spirituality, but rather that this theme is embedded in their writings. Thus, my purpose is not to analyse their writings in a systematic way, but to highlight them as models for a missional spirituality.

Evelyn Underhill's Tripartite Missional Spirituality

Evelyn Underhill (1875–1941) was influenced by the mysticism of St. Teresa of Avila (1515–1582), among others. Under the spiritual direction of F. von Hugel, she became a well-known English author on Christian mysticism as well as a spiritual guide and director. Later in life, she became an ardent pacifist.

In her brief classic, *The Spiritual Life*, she articulates an integrated vision of the spiritual life. Moreover, she makes the point that Christian mysticism is not an other-worldly form of escapism, a sort of "fenced-off devotional patch,"[6] but that "the Spiritual Life has everything to do with politics."[7] She sounds the warning that spirituality is not about the "mere cultivation of one's own soul; poking about our interior premises with an electric torch," but is "also intensely social."[8]

Under the rubric of a three-fold, inter-related paradigm of adoration, adherence, and cooperation,[9] which she takes on board from Cardinal Pierre de Berulle (1575–1629), she articulates the key contours of a missional spirituality (although that terminology is never used).

5. McFague notes that a "model is a metaphor that has gained sufficient stability and scope so as to present a pattern for relatively comprehensive and coherent explanation" (*Models of God*, 34). In other words, a model provides a productive framework and when "fleshed out" provides a narrative that is helpful for understanding and action.

6. Underhill, *The Spiritual Life*, 28.

7. Underhill, 91.

8. Underhill, 29.

9. Underhill develops similar themes in other writings. Her emphasis on adherence, communion, and cooperation is key to "a healthy spiritual . . . and natural life," which ushers us into "actual self-giving to His purposes" and the "throwing in of our whole spiritual weight on the side of His redemptive work" (*The Ways of the Spirit*, 191, 189).

First, through the practice of *adoration*, Underhill stresses that we are invited to delight in who God is and all that God does, which involves "attending to God,"[10] communion with God, and a life of prayer, where "our whole life [is turned] toward God."[11] Thus, we are attracted to God and awed by God, and so we celebrate who God is and seek to embrace all that God does, including God's mysterious ways with us and our world. This pulls us out of "our limited interests"[12] and calls us to surrender to God's way with us.

The language of delighting in God and God's purposes brings together both spiritual and missional themes. When we delight in *who* God is, we enter into the practice of spiritual friendship. When we delight in *what* God does, we enter into the mission of God.

Surely, we need to hear this theme in our day, when we so easily reduce God to serving our needs and wants. Some perceive God as a sort of divine "butler." Others cast God as a sort of "tribal" chief, who champions our narrow interests. Underhill reminds us of the freedom and magnificence of the God of the biblical narratives. Yahweh is not only Israel's God, but the God of the nations (Gen 17:4; 1 Chr 16:24; Ps 96:3; Isa 60:3).

Second, through the practice of *adherence*, we cling to the God who loves and sustains us as we constantly open our lives to God's presence, calling, and direction. If adoration is centrally about worship, then adherence has to do with spiritual growth in our lives. Underhill suggests that this calls us to "an attitude of humble and grateful acceptance, a self-opening [and] an expectant waiting."[13] In this posture, we experience God's nurture as well as God's call upon our lives. Underhill elaborates: "a spiritual life is simply a life in which all that we do comes from the centre, where we are anchored in God: a life soaked through and through by a sense of His reality and claim, and self-giving to the great movement of His will."[14]

This powerful vision of the action of God in our lives and our response to God's nurturing presence reminds us of our call to be anchored in, immersed in, and deeply sustained by the God who makes "home" with us. God is not an absent landlord, but an abiding presence. But being grounded in God involves being grounded in God's will. Here again, relationship and service are linked.

10. Underhill, *The Spiritual Life*, 59.

11. Underhill, 61.

12. Underhill, 70.

13. Underhill, 73.

14. Underhill, 36.

The inward movement of worship and nurture is complemented by the outward movement of service and witness.

Third, through the practice of *cooperation*, we acknowledge that God "made us in order to use us" for his purposes.[15] This means that we are called to join with God in God's love and concern for the world. Underhill goes on to say that this never involves a "limp resignation," but "a total concentration on the total interests of God," which "must be expressed in action."[16]

What is particularly significant in her articulation of this theme is her emphasis on the *total interests* of God. This is not a narrow vision of the Christian's engagement with the world, where the focus is on "soul saving" with the guarantee of a future heaven. Rather, God's interests are personal, social, creational, and global. While we are called to see things "from the angle of eternity," our engagement is to be "personal, social, and national."[17] This language implicitly frames a world-formative spirituality and missiology.

Underhill also strikes a helpful note of realism, reminding us that in the grand purposes of God – the restoration of all things in the new creation already begun in Christ – we are "*to take our small place in the vast operations of His Spirit*."[18] In this, she highlights the importance of knowing our particular calling and giftedness so that we can function out of who we are and what we have already received. Thus, our missional spirituality does not depend on us alone, but has everything to do with the ways in which we have been gifted and called. This implies that we will need to embrace both our calling and our limitations. As a consequence, ministry is not a "grinding" activity, but rather joyful and purposeful service – which is also costly.[19]

Furthermore, Underhill implicitly notes that this calling is for the whole faith-community, not simply a few heroic individuals. Finally, she highlights that when we join the purposes of God, God can choose to use us in different ways: "sometimes we are the currency used in some great operation," and "sometimes we are servants, left, year in year out . . . [in] the same monotonous

15. Underhill, 85.

16. Underhill, 87.

17. Underhill, 90.

18. Underhill, 89 (my emphasis).

19. The poet Czeslaw Milosz makes a similar point in that I play but "a diminutive part of a great totality" in the "small patch of time assigned to me" (*Second Space*, 59). However, being satisfied to find and play our small part in the bigger scheme of things, is not to everyone's fancy. As the poet Rainer Rilke notes, "You see, I want a lot. Maybe I want it all: the darkness of each endless fall, the shimmering light of each ascent" (*Rilke's Book of Hours*, 61).

job."[20] Though we may sometimes witness grandiose happenings, our keynote is faithful service.[21]

This reminder is particularly relevant for our time. In seeking to escape the bland social and cultural landscape of late modernity by pursuing heroic or celebrity status, we often transfer this nostalgia into the Christian life. In looking for significance,[22] purpose,[23] and noticeability,[24] we easily think that only grand projects are part of God's purposes for our lives. Instead, Underhill calls us to have a servant's, rather than a celebrity's, heart. In other words, she is encouraging us to embrace a major theme in Benedictine spirituality, namely, the blessedness of the ordinary.[25]

Though Underhill does not use the language of a "missional spirituality," she has clearly articulated such a vision for us.[26] She has also challenged the dualistic thinking that has marred so much of the Christian landscape, noting that "our favourite distinction between the spiritual life and the practical is false."[27] Moreover, she observes that "most of our conflicts and difficulties come from trying to deal with the spiritual and practical aspects of our life separately instead of realizing them as parts of one whole."[28]

Underhill's vision of integrating both a Godward and social orientation is a helpful starting point in thinking about a missional Christian spirituality.

20. Underhill, *The Spiritual Life*, 85.

21. During our street ministry in the early 1970s in Brisbane, when the Jesus Revolution was at its heyday, we saw hundreds of young people make a Christian commitment.

22. See Fukuyama, *The End of History and the Last Man*, xvi–xix.

23. See Warren, *The Purpose Driven Life*.

24. Elliott and Lemert, *The New Individualism*.

25. Ringma, "Drinking from Many Fountains," 78–81; Ringma, *A Fragile Hope*, 45–48.

26. Underhill's articulation is very much within the broad ambit of the Christian tradition. John Calvin points to the fact that "we must adhere to Him [God]" which is a "union of holiness" (*Institutes of the Christian Religion*, 682). This adherence is based on our adoption in Christ so that "the image of Christ may appear in our life" (683) and in "the depth of the heart" (684). This powerful inward movement results in the call to live "for His Glory" (685). This calls us to an inward posture and a practical outworking. Calvin writes: "you cannot find a person who practices gratuitous kindness toward people, unless he [sic] has renounced himself according to the Lord's command" (686–87). And there are no limits to this call. Calvin notes: we are "to do good to all without exception" (689).

27. Underhill, *The Spiritual Life*, 35–36.

28. Underhill, 37.

Mother Teresa's Eucharistic Spirituality

Mother Teresa was born as Agnes Gonxha Bojaxhiu (1910–1997).[29] Her Catholic theology is of a traditional, pre-Vatican II, vintage, and her ministry is best described as the practice of charity to the poorest of the poor. Unsurprisingly, she has been criticized on both counts. Particularly, she has been challenged to move toward a justice model of seeking to serve the poor.[30] When confronted in this regard, she has always challenged the challenger to do that precise thing rather than suggesting that Mother Teresa should do it. Her well-known comment in this regard is: "You change the world. In the meantime, I shall nurse it."[31]

My focus in this chapter is not on the overall nature of Mother Teresa's ministry, but rather the way in which she has integrated spirituality and service. In her lifetime, she often pointed out that she and her workers were not social workers, but *contemplatives in action*, seeking to serve the poorest of the poor through a radical identification with Christ, the poor One, who is hidden in the lives of the poor. Thus, in serving the poor, Mother Teresa and her sisters believe that they are serving Christ himself.[32] Mother Teresa summarizes her ministry as follows: "Our vocation is nothing else but to belong to Christ. The work that we do is only a means to put our love for Christ into living action."[33] More specifically, she says, "Whenever we offer shelter to the dying, we are sheltering Christ himself."[34]

These statements reveal how her ministry to the poor is intimately linked with her service for Christ and her being *with* Christ in acts of intimacy. She makes this connection between spiritual practices and ministry even more clear in referring to the Eucharist, noting: "[We are] called . . . to see Christ in the appearance of bread, and to see him in the broken bodies of the poor."[35] And

29. For more details about her life story, thinking, and ministry, see Spink, *Mother Teresa;* Ringma, *Wash the Feet of the World with Mother Teresa.*

30. See D'Abreo, *From Development Worker to Activist*, for his critique of welfare models (180–91).

31. Zambonini, *Teresa of Calcutta*; Ringma, *Wash the Feet of the World*, 175.

32. Dietrich Bonhoeffer makes a similar point: "Christ walks on the earth as your neighbor" and "He confronts you in every person that you meet" (Kelly and Nelson, *The Cost of Moral Leadership*, 197).

33. Mother Teresa, *No Greater Love*, 147.

34. Mother Teresa, 169.

35. Quoted in Ringma, *Wash the Feet*, 159.

again: "We see Christ in the Eucharist under the appearance of bread, while we see him in the poor under the distressing disguise of poverty."[36]

This simple correlation has vast implications. By connecting the chapel with people on the street and the sacrament of the Eucharist with practical service, Mother Teresa models a missional spirituality. Mother Teresa is not only making a creational connection between spirituality and service based on the biblical concept that we are all made in God's image and therefore are worthy of respect and care. Rather, she is making a Christological connection, where the Christ of the sacrament *is* the Christ of the poor, but under a different *gestalt*. Thus, the poor are not only God's creatures, as we all are, but they are "in Christ," and so we need to respond to them as Christ.[37] Thus, washing the feet of the poor is akin to washing the feet of Christ, not merely in a symbolical sense, but also in a spiritual and physical sense.[38]

While Mother Teresa makes no attempt to elaborate on this, or seek to explain this, we should. And the path I wish to take for this exploration is to engage the writings of Karl Rahner and Karl Barth. I, of course, have no idea whether Mother Teresa would approve of the course I am taking, but I am only taking her statements as a starting point.

Rahner's Perspective

Scholars have pigeonholed Karl Rahner (1904–1984) regarding his "philosophical anthropology," and so he asks readers to "be merciful," since he is neither a classical systematic theologian nor a professional philosopher.[39] Rahner's writings urge the church in the West to remain "responsible for the poor and the oppressed,"[40] emphasizing the freedom of the Spirit to spawn "grassroots communities" from below.[41] At the same time, he stresses that these grassroots communities need to remain within the ambit of the Roman Catholic Church so that they do not operate as "tiny sects" and erode "the

36. Mother Teresa, *One Heart Full of Love*, 27.

37. This, of course, raises the challenging question whether this in some way diminishes one's response to another human being. If we believe that we are serving the "hidden" Christ in the poor, are we basically serving the poor person or Christ?

38. In the novel *I Heard the Owl Call My Name*, Margaret Craven has the Bishop remark, "The church belongs in the gutter. It is where it does its best work" (82).

39. Rahner, *Theological Investigations*, vol. 17, 247.

40. Rahner, vol. 17, 171.

41. Rahner, vol. 17, 178.

substance of the Christian faith."[42] Clearly, Karl Rahner would give Mother Teresa's Missionaries of Charity a tick of approval, as they operate as an integral part of the Catholic Church.

From this basic starting point, we can probe deeper into Rahner's theology. First, he believes that the divine will is for the salvation of all. Second, he believes that revelation is everywhere because the Spirit is everywhere at work. Third, he believes that human beings are marked by both God's creational activity and God's grace. One sign of this grace is the "transcendental nature" of the human being,[43] which is evidenced in the human orientation towards faith, hope, and love, suggesting that "Christ is present and efficacious in the non-Christian" person.[44] This theological framing helps situate Mother Teresa's notion of seeing the hidden face of Christ in the poor, so that, by way of extension, we may see the hidden face of Christ in everyone. While some evangelicals might applaud Rahner for his spirit of generosity, others might express concern regarding the biblical grounding for this statement. Thus, we need to probe Rahner's biblical theology further and reflect on his ideas about "anonymous Christians."

First, Rahner is most clear about God's salvific will for all humanity (1 Tim 2:3–6), proposing that "Non-Christians have been touched in the depth of their being by the infinite grace of God in virtue of his universal saving purpose."[45] Thus, God's desire for all to be saved is not mere wishful thinking, but arises from God's purposeful initiation and provision. Peter's language – "you are a chosen people, a royal priesthood, a holy nation, God's special possession" (1 Pet 2:9 NIV) – was addressed to the particular "exiles scattered throughout the provinces of Pontus, Galatia, Cappadocia, Asia and Bithynia" (1:1), and while it was explicitly true for them, it is *provisionally* available for all humanity (Rom 5:17; 1 Cor 15:22).

Second, Rahner posits the ontological significance of the incarnation for the incorporation of all humanity into the purposes of God. In the coming of the God-Man, Jesus Christ, the status of the whole human race has changed because it has a new head – the new Adam. Thus, Rahner argues that the significance of the incarnation is "applicable to the human race as whole."[46]

42. Rahner, vol. 17, 224, 222.

43. Rahner, vol. 17, 40.

44. Rahner, vol. 17, 43.

45. Rahner, vol. 5, 11.

46. Rahner, vol. 5, 15.

He elaborates by saying that in Christ becoming human, we have "an idea of divine humanity."[47]

Third, Rahner reiterates that Christ's death and resurrection brought about "the reconciliation of the world" to God. As such, it is possible to speak of the "union of the spiritual creature . . . with God," and humans can now see themselves as "the *possible* self-expression of God."[48]

Rather than seeing Rahner's insights simply as "philosophical anthropology," it is far more accurate to see them as a theological anthropology, following the patristic idea that since God became man, humans become Godlike. As the Greek theologian, Irenaeus (c. 130–200) writes, "the Word of God was made man, and he who was the son of God became the son of Man, [so] that man [sic], having been taken into the Word, and by receiving adoption, might become the son of God."[49] And later, Augustine (354–430) announces in a sermon: "God wants to make you god – not by nature, as in the case of the One he gave birth to, but by his gift of adoption."[50] The contemporary Eastern Orthodox scholar, Paul Evdokimov (1901–1970) summarizes, "The Father is father without imposing his fatherhood. He offers himself in his Son, and every person is a son of God."[51]

Some people, particularly evangelicals, are concerned that this formulation seems to negate the mission of the church in history, for God has already finished the job, and so all we need to do is await the eschaton! But this flies in the face of the call to be the witnessing and serving community of faith, which is the heartbeat of the NT.[52]

Rahner also believes in the mission of the church. Though God has "done it all" in Christ, the church is still called to mission. How can this be? We might frame the answer to this question as follows: what is *already* true ontologically through the grand redemptive purposes of God in the salvation that Christ pioneered needs to be *existentially appropriated*. This appropriation can take place through the witness of the church by the power of the enlightening Spirit when the church lives as a sign, servant, and sacrament of the kingdom of God

47. Rahner, vol. 5, 13.

48. Rahner, vol. 5, 13, 14, 15 (author's italics).

49. McGinn, *Essential Writings of Mysticism*, 398.

50. McGinn, 401.

51. Evdokimov, *Ages of the Spiritual Life*, 51.

52. For a challenging rendition of the mission of the church in the light of the NT, see Arias, *Announcing the Reign of God*.

and boldly proclaims, "Look, the Lamb of God who takes away the sin of the world!" (John 1:29 NIV).

Rahner emphasizes that the role of the church "is the awakening of something which is already existent through grace."[53] As a result of God's free, redemptive activity, an inner light in the human being is spawned by "God's gratuitous grace,"[54] but humans have yet to become "what they already are."[55]

One way of thinking about this is that the witness and mission of the community of faith is not so much to *bring* the grace of God in Christ to the unchurched person, but rather to *awaken* what God has already placed in "embryonic" form within the human heart. This goes against some general evangelical sensibilities, where the core idea is that one brings the good news of grace into a world that is devoid of God's presence. Such thinking puts pressure on evangelicals to bring the gospel into the great void of the world – or, at worst, to drag a "reluctant" God into the world. Thus, some evangelicals think they are working *for* God rather than *with* God.

Rahner is realistic about the urgent mission of the church as well as the church's own vulnerabilities and weaknesses. Regarding the latter, he calls the church to renew itself constantly through "base communities," which should, first, be formed from below by the people; second, reflect a creative plurality; third, be both Eucharistic and missional. Further, he believes that these communities can sustain all the functions of gospel, sacrament, and service alongside, but in relation to, the institutional church. Such communities can become the carriers of a new evangelization,[56] which will result in a Christianity that "will have a deeper root, be more austere and more concentrated on essentials," and also be more personal and less dependent on institutional realities.[57]

At the same time, he recognizes that this vision is often not the reality in the "holy" church, which is in fact a church of poor sinners.[58] Moreover, he acknowledges that the church (and here he includes himself) is comprised of people who "obscure the light of the gospel by their mediocrity."[59] Thus, Rahner calls us to suffer for the sake of the church, since so many find it hard

53. Rahner, *Theological Investigations*, vol. 17, 231.

54. Rahner, vol. 5, 8.

55. Rahner, vol. 5, 11.

56. Rahner, *The Shape of the Church to Come.*

57. Rahner, *Theological Investigations*, vol. 3, 359.

58. Rahner, vol. 5, 16.

59. Rahner, vol. 5, 17.

"to manage the acceptance of the 'concrete Church.'"[60] He goes on to note that Christians live in a diaspora situation, estranged from family and friends who have abandoned the faith. As a result, "we have to carry the burdens" of those who have strayed, and "more than ever we will be strangers even among those we love."[61] But he goes on to encourage us to be full of "apostolic zeal," to fully appropriate the grace of God in Christ, and to proclaim that people are "saved only through the grace of Christ."[62] He concludes that it is imperative to make "anonymous Christianity" into "explicit Christianity."[63]

In this way, Rahner gives us a theological basis for seeing the hidden face of Christ in the poor (as Mother Teresa emphasized). Yet Rahner makes this even more explicit in his discussion of *caritas*, suggesting that the "love of God and the love of neighbour are one and the same thing."[64] He grounds this statement in Paul's claim that the love of others is the fulfilment of the law (Rom 13:8; see also Matt 25:34–46) and that love is the bond of perfection (Col 3:18). Rahner goes on to refer to John's sweeping claim that only the one who loves the neighbour can see God (1 John 4:20). Finally, Rahner suggests that "God in us" expresses itself in love of brother, sister, neighbour, stranger and that "the love of neighbour . . . is itself an act of this love of God."[65] In making this connection, Rahner is giving us a core theme for a missional spirituality: *If love of God is expressed in love of neighbour, and if love of neighbour is a way of loving God, then spirituality and mission are in "holy" union.*

This excursus of Karl Rahner helps us ground the praxis of Mother Teresa, who models service to the poorest of the poor as service to Christ. This means that our service to the poor is not simply an act of kindness, but rather a fruit of our spirituality, and so service is as much a part of our spirituality as prayer. Thus, when we limit the spiritual practices to prayer, fasting, journaling, reflection, and contemplation, we truncate the Christian life, for our service in and for Christ is also a spiritual practice.

My purpose in this section is not to engage Rahner's theology more broadly, but to highlight his insights as *one way* to ground Mother Teresa's assertion that we are serving Christ when we serve the poor. I would prefer a narrative, Christological approach more than Rahner's ontological orientation,

60. Rahner, vol. 3, 357.

61. Rahner, vol. 3, 357, 358.

62. Rahner, vol. 3, 370, 364.

63. Rahner, vol. 5, 21.

64. Rahner, vol. 6, 233.

65. Rahner, vol. 6, 236.

but Rahner can help us see God's "mark" on humanity as a connecting point for the church's mission to the world.

Barth's Perspective

In writing this book, I have a general Christian audience in view, and yet I am specifically concerned about my "fellow" evangelicals, as I was brought up in the Reformed faith and have worked in evangelical ministries and educational institutions all my life. Obviously, Karl Barth is more aligned with an evangelical perspective than Rahner, but Barth is not saying anything radically different, though he comes to these matters in a different way. Whereas Rahner is more ontological in his theological orientation, having being influenced by Martin Heidegger, Barth's orientation is more exegetical and Christological rather than philosophical.[66]

Barth points out that a person is a Christian when she/he partakes in the life-death-resurrection of Christ. He believes that the "history" of Christ is to become the "history" of each follower of Christ,[67] which has its starting point when a person is called. This calling, the *vocatio interna*, is the work of the Holy Spirit working in and with the *vocatio externa*, the ministry of witness and service.[68]

This work of the Spirit creates a special attachment between Christ and the believer, which Barth describes as *union* with Christ. He describes this union as Christ speaking, acting, and ruling in the life of the Christian, and the Christian responding to Christ and existing *for* and *with* Christ.[69] This profound link between Christ and the disciple is not simply for the benefit of the Christian. Rather, being called to be in and with Christ also "means being given a task."[70] Barth affirms this by saying, "the existence of the Christian is not an end in itself," but rather, "it is in principle and essence [being given] a ministry."[71]

Barth identifies this "task" as participating in the *prophetic* work of Christ, describing this life of witness and service as being an "accompanying and

66. Wood, *Barth's Theology of Interpretation.*
67. Barth, *Church Dogmatics*, vol. 4, part 3.2, 486.
68. Barth, vol. 4, part 3.2, 516.
69. Barth, vol. 4, part 3.2, 547.
70. Barth, vol. 4, part 3.2, 573.
71. Barth, vol. 4, part 3.2, 647–48.

confirming sign of the living word of God."[72] The specific expression of being this sign is to be "the reflection and echo of the prophetic work of Jesus Christ," which involves telling the world through word and deed that "a revolutionary alteration of the whole reality of the world" has taken place through the work of Christ.[73] This radical alteration is Christ becoming the head of the new humanity, the second Adam, taking upon himself the sins of the whole of humanity. As the initiator of the new creation, Christ is bringing in the reign of God, which is the "objective" change of the whole of humanity through Christ's death and resurrection.

Barth describes this reign as Christ living in Christians and non-Christians as the "Mediator, Head, and Representative of all, as the new and true Adam." Thus, in Christ, every person "is justified before God and sanctified for him." For the Christian, this "new and true Adam" has become a reality, whereas for others, it has not.[74] Barth reiterates that what Christ has accomplished in his salvific work "is already the reality of world history," but while the community of faith knows this, the world does not.[75]

Since all are elected for fellowship with Christ,[76] and all are caught up in the new Adam, the task of the church is to *tell* and *show* the world through its worship, proclamation, and service that the whole world is *already* redeemed in Christ. Though existentially lost in alienation and sin, every person is "one . . . [who] is already in process of becoming in virtue of the work and Word of God."[77] Thus every person must be seen as *christianus designatus*, moving from "a potential Christian to an actual" one.[78]

These insights can also help us understand Mother Teresa's dictum to see the hidden face of Christ in the poor. If everyone is already "objectively" in Christ, and thus all are to be designated as Christians, then it is most appropriate to see Christ in the other.

Like Rahner, Barth does not see the church as a wonderful instrument in being the prophetic word of Christ, demonstrating to the world what is already true about its transformation in Christ. Rather, he points out that its "witness has often been muffled and confused" and that the light of Christ "might

72. Barth, vol. 4, part 3.2, 609.
73. Barth, vol. 4, part 3.2, 622.
74. Barth, vol. 4, part 3.2, 604.
75. Barth, vol. 4, part 3.2, 713.
76. Barth, vol. 4, part 3.2, 535.
77. Barth, vol. 4, part 3.2, 810.
78. Barth, vol. 4, part 3.2, 810.

well be distorted . . . and falsified in the hands of the [church] community."[79] Therefore, Barth believes that the church can only fulfil its task towards the world if it is deeply rooted in Christ, if it lives the gospel in the power of the Spirit, and if it seeks to be God's prophetic word. Moreover, the church can only do this well when it embraces its marginal status rather than competing with the world for cultural, economic, and political power.[80]

From here, he goes on to describe what the church's attitude and mission to the world should look like. First, he says that there must be "a genuinely unlimited openness of the called in relation to the uncalled,"[81] which calls the community of faith to exhibit love, patience, and perseverance in its witness and service to and on behalf of others.

Second, he identifies the dialectical tension in which Christians must live out their engagement with society. Because Christians are bound to God and also bound to the neighbour,[82] they are both *for* the world as a healing presence and *over against* the world as a disturbing presence. In bearing the prophetic witness of Christ, they are to upset customs, the state, and particular forms of piety and religiosity.[83]

Third, the church as a faith-community is committed to the kingdom of God, and so it both sees and lives "the antithesis between the rule of God and the confusion of men [humanity]."[84] Thus, the church cannot support the "old man" (Adam as created and fallen) and the old form of the world (the world in idolatrous opposition to the way of God), but must be a reflection of the way of Christ.

Fourth, the church is called to reflect the incarnate Word, Jesus Christ, by living as an incarnational presence in the world. However, the church is not to conform to the way of the world, but to be an *other* presence in society – one that seeks to serve and attest to the Word of God.[85] Barth points out that Christians must see themselves as Christians, first and foremost, "and only then as members of this or that nation . . . participants in the work of this or that . . . society."[86]

79. Barth, vol. 4, part 3.2, 745, 812.
80. Barth, vol. 4, part 3.2, 747.
81. Barth, vol. 4, part 3.2, 494.
82. Barth, vol. 4, part 3.2, 609.
83. Barth, vol. 4, part 3.2, 623.
84. Barth, vol. 4, part 3.2, 716.
85. Barth, vol. 4, part 3.2, 736.
86. Barth, vol. 4, part 3.2, 741.

Barth argues that the church exists for God, and since God exists for the world, the church also exists for the world. Existing for the world means being in solidarity with it rather than conforming to it, which works itself out through our commitment to the world's renewal as we take responsibility for its failings, participate in its sufferings,[87] and cooperate with God by living toward the world that is to come in the light of Christ. Most basically, the church is called into the action of God, directing all that it does *extra muros* (literally, "towards the outskirts"), including its prayer, liturgy, theology, and service.[88] This call is not the task of the solo heroic Christian, but is equally binding on all the members of the faith-community. Although Christians will outwork this calling in different ways, we all have the responsibility for "calling the world to the service of God."[89]

In conclusion, Barth also helps us to see the neighbour with the eyes of faith, as he sees the world encapsulated in the redemptive work of Christ. Thus, the task of the church is to tell the world what is already true about its transfiguration through the death and resurrection of Christ. We can all enter this provision through the work of the Spirit, and so the faith-community must bear witness to this in every possible way.

One important theme in this extended discussion of Mother Teresa, Karl Rahner, and Karl Barth is that we are being invited to see the world and those outside of the community of faith in a new way, namely that "they are already part of us in a particular way." This new seeing is rooted in the all-embracing salvific work of Christ, which needs to become explicit and existential. This new seeing also has implications for spirituality and mission. First, those who do not identify as Christians already have a spirituality, but it is not yet Christologically explicit. Second, the prayer, witness, and service of the faith-community to the world should serve as a mirror, helping everyone see what they need to become in the fuller unfolding of the kingdom of God.

This rather extended discussion helps us clarify how we need to see the other. Rather than seeing the world as completely alienated from God or stubbornly blind and resistant to God's gracious provision, we need to recognize the connection between what God has *already* done in Christ and what God wants *us* to do for the world through our faithful witness and service.

---

87. Barth, vol. 4, part 3.2, 773.

88. Barth, vol. 4, part 3.2, 780.

89. Barth, vol. 4, part 3.2, 794.

Segundo Galilea's Double Movement of Contemplation

Segundo Galilea (1928–2010), a Chilean priest, pastoral worker, and spiritual and missional formator in Latin America, is best known for his integration of liberation theology and spirituality.

P. Pope-Levison gives us a helpful summary of Galilea's emphasis on communicating and demonstrating the good news of salvation through Christ. He identifies this in-breaking of the reign of God as a *first epiphany* that takes place within a person's inner being, an *interior liberation* that reflects the words of Jesus about the kingdom of God being within us, overhauling and reorienting our values, motivations, attitudes, and morals. This inner transformation is a metamorphosis, an ongoing conversion that moves us towards *exterior liberation.* This *second epiphany* involves the revelation of God in the social, economic, and political spheres of life as our interior liberation expresses itself through the transformation of relationships, communities, institutions, and aspects of society.

Galilea describes the process of interior and exterior liberation as *wholistic liberation*, which is initially expressed by serving the poor, since concern for the poor lies at the heart of Christ's compassion and should therefore find expression within the faith-community. Galilea suggests that this wholistic, integrated liberation is accompanied by certain signs. The first sign is the embrace of *evangelical poverty,* which involves freedom from the power of earthly attachments. This gives the community of faith the power to trust in God rather than in its own abilities and resources. As a consequence, the faith-community serves from the periphery of society rather than through centrally located power structures. Galilea offers Mary as an example of the power of service from the periphery.

Galilea identifies the second accompanying sign of wholistic ministry as *contemplative prayer.* In contemplation, we encounter Jesus through the practices of prayer, meditative reading, and reflection, and we also encounter our neighbours through the practices of service and action. This second sign integrates prayer and action, locating the subsequent outworking of prayer as service to the neighbour through political and prophetic action. Because this prayerful action is rooted in the good news of the gospel, it is prophetic; because it seeks to bring about societal transformation, particularly in terms of justice for the poor, it is political.[90]

Pope-Levison's assessment highlights Galilea's emphasis on evangelization, concluding that "Galilea's presentation of evangelization takes into account

90. Pope-Levison, *Evangelization from a Liberation Perspective*, 29–41.

the internal and external, transcendant [sic] and historical, and individual and communal basis [sic] for liberation."[91] Yet in this summary, Pope-Levison has not sufficiently focused on Galilea's integration of spirituality and service, which I describe as a *missional spirituality.*

In the following, I will focus on this emphasis. Galilea begins by pointing out that many Christians are dualistic in their thinking and action, separating prayer from service. He further observes that many Christians doubt the efficacy of prayer. Thus, he points towards an integration of prayer and service, warning that "if there aren't profound motivations and a stable mystique, the commitment will wither."[92] In other words, he argues that a sustaining and relevant spirituality must mark the work of witness and service in the world, particularly in the long journey of bringing shalom and justice to the poor.

In developing this integrated approach, Galilea seeks to overcome the bifurcation of two groups: "religious contemplatives" and "committed militants."[93] Put simplistically in my own words, the first group pray but are not committed to the work of justice, and the second group are concerned about changing the world but don't pray. Of course, this is an over-drawn typification, as many of us seek to be both, but often not in an integrated way. Many of us also fluctuate between seasons of activity and bouts of prayer, thereby lacking a life-sustaining dynamic.

Galilea, however, proposes a *double movement of contemplation*. The first movement is our encounter with Christ himself; the second movement is our encounter with Christ in serving the least (Matt 25:31–46). As Galilea points out, "[b]oth encounters are inseparable."[94] He goes on to highlight how the first movement "underlines the fact that Christianity transcends any temporal reality," and the second movement is "incarnate and inseparable from the love of neighbor."[95] In other words, "[t]he first encounter gives rise to contemplative prayer and the various ways of relating to God" and "the second to a temporal commitment."[96]

Thus, Galilea suggests that contemplation is both transcendental and incarnational. In *transcendence*, we contemplate the face of God through the practices of biblical reflection, prayer, and the disciplines of solitude, meditation,

---

91. Pope-Levison, 36.
92. Galilea, *Following Jesus*, 46.
93. Galilea, 55.
94. Galilea, 59.
95. Galilea, 59.
96. Galilea, 59.

and contemplation. In the movement of *incarnation*, we contemplate the face of Christ in our brothers and sisters in the faith-community and in the face of the neighbour, the poor, the stranger, and even the enemy. Prayer and service are both contemplative experiences.

Janet Ruffing, who writes from the perspective of spiritual direction rather than liberation theology, notes that "during contemplative prayer we find ourselves centered on God's reality instead of our own small egos."[97] This transcendental experience is transformative and extends itself into all "our concrete activity of care and creativity."[98] Andre Louf, who comes from the monastic tradition, notes similarly that both the contemplative and the activist "converge in the interior listening and looking," and these two "paths of believers cannot be opposed, much less [made] mutually exclusive."[99] These diverse voices confirm that Galilea's formulation of a double movement of contemplation resonates within the Christian tradition.

To put this central theme in my own words, when we move towards God, we never come alone, but bring our concerns and our world with us, including our passion for justice. Moreover, when we move towards God in prayer and meditation, God won't leave us on a spiritual "mountaintop," but will draw us towards the world, which God loves and wants to bring to the fullness of redemption. At the same time, whenever we move towards the needs of our neighbour, we are inevitably drawn back towards God in prayer as we seek God's shalom and blessing for them. Thus, *in the contemplation of God, we will come to see the neighbour in need, and in reflection on the neighbour in need, we will be moved to seek the face of God.* This latter movement is especially imperative, because in every form of ministry to others, we quickly realise our inadequacy in the face of so many great needs and our own need for the Spirit's wisdom and empowerment.[100]

Galilea makes a further important and somewhat startling point, noting that the contemplative experience also helps us to temporarily disassociate from the pervasive influence of our culture and society, which he describes as a "purification of cultural deformities."[101] Drawing near to God helps us to see life from a different perspective. As we inhabit the gospel, we see what is

97. Ruffing, *Spiritual Direction*, 108.

98. Ruffing, 108.

99. Louf, *In the School of Contemplation*, 85, 87.

100. Ministry to others is expressing the life of Christ to others through the Spirit. Ministry to others is not sustained by spiritual practices but through the Spirit's empowerment, which includes the way that the Spirit pours out the spiritual gifts, as enumerated in the NT.

101. Galilea, *The Way of Living Faith*, 92.

possible in the kingdom of God, and in that light, we can see the idolatries of our time more clearly. This insight is important for mission and ministry, as our missional task is not world-conforming, but rather world-forming. This focus requires us to go through a process of critical detachment, which is not a reactionary response to societal values, but rather formed by a renewed vision of the reign of God that results in a desire to heal our wounded world.

In this initial movement of disassociation or disconnection through prayer, we turn our face towards God and temporarily turn our backs to the world, which Galilea describes as going into the "desert."[102] This desert experience "transforms contemplatives into prophets and heroes of commitment."[103] Of course, this means that we must make *the return*. We move away from the world to be with God and his gospel, and then we re-engage the world, having heard from God. But we re-enter with a different perspective and possibly a different sense of calling.[104]

This movement of disengagement in order to re-engage is premised on the basic notion that the vision of the reign of God is different than the dominant values of society, even when – in the words of Reformed theology – that society is marked by God's common grace.[105] Since there is both goodness and "worldliness" in our world, which is expressed in various deformities, the Christian community needs to become a discerning community, able to step back in order to evaluate. In this context, the move to withdraw in prayer to listen to God enables us to see more clearly what to celebrate in our world, what to resist, and what to seek to change. And what we seek to change in the world must first be changed in us.

While this may sound counterintuitive, the contemplative may be the true radical in our world. Galilea speaks of the "politico-mystic,"[106] citing Moses as

---

102. Louf speaks of the desert as "a womb where, in the inevitable pangs of birth, a new being comes into light, the new man [sic] created in Jesus Christ in justice and holiness" (*In the School of Contemplation*, 73).

103. Galilea, *Following Jesus*, 63.

104. Rowan Williams makes the point that Christianity opened up a deep questioning about "how things were done" in the world, "the questioning of oneself," sowing "seeds of deep cultural unease," and promoting a "scepticism about existing situations and systems" (*Faith in the Public Square*, 67).

105. G. C. Berkhouwer notes that Abraham Kuyper "viewed common grace not as a power that renewed the heart, but as force that held sin in restraint." Berkhouwer sees common grace as an expression of the long-suffering of God, but this is indissolubly connected to the "call to repentance" (*The Providence of God*, 77).

106. Galilea, *Following Jesus*, 64.

an example,[107] and then describes Jesus's ministry as "pastoral-prophetic."[108] These typifications are clearly suggestive and open to debate, but we will discuss this topic in more detail in chapter 5 ("Mysticism and Mission").[109]

The history of Christianity demonstrates the integral relationship between spirituality and radical activism. As Christopher Rowland generalizes, "[t]he struggle against injustice remains at the heart of those committed to the good news of Jesus Christ, and that means to embark on a course of action, however inadequate it may seem to remedy it."[110] Many members of the community of faith throughout history were both activists and people of prayer: St. John Chrysostom, John Hus, William Wilberforce, Dietrich Bonhoeffer, Simone Weil, Dom Helder Camara, and Archbishop Oscar Romero, among countless others.[111]

St. Bernard of Clairvaux expresses the integration of spirituality and service in most basic terms, speaking of the need for the "healing ointment of devotion" as well as the need to "be nourished in labour with the food of good works."[112] Thus we are not nourished by devotion alone, but also through our service to others. Prayer renews us, and doing deeds of service nurtures us. Both practices will certainly enhance our life!

In conclusion, Segundo Galilea identifies prayer and service and contemplation and action as inter-related dimensions of the Christian life.[113] His notion of the double movement of contemplation is a key concept for a missional spirituality. For Galilea, contemplation is both transcendent and incarnational, drawing us into the love of both God and neighbour. In engaging this Latino scholar and practitioner, we have listened to other confirming voices. In conclusion, the double movement of contemplation is not an oddity

107. For a fully developed OT perspective, see Gorospe, *Narrative and Identity: An Ethical Reading of Exodus 4.*

108. Galilea, *Following Jesus*, 65.

109. For further reading, see Ruffing, *Mysticism and Social Transformation*; Soelle, *The Silent Cry*; Woods, *Mysticism and Prophecy.*

110. Rowland, *Radical Christianity*, 161.

111. See Ruffing, *Mysticism and Social Transformation*; Soelle, *The Silent Cry*; Woods, *Mysticism and Prophecy.*

112. Butler, *Western Mysticism*, 99.

113. This emphasis is supported by other liberation theologians. Sobrino writes: "The contemplation of God is simultaneously a contemplation of the world with God's eyes." And: "God and world alike are both the object of contemplation and of action." He continues: "a spiritual person is someone who sees the poor with God's eyes and deals with them as God does" (*Spirituality of Liberation*, 68–69).

from liberation spirituality, but may well lie at the heart of the Christian tradition.[114]

David Augsburger's Anabaptist Tripolar Spirituality

The Anabaptists, as a diverse movement, constituted the radical wing of the Reformation. This movement has been subjected to many differing interpretations, ranging from a proto-fundamentalist movement (John Horsch), a new vision of church and following Jesus (Harold Bender), a vanguard movement of the separation of church and state (C. Henry Smith), a prophetic counter-community (John Howard Yoder), and a distinct form of Christianity that is neither Roman Catholic nor Protestant (Walter Klassen).[115]

Walter Klassen's articulation identifies the following distinctive characteristics within the Anabaptist movement. First, it proposes a different spirituality that is based on living the Sermon on the Mount. Second, it offers a different ecclesiology, where the church-community is committed to mutual sharing. Third, it has a different understanding of discipleship based on following the suffering Christ into the world. Fourth, it proposes a different relationship to the world, where the community lives as a prophetic challenge to the world and refuses to be involved in managing society.[116]

This suggests that Anabaptists have a distinctive contribution, not only in the domain of ecclesiology, but also in the areas of spirituality[117] and mission.[118] Their missiology comes out of a communal vision of the body of Christ and is a subversive form of evangelization, which is expressed by being a counter-community that calls into question the dominant ethos of contemporary culture.[119] In this sense, Anabaptist mission is prophetic, demonstrating a whole new way to live within our consumer society.

Anabaptist spirituality is also profoundly Christological, as it is committed to following the suffering and wounded Messiah into the world. This commitment is based on the core concept of *Gelassenheit*,[120] which means "the

114. For a fuller discussion, see chapter 15 ("Liberation Theology: *A Spirituality and Praxis of Serving the Poor*").

115. See Weaver, *Becoming Anabaptist.*

116. Klaassen, *Anabaptism.*

117. Snyder, *Following in the Footsteps.*

118. Shenk, ed., *Anabaptism and Mission*; *The Transfiguration of Mission.*

119. Shenk, ed., *The Transfiguration of Mission*, 199–219.

120. A German word that was used in the mystical tradition to connote tranquil submission to the will of God.

readiness to yield one's life for Christ's sake."[121] This posture of yielding includes submission to the faith-community, resistance to the use of violence,[122] and the willingness to be sent into a hostile world and embrace a martyr's death.

Within this broad introductory frame, Augsburger's model of tripolar spirituality[123] can be distinguished from two other spiritualities. The first, monopolar spirituality, is purely inner-directed, which he defines as an "inner, subjective encounter with one's own inner universal self."[124] The second, bipolar spirituality, is inner-directed and oriented towards God, which he defines as an "inner, subjective experience of coming to know one's true self and an objective experience of existence before God."[125] Leaving to one side the problematical nature of his ideas about a "universal self" and "objective experience," we will discuss his model of tripolar spirituality. First, tripolar spirituality is inwardly directed, focusing on the journey of personal transformation. Second, it is upwardly compliant, highlighting the experience of having an encounter with God. And third, it is outwardly committed, emphasizing the relationship between integrity and solidarity with the neighbour.[126]

For Augsburger, these three dimensions are not consequential, in that one comes first and the others follow. This immediately removes the pressing question about why the experience of a divine encounter with God is not identified first (as I think it should be). Rather, he proposes that these three dimensions are always inter-dynamically related, and so one dimension is not fully valid without the others. Augsburger outlines their interdependency in the following three-step model. In the first step, the love of God transcends and transforms love of self. In the second step, the love of God and love of neighbour become one. In the third step, the love of neighbour and love of self, become one.[127] He concludes by observing that "[t]he Anabaptist form of tripolar spirituality is not the ordinary quest spirituality of individual discipline and discovery, but a communal spirituality of disciples . . . following a cluster of practices," which he identifies as "radical attachment, stubborn loyalty,

121. Snyder, *Following in the Footsteps*, 164.

122. See Ringma, "Franciscan Peacemaking."

123. There are others who also use a tripolar framework. Donal Dorr, using Micah 6:8 as key, identifies "structural justice," "interpersonal respect," and "personal responsibility and integrity" as three interlocking circles that reflect a "holistic spirituality" (*Integral Spirituality*, 1–2).

124. Augsburger, *Dissident Discipleship*, 11.

125. Augsburger, 12.

126. Augsburger, 13.

127. Augsburger, 13.

tenacious serenity, habitual humility, resolute nonviolence, concrete service, and authentic witness."[128]

I will discuss the details of this rather distinctive set of practices later,[129] but I am introducing Augsburger's tripolar spirituality here as a model of missional spirituality. While the practices that Augsburger identifies are classical Anabaptist concepts, the model of tripolar spirituality is "neither the invention nor the property of any one Christian group,"[130] for it shares similarities with those discussed above.[131]

Conclusion

In this chapter, I have highlighted a number of different but related models that are significant for understanding missional spirituality, though the authors did not set out to characterize them as such. These models demonstrate how the various dimensions of love of God and love of neighbour, spirituality and service, contemplation and action, prayer and the work for justice all belong together in a beautiful and dynamic mosaic.[132] Thus we can't engage Christ – who gave his life for the world – in the Eucharist without also seeing and engaging the hidden Christ in the face of the poor. And we can't embrace a transcendent spirituality that leads to attentiveness and worship without also embracing an incarnational spirituality that expresses itself in witness and service.

The logic of these models suggests that both prayer and service are life-sustaining, and we can't have one without the other. We pray in both contemplation and service. We are blessed in both service and solitude. We serve through both worship and the work of justice. Love of God and love of neighbour are one in Christ, who is the great bridge builder. At this point, we have only begun to explore the nature of missional spirituality. In chapter 3, we will explore some important *theological themes* that will further give shape to the richness and scope of this spirituality. Later in the book, we will return to some of these themes in more extended ways.

---

128. Augsburger, 20.

129. See chapter 13 ("The Anabaptist Vision of Community, Discipleship, and Service").

130. Augsburger, *Dissident Discipleship*, 19.

131. For a fuller discussion of Anabaptist missional spirituality, see chapter 13 ("The Anabaptist Vision of Community, Discipleship, and Service").

132. This notion fits with Trinitarian theology, which emphasizes that each member of the Trinity is wholly involved in the work of the other. Thus, creation includes the work of Christ and the Spirit, and is not the sole domain of the Father. Similarly, the work of redemption involves the Father and the Spirit.

3

Key Theological Themes

Introduction

This chapter engages many of the major themes of Christian theology to illustrate their relevance for missional spirituality. Returning to the earlier analogy, this chapter adds colour, depth, and more distinctive contours to the painting outlined in chapter 2. I trust it will give you a much deeper understanding of the richness of God's redemptive and restorative work and how that impacts us and calls us into the wonderful task of joining in God's purposes for renewing our world.

Some Personal Reflections

In chapter 2, I noted the importance of integrating the head, heart, and hand in living the Christian life. I also noted that we often don't do this integration well, since there is generally so much to do that prayer, reflection, and contemplation take the backseat – and may even disappear altogether in particular phases of our lives.

In the long journey of Christian service, I have been involved in far more planning meetings than prayer meetings. When prayer did take place, it was usually formulaic – a token move to open and close the meeting – and was more about confirming what we had in mind than seeking the direction of the Spirit. Though I have always found this unsatisfactory, prayer has never been easy for me, but has always been (and probably will continue to be) a challenge.[1]

1. There are multiple factors at play here. First, we tend to think that so much depends on us and our activities. Second, we are not altogether sure about God's intervention in human affairs, which reinforces the idea that we better do something in case God does not. Third,

Yet I have been greatly blessed in that very early in life, when I was barely twenty, I undertook seminary training. Upon completing this training and formation, instead of serving in the church, I began working on the streets of Brisbane as a detached street worker. In the early stages, I used to wonder – and sometimes complain – that my theological training was hardly relevant for the work I was doing. But as time went on, I became increasingly grateful, as I could see how my theological studies had provided a framework for my life, thinking, action, and spirituality.[2]

In this chapter, we will explore some key theological themes for a missional spirituality and how these themes can provide a framework for our thinking, praying, acting, and living in the world. While I have attempted to arrange these themes somewhat systematically, this order is not hierarchical, nor does one theme necessarily follow another. Moreover, I have gleaned these themes from reflection more than reading, and so they are suggestive rather than definitive. I have identified these key themes as follows: Trinitarian spirituality, incarnational spirituality, kenotic spirituality, communal spirituality, welcoming spirituality, spirituality of the Exodus, "reverse" spirituality, prophetic spirituality, contemplative spirituality, spirituality of the dark night, and spirituality of hope.[3]

Trinitarian Spirituality

Mainstream Protestant spirituality is fundamentally Christological[4] in its orientation, emphasizing the in-Christ relationship, the call to follow Jesus in

---

prayer is often seen as self-therapy, with little significance for the bigger dimensions of our social existence and engagement. And finally, prayer often feels like a waste of time.

2. The evangelical theologian, Donald Bloesch, speaks of the need for a "holy worldliness" that is "separated from the idolatries of the world" and of sculpting an "inner-worldly asceticism" that expresses itself in "self-mastery for the sake of service to God and our neighbor" (*Spirituality Old and New*, 92, 93).

3. In *Comprehending Mission*, Stanley Skreslet sets out the themes of pilgrimage, spiritual warfare, hospitality, and vulnerability (181–86). These themes are more practical, whereas mine are theological-practical.

4. In Sheldrake's discussion of Protestant and Roman Catholic spiritualities, he notes the following emphasis in the Protestant tradition: "the depravity of the human will, confronted by the unconditional love of God, are the two vital elements which enable us to understand Reformation spirituality." Then he links this to four key themes: "grace alone, faith alone, Christ alone, and Scripture alone" (*Spirituality and History*, 210). Clearly, this is Christo-centric. In Lovelace's discussion of evangelical spirituality, in contrast with Roman Catholic themes, he notes that "the genius of Reformation spirituality" is that "the simplest believer leaps to the top of the spiritual ladder simply by realistic faith in Christ." He goes on to note that "union with Christ, received by faith, is the foundation of evangelical spirituality, not the final achievement"

a life of obedience, and the challenge to be like Jesus in his life of service and prayer. Thus, we focus on being like Jesus in his ministry of proclamation, healing, pushing back the powers of darkness, serving the poor, and challenging the religious establishment, and we also emphasize his love relationship with the Father, his life of prayer and reflection, and his service in the power of the Spirit.[5]

These opening comments draw us into the *perichoresis* of Father, Son, and Holy Spirit, highlighting that any missional spirituality will be Trinitarian in its most basic orientation and will involve the good gifts of God's creation, the healing and restoring work of Christ, and the mysterious yet beautifying and empowering work of the Spirit. And so, creational care, redemptive healing, and both personal and institutional renewal are all part of our calling to serve God, who is Father, Son, and Holy Spirit.

But a Trinitarian missional spirituality does not start with what *we* do in terms of service, but with *who* God is, what God has done for us, and God's calling for our lives. Simply put, this Trinitarian God has unfolded the fullness of life towards all that has been called into being – the whole creation, including humanity – and will ultimately restore all things into the fullness of God's very being.

At the same time, humanity is called into a *relational union* with this Trinitarian God. Not only is God fundamental to our being, but we are called into a joyful love relationship. Most basically, becoming a Christian is not simply believing in Jesus, but being invited into the love, care, and mutuality of the Trinity – Father, Son, and Holy Spirit. Our greatest homecoming in this life[6] is to be welcomed home to God, who is both communion and community,[7] and this homecoming shapes our life, relationships, spiritual practices, and service to the world.

Many implications can be drawn from this joyful reality. First, the church is to be an icon of the Trinity,[8] which means that the people of faith gather for worship, teaching, sacrament, fellowship, and service in the joy of being

---

(quoted in Collins, *Exploring Christian Spirituality*, 216). While some of this language is not helpful, the Christological emphasis is noticeable.

5. See further discussion in chapter 4 ("Contemplation in a World of Action").

6. Ringma and Dickau point out that the greatest healing is "the spiritual restoration of our relationship with God." They continue: "This work of grace in Christ through the Spirit overcomes our alienation and brings us into a dynamic relationship with the Trinity" (*The Art of Healing Prayer*, 5).

7. Zizioulas, *Being as Communion*.

8. Volf, *After Our Likeness*.

in relationship with the Father, Son, and Holy Spirit. Moreover, the church is, first and foremost, a communion of persons in and through Christ rather than an institution.[9]

A second implication of our Trinitarian identity is that welcome, cooperation, and partnership should characterize our Christian presence in the world. Thus embrace – rather than exclusion – should mark our attitude toward others.[10] As Leonardo Boff points out, "the community of Father, Son, and Holy Spirit becomes the prototype of the human community dreamed of by those who wish to improve society and build it in such a way as to make it in the image and likeness of the Trinity."[11] This integral way of being and acting in the world reflects the life of the Trinity and invites us toward grassroots ecumenism and common strategies.

Third, the Trinitarian nature of God means that the church can be structured as a unity in diversity, which we can see in Christian families, the parish church, and forms of intentional Christian community.[12] Yet this formulation does not suggest that other forms of Christian organizing and institution-building are devoid of a Trinitarian vision. Rather, all the various modalities of corporate life in Christ through the Spirit are complimentary and reinforce one another.

Fourth, as an icon of the Trinity, the church is sent into the world by the Father and Son through the power of the life-giving Spirit, whose work is to bring Christ home to us in the very depth of our being, to bring the gospel to us as a living word, to form Christ's ways in the fabric and shape of our lives, and to empower us through our witness and service so that God's kingdom will blossom and flourish in the wider community. In light of this, the church is called to be creational, redemptive, renewing, and beautifying. As such, any ministry must be concerned with earth-care,[13] practice the reconciling and healing mission of Jesus,[14] and be empowered by the Spirit.[15]

---

9. Dulles notes: "the Church is not primarily [an] institution." He does, however, acknowledge that it has an institutional dimension, but this "should not be treated as primary." He believes that the church should fundamentally be seen as a "community of disciples" and as a "contrast society" (*Models of the Church*, 45, 205, 222).

10. Volf, *Exclusion and Embrace.*

11. Boff, *Trinity and Society*, 7.

12. Boff argues that the Trinitarian vision is most fully expressed "in religious orders" (*Holy Trinity*, xiii), but this, of course, is an overstatement. Wherever Christians express communion and community in Christ, a Trinitarian vision is operative.

13. Bouma-Prediger, *For the Beauty of the Earth.*

14. Gill, *Life on the Road.*

15. Suurmond, *Word and Spirit at Play.*

Finally, the kind of world that we are seeking to "build"[16] does not celebrate hierarchy but communion. If God were a mono-being, then we could easily conceive of a hierarchy with God in the heavens, the king on earth, the pope over the church, and the husband over the wife – as has been the case in much of the history of the Christian church.[17] Instead, the image of the Trinity conveys the beauty of mutuality. Boff uses the language of ecstasy to describe this communion, where we participate in "the celestial dance of the freed, the banquet of sons and daughters in the homeland and household of the Trinity."[18]

Thus, a Trinitarian theology helps us see the community of faith as diverse and mutually edifying, our ministry as comprehensive and inter-related, and our spirituality as rooted in Christ and empowered by the Spirit to the glory of God.[19]

Incarnational Spirituality

Within the Protestant tradition, the topic of mission and spirituality typically begins with the incarnation of Jesus and then immediately draws implications between the *imitatio Christi* and God's redemptive activity in the world. Yet this quick and simplistic move may leave us with a reductionistic understanding of incarnational spirituality, where we focus on emulating the *works* of Jesus alone. There is so much more to the biblical story!

Our key theological starting point does not begin with Christmas but in the very beginning of the biblical narrative, with the revelational God of Scripture, who creates the universe and world, acts into history, and is present with his people in a variety of ways. Though God's revelation comes to a fuller and more foundational expression in the Christ-child, its fullest expression will be in the new heavens and earth, when the glory of God will be fully revealed.[20]

16. We often use the language of "building." We talk of building faith-communities or the church. We also speak of building the kingdom of God. At this point, we need to be most careful. These are not our self-made projects, but the activities of God in relation to our participation, for good or ill. We can both further or harm God's activity in the world. But we are not the genesis of godly activity. We are participants in God's action.

17. Boff, *Trinity and Society*, 152.

18. Boff, 231.

19. Kallistos Ware makes the helpful and surprising observation that there is a "connection between our love for one another and our faith in the Trinity," resulting in "living sacrificially for the other" and struggling "against all forms of oppression, injustice, and exploitation" (*The Orthodox Way*, 49). This reflects the trialectic theme we are emphasising: God, self, and others.

20. Middleton, *A New Heaven, New Earth*.

The revelational God of the biblical story continually moves outward, from the fullness of who God is, to call all things into being and to be present in the world. Thus, God is both *beyond* this world, upholding all by divine power, and at the same time *in* the world and *in* sustaining all things. In the ancient biblical world, Yahweh embodied the sacred spaces of the tabernacle, temple, and Israel's feasts and celebrations. Through the roles of priest, prophet, and king, Yahweh sought to be present and accessible to his people. Yet however we might attempt to make sense of the presence of God in the world,[21] we must also bow before God's mystery and incomprehensibility.[22] For our so-called "knowability" of God may not lead us to worship, nor to obedience, but to the boring plateau of dull certainty or "domestication."[23] As Karl Barth puts it, God is both "wholly Other" and "wholly concerned," an acknowledgement that honours God's transcendence as well as God's immanence. Such an admission keeps us within the domain of paradox rather than predictability, prompting us to keep seeking the One we already know.[24]

In order to welcome all people and all things into the fullness of who God is, God draws near to us, speaks to us, and remains present with us, making himself known to us and imparting himself to others. This comes to astounding expression in Christ, the Word made flesh (John 1:14), who is the representation of God's very being, was with God from the very beginning (John 1:2), and is the culmination of God's self-giving love (Heb 1:3) for the whole world (John 1:4).[25] Hildegard of Bingen celebrates the incarnation in her *Symphonia*: "He delivered all things by his incarnation, whom God breathed forth without the chains of sin. In doing so, he cleansed and freed us from the greatest suffering."[26] And Gregory of Nazianzus, in his *Festal Orations*, casts the incarnation in terms of a great festival: "This is our festival, this is the feast we

---

21. McGinn, *The Presence of God.*

22. Meister Eckhart makes the paradoxical statement: "the more one seeks Thee, the less one can find Thee" (quoted in Ringma, *Hear the Ancient Wisdom*, 141).

23. Kierkegaard is reported to have made the statement: "Jesus turned water into wine, the church turns wine into water." In his *Attack Upon "Christendom"* he makes a similar statement: "the human race in the course of time has taken the liberty of softening . . . Christianity until, at last, we have contrived to make it exactly the opposite of what it is in the New Testament" (39).

24. Kallistos Ware makes the point that God is "not so much the object of our knowledge, as the cause of our wonder," and God's presence is both "hidden and revealed" (*The Orthodox Way*, 16, 18).

25. Schmemann, *For the Life of the World.*

26. Quoted in Ringma and Alexander, *Of Martyrs*, 117.

celebrate . . . in which God comes to live with human beings." Thus, we "[lay] aside the old human being, so we may live in Christ."[27]

As the people of God live in Christ (Eph 3:16–17), the faith-community embodies a secondary "incarnation,"[28] thereby becoming the body of Christ (1 Cor 12:27) so that the whole world might come to know the life-giving Son (John 1:12–13). In Orthodox theology, Christ is described as "the medicine of new life for us." Thus, salvation is not only a "forensic transaction that changes our *legal status* before God, but also a transformation of our *very being* . . . [so that we can] share in God's own Triune life."[29]

Just as Christ's incarnation upholds the mystery of his being both Son of God and Son of Man, the church embodies that mystery by living as both an institution and as the sacramental people of God through the Spirit. And just as Christ was a radical "other" in his culture[30] – neither priest, Pharisee, Essene, or political radical – the community of faith is called to live as a radical "other" in society. One of the marks of this "otherness" is radical inclusion and hospitality. Paul spells this out repeatedly, identifying the body of Christ as a place of welcome for Jews and Gentiles, slaves and free, women and men, rich or poor (1 Cor 12:13; Eph 2:19; Gal 3:28). Dietrich Bonhoeffer gives this a specific missional orientation in his recognition of "Christ as the Man for others,"[31] seeing his focus on "others" as a confirmation that *all* can come into the fullness of God's life.

Such an incarnational spirituality has many implications for those who follow the way of Christ. First, we are called to embody the basic movement of God, who moves from hiddenness toward activity, visibility, and presence. In other words, God unfolds himself/herself into the world.[32] We see the self-giving nature of God most clearly in the coming of the Messiah, who gives

---

27. Quoted in Ringma and Alexander, 387.

28. Karl Rahner makes the point that the church is a "'sacrament' of the kingdom for the world" and points out the danger of a "radical horizontalism," which reduces the gospel to secular meaning and an equally unhelpful "verticalism," where everything is spiritualized. Instead, he proposes that we need to be empowered by an "incarnational understanding of grace and salvation" (Dych, *Karl Rahner*, 105, 111).

29. Vigen Gurion, *The Melody of Faith*, 53 (author's emphasis).

30. Hans Kung describes this radical otherness as the fifth option man in *On Being a Christian*.

31. Bonhoeffer writes: "The experience that a transformation of all human life is given in the fact that 'Jesus is there only for others'" (*Letters and Papers from Prison*, 381).

32. Karl Rahner notes that grace has an "incarnational structure" in that it "descends into the world, but not to make the world unreal," but more real in terms of its God ordained purpose (Dych, *Karl Rahner*, 109).

himself for the light and life of the world. Similarly, incarnational spirituality calls us to give ourselves to others by being present to them. Second, Christ unfolds his life into us through the Holy Spirit. While we may want to give this or that to others, we are most basically called to give Christ to the world. His life in us is to be unfolded in others – not through coercion, but through the winsome movement of the Spirit, who brings about a synchronicity between human desire and God's purposes. Third, the Christ that we unfold into the world is neither anorexic nor self-made, but the Christ of proclamation and healing. This suffering and glorified Christ, who is both contemplative and activist,[33] is the head of the new humanity and the new creation rather than a popularized Christ of convenience.[34] Fourth, the embodiment of Christ in the faith-community suggests a whole *way* of life that is embraced by a people who are both gathered and scattered as they engage in prayer, play, and service.

This grand vision of living as a secondary incarnation of Christ is particularly challenging for our modern, nomadic world,[35] because it invites us into the pain and possibility of *particularity*.[36] When we are always ready to move to something bigger and better, to live everywhere and do everything,[37] we undermine our sacramental presence in the world. Thus, incarnational spirituality calls us to discern God's calling, to leave and go, to commit to inhabit and serve in a particular place in particular ways as we accompany a

33. See chapter 4 ("Contemplation in a World of Action") for a further development of this theme.

34. Vigen Gurion points out that "the Resurrection – not the Crucifixion – completes the purpose of the Incarnation." The Resurrection, he points out, "is the power of the Cross" (*The Melody of Faith*, 94, 97).

35. Wiesel is quoted as describing our modern world as "the age of the expatriate, the refugee, the stateless and the wanderer" (quoted in Bouma-Prediger and Walsh, *Beyond Homelessness*, 7).

36. There is something fascinating about this commitment to particularity. It can be the eventual move to generality. A specific ministry learned well in the slums of Manila may become a model for ministry elsewhere. The Jesus Movement as a renewal movement in Judaism becomes, in time, a global religion. The poet Rainer Rilke alludes to this, saying, "*Ich lebe mein Leben in wachsenden Ringen*" ("I live my life in widening circles") in *The Poetry of Rilke* (6–7). And everywhere there are the examples of ministries that started so small and have become global. Mother Teresa's missional order is but one contemporary example. The role of the desert fathers and mothers in the formation of Monasticism is a much older example.

37. In *Seeking God*, de Waal observes that "we are pulled apart by so many conflicting demands . . . that it often seems that the centre [of our lives] cannot hold." In commending the discipline of the Benedictine vow of stability, she notes that this allows us to "confront the basic questions of life" and to "know our true selves," because "without roots we can neither discover where we belong, nor can we grow" (56–57).

particular people. In the words of Eugene Peterson, if Christ "moved into the neighborhood,"[38] then we should as well.

One example of an incarnational spirituality is Ignatian spirituality. Its core concept, *in actione contemplativa*, combines prayer and action and focusses on discerning and participating in God's immanent activity in the world. George Lane notes that this leads us to collaborate with God, the Worker, and to participate in the great deeds that God does in the world.[39] Lane formulates the ideal of this spirituality, saying that "to find God's will is to find God, and to do God's will, even in total activity, is to be totally united with God."[40] This implies that both activity and prayer are part of our spirituality, and we need to contemplate both God and God's world. More contemporary Protestant and evangelical groups, such as Servants to Asia's Urban Poor[41] and Urban Neighbourhoods of Hope (UNOH),[42] attempt to live as an embodied presence in the slums of major Asian cities, and the New Monastic[43] movement seeks to live incarnationally within Western contexts. Yet this call to commit to particularity is a call for the church as a whole, not only a few special Christian groups.[44]

To conclude, an incarnational spirituality beckons us to be in Christ and like Christ as a second incarnation, calling us from the ideal world into the real world, from the universal world into the particularity of place. An incarnational spirituality also calls us to embrace the "death" of our ever-expanding egos and messianic notions,[45] inviting us to serve in our places over the long haul rather than looking for quick fixes and short-term gains.[46] We will need to experience a profound conversion, since we can no longer look for greener

38. Peterson, *The Message*, 1916.

39. Lane, *Christian Spirituality: An Historical Sketch*, 47–48.

40. Lane, 46–47.

41. Craig, *Servants Among the Poor.*

42. Barker, *Slum Life Rising.*

43. See Adam, *Cave, Refectory, Road*; Wilson-Hartgrove, *New Monasticism.*

44. One inspiring example is Grandview Calvary Baptist church in Vancouver, Canada, which has modelled this ideal for over twenty years (see Dickau, *Plunging into the Kingdom Way*).

45. Jon Sobrino stresses that "*evangelizers must recapitulate Jesus' own incarnation*" and "become, in a limited way, what Jesus became in an unlimited way" (*Spirituality of Liberation*, 136, 139, author's emphasis). This involves not only the call "in order . . . to give life, one must give of one's life," but that one may "even give one's life" through martyrdom (*Spirituality of Liberation*, 93). Both liberation theologians and Anabaptists experienced this call to martyrdom.

46. Andrew Goddard notes that for Jacques Ellul, being a Christian is "to be a faithful witness," which "must be lived out in the world for 'God became incarnate – it is not for us to undo his work'" (*Living the Word, Resisting the World*, 106).

pastures elsewhere, but must willingly embrace where we are, with all its pains and possibilities. Of course, the greatest possibilities are those which come through the fires of disappointment and difficulty, for the paschal mystery is at the core of a missional spirituality.

However, it is a profound misunderstanding to conclude that this calls us to stay put permanently, for the church is not called to group introversion. A commitment to neighbourhood on the part of a faith-community will mean that some will hear the call to move elsewhere, for the church is both an *embodied community* in a particular place as well as a *pilgrim community* on the road. Thus, there will always be "sent ones," who are called by the Spirit to embed themselves in other places. Yet there is a world of difference between a restless, nomadic lifestyle, where we are always searching for something better, and being sent by our church to relocate for the purposes of God in restoring the world. There is also a world of difference between becoming part of a neighbourhood to live as the servants of Christ in that place (while remaining open to be sent by the faith-community elsewhere in the future) rather than never rooting ourselves anywhere at all and always looking to be somewhere else.

Kenotic Spirituality

As we have already noted, spirituality in our contemporary world can mean almost anything, and the main concern is often with self-actualization. Christian spirituality, on the other hand, has to do with living the whole contour and shape of one's life in Christ through the Spirit. Thus, Christ is both existential and normative, which means that we live both *in* Christ and *for* Christ.[47] On this faith journey, our life *in* Christ must remain foundational so that it does not get lost in how we live *for* Christ. Simply put, our focus is not on *doing* something like Christ, but rather dwelling *in* Christ and thus becoming *like* Christ in our words and actions. As a consequence, our life, in the words of Karl Barth, is to be a small repetition of the life of Christ, where Christ is the great light, and we are "little lights."[48]

47. The songwriter Leonard Cohen, in his poem "There For You," writes: "I see my life / In full review / It was never me / It was always you" (*Book of Longing*, 201). While certainly not referring to living for Christ, Cohen does capture the sense of living *for* someone else.

48. Barth writes: "He himself [Christ] is the new event, the great light of hope that has already come and will come again after having shined provisionally in these little lights [Christians]" (*Evangelical Theology*, 70).

Kenosis refers to the self-emptying by Christ of godly power and privilege to live amongst us as a suffering servant in the power of the Spirit,[49] both in obedience to the Father (John 5:19) and as the revelation of the Father (John 12:45). As the gospel writers remind us, Christ could have come in a different way (Matt 26:53; Mark 14:62; Luke 22:24–30), yet rather than coming with a conquering sword, he came with the towel of a servant in his hand (John 13). The Christological hymn in Philippians 2 highlights this theme and outlines a pattern for how we are called to live in the world as we seek to follow Christ.

Yet in the long history of the Christian church, this way of following Jesus has not always been understood. With Constantine, the church sought to be powerful rather than living as the servant church in the world.[50] While this might make strategic sense, since those who are more powerful can theoretically use that power to benefit others, the reality is that by the time most people gain such power, they typically forget that it was supposed to be used to help others.

The theme of kenosis is significant for our theological and missional understanding,[51] as we are called to imitate Christ in this way as we carry out our mission and ministry. While we may be eager to follow the triumphant Christ into the world to achieve success, we are called to follow the servant Christ, and this path often leads us to suffer with and for others. Rather than being rational, straightforward, and programmatic, the Christian faith is paradoxical, counterintuitive, mysterious, and countercultural. Like leaven in a bowl of flour and water, its power works in hidden ways.

Yet kenotic spirituality can easily be misunderstood as an embrace of powerlessness, which can lead to ineffectiveness or a non-interventionist approach to life. But Jesus did not become *ineffective* by his obedience to a death on the cross (Phil 2:8). Rather, he demonstrated the power of suffering for and on behalf of others[52] – a suffering that brought life for the world[53]

---

49. In the Daily Office of Morning Prayer, we find the words, "lowly and meek, yet all-powerful," in reference to Christ (*Celtic Daily Prayer: Book Two*, 867).

50. Guder, *The Continuing Conversion*, 113. Huebner, drawing on the writings of Yoder, notes that "Constantinianism represents a fusion of church and state, clergy and emperor, Bible and sword, God and civil authorities" (*A Precarious Peace*, 58).

51. Nietzsche describes living "for the glory of God" and "for the salvation of the soul" as a "tyranny" and a "rigorous and grandiose stupidity" (*Beyond Good and Evil*, 101). He, of course, argues for self-assertion and the will to power as the authentic way to live. For him, anything other than that is a slave mentality.

52. Prior, *Jesus and Power.*

53. Vigen Gurion notes that a "mortally wounded humanity needs to be 'sanctified by the Humanity of God' in order to be restored to wholeness and perfected in God's true likeness" (*The Melody of Faith*, 49).

and led to his own resurrection. Paul understood this well and speaks of a desire "to know Christ and the power of his resurrection and the sharing of his sufferings" (Phil 3:10).

A second misunderstanding is to interpret kenotic spirituality as a form of negation instead of a decision to surrender to God and give ourselves to others. As we devote ourselves to the wisdom and purposes of God, we will become willing to make sacrifices for others.

Two major themes stand out in this regard. First, we need to be willing to embrace downward mobility for the sake of the gospel. Instead of seeking the power of ascendency, we are invited to embrace the *power of descent*. This might call us to lay aside our career path, plans for the future, or programs in order to walk a different road. The life of Henri Nouwen illustrates this path of moving from prestige to servanthood, as he left his work in academia to become a helper in the L'Arche Daybreak community in Toronto to work with persons with physical and intellectual disabilities.[54] In Nouwen's subsequent writings, we see some of the fruit that this move produced in his own life and within others. Many other Christians have made a similar journey, responding to God's call to leave their comfortable homes to embrace a different way of life for the sake of the gospel. The liberation theologians[55] have described this as the way of "evangelical poverty."[56]

Second, we may be called to a spirituality of asceticism.[57] While we may readily think that *fullness* is the most productive space for servanthood and ministry, kenotic spirituality involves ascetic practices, suggesting that places of *emptiness* are essential to our work of mission and ministry. This is counterintuitive, as we often think we need to be busy and productive in order to be effective, but we can't afford to neglect Sabbath, prayer, and staring out of the window and dreaming if we wish to be fruitful for the kingdom of God. Throughout the history of Christian spirituality, "the desert" plays an important part both in the quest to seek the face of God as well as the journey towards

54. Nouwen, *The Road to Daybreak*; Ford, *Wounded Prophet*, 149–56.

55. For a fuller discussion, see chapter 15 ("Liberation Theology: A Spirituality and Praxis of Serving the Poor").

56. Gutierrez describes "evangelical poverty" as living in "solidarity" with the poor, of "identification with . . . [their] interests," and making a "critique within a liberation praxis" of all that oppresses the poor (*The Power of the Poor in History*, 55).

57. For a fuller discussion, see chapter 16 ("Asceticism: Theological, Spiritual, and Missional Perspectives").

service. Simply put, by going through the "eye of the desert,"[58] we may gain a new vision of God, ourselves, and our calling in life.

Communal Spirituality

As Westerners, we tend to have little insight regarding the way in which our reading of Scripture, our way of doing theology, and much of our ministry has been shaped by Western cultural values. We seriously delude ourselves when we think that what we do is only shaped by the gospel. Usually, the "scales" fall from our eyes when we are immersed in another culture and begin to read the biblical narrative with very different "glasses." This terse observation highlights the great value in cross-cultural experiences. While a mono-cultural person is grounded in a particular place, a cross-cultural person has the opportunity to expand his/her horizons, grow in appreciating a different culture, and gain a more critical perspective regarding one's own culture.

Westerners have been particularly "blind" in their missional strategies, often celebrating the missionary as a solo hero.[59] This is a Christian variant to the cultural hero of USA society, with a lone ranger cowboy,[60] detective,[61] or superman (among many others) single-handedly fighting an enemy against all odds.[62] On this theme, culture has trumped theology, and so the contemporary church often fails to reflect a corporate identity. Yet Christian spirituality is fundamentally communal,[63] formed by the people of God through worship, prayer, and service – and thus any missional activity should be impregnated by that communal spirituality.[64]

A communal spirituality involves cooperating with the Trinity – Father, Son, and Holy Spirit – in renewing and healing the whole creation. Such a

58. See the life and ministry of Charles de Foucauld in Jones et al., eds., *The Study of Spirituality*, 419–23.

59. Think of the ways we speak of William Carey, David Livingstone, or Adoniram Judson.

60. See Clint Eastwood in the movie *The Pale Rider.*

61. See Al Pacino in the movie *Serpico.*

62. Bellah et al., in *Habits of the Heart*, calls this "mythic individualism" (144).

63. Gutierrez, *We Drink from Our Own Wells.*

64. Karl Rahner's position on the church is that it is "fundamentally a way of being and a way of life," which involves living the "faith and hope of Jesus himself" through the Holy Spirit (Dych, *Karl Rahner*, 83). Thus, the most basic reality regarding church is not its structures, but people's faith expressed in worship, fellowship, and service. Sadly, much theology does not engage the perspectives of the persons in the pew. See Ringma, *Catch the Wind: Church Where People Matter.*

Trinitarian approach calls for a team-based or community-based ministry[65] that will practise grassroots ecumenism (working with other Christians or Christian organizations) and also work with existing community groups and forms of communal infrastructure. Thus, no Christian ministry should be a solo venture.

Throughout the NT, mission and ministry is a communal activity.[66] Jesus quickly formed a missional community (Mark 6:7), and those who journeyed with him joined his kingdom of God endeavours and eventually formed a common-purse community (Mark 10:28–31; John 12:4–6) that consisted of both men (Luke 9:1–6) and women (Luke 8:1–3). In the first century, Paul conducted his mission to the Greco-Roman world in a similar fashion. While we often think of Paul as the great missioner, he forged a missional community on the road[67] as he journeyed with "his companions" (Acts 13:13; 17:1). Luke's narrative repeatedly uses the word "we" (Acts 13:32, 46; 16:16; 20:6, 13), along with the names of those who were part of Paul's activities (Acts 18:8–24).

Moreover, any mission team needs to be sustained by a communal and multi-dimensional spirituality that involves prayer, fellowship, support from sending churches, and shared spiritual practices, such as adopting a common lectionary.[68] These spiritual practices need to be forged with the people one is seeking to serve rather than "imported" from the outside. Communal prayer was also a common activity within the early church (Acts 2:42; 4:24; 13:3; 14:23; 16:25; 20:36), particularly in relation to its mission.

This communal focus does not undermine the importance of our personal relationship with God or practices of personal piety, nor does it erode our individuality or our specific sense of calling. Rather, when we live as the body of Christ in the world, we can reflect the communal glory of God – Father, Son, Holy Spirit – more fully. Rather than refusing to work with others and building our own little kingdoms, we can live as unique members of the body of Christ, working together as a witnessing, welcoming, and serving community

65. See Craig, *Servants Among the Poor.*

66. Jürgen Moltmann emphasizes that we are communally oriented in multiple ways: (1) we are "persons before God": (2) we live in the "community of creation"; (3) we live in the "community of generations"; (4) our fundamental personhood is relational and communal (*In the End – The Beginning*, 114).

67. Mellis, *Committed Communities.*

68. For example: *The Book of Common Prayer*; *Celebrating Common Prayer: A Version of the Daily Office, SSF*; *Celtic Daily Prayer*; *Common Prayer: A Liturgy for Ordinary Radicals*, or other spiritual resources for corporate use.

in the world.[69] Historical examples of a communal missional identity include mendicant orders (such as the Franciscans), the Anabaptists, and Moravians. More recent examples include the communities of the Jesus Movement in the early 1970s and contemporary forms of the New Monasticism.

Put most basically, if God is a community of persons living in dynamic mutuality, then those who are marked by the grace of God are called to reflect a common identity, spirituality, and service. This common identity reminds us, once again, of the significance of the Trinity in shaping our life together as well as the importance of sharing common spiritual practices that will keep us grounded in Christ and encourage us in the life of faith.[70]

Welcoming Spirituality

Theologians have rightly emphasized that mission lies in the very nature of God.[71] But before we engage in missional activity, we must begin with the welcome that God extends to us. Through the ministry of the faith-community (and sometimes apart from it), we are welcomed by the Holy Spirit into the heart of God and into the blessed communion of the Trinity (John 14:20). This multi-dimensional and multi-directional welcome should be paradigmatic for how we engage in mission rather than seeing it as a project we take on to try to move people from one point to another.[72]

Thus, we need to begin by being welcomed into a community and into relationship with those we are seeking to serve. To put this another way, the gratuitous gift of welcome does not begin with us, but with the other – even the stranger or the enemy, however tenuous that welcome may initially be. Though it may take a long time, when we receive this gift of welcome from others, it is a sign that the Spirit is moving amongst us. This highlights the fact that we can't just crash into people's lives with our mission, no matter how valuable, important, and pressing we may believe it is. Rather, we have to give others the gift of time so that openness, trust, and receptivity can grow. This can occur in a variety of ways, including our practice of hospitality.

---

69. Rowan Williams stresses the corporate nature of Christianity. He speaks of "religious lives" (plural) as lives "inhabited by God's meanings" and as "a narrative that seeks to embody God," and, as such, they should be lives "of testimony" (*Faith in the Public Square*, 314, 320, 323, 319).

70. Ringma, *Catch the Wind*.

71. Hastings, *Missional God, Missional Church*.

72. Pohl, *Making Room*.

Luke's gospel, in particular, highlights the importance of welcome and hospitality as the way of Jesus and the way of the kingdom. In Luke 10:29–37, the cultural "outsider," the Samaritan, demonstrates the gift of hospitality by caring for the battered person he finds by the side of the road and bringing him to an inn (v. 34). This narrative is followed by a reference to the home of Mary, Martha, and Lazarus, where Jesus and his disciples are given hospitality and welcome (v. 38). In Luke 14:1–14, when Jesus visits the Pharisee's house, we encounter hospitality practices that are shaped by culture rather than the kingdom of God. This story is immediately followed by the parable of the Great Banquet, where radical hospitality is extended to the poor (vv. 15–24).[73]

The parable of the Lost Sheep (Luke 15:1–7) and the parable of the Lost Son (vv. 14–32) both call us not to give up on those who wander from the community of faith, but to extend welcome and hospitality through all seasons of life and all the contours of the faith journey. Over the course of our many years of working with drug addicted young people, we encountered the painful experience of extending hospitality and then later having it spurned. In the face of heartbreaking disappointment and loss, we had to learn how to extend the welcome of God over and over again.[74]

One of the most compelling narratives about welcome and hospitality in Luke's gospel is the story of Zacchaeus (Luke 19:1–10). After Jesus is welcomed into the home of Zacchaeus, who is described as a rank outsider, a "sinner" (v. 7), the Greek says that Jesus wishes "to remain" there (v. 5). This suggests that the brief scenario sketched in Luke's narrative may have involved an extended stay. During this time, Jesus may have engaged in a time of instruction with Zacchaeus, but whatever transpired, we know that a profound conversion and transformation took place. For Zacchaeus makes a commitment to the poor, a vow of restitution, and is restored to the faith-community so that "he too is [now] a son of Abraham" (v. 9).[75]

And so, a welcoming spirituality involves being welcomed into the lives and homes of those we are seeking to serve as well as welcoming others into

73. Hendricks points out that "Jesus granted to his critics that the banquet was prepared for them." Thus, grace is extended to them. He continues, "the reason for the exclusion of the first invitees being their refusal of the divine call" (*Parables of Jesus*, 134).

74. Grant-Thomson, *Jodie's Story*.

75. John Driver, "Messianic Evangelization," suggests that Zacchaeus's conversion reflects the theme of "Jubilee restoration" (in Shenk, *Transfiguration of Mission*, 208).

our lives and homes.[76] The faith-community is to be known by this spirit of hospitality, where even the outsider and stranger can find welcome.[77] Thus, the church is not an exclusive club or gated community, with closed doors and windows. In the ethos of the Northumbria Community in the UK, the church should be strongly grounded at the core and loose at the edges, vigilantly removing any unnecessary barriers. Therefore, racism and sexism have no place in the church.

Most basically, the church is to be a sign, servant, and sacrament of the reign of God so that people will be moved to say, "come and see."[78] This is especially relevant in our day, when so many people are estranged from the church and have no real understanding of the Christian story. Though they may have heard the gospel, we need to help them *see* the gospel being lived out in the world and give them time and space to respond to the welcome of the Spirit to enter into a liaison with Christ.[79] In this way, the community of faith lives as an echo and reflection of the Spirit's invitation to all seekers and strangers to find home in the generous heart of God and to encounter healing and renewal in Christ.

Yet the community of faith often comes across as superior, exclusive, and judgemental, which is hardly a posture of welcome. Clearly, the church itself needs to be transformed through a second conversion to the wide and gracious welcome of Christ! All who have been welcomed home in God are called to bend strenuously towards others so that they, too, might find the love of God in Christ Jesus.

Spirituality of the Exodus

As we have noted, missional spirituality is multi-dimensional, involving both prayer and action, homecoming and sending. It also involves responding to the Spirit, who is always moving ahead of each of us and ahead of our faith-community. Paul and Barnabas were sent by the church at Antioch to

---

76. For much of the first several decades of marriage and family, we had needy people with addiction issues live in our home. See Ringma, "Lower the Drawbridge: Bringing Social Justice Home."

77. Ringma, *Catch the Wind.*

78. Karl Rahner believes that the church is to be "the enduring presence of the Christ in the world." As such, it is a sacramental reality, since "the church comes from the death and resurrection of Christ" (Dych, *Karl Rahner*, 84, 89). The church's calling, then, is to help people find "a new and fuller way of being [of] what one already is" through God's provision in "the universal call to grace" (*Karl Rahner*, 85, 84).

79. See Dickau, *Plunging into the Kingdom Way.*

engage in missional activities (Acts 13:2–4), but Philip's encounter with the Ethiopian eunuch (Acts 8:26, 29) and Peter's involvement with Cornelius (Acts 10:23–48) were inspired by the Spirit well before the church was "ready" for these activities.[80] Hence Peter had to explain to the leadership of the church in Jerusalem why he had eaten with the Gentiles (Acts 11:1–18). These narratives reveal how sometimes missioners are sent *by* the community of faith, and sometimes they are sent *ahead* of the community, empowered by the Spirit to bring God's transforming mission of love and welcome back into the church.

In Genesis, God called Abram away from his land and people, saying, "I will show you" where you are to go (12:1). Though the call to leave was clear, Abram did not know where he was being sent. Being sent in this way is risky and may bring about unexpected outcomes of ministry. Yet when surprising things take place in outreach, the faith-community may not support missionaries and may leave them hanging out on a limb, so to speak.

Whenever we leave what is familiar and enter a territory that is unknown and unexpected, we experience a deep sense of "unbelonging,"[81] where we are no longer a part of our former community, nor a part of the community we are seeking to serve.[82] In this difficult space of transition, we are stripped bare and often feel painfully vulnerable. The most basic temptation at this point is to doubt seriously that we have heard the whispers of the Spirit or the voice of God and to assume that we have been foolish and impulsive. When we find ourselves in this space, we are wandering in the terrain of liminality, and we will need a spirituality of the Exodus to sustain and guide us.[83]

After seminary, when I felt impelled by the Spirit to work on the streets of Brisbane as a detached street worker rather than serving in a regular parish, I remember walking around the streets at night, feeling deeply alone. During this season, I often handed in my "resignation" to God, but God did not seem to accept it. To compound matters, nothing much seemed to be happening in this new ministry. While Both Philip and Peter had immediate evidence that God was blessing their risk-taking steps, I did not. Though I could sense, feel, and smell what I was moving towards, it was only vaguely in the distance. Because I couldn't articulate what this new ministry was all about, I was left with a nagging sense of stupidity.

---

80. Mendoza, "Faith on the Border, Faith on the Move," 253–67.

81. Lee, *Marginality.*

82. Rowan Williams notes that the very nature of conversion to Christ involves becoming different and is a "step out of the culture you once belonged to" (*Faith in the Public Square*, 66).

83. Lee, *Marginality*, 152–54; Gorospe, *Narrative and Identity*, 197–98.

During these seasons, a spirituality of the Exodus reminds us that we are traveling as guests and outsiders as we seek to befriend, join, learn from, and journey with the stranger – or those who are insiders within another culture.[84] The Israelites wandered in the desert for some forty years, and so an Exodus spirituality also reminds us this is not a quick process and may well take a lifetime. Moreover, Neno Contran soberly reminds us that this move is often an "exodus from oneself through renunciation, failure, and misunderstanding."[85] Pope John Paul II notes that mission "is an emptying of self which is permeated by love and expresses love," and he observes that this "leads to the foot of the cross."[86]

Whether we are going overseas and beginning the journey to learn another language and culture, or we are trying to pluck up enough courage to start a conversation with a new neighbour or colleague at work, the move toward the other is similar. Though we do not know the outcome, we make the move in hope that something good will come from any small – or large – journey towards serving the other. Thus, *provisionality* characterises a spirituality of the Exodus.

Having made a number of these larger "journeys" to other cultures, including service in the Philippines and Myanmar, I have learned a most basic lesson. Though it may not be immediately clear *why* we are in a particular place, or *what* we are to do, or what *role* we can play, we need to live through liminal spaces with patience. In time, clarity will come – though it is typically not what we might have expected! Thus, *emergence* is a core aspect of an Exodus spirituality. Jesus's kenosis – the journey from the bosom of the Father to inhabit a Galilean culture and identity – is the most radical form of this exodus journey.[87]

"Reverse" Spirituality

Early on in our decades of work with street people, drug addicts, and those involved in prostitution, we were surprised to learn an important and beautiful lesson. Like many young people, we had begun our work assuming that we had

84. Lee provides a helpful discussion in that becoming an insider does not mean that one loses one's earlier cultural identity. Thus, it is more helpful to speak of outsider/insider. Lee speaks of being "in-both" (*Marginality*, 47–53).

85. In Karotemprel, *Following Christ in Mission*, 135.

86. *Redemptoris Missio*, 146.

87. Costas, *Liberating Good News*, emphasizes Jesus's missional journey from the rogue province of Galilee to confront the powers in Jerusalem.

something to give to those in need. But over time, we slowly discovered that we had many previously unidentified needs – and the very broken people whom we were seeking to serve mirrored back to us with astonishing brightness the vulnerability and transparency that we were lacking. Archbishop Oscar Romero learned a similar lesson as he realized that he had learned a lot from the world of books, but he had even more to learn from the poor people he was seeking to serve.[88]

This wonderful discovery has two key components: the conversion of the missioner and the fact that ministry is a two-way street. Regarding the first, I usually identify myself as having had at least four major conversions. The first was my conversion to Christ. The second was my conversion to the poor while I was working with Indigenous communities in Western Australia, where I came to realize, among many other things, that I had been shaped by middle-class suburban values and had typical biases to marginal groups of people. The third conversion came during my long stint of working with those with addiction issues, when I came to see areas of brokenness in my own life. The fourth conversion came during my many years in South Asia, as I came to realize how my values, theology, and understanding of God had been shaped by Western culture. This conversion was probably the most significant upheaval, but I am not at all suggesting that my need for ongoing conversion stopped there – or should stop anywhere!

Though I have met some missionaries who have not seemed to change at all during the course of their ministry. They usually operated out of a "compound" mentality, which set them apart from the people they were seeking to serve. Most missioners, who engage in cross-cultural and incarnational experiences have been powerfully transformed in a variety of ways – particularly through the growing realization that mission is not simply a move "from us to them," but also a move "from them to us."

Anthony Gittens has developed a helpful paradigm that traces this movement in a fuller way.[89] The first movement is the bread that we *bring*. The second movement is the bread that is *received*. The third movement is the bread we *break together*. At this point, the desire to do something *for* others is transformed into something we do *with* others.[90] The fourth movement is gathering up all the leftover, broken fragments of bread, which we *distribute*

88. See the movie, *Romero*, and Romero, *Violence of Love*.

89. Gittins, *Bread for the Journey*, 57.

90. May, *Power and Innocence*. May speaks of the negative "power over," the reality of "power for" (or "nutritive power") and the need to move to "power with."

together to others. In this final movement, what were once called "younger churches"[91] take on the missional challenge for themselves.

The past hundred years or so of global missional activity, which moved primarily from the West to the rest of the world, has been marred by two key sins. First, the Western missional efforts often went hand in hand with Western colonial expansion and therefore involved the subjugation of native peoples as well as the arrogant impulse to bring them a "superior" culture and religion. Second, these missional efforts often sought to keep the so-called "younger churches" in an "infantile" state. As a result, it has taken far too long for these churches to become self-determining, self-governing, and self-propagating.[92] And it has taken even longer for them to construct their own local theologies.[93]

These unfortunate circumstances highlight the fact that those in power typically prefer to hold onto control rather than give it away. Yet those who have power need to *empower* others rather than trying to maintain control.[94] Maturity comes by gaining self-determination, which leads to cooperation, so that we can all work together as equal partners in the grand scheme of the global church living as God's missional people.[95] From this perspective, the missioner does not have all "the goodies." Rather, the most broken and vulnerable can bless us and enrich us and also challenge our lives.

In a course on Christian communities that I have taught for over twenty-five years,[96] I often surprise students when I tell them that I did not learn the importance of Christian community in church, but through working on the streets with alcoholics and drug addicts, whose sense of community forced me to reread the NT regarding this topic. This highlights the importance and beauty of "reverse spirituality" in any ministry. This dynamic of giving and receiving is now playing itself out on a global scale as missioners, clergy, and

91. The "younger churches" were spawned by the Western mission project. For far too long, they were regarded by Western mission agencies as "younger churches" rather than full partners in the task of the global mission project. Much of this paternalistic thinking began to change after World War II. Today, Christian expansion is taking place most significantly in Asia, Africa, and Latin America.

92. Bosch, *Transforming Mission*, 450.

93. Schreiter, *Constructing Local Theologies*.

94. Freire, *Pedagogy of the Oppressed*.

95. Jenkins, *Next Christendom*.

96. "Building Christian Communities," which is available from Regent College, Vancouver, Canada.

educators from the Majority World are contributing to the life of churches and other institutions throughout the Minority World.[97]

Prophetic Spirituality

Without an integrated understanding of missional spirituality, one might assume that spirituality is only concerned with one's inner life of worship, prayer, and reflection and has nothing to do with the more "dangerous" work of prophetic justice. This is a serious misunderstanding, for any spirituality that is not prophetic[98] may become self-enhancing and narcissistic.

Any missional spirituality will be committed both to the love of God and love of neighbour, which is never an abstraction. Rather, we love particular neighbours in the midst of their particular life circumstances and the ways they are impacted by larger cultural and economic forces. Thus, the gospel is not only good news for our inner life, but for the whole of life. And that good news is not simply about going to heaven, but experiencing God's shalom here and now on earth – as it is in heaven. In this light, proclaiming the good news involves the *annunciation* of our salvation and redemption from personal sin and our healing from the impacts of structural evil as well as the *denunciation* of all that distorts life.[99] As a consequence, our missional task is prophetic and will include the work of prophecy.

However, I am not referring to prophecy in its more popular sense as a prediction of the future, but rather to the broader biblical sense as the annunciation and demonstration of the word of God to the faith-community, calling them to "change" their ways and giving them a vision for God's renewing future.[100] In this sense, the prophet looks at the present through the future perspective of God's reign, both correcting and casting a vision for

97. In the city of Brisbane, where I presently live, many churches now have Asian and African clergy.

98. See Ringma, *Let My People Go*, which looks at major justice themes in the life and ministry of Martin Luther King Jr.

99. While liberation theologians see both annunciation and denunciation as part of Christian ministry, evangelicals have found this more difficult. While evangelicals do raise matters of personal morality and issues such as abortion, they are generally weak in their analysis and engagement of structural evil.

100. Frank Jehle, in his discussion of Karl Barth's social and political orientation, notes that Barth had a profound grasp of the biblical story and a deep awareness of the issues in society. Barth read society with "critical engagement," recognizing that politics stands under the "eschatological proviso" (Jehle, *Ever Against the Stream*, 100, 101). This means that politics is not self-authenticating, but needs to be accountable to God!

what could be.[101] We see this prophetic perspective most clearly in Isaiah's lilting annunciation:

> He shall judge between the nations
> and shall arbitrate for many peoples;
> they shall beat their swords into plowshares,
> and their spears into pruning hooks;
> nation shall not lift up the sword against nation,
> neither shall they learn war any more. (Isa 2:4)

Yet this future vision is not only for Israel, but also for the surrounding nations. God's concern is never simply for his own people, but for all who hear the words of welcome that pass through the "eye" of repentance to come to the banquet table and taste God's goodness.

Just as the Word *becomes* flesh in the incarnation, the community of faith *embodies* the prophetic word to the world, inviting it to "come and see" what *can be* in the purposes of God.[102] Christ, the prophet par excellence, brought a prophetic word of healing and hope into the world about the kingdom of God. In this new world order, the followers of Christ live the way of Christ in the world through the Spirit. For as we live *in* Christ – the icon of the new humanity, "the surgeon who removes the sting of death" – he "restores the image [of God] to its full integrity and returns humanity to complete health."[103] But our identification with Christ also has political and economic implications, for the way of Christ is for the healing of the whole world, demonstrating a new social order that crosses all social hierarchies and privileges, calling us beyond self-seeking to economic sharing.[104] For as the faith-community is conformed to Christ in the power of the Spirit, it *becomes* a prophetic word and embodies a new future.[105]

---

101. Given this vision of prophetic spirituality, it is appropriate to see this as belonging to political theology in that this theology does not only deal with the creation mandate, but also with the corruption of the principalities and powers (Phillips, *Political Theology*, 155).

102. For a more pastoral rather than scholarly discussion of prophetic spirituality, see Jones, *Sharing God's Passion.*

103. Gurion, *Melody of Faith*, 56.

104. In particular, see the accounts of economic sharing in Acts 2 and 4.

105. William Dych points out that while Karl Rahner holds that "the Church must not only teach the world, but also learn from it," Rahner's fundamental vision is that the church must "imprint its eschatological hope upon the structures of worldly life" (Dych, *Karl Rahner*, 106, 108).

Though John and Charles Wesley called the church to such an integrated vision of both personal and social holiness during their lifetime,[106] this understanding has fallen into disrepair in our present-day consumer Christianity, which seems to be concerned with self-enhancement and survival rather than prophetic engagement with the contemporary culture.[107]

A prophetic spirituality does not spring from "holy" detachment, but calls the faith-community to identify with the grieving heart of God for the wounded world, which is marked by conflict, war-mongering, and idolatry, and then to discern how we can respond. This process of identification leads us to engage in loving service and to advocate on behalf of the marginalized and oppressed in their quest for justice. This most precarious and painful journey is our *via dolorosa*.

To give an example from our ministry with troubled youth, drug addicts, and men and women in prostitution, we had no difficulty gaining support from churches, the general community, or the business world in our counselling work, drug prevention programs, rehabilitation, and training for meaningful employment. However, we were living in a city with a corrupt police drug squad, and we knew many people who had their doors bashed down at 5 am, been dragged out of bed, herded into a room, and guarded while other police searched the place and "found" guns, money, and loads of drugs, leading to an impressive arrest for the police force. Yet in many cases, the police had planted the drugs, as they were some of the key drug dealers in the community. Each police "success" put people we knew behind bars for several decades. As we learned of these unjust practices, we began to support our friends with legal help. But as soon as we raised the issue of police corruption, the churches and community sent us a clear message: heal, but don't advocate; evangelize, but don't work for justice; counsel people, but don't engage political issues. In other words, we should try to "save people from their personal sins," but we shouldn't engage their oppression and victimization.

Yet prophecy and the work of justice are dynamically interrelated. The whole prophetic impulse is eschatological,[108] as it seeks to bring "heaven" to earth (as illustrated by Isaiah's vision above). However, this vision is not established by revolutionary force, but rather comes to earth through God's action within the

106. Hynson, *To Reform the Nation*.

107. Alexander Schmemann makes the point that the object of mission is not the person in isolation but "in the whole of life." This means that the "State, society, culture, nature itself are real *objects* of mission" (*Church, World, Mission*, 216).

108. Thus it bears similarities with millenarian movements (e.g. Burridge, *New Heaven, New Earth*; Worsley, *Trumpet Shall Sound*).

community of the peaceful dove.[109] If we are seeking God's peaceable kingdom, we must, in the words of Gandhi, seek a correlation between the means and the ends. Peaceful means alone will establish a peaceable kingdom.[110]

The prophetic impulse has three important dimensions. First, prophecy is not a negative force, but seeks to *affirm* what is good in a community and in a tradition.[111] In this sense, it has a *preservative* orientation. Second, prophecy is a *critical* force that seeks to bring about correction, change, and transformation.[112] In this sense, it has a *renewing* function. Third, prophecy casts a *vision of hope for the future.* It calls for what may yet be – not only in God's final future, but in the present struggling domain, where good and evil continue to jostle together in a most awkward dance.[113] These dimensions reveal the dynamic quality of prophecy, which is a word from the heart of God that is spoken through the mouth of the prophet and embedded in the faith-community for the life of the world. Thus, a prophetic spirituality casts a visionary corrective for what *is* in the light of what *can be* according to the purposes of the restoring God.

A prophetic spirituality attends to God's heart for the world while recognizing both the goodness and failure of the community of faith as well as one's own stupidities. It sees the world with eyes of longing as well as a heart of grief. It dares to speak truth to power, and it endures in the face of opposition and failure. The prophet has a most unenviable task in following the paschal road, constantly torn between what is and what could be. The journey through this valley of grief is profoundly lonely and is marked by deep sorrow.[114]

Contemplative Spirituality

In the previous chapter, I touched on the contemplative dimensions of the missional Christian life, particularly in the discussion of Segundo Galilea.[115]

109. Huebner, *Precarious Peace.*

110. Ringma, "Franciscan Peacemaking."

111. See Gadamer, *Truth and Method*, for a hermeneutics of affirmation.

112. Smith notes that one of Ricoeur's "signal accomplishments has been his analysis and interpretation of what he calls the hermeneutics of suspicion, the masters of which were Freud, Marx, and Nietzsche" ("Freud, Philosophy and Interpretation," 147).

113. See chapter 18 ("Hope: A Magnificent Mosaic") for such a hermeneutics of hope.

114. For a further discussion of this theme, see chapter 6 ("A Vision of God and a Passion for the World").

115. See chapter 2 ("Towards a Missional Spirituality").

In this chapter, I will elaborate on this recurring theme and will then return to a further discussion of contemplation and action in the next chapter.[116]

To begin, it is important to make a distinction between contemplation as a spiritual *practice* and contemplation as a *gift*, which Thomas Merton describes as *infused* contemplation.[117] The challenging and liberating concern here is that the practice of contemplation doesn't necessarily lead to the gift. In other words, we may employ the practices of stillness,[118] solitude,[119] reflection, *lectio Divina*, worship, prayer, meditation, journaling, among others, and not gain inner peace, insight, inspiration, or any other sense of God's presence or direction. In fact, we may engage these practices and experience a seeming emptiness or even a dark night of the soul,[120] or these practices may become a lifeless routine.

This wonderfully liberating insight resists the impulse to import an *instrumentality* into our spirituality and rejects the outcome-based orientation of our age. This radically countercultural perspective also challenges our contemporary *quid pro quo* attitudes and the utilitarian and programmatic bent of our Western culture. We cannot coerce or manipulate our Sovereign God, who is radically free, and so we should not try to master some technique or engage a particular practice in order to make God "show up." Such an approach would quickly eliminate God and exalt ourselves – what a miserable idolatry!

Thus, we need to receive any revelation, inspiration, or direction in contemplation as a *gift* rather than the product of our own doing. From this

116. See chapter 4 ("Contemplation in a World of Action").

117. Merton notes that "contemplation is always beyond our own knowledge, our own light, beyond systems, beyond explanations," and continues that it is "a sudden gift of awareness" (*Seeds of Contemplation*, 2).

118. Henri Nouwen points out the many challenges we face in coming to stillness, but he says, "being useless and silent in the presence of God belongs to the core of prayer." He continues, "slowly . . . we discover that the silent time makes us quiet and deepens our awareness of ourselves and God" (*Seeds of Hope*, 70–71). Elsewhere, Nouwen notes that "silence is primarily a quality of the heart that leads to ever-growing charity" (*The Way of the Heart*, 64). Thus, the practices of silence have everything to do with ministry and mission.

119. Nouwen notes that solitude is one of the "most difficult disciplines." It "begins with a time and place for God," and "in solitude we develop an attentiveness to God's voice in us" (*Seeds of Hope*, 14–15). Wil Hernandez notes that for Nouwen, solitude is the "furnace of our inner transformation . . . from which real compassionate ministry freely flows" (*Henri Nouwen and Spiritual Polarities*, 53). Thomas Merton notes that "solitude is therefore at the same time a vocation to silence, poverty, and emptiness. But the emptiness is for the sake of fullness" (*The Monastic Journey*, 152). Lawrence Cunningham notes that for Merton, the practices of solitude not only created "purity of intention and clarity of purpose," but also a "prophetic character" and a "concern for the illusions and sins of the world" (*Thomas Merton and the Monastic Vision*, 78).

120. Merton writes, "the deep, inexpressible certitude of the contemplative experience awakens a tragic anguish and opens many questions in the depth of the heart like wounds that cannot stop bleeding" (*Seeds of Contemplation*, 9–10).

insight, we can infer the following about the relationship between God and ourselves. First, God is the initiator, always wooing us, drawing us, and nudging us long before we ever know God, respond to God, or do something for God.[121] Second, God is the enabler, always enlivening and empowering us through the Spirit. Third, God invites our response of faith, love, and hope through prayer and service, but this is not something we can generate ourselves. Finally, God is full of surprises and cannot be contained by our expectations and strategies. As Isaiah proclaims:

> For my thoughts are not your thoughts,
> nor are your ways my ways, says the Lord.
> For as the heavens are higher than the earth,
> so are my ways higher than your ways
> and my thoughts than your thoughts. (Isa 55:8-9)

Therefore, the dynamic in contemplative practices is not to work towards certain outcomes, but rather to cultivate a posture that has the following contours: *relationship*, *waiting*, *attentiveness*, and *expectation*.[122] In this posture, we enter God's presence with open hands,[123] and we wait for God to act – not by magically writing messages on the wall, but through inner inspiration that must pass through the vortex of discernment.

Though we may sometimes wish that God would make things easier and more immediately obvious, God is constantly holding divine sovereignty in creative tension with human participation. If we focus too much on our own participation, we become gods. If we focus exclusively on God's sovereignty, we become mere robots in the machinations of an oppressive God.[124] Thus contemplative practices create a *relational* space where we can live in this creative tension with God.[125]

Contemplative practices also pull us away from our much-doing so that our work does not become a god or an uncontrollable beast of burden.[126] In this way, they are a form of self-care that ensure our well-being and help us

---

121. Wesley's concept of prevenient grace.

122. These contours will be expounded more fully in chapter 4 ("Contemplation in a World of Action").

123. Nouwen, *With Open Hands*.

124. de Vries, *Religion and Violence*.

125. John O'Donohue highlights that contemplative practices involve an "ascetic solitude" in which silence plays a key role. He goes on to note that: "words that have a depth, resonance, healing, and challenge to them, are words loaded with ascetic silence" (*Anam Cara*, 108, 110).

126. In *Seek the Silences*, I make the point that "it is not possible only to live an activist agenda. It will lead to burnout or disillusionment. It does not empower, but fragments" (180).

embrace a spirituality of Sabbath.[127] These practices also draw us into a valuable space of reflection so that we can re-evaluate our life and ministry and make any necessary adjustments. But the most important aspect of contemplative practices is that they help us cultivate a *friendship* with God,[128] which generates and empowers our life of service.

Sadly, we have adopted the "Great Commission" in Matthew's Gospel as the sole *raison d'etre* for our missional activity.[129] In so doing, we have neglected the missional vision of union recorded by John, where Jesus teaches his disciples, "Those who love me will keep my word, and my father will love them, and we will come to them and make our home with them" (14:23). Then he prays, "As you have sent me into the world, so I have sent them into the world" (John 17:18). In John's account, *union* with God is a promised *gift* rather than a command. Yet we can easily misread Matthew 28 as prioritizing Jesus's "authority" (v. 18) and his command to "go" (v. 19) over the gift of his promised presence ("I am with you always, even to the end of the age," v. 20).[130] Such a formulation seems to suggest that work precedes grace, but this undermines the emphasis of the whole biblical narrative. We see this in God's call to the prophet Isaiah, where God first declares, "Do not fear; I have redeemed you," and then says, "I have called you by name; you are mine" (Isa 43:1).

Contemplation lies at the heart of a missional spirituality, because it draws us into a relationship (union) with both God and the world. For as we contemplate the "face" of God, we will begin to see the face of our neighbour differently. Put starkly, anyone who has gazed into the face of God, or tasted forgiveness in Christ, or has been touched by the gentle Spirit cannot torture another human being, oppress someone – let alone a whole nation – or neglect a starving person. The lack of humanity in our world is directly related to the fact that the face of God has become obscured to us. How greatly we are to be pitied!

In contemplating the face of God through prayer, solitude, reading, and reflecting on Scripture and our world, we *cultivate friendship with God* and

127. Dawn, *Keeping the Sabbath Wholly*; Nouwen, *Sabbatical Journey*; Ringma, *Sabbath Time*.

128. Houston, *Transforming Friendship*.

129. "Jesus came up and spoke to them, saying, 'All authority has been given to Me in heaven and on earth. Go therefore and make disciples of all the nations, baptizing them in the name of the Father and the Son and the Holy Spirit, teaching them to observe all that I commanded you; and lo, I am with you always, even to the end of the age'" (Matt 28:18–20).

130. For a discussion of this theme, but in a different context, see Huebner, *Precarious Peace*, 83–95.

we *seek God's will* for our time. This will involve a hermeneutics of both text and context.[131] Understanding our world will also involve the work of exegesis, theology, and the historical and social sciences.[132] In our contemplation of the world through the cycle of action and reflection, we seek to understand both the goodness of God in our social fabric and institutions[133] as well as the idolatries of our society and culture.[134] Amidst this interplay,[135] we seek to discern how God is inviting us to participate in God's passion for the healing and reconciling of all things through Christ.

Thus, the contemplation of both the face of God and the world belong together. For in seeking God, we find the One who turns our face to the world.[136] And in contemplating the beauty and madness of our world, we are driven to seek the face of God, who alone can sustain us in the journey of love, hope, and service.[137]

Spirituality of the Dark Night

The core idea of "the dark night" in Christian spirituality is that God's presence has become an *active absence* in order to help the pilgrim move from the certainties and securities of living in God's presence to embrace more fully the great mystery of God's way.[138] Though the language of the spirituality of

131. Thiselton, *The Two Horizons*; Thiselton, *New Horizons in Hermeneutics*; Maggay, *Gospel in Culture.*

132. Apart from the newer theologies (black, liberation, feminist, political, and green), theology has not always been strong enough in understanding its context. Thus, there is a greater need for contextual theologies.

133. Mathewes, *Theology of Public Life*. The importance of Mathewes' work lies in its major focus on how to understand culture theologically rather than first of all looking at the church's engagement with culture.

134. Ellul, *New Demons*; Smith, *How (Not) to Be Secular.*

135. See Jürgen Moltmann's discussion of Trinitarian hermeneutics as a wonderful interplay of the relationship between Father, Son, and Holy Spirit (*Experiences in Theology*, 139–48).

136. Martin Luther is rather negative about monks and their contemplative practices. He writes: they are waiting for "extraordinary illuminations without external means" and thus "were frequently deceived by delusions of the devil" (*Luther's Works*, vol. 3, 275). Elsewhere, he charges monks with living a "speculative life" (*Luther's Works*, vol. 5, 345). However, Luther is not opposed to contemplation as such and suggests that the right way for the Christian to contemplate is to "reflect on his [her] Baptism, let him read his Bible, hear sermons, honor father and mother, and come to the aid of a brother in distress" (*Luther's Works*, vol. 3, 275). Thus, Luther acknowledges that contemplation involves an orientation to the Word and to the world, to prayer and action.

137. For a further discussion of this theme, see chapter 4 ("Contemplation in a World of Action").

138. St. John of the Cross, *Dark Night of the Soul.*

the dark night has largely been confined to the inner life of the individual,[139] there is no reason why this concept cannot be applied to the corporate and communal aspects of the Christian life as well.

For example, one may speak of a communal spirituality of the dark night in a church that has been traumatized by clergy child abuse.[140] Or one may think of a community that has been shattered by a typhoon or earthquake.[141] Or one may think of Israel's songs of lament during the Babylonian captivity[142] or the present-day lament of Christians in the West in light of the increasing marginalization of the church and Christian values in society.[143] Another example is St. Augustine's lament toward the end of his life (as recorded by Possidius) in response to the Barbarian invasions, which resulted in the murder of Christians and the desecration of the basilicas:

> These days, therefore, that he [St. Augustine] lived through and endured, almost at the very end of his life, were the bitterest and most mournful of all of his old age. For he had seen cities overthrown and destroyed . . . He saw churches denuded of priests and ministers; holy virgins and men vowed to monastic life dispersed . . . [some] perished by the sword . . . churches . . . in many places burnt down . . . the holy sacraments no longer wanted.[144]

Applying the communal concept of dark night spirituality more directly to mission, there is often a noticeable cycle in missional activity, which begins with initial enthusiasm, then moves toward consolidation, and eventually falls into some form of deterioration or entropy, where the dark night often occurs. This leads to the subsequent need for renewal and revitalization. Within this cycle, missioners can lose their way if they become self-focused and self-serving, trying to prop up the ministry instead of being empowered by the Spirit. Such a loss of focus causes a deep rift in the heart of a church or ministry and may launch its parishioners and missioners into the psychological darkness of cognitive dissonance. Another misdirection occurs when charismatic leaders, who are the vanguard of new missional activities, overreach by promulgating

139. Mother Teresa's reluctant testimony in *Come Be My Light* is a good contemporary example.

140. Mouton, *In God's House.*

141. Gorospe et al., *Why, O God?*

142. Westermann, *Praise and Lament in the Psalms*; Brueggemann, *The Psalms and the Life of Faith.*

143. Newbigin, *The Gospel in a Pluralist Society*; Foust et. al., eds., *A Scandalous Prophet*; Hunsberger and Van Gelder, *The Church Between Gospel and Culture.*

144. Stevenson, *Creeds, Councils and Controversies*, 225–26.

utopian visions and trumpeting Christian triumphalism. Expecting too much, they promise a "new" world while their unthoughtful strategies disintegrate in the face of the persistence of evil in the world, plunging their followers into a communal dark night.

Another unexpected dysfunction may occur at the peak of a ministry's success.[145] As the ministry begins to rely on programs and strategies, humility and prayer may become scarce. Slowly, idolatry begins to take shape, darkening the landscape at the very time when many people think that things are going well, and all the talk is about expansion and multiplication. Thus, in the full sunshine and maturity of a ministry project, the seeds of death may lie unnoticed. For in the experience of the dark night, it does not grow suddenly dark, but as the light begins to fade, we may not notice.

Apart from such times of misdirection, the spirituality of the dark night is an intrinsic part of mission. First of all, our missional activity may be singularly unsuccessful.[146] Thus, we need to acknowledge this reality and drop the inflated language that we use to cover it up. Second, mission often involves long years of preparation and sowing. The land may lie fallow for a long time, and there may be a long, dark winter before the springtime of the kingdom of God sprouts in a particular place. Third, a ministry may suddenly be decimated through external factors. For example, a slum community in which a missional team has worked for many years may suddenly be "mysteriously" burnt to the ground or bulldozed while police wearing balaclavas stand by and supervise the illegal operation.[147]

As Karl Rahner looked down the road and saw the first signs of Western de-Christianization, he spoke of the Western church entering a communal dark night, which he described as our *diaspora* status, observing that we would "have to carry heavy burdens" because "more than ever we will be strangers even among those we love."[148] Thus, many writers are now speaking of a "new" dark ages[149] amidst the uncertainties and tribulations of our age – global warming, the corona pandemic, the rise of new fascisms, employment insecurity, global political changes, among many other concerns.

145. The Dutch poet Alice Nahon makes this point: *van het zone-zoenen, die een roze sterven doet* ("the kiss of full sunshine is what eventually kills the rose") in *Vondelingskens* (16). Similarly, in the full sunshine and maturity of a ministry project, the seeds of death lie unnoticed.

146. Elliot, *No Graven Image.*

147. Duncan, *Costly Mission.*

148. Rahner, *Theological Investigations*, vol. 3, 357–58.

149. Colson, *Against the Night*; Jacobs, *Dark Age Ahead.*

Just as we are called to live the paschal mystery of the dark days of the cross and the joy of resurrection in our personal lives, this paschal mystery will also play itself out in our ministries and missional strategies, churches and institutions. Yet this dark night is a transitional phase rather than the end of the story. Though it might "throw" us, it has a purgative and transformative dimension, which does its mysterious work. We cannot exploit or manipulate the dark night, for it has its own logic and *modus operandi*, takes its own time, and produces its own fruit. Thus, we are called to wait[150] while keeping our "hands off" as we enter a season of lament.[151] Though we cannot anticipate the specific fruit of the dark night, it carries us away from our familiar certainties, liturgies, and religious support-structures into the mystery of God's strange way with us. This strange way teaches us to rely on God, even when God seems to be completely absent. As we inhabit the strange territory of this contradiction, we begin to perceive the *blessings* of the *absent-present God*!

Spirituality of Hope

Faith, hope, and love are three core, intimately related theological themes, for one can't have one without the others. Faith is both *that* we believe and *what* we believe. An important theme in our faith is our hope in what God will *yet* do and what we may anticipate as we enter into God's final future.[152] And love is the ground of both our faith and hope as well as its practical outworking.

Yet hope is often misunderstood, as some see it as mere wishful thinking and others push it totally into the future, with no practical implications for the here and now. In Christian spirituality, hope is both *grounded* and *fragile*. It is grounded in the redemptive purposes of God throughout history, culminating in Christ's death and resurrection[153] and God's promises for the final restoration of all things. However, Christian hope is not only for the *culmination* of all things, but also for the *renewal* of all things in the here and the now.[154] Thus, as N. T. Wright observes, "a mission-shaped church must have its mission shaped by hope."[155] Wright also points out that "to hope for a better

150. Weil, *Waiting on God.*

151. Weems, *Psalms of Lament.*

152. Jürgen Moltmann, *The Crucified God*, makes the point that Christian hope "is the anticipation of God's future in the resurrection of the *crucified* one that inspires and enables Christian hope for a liberated world" (Hebblethwaite, *The Christian Hope*, 180).

153. Wright, *Surprised by Hope*, grounds Christian hope in the resurrection of Christ.

154. See Wright, 269.

155. Wright, 269.

future in this world – for the poor, the sick, the lonely and depressed, for the slaves, the refugees, the hungry and homeless, for the abused, the paranoid, the downtrodden and despairing"[156] – is intrinsic to the good news of the gospel. And he notes that working for this "intermediate hope," which gains its inspiration from "God's ultimate future . . . *will last into God's future*."[157]

In other words, God's future hope for healing and restoration is already alive in the present through God's action in and through the faith-community. Thus, the mission of the church is grounded in the church's participation in the restorative work of God and is an overflow of its life into the world. This work of the people of God is carried out in the present, with the hope and faith that through the purifying grace of God in Christ, it will last into eternity. Inspired by the grace of Christ, we are moved by the brokenness of our world to act, trusting that God will use our witness and service to bring healing and restoration to individuals, communities, and institutions.

Segundo Galilea also roots the present hope of the church in the resurrection of Christ, noting that "the resurrection is the work, the act, of Christ, which sums up all his life's deeds of promise."[158] He continues: "the resurrection gives the reason for our hope" in that this "is not a life and world of pure spirits," but a new life in the here and now. Thus, "the risen Christ inaugurates a new world, a new justice, a new fellowship, a new reality totally humanized and renovated."[159]

The church acts into the world in hope – not in what we will be able to achieve, but in what God, by the Spirit, will do through us and inspite of us. Yet living and acting in hope draws us into a life of fragility, because there is often so little to be hopeful about in our circumstances or in the general shape of our world. We are so easily discouraged, often frustrated with the church, and may feel hopeless that things will ever change amidst the persistence of evil and folly in the world.[160] Moreover, we are living in between the first and second coming of Christ, in the middle of the yet and not-yet nature of God's kingdom. And our witness and service seem so feeble in the midst of the world's powers, governments, and multi-national corporations. So, we doubt

156. Wright, 191–92.

157. Wright, 192–93 (author's italics).

158. Galilea, *Spirituality of Hope*, 21.

159. Galilea, 22–23.

160. Ellul goes so far as to suggest that God perhaps "still speaks in the heart of a person," but it is "from our history, our societies, our cultures, our science, and our politics that *God is absent*" (*Hope in Time*, 72, my italics).

that proclaiming the gospel or offering loving service to our neighbours and community can have any significant influence.

Hope is never utopian, nor is it rooted in our abilities. Rather, our hope is in God's work in, through, and beyond us. As we walk this precarious road, we are called to remain faithful amidst our uncertainty – and amidst the seeming absence of God. A missional spirituality of hope commits itself to ongoing prayer and service, even in the face of the existing realities in our own life, the church, and the wider society. Thus, our hope is readily threatened and needs to be rooted in Christ, empowered by the gospel, and sustained by the presence of the Spirit – and the hope of what God will *yet* do amongst us and what will eventually take place in God's final future. Our hope does not deny present pain or injustice, but recognizes that we have been marked by the cross of Christ, and so we will each need to bear our own cross.

Finally, our hope anticipates God, who is always moving ahead of us while calling us to live in the here and now. As we look towards God's final restoration, our status in the world is both provisional and penultimate.[161]

Conclusion

This chapter has sought to overcome the fragmentation of much theological discourse.[162] The particular theological themes that we have explored are central to the biblical narratives and the Christian story of the church in history. Yet all biblical and theological themes are fundamentally missional, because God is revealed in both word and deed, in the work of creation and the work of redemption, in Christ's embodied action and reflection in the world. The themes of creation, redemption, and the theology of the Trinity cannot be separated from Christian mission, which engages the head, heart, and hand – the theological, spiritual, and practical – in a rich mosaic of life and service.[163] Missional spirituality is a way of living *in* God and *with* God through worship, prayer, biblical reflection, and our participation in a faith-community that is seeking not only to understand God's ways, but also to live and do them through our service in the world.

---

161. For a further discussion of this theme, see chapter 18 ("Hope: A Magnificent Mosaic").

162. Farley, *Theologia*.

163. For a further discussion of these themes, see chapter 8 ("Grand Design and Fragile Engagement: The Church's Calling in a Troubled World").

4

Contemplation in a World of Action[1]

Introduction

In this chapter, we will further explore the inter-relationship of prayer and service, contemplation and action. We will root our reflections in the biblical narratives, particularly the Gospels of Mark and John, to locate the dynamic of contemplation and action in the life and ministry of Jesus, who is both our Saviour and a normative human being, and the model for our action in the world. Then we will explore some perspectives of the church in its long march through history regarding the *gestalt* of the contemplative experience. We will conclude with the recognition that we need to be *pregnant with the holy*[2] and carry the seeds of the kingdom of God within us. As mystics and contemplatives, we are impacted by what Merton describes as the "'mercy of God,'" which is "revealed to us by the secret missions" of God "in which He gives Himself to us and awakens our identity as sons [daughters] of His kingdom."[3]

In response to God's gratuitous and merciful move towards us, we are called to gaze into the heart and mind of God to discern the movement of the Spirit. We are also called to gaze into our world, with all its beauty as well

1. This title is borrowed from Merton's *Contemplation in a World of Action*. See also Barry and Doherty, *Contemplatives in Action*.

2. To be pregnant with the holy is not only to be overshadowed by the brooding Spirit, but, as John O'Donohue points out, "to be natural is to be holy." He means by this that we are "to be at home with [our] own nature," which involves the "integrity of [our] solitude" (*Anam Cara*, 101). In other words, we have to move deeper than our social self and beyond our fears into the realm of our soul, which is created and loved by God.

3. Merton, *Seeds of Contemplation*, 33.

as its pain and injustice. Moreover, we are called to gaze into our own lives – our good purposes and lofty ideals as well as our stupidities and sins. If we wish to impact our world, we need to direct our gaze toward God and our inner life as we seek to engage the world. Mere activism points us towards our own plans and strategies, whereas mysticism guides us into prophecy and the work of justice. And so, our activism must be nourished and sustained by contemplation, and our contemplation should lead to service, and our service should return us to contemplation.

Contemplation: Resistance and Renewed Interest

Yet some Christians, who have been shaped by the *activist* traditions of Protestantism and evangelicalism, may be nervous with the language of mysticism and contemplation. Our traditions hold up missionaries and social reformers as heroes rather than men and women of prayer. Some may think that contemplation belongs to the world of the monastery and that monks have "dropped the ball" because they are more concerned with piety than social transformation. Therefore, this chapter will begin by seeking to correct some of these persistent misunderstandings while highlighting some key reasons for our contemporary world's renewed interest in the spiritual, mystical, and prophetic life.

First, we are being encouraged to think and act in more wholistic ways. One expression of this is to speak of our formation in terms of the head (theological), heart (spiritual), and hand (mission). In other words, vision, passion, and action belong together.[4]

Second, we are being invited to move beyond dualistic ways of thinking and acting. In ancient Christianity, the soul was elevated over the body, virginity over marriage, and piety over service. In modern Christianity, we turned these around and prioritized the body, marriage, and service. But now, in the twenty-first century, we are being encouraged toward both piety and service, both body and soul as we seek to integrate the cave (the place of prayer and meditation), the canteen (the community of faith), and the journey on the road (the place of service and mission).[5]

4. See chapter 8 ("Grand Design and Fragile Engagement: The Church's Calling in a Troubled World").

5. See Adams, *Cave, Refectory, Road.*

Third, we are being encouraged to develop a comprehensive vision of the reign of God[6] rather than an ecclesiastical vision for acting into our world. Thus, our focus is not so much on church programs and outreach activities, but on our intention to be the servants of Christ in the world and to be actively caught up in God's purposes for our time.

Fourth, we are being invited to develop spiritual practices – including prayer, *lectio divina*, meditation, centering prayer, contemplation, fasting, journaling, spiritual direction, among others[7] – not to gain credit in God's "bank," but to sustain our friendship with God,[8] grow in spiritual insight, enhance our self-care, and be more fully empowered for service in the world.

Fifth, we are discovering that the evangelical focus on the *word* as witness and the more contemporary focus on *deed* as service don't quite cut it. Though our presence in the world should involve both word and deed – both words and acts of love and forgiveness – we will continually experience labour pains as God's new world springs forth (Rom 8:22–23; Gal 4:19; Eph 1:17–23). Thus, if we are going to be *pregnant with the holy*, we need to be nourished by an inner life of prayer and contemplation.[9] Yet this is the domain we most readily neglect. As the Latin American theologian Segundo Galilea warned, our first temptation is to abandon prayer.[10]

Jesus: the Contemplative and Missionary God[11]

We will begin this exploration by grounding the above reflections in Scripture. For evangelicals,[12] Scripture is the normative narrative that forms our Christian

---

6. See Stanley Jones, *The Unshakable Kingdom*; Stassen and Gushee, *Kingdom Ethics*.

7. Merton, *Contemplative Prayer*; Nouwen, *Clowning in Rome*; Byrne, *Traditions of Spiritual Guidance*.

8. Ellithorpe, *Practical Theology of Friendship*.

9. Thomas Green warns us about running "out of steam" in *When the Well Runs Dry*.

10. Galilea, *Temptation & Discernment*.

11. St. Gregory the Great notes: "Christ set forth in Himself patterns of both lives, that is the active and the contemplative, united together" (quoted in Butler, *Western Mysticism*, 176).

12. What we mean by this term is increasingly difficult to determine. Editors Ford and Higton rightly point out that "Evangelical Christianity is a huge [and] varied movement" (*The Modern Theological Reader*, 366). This statement poses a challenge about how we can gain greater clarity regarding this movement. For some further discussion around this issue, see Bloesch, *The Future of Evangelical Christianity*; Noll, *The Scandal of the Evangelical Mind*; Stackhouse, *Evangelical Ecclesiology*; Webber, *Ancient-Future Faith*. It is rather curious, however, that McGrath, in the first edition of his *Historical Theology*, includes a discussion on evangelicalism (249–52), but not in the second edition (see bibliography). Evangelicalism in the US, in particular, is facing an identity crisis in the light of the political developments in that country.

identity, shapes our communities of faith, and guides our Christian life and practice as we seek to engage our world in ways that reflect God's restorative action. Both God's word and God's way give us life, wisdom, inspiration, and direction.

We could begin our journey by turning to many places in the biblical narrative. We might look at Leviticus 19, which links holiness with right conduct, calling God's people to "love the alien as yourself" and to have "honest balances, honest weights" (Lev 19:34–35). Or we could turn to the prophetic tradition and hear Isaiah's call: "this is the fast I choose: to loose the bonds of injustice . . . [to] bring the homeless poor into your house" (Isa 58:6). Or we could go to the wisdom literature, where the psalmist calls the people to "extol . . . [our] God and King and bless your name forever and ever" and then to emulate the "Lord [who] upholds all who are fallen and raises up all who are bowed down" (Ps 145:1, 14). Or we could look at Matthew 25, where service to the least is as an act of worshipping Christ himself (Matt 25:40). Or we could be guided by the wisdom of the author to the Hebrews, who instructs the followers of Christ to "continually offer a sacrifice of praise to God, that is, the fruit of lips that confess his name," and also "to do good and to share what you have for such sacrifices are pleasing to God" (Heb 13:15–16). All these passages clearly connect spirituality with service.

But rather than stringing verses together, let us turn to the great normative narrative, Christ himself, the Word made flesh and the icon of the new humanity, for Christ is both our redeemer and our model. Being a Christian is not simply about believing in Jesus, but allowing Christ to shape and form our lives (Gal 4:19). We are all called to take on the *gestalt* of Christ – and, in the words of Karl Barth, to be a small repetition of the life of Christ. In this sense, Christians are to be a "second incarnation," and therefore Christ-conformity is crucial to our witness and service in the world. Yet the contemporary church in the West, with its consumer mentality and lack of spiritual formation, has separated Christ conformity from service. In many ways, we have become "do-gooders" in the world rather than radical disciples who follow the new way of the Messiah.

The Activist Jesus in Mark's Gospel

Our model, Jesus, is both an activist and a contemplative. We see the activist Jesus most clearly in Mark's gospel, where one scene moves quickly to another, leaping from "then" Jesus did this to "then" Jesus said that. Mark's Jesus is in a hurry. Jesus's activism can be identified by the following contours.

First, Jesus's central concern is the presence, rule, and restorative work of the kingdom of God.[13] Thus Jesus proclaims the reign of God and mirrors it through his life and actions. He is so committed to the reign of God that he gives his life for it, suffering and dying on the cross to make God's way a reality for all who are touched by his redemptive sacrifice. His costly death reminds us that *working for the reign of God involves sacrifice.*

Second, in his kingdom mission, Jesus calls people to conversion and repentance and then invites them to follow him. While he ministers to crowds of people, he also makes time for individuals, such as Zacchaeus and Bartimaeus, along with many other named and unnamed individuals. This practice reminds us that *people are more important than causes.*

Third, throughout his life on earth, Jesus draws others into his ministry. Those who are blessed by his ministry become compatriots and seek to bless others. Thus, Jesus does not operate as a solo hero, but intentionally replicates himself in others. This practice reminds us that *Jesus is committed to building a community.*

Fourth, in his ministry of healing,[14] Jesus seeks to restore broken relationships and to bring wholeness and well-being into people's lives. The healed person is no longer an outcast, but is made whole and welcomed back into the family and broader community. Jesus is not only concerned with the inner life, but the whole person, and so he seeks to restore people to God, to their inner well-being, and to a call to serve others. Throughout the Gospels, the healing narratives remind us that *Jesus restores people to community.*

Fifth, in his ministry of exorcism, Jesus pushes back the powers of darkness.[15] These narratives remind us that *Jesus wants to bring those who are oppressed by dark forces and entities to freedom and wholeness.*

Sixth, the community of men and women who follow Jesus not only share a common faith and ministry, but also a common purse.[16] This community, which is a precursor of the church, models a way of sharing faith and being in the world. This model reflects a *communalism that is rooted in Christ.*

Seventh, Jesus's confrontation with the religious leaders of his day is not about an ideological conflict, but a whole new way of life that is defined by the *shalom* of God. While Jesus acknowledges the good in the Judaic practices of his day, he is deeply concerned about the way that these rituals burden

13. Snyder, *Models of the Kingdom.*

14. Wilkenson, *Bible and Healing.*

15. Israel, *Exorcism.*

16. Janzen, *Intentional Christian Community*, 223–31; Moore, *Called to Community*, 36–42.

people rather than leading them into freedom and life. This reminds us that *our religiosity, rules, and programs should never replace the most precious dynamic of grace, forgiveness, and restoration.*

Eighth, though we don't know if Jesus was intending to start a popular movement among the poor,[17] the Gospels make it clear that the poor hear him gladly and that he freely ministers to them. Thus, Jesus is not only concerned about his inner circle of disciples, but the wider community, including the religious establishment and the poor. This reminds us that *any mission of Jesus is not narrow, as all stand in need of grace and renewal.*

Finally, Jesus practices religious and civil disobedience[18] by healing on the Sabbath. This reminds us that Jesus can hardly be called a social conservative, for *Jesus is a radical in every sense of the word: he goes to the root of things and forges a new way.*[19]

Ched Myers notes that the Gospel of Mark is "a story by, about, and for those committed to God's work of justice, compassion, and liberation in the world."[20] He goes on to say that Mark's gospel is "the manifesto of an early Christian discipleship community"[21] which was seeking to live as a contrast society ". . . from below."[22] Mark's gospel depicts a radical Jesus with a radical manifesto forming a radical community that has a dove in the hand, reconciling love in the heart, and a generous welcome for all. Mark also makes it abundantly clear that the *words* of Jesus are continually expressed through the *deeds* of the kingdom – forgiveness, healing, and restoration.

All this has broad implications for the way in which we are called to witness and serve. Yet some Christians emphasize proclamation and may be uncomfortable with healing and deliverance ministries. Others don't see any connection between the community that Jesus formed and the nature of his ministry. Some downplay that Jesus confronted the religious establishment of his day, claiming that Jesus was not a revolutionary. Others argue that Jesus could not have practised civil disobedience because other parts of the NT advocate obedience to civil and political authority at all times. All these perspectives depict Jesus as a benign figure who loved children and nature,

---

17. See Mangalwadi, *Truth and Social Reform.*

18. Washington, *Testament of Hope*, 43–53.

19. Smith, *Going to the Root.*

20. Myers, *Binding the Strong Man: A Political Reading of Mark's Story of Jesus*, 11.

21. Myers, 31.

22. Myers, 40.

lived outside the demands of work and politics, and was socially irrelevant.[23] This Jesus is only concerned with our inner life and our future life in heaven.

While this serious misreading of the Gospels helps explain the contemporary Christian focus on piety, it does not bear salt and light into a world that desperately needs redemption, healing, and restoration. We will pick up this discussion again in chapter 7 as we explore the missional orientation of the church and the people of God.[24] Here, we will return to our model, Jesus, and explore the contemplative nature of his ministry on earth.

The Contemplative Jesus in John's Gospel

While Mark's Gospel gives us only brief glimpses of Jesus as a contemplative,[25] we meet the contemplative Jesus most fully in John's Gospel. Contemplation involves attentiveness, gazing, joining, abiding, and union, and John's gospel highlights the intimate relationship between Jesus and his Father, their mutual indwelling, and their common participation in all that Jesus is seeking to do. Jesus does what the Father wants him to do, and their bond is so close that Jesus says, "the Father and I are one" (John 10:30). These words reflect a mysterious merging, where one reflects the other more fully.

Following are some of the key contemplative themes in John's Gospel. First, Jesus speaks of *knowing* the Father: "but I know him" (John 8:58; 17:25). This implies intimate knowing, not simply intellectual knowing. Jesus also speaks of mutual knowing: "just as the Father knows me and I know the Father" (John 10:15). To know and to be known is foundational to any relationship. Knowing and being known by God is our existential homecoming, our place of final security.

Second, Jesus celebrates the Father's *love* for him: "the Father loves me" (John 10:17).[26] Knowing that we are intimately loved is foundational to our sense of identity and security.

Third, Jesus acknowledges a *mutual indwelling*: "the Father is in me and I am in the Father" (John 10:38. See also John 14:20; 6:57). For Jesus, this sense of mutuality is foundational to his sense of identity and purpose. Jesus is not

---

23. See Yoder's challenge to this way of thinking in *The Politics of Jesus*.

24. See chapter 7 ("The Heart and Scope of Integral Mission").

25. Jesus's testing in the desert (Mark 1:13), Jesus praying at the beginning of the day (Mark 1:35), Jesus going to a deserted place to rest (Mark 6:31), Jesus's experience of transfiguration (Mark 9:1–8), Jesus in Gethsemane (Mark 14:32), and Jesus's prayer of forsakenness on the cross (Mark 15:34).

26. See also John 3:35; 5:20; 15:9.

simply committed to the purposes of the Father, but is *one* with the Father in being and purpose.

Fourth, Jesus testifies that he is doing the *work* the Father has given him to do: "I have not spoken on my own" but the Father has "given me . . . what to say" (John 12:49).[27] Jesus also speaks of doing "the works that the Father has given me to complete" (John 5:36).

Fifth, Jesus constantly acknowledges that the Father has *sent* him (John 5:36; 7:16; 8:16; 14:24).

Sixth, Jesus confesses that he has fully *revealed* the Father: "I have made known to you everything that I have heard from my Father" (John 15:15).

Finally, Jesus asserts that he is the *embodiment* of the Father: "If you know me, you will know my Father also" (John 14:7).

This language reflects a most amazing union of intimacy and purpose in the relationship between Jesus and his Father, where love leads to service, and loving service leads to the ultimate self-giving by Jesus in order to fulfil the purposes of the Father to redeem and restore the world.

We completely "miss the boat" when we seek to follow the Jesus of Mark's gospel while neglecting the Jesus of John's gospel! For in John's gospel, we see the contemplative Jesus, who lives in the background of the activist Jesus in Mark's gospel. To use psychological language, Mark reveals Jesus's public persona, while John reveals the inner and relational self of Jesus.

And so, if we want to follow Christ, we need to follow the *whole* Christ, who is both activist and contemplative. This is a particular challenge for Protestant evangelicals who have grown up hearing that becoming a Christian is about *believing* in Jesus rather than being invited into the loving intimacy of the Trinity. Jesus describes this relationship by saying, "Those who love me will keep my word and my Father will love them, and *we* will come to them and make our home with them" (John 14:23). The Spirit, whom the Father will send through the Son (John 14:26; 15:26), joins us in this mutual indwelling.

Thus, cultivating an intentional inner life needs to be a central aspect of our missional praxis. John's gospel brings this home with a core missional statement: "as the Father has sent me, *so I send you*" (John 20:21). Yet we often neglect these words, because we have become so enamoured with the missional statement of Matthew 28:19: "Go therefore and make disciples of all the nations." In seeking to imitate Christ, both his praxis and his inner life of love and obedience with the Father must become normative for us.

27. See also John 7:16.

The Witness of the Church in History

We will continue our exploration of the inter-relationship between contemplation and action by turning to the wisdom and practice of the church in its two-thousand-year journey.[28] Though some periods in the history of the Christian church have emphasized the inner life, while neglecting a life of witness and service, more contemporary Western Christianity has tended to emphasize the outer life without paying sufficient attention to the inner life. Such pendulum swings are part of history – including the history of the church.

But the overarching picture traced throughout the biblical narrative is that *love of God involves love of neighbour.* John Cassian (360–435), the great formator of early monasticism, highlights how "the ultimate goal of our way of life is . . . the kingdom of God" and "the immediate aim is purity of heart," but "so long as injustice prevails in the world works of mercy are needed."[29]

In *Hear the Ancient Wisdom* I cite other confirming voices. St. Maximus the Confessor (c. 580–662) says, "we shall be judged for the evil we have done, but especially for the good we have neglected, and for the fact that we have not loved the neighbour" (101). The Dutch Catholic Geert de Groote (1340–1384) prays, "let me first seek the kingdom [of God] and then I shall so much the better be able to serve my neighbour" (8). Meister Eckhart (c. 1230–1628), the German Catholic theologian and mystic, instructs, "do all you can in the way of good works, solely for the praise of God" (136). And the English mystic Walter Hilton (c. 1340–1396) observes, the "contemplative life lies in perfect love and charity . . . by a true knowledge and sight of God in spiritual things" and the "active life lies in love and charity shown outwardly in bodily works" (341). And St. Catherine of Siena (1347–1380), a Dominican mystic and activist, declares that "no virtue . . . can have life in itself except through charity and humility" (283). Thus, throughout history, many voices in the church have understood the inter-relational nature of the inner and outer life of the community of faith.

Moreover, many prominent figures in the Christian church have called followers of Christ to nurture both friendship with God as well as loving service to neighbours. In this section, I will highlight three key voices that describe the dynamic interplay of the inner and outer life for the Christian: St. Augustine

28. See Ringma, *Hear the Ancient Wisdom* and *In the Footsteps of an Ancient Faith*; see also Webber, *Ancient-Future Faith.* As evangelicals, we need to be reminded that our tradition did not begin with Wesley or the Reformation – the fifteen hundred years prior to the Reformation are part of our tradition as well.

29. Cassian, "The Conferences of Cassian," 194, 201.

(354–430), St. Gregory the Great (c. 540–604), and St. Bernard of Clairvaux (1090–1153).

St. Augustine notes that there are three "forms" of the Christian life. The first is a life of "contemplation and examination of truth." The second is being "buried in carrying on human affairs." The third "combines both of these."[30] However, Augustine goes on to point out that one should not be so caught up in reflection so as "not to think of his neighbour's welfare," nor so busy with the ordinary affairs of life "not to seek after contemplation."[31] And he gives the warning that in the active life one should not seek honour and power, but to do the work of mercy and justice for its own sake. He explains that the obligations of charity make us undertake righteous business, while the love of truth calls us to contemplation. He concludes with a testimony about the power of inner communion with God through the practice of meditation: "this I often do, this delights me, and as far as I may be freed from necessary duties, unto this pleasure I have recourse. And sometimes Thou dost admit me to an interior experience . . . [of] a wondrous sweetness."[32]

St. Gregory strikes a similar note, writing that "everyone who is converted to the Lord, desires the . . . contemplative life . . . but first it is necessary that in the night of the present life, he [she] work that good he can, and exert himself in labour."[33] He continues, "it is the right order of living to pass from the active life to the contemplative" and "for the mind to turn back from the contemplative to the active."[34] Then he points out that "the active life is by necessity, the contemplative [is] by choice."[35] Gregory further observes that it is necessary to "put aside the tumult of temporal activities" and in one's "contemplation [to] search out . . . the divine will." Thus "we hear inwardly and in silence what we must do openly."[36] Like Augustine, Gregory also speaks of the wonder and significance of the contemplative experience: "the voice of God is heard when, with minds at ease, we rest from the bustle of this world, and the divine precepts are pondered by us in the deep silence of the mind."[37]

30. Quoted in Butler, *Western Mysticism*, 164.
31. Butler, 165.
32. Butler, 165.
33. Butler, 172.
34. Butler, 173.
35. Butler, 174.
36. Butler, 182.
37. Butler, 183.

Finally, St. Bernard of Clairvaux reminds us that contemplation and action "are intimately related, they are chamber companions and dwell together." He also notes that to find adequate time for contemplation is difficult "because the duties of office and usefulness of work press upon us more urgently." Therefore, it is easy for us to "fall from the state of contemplation . . . [and] resort . . . to action."[38] Yet fruitful action is sourced by contemplation, and so he warns that it is not good to "desire the repose of contemplation" without bringing forth the "blossoms of good works."[39]

These important voices from the Christian tradition all highlight how prayer and service, contemplation and action belong together. Yet the church's praxis has tended to pull these two dimensions of the Christian life apart, elevating spiritual practices over one's engagement with the ordinary affairs of life. Such polarization is always a challenge in the Christian community, but these dimensions need to be integrated so that prayer can be recognized as both a spiritual activity and a work, and service can also be seen as both a spiritual activity and a work.

The Gift and Practice of Contemplation

As noted earlier, contemplation involves attentiveness and gazing – what we might describe today as "mindfulness."[40] We are thinking more about mindfulness in our contemporary age because of our "overly-connected" and "distracted" lifestyles, with many people on call 24/7, some suffering from "attention deficit disorder," and others feeling pulled in so many directions that they claim to be "time poor." Still others do not feel loved in their work or appreciated for ways they seek to serve others.

As we try to juggle so many commitments within our functional and pragmatic world, we often find ourselves longing for relationship, intimacy, union, and homecoming. And though we may say that God is our "dwelling place" ("Lord, you have been our dwelling place in all generations," Ps 90:1), our church activities, programs, and service to the world often leave us aching for a sense of belonging and connection. Amidst our much-doing, we may long to abide in the life of Christ (John 15:4), but feel more like "religious refugees" and exiles. And though we may talk about seeking God's presence,

38. Butler, 193. St. Bernard does not mean that contemplation must not flow into action, but that action should not be a substitute for contemplation.

39. Butler, 194.

40. Thompson, *Christ-Centered Mindfulness.*

we may actually feel that God has abandoned us. Sadly, we may think that we are working *for* God or for our religious institution rather than working *with* God. In all these ways, our work can become a "beast of burden."

In light of these realities, we will explore two inter-related themes in the art of contemplation: contemplation as a *gift* and contemplation as a *spiritual practice*. We touched on this theme in the previous chapter, but will explore it more fully here.

Most of us are familiar with contemplation as a *spiritual practice,* which for many people means setting time aside to be still in the presence of God.[41] In this time of stillness, we lay down our agendas and issues and whatever we think we should do, and we open ourselves to behold who God is and to listen to God's heart for our lives and our world. The stillness of surrender can lead to a new attentiveness, where we seek to hear the voice of God within our very being as a voice of friendship and direction. Since such a connection cannot be orchestrated, the contemplative experience calls us to wait in hope. Thus *surrender*, *expectancy*, and *waiting* are core elements of contemplative practices. Many different practices play a part in the contemplative experience, but some include journaling, practicing art, *lectio Divina*, other forms of engaging Scripture, meditation, being in nature, and prayer. The list, however, is endless, as many activities can heighten our sense of God's presence based on our particular culture and personality.

The concept of contemplation as a *spiritual gift* may be less familiar. In this posture, we open ourselves to how God, through the Spirit (who is beyond gender), might reveal himself/herself to us. God may come to us as the God of comfort and nurture, or the God who seeks to affirm or consolidate something in our lives, or the God who confronts us and calls us to repentance, or the God who heals, or the God who guides and directs us.

While a great gift in contemplation is to nurture friendship with God and to know that we are loved, a secondary gift is to be *undone* in order to gain a new self and new perspectives about life and the world around us. When we are immersed in daily life and shaped by the dominant values of our culture (Rom 12:1–2), we need to withdraw into "the cave," the "desert," or the "closet" in order to be denuded – stripped bare – from our contamination, illusions, and self-made plans. In this posture of "nakedness," we need to be "reborn" so that

41. Nouwen points out: "Silence is the way to make solitude a reality" (*Way of the Heart*, 43). Thus, silence is a step towards solitude, and solitude is the great gift, the place of encounter in meeting the Lord (30). This encounter, while it may be one of comfort, may also be "the place of purification and transformation" (31).

we can see ourselves in a different light and see God's purposes more clearly. When God comes to us through this secondary gift, we find our unique place in the vast operations of the Spirit in renewing the world and often discover a new way of engaging our world. Put simply, *contemplation facilitates action.*

This concept of being undone in order to be remade is well-illustrated in the work of Victor Turner, who speaks of the dynamic of moving from order (one's present *gestalt* of life) to a time of disorder or liminality.[42] This may occur through a major crisis, a relocation, or a phase in one's psycho-social development, but it can also occur through prayer and reflection. In this in-between stage, we are undone so that a new sense of self, purpose, and calling may emerge.

The Asian NT scholar, Noli Mendoza, illustrates this well through the story of Peter's undoing and remaking in his vision of the large net with all kinds of creatures that he is ordered to kill and eat. This powerful experience calls Peter to embrace a mission to the Gentiles (Acts 10).[43] Most basically, prayer and contemplation is a place of transformation that can have significant implications for our mission to the world.

Voices from the Contemporary Contemplative Tradition

In this concluding section, I will attend to more contemporary voices within the contemplative experience: Diogenes Allen (1932–2013), Basil Pennington (1931–2005), Henri Nouwen (1932–1996), Thomas Merton (1915–1968), and Carlo Maria Martini (1927–2012).

Diogenes Allen, who was an American professor of philosophy at Princeton Theological Seminary in the USA, notes that the contemplative orientation is multi-faceted. First, it involves the quest to "discern God's presence in the entire created universe,"[44] which includes attentiveness to "people, situations, and one's actions and motives."[45] Thus, while the central impulse is to rest in God and to become "like God through knowing God's wisdom,"[46] the outworking of this is the active life, where one becomes "like God by acting like God."[47]

---

42. Turner, *Ritual Process.*
43. Mendoza, "Faith at the Border."
44. Allen, *Spiritual Theology*, 11.
45. Allen, 103.
46. Allen, 97.
47. Allen, 97.

Allen notes how various practices can facilitate the contemplative experience, such as reading Scripture, meditating, and praying. He also points out the challenge of growing in the blessing of *apatheia*, where one becomes free from inner distractions and comes to "purity of heart."[48] In this, he notes the difference between contemplation as a task and a gift. He calls the latter "infused contemplation," which is the gift of God's "habitual presence."[49] In this, "we are receptive rather than active."[50]

Allen also helpfully notes that while we are invited to contemplate the Scriptures "to gain knowledge of God,"[51] we are also invited to contemplate the natural world and human nature as "a way to increase . . . love and knowledge of God."[52] This understanding of contemplation means that we gaze into the face of God as well as our own hearts, the human condition, and our world. As we gaze and attend to the face of God, we are transformed and impacted by the presence and wisdom of God, which brings forth our active service in the world. This vision approximates that of St. Ignatius of Loyola, which Allen describes as a tradition where "contemplation is used to form oneself spiritually so that one is better able to discern and do God's will in daily life."[53]

Basil Pennington, an American Roman Catholic Trappist monk and priest, is well-known for his popular book *Centering Prayer*.[54] While Pennington prefers to speak of "centering prayer" rather than meditation or contemplation,[55] he later says that "whenever anyone asks me how I manage to get so much done," he always replies, "by giving several hours a day to contemplative prayer."[56] Elsewhere in the book, he uses contemplative prayer and centering prayer synonymously.[57] Thus there is no substantive difference between these two terms.

---

48. Allen, 80.
49. Allen, 30.
50. Allen, 11.
51. Allen, 125.
52. Allen, 111.
53. Allen, 156.
54. While Pennington's book is grounded, it is more of a "how-to" book. See also the practical wisdom of John Main, *Way of Unknowing*, which focuses on Christian meditation as an exploration of "faith, active in love," that seeks "'union with Jesus Christ'" (53).
55. Pennington, *Centering Prayer*, 13.
56. Pennington, 130.
57. Pennington, 85, 96.

His core concept is that centering prayer is a "response to God's great love," where we give our hearts to God and "the rest is inconsequential."[58] Pennington then elaborates that this form of prayer "is the simple enjoyment of God," where we are attentive to God's "wonderful Presence" and "sink down into the quiet depths, where there is only a simple flow . . . into the Ocean of Infinite love."[59] The fruit of this life of prayer is that we become aware of "our sins and miseries, our backsliding and infidelity," and "the entanglements of . . . [our] false, superficial selves," and then we can come to a "reintegration," where our true self can "come forth from God's love."[60] While Pennington does not draw missional implications from this life of prayer, he believes that if the entire Christian community engaged in these practices,[61] a world of peace would be possible "through the loving and nurturing Presence of God in all."[62]

Henri Nouwen, a Dutch Catholic priest, professor, and writer, briefly joined the Maryknoll missionaries in Lima, Peru (1981)[63] and also spent time in Mexico and Nicaragua while juggling teaching duties at Harvard University (1983).[64] Then, in 1986, he resigned from academia to become a pastoral care worker at the L'Arche Daybreak community in Toronto, Canada.[65] By virtue of all these different callings in his life, Nouwen demonstrates an integration of spirituality and service to others.

Nouwen's biographer, Jurjen Beumer, rightly points out that Nouwen struggled with his life of upward mobility and prestige "most starkly during his short period at Harvard University." His desire for downward mobility, as a way of following Jesus and seeking to be a sign of the kingdom of God, eventually led him to the L'Arche Daybreak community, where he embraced, as Beumer points out, a "kenotic ethic" of self-emptying in the way of Christ.[66] Thus compassion and caring were major themes in Nouwen's life and writings.[67]

Throughout his writings, Nouwen makes it explicitly clear that the spiritual disciplines are intrinsic to his life of faith and service. He writes extensively

58. Pennington, 76.
59. Pennington, 83, 50, 54.
60. Pennington, 135, 134, 96, 97.
61. Pennington, 134, 217.
62. Pennington, 215.
63. See Nouwen et al., *Compassion.*
64. See Nouwen, *¡Gracias!*
65. See Nouwen, *The Road to Daybreak.*
66. Beumer, *Henri Nouwen*, 125.
67. Beumer, *Henri Nouwen*, 132–36.

about solitude,[68] prayer,[69] and contemplation, which he conceives as *a new way of seeing*. Following the desert father, Evagrius Ponticus, Nouwen says that contemplation is about seeing "things for what they really are" and moving from "opaqueness to transparency."[70] Thus, the "contemplative life is a life of vision."[71] This new way of seeing involves seeing all things bathed in "the Creator's love"[72] and in the light of "the hand of God with us" in all that we are and do.[73] However, this way of seeing life and the world is not based on a few extraordinary moments, but a whole way of life that is possible when the "God within us recognizes God in the world."[74] Nouwen observes that when we see "ordinary life with its daily routines and responsibilities with a 'deeper vision of life,'"[75] it has consequences for how we see others. He writes, "our time of being with God gives us new eyes to see the beauty and gifts in those for whom we care."[76]

A key summary of Nouwen's understanding of contemplation is that "the movement from loneliness to solitude is not a movement of growing withdrawal, but instead a movement toward a deeper engagement in the burning issues of our time."[77] Nouwen continues, "if you are really praying, you can't help but have critical questions about the great problems the world is grappling with."[78] Thus, he concludes that contemplatives are "the ones who enter the center of the world and pray to God from there,"[79] noting that "as prayer leads us into the house of God and God's people, so action leads us back into the world to work there for reconciliation, unity, and peace."[80]

At this point, it is imperative to bring Thomas Merton, a French-born American Trappist monk and prolific author, into the conversation. Though Merton lived for most of his life as a monk within the confines of a monastery

68. Beumer, 84–91.
69. Beumer, 92–103; see also Ringma, *Dare to Journey* and *Hear the Heartbeat*.
70. Nouwen, *Clowning in Rome*, 85.
71. Nouwen, 84.
72. Nouwen, 88.
73. Nouwen, 93.
74. Nouwen, 101.
75. Nouwen, 93.
76. Nouwen, 96–97.
77. Quoted in Ringma, *Dare to Journey*, reflection 7.
78. Quoted in Ringma, reflection 157.
79. Quoted in Ringma, reflection 153.
80. Quoted in Ringma, *Hear the Heartbeat*, 38.

in rural Kentucky, he was actively engaged with the world and the issues of his time.

Merton observes that the monastic vocation is "a life of renunciation and total, direct worship of God for his own sake."[81] He elaborates that the monk "unites himself with the hidden years of labour spent by Jesus in Nazareth, or he follows Jesus into the desert sharing the Master's solitary prayer."[82] The heart of the monastic journey is a "life in Christ," and by living *in* Christ, the monk "prolongs the mystery of the incarnation on earth."[83] At the same time, Merton observes that because the monk is concerned about God, he is necessarily deeply concerned about the world and the realities of "human conflict, hate, aggression, destruction, subversion, deceit, [and] the unscrupulous use of power."[84] He further clarifies that "far from being exempted from service in the battles of his age, the monk, as a soldier of Christ, is appointed to fight these battles on a spiritual, hidden front – in mystery – by prayer and self-sacrifice."[85]

In the classics, *Seeds of Contemplation* and *Contemplative Prayer*, Merton has a general audience in view rather than members of monastic communities. In *Seeds of Contemplation*, after giving a long articulation about what contemplation is *not*,[86] Merton offers the enlightening observation that contemplation is the very core of our being. When we know we are blessed "with the majesty and mercy of the Hidden and Living One,"[87] we gain a "certitude of God's creative and dynamic intervention in our daily life."[88] Thus, we know and love God "for His own sake alone,"[89] and in this place, "your mind can be idle, and forget its concerns, descend into silence, and worship the Father in secret."[90] Yet Merton also highlights how the contemplative experience not only draws us into a fuller encounter with God, but also with ourselves. In this place, we are stripped bare of our stupidities and illusions so that we can "be saved above all from the abyss of confusion and absurdity which is our own worldly self" and delivered from "the false self in me."[91]

81. Merton, *The Monastic Journey*, 4.
82. Merton, 6.
83. Merton, 15.
84. Merton, 4–5.
85. Merton, 35.
86. Merton, *Seeds of Contemplation*, 5–11.
87. Merton, 3.
88. Merton, 4.
89. Merton, 208.
90. Merton, 64.
91. Merton, 30, 33.

In *Contemplative Prayer* Merton provides a more sustained discussion of contemplation, emphasizing that this spiritual discipline is not about a "method" or "system" but our "attitude."[92] Our central concern is to cultivate a "watchful listening of the 'heart'" – not as a way of *finding* God, but rather as a way "of resting in Him."[93] Moreover, contemplation is not concerned with having "extraordinary experiences,"[94] personal security, or arriving at some sort of perfection,[95] but rather with "self-denial and sacrifice," "humble surrender," and patience in "the weary and arid path that takes us through dry places in prayer."[96]

Moreover, Merton makes it very clear that contemplative prayer is not simply for monks,[97] and he further emphasizes that it is not a way of escaping from life's realities. In fact, the contemplative is always "searching . . . his [her] own heart" while at the same time plunging "deep into the heart of the world."[98] This form of prayer and reflection "does not blind us to the world, but . . . transforms our vision of the world,"[99] so that we can see the love of God upholding our world and gain insight into the "falsity and illusion" of much of life, along with "exposure to what the world ignores about itself – both good and evil."[100]

Referring to St. Gregory, Merton links contemplation with service, as both are "demanded by charity, since man [woman] is commanded to love both God and his [her] neighbor."[101] He also quotes St. Bernard, arguing that Mary, the contemplative, and Martha, the activist, "dwell together in the same household."[102] Merton pushes this even further, observing that "action and contemplation are fused in one entity by the love of God."[103]

Merton concludes by saying "without contemplation and interior prayer the church cannot fulfil her mission to transform and save mankind

92. Merton, *Contemplative Prayer*, 39.
93. Merton, 33, 32.
94. Merton, 21.
95. Merton, 47, 43.
96. Merton, 89, 83, 94.
97. Merton, 20.
98. Merton, 25.
99. Merton, 139.
100. Merton, 27.
101. Merton, 63.
102. Merton, 65.
103. Merton, 143.

[humankind]."[104] Thus, he sees the contemplative experience as central to the mission of the faith-community. We might describe this as a missional spirituality, though Merton does not use this terminology.

As noted previously, some Christians throughout history have elevated spiritual practices and neglected practical care, but in our time, the opposite seems to be the case. In following the dominant ethos of our culture, we have become so functional and practical that prayer, reflection, and contemplation have become marginal – and sometimes irrelevant. Thus, the crisis of prayer in the contemporary church reflects a weakness in the life of the church and its mission in the world. Though we have championed the importance of relevance, we have failed to stress that we are to live as God's peculiar people in the world. Though we have rightly stressed the call to practical service, we have not equally stressed the need to turn to God for nurture, direction, and empowerment.

A Model for Contemplation and Action

The dynamic between contemplation and action is both interactive and personal, and so we will need wisdom as we seek to develop our own practices. Carlo Martini, an Italian Jesuit who became the Archbishop of Milan, offers a helpful model for integrating contemplation and service in our daily life. This model has four inter-related dimensions.

In the first, *consolatio*, we gain hope, courage, and renewal through the comforting and healing presence of God. This is where we hear the words: "you are my beloved son/daughter." As we come home to the Father-heart of God, in Christ, through the Spirit, we find our true centre and receive the consolations that we need to sustain us in our life's journey and service.

In the second, *discretio*, the Spirit nudges us and prompts us to make new life and ministry choices. This is where we hear: "this is how you need to live and act." In this dimension, we gain a new openness to the voice of God as we hear the call to repentance. This dimension also ensures that our *consolatio* does not remain "stuck" in an introspective self-preoccupation.

In the third, *deliberatio*, we wrestle with the voice of God and the leading of the Spirit as we seek to come to a place of surrender and obedience. This is where we say, "Yes, Lord, I love to do your will." Being comforted by God, then stripped bare and re-directed is not a five-minute journey. If it is, we may well be "missing the boat." Instead, it is a struggle of faith to *hear* and *do* the

104. Merton, 144.

particular calling that God places on our life. Let us not be too quick to say: "Yes, Lord." We need to count the cost, as we may well be called to walk the long road of a new obedience.

In the fourth, *actio*, we live out our commitment to the call of God in the world. This is where we say, "Lord have mercy upon me and empower me to do your will."[105] Both dimensions in this response are important. Our doing the will of God will continue to be marked by our ongoing struggles and imperfections. Hence, we cry, "Lord have mercy." And our need to be empowered by God is constant, because the task will always be greater than our resources.

To clarify the dynamic interplay of contemplation and action, let us return to the wisdom of Segundo Galilea, who observes that contemplation is always two-directional. In the move of transcendence, we contemplate the face of God. In the move of incarnation, we contemplate the hidden face of Christ in those whom we seek to serve. When we seek the face of God, God will remind us of the neighbour in need. When we serve the neighbour in need, including the enemy, we will be reminded to seek the face of God on their behalf.

Conclusion

In this chapter, I have sought to situate the relationship between contemplation, mission, and service in the life of Jesus by engaging the Gospels of Mark and John as well as older traditions of the church and a number of contemporary voices. My primary concern has been to reinforce the theme that contemplation is no stranger to the biblical story, is rooted in the church's long tradition, and is essential to the missional work of the church. Thus, the mission of the community of faith will be weakened if it neglects the spiritual disciplines, including prayer, meditation, and contemplation, as it seeks to engage society with a vision of the reign of God.[106] This challenging task is awakened by the voice of Love, sustained by the grace of Christ, and empowered by the Spirit – and so it is born in prayer and must be continually nourished by prayer.

Let us conclude by listening to the winsome and challenging words of St. John of the Cross:

---

105. The bare-bones skeleton of this model is in Cunningham and Egan, *Christian Spirituality: Themes from the Tradition* (39). I have considerably elaborated on this model.

106. Arias, *Announcing the Reign of God.*

If you want
the virgin will come walking down the road
pregnant with the holy,
and say,
"I need shelter for the night,
please take me inside your heart,
my time is close."
Then under the roof of your soul,
you will witness the sublime intimacy,
the Christ
taking birth.[107]

107. Quoted in Ladinsky, *Love Poems from God*, 306.

5

Mysticism and Mission

Introduction

In this far-reaching chapter, I will trace a direct link between mysticism and mission, but I must first make a few observations. First, because mysticism is often seen as inward or overly concerned with extra-ordinary spiritual experiences[1] that pull people into an esoteric realm and away from orthodox Christianity or social responsibility,[2] it is sometimes perceived as a threat rather than a blessing. I will argue that mysticism can enhance our missional task and serve to deepen the church's witness and service in the world.

Second, this chapter will broaden and deepen the previous chapter's discussion of the relationship between contemplation and action, highlighting how mysticism is not a sub-category of the contemplative experience. Rather, contemplation fits under the umbrella of mysticism.[3]

1. The Jesuit philosopher and spiritual director, Father Thomas Green, while emphasizing the transcendence and otherness of God, notes that "God is really the most sensible person that I know" (*Prayer and Common Sense*, 9). What he means by this is not a denial of the mystery of God in the life of faith, but that living the Christian life is also about responding to and living normal life realities. He notes that "this world - and our human experience - is not a dream, to be rejected as illusory or unreal. Rather, we are called to see it from a new vantage point, in a new light" (57).

2. Allen Brent notes that one danger of the very early Christian communities was a "retreat from social engagement . . . into individual mysticism" (*Political History of Early Christianity*, 128). However, he goes on to highlight various emphases on the relationship between church and society in early Christianity, including the Lucan tradition and that of Clement and Ignatius, with its core idea that "contemporary society was to be embraced, engaged with, and transformed" (167).

3. In *The Essential Writings of Christian Mysticism*, McGinn provides an extensive panorama of the various dimensions of Christian mysticism, including sections on "Vision, Contemplation, and Rapture" (309–64) and "Contemplation and Action" (519–51). In this, he identifies contemplation as a sub-theme of Christian mysticism. Some of the major themes of mysticism include union with God, birthing, deification, endless desire, vision, and so on (xv). In

Third, I am particularly interested in addressing this chapter to my evangelical friends, since mysticism continues to be neglected by this tradition. For example, the missional documents of the Lausanne Movement[4] – with the single exception of the Cape Town Commitment[5] – do not make clear connections between spirituality and mission or mysticism and the ministry of the church in the world.[6]

Finally, I will draw some general conclusions that have practical implications for the Majority world[7] – particularly Asian Christians, as I have served various faith-communities in Asia for over thirty years. However, these implications may well be relevant for Christians elsewhere.[8]

Personal Reflections

I see myself as rational and pragmatic and often say that I drank in the Protestant work ethic with my mother's milk. I have also worked in secular employment, urban ministry, and education, and I have had a lifelong struggle with integrating prayer and work. Thus, I certainly do not see myself as a mystic!

And yet, I have had a number of unusual experiences that resulted in my becoming involved in particular areas of ministry. In sharing these stories, I do not wish to draw attention to myself, for I am too much of an introvert for that! Nor do I wish to suggest that my experiences were somehow special. Rather, I recount these experiences to highlight the direct link between mysticism and ministry.

The first experience was in a hospital setting, where I was undergoing treatment for lead poisoning (I was possibly not yet as mad as a hatter!) from my work as a compositor in the printing and publishing industry. Several days before my discharge, I had an inner impression that my girlfriend and I would receive a call to work with Australia's Indigenous peoples. This impression came from left field, as I had not been thinking about this at all and had no prior

---

Christian Spirituality, Cunningham and Egan discuss "Meditation and Contemplation" (84–104) and "Living in the Presence of God: The Way of the Mystics" (123–42) in separate chapters.

4. Stott, *Making Christ Known*.

5. http://www.lausanne.org/content/ctc/ctcommitment.

6. See Nicholl, "Towards Integrated Mission for the Evangelical Lausanne Movement."

7. In terms of global Christianity, we now speak of the Minority World (the West) and the Majority World (basically the rest of the world). The latter constitutes 70 percent of global Christianity.

8. We need to be careful that we do not overdraw the distinctive features of Christianity in the Minority and Majority Worlds.

connection with such a ministry. I told my girlfriend about this impression, but said it might be best not to mention it to anyone else and to wait and see what would unfold. This we did. Sure enough, several months later, an invitation came "out of the blue" from Western Australia for us to volunteer for such a ministry, which we accepted. This proved to be an incredibly formative experience for us.

The second experience was equally surprising. I had completed my theological studies. We were unable to return to serve in Western Australia, and then an overseas position in Indonesia fell through, leaving me in "no man's land." One morning, I heard an inner voice saying, "you are on the street so start working on the street!" Simple! Penetrating! A crystal clear voice I could neither ignore or resist! After securing a normal 9am to 5pm job to care for my family, I began to work on the streets in a notorious part of Brisbane's inner city from 9 at night to 1 or 2 in the morning. This eventually led to the founding of Teen Challenge here in Australia, a ministry with street people, drug addicts, and men and women in prostitution.

Lastly, I have never talked about this experience with others or put it into the public domain, and I do so now with some reluctance. Yet I think it is appropriate to this chapter and, more broadly, that it is important during this time, when so much of life – including the church – has become functional, pragmatic, and rational. In an age when clergy are pursuing MBA's rather than Master's degrees in Spiritual Theology or Spiritual Direction, I believe we need a recovery of the Spirit, who animates our lives and service.

This third experience occurred after years of overwork in ministry, when I had a physical breakdown. Doctors recommended a complete six-month break, and I complied. Nothing too untoward happened during this recovery time. I walked a lot and regularly swam in the nearby surf. I fished endlessly, mainly fruitlessly. I read little. As the months went by, I regained strength and energy. There was only one dark cloud in all of this – a sense that God's presence had fully departed and the heavens seemed as brass. What made this all the more pressing was that I was about to return to my involvement in urban ministry.

One afternoon, I was sitting in the lounge room on my own. I was not praying, just sitting there. Suddenly a person appeared to me in a wide-awake vision – a person who was bathed in subdued light, but radiating love. He came over to me, embraced me, and was gone. The impact was electric. I felt love pulsating through me and felt wholly renewed in my inner being. I had never felt so cared for, understood, and accepted, and I felt alive in a whole new way. I assumed that the person who appeared to me was Jesus, and in the following days, I had the simple conviction of a salient lesson: we are well-loved and embraced first, and out of this embrace, we serve the world. This lesson completely torpedoed the other narrative that so often dominates our service: we serve in order to be accepted or respected.

I need to add that neither life in general, nor my work in urban mission, magically changed forever after this revelation.[9] The blessings of God do not come to us as a permanent state of spiritual existence. The Pauline epistles are clear: we are *always* called to put on the new in Christ and to put off our old ways of being and doing. My challenge was how to re-appropriate this visionary experience and *live* my new mantra: *well-loved in the grace of Christ, service spawned as an overflow of that love.*

The Christian Mystical Tradition and the Art of Contemplation[10]

While we are about to enter a terminological minefield,[11] it is necessary to discuss the relationship between mysticism and contemplation. It may be helpful to make the initial point that the above personal experiences may be typified as belonging to Christian mysticism. Moreover, these experiences had nothing do with certain contemplative practices, as spiritual practices played no part.

Dictionaries define contemplation as concentration on spiritual things, deeply reflective thought, and thoughtful observation. They define mysticism as union with the divine through contemplation, self-surrender, direct communion with ultimate reality, and the soul's communion with God through contemplation or ecstasy. From this basic starting point, one may surmise that contemplation may simply be *one* of the means through which mystical union takes place. However, we can progress further by drawing on the works of a number of scholars who have made Christian mysticism a particular focus of study.

First, Christian mysticism has a wide and varied history, with at least five major periods: the mysticism of the early church fathers, Monastic mysticism,

9. More recently, I spent six months in a hermitage, and nothing revelatory took place. See Ringma, *Sabbath Time.*

10. Part of this chapter was first published as "Hear the Ancient Wisdom: Medieval Christian Mystics Speak to Present-Day Asian Evangelicals," in *Walking with God*, ed. Ringma and Hollenbeck-Wuest, 112–26 (used with permission).

11. Louth, *The Origins of the Christian Mystical Tradition,* notes the "difficulty of precise definition" for the term, "mysticism" (203).

later Medieval mysticism, the Reformation and Catholic Reform, and the modern period.[12]

Second, Christian mysticism has had various emphases throughout the history of Christianity, including: (1) the "desire to know and to love God as deeply as possible through contact with Christ hidden in the Scriptures";[13] (2) the "bridal mysticism" of the monastic movement[14] and that of the medieval Christian women mystics;[15] (3) the emphasis on the soul's ascent to God in the later medieval period and the Franciscan mysticism of bearing "the naked and crucified Christ"[16] in one's inner being and in one's outer expression of serving the poor; and (4) the Catholic reform movement, with Teresa of Avila's emphasis on the "journey to spiritual marriage" and its outworking in "growth in love of neighbor,"[17] along with the Ignatian spirituality of service that is "rooted in contemplative prayer."[18]

Third, despite these different emphases, there is an underlying commonality to Christian mysticism, which Andrew Louth describes as the "experience of immediacy with God" and the "soul's longing"[19] for "direct apprehensions of the God who has revealed himself in Christ and dwells within us through the Holy Spirit."[20] He goes on to point out that this mysticism, while personal, is also "ecclesial and sacramental," and while there may or may not be ecstatic experiences, its heartbeat is the "radical opening of ourselves to God."[21] Bernard McGinn adds a transformational dimension to the mystical experience, observing that Christian mysticism is a "consciousness of and the effect of . . . a direct and transformative presence of God."[22] He goes on to note that this leads

---

12. Cunningham and Egan, *Christian Spirituality*, 128–42. See also Wiseman, "Mysticism," 681–92. For the most extensive discussion of Christian mysticism to date, see the works of Bernard McGinn: *Foundations of Mysticism*; *Growth of Mysticism*; *Flowering of Mysticism*. See also Louth, *Origins of the Christian Mystical Tradition*, which covers the period beginning with Plato and his influence on the early church fathers through Denys, the Areopagite, and St. John of the Cross.

13. Cunningham and Egan, *Christian Spirituality*, 128.

14. Cunningham and Egan, 133.

15. See Spearing, *Medieval Writings on Female Spirituality*; Madigan, *Mystics, Visionaries and Prophets*.

16. Cunningham and Egan, *Christian Spirituality*, 134–35.

17. Cunningham and Egan, 137.

18. Cunningham and Egan, 136.

19. Louth, *Origins of the Christian Mystical Tradition*, xiv.

20. Louth, x.

21. Louth, 201.

22. McGinn, *Essential Writings*, xiv.

to "new ways of knowing," where God becomes "the direct and transforming center of life."[23] Clearly, this experience of inner transformation has all sorts of implications for one's life of faith, prayer, and service. McGinn notes that mysticism is meant "to spill out and over into a new mode of living," because the Christian is called upon "to serve his [her] neighbor in love."[24] Thus the Ignatian mantra, *in contemplatione activus*, is a core theme.

In light of the above, we may conclude that Christian mysticism is a complex and varied movement within Christianity that significantly and existentially brings the Christ follower into a more direct encounter with God, which deepens his or her love of both God and neighbour. This mystical encounter leads the Christ follower to engage the world in ways that have been formed, inspired, and shaped by God's love and wisdom. Such loving and wise engagement will have critical and transformative consequences for the world. Moreover, this existential encounter with God that leads to a passion for the world actually operates as a hermeneutical circle, for our ministry in the world will inevitably lead us back into the bosom of the Father's love for refreshment and further direction.

While it is possible for the Christian mystic to get marooned in the eddies of one's own spiritual experiences, this is not the hallmark of the Christian mystical tradition. Rather, its orientation is rooted in the inextricable connection between the love of God and the love of neighbour. As such, there is a direct link between mysticism and ministry, and thus evangelicals have much to learn from the Christian mystical tradition.

To clarify the intimate connection between contemplation and mysticism,[25] we might say that Christian mysticism is a broad movement within Christianity that has many dimensions, whereas contemplation is a spiritual practice and therefore a sub-category of mysticism. Contemplative practices – particularly "infused contemplation," or contemplation as a gift rather than a discipline – may lead to mystical experiences, but this is not the only road. Any longing heart that is moved by the generative Holy Spirit can experience mystical union with God.

---

23. McGinn, xvi.

24. McGinn, 519–20.

25. Shannon observes that contemplation is "often used interchangeably with *mysticism*," but then unhelpfully focuses on mystical prayer while acknowledging that mysticism includes "a number of phenomena that relate human creatures to God" ("Contemplation, Contemplative Prayer," 209).

Evangelicals and the Christian Mystical Tradition

Present-day evangelicals and those in the Christian mystical tradition may think they have nothing to say to each other.[26] Many present-day evangelicals tend to think of Christian mystics as people with strange ecstatic and visionary experiences that take them away from a singular focus on Christ and the Scriptures.[27] Moreover, mystics are often seen as self-absorbed and disengaged from serving their neighbours and caring about the world – so heavenly minded that they are of no earthly good! And some evangelicals may trace the roots of our faith, theology, and spirituality through various revival and holiness movements back to the Reformation – but no further. From this perspective, just as the Reformers put an end to monasticism, they also put an end to mysticism.[28]

But many scholars have identified numerous Protestants – and even evangelicals – as part of the Christian mystical tradition, including Johann Arndt (1555–1621), George Fox (1624–1691), William Law (1686–1761), Jonathan Edwards (1703–1758), and John Wesley (1703–1791), among others.[29] To give a particular example, Johannes Tauler (c. 1300–1361), who belonged to the Rhineland mystics headed by Meister Eckhart (1260–1327), had a huge influence on Martin Luther. Tauler wrote about the soul's insatiable hunger for God, the experience of the dark night of the soul, and the *via negativa*: "finding God in withdrawal and the wilderness."[30] The Reformers, moreover, were deeply influenced by the church fathers, many of whom were regarded as early Christian mystics, including Clement of Alexandria (c. 150–c. 215) and Gregory of Nyssa (330–395). The most important influence on the Reformers was Augustine of Hippo (354–430), who is regarded as one of the great Trinitarian Christian mystics. Augustine speaks of God "powerfully blazing

26. The Asian evangelical scholar, Simon Chan, notes in *Spiritual Theology* that among "Protestants who developed the mystical theme in their theology the most notable were the Puritan ascetics," and the most prominent person was Richard Baxter (99).

27. It should be noted that throughout this book, the focus is *Christian* mysticism, but I acknowledge that other religions also have their mystical traditions.

28. Cunningham and Egan in *Christian Spirituality* make the broad statement that "Luther's opposition left Protestantism without much access to the mystical tradition" (136). However, Philip Sheldrake in *Spirituality and History* qualifies this with the observation that the Reformers "had a great esteem for *some* medieval spiritual thinkers such as St. Bernard, Meister Eckhart, Tauler and a Kempis" (211). And Hoffman in "Lutheran Spirituality" concludes that "mystical knowledge *was* part of Luther's spirituality, but it was not free-floating; it was rooted in the justifying *kerygma* of Scripture" (128).

29. Fanning, *Mystics of the Christian Tradition*.

30. King, *Christian Mystics*, 117.

into me; and I trembled with love and dread" and "the brightness of the Lord will be seen . . . through direct appearance."[31]

Many scholars also point out that Christian mysticism, which was influenced by Jewish mysticism and Neoplatonic thinking, also has deep biblical roots, citing Jacob's vision of the ladder to heaven, Moses's visionary experience at Mt. Sinai, Isaiah's vision of the holiness of Yahweh, St. John's gospel of sacramental Christology, and Paul's emphasis on Christo-mysticism in the in-Christ relationship (Col 1:26–27; Gal 4:17) as well as his use of the language of mystery (Eph 3:4; Col 1:26–27; 1 Cor 4:1; 1 Cor 2:7).

Some may assume that if one does not experience extraordinary mystical phenomena, such as visions and other ecstatic experiences, one is not a mystic. Yet mysticism is not primarily about ecstasies, but about "self-abandonment in naked faith" through the cross of Christ to become "one with the very love of the crucified God."[32] Said another way, the Christian mystic "is one whose experiential awareness of Jesus Christ enables life to be lived with an increasing depth of faith-vision and love-dynamism."[33] Most simply, mysticism is the "direct and transformative presence of God" and the "journey to God," and while this may come in unmediated ways, it may also come through spiritual practices.[34] Thus, the concept of Christian mysticism fits clearly within the evangelical tradition, particularly its charismatic expression. Moreover, John Calvin emphasizes the Christian's mystical union with Christ, which he calls a "sacred marriage," language that places him alongside the bridal mysticism of Bernard of Clairvaux.[35] Nevertheless, the experience of mystical phenomena cannot be completely excluded from the definition of mysticism, since it fits within the biblical tradition and the experience of many church leaders, including Augustine, St. Francis, Bernard of Clairvaux, and Julian of Norwich.

Revitalization within Evangelicalism

Some present-day voices within the evangelical community charge evangelicals with being too pragmatic, further splintering the church by creating solo independent churches, and treating the church like a corporation. Moreover, they criticize evangelicals for not living Christlike lives that are shaped by

31. McGinn, *Essential Writings*, 317, 323.

32. In Downey, *New Dictionary of Catholic Spirituality*, 682.

33. Madigan, *Mystics, Visionaries, and Prophets*, 3.

34. McGinn, *Essential Writings*, xiv, xvii.

35. In Scorgie, *Dictionary of Christian Spirituality*, 180.

the spiritual practices and disciplines. Thus, they are calling for revitalization within evangelicalism.

First, Richard Lovelace suggests that evangelicals need to embrace a more "ascetic model of spirituality" and to rediscover the early church fathers, Reformation leaders, the leaders in modern spiritual awakenings, and "the medieval mystics."[36]

Second, Robert Webber suggests that evangelicals need to overcome their "strong bias against the history [of the church] preceding the Reformation" and rediscover "the great treasury of spiritual resources in the history of the church." Moreover, they need to recover "the mystery of the transcendent" and recognize mysticism as a "protest movement" for renewal rather than writing it off as a movement of spiritual escapism.[37]

Third, G. G. Scorgie reminds us that the mystical writers call us to a "deep communion with God" through their emphasis on Christ. He suggests that evangelicals need "inspirational models and heroes," such as St. Francis of Assisi, Thomas à Kempis, and Julian of Norwich. Moreover, he calls evangelicals to resist the "pervasive pressures to downsize Christian spirituality," to recover "intentionally cultivated virtues," and to embrace the "spiritual disciplines" in a transforming friendship with God.[38]

Challenges from Medieval Mystics

In light of these encouraging words from present-day evangelicals, we will listen to challenges from several medieval mystics, including St. Francis of Assisi (c. 1181–1226), Bonaventure (1221–1274), St. Catherine of Genoa (1447–1510), St. Catherine of Siena (1347–1380), St. Bernard of Clairvaux (1090–1153), Hildegard of Bingen (1098–1179), and Julian of Norwich (1342–1420).

St. Francis of Assisi and Bonaventure

St. Francis[39] (c. 1181–1226) shifted the spirituality of the monastic life into a spirituality of "the instability of life on the road."[40] His Trinitarian theology

---

36. Quoted in Collins, *Exploring Christian Spirituality*, 223, 224.

37. Webber, *Ancient-Future Faith*, 76, 107, 135, 129.

38. In Scorgie, *Dictionary of Christian Spirituality*, 30, 31.

39. For more on Franciscan spirituality, see chapter 14 ("Franciscan Peacemaking: *A Key Theme in a Missional Spirituality*").

40. King, *Christian Mystics*, 72.

had a strong Christological focus in following the suffering Christ into the world. His passion was to live the gospel and not simply preach it. He challenged followers of Christ to: (1) reject a "culture of violence" and live a life of peacemaking through the gospel; (2) rebuild God's "house" (the church, Christian institutions and the wider society) rather than abandoning or further fragmenting it; (3) "Kiss the leper" (that is, expect to find God in the most unlikely places, including among the poor); (4) go beyond belief in Christ to "become Christ," that is, pattern our lives on Jesus so that he becomes replicated in our own lives, even to the point of having the stigmata; (5) worship the Creator by caring for his creation; and (6) create a faith-community that overcomes hierarchy, the misuse of power, and the spirit of possessiveness.[41]

Bonaventure (1221–1274), a professor of theology at the University of Paris, became a Franciscan at age twenty-one. In 1257, he became Minister General of the Franciscans and later became a cardinal in the Roman Catholic church. His great work on mystical theology, *The Mind's Journey to God*, traces this journey as follows: first, "prayer in the service of reforming grace"; second, "by one's manner of life for purifying justice"; third, "by meditation for illuminating knowledge"; fourth, "by contemplation for perfect wisdom."[42] He goes on to suggest that we see God in three ways: first, through creation because "the world bears the traces of God"; second, through reflecting inwardly because we bear the image of God; third, through reflecting on God himself as Trinity.[43] This ascent of the heart can only occur "through the blood of the Lamb" by "divine grace." He further argues that no one "receives [the contemplative rapture] who has not desired it," having been "set aflame within by the fire of the Holy Spirit."[44] To see God in these ways, we are to "ask grace, not instruction; desire, not intellect; the cry of prayer, not the pursuit of study; the spouse, not the teacher; God, not man; darkness, not clarity." The purpose of this ascent of the heart is to "have one heart with Jesus."[45]

Despite these emphases, none of Bonaventure's writings suggest a self-indulgent, esoteric form of Christian spirituality that takes us away from the concerns of our world. Rather, on this journey to God, we are drawn more fully into the life of God in order to penetrate the world more effectively through

41. Crosby, *Finding Francis, Following Christ*.

42. McGinn, *Essential Writings*, 168.

43. King, *Christian Mystics*, 77.

44. McGinn, *Essential Writings*, 164–69.

45. King, *Christian Mystics*, 78.

the presence of Christ. As a Franciscan, service to the neighbour and especially the poor is a mark of being connected to Christ.

This understanding was also clearly articulated by Richard of St. Victor (1120–1173), who was the prior of an abbey near Paris. He developed a circular understanding of the relationship between contemplation and action, where meditation as a discipline leads to an ecstatic experience of the presence of God, which in turn must lead to fruitful service, a journey he describes as contemplation "bringing forth its children" (i.e., bearing fruit in compassionate witness and service).[46]

St. Catherine of Genoa and St. Catherine of Siena

Two women mystics who particularly embodied this form of Christian mysticism were St. Catherine of Genoa (1447–1510), whose life of prayer and contemplation led her to found the first hospital in Genoa, and St. Catherine of Siena (1347–1380), who worked tirelessly for political change in Florence and also for church reform.

St. Catherine of Genoa was particularly active in serving the poor and needy "when the plague struck Genoa in 1493 wiping out much of the population."[47] McGinn notes that Catherine's "'writings' . . . from the pen of her followers" emphasize the themes of "God as the overwhelming force of Pure Love" and the need for God's "purifying fire" to deal with human sin to prepare the soul for "union with God."[48] But Catherine's orientation toward God was matched by her service to the wider community. As McGinn puts it, "this married mystic . . . was able to combine action with contemplation so effectively."[49]

St. Catherine of Siena's writings describe how Christ's feet enable us to move upward; Christ's heart calls us to loving union; and Christ's mouth calls us to apostolic action. She also describes a vision of a soul in loving union with Christ. Though the soul "has lost . . . her own will," Christ tells her, "I have put you in the midst of your neighbor, so that you can do for him [her] what you cannot do for me."[50]

46. King, 71.

47. McGinn, *Essential Writings*, 65.

48. McGinn, 66.

49. McGinn, 65–66.

50. McGinn, 541–43.

St. Bernard of Clairvaux and the Beguines

During the Patristic period, the early church fathers connected mysticism with the Word of God and the sacraments. After this period, mysticism was primarily connected with the communal life and the spiritual practices of monasticism. John Cassian, St. Benedict, and St. Augustine all shaped monastic mysticism, but St. Bernard of Clairvaux had a more profound and lasting influence.

St. Bernard, Abbot of Clairvaux, played a key role in Cistercian reform and the theological disputes of his time, and he also founded sixty other monasteries. He speaks of his own mystical experiences, but acknowledges that "where [God] comes from when he enters my soul, where he goes when he leaves it . . . I frankly do not know." One of Bernard's key concepts is that just as the wisdom of God builds a house within Mary for the incarnation of Christ, God seeks to build a house within each of us. Yet God does not come from within, for God is good, and there is "no good in me." And when God comes, there is no sound, no glimpse, no footfall, but only "the warmth of my heart," which he describes as "the spiritual kiss of Christ."[51]

In *On Loving God*, an outstanding work drawn from the Song of Songs, Bernard identifies four stages of love in our response to God's gratuitous love for us. First, we love ourselves for our own sake; second, we love God, but for our own sake; third, we love God for his sake; fourth, we love ourselves for God's sake.[52] Bernard describes the fourth and most profound way of love as having the consequence that "all human feelings melt in a mysterious way and flow into the will of God." Yet this final stage is a gift from God alone and "is not obtained by human effort."[53]

Bernard's "bridal mysticism" is a metaphor to describe the ancient quest towards deeper union with God. While Meister Eckhart's language of union with God tends to lose the distinction between the human person and God ("that I and God are one"), Bernard is clear in maintaining the ontological distinction between God and humans. His focus is on uniting our will and love with God, not our being.[54]

St. Bernard's "bridal mysticism" flourished in the twelfth to fourteenth centuries amongst the Beguines, laywomen who formed intentional Christian communities for the purposes of prayer, contemplation, and practical service.

51. Fanning, *Mystics of the Christian Tradition*, 81.
52. Griffin, *Bernard of Clairvaux*, 73–81.
53. McGinn, *Essential Writings*, 436.
54. McGinn, 427–31.

In the city of Cologne, between 1250–1350, there were over one hundred such communities involving more than a thousand women.

Among the Beguines, the most famous were Mechthild of Magdeburg (1210–1297), Beatrijs of Nazareth (1200–1268), Hadewijch of Brabant (thirteenth century), Marguerite of Porete (d. 1310). They wrote in vernacular languages rather than Latin, often in poetic form, focusing on a "lyrical love mysticism."[55] Their spirituality was not simply of the mind or will, but one of affectivity, body, and feeling. They write of total spiritual "nakedness" before God, losing all in God, and utter abandonment in entering the darkness of a boundless unknowing. The language that these women use is sometimes sexual in orientation. Hadewijch, for example, speaks of Christ as "the Bridegroom of the soul" and says that Christ "gave himself to me in the form of the sacrament," and "I remained in a state of oneness with my Beloved so that I melted into him." But she immediately qualifies this language with being "completely virtuous in every virtue."[56]

While this kind of language may make some of us a bit uncomfortable, we need to remember that men, besides St. Bernard, also use this language. William of St. Thierry (c. 1075–1148) exhorts us not only to keep God's commandments, but also to "anticipate God's wishes," and not only to believe in God, but "to taste and comprehend him."[57] He describes a movement in our relationship with God, where "the thinker's understanding becomes the lover's contemplation."[58] Richard of St. Victor (c. 1120–1173) speaks of the surprising charity of Christ that conquers all other loves. This love of Christ in us "wounds . . . binds . . . makes ill," which births an "insatiable love" for God. In this love dynamic, "the beloved soul is frequently visited"; "she is led to marriage"; "she is joined with her Lover"; "she is made fruitful," but "for her neighbor's sake."[59] In the previous sections, these medieval mystics focus on the connection between contemplative practices that draw us into the love of God and lead us to action. In the final two sections, the medieval mystics focus on nurturing a profound relationship with God in Christ, which spills over into love for the community of faith, friends, and the neighbour.

55. King, *Christian Mystics*, 90.

56. McGinn, *Essential Writings*, 102–4.

57. Colledge, *The Mediaeval Mystics of England*, 29.

58. McGinn, *Essential Writings*, 255.

59. McGinn, 158–60.

Hildegard of Bingen

Hildegard came from a German aristocratic family. At age eight, she was sent to a Benedictine convent; at age forty, she became an abbess. At the ages of three, fifteen, and forty-two, she experienced spiritual visions. She writes, "Heaven was opened and a fiery light of exceeding brilliance came and permeated my whole brain, and inflamed my whole heart."[60] She speaks of this as a mystical and wondrous vision and says that "my insides were disturbed and my body's power of sensation extinguished."[61] But she was wide awake, in her right mind, and able to remember and write down all she had seen. Though she was afraid to say anything to anyone about these visions, she finally sought approval from St. Bernard of Clairvaux, who gained permission from the pope for Hildegard to disseminate the teachings of her visions.

Over time, her writings and teachings made her famous throughout Europe. She became an advisor to emperors, popes, bishops, and the general clergy, and was a spiritual director, healer, writer of morality plays, musical creator, expert in medical and science issues, and conducted preaching tours throughout Germany between 1159–1170.

Her visions received "from above" were profoundly theological and gave her insight into the meaning of Scripture. She comments, "immediately I knew the meaning . . . of the Scriptures."[62] Her visions had four central themes: the Trinity, Christology, the Holy Spirit, and the church.

Emphasizing mutual cooperation within the Trinity, she writes, "The Word [Christ] is the fullness of fruitfulness, but is not without God and the Holy Spirit;" and "The Holy Spirit is the attendant of faithful hearts, but is not without God and the Word."

In focusing on Christ, she writes: "The Word [Christ] was begotten before time according to the divinity of God, but the Word was made flesh afterward in time according to the humanity of the world." She says that the Word was sent because of the Father's great love for humanity and that the Word saves us and also "washed and dried off our wounds."[63] She speaks of Christ having "the colour of sapphire" and describes him as the "fullness of fruitfulness." She describes the Son of God as the true cornerstone and "the habitation of the faithful people," protecting them from all harm.[64]

---

60. Fanning, *Mystics of the Christian Tradition*, 83.
61. McGinn, *Essential Writings*, 334.
62. Fanning, *Mystics of the Christian Tradition*, 83.
63. Madigan, *Mystics, Visionaries, and Prophets*, 100–2.
64. Hildegard of Bingen, *Selected Writings*, 24, 26.

She describes the Holy Spirit in her vision as "red-burning fire" and says that the Holy Spirit "inflames the heart of the faithful," but is not without the Father or the Son. The Spirit lights up the darkness and "puts unbelief to flight, removing all the rust of iniquity."[65]

She speaks of the church as being "espoused to my Son in a heavenly marriage" and giving "birth to her children." She also sees Christ speaking to the church: "take care of the Christian people whom I have redeemed with my blood and entrusted to you; and take care lest they lack what pertains to life and wander from the path."[66]

Hildegard is clearly a mystical visionary figure, but her teaching – while cast in the language of metaphors and colours – reflects the teachings of Orthodox Christianity. Yet her teaching has such vitality that many of her preaching tours were almost revivalist in nature. Of all the medieval Christian mystics we have considered so far, the writings, poetry, and music of Hildegard – along with St. Francis – are experiencing a significant modern revival.

Julian of Norwich

Julian was an English anchoress, a female hermit. Little is known about her, but she was probably attached to the church at Norwich. The time in which she lived was a dark time, with the Hundred Years War, the bubonic plague, and much general violence and fear. She received her visions, which she called "showings," when she was thirty years old, and she wrote them down immediately. Twenty years later, she rewrote them with more reflective depth.

Julian is best known for her feminine language in relation to God. The maternal image of God was used by the patristic writers, St. Bernard of Clairvaux, and the Beguines. But with Julian, the "motherhood" of God operates as a metaphor for the self-giving nature of God. We are born in the "womb of God"; birth pangs cause suffering and the cross, but we are carried in love to eternal life.[67]

She explains that her visionary experiences involved "physical sight, by word formed in my intellect, and by spiritual sight." But of the latter, she says, "I can never describe it fully."[68] However, this vision bound her more fully to Jesus so that she asked of God a threefold favour: "The first was [a] mind of

65. Hildegard of Bingen, 24, 26.

66. Hildegard of Bingen, 74, 73, 76.

67. Madigan, *Mystics, Visionaries, and Prophets*, 193–94.

68. Julian of Norwich, *Revelations of Divine Love*, 191–92.

his [Jesus'] passion." In this she wanted to join those who stood at Calvary's cross to suffer with Jesus. "The second was bodily sickness in youth" so that "purged by the mercy of God" she might live "to the worship of God." And, "The third was to have God's gift [of] three wounds." These were the "wound of . . . contrition," the "wound of kind compassion," and the "wound of willfull longing towards God."[69]

As with Hildegard of Bingen, the visions of Julian of Norwich do not lead us towards strange, esoteric knowledge that is unsubstantiated by Scripture or the tradition of the church. Rather, we receive from her a vibrantly fresh way of talking about faith. And as scholars have pointed out, Julian's theology is firmly rooted "in Paul's theology of sin, grace, and redemption."[70] Her writings touch on five key theological themes: redemption, the Christian life, the Trinity, the ongoing brokenness of the world, and Jesus as our mother.

In writing about redemption, she describes Adam as the servant of God who fell into wretchedness and woundedness, but the new servant, God's Son, fell into "the valley of the womb of the maiden [Mary]" and brought us to new life. She writes that God "permitted his own Son in human nature to suffer all humanity's pain without sparing him."[71]

In writing about the Christian life, she recognizes the ongoing conflictual nature of our life in Christ, because we have within us both "our risen Lord Jesus Christ" and also "the wretchedness and harm of Adam's falling." Thus, we experience a "mixture," and "we [remain] in this mixture all the days of our life." But we also have the confidence that God is "drawing us up" through the "sweet touching of grace."[72]

In writing about the Trinity, she describes the Trinity as Maker, Keeper, and Lover, explaining that "Our Father decides, our Mother [Jesus] works . . . the Holy Spirit strengthens."[73] She observes that in the Father, we have our being; in the Son, we have our increasing; and in the Holy Spirit, we have our fulfilment. Thus, through the Son, we have our salvation, restoration, and perfection, and through the Spirit, "we have our reward, and our gift for our living and our labor."[74]

---

69. Julian of Norwich, 28.
70. McGinn, *Essential Writings*, 239.
71. Madigan, *Mystics, Visionaries, and Prophets*, 198.
72. Madigan, *Mystics*, 199–200.
73. Julian of Norwich, *Revelations of Divine Love*, 168.
74. Madigan, *Mystics, Visionaries, and Prophets*, 201.

In her visions, she recognizes the ongoing nature of evil in our world: "we see deeds done that are so evil and injuries inflicted that are so great."[75] But she believes that everything is going to be all right, because in Christ "a glorious reparation" has happened and is happening. Jesus has made full amends, and this is "incomparably greater" than Adam's sin.[76] She writes that just as the "Trinity made everything out of nothing," so "in the same way shall he [Christ] make all that is wrong" turn out all right.[77]

She speaks of Jesus as "our Mother, Brother, and Savior," often using feminine terms to emphasize Christ's generativity and to highlight how Christ brings us forth into new life. She writes, "in mercy he reforms and restores," and through his life, death, and resurrection, "he unites us to his substance."[78] She concludes, "And so Jesus is our true mother by nature . . . and he is our true mother in grace."[79]

Mysticism's Orientation to the Other

Thus far, this chapter has drawn on a small but significant part of the ancient wisdom of the Christian tradition to demonstrate that Christian mysticism is not world-denying, but rather world-engaging. In this section, I wish to establish a clear link between mysticism and ministry, but I must first make some initial points.

First, I am not in any way suggesting that a mystical experience is the *only* thing that can lead to ministry and a concern for the other. Many impulses can move someone toward service. I am only suggesting that mysticism can be a motivating factor. Second, any spiritual practice or experience can lead someone to inwardness and selfishness. Prayer can lead to self-focus, and mysticism can lead to a focus on the ecstatic and bizarre in one's religious experience. But this need not and should not be the case. Finally, much of the Christian story has been impacted by dualistic thinking, and so we should not be surprised that Christians have elevated the spiritual over the practical. Sheldrake notes how "Classical spiritual texts, such as the fourteenth-century English mystical work, *The Cloud of Unknowing*, assume a conscious choice

75. Julian of Norwich, *Revelations of Divine Love*, 109.
76. Julian of Norwich, 106.
77. Julian of Norwich, 110.
78. Madigan, *Mystics, Visionaries, and Prophets*, 201–2.
79. McGinn, *Essential Writings*, 243.

of the contemplative life over the active."[80] Sheldrake continues that this preference is "based on a Platonic ascent away from the natural world towards the purity of ideas or intelligibility which is God," and this emphasis passed into Western Christianity through the writings of Pseudo-Dionysius.[81] But many other voices have made the connection between prayer and service, contemplation and action, and mysticism and ministry, and so I would like to explore this connection further.

The Christian mystical experience – whether in a dream, vision, impression, revelation, or any other experience of the presence of God – is always a gift and a surprise. It may come in any way, not only through certain spiritual practices, and so it is a *revelatory* encounter. Moreover, it is profoundly relational in that it is an encounter with the God whom we already know, the One who longs for and seeks us. This means that mysticism is not a culmination point in an ascent up a ladder towards God. Rather, *mysticism apprehends the descending God, who moves towards us in creation and redemption.* Mysticism attends to the God who wishes to draw near to us in order to nurture us, correct us, heal us, and engage us in God's renewing purposes for the world.

While this revelatory encounter may be intensely personal, it is never idiosyncratically individualistic. Christian mysticism is rooted in the life of the faith-community in its particular historical setting, and it draws on Scripture and is spawned by the life-giving Spirit. Therefore, Christian mysticism has various traditions, foci, and emphases, and we can locate ourselves somewhere within this rich and vast tradition. This provides a sense of safety and also confirms the Spirit's work in particular ways within the community of faith. Just as conversion has a particular *gestalt* in the Christian tradition, so has mysticism.

The initial impulse of Christian mysticism is not towards knowing the future, but rather experiencing a fuller or more particular sense of the presence of God. While this presence may be overwhelming, it is essentially energizing, nurturing, and life-giving, and it brings hope and vitality.

All of this means that Christian mysticism is an act of God that draws us out of ourselves and beyond ourselves, inasmuch as we have been shaped

80. Sheldrake, *Spirituality and History*, 71. However, important qualifications are made of the elevation of the one life – the contemplative – over the other. The unknown author of *The Cloud of Unknowing* writes, "My friend, do you see that this whole incident concerning Jesus and the two sisters was intended as a lesson for active and contemplative persons of the Church in every age?" (McGinn, *Essential Writings*, 536–37).

81. Sheldrake, *Spirituality & History*, 71.

by our dominant culture and general socialization.[82] The mystical encounter opens up new ways of knowing and seeing, and so it "undoes" us, renews us, and enlightens us. As such, the mystical experience is transformative. Some may talk about how the mystical experience creates a new self,[83] but I think it is far closer to the truth to say that it creates an invigorated self that is more closely attuned to the ways and wisdom of God. Our impulse, then, is to live this wisdom out in a prophetically world-engaging way.

At this point, the interplay of the relationship between God and humans becomes challenging. Though the Christian mystical encounter comes as a gift, it is a gift that needs to be received. One can dismiss this encounter, or deny it, or misuse it by appropriating it for one's self and one's ego. Or, one can embrace this encounter in faith and humility as a further step in one's relationship with the God who, in Christ, through the Spirit, continues to empower us and call us into the fray of life, the joy of the kingdom of God, and service to the world.

In Christian mysticism, discernment remains a permanent dimension. God's encounter is not to tantalize us, but to renew and direct us. Thus, the mystical experience opens us to fresh ways of seeing and engaging the world. *If one has received and embraced such an encounter, this does not in any way suggest that the fruit of this encounter will be the success of one's missional call and service.* One can have a profound mystical experience, but that does not guarantee the success of what follows. All our service to the world, whatever its core motivation, is marked by fruitfulness, weakness, and resistance – and some missional projects clearly end in failure.

We have already seen the link between mysticism and ministry in the key medieval mystics we have engaged in this chapter, but now we will draw some more contemporary figures into the discussion.

Dorothee Soelle, in her discussion of the relationship between mysticism and resistance in *Silent Cry*, refers to Dag Hammerskjold, John Woolman, Dorothy Day, and Dom Helder Camara, among many others.[84] Soelle makes

82. We need to be careful, however, that we do not "demonise" our culture and world. We need to resist the *worldliness* of the world, not the world as gift from the creator and sustaining God. Mathewes, *Theology of Public Life*, does well in helping us to see the world as gift. At the same time, however, we need to discern the idolatries of our time and the ways in which Christians are implicated so that we may resist that which is "death-dealing" and embrace that which is "life-giving."

83. The language of "true self" and "false self" that is so prevalent in contemporary spiritual literature needs to be framed, first and foremost, in the Pauline language of continuing to put off the "old self" and to put on the "new self" (Col 3:5–17) as well as Luther's description of the Christian as a sinner/saint.

84. Soelle, *Silent Cry*, 191–298.

the initial point that many think that mysticism is "more a flight from the world, an introversion and concentration on the well-being of one's soul."[85] But she counters this presumption, observing, "Most of the great men and women of mystical movements have . . . spoken clearly . . . against a complete withdrawal from the world."[86]

She notes that the basic movement in the NT was the formation of groups "that set out a new way," which involved an appeal to the "justice of God against that of the emperor."[87] This new way, which was the "experience of bliss," was at the same time the experience that made the Christian "homeless."[88] This homeless and marginalized status meant that Christians lived in "abstinence, separation, dissent, opposition, and resistance."[89]

One of Soelle's key points is that the very nature of Christian experience, which draws us *out* of our "false" or social self, draws us *into* the ambit of God's life and wisdom. Being captivated by that wisdom, we are "undone," which is possibly the most basic meaning of conversion. Thus, we become "alien" to the ways of the world. This alienation causes us to long for a new "homecoming" – not in the world to come, but in this world. Having turned to God, we return to our families, work, and society with new eyes and a desire to see the wisdom of God imparted to our "wounded" world.

In *Mysticism and Social Transformation*, Janet Ruffing points to St. Francis, Meister Eckhart, St. Teresa of Avila, and St. Ignatius of Loyola in her discussion of the relationship between mysticism and social transformation, but she also deals with mysticism in relation to the activism of the Quakers, African American women, and those involved in the ecology movement. Within Christianity, Ruffing makes the observation that "certain mysticisms emphasize the intellect, others emphasize the heart, and still others emphasize dedicated action in the world."[90] While this is helpful in some ways, it is also problematical in that all three elements may be at play. For example, Ruffing places Franciscan mysticism in the "*affective mysticism*" camp and Ignatian spirituality in the domain that "the path to God [is] through action in the world,"[91] but these typifications are clearly overdrawn, for both movements

85. Soelle, 196.
86. Soelle, 196.
87. Soelle, 193.
88. Soelle, 196.
89. Soelle, 193.
90. Ruffing, *Mysticism and Social Transformation*, 4.
91. Ruffing, 4.

involve the heart and action – and who would dare to say that the intellect is not also in play in these movements?

More helpfully, she draws on Martin Buber's notion that in the Bible, the religious orientation is not "realization and rapture, but vocation and mission."[92] She also highlights Bernard McGinn's concept that mysticism "includes prophetic consciousness," which shows "the relationship between mysticism and social transformation."[93] And she points to Karl Rahner, Johann Baptist Metz, and David Tracy, who use the category of the "mystical-prophetic"[94] as a way of understanding the social relevance of Christian mysticism.

Drawing on the work of Robert Egan, Ruffing notes the various ways in which individuals and their communities can become prophetically enlightened. First, the experience of engaging "the stranger" can reveal to us something of "God's radical otherness." Second, we can make ourselves a "stranger" through art, a religious experience, or other ways of social disengagement and reengagement. Third, we can experience a change of consciousness through our experiences of "misery, deprivation, suffering, protest, conflict." These "contrast experiences" may be precursors to our hope and longing for a better and more just world.[95]

All these contemporary voices confirm that we cannot engage society as an agent of transformation without undergoing a significant change of consciousness and perspective ourselves. Why work for change when all is well or when we feel indifferent? Some rupture needs to take place in the societal narratives that keep spinning the tale that "all is as it should be," or that "this is the best we can expect." And while one's own need or the need of the other may be compelling factors in moving us to work for social change, a religious conversion, revelatory encounter, new calling, experience of renewal, or prophetic vision may well "strike" the inner change that leads to the work of justice and transformation.

Reflections

We have merely "gotten our toes wet" in the deep pool of medieval Christian mysticism, as there is such a vast treasure-house of primary writings, along with many diverse and colourful figures. There are also many themes that we have

92. Ruffing, 8.
93. Ruffing, 7.
94. Ruffing, 7.
95. Ruffing, 21.

not touched upon, such as asceticism and purgation, the role of the sacraments, kataphatic and apophatic mysticism,[96] and distress and dereliction in the dark night of the soul.[97] Nor have we explored the flaws and dangers in the history of medieval mysticism, including body-soul dualism, an overemphasis on ascetic practices, and an overemphasis on merging the human and divine through the Christification process.[98]

But we have discovered many rich treasures in these different forms and expressions of Christian mysticism. While some had visionary experiences (Julian of Norwich), others had more reflective mystical experiences (St. Bernard of Clairvaux). None of the mystics we have engaged advocated love of God at the expense of love of neighbour, and some – such as St. Francis and Hildegard of Bingen – were strongly evangelistic. All were deeply involved in the life of the church and had reformist impulses in wanting the church to live more fully in the light of the gospel and the love of God. While some were hermits (Julian of Norwich), most held key positions in the church (Hildegard), in monastic communities (St. Bernard), or in religious orders (St. Francis). All brought fresh insights about how to live the gospel and grow in the Christian life. But finally, and most importantly, the medieval Christian mystics demonstrate that they are the troubadours and lovers of God, who carry a profound concern and love for the world.

Medieval Christian mystics pose many challenges for all evangelicals, including my Asian Christian evangelical friends, which may be summarized as follows. First, our programmatic and action-oriented Christianity can easily run out of steam, and so we need deeper roots in the love of God in Christ through the Spirit. In other words, spiritual practices need to become a more integral part of our lives, and we need to be more open to the workings of the Holy Spirit.

Second, our emphasis on intellectually understanding the Word of God can lead us away from the need to grow in a love relationship with the Word made flesh and to grow in the wisdom of God. This means that we need to engage the ancient practice of *lectio Divina* and other meditative ways of engaging Scripture so that the Word can penetrate our hearts and move our hands.

---

96. Apophatic (negative) spirituality stresses interiority and the absence of images and words in understanding God. Kataphatic (positive) spirituality draws on analogies and images to understand God.

97. McGinn, *Essential Writings*.

98. McGinn, 481–517.

Third, our relationship with the church tends to be practical and programmatic, lacking a sacramental understanding of the "communion of the saints." Thus, we need to grow in the understanding that the church is not simply a sociological entity, but also the mystical body of Christ.

Fourth, our good understanding of justification by faith in what Christ has done on our behalf needs to grow into a Christo-mysticism and an experiential understanding of the in-Christ relationship. This means that Christ is to take shape in us and form us into the new humanity.

Fifth, our emphasis on prayer needs to be further enriched by the spiritual practices of meditation and contemplation.

Finally, in keeping with Asian culture, we need to be far more open to the mysterious, visionary, and surprising workings of the Holy Spirit. We need evangelical Christian mystics who can lead us more deeply into the heart of God and into prophetic engagement with our world.

We explored this final theme in our discussion of the relationship between mysticism and ministry. One of the particular challenges for Asian Christians is the notion of the prophetic. In a hierarchical society and within hierarchical institutions – including the church – it is important for prophetic mysticism to gain fuller exposure. Clearly, the church is not simply a maintenance institution in society, but is a prophetic and transformational community. Its task is to dwell in the rich resources of the biblical narratives that speak of shalom, justice, the reign of God, the healing of the nations, and the renewal of all things.[99] These narrative themes need to be woven into the lives and praxis of the faith-community, calling for *faith* to embrace God's way, *inspiration* to be empowered by God's way, and *courage* to live this out in a contrary and challenging world. Welcoming greater sources of inspiration into our minds, hearts, and lives opens the door to the mystical and transcendent.

Conclusion

In this chapter, I have suggested that Christian mysticism is part of the Protestant tradition, but this connection needs to be stronger. This chapter is a small response to the contemporary evangelicals who are calling us to look at the Christian mystical tradition as a source of inspiration. By engaging some

---

99. Donal Dorr constantly emphasizes the two-dimensional nature of the Christian life: a "living relationship with God" and a "practical . . . commitment to human liberation." Dorr also suggests two levels of transcendence: "in touch with the underlying moral or political values that shape our lives" and the willingness to respond to God's call and empowerment (*Integral Spirituality*, 271–72).

key figures of the medieval period, I have sought to overcome the present-day fears or misunderstandings that evangelicals may have regarding this tradition. My purpose has not been to justify everything in the mystical tradition, but to suggest that we simply have a look, listen, and taste. In our time, we urgently need deeper spiritual roots if we are going to grow in Christ, renew the church, and prophetically impact our world. The mystical tradition may help us grow these roots by deepening our friendship with God so that we can grow in spiritual wisdom, envision new life in Christ, and participate more fully with the Spirit. We may well come to the same conclusion as Ursula King, which is that "the deepest renewal of Christianity can only come from a deeply spiritual and mystic renewal."[100]

But the renewal of Christianity is not our only concern, for the church is not an introspective institution, but a world-engaging and a world-formative movement. Its concern is not simply the wellness of a person's inner life, but goodness in the whole gamut of life, including its economic and political dimensions. To engage the world prophetically, by *living* the wisdom of God, calls for deep-seated courage that must be grounded and sustained by an encounter with the living God and the power of God's Word. Thus mysticism, this revelatory encounter with God's presence, needs to become part of the dance of God's mysterious way with us.

100. King, *Christian Mystics*, 248.

Section II

Biblical Themes

6

A Vision of God and a Passion for the World

Introduction

In exploring the broad themes of mission and spirituality, it is important to remain attentive to the biblical narratives, for in contemporary Western culture, spirituality can mean almost anything that has to do with inwardness and mindfulness, and mission is often seen as a cultural change project rather than a kingdom of God project. Thus, this chapter will focus on Christian spirituality in the light of Scripture while also drawing missional implications.[1] In pursuing this path of exploration, it is not as if we are trying to draw blood out of a stone, for Christian spirituality is about living the whole of one's life in and through Christ, which clearly involves both prayer and service. Moreover, both mission and spirituality are deeply rooted in the major themes of both the OT[2] and the NT.[3]

It is also important to note that Christian spirituality does not have its beginnings in the desert fathers and mothers, who went off into the Egyptian desert to pray and fight with Satan.[4] Rather, in the ebb and flow of the church's journey through history, the desert fathers and mothers, various monastic traditions, Reformers, Methodists, parish ministers, among many others each gave biblical themes a particular nuance in developing their renewal movements

1. In chapter 7 ("The Heart and Scope of Integral Mission"), we will reverse the focus and explore missional themes in the light of Scripture while, of course, including spiritual perspectives.

2. Collins, *Exploring Christian Spirituality*, 311–26.

3. Collins, 327–51.

4. Waddell, *The Desert Fathers*.

or respective spiritualities.[5] Of course, distortions sometimes occurred, including various forms of dualism and the tendency to place contemplation above service. But the various spiritualities that emerged in the life of the Christian church often emphasized a central theme of Scripture. For example, the church father St. Ignatius made the spirituality of the faithful following of Christ synonymous with martyrdom.[6] St. Francis made it synonymous with embracing poverty.[7] And Dietrich Bonhoeffer connected the spirituality of the *imitatio Christi* with resisting political tyranny.[8]

While some of these rich themes have been emphasized at particular points in the history of the Christian church, they may have faded over time. Therefore, these themes need to be recovered, and so our challenge is to return to the history of these traditions and seek to reread the biblical narrative in the light of these themes. The following overarching framework can guide us in this process: first, the pattern of creation–fall–re-creation in the biblical narrative; second, God's call of a particular people to be a universal blessing (Gen 12:3; Isa 42:6; Matt 28:19); third, the recurring themes of salvation, community, and mission through which God reveals "himself" to redeem a people, who are then called to offer their lives in worship to the glory of God and in service to their neighbours.

Before engaging the biblical narratives, I offer a brief personal reflection on reading Scripture while drawing on my own practices.

Reading Scripture: A Personal Reflection

I have been deeply shaped by reading the biblical narratives. In my family of origin, we read a chapter from Scripture at mealtimes, and within our Reformed tradition, sermons were usually an hour long and were always rooted in the biblical text.[9] I have read Scripture ever since – not in isolated verses here or there for personal comfort or direction, but rather whole sections of Scripture have been my diet.

---

5. Sheldrake, *Spirituality and History.*

6. Ringma, *Hear the Ancient Wisdom*, 114, 180.

7. "The Earlier Rule," in *Francis and Clare*, 110.

8. Green, *Bonhoeffer*, 139–40.

9. Of course, the Reformed faith, as a confessional denomination, reads the biblical text through the confessional lens of the Heidelberg Catechism, among other doctrinal formulations.

In coming to a living faith in Christ during my mid-teens, Scripture became more alive and challenging for me as I began to see it as a *living* word[10] that was shaping my life and worldview. During times of personal renewal, Scripture seemed to have an even more vibrant impact. As I have taught hermeneutics and practised both a scholarly and a *lectio Divina* reading of the biblical text, I have continued to be fascinated and challenged by the biblical story, and I continue to seek to live the wisdom of this remarkable book.

Along with Karl Barth, I see Scripture as historical, literary, and theological. Though I am familiar with most interpretive strategies, I have primarily engaged Scripture as the wisdom of God that has been revealed in various historical contexts and also has relevance for our time.[11] Thus, I do not read Scripture primarily to gain insight into an ancient world, nor because of its literary qualities, but rather as a living and active word that challenges me to live according to its wisdom. But of course, in seeking to understand Scripture, I need to be aware of its literary and historical qualities.

Moreover, I do not engage in a flat reading of Scripture, where every word and sentence carries equal weight. Rather, I take a mountain and valley approach, where certain sections of Scripture hold greater weight than others. I certainly don't believe that disobedient sons should be stoned to death (Deut 21:18–21), but I do believe that this OT book, which speaks of the importance of worship, obedience, and the practice of justice, rings with contemporary relevance, particularly its two key themes: to love God "with all your heart . . . soul, and . . . might" (Deut 6:5) and to "love the stranger, for you were strangers in the land of Egypt" (Deut 10:19).

Traditionally, this way of reading has been described as the canon within the canon, meaning that certain portions of the text are given more weight than

10. I have appreciated the emphasis that Emil Brunner places on the word of God as an encounter. He writes: "It is not a matter [I would say: "it is not *only* a matter"] of assent to a particular doctrine, not correct ideas, [not] so-called dogmas; in the Bible . . . everything is personal. What is at stake is that I should place my person completely under the lordship of the person of God, as he apprehends me in the person of Christ, through my acknowledging that God's hand in Christ is grasping . . . me" (*The Word of God and Modern Man*, 63). Elsewhere, Brunner speaks of our "reception of God's earnest voice," which leads to conversion that "God alone can do" and also leads to our seeking the kingdom of God, which issues in "service to the neighbour" (*Our Faith*, 85).

11. It is striking how critical Jacques Ellul is of contemporary hermeneutics. He writes, "the passion for language analysis and hermeneutics is the unintentional expression of God's silence" (*Hope in Time of Abandonment*, 141). This is an overstatement, as one can be hermeneutically attuned in order to hear the text as the word of God more clearly. But Ellul is right in his concern about losing the message of the text if there is too much focus on "the diversity of authorship, schools of thought, and literary forms" (142).

others.[12] But this may be consistent with Scripture's own internal movement toward greater clarity in light of the Christ event, the coming of the Spirit, and the formation of the faith-community. Yet this does not relegate the OT to irrelevance, for it, too, is the word of God, and yet it needs to be interpreted theologically in the light of the NT. And of course, both the OT and the NT need to be read as a reflection of the culture of their particular time.

But this way of reading Scripture runs the risk of selecting only what suits the present-day reader. Through a hermeneutic of correlation,[13] for example, one may turn to Scripture merely to find echoes of contemporary concern. While this strategy may make Scripture relevant to our time, it does not do justice to the biblical text, which does not merely answer the pressing questions of our time, but also confronts us with its own *strange* voice, calling us to ask questions that we may otherwise neglect or to reframe the questions we are asking. Thus, we can read Scripture as a reflection on God's revelation and action in history, the shaping of a people who have been impacted by that revelation and action, and the calling of a people to serve the world in light of their own ongoing transformation and healing.

The central issue, then, is not about correlation, but *transformation* as the biblical narratives draw us, through the Spirit, into their wisdom. The core theme of that wisdom is God's restorative love for humanity and the whole created order. This theme is embedded in both testaments, but it finds

---

12. This was a hermeneutical theme developed by Martin Luther. Duncan E. Ferguson notes that Luther read Scripture as a Christocentric book but that he questioned "the canonicity of Hebrews, James, Jude and Revelation" (*Biblical Hermeneutics*, 158). This questioning is not my position, nor my concern. Mine is much more along the lines of a feminist critique, where I preference those themes in Scripture that emphasize God's new salvific order as undermining all forms of ceremonial and cultural practices along with patriarchal and other oppressive values still reflected in the canonical text.

13. This is not the place to enter into a full discussion of Paul Tillich's hermeneutic of correlation, which has to do with the interface between the questions that a philosophy of human existence raises and the "answers" that theology provides. As John Macquarrie notes, Tillich "takes the existential of man [woman] on the one hand and the message of the Christian revelation on the other, and 'tries to correlate the questions implied in the situation with the answers implied in the message'" (*Twentieth Century Religious Thought*, 366). While this method may produce a vitally relevant theology, there is always the risk that the questions raised by the human condition may dominate the horizons of the biblical narratives. Critics have noted, "While the idea of the method of correlation is valuable and even necessary, as Tillich developed it, modern culture rather than the Christian tradition was really the controlling factor" (Grenz and Olson, *Twentieth Century Theology*, 120). This analysis is open to further discussion, but the problem is clear enough. Questions do pre-set answers, and therefore this hermeneutic runs the constant risk that the wisdom of the biblical narratives becomes skewed in directions set by modernity. And it is rather obvious that the church has been impacted much more by modernity than it realizes. Taylor's *A Secular Age* provides ample evidence of this.

greater clarity in the incarnation, death, and resurrection of Christ, who is our Saviour, a normative human being, and the revelation of the Father. Our identification with him through the work of the Spirit becomes the heartbeat by which we engage the biblical text and seek to live its all-embracing wisdom in the world. This does not mean that we stand aloof from the world with our answers. Rather, we are deeply embedded in the world amidst both its beauty and madness. As we fully partake of the human condition, we open ourselves to the brooding Spirit and the living word, Jesus Christ, who is revealed in Scripture, and we also trust in Scripture's power as *kerygma* (the "proclamation" of the gospel) to confront and transform us.

Thus, we come to Scripture with our issues and concerns as well as a love for the whole world, and we also come to the biblical story to hear its challenging wisdom. While we may interrogate Scripture, Scripture also seeks to interrogate us and to call us into a new way of being and living as Christ, the living word, takes form and shape within us. This transformation happens through our participation in the community of faith, our personal spiritual practices, our family life, our daily work, and our various forms of Christian service.

While much more could be said regarding our engagement with the biblical narrative, I trust that this personal reflection has made it clear that I take Scripture seriously. I believe that it provides the vision and roadmap for God's revelation of redemption and the renewal of all things, and so we do well to seek its wisdom and direction.

Old Testament Spirituality Themes[14]

A Spirituality of the Vision of God

One of the remarkable themes in OT spirituality is the *vision of God.* Abram receives an assurance from God regarding his offspring, which takes place in the form of a visionary experience: "the word of the Lord came to Abram in a vision" (Gen 15:1). This promise is made concrete in the visit of the three "men," but the text makes clear that "*the Lord* appeared to Abraham by the oaks of Mamre" (Gen 18:1, emphasis added). Abram's desire for the vision of God is not just so he can have an ecstatic experience. Rather, Abram needs a promise from God for the future.

---

14. I am partly indebted to the fine summary in John Barton, "The Old Testament." For another treatment of OT spirituality, see R. Paul Stevens and Michael Green, *Living the Story*, 47–93.

Similarly, Moses needs assurance that the wisdom and presence of God is with him as he continues to lead the people of Israel. And so, Moses asks God to "show me your ways" (Exod 33:13) and "show me your glory" (33:18). In response to this request, God tells Moses that he cannot see God's "face," but "you shall see my back" (33:23), and "all my goodness [shall] pass before you" (33:19). In this remarkable interplay, God assures Moses that "you have found favor in my sight, and I know you by name" (33:17), and I have made myself known to you as "The Lord," who is the gracious and merciful one (33:19).

In another visionary experience of God, Job hears the word of God "out of the whirlwind" (Job 40:6). And in Isaiah's vision of the Lord, the Seraphs proclaim, "Holy, holy, holy is the Lord of hosts; the whole earth is full of his glory" (Isa 6:3). This proclamation is followed by Isaiah's confession, "I am a man of unclean lips" (6:5), and exhilaration, "my eyes have seen the King, the Lord of Hosts" (6:5). Then God calls Isaiah to "Go and say to this people . . ." (6:9).

In these visionary encounters in the OT, we see the following dynamics. First, God *initiates* these encounters. God reveals "himself" and makes "herself" known. Second, God's servants *desire* the presence of God. They want to be known, and they want to know this God. Third, God makes "his" purposes known. God's revelation is nurturing and comforting, but it is also directional.[15] Fourth, God's revelatory presence calls "her" servants to become actively involved in God's redemptive purposes for humanity.

This OT dynamic of encountering the vision of God poses some challenges for us. First of all, we tend to orient ourselves towards seeking God's *purposes* rather than God's *presence*. Because we tend to orient ourselves functionally rather than relationally, the task at hand seems to be our unfortunate first move rather than seeking to love and to be well-loved. This tendency seriously distorts the way we live the Christian life and commit ourselves to mission.

Second, our contemporary Christianity tends to be rationally rather than mystically[16] oriented. Yet in both the biblical narratives and the biographies of many Christians, the nature of one's *encounter* with God determines how one seeks to live and to serve others. Janet Ruffing notes, "A mystical path of action is exemplified in the Christian tradition by Ignatius of Loyola and others

---

15. In *Evangelical Theology*, Barth makes the point that what Israel needed to heed was "the sovereign voice of the *God of the Covenant*: 'Thus says the Lord'" (27). And it was this word and wisdom that the servants of God were "enabled, permitted, and called to echo" (27).

16. Ruffing, *Mysticism and Social Transformation*. See also the discussion in chapter 5 ("Mysticism and Mission").

whose *mystical apprehension* of God sent them on particular *missions* into the world."[17] This relationship between mysticism and mission can be reworded as the relationship between *gift* and *task*, but in this reciprocal configuration, it is important that we don't see our task as a repayment for the gift, which would in effect nullify the gift.[18] Rather, the task is our gratuitous response to the gift of God's creational and salvific work in our lives. We continue to live and serve out of our joy for this gift, which is imparted by the Holy Spirit, who was present in the work of creation, enabled the ministry of the prophets, empowered Christ and his ministry, and continues to dwell in the church. Barth's language is ecstatic at this point: "The Spirit *himself* was present . . . This was his invasion, incitement, and witness to 'what is in God' and what has been given us by God, his power arousing and begetting the confession 'Jesus is Lord!'"[19] On the basis of this confession, the faith-community seeks to be a witness to the world.

A Spirituality of Liberation

In an earlier chapter,[20] we gained a foretaste of a contemporary spirituality of liberation through the work of Segundo Galilea. In a later chapter,[21] we will highlight a Latin American spirituality of liberation more fully. In this chapter, we will explore the central theme of redemption or liberation in the OT. This theme is clearly revealed in the song of Moses: "In your steadfast love you led the people *whom you redeemed*; you guided them by your strength to your holy abode" (Exod 15:13, emphasis added). The account of the Ten Commandments begins with God saying, "I am the Lord your God, *who brought you out of the land of Egypt*" (Exod 20:2, emphasis added). And the central confession of the Israelite community includes the words, "the Lord *brought us out of Egypt* with a mighty hand and an outstretched arm" (Deut 26:8, emphasis added).

As the OT scholar J. Croatto observes, biblical liberation is not only about interior redemption, but is multi-dimensional,[22] involving a renewed vision of God, new practices (such as Passover), and sociopolitical liberation. Croatto goes on to point out how God's liberation in the Exodus event later

17. Ruffing, 4 (my emphasis).
18. For a discussion of gift in postmodern thinking, see Hart, *Postmodernism*, 161–93.
19. Barth, *Evangelical Theology*, 55.
20. See chapter 2 ("Towards a Missional Spirituality").
21. See chapter 15 ("Liberation Theology: A Spirituality and Praxis of Serving the Poor").
22. Croatto, *Exodus: A Hermeneutics of Freedom*.

becomes central to Israel's confession, their ethical life, and the prophetic call for renewal. Thus, the Israelites are the happy recipients of God's all-embracing liberating action, and the ethical life of their community flows out of this central, defining moment of redemption. In the most basic terms, the way that God has acted towards the Israelites is the way in which they, in turn, are to treat the vulnerable members of their own community and the stranger in their midst. For example, the biblical command to free Hebrew slaves in the seventh year and to empower them with resources for a new beginning is rooted in the Exodus event: "remember that you were a slave in the land of Egypt, and the LORD your God redeemed you; for this reason I lay this command upon you today" (Deut 15:15).

While everyone is expected to care for one's own, the ethical stance of the Israelites, as God's redeemed people, is to extend that care to resident aliens: "you shall love the alien as yourself, for you were aliens in the land of Egypt" (Lev 19:34). Concern for the alien is further expressed in the broader call for justice: "you shall not deprive a resident alien or orphan of justice" (Deut 24:17). Once again, this call is rooted in the Exodus event: "you were a slave in Egypt and the Lord your God redeemed you from there" (24:18).[23]

In drawing some broad conclusions from this fundamental theme, we may note the following. First, a biblical spirituality of liberation and its subsequent expression in ethical behaviour is not rooted in certain practices but in the gratuitous work of God. Second, God's liberation forms a people or community and gives them a particular identity. Third, a people or community that is marked by God's redemption is to reflect the generous nature of God's concern in the way they relate to others. Put simply, the faith-community is to be a "small" repetition of God's bountiful goodness. Thus, a biblical spirituality of liberation is not only inward, but also outward, practically seeking to serve the other, including the stranger.

Personal Prayer and Corporate Spirituality

We live in a time when personal prayer is a problem, as we are no longer sure about God's interaction with our modern world. We may worry about the seeming "weakness" of God in human affairs, and thus we may live with a sense that so much depends on us. At the same time, we may be suspicious of

23. For an extended discussion of the OT concept of stranger/alien (*ger*), with application to contemporary migration issues, see Gorospe, "What Does the Bible Say about Migration?"

any corporate or liturgical spiritualities.[24] Thus, our contemporary challenge is to remain open to the witness of the OT, as many of its key characters are identified as people who pray: Abram (Gen 15:2), Samuel (1 Sam 3:10), King Hezekiah (2 Kgs 19:14–19), Nehemiah (Neh 1:4–11), and King David (Ps 51:1–2). Some may lament, "I say to God, my rock, 'Why have you forgotten me?'" (Ps 42:9), and some may boldly proclaim, "Hope in God; for I shall again praise him, my help and my God" (Ps 42:11). But throughout the biblical narrative, amidst this vast cast of praying characters, God is depicted as the one who *hears* (Ps 69:33), *answers* (Ps 65:2), and *acts* (Hos 11:3).

In light of this witness, we need to recover the centrality of personal prayer in both our spirituality (inner life) as well as our mission (the outward expression of our inner life). Through prayer, we become animated by the energy, breath, and impetus of God. Without prayer, we will become diminished in our inner life and service as we focus only on our outward performance rather than also on our *relationship* with God.

But the OT also bears witness to the importance of corporate prayers and practices, including the many festivals in the life of the community as well as occasions of corporate worship, celebration, and prayer. Jeremiah's anguished prayer becomes a public prophecy (Jer 4:19–21), and the Israelites make a public cry for help to the Lord over and over again (Judg 3:9, 15; 4:3; 6:7). In Nehemiah, the people publicly confess their sins (Neh 9:6–36), and many of the prayers recorded in the psalms are corporate (Ps 67:1–2). Though a psalm may start with a personal declaration, "I will extol you, O LORD, for you have drawn me up" (Ps 30:1), it soon shifts into a corporate proclamation, "Sing praises to the LORD, O you his faithful ones" (Ps 30:4).

Just as spirituality is both personal and communal, so is the missional task. While personalism is an important theme in our contemporary world, individualism is a deep concern. And though we need to be careful not to reduce complex issues to singular themes, we can observe how the fragmentation of corporate prayer has led to the fragmentation of our mission. Thus, we need to recover a corporate sense of our Christian identity.[25]

---

24. For a somewhat overstated but penetrating discussion of this present-day vulnerability/insecurity regarding our sense of the presence of God, see Ellul, *Hope in Time of Abandonment*.

25. See Volf, *After Our Likeness*, where he argues for a more "catholic" (or corporate) understanding of the nature of the church and Christian identity.

A Spirituality of Wrestling with God

With all the religious infrastructure in the OT, one might readily assume that God is very accessible to the Israelites. To some extent, this is true. There is the tabernacle and later the temple. There is the law and all the extensive legislation regarding Israel's identity and its corporate and ethical life. There are the priests, Levites, kings, and prophets. And there are the many religious festivals that cement and celebrate Israel's life with God. Though the OT stresses God's majesty and sovereignty (Pss 99:1; 146:10; Isa 24:23), it also emphasizes the God who draws near. The God of Israel not only reigns over all the earth (Ps 146:6–7), but also "raises up all who are bowed down" (145:14; 146:8) and is "near to all who call on him" (145:16). This "double movement" of God is most clearly expressed in the words of the psalmist: "for though the LORD is high, he regards the lowly" (Ps 138:6).

This sense of God being exalted, yet close, is an important OT theme.[26] And because God is close, we see many characters wrestling with God. Abraham pleads with God to withhold judgement on Sodom (Gen 18:16–33). Moses pleads with God to withhold judgement on the disobedient and unfaithful people (Exod 32:11–14; Num 14:11–19). Job wrestles with God to vindicate himself and to provoke God to reveal "himself" to Job (see Job 40:2–4). The psalms are full of these pleading encounters with God: "Lord, where is your steadfast love of old" (Ps 89:49); "turn, O LORD! How long? Have compassion on your servants" (90:13); "will you not revive us again, so that your people may rejoice in you?" (85:6).

These representative references reveal the living and dynamic relationship that God has with "his" people. Rather than being removed and unapproachable, God has a close and gracious relationship with Israel. This is clearly spelled out in Hosea's prophetic word, where God's judgement – "there is no faithfulness or loyalty in the land" (4:1); "they are greedy for their iniquity" (4:8) – is followed by God's promise – "I will heal their disloyalty; I will love them freely" (14:4). The people respond to God's gracious initiative by declaring, "the way[s] of the LORD are right, and the upright walk in them" (14:9).

These narratives have important implications for us today. While God is certainly not at our beck and call, God is also not separated from us in ironclad immutability or indifference. Rather, God is relational, and so we are encouraged to seek God's "face" and to make our prayers and concerns known. Moreover, God seems to be most moved when our concerns are not for the

---

26. Karl Barth is, therefore, right with his dialectic of God the Wholly Other and God the Wholly Concerned.

"petty" things in our own lives, but for the glory of God and the well-being of our neighbours, especially the poor.

Rather than living in sullen silence before God, the OT invites us to live the whole of our lives in the light of God's presence as we wrestle with God about the ambiguities and challenges of our existence while also seeking to serve the world. Unfortunately, most churches today say very little on this theme. If God blesses us, well and good; if God does not bless us, too bad! Yet the OT gives us a very different picture of people questioning God and pressing God for answers. We could learn a lot from these OT characters, who pressure God to act because they long for blessings to come to the people – particularly the poor and oppressed – rather than passively resigning themselves to unjust circumstances.[27]

A Spirituality of Continually Seeking God

While the presence of God in the OT was institutionalized in the tabernacle and the temple and mediated through the roles of priests, prophets, and kings, the biblical narrative also depicts characters with longing hearts actively seeking the presence of God. We see different kinds of individuals prayerfully seeking the "face" of God, including Jacob (Gen 28:20–22), Moses (Exod 32:11–14), Gideon (Judg 6:36–40), Hannah (1 Sam 1:9–11), and many others. These narratives suggest that the presence and blessing of God cannot be controlled through certain rituals and formulas.

For example, in Solomon's dedication prayer of the temple, he does not assume that God is there, as if God's presence is something he can invoke or take for granted. Instead, he declares, "the highest heaven cannot contain you, how much less this house that I have built!" (2 Chr 6:18). Then he goes on to plead for God's "eyes [to] be open day and night towards this house" and for God to "hear the plea of your servant and of your people Israel, when they pray toward this place" (6:20, 21). This narrative suggests that our relationship with God is never automatic, but is continually relational, existential, and dynamic. Thus, prayer is always necessary.

If the presence of God must be sought continually, then prayer, seeking, and longing are intrinsic to our relationship with God. Sadly, we can neglect

27. Jacques Ellul believes that we should "provoke" God (*Hope in Time of Abandonment*, 179). He writes that through hope we need to enter into "conflict with God" (180). Thus, "hope is protest before . . . God." Ellul goes on to say that while we must always repent of our follies, "we must also arouse God" (182).

this relationship, and there will be times when God may seem to be absent. In the dynamics of all of this, we can make the following observations. First, when God's people do evil, God says, "I will hide my eyes from you," and "even though you make many prayers, I will not listen" (Isa 1:15). This challenges us toward *repentance*. Second, when God withdraws, we are more likely to sin. As Isaiah notes, "because you hid yourself, we transgressed" (64:5). This challenges us toward *faithfulness*, even when God's active presence does not seem to be with us. Third, the psalmist cries out to the seemingly absent God, "How long will you hide your face from me?" (Ps 13:1). This posture challenges us toward *active seeking*.

In the life of faith in the Christian community, it is important to note that this complex dynamic of God's presence and absence is a blessing rather than a difficulty. Because of our human propensity towards control and creating systems, our relationship with God can take on a stultifying predictability or even a form of idolatry if we think that we have God – or the ways of God – in our grasp. Thankfully, the ways of God are far beyond our comprehension, and so it is a blessing to remember that God is God, and we are not. Embracing this dialectic of God's presence and absence is necessary to any movement of renewal or revitalization within the church.

Bernard McGinn points out that in the history of Christian spirituality, there is an overwhelming witness to the fact that Christians have not only experienced the "fear and distress that the overwhelming majesty of God brings to those . . . who draw near to him," but that "those who dedicate their lives to the pursuit of God have so often been visited with periods of abandonment and dereliction."[28]

Just as this is true in our life of prayer, it is equally true in our life of witness and service. There will be times when our service is more overtly empowered by the Spirit, and its fruit will be evident as people come to faith, new ministries come into being, people are healed, and the work of justice progresses. But other times, we have to persevere through long, arduous seasons of maintenance rather than creativity, when nothing seems to be happening. Therefore, the work of social transformation, in particular, needs deep, sustaining roots. During these times of drought, our faith may be sorely tested, and we may be tempted to abandon prayer altogether as we journey through the "dark night"

---

28. McGinn in *Essential Writings of Christian Mysticism*, 365. This, of course, has significant implications for the teaching and pastoral life of the church. The idea that the Christian life is simply an upward trajectory is idealistic and unfounded. The movement in the Christian life is not only from darkness to light, but also from light to darkness, in the sense of always moving into a greater sense of the mystery of God.

or the "desert," with all its temptations and possibilities of purgation. In these seasons, Segundo Galilea challenges us to keep ourselves open to "an irruption of the transcendent, of the Gospel," and he notes that it is prayer that "brings this about." He continues, if this irruption does not take place, "one becomes merely a pragmatist."[29] Such pragmatism places us and our activities at the centre, focusing on what we do and thereby making God unnecessary.

In conclusion, the reality of God's absence in the OT is both a temptation and a possibility. As a temptation, it can lead us to become discouraged and to lose our faith. As a pregnant possibility, it can lead us toward deeper faith, even amidst a "dark" and difficult time, as we seek the God who is faithful and trustworthy beyond our feelings and sense – the one who remains with us, even in the "desert" places.[30]

A Prophetic Spirituality

The prophetic tradition is a pervasive presence throughout the OT. The prophets formed "schools," played a role in the central life of the nation, had perspectives regarding the "global" realities of their time, proclaimed the pathways of correction and renewal, and were visionaries of an age to come.[31]

In summarizing the prophetic tradition, Walter Brueggemann identifies the "prophet as mediator."[32] The prophets were out of the ordinary spokespersons for Yahweh, whose challenging perspectives could not be silenced in the national life of Israel, although many attempted to do so. Their prophetic messages produced crises and controversy as well as the possibility of healing and restoration. The prophets denounced the abuses of power and privilege around them, not on the basis of their own authority, but in the light of the

29. Galilea in *Following Jesus*, 57. One frequently hears that Western Christians have become functional atheists. What is meant by this is that we live the Christian life as if it all depends on us, and thus we don't really need God's presence and intervention. Within this framework, prayer surely dies!

30. Meister Eckhart raises the question: "When you are in low condition, and feel forsaken, see if you are just as true to him [God] as when your sense of him is most vivid, and if you act the same when you think all help and comfort [is] far removed as you do when God seems nearest" (quoted in Ringma *Hear the Ancient Wisdom*, 6).

31. L. L. Grabbe highlights some key emphases in the OT prophetic tradition: proclaimers of a worldview of Yahweh as the powerful God of heaven and earth; proclaimers of a moral vision; and those who critiqued false religion. Grabbe also notes that some prophets had priestly roles (Jeremiah and Ezra), some were close to the King (Isaiah to King Josiah), some were war leaders (Samuel), and some formed prophetic "groups" (Grabbe, "Shaman, Preacher or Spirit Medium," 125–27).

32. Brueggemann, *Theology of the Old Testament*, 622–49.

visionary word Yahweh proclaimed to them. The message of each prophet was stylized in the form of an accusatory "lawsuit speech," identifying the people's wrongdoing, a call to repentance, and "oracles of promise."[33]

Brueggemann notes that the prophets always looked back to the Mosaic vision and its practices of justice while also looking forward to the "age to come." In looking back, Brueggemann concludes that "the core of this prophetic accent" is "that all members of the community, rich and poor . . . are bound to each other in a common historical and social enterprise."[34] Thus the nation's common lot is located in a "covenantal communitarianism," with the vision that "justice and righteousness" will prevail for all.[35] In looking forward, Brueggemann notes that the prophets celebrate how Yahweh will bring all of creation into "Yahweh's sovereign intention."[36]

Brueggemann further observes that there was a tendency during the period of the Israelite kings to move towards the totalization and institutionalization of God's delegated power,[37] particularly in the Solomonic dynasty. Any such movement towards totalization and institutionalization closes the future against the purposes of Yahweh and "militates against hope."[38] As Brueggemann observes, the "kings . . . could not cope with the thought that an end might come" and "could not imagine a new beginning."[39] Moreover, the hegemony between king, priest, and false prophet gave rise to forms of power in Israel's communal life that brought about both spiritual and economic corruption. Thus, those in power resisted the very problems that the prophets sought to address.[40]

This brief historical overview reveals some core features of a prophetic spirituality. First, the prophets had visionary experiences of Yahweh that gave

---

33. Brueggemann, 635–39.

34. Brueggemann, 645.

35. Brueggemann, 645.

36. Brueggemann, 646.

37. Brueggemann, *The Prophetic Imagination.*

38. Brueggemann, 60.

39. Brueggemann, 61.

40. We will leave to one side the discussion of the prophet's social location. While much has been made of prophets who are centrally located and those at the periphery, Hutton concludes that one "cannot simply align 'central' and 'peripheral' prophecy . . . with social maintenance and social disruptive functions" of the prophets (*Charisma and Authority in Israelite Society*, 124). Hutton also notes that the distinction between "charismatic" and "institutional" features of the prophetic movement are overplayed, observing that "the prophet represents not a shattering of the social consensus from the outside in, but rather a stretching of that consensus to its limits from the inside out" (136).

them a profound sense of divine calling. Second, this calling brought them great hope as well as ongoing suffering as they sought to proclaim a message that often ran counter to the prevailing values of their time. Thus, as mystics, visionaries, and poets, the prophets were the troublemakers of their time, agitating people to listen and respond to Yahweh's purposes for his people and God's vision for the world, even when that made them unpopular.

The OT prophets cannot be regarded as social workers or change agents in the way that we understand these functions today, as their primary concern was not to change society, but to bring the nation, particularly its leaders, back into the worship and ways of Yahweh. Clearly, this call had social implications, since the biblical narrative continually identifies Yahweh as the God of the poor and the God of justice.

While some scholars do not include prophetic spirituality in their discussion of mission,[41] Donal Dorr has written extensively about how we might understand the prophetic task. First, he identifies prophetic contemplation as a process, where persons are "brought into the conjunction [of] the mystery of God's love and the reality of the world around them."[42] Second, he identifies prophetic witness as an action that is committed to a "*different* and better future which is bound to seem unrealistic in present-day terms."[43] Third, he notes that prophetic witness and action cannot be the task of individuals alone, but need to find "support within the wider church."[44] Dorr believes that the "call of the Spirit is most likely to be heard first 'on the prophetic edge' of any given group."[45] Moreover, he believes that the prophetic task is "Spirit-given," empowering people to exercise a ministry "beyond . . . everyday experiences or concerns," thereby opening up the "marvellous and mysterious aspects of life."[46] Simply put, the prophet has the ability to see things in a new light and can therefore inspire others to live now in the light of the new.

Whatever contemporary application we may draw from the OT prophetic tradition, we need to remember that OT perspectives are much richer than

41. Prophetic spirituality is not featured in David Bosch's important work, *Transforming Mission*, but Bevans and Shroeder mention mission as "prophetic dialogue" (*Constants in Context*, 348–95), which they identify elsewhere as involving an authentic life (speaking without words), proclamation (speaking with words), a vision of a contrast society (speaking against), and speaking truth to power (*Prophetic Dialogue*, 40–55).

42. Dorr, *Mission in Today's World*, 176.

43. Dorr, 154 (author's emphasis).

44. Dorr, 284.

45. Dorr, 213.

46. Dorr, 169.

ours. Our application tends to be limited to a vision and action for justice, whereas the OT prophetic vision, which was framed by Yahweh's covenant with his people, was concerned with national restoration, both spiritually and socially. The OT prophets were called to bring light to the surrounding nations and to announce a visionary future, a "new" world of peace and well-being for all – a grand vision, indeed! The OT perspective continues to challenge us to enter more deeply into a prophetic spirituality, particularly since the primary concern is not with justice, but rather entering into a more worshipful and obedient relationship with the Lord. In other words, the OT prophetic inspiration is that as we become more like Yahweh in our daily lives, we will see the renewing of the nation as we practise justice, use power differently, serve the poor, and live towards a new future with a fuller coming of God's *shalom.*

The Spiritual Disciplines

The pages of the OT recount the ongoing struggle of the people of God to live out their "national" identity and the ways of Yahweh consistently in the world. What a painful struggle! Amidst the constant cycle of obedience and disobedience, renewal and repentance that leads to new obedience,[47] the people of God engage in a kaleidoscope of different spiritual practices, including fasting, keeping the Sabbath, worship, prayer, confession, and restitution. These practices are most clearly reflected in the psalms, which continue to be a rich resource for contemporary spiritual practices.[48]

Throughout the OT, we hear the call to fast at both personal and national levels (Lev 16:29–30; Neh 1:4; 2 Chr 20:3; Isa 58:6). Joel highlights this call: "return to me with all your heart, with fasting, with weeping, and with mourning; rend your hearts and not your clothing. Return to the LORD, your God, for he is gracious and merciful, slow to anger, and abounding in steadfast love" (Joel 2:12–13). In this call, fasting is a spiritual practice that has a healing dimension, as it is concerned with reinstating the people's relationship with Yahweh.

Sabbath spirituality is also important for missional practice. However, its core concept is not that we seek rest in order to do more work, but rather for the purpose of cultivating a new attentiveness towards God, self, and others so

47. See in particular the book of Judges (Gorospe and Ringma, *Judges*).

48. See Peterson, *A Long Obedience*; Brueggemann, *The Psalms and the Life of Faith*; Stuhlmueller, *The Spirituality of the Psalms.*

that we can worship, give thanks, and reflect.[49] In practicing Sabbath, we enter another "zone" for its own sake. There are myriad benefits that flow from this time, including nurturing friendship with God, rediscovering oneself beyond one's work identity, gaining new inspiration and insight, and experiencing life-sustaining rest.

Even more importantly, the spiritual disciplines in the OT serve to remind us that the *whole* of our life, both personal and communal, is to be lived out in the presence of Yahweh. Thus, *all* of life is a spiritual practice, not simply a list of particular practices, and the God of the OT is the God of the whole world and all people. This God has a concern for the stranger and the alien, and God's people are to mirror this concern to the world and so be a light to the nations (Isa 42:6–7; 60:3).[50]

New Testament Spirituality Themes

Introduction

Many of the spirituality themes in the OT are repeated in the NT, and yet they are placed within a new framework: the person and work of Christ, the coming of the empowering Holy Spirit, and the birthing of faith-communities in early Christianity.[51] This new framework emerged over a relatively short period of time as the Jesus movement spread from Palestine to the Greco-Roman world through the Pauline mission. Thus, all of these NT themes were forged within a missional context and therefore remain key in the construction of any missional spirituality.

I engage the discussion of NT spirituality in a similar fashion to the above discussion of OT spirituality, though this admittedly involves too much simplification and schematization. Spiritual themes are embedded in the very fabric of all the NT narratives, and the larger narratives regarding the person and work of Christ as the word made flesh, proclaimer of the kingdom, Saviour of the world, icon of the new humanity, and hoped-for carrier of God's eschatological future, must frame all Christological spiritual practices, along with the doctrines of pneumatology and ecclesiology in painting a fuller picture. Nevertheless, I will highlight some core NT spiritual themes.

49. The practice of meditation is also found in the pages of the OT (Pss 119:15; 145:5).

50. See Wright, *The Mission of God.*

51. For another treatment of NT spirituality themes, see R. Paul Stevens and Michael Green, *Living the Story*, 97–207.

Spiritual Themes in the Synoptic Gospels

The gospels tell the theological story of the Jesus movement as a renewal movement within Judaism. Thus, we see a continuation of temple and synagogue worship, along with the development of more distinctive practices. As is typical with any renewal movement, we can note the charismatic[52] and sect-like[53] characteristics of the Jesus movement in the form of enthusiasm, great commitments, egalitarian sentiments, community, and the hope for a final future. Centred on the person and work of Christ, the followers of this Jesus movement often find themselves at the centre of a domain of conflict between the surprise and excitement that Jesus brings in light of his new vision of the kingdom of God, on the one hand, and the persistence of old traditions and the understandings in which they were forged and schooled, on the other hand. While some of these traditions can be retained, some have to be reinterpreted. This position of tension between the old and the new perspectives highlights several important spiritual themes.

Spirituality of Awakening

Jesus awakens new longings and hopes within the people that meet him and hear him teach, which we might describe as a *spirituality of awakening.* Before Jesus begins teaching, John the Baptist points out that Jesus "will baptize you with the Holy Spirit and fire" (Luke 3:16). And at the very beginning of his mission, Jesus makes it clear that he has assumed the mantle of the one who will "let the oppressed go free" (Luke 4:18). Throughout his preaching and healing ministry, Jesus proclaims and demonstrates that his work is one of forgiveness (Mark 2:5) and healing (Mark 2:11). Thus, Jesus *awakens* new life in people.

Spirituality of Discernment

Jesus calls aspects of the old into question and beckons people toward a new way, a call we might describe as a *spirituality of discernment*, since those who meet and hear Jesus have to *discern* the truth and goodness of his mission. The gospels are full of situations of conflict, where the practices of Jesus deviate from those of the current religious leaders. In one such conflict, Jesus heals people on the Sabbath day (Mark 3:1–6), and amidst the scorn and criticism of the religious leaders, those around him have to make difficult choices. In this tense situation, we can take note of Peter's statement, "Look, we have left everything and followed you" (Mark 10:28).

---

52. Gerth and Mills, *From Max Weber*, 245–52.

53. Christopher Rowland, *Christian Origins.*

Spirituality of Formation

The Jesus movement is marked by a *spirituality of formation*. Jesus does not simply give people new ideas, but seeks to form people into a whole new way of life. In translating the core religious values into this new way of life, Jesus constantly shifts the focus away from religious observances to the central concerns of one's heart and life. In one critique of the Pharisees, Jesus proclaims, "But what comes out of the mouth proceeds from the heart, and this is what defiles" (Matt 15:18).

The NT scholar Ernest Best also notes this theme of formation or discipleship in Mark 8–10,[54] highlighting how the disciples' "understanding of discipleship" does not arise first and foremost out of Jesus's teaching, but rather from "what he did."[55] Best further observes how the way of Jesus, both in terms of the contours of his life and actions – including his journey from rural Galilee to confront the centre of power in Jerusalem – "is not just a literal journey to Jerusalem, but is intended also to be understood spiritually."[56] Best notes that the notion of "way," or pilgrimage, should not simply be understood as a Christian's journey to heaven, but rather a call to live the "way" of Jesus in one's daily life.[57] Thus, the goal of our pilgrimage "is Jesus."[58] Best continues, "Christians go the same way as their Lord but always in the position of those who follow, never of those who have arrived."[59] However, as Best notes in his discussion of Mark 8–10, the disciples frequently misunderstand their relationship to Jesus and their calling. The NT scholar Athol Gill concurs, observing how "the disciples, as Mark portrays them, continually fail to understand the meaning of faith . . . they feel that they have arrived and that security is theirs."[60]

Identificational Spirituality

The gospels also highlight an *identificational spirituality*, though the primary concern is not with the *imitatio Christi* or identifying Jesus as a model for

54. I have written my own version of Mark 8–10; see Ringma, "Discipleship: The Magnificent Mosaic."

55. Best, *Following Jesus*, 15.

56. Best, 15.

57. Best, 16.

58. Best, 247.

59. Best, 248.

60. Gill, *Life on the Road*, 222.

our lives. Rather, these themes focus on what *we do*,[61] and though they are important, the fundamental nature of an identificational spirituality grounds us in the reality that *Christ is within* us. We see this dynamic when Jesus says, "The cup that I drink you will drink; and with the baptism with which I am baptized, you will be baptized" (Mark 10:39). Or, during the institution of the Lord's Supper, Jesus invites, "Take, this is my body" (Mark 14:22). As followers of Jesus, we are grafted into God's revelatory power, for as Jesus testifies, "no one knows who the Son is except the Father, or who the Father is except the Son and anyone to whom the Son chooses to reveal him" (Luke 10:22). John describes the nature of this spirituality most clearly in his gospel when Jesus declares, "On that day you will know that I am in my Father, and you in me, and I in you" (John 14:20); "I am the vine, and you are the branches" (John 15:5); "I will send [the Advocate] to you" (John 16:7); "As you, Father, are in me and I am in you, may they also be in us" (John 17:21). Thus, an *identificational spirituality* is not simply about taking up certain practices, but constitutes the fundamental reality that because Christ is within us, we are empowered to live the *imitatio Christi.* Put another way, being *in Christ* is more fundamental than being *with Christ*, and the Holy Spirit is the source of all that we do *for* Christ. Thus, ontology energizes pragmatics!

Participatory Spirituality

The gospels reflect a *participatory spirituality.* Throughout this section, I have deliberately been using the phrase, "the Jesus movement," for Jesus employs a participatory structure with his followers throughout the gospels. As Matthew makes clear, Jesus calls his disciples into his ministry: "As you go, proclaim the good news, 'The kingdom of heaven has come near. Cure the sick, raise the dead, cleanse the lepers, cast out demons'" (Matt 10:7). And so, we might describe Jesus as a community-builder who forms a common-purse-community (Luke 8:1–3; John 12:1–7). Yet along with the "full time" disciples who accompany Jesus in his ministry, many followers continue to live "normal" lives, including Mary, Martha, and Lazarus. Moreover, some of Jesus's ministry does not take place "on the road," but in the homes of his followers (Mark 2:1). Gerd Theissen typifies these two distinct "groups" of disciples as the "wandering charismatics" and the "stay-at-home sympathisers."[62]

61. This is most clearly expressed in Jesus's statement: "If any want to become my followers, let them deny themselves and take up their cross and follow me" (Mark 8:34).

62. Gerd Theissen, *Sociology of Early Palestinian Christianity.*

Suffering Spirituality

The gospels also emphasize a *suffering spirituality*, a theme that flows out of the previous discussion of identificational spirituality. If we are to be like Jesus, then the life of Jesus will be "repeated" in us. In this sense, Jesus is the iconic servant of God, and his way of life will shape ours. Thus, the call to discipleship is clear: "Whoever does not carry the cross and follow me cannot be my disciple" (Luke 14:27). This means that persecutions will come to all who follow Christ: "they will hand you over to be tortured and will put you to death" (Matt 24:9).

The NT scholar Athol Gill writes extensively on NT discipleship themes, the work of justice, community-building, and the life of prayer.[63] He notes how the "outward journey in the mission of grace and love was to develop its necessary counterpart in the inner journey of prayer and dependence upon God."[64] He goes on to observe how the disciples of Jesus have to remind themselves that they are only ever "disciples and it is only as they recognize their dependence upon God that they are able to maintain their mission in the world."[65] Moreover, he highlights how prayer "is found in the context of discipleship and Christian community,"[66] and he also recognizes the formative nature of the Sermon on the Mount in shaping the inner and communal life of the faith-community.[67] Gill concludes his reflections on the synoptic gospels with Mark's story of the epileptic boy (Mark 9:14–19), noting how prayer exists "within the context of missionary struggle in the world."[68] Then he observes how Matthew wanted to make sure that the praying communities continued "the relationship with their neighbours"[69] in terms of witness and service and how Luke "had to encourage his church . . . to keep on praying."[70] In conclusion, Gill notes that "God provides streams of prayer and communal spirituality in the desert"[71] and so the present-day church as a messianic community in

63. Gill, *Life on the Road.*

64. Gill, 215.

65. Gill, 224.

66. Gill, 224.

67. Gill, 228–33.

68. Gill, 243.

69. Gill, 243.

70. Gill, 243.

71. It is interesting to note that in a book of essays honouring Athol Gill, the comment is made that Athol was "steeped in worship and prayer," along with his commitment to NT scholarship and social activism, and yet there are various references to failing to keep the spiritual practices (*Prophecy and Passion*, 4). John Hirt notes that "having survived the 'death of God'

the long march towards justice needs to come "before God with empty hands and broken hearts" to rediscover the power of the "crucified and risen Jesus in its midst."[72]

Spiritual Themes in the Pauline Epistles

Paul's letters to the house churches in the Greco-Roman world were occasional writings of encouragement and correction for the faith-communities he had founded as part of his mission. The basic structure of these letters includes two basic elements. First, the letters highlight key theological themes that ground the basis of these communities of faith in the redemptive work of Christ as the crucified and risen Lord. Second, the letters discuss the practical and ethical implications that flow from the faith-community's beliefs to help guide the internal life of the house churches as well as their posture in the world as servants of Christ. Following are several key spiritual themes that we can identify in the Pauline epistles.

Christological Spirituality

One of the most fundamental themes in Paul's letters is a Christo-mysticism or *Christological spirituality.* In reflecting on the nature of salvation, Paul highlights the centrality of the "in-Christ" relationship.[73] The salvific work of Christ, as a free gift from the loving heart of God through the empowerment of the Spirit, not only brings us into the benefits of Christ's work on the cross (reconciliation, forgiveness, and healing), but more fundamentally into *union* with Christ. Paul frequently speaks of those "who are in Christ" (Rom 8:1), how "Christ is in you" (Rom 8:10), and how "you are in the Spirit" (Rom 8:9).[74]

By way of application, a *Christological spirituality* cautions us from the overschematization of the *ordo salutis* (the way of salvation) in terms of faith, justification, and sanctification. Furthermore, we must be careful not to

---

many of us have not survived the 'death of devotion'" (*Prophecy and Passion*, 317). And Rowena Curtis laments, "we found it difficult to reflect, to take time out, to make room for solitude, to allow time for God's healing and refreshment in our own lives as individuals and as a group" (*Prayer and Passion*, 387). It should also be noted that none of the chapters deal with spiritual themes in a significant way.

72. Gill, *Life on the Road*, 244–45.

73. The medieval Christian mystic, Richard Rolle, states "that Christ may stable [in] us" (quoted in Ringma, *Hear the Ancient Wisdom*, 287). See also Michael Gorman, who understands the "in-Christ" relationship as reflecting a "resurrectional cruciformity" (*Participation in Christ*, 259).

74. See also 1 Cor 3:16; Gal 4:6; 2:20; Eph 3:17.

functionalize the work of Christ on the cross simply in terms of its benefits to us.[75] The salvation that Christ initiates invites us into a living relationship with Christ in the Spirit, which leads to a mutual indwelling: *Christ in me and I in Christ.* This understanding has profound spiritual and missional implications, for the Christian is always in a dynamic relationship with Christ, and this relationship is nurtured and upheld by the Spirit as we remain attentive and obedient to the Spirit's leading. Thus, our mission does not come from well-meaning projects that we construct, but from the unfolding of the life of Christ within us through the Holy Spirit.[76]

Incarnational Spirituality

Paul's letters also highlight the importance of an *incarnational spirituality.* In the following, I will explore two distinct senses of incarnational spirituality. First, throughout Paul's epistles, there is an interesting double movement. On the one hand, the author writes that Jesus "was born in human likeness" and was "found in human form" (Phil 2:7); on the other hand, he notes that believers were "predestined to be conformed to the image of his Son" (Rom 8:29). Very simply, this means that Jesus has become like us so that we can become like him. Put more strongly, Jesus is the icon of the new humanity, and therefore we should seek to resemble him.[77] In this sense, Jesus is the "last Adam" (1 Cor 15:45) and thus the normative human being for all humanity. Moreover, Jesus became the "life-giving spirit" (1 Cor 15:45) so that we could become like him.

The implication of this is that the life of Jesus is to be repeated in us, and therefore Jesus is the great mirror in which we can see the spiritual pattern of our life, our purpose, and destiny. Jesus was baptized, and thus we should be baptized as well. Just as Jesus lived and served in the power of the Spirit, we should as well. Because Jesus was tempted, we will be tempted. Just as Jesus

75. This is a particular challenge at this point in the twenty-first century, as our Western culture is very self-focused, and this self-focus has made its inroads into the life of the church. So much church participation is about what *we* can gain, and thus we forget Karl Barth's mantra that the Christian life is about gift, calling, grace, and responsibility. Sadly, contemporary Christianity has become the *cultus privatus* in that "faith is the receiving of one's self from God," and we have lost, according to Moltmann, the "*cultus publicus*," where faith is the "integrating centre of modern society" (*Theology of Hope*, 314, 310, 311).

76. I believe that one may safely say that the concept of Christo-mysticism can most basically find its frame within a high Christology rather than the low Christology of the historical Jesus.

77. St. Cyril of Alexandria writes, "Christ is for us a pattern and beginning and image of the divine way of life, and he displayed clearly how and in what manner it is fitting for us to live" (Ringma, *Hear the Ancient Wisdom*, 158).

loved the Father and lived to bring in the reign of God, we should seek to do the same. Because Jesus suffered, we will suffer.[78] This repeating pattern is not simply premised on our attempts to imitate Christ, but rather on Christ in faith being *ontologically* "formed in us" (Gal 4:19). In other words, this process of *Christification* is the grand finale of all things, since "all things have been created through him and for him" and "in him all things hold together" (Col 1:16–17).[79]

Throughout the pages of the NT, we find a rich, normative narrative about the life and mission of Jesus, which is the narrative in which we need to find ourselves. To find ourselves in this narrative, we first need to be found by the seeking God, who brings us home to God's presence, healing, and restoration through Christ in the power of the Spirit. Thus, as disciples of Christ, we become a second incarnation when we reflect and unfold Christ into the world. This understanding is reflected in Paul's emphasis on the church being the body of Christ (1 Cor 12:27).

The second sense in which we may understand *incarnational spirituality* is that we, like Christ, are called to embrace a particularity of place in which we witness and serve. Jesus, a Palestinian and Galilean, served his particular community. Though he did not come as a global, transnational man, his particularity had universal significance. In the same way, we are called to serve wherever we are – in our neighbourhoods, our places of work, and the spaces of our immediate influence. But this is not to say that our service will not have wider implications, particularly when a charism of the Spirit brings forth a *model* of ministry that can be creatively and thoughtfully replicated elsewhere.[80]

---

78. Paul writes, "you were buried with him [Christ] in baptism, you were also raised with him through faith in the power of God" (Col 2:12).

79. The concept that the life of Jesus will be creatively repeated in us is hinted at throughout the NT. Jesus notes in multiple places that it "is enough for a disciple to be like the teacher" (Matt 10:25; Luke 6:40; John 13:16; 15:20). Mark records that Jesus said, "The cup that I drink you will drink; and the baptism with which I am baptized you will be baptized" (Mark 10:39). There are also many exhortations to have the same "mind" as Christ (Phil 2:5), to "follow in his steps" (1 Pet 2:21), to take a servant role – "you should also do as I have done to you" (John 13:15), along with the Pauline injunction, "each of us must please our neighbour . . . For Christ did not please himself" (Rom 15:2–3). Finally, Paul's significant challenge is to "be imitators of me, as I am of Christ" (1 Cor 11:1).

80. One example would be the contemporary L'Arche communities (Spink, *Jean Vanier and L'Arche*).

Communal Spirituality

The Pauline epistles also reflect a *communal spirituality.* While each person is important and brings his or her own individual gifts and contributions, both the NT and the OT celebrate the theme of community. A core theme in Paul's letters is that being baptized into Christ by the Spirit has the corollary of being baptized into the body of Christ, the faith-community. Paul speaks of being "baptized into Christ Jesus" (Rom 6:3), and he also says that "in the one Spirit, we were all baptized into one body – Jews or Greeks, slaves or free – and we were all made to drink of one Spirit" (1 Cor 12:13). In this context, Paul is speaking about the beauty of the unity of the community of faith in the midst of a diversity of people with different ethnicities, status, and gifts (1 Cor 12:12–26).

This *communalism* has Christ as its heart, is blessed by the unifying Spirit, and expresses itself in common word, worship, sacrament, fellowship, and service. This grounded community in Christ, with all its nurturing and sustaining practices, is to be a missional entity and a second incarnation of Christ – an embodied word and a sign, a servant and a sacrament of the kingdom of God. Thus, the church reflects the richness and beauty of Christ in its life together and also in the outpouring of its life through prayer and sacrificial service. Obviously, this communalism cannot be formed through a one-hour Sunday worship service, but must be shaped through a shared life[81] as the community of faith seeks to love and serve the wider community.[82]

Spirituality of the Holy Spirit

The entire NT celebrates a *spirituality of the Holy Spirit.* Because spirituality in our contemporary culture can almost mean anything relating to the enrichment of one's inner life, spirituality has often become self-focused and self-generated. Yet Christian spirituality is rooted in the salvific work of Christ and one's ongoing growth into the likeness of Christ, which transpires through the work of the Holy Spirit, who brings the grace, blessings, and presence of Christ home to us (John 16:14). Thus, our life *in* Christ is life *in* the Spirit. As Paul puts it, "God has sent the Spirit of his Son into our hearts" (Gal 4:6). Not only does the Spirit impart gifts (1 Cor 12; Rom 12) and weave graces into our lives (Gal 5:22–25), but the Spirit is also missional (Luke 24:49; Acts 2:1–4; 4:31; 5:32;

81. See Bonhoeffer, *Life Together*; Vanier, *Community and Growth*; Moore, *Called to Community.*

82. Guder, *Missional Church.*

7:55; 8:17; 9:17).[83] While we may wish to emphasize the importance of spiritual disciplines in the Christian life, these practices should never be divorced from a life of faith in Christ and the gift of the empowering Spirit, for it is the Spirit that gives life (John 6:63).

Spirituality of Servanthood

The entire NT celebrates a *spirituality of servanthood.* Rooted in the beauty and love of God, which has been incarnated in the world through Christ, Christians are called to wash the feet of the neighbour.[84] As Christians seek to be formed in Christ, they are called to reflect the ministry of Jesus by proclaiming the kingdom of God, healing, exorcising, confronting those who abuse power, building the new community, empowering the poor, and holding the hope of God's final future. As such, a Christian spirituality of servanthood knows the reality of sacrifice and is willing to suffer on behalf of others. A spirituality of servanthood reflects the central tenant of Jesus's ministry: "the Son of Man came not to be served but to serve, and to give his life a ransom for many" (Mark 10:45).

Ascetic Spirituality

We can also describe the spirituality in the NT as an *ascetic spirituality.*[85] This does not mean that Christianity should be characterized by strange esoteric practices, but rather by prayer (Phil 4:6), fasting (Matt 6:17), visionary experiences (2 Cor 12:1), and generous giving (Rom 12:13).[86]

Yet there is something more fundamental at play here, for an ascetic Christian spirituality is also marked by a certain "detachment" in the midst of life's full engagement. In Paul's epistle to the Corinthians, he describes this as being engaged with the world in our daily life, and yet we are not caught up

---

83. Along with the rest of the book of Acts.

84. See Ringma, *Wash the Feet of the World.*

85. See chapter 16 ("Asceticism: Theological, Spiritual and Missional Perspectives") for a fuller discussion.

86. The fundamental dialectic in the Christian life is, on the one hand, being oriented towards God and the life to come while, on the other hand, engaging in the affairs of daily life and the issues of our time. Sometimes the dialectic is severed, and we stress one while neglecting the other. Thomas à Kempis runs the risk of being so heavenly minded that he is of no earthly good when he writes that we should "Live as a *pilgrim and stranger on earth*, unconcerned about the world's cares, and keep your heart free and raised to God, for this earth of ours is *no lasting city*" (quoted in Ringma, *Hear the Ancient Wisdom*, 13). Or we can be so immersed in the issues of our time that we over-identify with its values and lose the radical nature of the gospel. See Niebuhr's discussion of the Christ *of* culture (*Christ and Culture*, 83–115).

in the world's power or idolatry (1 Cor 7:29–31). We can engage the world with this sense of detachment because we carry a vision of a world and life that is to come. And so, an ascetic Christian spirituality is born out of an eschatological vision, and yet we do not seek to bypass the here and now. Rather, we live in the world and act in the world, but we remain mesmerized by what will yet be in God's final future.

Conclusion

In this chapter, I have sought to demonstrate how many of the spiritual themes that we find in the history of Christianity are deeply rooted in both the OT and the NT. Thus, we must re-inhabit the biblical narratives so that we can learn to live their story. In this, we reaffirm that the Scriptures are creatively normative in shaping our beliefs, worldview, values, and therefore our witness to the world.

While our focus has been on spiritual themes, and we will discuss missional themes in the next chapter,[87] the spirituality of Scripture has everything to do with our witness and service.[88] In both the OT and the NT, we see God's concern for forming a people in his likeness so that they will display the goodness of God in the world.

Throughout the biblical narratives, the people of God are called to live in the grace and goodness of God, so that both the messenger and those whom the messenger is seeking to serve, can be healed. Thus, we can say that our personal salvation connects us to all who receive this grace, and together we seek to extend the flow of goodness through the Spirit to a waiting and watching world. Though the world may not seem to be waiting or watching, it is already marked by Christ's salvific self-giving for the whole world. For having been shaped by a loving creator and redeemer God, the world is already nestled in the love of God. This love is most clearly revealed in the death and resurrection of Christ, who took the pain, shame, and sin of the world into his very heart so that forgiveness, healing, and restoration might flow from the horror of Golgotha's brutal madness over the entire creation.

---

87. Chapter 7 ("The Heart and Scope of Integral Mission").

88. The fact that spirituality and mission are so intertwined in the biblical narratives has led to some repetition in various chapters of this book, but we have a lot of work to do in order to overcome the fracturing that has occurred in our biblical and theological studies.

7

The Heart and Scope of Integral Mission[1]

Introduction

Whereas the previous chapter focused on spirituality while highlighting some missional implications, this chapter seeks to set out a missional theology while acknowledging some spiritual dimensions. To some extent, this book is a bit of a balancing act, particularly in light of its overarching focus on the integration of mission and spirituality. While it is important to give equal weight to both of these themes, it is always possible for one theme to dominate the other, so that in emphasizing spirituality, we might become personally inward and lose sight of our love for neighbour. Or, in emphasizing mission, we can easily become entrapped in an evangelical activism that becomes a "beast" of burden. Before exploring the dimensions and challenges of integral mission, I will begin with some personal reflections.

Personal Reflections

Though I have worked in Indigenous communities in Western Australia, in urban mission in Brisbane, and in cross-cultural mission in the Philippines and Myanmar, I have never regarded myself as a professional missioner. Rather, I have continued to see myself as a follower of Jesus, which always involves serving others, particularly the poor and those without justice.

I see nothing special in any of this, but rather a normal response to my having been impacted by the grace and Spirit of God. Just as being a Christian

1. Elsewhere, I have explained my use of the term "integral" rather than "holistic," which is more common in current missiological literature (see Ringma, "Holistic Ministry and Mission").

involves prayer and worship, so it involves service to others. This service, while highly diffused, has a particular shape that has to do with encouraging others to embrace God's healing grace, build Christian community, serve the common good in our world, and raise a prophetic voice in the cause of justice and transformation.

Thus, mission is not some grand Christian empire building project,[2] nor a plan to overtake the world as if Christians have all the answers to the challenges facing our world.[3] Rather, mission is simply about bearing a *faithful* and *subversive* witness to those around us. Christian presence in society is not a utopian answer, nor an echo of the dominant values of contemporary society, nor a brake to curb human sinfulness. Rather, the distinctive aspect of the Christian presence in the world can best be expressed in terms of the people of God seeking to be a healing and eschatological presence in society.[4] This means living as a *curative* in the body politic – not simply an antibiotic, but a *stimulant* to help bring about a more wholesome way of being and living in the world.

This more integrated way of being and living is not an end goal, however, but something that is formed *on the way*. Our vision, hopes, and dreams are always ahead of us.[5] Thus we continue to pray, long, and work for what may *yet* be at some point down the road. God's final future continually draws us forward, even though our present work is far from complete. More basically, this will include the ongoing conversion of the faith-community[6] so that we might more fully become what God is calling us to be.[7]

---

2. Jonathan Ingleby writes about the challenges of post-colonial Christianity, arguing that we need to desist from empire building while calling us to identify and resist "the Domination System" – the worldliness of the world – and to live a Reign of God alternative amongst a "community" of friends (*Beyond Empire*, 234).

3. Miroslav Volf is equally realistic on this point. He writes: "Christian communities can exert influence . . . mainly from within, in a piecemeal fashion, and without being able to control the results of their engagements." He continues, Christian communities are "to work vigorously for the limited change that is possible" (*A Public Faith*, 83). He further notes that while "no total transformations are possible" and cultural accommodation should be resisted, Christians should engage "*all dimensions of a culture*" (93–97).

4. See Rudolf Bultmann's insistence that the Christian life is fundamentally an "eschatological existence," a future hope and present reality (*Theology of the New Testament*, vol. 1, 279).

5. For further elaboration, see chapter 18 ("Hope: A Magnificent Mosaic").

6. Segundo Galilea speaks of conversion as a greater fidelity to the purposes of God and greater "affective maturity," which draws us into a "critical distance from its cultural context in order to break with the attitudes, norms, and criteria that are incompatible with . . . evangelical life" (*The Way of Living Faith*, 89, 91).

7. Hauerwas and Willimon, *Resident Aliens*.

In reflecting on my own missional engagement in the world, I can observe the following contours. First, I have always worked together with others. Second, projects have always started small and evolved over time, which resulted in much learning and modifying along the way. Third, visioning, praying, and planning were key starting points for any endeavour, always in concert with others. Fourth, the focus was always on missional *action* rather than on creating structures or institutions. Fifth, our intention was to help bless a few people rather than setting out to change the world. Sixth, we expected difficulties and resistance, including within our own group. Seventh, we believed that in the long haul, over many years, we would gain some wisdom that could be replicated elsewhere. Finally, our work was always less than what we had hoped it would be. This called us to internal renewal and reassessment as well as a willingness to let the work go to allow others to carry it forward.[8]

While I have experienced many difficulties and disappointments over the years, my missional service overall has been a joy and a great learning experience. At the same time, my sense of what it means to work well in the purposes of God, live the *imitatio Christi*, or embrace the leading of the Spirit remains as elusive and challenging as ever. Though I have seen the Spirit work dramatically in conversion and healing, I have also known long years when the work seemed extremely hard and the blessings few.

In concluding these personal reflections, I would like to add that I believe mission belongs as much to the "scattered" people of God as to the official programs of the church.[9] I have always been part of the church and also part of intentional community existing alongside of the church in order to support and amplify its witness and service. With other "laity,"[10] I have initiated ministries in service of the purposes of God when the church has seemed disinterested. But there have been times when these initiatives have later been taken up by the church as part of its official programs. As a consequence, I have come to perceive the ongoing *dialectic* between organizational commitment

8. I have never had the idea that a particular ministry project or structure should last forever. It is okay for something to die, as it may become a seed for something better. The dominant metaphor for me in relation to ministry has been to act as a "midwife." See Ilia Delio's discussion of the life and ministry of St. Francis as one who sought to bring "[souls] to birth in Christ" (*Franciscan Prayer*, 153).

9. In our time, as the government calls for increasing compliance, perhaps churches should give greater attention to empowering the laity for their "informal" work of love and service.

10. See Stevens, *Abolition of the Laity*. The clergy/laity distinction makes organizational sense, but is theologically unsound. We are all the people of God – *laos tou theou* – with differing gifts and ministries. Institutional distinctions involving hierarchy violate our commonality in Christ through the Spirit and our identity as the body of Christ.

and spontaneous "lay" involvement. Understanding this dialectic can help us appreciate the many renewal movements that have sprung up in the life of the church, along with the role of prophets and initiators, such as St. Francis, St. Ignatius of Loyola, St. Teresa of Ávila, Martin Luther, and Martin Luther King Jr., among many others.

Framework for Exploring Integral Mission

I will use the following approach to frame our exploration of integral mission. First, I will thematize some *paradigmatic* sections of biblical passages to help construct a missional theology.[11] These paradigms are not meant to provide a controlling function,[12] but rather are a mosaic, a larger picture, by which to gain a sense of our participation in God's purposes for humanity. Thus, I am not arguing for repetition, but rather creative appropriation. Second, I will approach missional theology from a *parabolical* (or metaphorical) perspective, drawing on particularly suggestive biblical concepts, such as the kingdom of God. Third, I believe that a *personal* God called each of us and is transforming us *as a people* so that we might join God's purposes in history and participate in the forward movement of God's Spirit. Thus, I will focus on the *personal* and *peoplehood* dimensions of our missional call to witness and service. Finally, I will engage the *paradoxes* and *perplexities* of our engagement with society.[13] The mission of the church should also be marked by a vulnerable stumbling in the dark as we seek to trust the guiding and upholding of the Spirit rather than a clear-eyed strategy of social transformation.[14] Or, to put this differently, the church can only exercise invitational power through its prayer, witness,

11. Let me explain. I am concerned that in some missional circles, there is a tendency to isolate certain texts (particularly Matt 28:19–20) in grounding the missional mandate and vision. Clearly, this passage is important, but we find an even fuller missional mandate in Jesus's Nazareth manifesto (Luke 4:18–19). An even broader vision swims into view in Jesus's priestly prayer: "as you have sent me into the world, so I have sent them into the world" (John 17:18). Rather than proof-texting particular passages of Scripture, the *whole* narrative of Jesus's life should be a paradigm for the church's mission in the world. Thus, we need to take a more narrative approach in understanding the church's calling in society by engaging the entire biblical story. Christopher Wright does this extensively in his monumental work, *The Mission of God*, but I am puzzled by the way that David Bosch begins with the NT (overlooking the OT) in his classic book, *Transforming Mission*.

12. Terry Eagleton rightly points out some concerns with postmodern thinking, writing that "those who believe that normativity is always negative are also likely to hold that authority is always suspect" (*After Theory*, 15).

13. Sadly, this topic is missing in most missiological literature.

14. See chapter 8 ("Grand Design and Fragile Engagement: *The Church's Calling in a Troubled World*") for a much fuller treatment of this theme.

and service. It cannot politically mandate its vision for the world, for the faith-community is not a political solution, but rather a prophetic sign of God's transformative passion for our world.

While some may argue that the Bible lacks coherence,[15] I see the Scriptures as containing grand, overarching narratives that reflect vast historical and cultural diversity.[16] Put simply, one grand narrative is about the renewing work of God in the restoration of all things so that the world can become what God intended it to be – not only in terms of restoring its initial goodness, but also in the light of God's final future. In the interim before that final future, God invites all of humanity to cooperate with God in that renewing work. While those who have been touched by God's renewing work are uniquely called to bear God's love and passion for the world, God can and will use anyone to bring forward God's purposes.[17]

The biblical paradigms that we will identify in both the OT and the NT[18] are primarily about what God is seeking to do through this restorative work, and how those who have been impacted by the grace of God, are invited to join God in this renewing work through witness and service. In entering these narratives, it is important to remember that Scripture is not filled with "abstract" speculations about the nature of God, but rather particular stories that reveal who God is through God's speech and actions.[19]

These preceding introductory paragraphs highlight three important dimensions of integral mission. First, any mission should be concerned with *God's* ideas, plans, and purposes. As the initiator and sustainer of any mission, we might say that God is a "missional God."[20] David Bosch reminds us that the notion of *missio Dei* surfaced at the famous Willingen International Missionary Council in 1952, with the core idea that mission is "derived from the very

15. I am deeply concerned that one of the unfortunate impacts of postmodern thinking has been to further fragment the biblical narratives. Our piecemeal approach to Scripture and our propensity to garner our favourite texts has left us with little sense of coherence. See Kevin Hart, *Postmodernism*, for a discussion of a postmodern Bible and postmodern religion (109–33, 134–60).

16. Wolters, *Creation Regained.*

17. Plantinga writes, "even if the Christian church is a primary instrument of the kingdom on earth, God also uses an array of other organizations" (*Engaging God's World*, 109). One example in the OT is Yahweh's use of King Cyrus (Isa 45).

18. As mentioned, it is most surprising and somewhat disconcerting that the comprehensive work by David Bosch, *Transforming Mission*, begins with the NT and neglects the OT.

19. Theologians speak about this as the "Economic Trinity," where we know who God is by what God says and does. See Tan, *Fullness Received and Returned*, 97–100.

20. Hastings, *Missional God, Missional Church.*

nature of God," and thus mission is about "participating in the sending God."[21] Second, our participation in the mission of God does not begin with a task, but with the grace and the calling of God. Having been impacted by the healing and restorative work of God, we carry that healing into the world through the sustaining presence of God. Third, this task is not simply the province of individuals, for God is calling a *people* who are to reflect the very nature of God and carry God's restorative passion into the world.[22] Thus, mission is rooted in relationship and community, a model that is most fundamentally displayed in the Trinity, which we might speak of as the *sender* (Father), the *sent one* (Son), and the *sending* (Holy Spirit). Of course, the faith-community continues to be *sent* by the *sending* God.

Before we turn to particular biblical paradigms or "models,"[23] let me explain the use of the term "integral" in relation to mission. While "holistic mission" is a more dominant term at present, I prefer "integral" because "holism" is "based in idealistic philosophy and assumes that we work from the whole to the part, a move that falsely assumes that we know the whole in the first place."[24] The term "integral," which is derived from the Latin *intergare*, means to work from the parts towards the whole. This movement expresses the *functional reality* of mission, as we begin by making some response to God's grace in our lives through our witness and service, and this response usually calls us toward greater involvement, which often seems to unfold by itself. For example, one does not start with some grand scheme to solve the drug problem in contemporary society. Rather, one starts by befriending those in the drug scene, and those friendships may stir us to create counselling and rehabilitation services or educational and work-placement programs, which may be complemented by drug prevention programs or efforts to challenge

21. Bosch, *Transforming Mission*, 390.

22. Hanson, *People Called*.

23. T. F. Carney explains that models "are *selective* representations that focus our attention on *major* components of interest and their *priority* of importance" (author's emphasis), while Ian Barbour argues that a "model is a symbolic representation of selected aspects of behaviour of a complex system of particular purposes" (quoted in Ringma, *Gadamer's Dialogical Hermeneutic*, 172). I acknowledge that any model is an abstraction and an author's configuration, and thus it always runs the risk of unhelpful generalization. The reader will notice that I use various terms – paradigm, model, mosaic, and perspective – interchangeably.

24. Ringma, "Holistic Ministry and Mission," 441.

current legislation regarding drug use. This unfolding path depicts how integral ministry often moves from the parts towards a more fully orbed approach.[25]

Old Testament Paradigms

The Genesis Mandate

The first general missional mandate in the Bible is found in the particular calling of the Genesis narrative (1:27–28), which is set within a broader narrative about the God of the Scriptures as the Creator God. This creational theme, with its vision of the good earth sustaining life and facilitating human flourishing, is sustained throughout the biblical narratives, and culminates in the vision of a new heaven and a new earth.[26]

I will return to this broader biblical narrative, but will first turn to the particulars of the Genesis mandate. In this colourful, compact mosaic, we learn that humans are made in God's image and invited to share in God's purposes and creativity. We also learn that this calling is intended to be a partnership between men and women that involves the building of a human community. This calling is also expansive, as the whole world is marked by goodness, and its resources are meant to be used and preserved under the impulse of God's blessing and guided by our responsible stewardship. One could, of course, write an entire book on this rich and beautiful mosaic![27] But for the purposes of this chapter, we will draw some contemporary implications so that we can creatively appropriate this text for our context.

First, this passage makes clear that God is the one who creates and sustains life and that humanity is called to live *in* the blessing of God and also in *response* to God's community-shaping call. Emil Brunner draws a basic pastoral implication from this mandate, which is that *belief* in God the Creator means that God the Lord is to be *obeyed*.[28]

---

25. In *Integral Spirituality*, Donal Dorr uses Micah 6:8 to thematize the call to work for "structural justice," "personal integrity and responsibility," and "interpersonal respect" (2). Throughout the book, he uses the terms "integrated spirituality" and "holistic spirituality" interchangeably. He emphasizes the two-dimensional nature of the Christian life as "living in relationship with God" and the "practical . . . commitment to human liberation" (271). Evangelical missional scholars in Latin America also use the terms "holistic" and "integral" interchangeably (Escobar, *In Search of Christ in Latin America*, 264, 275).

26. See Rev 21.

27. See Neville Carr, "The Creation Story – Questions for Today's Church," which demonstrates the wide relevance of this story.

28. Brunner, "Geloven in de Schepper betekent: God de Heer gehoorzamen," (*Ons Geloof*, 24), "belief in the Creator God means to obey God," my translation.

Second, this passage suggests that all of the dimensions of our social life, including its emerging institutions and our awareness of the sustaining environment of our world as a gift, are part of the purposes of God. Therefore, it is a most unfortunate narrowing of the arteries of human life if we simply see God's missional purpose as seeking to impact our spiritual interiority and prepare us for an afterlife, without any real concern for *this* life. The Genesis mandate conveys that we need to be concerned about *all* of life – and that *all* life is to be shaped under the beneficence of God.

Third, the call to be fruitful, multiply, fill the earth, and have dominion[29] implies that God intends for humans to shape the social order and create sustaining institutions. Nicholas Wolterstorff reminds us that "government" did not come into being simply as a "remedy for sin," but as part of "God's providential care for us finite and limited creatures"[30] from the very beginning.[31] In the purposes of God, we are not only called to impact individuals, but also to create life-sustaining institutions. Thus, a world-formative Christianity is a part of God's calling. However, this does not suggest any sort of Christianization by imposition or force. Rather, world-formative mission that is inspired by the creation mandate calls us to seek to penetrate and influence every domain of life with the loving and healing values of the kingdom of God.

Fourth, creation-care is part of our calling,[32] which is implied when God places humankind in the life-sustaining garden in order to care for it (Gen 2:15). Christopher Wright has given sustained attention to this challenging topic. He speaks of "the suffering of the earth itself" and goes on to suggest that "taking good care of the earth . . . is surely a fundamental calling of all God's people," noting that this brings together "compassion and justice." He concludes

---

29. Christopher Wright points out that "human dominion over . . . creation is to be an exercise of kingship that reflects God's own kingship. The image of God is not a license for abuse based on arrogant supremacy, but a pattern that commits us to humble reflection of the character of God" (*The Mission of God*, 427). Reflecting God's way means that any rulership should sustain rather than exploit.

30. It should be noted that some Christian thinkers, such as Jacques Ellul, don't believe in God's providence. He says that if God was providentially involved with the world, "then God's will is necessarily done in every situation." He continues, "praying for God's kingdom and will shows that there is no such thing as providence" (*What I Believe*, 156). Furthermore, he notes, "there is no question here of a set divine plan," but instead, "God accompanies us, imposing nothing by force, and not doing everything" (157).

31. Wolterstorff in *Hearing the Call*, 356. He elaborates, "properly functioning government is part of God's providential care for God's creation *qua creation*" (356).

32. It is interesting to note that neither Bosch (*Transforming Mission*, 1991), Van Engen (*Mission on the Way*, 1996), Plantinga (*Engaging God's World*, 2002), Bevans and Schroeder (*Constants in Context*, 2004), nor Volf (*A Public Faith*, 2011) deal with creation-care as part of the mission of the faith-community.

that "Christian environmental action" is "evangelistically fruitful" because it demonstrates "the Creator's limitless love for the whole of his creation."[33]

In summary, the overarching missional reminder in the Genesis mandate is that the building of the human community is a complex affair, and thus all the dimensions of life and culture are to be lived under the blessing of God and marked by shalom.[34] This Genesis mandate calls us to diverse human activity, but not human autonomy.[35] For the great sin of humanity is not simply disobedience, but the desire to be god through self-effort. Thus, idolatry is one of our greatest temptations.[36] Put most basically, the God of the biblical narratives is the God who is profoundly concerned about people, family, institutions, and the earth. All of life comes into focus in any missional mandate – and this includes discipleship-making, community-creating, as well as earth-keeping.[37]

We can now come back to the broader biblical narrative about the nature and action of the creator God and the creational motif that speaks of a blessed, fertile, and life-enhancing land as God's gift for human well-being. Both the OT and the NT reiterate and expand on this theme, which is framed within

---

33. Wright, *The Mission of God*, 412–20. As a helpful vision of creation-care, see also Bouma-Prediger, *For the Beauty of the Earth*, as well as Andrew Kirk, "Care for the Environment," in *What is Mission?* (164–83).

34. Wolterstorff has written extensively on the topic of shalom, noting that shalom involves "right relationships to God, to nature, and to oneself" as well as "right relationships to other human beings." He asserts that this vision of harmony and well-being involves both "development and liberation" (*Hearing the Call*, 111–13).

35. In the introduction to Karl Barth, *Community, State and Church*, Will Herberg notes that Barth's opposition to Nazism identifies its fundamental orientation in terms of "its self-divinizing pretentions," thereby losing its basic nature to the point that it is no longer the state as reflected in Romans 13, but is the "beast out of the abyss" of Revelation 13 (*Community, State and Church*, 45). The point is that human autonomy without external referents can easily devolve into serious distortions and may well be a form of idolatry.

36. See Christopher Wright, *Here Are Your Gods.*

37. From the Genesis mandate, traditional Christian theology has sourced three "orders of creation" – family, work, and governance – but there have been problems with the way these orders have been understood. First, these orders have often been seen as independent of God's redemptive work and thus have been given an independent status, which has led to the world of politics as a self-sufficient authority. See the Barmen Declaration as a critique of this perspective (*Creeds of the Churches*, 517–22). Second, there has been a tendency in conservative evangelical circles to say that the Genesis mandate has nothing to do with the church's missional task. For example, George Peters writes that the first mandate, with its concern for the human "habitat, agriculture, industrialization, commerce, politics," among other endeavours, is based on a "revelational theism," while the second mandate, with its focus on "the spiritual liberation and restoration" of humanity and the task of "evangelization, discipleship training, church planting, church care and benevolent ministries," is alone "considered missions" (*A Biblical Theology of Missions*, 166–70).

our call to obey God the Lord and to steward all that has been gifted to us. The biblical narratives also cast an eschatological vision of the earth, which is marked by shalom[38] and "groaning" for full liberation,[39] as well as the new heaven and new earth in God's final future.[40] Thus the Genesis mandate is not a stand-alone passage, but is sculpted more fully throughout the OT and NT.[41] Moreover, creational motifs need to be theologically located in what Jonathan Wilson describes as a "trinitarian grammar."[42] In the work of both creation and redemption, Father, Son, and Holy Spirit join together to participate in an ongoing, unfolding divine dance.

The Exodus Paradigm

While it is a most open and speculative question whether God's action in the world was only a response to the problem of human wrongdoing, or whether God's action in the world would have occurred anyway, the biblical narratives are clear that the work of God is healing and restorative. Moreover, the Genesis narratives clearly highlight the need for the world to be healed and restored.

The Exodus narratives provide us with another "picture" of the scope of Yahweh's redemptive and liberating activity.[43] This richly textured narrative depicts God's liberation of a people from oppression, their arduous journey to the land of promise, and their call to reflect to others, particularly the poor and the stranger, the goodness that Yahweh has extended to them. This means then, in the words of Karl Barth, that this faith-community is intended to be "little lights"[44] to others, bearing God's love and concern for all.

---

38. While I cannot develop this more fully here, Brueggemann is clear about the scope of the "hope for creation" in the OT through YHWH's "ordering, empowering, and blessing" occurs in the face of the constant threat of chaos and "covenantal infidelity" (*Old Testament Theology: An Introduction*, 323, 326, 333–34). This hope includes the prophetic projection of earth restoration and the land's eschatological flourishing (see Hos 2:18; Isa 11:6–9; 65:17–25; Ezek 36:29–36). Brueggemann concludes: "the hope of new creation as it is voiced in the prophetic tradition, enunciated a moral accountability in creation" (340).

39. Rom 8:22.

40. Rev 21–22.

41. Jonathan Wilson cites numerous NT passages (Rev 21–22; Heb 1:1–3; Col 1:15–20; Rom 8), noting the Trinitarian dynamic of "God's work of redeeming creation" and this "work of creation is for life" (*God's Good World*, 133–46, 129, 133).

42. Wilson, 77.

43. Brueggemann refers to Exodus as "primal revelation" (*Old Testament Theology*, 23–71).

44. Barth, *Church Dogmatics*, vol. 4, part 3:2, 654.

The OT liberation theologian J. Severino Croatto spells out several key elements in the Exodus narrative.[45] First, Yahweh is a seemingly slow God, who accompanies the people through long periods of suffering and then actively participates in their liberation. Thus, God enters history on the *side* of the oppressed, even while offering "grace" to Pharaoh. Second, liberation in Exodus is not simply cast as being freed *from* oppression, but in becoming more fully free *for* Yahweh. In other words, liberation includes the revitalization of the faith and life of God's people. In this light, we see the role of Moses not simply as a voice of critique to Pharaoh, but also as a voice of renewal to his own people. Part of Moses' call is to liberate the people so that they can worship God (Exod 3:12; 5:3, 8) and also to institute the Passover feast as a permanent memorial to the Lord for all generations (Exod 12). Croatto then makes the important point that the purpose of this renewal is not inwardly focused, but rather outwardly oriented in that the Hebrew slaves actually experienced deliverance from oppression. Croatto refers to this as "socio-historical practice."[46] In other words, God's work of redemption in the Exodus narrative is concrete and multifaceted.

Similar to the Genesis mandate discussed above, Exodus functions as a paradigmatic event that is creatively repeated in other biblical narratives. Croatto makes the following observations in light of this paradigmatic event. First, the Exodus event becomes the central confession of Israel's faith and identity for all future generations (Deut 26:5–9). Second, the Exodus reflects a key aspect of Israel's ethical life in that the liberation spirit of Exodus is to be repeated in the way in which the Hebrew people treat others (Deut 15:12–15; 24:14–22). Third, the OT wisdom literature celebrates the Exodus event as foundational to Israel's life (Ps 105:23–45).[47] Fourth, the OT prophetic tradition repeats the Exodus theme in its vision of social justice.[48] Moreover, Croatto argues that the Exodus theme is also reflected in both the ministry of Christ and Paul's writings, given their "emphasis on radical human 'liberation.'"[49] In other words, a much wider set of biblical readings reflects the paradigmatic nature

45. Croatto, *Exodus: A Hermeneutics of Freedom.*

46. Quoted in Ringma, *Gadamer's Dialogical Hermeneutic*, 241.

47. Throughout the psalms, there is a constant reminder to remember what God did for his people in the past by delivering from Egypt as a sign of God's *present* faithfulness (Pss 81:10; 106:21).

48. Croatto, *Exodus: A Hermeneutics of Freedom.* In particular, see Jer 7:22; 23:7; 32:21; Ezek 20:10; 30:18; Hos 2:15; 11:1; Amos 2:10; Mic 6:4.

49. Quoted in Ringma, *Gadamer's Dialogical Hermeneutic*, 244.

of this central biblical event and theme.[50] Moreover, Croatto methodologically identifies the Exodus event as a "kerygmatic paradigm."[51] Using Ricoeur's concept of the "production of meaning" in narrative interpretation, Croatto goes on to make the point that the Exodus theme has been productive for generating *new* events, both within the biblical narratives as well as in contemporary history.[52]

From this, I will draw some positive implications while also raising some troubling concerns. The first positive implication is that the God of the Bible is a promise-keeping God who acts in history to revitalize, redeem, and liberate people. Carrying the Exodus theme into contemporary ministry would lead us to engage in spiritual renewal, confront systemic oppression, and seek pathways to freedom. Second, the Exodus story reflects a profound understanding of the nature of oppression, abuse, and genocide.[53] For contemporary ministries, this highlights the importance of gaining a deep understanding of the complex situation in which the people among whom we are seeking to minister, find themselves. It is far too easy to bring our own assumptions and presumptions into our work with those whom we are trying to help without perceiving the nature of systemic oppression.[54] Third, Exodus tells the story of an agonizingly belated salvation. In our contemporary context, this reminds us that we must not over-promise, for the road to justice is long and circuitous.[55]

In terms of the troubling implications of the Exodus narrative, some have used the "conquest" of the promised land to justify colonial expansion, oppressive uses of power, and modern forms of cultural oppression.[56] Though

---

50. For a much fuller discussion of Croatto, see West, *Biblical Hermeneutics of Liberation*, 154–73.

51. Ringma, *Gadamer's Dialogical Hermeneutic*, 241.

52. Ringma, 241.

53. See Tamez, *Bible of the Oppressed.*

54. In some of the socially oriented courses that I taught at Asian Theological Seminary in Metro Manila, I noticed that many students did not have any problem understanding the various challenges that the urban poor were facing, but they had great difficulty grappling with the implications of the minimum wage, which was only half of what it needed to be for people to live above the poverty line. We can remain blind to such forms of systemic oppression in our efforts to help others.

55. Martin Luther King Jr. says: "I am convinced that we shall overcome because the arc of the universe is long, but it bends towards justice" and "every step toward the goal of justice requires sacrifice, suffering, and struggle" (quoted in Ringma, *Let My People Go*, 77, 89).

56. For challenges to these ideological readings of the Bible, see West, *Biblical Hermeneutics of Liberation* and Swartley, *Slavery, Sabbath, War and Women*. Yet the history of mission and colonialism has always been complex. In reference to Gustavo Gutierrez, Samuel Escobar points out how there are "profound tensions between those who converted the message of Christ into

a more careful consideration of this is not possible here, David Bosch rightly points out that "modern" mission "is historically linked indissolubly with the colonial era" and is thus "an attendant phenomenon of European expansion."[57]

In concluding these reflections on the Exodus paradigm, several voices can help sharpen our focus. First, Leonardo and Clodovis Boff appeal to the Exodus to make the point that God is "impelled to come to the help of the oppressed poor" and that God "*sides with the oppressed against the pharaohs of this world*."[58] Therefore, they argue, all Christians "need to make an option for the poor" and to transform "society in the direction of greater justice and fellowship."[59] To underscore the relevance of the Exodus, they quote from the bishops' conference in Medellín, Columbia: "Israel experienced the saving presence of God when he set them free from slavery in Egypt . . . so we too . . . cannot fail . . . [to see] deliverance for each and every one from less human to more human conditions of life."[60]

A second voice, Richard Middleton, speaks of the Exodus as a "model or paradigm," which evidences "salvation in the rest of the Old Testament (and in the New Testament too)."[61] Middleton places the Exodus motif in the "overall biblical vision" of "earthly flourishing as the very purpose of salvation," identifying two key themes: "God's *deliverance*" and "*restoration* to wholeness,"[62] which involves "the gift of [the] land."[63] Middleton then draws a range of practical implications. First, he identifies the "cry for help" as "Israel's most typical form of prayer."[64] Second, he identifies YHWH as the liberating and judging God "fighting on behalf of his people."[65] Third, he observes how the Exodus narrative showcases the "interplay of divine and creaturely freedom in bringing salvation."[66] Fourth, he notes how the Exodus functions "as the historical ground for Israel's allegiance to YHWH," which therefore calls Israel to "obedience to YHWH's Torah," and this involves protection and care for

rhetoric to justify military conquest and other figures . . . who in the name of Christ opposed the abuses with intelligence and force" (Escobar, *In Search of Christ in Latin America*, 2).

57. Bosch, *Transforming Mission*, 228.

58. Boff and Boff, *Introducing Liberation Theology*, 44, 50, authors' emphasis.

59. Boff and Boff, 46.

60. Boff and Boff, 51.

61. Middleton, *A New Heaven and A New Earth*, 78.

62. Middleton, 78, 79.

63. Middleton, 86.

64. Middleton, 80–81.

65. Middleton, 82–83.

66. Middleton, 84.

"aliens, widows, or orphans."[67] The overall conclusion that Middleton draws is that the Exodus "resists any 'spiritualizing' of salvation, keeping it firmly rooted in life in this world."[68]

Finally, Gustavo Gutierrez also describes the Exodus as "paradigmatic,"[69] placing his discussion of Exodus within the broader context of the connections between creation and salvation, on the one hand, and historical outworking and eschatological vision, on the other hand. He signals that the "center of God's salvific design is Jesus Christ, who by his death and resurrection transforms the universe and makes it possible for the person to reach fulfilment as a human being."[70] Bringing this salvific theme back to the Exodus, Gutierrez notes that the "God who makes the cosmos from chaos is the same God who leads Israel from alienation to liberation."[71] Having been impacted by this liberation, humans are to find a "place for active participation in the building of society."[72] In linking the Exodus, the OT prophetic tradition, and the person and work of Christ, Gutierrez gives us a sweeping sense of salvific-liberation in the biblical narrative. He concludes, "salvation embraces all persons and the whole person," and he proclaims, "the Christian life is passover, a transition from sin to grace, from death to life, from injustice to justice, from the subhuman to the human."[73]

This discussion reveals the "pregnant" nature of the Exodus paradigm, which is both directly and indirectly reflected in other biblical narratives. Its main symphonic theme is that God is wholly concerned and engaged in bringing about a redemption that involves freedom from sin, discouragement, alienation, and oppression.

The OT Social Justice Model

Throughout the biblical narrative, God's redemption and liberation impacts people and forms them into a common identity that has been "marked" or "formed" by God. This corporate identity is not first and foremost political, but salvific-historical as God's people "repeat" for others what God has done

67. Middleton, 87, 88.
68. Middleton, 80.
69. Gutierrez, *A Theology of Liberation*, 90.
70. Gutierrez, 85.
71. Gutierrez, 89.
72. Gutierrez, 90.
73. Gutierrez, 97, 103.

for them. Thus, those who have been blessed and transformed by God's grace and love are called to bless others in similar ways, especially the poor, marginalized, and oppressed. In this way, the earlier actions of God as they have been encapsulated in the biblical narrative become an ethical embodiment in the lives of God's people. Put differently, the word becomes flesh as the people of God embody the love of God to the rest of humanity. As with the creation, this pattern of redemption prefigures Christ's incarnation and the witness of the first communities of early Christianity.

There are a number of OT social justice laws that reveal the sober "realism" of the biblical narratives in that, within the tribal confederacy of Israel's corporate life, things would not always be well.[74] These OT laws anticipate times of drought, "military" battles, and forms of injustice and also how the poor, in particular, would suffer, for all of these laws were meant to mitigate suffering through the provision of just redistribution. First, the law regarding the Year of Jubilee called for ancestral lands to be returned to the original owners within the tribe every fifty years (Lev 25:10–24; Num 36:4). Second, the law regarding the Sabbatical Year called the land to be left fallow every seventh year to allow it to recover and to allow the poor to help themselves to its produce (Exod 23:10–11; Lev 25:1–7); moreover, Hebrew bond slaves were to be set free every seventh year and given provisions so that they could start life anew (Deut 15:12–18); finally, all debts were to be cancelled every seven years to offer debtors a new beginning (Deut 15:1–16). Third, the law regarding tithing stipulated that every third year, the tithe was to support the Levites and the poor (Deut 14:28–29). Fourth, a law commanded no interest to be charged to the poor (Lev 25:35–38). Fifth, the law of gleaning forbade farmers to over-harvest and allowed the poor to access whatever was left behind in the fields (Lev 19:9–10).

These OT mandates are the practical expression of the Exodus paradigm, as they make repeated references to the God who delivered the people from oppression in Egypt as the same God who is now instructing the people to extend just provision to others, including the aliens and foreigners in their

74. I continually find the Bible surprising. Normally, we expect any founding documents, whether religious, social, or political, to be foundational and normative and thus promote the ideals of that group or movement. We see this in the contemporary mission statements of corporations, businesses, and ministries, which typically state the good that they seek to do. Yet the Bible speaks of a generative God in creation and redemption, who sustains all that has been made, but it also speaks of a wayward humanity and a refractory world. It is amazing that the Bible is so clear about failure and folly – and at the same time so winsome in its vision of the restoring God, who continues to search us out and heal us. Realism and hope are at play, not idealism.

midst (Lev 19:35; Deut 15:15). These mandates reflect more than charity, which is premised on the generosity of a giver/donor in response to a specific situation of need. In situations of charity, the power lies with the giver in terms of what will be given. But these OT mandates reflect a social justice model because the donor does not determine what should be given or who the recipients should be, but rather *YHWH* indicates what should happen at which particular times. This model of structured generosity befits the notion of justice.

Ronald Sider first made the contemporary Christian public aware of these biblical mandates in 1980 as a matter of urgent relevance,[75] and he has since provided further reflections on the implications of these social justice laws.[76] Sider believes that these life-giving strategies in the OT reflect "distributive justice," which "gives special consideration to disadvantaged groups by providing basic social and economic opportunities and resources."[77] Sider elaborates that justice in the Bible "does not mean we should merely help victims cope with oppression; it teaches us to remove it." Moreover, he insists that "Biblical justice does not merely require fair procedures for the poor: it demands new opportunity!"[78]

Sider concludes with some hard-hitting challenges at the pastoral and practical level. First, if we get rich "by oppressing the poor or if we have wealth and do not reach out generously to the needy, the Lord of history," who is committed to the poor and needy,[79] "moves against us."[80] Second, he points out that "God identifies with the poor so strongly that caring for them is almost like helping God."[81] Put differently, we reflect in our behaviours who God is and what God is like. Third, the biblical notion of justice "includes restoration to community,"[82] which includes the long and challenging work of community work and community transformation.[83]

---

75. Sider, *Rich Christians in an Age of Hunger.*

76. Sider, *Just Generosity: A New Vision for Overcoming Poverty in America.*

77. Sider, 55.

78. Sider, 56.

79. See chapter 9 ("God's Heart for the Poor: A Missional Focus").

80. Sider, *Just Generosity*, 58.

81. Sider, 58.

82. Sider, 59.

83. For a fuller biblical perspective, see Dorr, *The Social Justice Agenda.* For a practical handbook, see Andrews, *Compassionate Community Work.* For two grounded books from those working among slum communities in Southeast Asia, see Craig, *Servants Among the Poor* and Jack, *The Sound of Worlds Colliding.*

Writing from a Majority World context, Andrew Kirk offers various perspectives regarding the causes of poverty,[84] concluding that "the biblical view of justice is that of bringing harmony to the community through the establishment of right relationships."[85] He highlights that justice "is what God does, for justice is what God is,"[86] and that it is "an active concept" because it seeks to "put right" what is a disordered or disproportionate state of affairs.[87]

If justice has to do with a *communal* reality, then it has everything to do with the "common good." Thus, I will conclude this section on OT social justice models by elaborating on the nature and scope of the "common good" and how this theme, as Dennis McCann and Patrick Miller put it, "is intrinsic to the very character of Christian faith."[88] As Jacqueline Lapsley writes, the Bible calls the church "to participate in what is . . . good for all."[89] Moreover, Christians, as "citizens of a heavenly commonwealth," are also "citizens of the wider society" and therefore have accompanying responsibilities.[90] Referring to the Pauline epistles,[91] Victor Furnish concludes that Paul holds believers "responsible for contributing to the public good" and emphasizes that the church is not "an island of one culture in the middle of another," but is a "witnessing community" that is "caught up in the life of the wider civic community."[92]

While Dennis McCann acknowledges that the notion of the common good is "an eschatological concept," he argues that it includes the concern for and implementation of "social justice, human rights, integral human development, the common welfare, public good, and . . . option for the poor."[93] Similarly, Robert Jenson makes the helpful point that the common good is fundamental to any society, writing that "every commonality is united by some good."[94] But he goes on to explain that within the Christian tradition, the common good has everything to do with who God is and what God does, and therefore it is an "*analogous* term which applies to God and to us who derive our life from

84. Kirk, *What is Mission?*, 99–101.

85. Kirk, 105–6.

86. Kirk, 104.

87. Kirk, 105.

88. McCann and Miller, *In Search of the Common Good*, 8.

89. Lapsley, "Biblical Dimensions: Introduction," 11.

90. Lapsley, 12.

91. In particular, Rom 12:7; 13:13; 1 Cor 5:9–10; 10:32; 2 Cor 8:21; Gal 6:10; 1 Thess 4:12; Phil 4:5.

92. Furnish, "Uncommon Love and the Common Good," 83, 86.

93. McCann, "The Common Good in Catholic Social Teaching," 143, 146.

94. Jenson, "The Triunity of Common Good," 336.

God."[95] This theme is developed by Jonathan Ryan, who draws on the writings of Augustine to demonstrate that as we nurture a "common love for God,"[96] a common love of neighbour comes into play. In reflecting on Matthew 25:31–46, Augustine teaches that by loving the neighbour, "*whom you can see*," love for God "is expressed."[97] In this passage, Augustine recognizes Christ as present in the poor and exclaims, "'Recognize him here needing charity.'"[98] Thus, our concern for the common good must be expressed within the faith-community and also in the church's involvement in the world. Augustine challenges our "much-having" and attendant avarice desires, calling us to share "'even . . . things which are called your own,'"[99] concluding that we are to "'hold onto what you have in such a way that you provide for the needy.'"[100]

While some of the contemporary implications that we have drawn from the OT social justice model move beyond the specifics of the texts, the underlying theme of these narratives is that the faith-community is called to repeat the liberating good of the Exodus in the life of the present community whenever people suffer deprivation. Moreover, the various forms of help are intended to be structured realities, rather than only one-off forms of charity, so that the common good will be fostered among those in the community of faith as well as the strangers and aliens in their midst.[101]

The OT Prophetic Movement

I have already touched on the prophetic movement in a number of places in this book[102] and will refer to it again,[103] but it is an important theme. The spiritual and missional themes throughout the biblical narrative reflect an eschatological vision of God's healing goodness breaking into our world, bringing about change and transformation, and this vision calls "what is" to be held within

95. Jenson, 341.

96. Ryan, *Love Does Not Seek Its Own*, 232.

97. Ryan, 234.

98. Ryan, 235.

99. Ryan, 236.

100. Ryan, 236.

101. For extensive discussions on justice and the common good, see O'Brien and Shannon, eds., *Catholic Social Thought*.

102. See chapter 3 ("Key Theological Themes") and chapter 6 ("A Vision of God and a Passion for the World").

103. See chapter 18 ("Hope: A Magnificent Mosaic").

the counter-perspective of "what can yet be." This ability to perceive the "not yet" within the present is a hallmark of the prophetic movement in the OT.

While I acknowledge that there is great complexity and diversity in the OT prophetic movement,[104] my limited task in this section is to highlight the themes that stand in continuity with the paradigms discussed above. Once again, I will draw on several authors who reflect on the contemporary implications of the prophetic tradition.

While Israel's prophets were often disquieted about the nation's kingship,[105] they were persistently hopeful about the vision of Israel's kings exercising God's royal rule as the stewards of God's royal power. As such, Israel's kings were intended to serve the nation as wise shepherds, protecting the people from enemies and promoting justice (2 Sam 3:18; 1 Kgs 3:9; Prov 31:9).[106] However, the kings failed this God-given responsibility again and again, and so the prophets served as a hopeful voice of restoration[107] as well as a corrective voice of rebuke. They were spokespersons on behalf of the poor, and they called the people towards repentance and a just way of life for all.

The prophets raised repeated concerns about three areas of life within Israel. First, the rich and powerful seized property, often leaving people without a sustainable future (Mic 2:1–2; Amos 8:4–6; Ezek 22:29; Isa 5:8–10). Second, traders favoured the rich and exploited the poor (Mic 6:10–12; Hos 12:7; Amos 8:5; Isa 3:13–15). Third, many judges were corrupt, and so the oppressed could not turn to anyone to receive justice (Amos 5:7; 6:12; Mic 3:9–11; Jer 22:13–17; Isa 5:23; 10:1–2).[108]

Richard Middleton notes that the "two main targets of prophetic critique are . . . idolatry and injustice," reflecting Israel's failure to live the vision of "the God of the exodus."[109] He goes on to emphasize that living this vision involves "a life that embodies righteousness and justice, since these are central to the

---

104. Some of these themes include restoration, human flourishing and justice, a new creation, giving advice to kings, engaging in the politics of the surrounding nations, and casting a vision of a future age to come.

105. Middleton refers to the "complex narrative of mostly failed kings" and their failure "in restoring Israel to its mission of bringing blessing to the world" (*New Heaven and New Earth*, 66).

106. See Weber, *Power.*

107. Brueggemann points out that in the "rich variety" of prophetic voices, there was a "single, glad affirmation that YHWH is actively at work to assure the return of deported Israel to its homeland" and the glorious future that awaited the nation (*Old Testament Theology: An Introduction*, 295).

108. See Boerma, *The Rich, the Poor, and the Bible.*

109. Middleton, *New Heaven and New Earth*, 103.

interhuman flourishing that God desires."[110] Middleton concludes by setting out the broad parameters of the prophetic restorative vision: the people were to "return to the land," and there was to be a "restoration of God's people in society" as well as a "flourishing in the natural world," with Zion as the centre for blessing the nations.[111] Moreover, the people would receive the gift of a "new heart" to facilitate obedience, and they would be restored through God's presence in "the renewed land."[112]

In liberation theology, prophecy is an implicit feature in the work of evangelization, which is understood as both the annunciation of good news and the denunciation of all that is death-dealing. When evangelization is cast in terms of the reign of God, the prophetic impulse anticipates God's final future.[113]

Ignacio Ellacuria makes clear connections between the kingdom of God and prophetic witness, noting how the "church as institution tends to be more conserving of the past than renewing of the present and creative of the future."[114] He argues that the church itself needs to hear the prophetic witness and undergo transformation because it "has picked up as dead weight" so much baggage "on its way through history."[115] Thus he calls the church to listen to the Hebrew prophets, the Sermon on the Mount, the Last Supper discourse and the book of Revelation, along with other inspirational voices.[116] Yet Ellacuria also stresses that the transformation of the church and its prophetic witness to the world can only take place when it lives out God's preferential option for the poor. He believes that "it is in the poor that the greatest real presence of the historical Jesus is found," and therefore among the poor is "the greatest capacity for salvation."[117] This salvation will only occur when the poor are "active" subjects of history, rather than simply passive-receptive subjects.[118] When history is viewed from the perspective of the poor, it calls for a critique of all "pseudo-utopia" visions, including development, socialism, and capitalism,

110. Middleton, 103.

111. Middleton, 105–6.

112. Middleton, 106–7.

113. It is surprising that Guiterrez, in his chapter on "Eschatology and Politics," discusses the themes of annunciation and denunciation within the framework of a utopian vision, and yet he does not refer to prophecy (*A Theology of Liberation*, 136).

114. Ellacuria, "Utopia and Prophecy in Latin America," 326.

115. Ellacuria, 301.

116. Ellacuria, 290–91.

117. Ellacuria, 302.

118. Ellacuria, 303.

and a vision for a new sociopolitical and cultural order that will reflect the prophetic impulse.[119]

However optimistic this may be, Ellacuria demonstrates the centrality and universal implications of the prophetic vision and its connection to the kingdom of God. He writes, "Without prophecy there is no possibility of making a Christian concretion of utopia and, consequently, a historical realization of the Kingdom of God."[120] Moreover, he says that "Christian utopia" cannot function without "prophecy to inspire it."[121] This inspiration is "nourished by the intercession that the Spirit makes throughout history."[122] In this light, prophecy must be a permanent feature of the life and mission of the church, which means that the mission of the church includes prophetic discernment. The outworking of this prophetic discernment is a "critical contrasting of the proclamation of the Kingdom of God with a definite historical situation,"[123] which implies a careful analysis of one's sociocultural setting in the light of Scripture. Thus, the prophetic impulse is multi-directional, for it looks to the biblical narratives for its life-giving themes, and it both critiques and inspires the faith-community as it seeks to bring about societal change in light of the kingdom of God and in solidarity with the poor.

While much more could be said about the prophetic movement and its implications for the church and its mission,[124] I will conclude this section with a summary of the key points. First, the missional task of the church is to bring the good news of God's redemption to the world. Therefore, the church needs to *be* good news and to *resist* all that is bad news. Second, the prophetic task of the church can only come from a place of repentance and humility, since the church needs to be what it proclaims as it points out the idolatries in the world. Third, the prophetic task can only come from a life of deep fidelity to God and God's way in the world. Fourth, prophecy involves a profound spirituality in listening to God and being willing to follow God's ways, even when others (or an entire nation) do not. Fifth, the prophetic vision is always both corrective and visionary, for its ultimate goal is the new that God will bring into the world.

---

119. Ellacuria, 296–300, 309–28.

120. Ellacuria, 291.

121. Ellacuria, 293.

122. Ellacuria, 293.

123. Ellacuria, 292.

124. See the way that Christopher Wright has extensively woven the prophetic vision throughout *The Mission of God*.

The Model of God–People–Land

All these paradigms or models are comprehensive in nature, as they are concerned with God's salvific work, the formation of a people who are redeemed by God's healing presence, and the call to reflect God's goodness to the whole world. These paradigms all move from particularly to universality, for the creator God is Israel's God, who has given Israel the task of being a light to the nations. These paradigms are wonderfully wide in scope, as they are not simply concerned with internal spiritual realities ("saving souls" in contemporary terms), but with the renewal of persons, a people, and the nations. The work of renewal draws us into nation building, justice, peacemaking, creation-care, as well as worship, prayer, and celebration.

This rich vision is also reflected in the biblical model of the triangle of God–people–land.[125] The first dimension is *theological*: God calls into being a particular people who are marked by his redemption and covenant faithfulness. Though God's faithfulness knows no bounds, it often takes a recalcitrant people through the vortex of judgement and purgation towards restoration. The second dimension is *sociological*: God places himself/herself in relationship with a people. Through calling and liberation, God's people come into being as a reflection of who God is and what God does. Thus an "incarnation" not only occurs in the creation but also in a people who are marked by God's presence. The calling of this people in relation to God is to worship, obey, embody, and bear witness. The third dimension is *economic*: the creator-redeemer God provides for the sustenance and well-being of people through the resources of the land.[126] Thus, the God of the Bible is a "material" God. The land is God's creation and possession, and it is given as a generous gift to sustain a people who are called to responsible stewardship and care.[127]

Christopher Wright helpfully expands this vision to the NT, noting that the OT triangular model consists of God–church–*kononia* in the NT[128] and highlighting how the economic angle is not lost in the faith-communities of the NT. The Jerusalem church functioned as a form of communitarianism, and the house churches of the Pauline mission practised practical care for needy

125. For this triangular model, I am wholly dependent on Christopher Wright, *Living as the People of God* (19, 90, 100).

126. Brueggemann highlights that just as God is the "lord of events," so God is the "fructifier of the land," and thus this land is "never only land possessed and managed," but always "land of gift and promise" (*The Land*, 185, 191).

127. See Lev 25:5.

128. Wright, *Living as the People of God*, 100.

members as well as for neighbours. Finally, Wright draws this paradigm into the vision of a new heaven and a new earth.[129]

In reflecting on this most basic model, we note again the dynamic relationship between creation and redemption and the provision of God both for this life and the life to come. When we fail to live in this way by denying care and resources to the poor and alien, the implication is that this violates the image of God in people and thus fractures God's purposes for humanity. The biblical narratives are very cognisant of human creatureliness and vulnerability – and therefore perceive the profound need for resources and safety for human well-being. Thus, in the biblical vision, spirituality and economics are intimately related, and any mission of the church must reflect this comprehensive vision.

OT Shalom

The OT engages many broad themes, including salvation, justice, righteousness, redemption, among others, but the most comprehensive term for understanding the work of God among the people of Israel and their corresponding task in the world is *shalom*, which can mean inner peace or tranquillity along with overall well-being, wholeness, security, safety, and prosperity, among many other nuanced shades of meaning. When the concept of shalom is applied to individuals, we note the following. First, the gift of peace relates both to personal goodness and overall well-being. Proverbs 3:2 speaks of "abundant welfare" as a gift from God for those who keep the commandments. A similar promise of "great peace" is made for those "who love your law" (Ps 119:165), and the prophet declares that God will "keep in peace" those of a "steadfast mind" and those who "trust" in God (Isa 26:3). Second, this gift of peace is untroubled. The psalmist speaks of being able to "sleep in peace" because the Lord makes "me lie down in safety" (Ps 4:8). Third, the gift of peace is connected to God's covenant. Phinehas is promised, "I hereby grant him my covenant of peace," and this covenant will be passed on to his descendants (Num 25:12–13). This covenant of peace is also mentioned elsewhere in the OT, where it is applied to the people as a whole (Isa 54:10).

The OT emphasizes this concept of shalom being a blessing from God that has a communal dynamic. First, in the Aaronic blessing, peace is extended to the nation of Israel: "'the LORD lift up his countenance upon you, and give you peace.' So shall they put my name on the Israelites, and I will bless them"

129. Wright, 100.

(Num 6:26–27). Second, the blessing of obedience brings about God's gifts of abundance in that "the land shall yield its produce," and you will "live securely in your land," and "I will grant peace in the land" (Lev 26:4–6). Third, there is a general benediction of peace for God's people: "May the LORD give strength to his people! May the LORD bless his people with peace!" (Ps 29:11).[130] Fourth, there is peace because of the absence of war (1 Chr 22:9). Fifth, Scripture speaks of the relationship between moral well-being and social and political security, for "the effect of righteousness will be peace . . . And my people will abide in peaceful habitation, in secure dwellings, and in quiet resting places" (Isa 32:17–18).

It is now appropriate to put these diverse verses about shalom into a wider frame.[131] First, while Genesis does not mention "shalom," the concept is implicit in Genesis 1, as it mirrors the work of completion in creation, and shalom holds the notion of completeness in its heart. Second, Genesis 2 speaks of the relationships between God and humanity, man and woman, humans and the earth, and humans and animals, reflecting another important theme of shalom: harmony in all relationships. Third, Genesis 3 and 4 highlight how shalom is threatened and falls into chaos. This slide into chaos is most vividly expressed in the Noah narrative (Gen 6:11–13). Thus, shalom is both a generative gift from God and also a task for humanity, as our calling is to imbibe this gift and live it out in the joyful task of peacemaking. Fourth, the major emphasis throughout the OT is the restoration of the relationship between God and humankind, between humans (including the stranger or alien), and between humans and nature. This is the central impulse of shalom, and is, therefore, often cast in eschatological terms (Isa 2:1–4; 55:12–13; 65:17–25).

Brueggemann summarizes the "themes of *created order for life, jeopardy*, the *restraint of chaos*, and *responsive doxology*" as "constitutive of Israel's creation faith" and argues that living this faith will result in the "maintenance of the created order" through God's covenant faithfulness and the dynamic of a "mutual fidelity."[132] He goes to make the applicational point that the persistent theme of the OT – "creation-new creation" – leads us away from "*commoditization*" so that we understand "*creatureliness* in terms of dialogic-covenant categories."[133] This insight touches on the very heartbeat of shalom,

130. See also Ps 147:14.

131. For what follows, I am indebted to Prof. Athena Gorospe at Asian Theological Seminary in Metro Manila, with whom I team-taught the course, "Transformation Theology."

132. Brueggemann, *Old Testament Theology*, 331, author's emphasis.

133. Brueggemann, 340, author's emphasis.

which has everything to do with the harmony of life, overcoming chaos, God's ongoing gift of human well-being, and the call to extend the blessings of God's good gifts towards others. In other words, all who have been marked by God's shalom are to be peacemakers in our world. This calling is not peripheral to the life of faith, for as Jonathan Wilson points out, "creation cannot be rightly understood apart from peace. The story of God's creative work and the story of God's consummation of that work is one that can only be understood as shalom."[134] In later chapters, I deal more fully with the theme of peace,[135] where I include more practical applications.[136] But to summarize, peace is God's gift, and it is intrinsic to human well-being. As such, it is part of our mission as the people of God to be peacemakers.

To conclude this overview of OT paradigms, we can see how these interrelated models form a colourful mosaic, where God initiates redemption, and those who are shaped by God's grace are called to extend that grace into the world as they relate to others. All of these paradigms are interwoven and must be outworked in daily life while looking toward an eschatological future. As such, they have ongoing relevance and are part of the missional calling of the present-day community of faith.

New Testament Paradigms

As noted previously, both the OT and the NT are important in helping us to understand God's salvific work and the calling of the people of God as a community of witness and service. The NT celebrates the person and work of Christ through the Spirit, and this forms a new culminating centre for the previous narratives.

Since the central concern of this chapter is integral mission, my focus will be on the missional implications of the person and work of Christ as they were embodied and became normative for the faith-communities of early Christianity. In emphasizing this, it is important to highlight that the power of the NT is not so much in the *imitatio Christi* (though this is important), but rather in *Christo-mysticism*.[137] In other words, our in-Christ relationship through the Spirit becomes the energizing centre that impacts our missional

---

134. Wilson, *God's Good World*, 26–27.

135. See chapter 13 ("The Anabaptist Vision of Community, Discipleship, and Service") and chapter 14 ("Franciscan Peacemaking: A Key Theme in Missional Spirituality").

136. For further practical application, see Fahey and Armstrong, eds., *A Peace Reader*.

137. See Gorman, *Participating in Christ*.

engagement with the world. Thus, who we *are* in Christ determines what we are called to *do* as we live and serve in the way of Christ in the world.

Various missional theologians have different starting points when it comes to engaging the NT, and some have given much more attention to Scripture than others.[138] But David Bosch has engaged the NT most extensively in laying a foundation for mission.[139] He proposes that Matthew's paradigm of mission focusses on discipleship in "living out the teachings of Jesus" in commitment "to God's reign, to justice and love, and to obedience to the entire will of God."[140] He also suggests that the Luke-Acts paradigm has a rich texture of missional themes, including the following: the universality of God's redemption and the ever-widening circles of witness; the power of forgiveness, healing, witness, and service in the Spirit; a concern for the poor; and the way the faith-community lives out a radical hospitality. Bosch concludes, the "intimate linking of pneumatology and mission is Luke's distinctive contribution to the early church's missionary paradigm."[141]

Bosch's articulation of the "Pauline Missionary Paradigm" includes the following features: the church as the new community, a concern for Israel's

---

138. Dorr, *Mission in Today's World*, makes no attempt to entertain either the OT or the NT and mainly focusses on themes, such as evangelization, inculturation, reconciliation, justice for the poor, among others. In his discussion of the purpose of mission, he acknowledges that it involves church planting as well as the work of building a more just society (193–201). Amaladoss, *Making All Things New*, does not engage Scripture either as he wrestles with how to understand Christ in the world of Asia's religious pluralism. Ramachandra, *The Recovery of Mission*, also wrestles with an Asian context, but grounds his work in Christology, concluding that "the normativeness and ultimacy of Jesus Christ in God's salvific dealings with his world . . . is *intrinsic to Christian praxis and self-understanding*" (216, author's emphasis). Kirk, *What is Mission?*, grounds this question in the theme of "mission in the way of Jesus Christ," which he argues has to do with Christ's "own life work" and the "conduct of his disciples," and which involved Jesus in forming an "alternative community" as a sign of the reign of God and involved the disciples in a life discipleship and the work of "evangelism, justice, compassion, and non-violence" (38, 47, 53). Newbigin, *The Open Secret*, is deeply rooted in Scripture and has a vibrant Christology. He grounds his missional theology in the following Trinitarian frame: "Proclaiming the Kingdom of the Father," "Sharing in the Life of the Son," and "Bearing the Witness of the Spirit." His main point is that the church is to be a hermeneutic of the gospel: "the church is a movement launched into the life of the world to bear in its own life God's gift of peace for the life of the world" (48). Hastings, *Missional God, Missional Church*, develops his missional theology within a strong Trinitarian orientation, which shapes the identity and mission of the church in living out the "great cultural mandate," the "great commandment," and the "great commission" (157). Reflecting a thorough engagement with Scripture, Hastings concludes that the "commission" of the church is "to bring God's forgiveness to people in every situation, through word and action," which makes the church a bearer of the "shalom of God" (321).

139. Bosch, *Transforming Mission*, 15–178.

140. Bosch, 81.

141. Bosch, 114.

redemption, the imminent return of Christ, the transformation of society, and the centrality of weakness.[142] Bosch concludes that in the Pauline corpus, mission is concerned with the church's role in "God's cosmic-historical plan for the redemption of the world"[143] and the restoration of all of creation.

In the light of the above, I will suggest some paradigms that are reflective of an integral mission. To clarify, my task is not to set out a fully orbed theology of mission, but to look to Scripture for larger configurations that outline the scope of our mission. Thus, my focus will be on the *praxis* of mission, which refers to the way that these ideas are lived out and operationalized in the world.

The Jesus Movement: a Transformational Model

I am using the phrase, "Jesus Movement," deliberately to acknowledge the normativity of Christ and how Jesus called people to follow him and become part of his mission. Jesus set out to form a community that would reflect new values – the values of the kingdom of God – in order to make an impact on the Jewish society of his day.[144]

We need not linger on questions about the sort of community that Jesus formed, but we can observe that it was a common purse community[145] that was supported by wealthier people who were also part of the movement.[146] Applying the sociological categories of introversionist, conversionist, utopian, reformist, and transformational communities,[147] we can also observe that the Jesus community had some of all these features, for its inner-life orientation included prayer and formation; its proclamation included a call to repentance and conversion; it had a utopian outlook framed by the hope of the coming kingdom of God;[148] and it certainly had a reformist agenda in that it sought to be a renewal movement within the Judaism of that time;[149] but its dominant

142. Bosch, 172–77.

143. Bosch, 178.

144. See also chapter 6 ("A Vision of God and a Passion for the World").

145. See John 12:6 and the reference that Judas kept the common purse, but he was a thief.

146. Luke 8:1–3 and the reference to wealthy women who supported the Jesus movement. See also Theissen, *Sociology of Early Palestinian Christianity.*

147. Wilson, *Religious Sects: A Sociological Study.*

148. John Gager's work on the NT, while more complex, has drawn on the study of millenarian movements in an attempt to describe the Jesus movement. He identifies the following characteristics: (1) promise of heaven on earth; (2) reversal of the present social order; (3) release of emotional energy; (4) brief lifespan of the movement; (5) central role of a charismatic leader (*Kingdom and Community*, 21).

149. See the work of Christopher Rowlands, *Christian Origins.*

feature was transformational in that it sought to bring about a new people in a new world that would be formed by the reign of God.[150]

By describing the Jesus movement as a *transformational* community, I am referring to its trilectic orientation in that it is inward, upward, and outward. First, Jesus and his disciples sought to bring about inner restoration through processes of forgiveness and healing. Second, they sought to bring about a restored relationship with God and an orientation towards God and God's kingdom purposes. Third, they sought to live as light, leaven, and salt within the society in order to affect social change. This meant that as a community, they sought to live differently with new attitudes towards women, children, marginal persons, and the poor. Moreover, theirs was an ethic of both spiritual sharing and economic generosity. And in their witness, they not only called others to embrace the way of Jesus, but they also critiqued existing religious power structures. In light of our focus in this chapter, we can also say that this transformational dynamic reflects an integral orientation. In the present day, if we seek to follow the example of Jesus by living and serving in the way of Jesus, then our faith-communities will need to be concerned with spiritual renewal, healing, community building, evangelization, as well as prophetic witness.

In the light of the above, we can note some basic characteristics of the *praxis* of the Jesus movement. First, the movement was captivated, renewed, and empowered by Jesus. Second, its followers were disciples of Jesus, and so they were nurtured and trained in the vision of God's reign and God's restoration of all things. Third, its followers learned the ministry of witness and healing through a cyclical process of doing, reflecting, and more doing. Fourth, the Gospel accounts are filled with stories of individual people receiving the blessings of faith, repentance, and healing. Thus, we can say that the Jesus movement is person-focused. Fifth, Jesus and his disciples ministered to crowds of people through both word and deeds of power. Sixth, Jesus and his disciples demonstrated both an inner and outer dynamic. They made time for rest, prayer, teaching, correction, and they also made time to be on the road, proclaiming the good news of the kingdom of God. Seventh, the first formative expressions of the community's life together, as reported in Acts 2 and 4, reflect the DNA of the Jesus movement. Eighth, there is evidence in the Gospels that the message of Jesus and his disciples (who included both men and women) started as a movement of hope among the poor. Ninth, the voice of Jesus as it

---

150. There are NT scholars, such as George Pixley in *God's Kingdom*, who read transformation in political and economic terms. Pixley sees the Jesus movement as a revolutionary group seeking to overthrow the unjust economic system of the Jerusalem Temple elite.

is portrayed in the Gospels included a sustained critique of the Pharisees and the temple leadership regarding their oppressive religious practices. Tenth, the Jesus movement practised "civil disobedience" by continuing to heal on the Sabbath day. Eleventh, the movement's vision of the reign of God gave it an eschatological orientation that no amount of opposition (including death) could dampen.

In applying these characteristics of the Jesus movement to the missional calling of today's church, we face a profound challenge in seeking to overcome our present-day polarities. Whereas some Christian groups stress evangelism, others stress the work of justice. Whereas some see ministry in terms of apologetics, others see it primarily as healing. Yet the above mosaic of the Jesus movement reflects a much more profound and comprehensive vision of mission and ministry.

Some NT scholars have used the Synoptic Gospels to forge a missional vision that is grounded in the messianic narrative rather than in a few isolated texts. For example, in *Life on the Road*, Athol Gill emphasizes costly discipleship, joyous community, kingdom-oriented ministry, and spiritual practices. Gill's closing challenge is that as new creations in Christ, we are called to discipleship through both community and pilgrimage, and so we will be called to walk the road to Jerusalem, the cross, and the resurrection, awaiting "that day when his kingdom will be revealed in all its glory as his will is accomplished on earth as in heaven."[151] In *Liberating News*, Orlando Costas also provides a broad NT vision of contextual evangelization, highlighting one aspect of the Jesus movement that deserves more attention: how Jesus moved from the periphery of society (in terms of his Galilean origins) to the centre of society (in Jerusalem) in order to call for its radical renewal.[152] This missional shift from the periphery to the centre is also part of the vision of Anabaptists and liberation theologians, and it is a focus we need to recover in light of the collapse of Christendom in our age and the challenge of the now-marginalized church to seek to become a more fully prophetic community by resisting the dominant powers of this age.

The Model of Luke-Acts

In highlighting Luke-Acts, my intention is not to make these texts more important than other parts of the NT. Rather, Luke-Acts provides a helpful

151. Gill, *Life on the Road*, 293.
152. Costas, *Liberating News*, 49–70.

illustration of integral mission, not only by linking evangelization and the work of justice, but even more fundamentally by highlighting who God is and what God does and then applying that to who we are called to be and what we are called to do as a result of God's transformative work in us. This OT theme is repeated most amazingly in Luke-Acts. The events recounted in the Gospel of Luke are in many ways repeated in the book of Acts, highlighting the simple theme that the faith-community is called to repeat who Jesus is and what Jesus does, thereby becoming a creative recapitulation of the ministry of Christ. We see evidence of this repetition in the following.

First, Luke-Acts demonstrates a continuity with Israel. Luke refers to a continuity with David (1:32), and Simeon exclaims that he has seen God's salvation as a "light for revelation to the Gentiles and for the glory of your people Israel" (2:30–32). We also see evidence of this continuity in Peter's preaching in Acts, where he says that "David spoke of the resurrection of the Messiah," and he proclaims that the Lord is seated at God's "right hand" (2:30, 34). Elsewhere, Peter alludes to the prophetic tradition as depicting the coming of Christ,[153] and in Acts, Peter exclaims, "you are the descendants of the prophets and of the covenant that God gave to your ancestors" (3:25). This emphasis is important in integral mission, for God's salvation is for *all* – the old community and newcomers, both insiders and outsiders.

Second, the heart of mission is for others to experience God's bounteous salvation, which brings forth the joy and freedom of forgiveness. This blessing of forgiveness also brings forth redemptive change and new life (Luke 5:20; 7:1–10; 19:1–10; Acts 2:38; 3:19; 10:43).

Third, the good news of forgiveness is accompanied by signs of profound transformation. Word gets translated into deed. Forgiveness is enriched by acts of healing and exorcism, where the powers of darkness are exposed and light shines (Luke 13:10–17; Luke 11:20; 13:32; Acts 2:43; 5:12–16; 16:16–19).

Fourth, the heart of Luke-Acts is the Nazareth manifesto (Luke 4:18–19), which proclaims the great OT theme[154] of God's salvation, restoration, healing, and deliverance, especially for the poor and oppressed. This passage illustrates integral salvation, for it casts a vision of new life and freedom for the whole

153. 1 Pet 1:10–12.

154. See Isa 61:2.

person, despite their prior bondage and oppression. When we are set free in the freedom and generosity of a God of love and grace, this is truly great news![155]

Fifth, Luke-Acts highlights the work of the Spirit. In Luke's Gospel, the Spirit comes upon Zachariah (Luke 1:67), Simeon (Luke 2:25–32), Jesus (Luke 3:22; 4:1, 18; 10:21), and on the community of disciples (Acts 1:8; 4:31; 6:3; 10:44–48; 13:2–4; 16:6–10). This emphasis highlights how the work of bringing people into the realm of restoration is inspired by the Spirit, and thus any missional activity must be both Spirit-led and Spirit-empowered.

Sixth, the Luke-Acts paradigm also highlights the importance of community formation (Luke 8:1–3; 19:1–10; Acts 2:42–47; 4:32–47). Those who are part of the Jesus movement share a communal identity, for we become one with Christ and one another as we share a common life with Christ at the centre. At the same time, our shared life together in and with Christ and one another is the basis of our witness and service. As such, the faith-community becomes an embodied word. In the Acts narrative, we can note how entire households came to faith in Christ (Acts 16:15).

Seventh, Luke-Acts portrays a movement that is both radical and transformative in the way it depicts boundary-breaking behaviour. This is expressed in the ministry of exorcism (Luke 4:40–41; Acts 16:16–18), the practice of healing on the Sabbath (Luke 6:6–11; 13:10–17), the ministry extended to a Roman army officer – an "outsider" (Luke 7:1–10), the example of the good Samaritan (Luke 10:25–37), the critique of the rich (Luke 1:53; 16:19–28), ministry to all sorts of culturally marginal and suspect people (Luke 7:36–50; 19:1–10), and the inclusion of the poor at God's banqueting table (Luke 14:21).[156] Acts extends the Jesus movement beyond Jerusalem into Samaria and Asia-Minor, highlighting the conversion of households, household-based ministry, and broadening the ministry of proclamation and healing.[157]

Thus, we can identify the Jesus movement and the models in Luke-Acts as part of the same biblical mosaic, revealing several core themes about integral

---

155. Whether the Nazareth manifesto includes an allusion to the OT Year of Jubilee, with its reference to the "year of the Lord's favor," remains an open question. See Ringe, *Jesus, Liberation, and the Biblical Jubilee.*

156. See Koenig, *New Testament Hospitality.* Koenig notes that in Luke-Acts there are "an impressive number of references to meals" (89) and that meals are "bridge building" in the ministry of hospitality (87). Thus "for Luke partnership with strangers becomes a natural feature of mission" (87).

157. Koenig highlights the nature of "house church hospitality" in the Pauline mission (61–65). See also Robert Banks, *Paul's Idea of Community.*

mission. First, the incarnation of Christ is expressed in and through the faith-community. Thus, the followers of Christ are to be a second incarnation by becoming an embodied word that reflects Jesus Christ, the living word. By implication, we can say that any integral mission is *incarnational*. Second, the followers of Christ are disciples, who seek to become more like Christ and to do what Christ did. Christ-formed disciples will live out a life of obedience, witness, and service "on the road." Thus, any integral mission will involve ongoing *discipleship* and *service*. Third, the followers of Christ live as a community of radical hospitality and welcome in their service to the world. Thus, we can say that any integral mission is *communal*. Fourth, having been impacted and formed by the kingdom of God, the Christ community always points beyond itself to the in-breaking of the reign of God. Thus, any integral mission is *eschatological*. We will explore this fourth theme more fully in the next model.

Kingdom of God Models

A central theme in Scripture is the sovereignty of God, which has everything to do with the kingdom of God. Most basically, the kingdom of God describes how God's presence and rule are made evident in the lives of individuals, movements, and institutions. The heartbeat of this kingdom is salvific and restorative, a manifestation of God's eschatological purpose in making all things new. As a consequence of this grand purpose, the kingdom of God exposes all that is not part of God's renewing purpose for the world. Thus, the kingdom of God is inherently redemptive and prophetic, always bringing in the new while rejecting the contra-realities of the old.

My purpose in this chapter is limited, as I am engaging this model to illustrate the nature and scope of integral mission. To begin, I will provide a summary of Howard Snyder's *Models of the Kingdom*, which demonstrates the many dimensions of the kingdom of God, and then offer my own reflections on this helpful work. Rather than overplaying a particular aspect of the kingdom of God (such as the *heavenly* kingdom), Snyder concludes that "no one model is fully adequate" and all models are only a "partial representation of a deeper and broader truth."[158] His main purpose is to demonstrate the different theological and historical understandings of the kingdom of God that have emerged among those who have sought to live out the vision of the kingdom,[159] particularly how

---

158. Snyder, *Models of the Kingdom*, 131, 143.

159. Snyder, 22.

they came to terms with the tensions between present/future, individual/social, spirit/matter, gradual/climatic, divine/human action, and church/kingdom dimensions of the reign of God.[160] Snyder's most basic point is that when we accent a particular model and underplay its inherent tensions, we end up with a partial and sometimes distorted view about how we are to live the Christian life and how the church is called to serve the world.[161] Following is a brief description of Snyder's eight models.

First, the *interior kingdom* model stresses the personal salvation experience and sees the kingdom mainly in terms of inner change and personal benefits. This model is inspired by Luke 17:21: "the kingdom of God is within you."[162] While this interior emphasis is appropriate, it is inadequate, as it overlooks the broader dimensions of the kingdom in terms of forming community and impacting the world. On the other hand, if we only understand the kingdom in terms of the rule of justice and peace in our world, then we will overlook the inner, spiritual dynamic of the kingdom that empowers us to walk the long road in the quest for justice.

Second, the *future kingdom* model takes note of Jesus's statement, "my kingdom is not of this world" (John 18:36 NIV).[163] Taken out of context, this verse can readily give the impression that God's concern is wholly for the age that is to come in God's final future rather than this world. This focus can result in a world-denying form of Christianity. While a focus on the *interior* kingdom can lead to a cultic personalism, a focus on the *future* kingdom can lead to societal indifference as we lose sight of the eschatological nature of our Christian existence and ministry. The Christian who is marked by God's kingdom of forgiveness and freedom and who is sustained by the presence of the Spirit will become a person of prayer and ongoing longing[164] for the full expression of God's kingdom. This longing is not only for the *future* kingdom in the age to come, but for God's kingdom to come amongst us more fully in the *present*, the here and now. Hence Jesus teaches us to pray, "your kingdom come, your will be done, on earth as in heaven" (Matt 6:10).

Third, the *heavenly kingdom* model takes its inspiration from Luke 22:29–30: "I confer on you, just as my Father has conferred on me, a kingdom, so

160. Snyder, 16–17.

161. As Snyder writes, the "greatest challenge" that these models of the kingdom of God raises is "how to be authentically Christian in our present environment" and "how to lead the kind of life that gives credibility to the theology we affirm" (131).

162. NIV: "within you"; NRSV: "among you"; ESV: "in the midst of you."

163. NRSV: "my kingdom is not from here"; ESV: "my kingdom is not from the world."

164. See Smith, *Desiring the Kingdom*.

that you may eat and drink at my table in my kingdom." Snyder interprets this passage with a highly sacramental view, identifying the faith-community as sharing a mystical communion. He notes connections between the heavenly kingdom and the future kingdom (model 2, discussed above), along with the ecclesiastical kingdom (model 4, discussed below).[165]

Fourth, the *ecclesiastical kingdom* model finds its inspiration in the authority bestowed on the faith-community by Christ: "I will give you the keys of the kingdom of heaven, and whatever you bind on earth will be bound in heaven, and whatever you loose on earth will be loosed in heaven" (Matt 16:19). This proclamation suggests a close connection between the church and the kingdom, along with the authority structure of the church and the power that the church possesses in the purposes of God for the world. This connection suggests that the church is not merely a religious-sociological entity, but rather the bearer and embodiment of the reign of God as a servant and sign of God's kingdom. This model places a great responsibility on the community of faith to be renewed by God as it seeks to bear witness to the kingdom in its service to the world. The danger of this perspective is that the church and the kingdom can become synonymous so that whatever the church is and does is a reflection of God's kingdom. Yet this collapses the kingdom of God into ecclesiology, which is a most dangerous move if the church forgets its cruciform nature and servant status. To some extent, this model resulted in the Christendom vision, with its notion of a powerful church as a significant influence in society.

Fifth, the *subversive kingdom* model receives its inspiration from verses such as Luke 6:20: "Blessed are you who are poor now for yours is the kingdom of God." Such passages suggest that God's kingdom is not a conservative, middle-class dynamic, but rather an irruption from the bottom up. This model demonstrates God's heart for the poor and calls the church to be a community of hospitality for the marginalized, a concern that is particularly pressing in our self-focused, consumer-driven age. Thus, the church not only has a conserving influence on society, but becomes a transformational community that is committed to seeing grace, healing, restoration, and justice for *all*, particularly those on the ash heap of life. This model calls the church to commit to an upside-down kingdom.[166]

Sixth, the *theocratic kingdom* model gains its impulse from verses such as Revelation 1:5–6: "from Jesus Christ, the faithful witness, the firstborn of the dead, and the ruler of the kings of the earth. To him who loves us and frees us

---

165. Snyder, *Models of the Kingdom*, 66.

166. Kraybill, *The Upside-Down Kingdom*.

from our sins by his blood, and made us a kingdom, priests serving his God and Father."[167] This emphasis can suggest that the church itself has a kingly task, which can be interpreted as a form of governmental rule set by ecclesiastical authority.[168] This Constantinian concept has been repeated in the history of the Christian church[169] and assumes that all ecclesiastical concerns can be applied politically or, in a much milder form, that a Christian will make a better political leader. Of course, elements of this model persist in state churches and wherever churches are aligned with political realities. The grave danger of this kind of alliance is that it will undermine the prophetic nature of the church.

Seventh, in the *utopian kingdom* model, its proponents believe that heaven can come to earth. Such groups may be based on political ideology[170] or millenarian beliefs.[171] In the history of Christianity, this generalized vision has been expressed in many attempts to create some form of "perfect" community.[172] In referring to Scripture, Snyder cites Isaiah 11:6, which gives an idyllic picture of the animal kingdom living in perfect peace, a vision that has been projected onto a new world of joyful habitation. While eschatological beliefs are part of the Christian story, Scripture makes it clear that we still live in a fallen world and that God's final kingdom still awaits us.

Eighth, the *transforming kingdom* model is most clearly set out in the parables in Matthew 13, which emphasize both sudden growth and transformation. This model suggests that the word and the Spirit – and therefore the people of God who have been impacted by God's grace – can live as salt, light, and leaven in society, and can therefore become agents of transformation. In *Christ and Culture*, H. Richard Niebuhr suggests that the transformation motif has been a dominant model in the history of Christianity, citing in particular John Calvin, who stresses the "permeation of all of life by the gospel" through the laity outworking their faith in all the dimensions of

---

167. For similar verses, see Rev 5:10; 11:15; 12:10.

168. The Roman Catholic encyclical, *Redemptoris Missio*, clarifies: "while remaining distinct from Christ and the Kingdom, the Church is indissolubly united to both" (32).

169. Herrin notes that the Frankish king, Charles, was seen as "the divinely commanded leader of the churches within his dominions," was acclaimed as "king and priest (*rex et sacerdos*)," was "anointed by God," and "was charged with responsibility for the salvation of his people as a New David" (*The Formation of Christendom*, 435).

170. Hardy, *Alternative Communities*.

171. Burridge, *New Heaven, New Earth*.

172. Knowles, *Christian Monasticism*; Hyma, *Brethren of the Common Life*; Rausch, *Radical Christian Communities*; Zablocki, *The Joyful Community*. However, the extent of a realized eschatological view is varied in these and other groups, while some groups became cultic. See Faubion, *The Shadows and Lights of Waco*.

life.[173] The theme of transformation is an important concept in present-day missional thinking.[174]

To summarize, we might observe that in our mosaic of integral mission, the subversive and transformational models are dominant colours while the others add texture and contrast. Moreover, the future and heavenly models need to be carefully calibrated in order to reflect Scripture's eschatological vision of the new breaking into the world through the salvific work of Christ in the Spirit rather than offering an escapist option. While the interior kingdom can highlight the importance of a sustaining spirituality, the utopian model can cast a vision for what is best in the vision of God while avoiding illusions about what we can create. Finally, any understanding of the relationship between the church and the kingdom of God should identify the church as a community of faith that is spawned and shaped by God's kingdom and is therefore called to bear witness to the values of that kingdom as a servant to the world.

I will conclude this discussion of various kingdom of God models by drawing on some other voices. First, in *Announcing the Reign of God*, Mortimer Arias challenges the church to live out the subversive memory of Jesus in discipleship communities that proclaim the gospel by engaging "collective sins [and] structural powers" and that also bear prophetic, contextual witness by engaging in incarnational, humanizing, conscientizing, liberating activities, recognizing that through the "announcement of the reign of God," these activities will inevitably be "conflictive."[175]

E. Stanley Jones makes the basic point that the "entrance into the kingdom is personal and by a new birth, but the nature of that kingdom is social; everything comes under its purview, for all life, individual and collective, is to become subject to the Kingdom."[176] Jones describes Luke 4:18–19 as a "kingdom manifesto," which calls us to live as servants to others.[177] Moreover, Jones asserts that living the kingdom way is how we were made to live – "the built-in way to live" – and that to live any other way is "to live life against itself."[178]

---

173. Niebuhr, *Christ and Culture*, 217.

174. Tizon, *Transformation after Lausanne.*

175. Arias, *Announcing the Reign of God*, 117, xvii. See also Ekblad, *A New Christian Manifesto*, for a profoundly grounded vision of kingdom service.

176. Jones, *The Unshakable Kingdom and the Unchanging Person*, 81.

177. Jones, 115, 137.

178. Jones, 220, 209.

Finally, I return to Howard Snyder, who grieves for the way that "too many Christians" today have "put their national, racial or economic identity above their identity as citizens of Jesus' new order."[179] Rather than supporting these other priorities, Snyder calls us to become "one people, one nation, one new race throughout the world," living as "God's kingdom community."[180]

A Pauline Trajectory

With this final model, I am proposing that our missional vision should never be based on isolated texts, regardless of how important we might consider them to be. For mission is never simply a program or strategy, but a whole *way of life*. Therefore, we need to capture the rich tapestries in Scripture that give us a deep and broad perspective about how to be with God, how to live in God's way, and how to serve others in light of the ways that God has blessed, formed, and called us into God's kingdom purposes.

At best, I can only outline some key features of the Pauline perspective, which is so rich, deep, and comprehensive. The fundamental structure is clear: Paul first sets out his Christology and then draws all sorts of pastoral, ethical, and missional implications. Moreover, both his theology and its *praxis* are also clear: his theology is contextual and arises out of his missional engagement. Finally, we can clearly identify an underlying theme: because of the new provision in Christ, a new people (new faith-community) can live out a new way of life and bear a new witness to the world. Following are ten key features of the Pauline model.

First, the heartbeat of Paul's trajectory is the transforming gift of grace through Christ: "If, because of one man's trespass, death exercised dominion through that one, much more surely will those who receive the abundance of grace and the free gift of righteousness exercise dominion in life through the one man, Jesus Christ" (Rom 5:17). Moreover, "if anyone is in Christ, there is a new creation: everything old has passed away; see, everything has become new!" (2 Cor 5:17).

Second, in Christ, though perfection awaits us, we have to put aside old ways and passions and grow in Christlikeness, and yet "sin will have no dominion over you, since you are not under law but under grace" (Rom 6:14).

Third, this new life in Christ is sustained and empowered by the Spirit: "you are in the Spirit," and the "Spirit is life," and it is "his Spirit that dwells in

179. Snyder, *Kingdom, Church, and World*, 119.

180. Snyder, 119.

you" (Rom 8:9–11). And so, Paul calls us to be filled with the Spirit (Eph 5:18) and admonishes us to dance, rejoice, and serve with the abundance of special gifts that the Spirit bestows (1 Cor 12).

Fourth, the life in Christ through the Spirit is communal. God is a community-forming God, and thus any Christian life is formed by our life together: "in the one Spirit we were all baptized into one body – Jews or Greeks, slaves or free – and we were all made to drink of one Spirit" (1 Cor 12:13). In Christ, we also have a common corporate identity and a common purpose to love and worship God, to share a life together, and to serve the world as a prophetic and healing community.

Fifth, life in this community is governed by the grace and lordship of Christ, which makes us all servants of Christ, of one another, and of the whole world: "Each of us must please our neighbor for the good purpose of building up the neighbor" (Rom 15:2).

Sixth, the faith-community in Christ is God's radical insertion in the world as a healing and restorative provocation. This community no longer prioritises ethnic, economic, or gender distinctions, for in Christ, there "is no longer Jew or Greek, there is no longer slave or free, there is no longer male and female; for all of you are one in Christ Jesus" (Gal 3:28). As a new peoplehood formed through Christ's redemptive work, the faith-community calls all of our social biases and all forms of exclusion into question. Moreover, it casts a vision for a new common humanity that is centred in Christ.

Seventh, the community of faith seeks to bear witness to God's vision for a new humanity in Christ through the power of suffering love rather than any form of coercion: "the only thing that counts is faith working through love" (Gal 5:6b), and though there is a call to faith and hope, "the greatest of these is love" (1 Cor 13:13b).

Eighth, the church's unity and solidarity exists through "one Spirit" and is expressed in "one hope" and "one faith, one baptism," because there is only "one Lord" and "one God and Father of all" (Eph 4:4–6). This unity leads the community to common worship, mutual care, and common service, but this solidarity is also expressed in economic sharing. Paul speaks of "a fair balance between your present abundance and their need" (2 Cor 8:13–14).

Ninth, though the members of the faith-community were previously marked by personal "trespasses and sins" and shaped by the culture, "following the course of this world" and subject to the "ruler of the power of the air" (Eph 2:1–2), the community is now called to resist the power of these powers through Christ's disarmament "of the rulers and authorities" (Col 2:15) and to "struggle" against "the rulers . . . authorities . . . cosmic powers of this present darkness" (Eph 6:12). This call suggests that the faith-community is to be a discerning and prophetic presence in the world by resisting and seeking to overcome all forms of systemic, ideological, political, and spiritual powers that do not reflect the ways of God's kingdom.

Tenth, this way of living in the world in the name of Christ for the sake of redeeming the world calls the faith-community to a radically new, eschatological form of human existence. Paul touches on this way of living *in* the world but not *of* the world through his reference to "those who buy as though they had no possessions" and "those who deal with the world as though they had no dealings with it" (1 Cor 7:29–31).

These ten core realities form the basis of the church's calling in the world as a "new society" that is rooted "in God's love and grace" and as a "'purposive social-group' representing the new order that God intends."[181] As "a manifestation of the Reign of God" and as a "counter-community,"[182] the church lives out the change it seeks in society in the following ways. First, it points to the new in the kingdom of God. Second, it does not conform to the "worldliness" of the world nor the values shaped by that "worldliness." Third, it seeks to unmask the idolatry of the present world order. Fourth, it actively seeks to be and bring good news to the world through prayer, witness, service, hospitality, and prophetic annunciation and denunciation.

Many different scholars, denominations, and Christian movements have attempted to define the missional task of the church. As Andrew Kirk writes, in response to the *missio Dei*, the faith-community lives by "bearing witness to God's activity in the world" through sharing "the good news of Jesus Christ in word and deed."[183] Ross Hastings identifies mission as our participation "with the triune God in his mission to the world, by being the image of the Trinity in the world" and through our "engagement with . . . people . . . the public square . . . culture-making and creation care."[184] In the "Manila Manifesto," the Lausanne Movement defines mission as the task of the "whole church" to take "the whole gospel" to the "whole world," which is to be carried out with "urgency, unity, and sacrifice."[185] *Redemptoris Missio* maintains that the "Church's universal mission is born of faith in Jesus Christ," that the church "is missionary by her very nature," and that the "ultimate purpose of mission is

---

181. Mott, *Biblical Ethics and Social Change*, 129.

182. Mott, 131, 133.

183. Kirk, *What is Mission?*, 31.

184. Hastings, *Missional God, Missional Church*, 15.

185. Stott, ed., *Making Christ Known*, 248.

to enable people to share in the communion which exists between the Father and the Son."[186] In the 1982 document, "Ecumenical Affirmation: Mission and Evangelism," the World Council of Churches affirms that the church's "vocation in the world is the proclamation of the kingdom of God inaugurated in Jesus the Lord, crucified and risen," and that it seeks to live its missional calling through the maintenance of a eucharistic life of prayer and service in "solidarity with the poor" by confronting "the powers that oppress" humans.[187] The 1986 document, "Go Forth in Peace: Orthodox Perspectives on Mission," holds that the "final goal of evangelistic witness" is "conversion and baptism," but it also includes dialogue with those of other faiths, "interpenetration of the structures of society," as well as confronting "injustice" and being a "prophetic challenge to the world's values."[188] Finally, David Bosch identifies mission as "a multifaceted ministry, in respect of witness, service, justice, healing, reconciliation, liberation, peace, evangelism, fellowship, church planting, contextualization, and much more,"[189] while also helpfully reminding us that the way we understand mission is "a continual process of sifting, testing, reformulating, and discarding."[190]

Notwithstanding the many diverse and helpful paradigms, models, and trajectories that can help define the profound scope and depth of our missional calling, we constantly need to appropriate our missional calling and task within the context of three narratives. First, the biblical narratives give us a magnificent mosaic of who God is, what God does, and therefore who we are called to be and what we are called to do far beyond any definitions or paradigmatic propositions. Second, the narrative of our own lives and the narrative of the faith-community remind us of who God calls us to be and what God calls us to do while locating that call within ever-changing circumstances. Third, the narrative of contextualization and inculturation is concerned with the hermeneutics of context, where we have to make sense of our place in the ever-changing world in which we seek to bear witness to the transforming love of God for the whole world.

186. *Redemptoris Missio*, 9, 12, 40.

187. Scherer and Bevans, eds., *New Directions in Mission and Evangelization*, 39.

188. Scherer and Bevans, eds., 222.

189. Bosch, *Transforming Mission*, 512.

190. Bosch, 511.

Conclusion

In this chapter, I have sought to be attentive to entire biblical narratives in terms of the overarching picture that both the OT and NT provide about God's redemptive and restorative passion throughout history – and how that passion calls us to reflect God as we seek to live as God's witnesses in the world, whether the world is watching or indifferent.

At the same time, I have emphasized that any models we create are our own constructions and thus need to be implemented with care. While models and paradigms can create room for us to move, they can also be appropriated in unhelpful ways. The Exodus can be wrongly used to justify conquest, and the future kingdom can be wrongly used to advocate a world-denying form of Christianity. Whatever God has done in the past must not be frozen in the past, for God is also active in our present time, calling people to live full lives within their particular communities while bearing the love of God to the entire creation through faithful witness and service. God is also always going ahead of us, calling us forward in anticipation of a fuller in-breaking of God's presence and kingdom in the world. Thus, the particular contours of any integral mission will need to be enriched by the mosaics of Scripture as well as the unique challenges of our time.

8

Grand Design and Fragile Engagement

The Church's Calling in a Troubled World

Introduction

This chapter is based on a talk that I gave at an Asian Theological Seminary forum on "The Church as Agent of Community Transformation" in Metro Manila in 2017. By "grand design," I am not referring to some impersonal, cosmic infrastructure. Rather, I believe that the universe and planet earth are the result of God's creative activity and are therefore marked by love and personalism. Thus by "grand design," I am referring to the meta-narrative of Scripture, which speaks of God's creative and redemptive activity as summarized in the paradigm of Creation–Fall–New Creation.[1]

The church is called to be the servant of God by participating in God's renewing and healing activity in the world. In this participation, the church knows by faith what God's final future will be like. Thus, we are not working *towards* an uncertain future, but we are living and serving in the light of a grand future that has already, partly, come *towards* us.

When I speak of "fragile engagement," I do not mean that the church is an impotent force in the world. Rather, I am referring to the nature of its engagement with society. The *nature* of that engagement is fragile: the church does not act in the world with guns or political power, but with persuasion and

1. For a very accessible discussion of this paradigm from a Reformed perspective, see Plantinga, *Engaging God's World*, 17–100.

acts of care and kindness that seek to proclaim and express God's redemptive love in Christ for the whole world. The fruitfulness of the church will not be determined by its programmatic endeavours, but rather by how it lives as a community marked by the grace of Christ, its conformity to the way of Christ, and how it lives and serves in the power of the Holy Spirit. These powerful spiritual dynamics are the impetus for the church's witness and prophetic presence in society, calling the world to enter into God's shalom and justice.

In describing our world as a "troubled world," I am not suggesting that society is only marked by sin and dysfunctionality, for it is also marked by God's maintenance and common grace.[2] "Common grace" reflects the long-suffering nature of God's involvement with humanity. But amidst this long-suffering story, the central and over-riding message is always that *this* "is the time of salvation."[3] Thus, special revelation continually seeks to disrupt the flow of common grace and bring it to a fuller manifestation.

I cannot remember ever feeling so vulnerable and uncertain in setting out to write a chapter. There are several reasons for this. First, the older one gets, the more one is marked by ambiguity and mystery[4] rather than the earlier, easy certainties that one might have held about changing the world. The impulse of the kingdom of God constantly meets the persistence of the worldliness of the world,[5] and so there is no simple way to solve the world's problems. Second, as time has gone on, I have become more aware of the precarious nature of being an outsider/insider within a particular culture.[6]

---

2. For a Reformed perspective on common grace, see Berkouwer, *The Providence of God*, where the core idea is that God's creative activity moves into God's sustenance and maintenance activity (54). However, "common grace" should not be viewed "as a power that renewed the heart" (77), but rather "the restraining work of God" that "does not lessen the guilt and responsibility" of humans (79).

3. Berkouwer, 81.

4. Some spiritual writers suggest that the movement of grace is first from darkness into the light of Christ. Then there is a movement into the "darkness" of the mystery of faith. Jürgen Moltmann makes the point, "The more we know of God, the more we perceive that we know nothing of God" (*Experiences in Theology*, 160). See also St. John of the Cross, *Dark Night of the Soul*, and Mother Teresa, *Come Be My Light*.

5. In *The Presence of the Kingdom*, Jacques Ellul writes: "in this preservation of the world, the Christian ought to place himself [herself] at the point of contact between two currents: the will of the Lord and the will of the world" (27). See also Ringma, *Resist the Powers with Jacques Ellul*, 83. Such placement means that we are constantly in the midst of conflict and decision. The conflict is between the pull of the kingdom of God and the worldliness of the world. The decision, which needs to be made again and again, is to choose the reign of God.

6. In *Missions*, van Rheenen helpfully discusses the various phases that one goes through in entering a new culture (77–96), noting that "effective adaptation takes place only when . . . missionaries critically evaluate *their* reactions to the people and customs of the new culture" (91, my emphasis).

We may think we understand a context, but we often miss the mark, and so the boundaries between interference and assistance are often blurred. This challenge also exists for those seeking to serve within their own communities given the multicultural realities of modern cities. Third, we are living in rapidly changing and challenging global times.[7] Though no one can predict where these global changes will lead, they will undoubtedly impact each of us,[8] as we cannot impact the world without the world also impacting us.[9] Fourth, in terms of the local context here in Metro Manila, we are not only facing the ongoing challenges of poverty, under-employment, and corruption, but also how to make appropriate responses to present government policy, including the extra-judicial killings of those in the drug scene.[10] Finally, the church's response to human need is such a huge topic that the challenge is not only what to say, but more appropriately what *not* to say. It is important to discern what to highlight, but who knows whether one has chosen the most relevant themes?

---

7. Farrely, in her 2016 article, "There is still hope in a horrible year," refers to *Dark Age Ahead* by Jane Jacobs, which makes the point that we are living in a time of "social amnesia in which we simply forget how to be civilised" (*Sydney Morning Herald*, 31 December 2016–1 January 2017: 21). And Mishra, in *Age of Anger*, speaks about the major social, political, and environmental convulsions impacting our world.

8. We need to acknowledge that any changes in society also impact us. David Kettle, "Gospel, Authority and Globalization," notes the "marginalization of Christian belief [in the West] as now a private value and no longer a publically acknowledged truth, with today many established public values fading in the same way." He goes on to ask whether this erosion of values will also impact societies in the Majority World (Foust, *A Scandalous Prophet*, 202).

9. More than likely, the contemporary church has failed to form its members into the way of Christ. To the extent that the church becomes more self-preoccupied and programmatic and less prayerful, it will become more conformed to the dominant values of society.

10. This refers specifically to a policy of the current government in the Philippines. More generally, the task of the church has always been to live as a redemptive, humanizing, and healing force in society, which includes the call "to follow Jesus in identification and sharing with the weak, the marginalized, and poor of the world" (Kinnamon, *The Ecumenical Movement*, 379). This calls the church to engage the work of justice and the option of the poor, to oppose the "structures of sin," and to commit itself to "integral human development" by living in solidarity with the despised of the earth ("Sollicitudo Rei Socialis," in O'Brien and Shannon, eds., *Catholic Social Thought*, 425, 419, 399). The evangelical Manila Manifesto reminds Christians that "as we preach the kingdom of God, we must be committed to its demands of justice and peace" (quoted in Stott, *Making Christ Known*, 236). In this, Christians are called to make a stand: "Among the evils we deplore are destructive violence, including institutionalized violence, political corruption . . . and the abuse of human rights" (quoted in Stott, *Making Christ Known*, 236). Thus, it is impossible to be a Christian and to support extra-judicial killings, which means that Christians should oppose the present governmental policy in Manila.

Given the uncertain nature of these opening reflections, I proceed with deliberate caution while also recognizing the relevance of this topic.[11] My title is meant to suggest that Scripture gives us a mega-picture[12] of God's purposes for our world while also reminding us that our engagement with the world in terms of our witness and service is often only a meagre offering.[13] After laying the groundwork for a common understanding of the church's calling in the world, my limited task in this chapter will be to highlight three important themes regarding our "fragile" engagement with a "troubled" world: first, the dialectical nature of our Christian existence and presence in the world; second, the importance of the dynamic relationship between orthodoxy, orthopathy, and orthopraxis; third, the fruitful relationship between mysticism and prophecy.

A Common Understanding of the Church's Calling in the World

I begin this section in hope, as I believe it is possible for the evangelical church to come to a common understanding regarding the role of the church and Christians in society.[14] My hope is partly based on the belief that as the church faces greater difficulties and challenges, greater cooperation will be possible. My hope is also based on the more than a thousand student papers that I have read over the past thirty years, which have identified a wide array of theological perspectives and impressive practical ministry initiatives of many churches

11. In my introductory comments for my presentation at this forum, I acknowledged the following: "Given these remarks and the attitude undergirding them, I proceed with deliberate caution, while at the same time recognizing that the choice of the theme of this forum, 'The Church as Agent of Community Transformation,' can only be seen as being auspicious and most relevant. This conference can be a *kairos* moment in the evangelical movement in the Philippines and beyond. It is my hope, therefore, that all of us will think wisely, pray much, speak boldly, and act prophetically as a result of having spent these two days together."

12. Postmodern culture resists such constructions, promoting instead a fluid relativism. But as Andrew Kirk argues, "Christian faith is necessarily based on a 'grand narrative' whose message counters the possibility of manipulation in the interests of sectarian concerns" (Kirk, *What is Mission?*, 10). One of the themes in this meta-picture is that all human beings are made in God's image and are therefore candidates for God's healing and redemption. As a consequence, all humans are to be treated with dignity, care, and justice, no matter what Adolf Hitler, or a Ku Klux clan member, or President R. Duterte may say or do.

13. In the Manila Manifesto, there is an acknowledgement "that many of our congregations are inward-looking, organized for maintenance rather than mission," and that "we have been indifferent to the plight of the poor" (quoted in Stott, *Making Christ Known*, 242, 235).

14. For a book that sets out the strategic missional thinking on the part of evangelical churches in the Philippines, see Tizon, *Transformation after Lausanne*.

here in the Philippines.[15] There is little doubt that the evangelical community in the Philippines is seeking to be a blessing to the wider community.[16] But my greatest hope lies in the ever-brooding Spirit, who builds community and unity within the faith-community and makes a practical, grassroots ecumenism possible.

The Witness of Scripture

Let me begin by stating a most basic Christian concept: to the extent that we have been impacted by the love, grace, and healing presence of God, we are thereby called to live to the glory of God, serve the community of faith, and do good to others. Throughout the biblical narrative, these three domains of life are deeply connected,[17] and so our love of God and our love of neighbour are inter-related (Matt 22:34–40; 1 John 4:11; Luke 6:27–28) – so much so that our love for and service to the needy is actually a reflection of our love for God (Matt 25:31–46). Therefore, our witness and service to others is expressed in both word and deed (Jas 1:22; Rom 12:20) as we seek to bring the good news of the gospel to the world (Rom 10:15; Eph 6:15), do deeds of love (1 Thess 5:12; Gal 6:10; 1 Pet 3:9), and engage in the work of justice (Ps 106:3; Prov 21:3; Amos 5:24; Matt 12:18–21; Luke 11:22).

Moreover, the NT sets out a clear framework for how our ministry to others should be lived out within the broader frame of our Christian life. For example, Scripture instructs Christians to form families (Eph 3:14–15; 1 Tim 5:4), be a gift to the faith-community (Rom 12:3–8; 1 Cor 12:1–31), be involved in daily work (1 Thess 2:9; 4:9–12; 2 Thess 3:10–12), be good citizens in the broader community (1 Pet 2:12; 3:15–16) and submit to political authority (Rom 13:1–7; 1 Pet 2:13–17). Yet both the OT and NT make it clear that our *obedience* is always to God, first and foremost (Deut 27:10; Ps 119:17; Jer

15. These papers came from courses that I taught over this thirty-year period at Asian Theological Seminary in Manila, often with national faculty, including "Transformation Theology," "Urban Anthropology and Mission," "Holistic Ministry," and "Building Christian Communities." All of these courses had a significant fieldwork component.

16. There are many churches and ministries that are seeking to bring God's shalom into the world, including the work of the Institute for Studies in Asian Church and Culture (ISACC), Focig, the Center for Community Transformation, Samaritana Transformation Ministries (a psycho-spiritual healing ministry), and Onesimo (a church-based ministry), among many other ministries. For the story of just one of these ministries, Center for Community Transformation, see Palugod, *Toward the Abundant Life*. And for something of the church's response to the devastation of Typhoon Yolanda (international name, *Haiyan*), see Gorospe, *Why, O God?*

17. Deut 10:17–20; Gal 6:10.

11:4; John 15:10; Rom 16:26), as "We must obey God rather than any human authority" (Acts 5:29).[18]

However, before we can outline a common ground and purpose in fulfilling our calling to live to the glory of God, serve the faith-community, and do good to others, it is important to make theological sense of these basic scriptural principals within the broader framework of the biblical narrative. The following themes within the biblical narrative highlight some of the key traits of our distinctively Christian presence in the world.

First, Christians are a restless and uneasy insertion in the world, for as pilgrims,[19] we are never calmly settled. Though we have a heavenly vision, we are deeply engaged in society and the issues of our time. This makes us a *disruptive presence*[20] in the world, since our primary commitment is not to world maintenance, but rather world transformation.[21] Moreover, our disruptive presence is not political or revolutionary, but rather restorative and healing as we seek to bear witness to others in word and acts of loving service and also as we pray and seek to transform all that is distorted and corrupted in our world, including the political sphere.

Second, our distinctively *Christian presence* in the world is shaped by our participation in the healing grace of God in Christ, our embrace of Christ as our model for our action in the world, our ever-growing conformity to Christ's way, our reliance on the Spirit, our commitment to a life of prayer, and our practical cooperation with others in the faith-community to work together for the sake of the kingdom of God.

Third, our primary task as Christians in society is to carry God's values into the world. This means that we are called to live as a *cooperative presence* as we join with all that God is seeking to do[22] in bringing about the restoration and healing of the world. Thus, the church is not merely a corrective presence in the world, but one that casts a new vision of what humans and our society can be like in the restorative grace of God.

---

18. For important texts on the relationship between church and state, see Villa-Vicencio, *Between Christ and Caesar.*

19. For a discussion of the church's nature as the pilgrim people of God, see Flannery, "Lumen Gentium," in *The Basic Sixteen Documents, Vatican Council II*, 72–78.

20. Jürgen Moltmann points out that Christian hope "makes the Christian Church a constant disturbance in human society" (*Theology of Hope*, 22).

21. See Wolterstorff, *Until Justice and Peace Embrace*, for his idea that the people of God are not simply involved in a world-engaging Christianity, but a world-formative Christianity.

22. Our mission is the *missio Dei*, and as such it is rooted in who God is and is "God's very own work." Thus, the church is called to participate in all of God's redemptive work in the world (Muller, *Mission Theology*, 46).

Fourth, because Christians are called to be a second "incarnation"[23] in the world, we are to live as an *embodied* and *embedded presence* within the shape and context of the world. This means that we are called to subvert the human march towards self-exaltation and to restore a vision for humanity and society in light of the glory and purposes of God's reign.

The Voice of the Lausanne Movement

Turning to some historical documents from the Lausanne Movement, which seek to speak for global evangelicalism, we find several resonating themes that can provide further basis for our common and cooperative action in society.[24]

First, the 1974 Lausanne Covenant makes it clear that our "Christian presence in the world is indispensable to evangelism . . . and responsible service in the world."[25] While holding that "evangelism is primary,"[26] the Covenant calls us to "share his [God's] concern for justice and reconciliation throughout human society."[27]

Second, the 1982 Grand Rapids Report on Evangelism and Social Responsibility seeks to clarify the relationship between evangelism and social concern, noting that "in practice . . . the two are inseparable."[28] Yet it suggests that "social activity is a *consequence* of evangelism," in that people who are touched by the grace of Christ will want to serve others, and that it is also "a *bridge* to evangelism," in that care for and service to others can open the way for gospel proclamation. Thus, social concern "accompanies" evangelism "as its *partner*."[29]

Third, the 1989 Manila Manifesto highlights how "we must demonstrate God's love visibly by caring for those who are deprived of justice, dignity, food,

23. We are called to be in Christ, and Christ is to be formed in us, and so our core "Christian vocation . . . [is] 'putting on Christ in one's own life'" (Delio, *Franciscan Prayer*, 149). However, this does not mean that we become carbon copies of the historical Jesus, as we are to "embody something of the Word [Jesus Christ, the Living Word] in ourselves in a distinctive and personal way" (Delio, *Franciscan Prayer*, 155). In this secondary sense we are to be a second incarnation of Christ.

24. For an extended discussion of Lausanne's missional vision, see Nicholl, "Towards Integrated Mission for the Evangelical Lausanne Movement."

25. Stott, *Making Christ Known*, 20.

26. Stott, 28.

27. Stott, 24.

28. Stott, 183.

29. Stott, 181–2.

and shelter."[30] The Manifesto's "Twenty-One Affirmations" go on to declare that Christian service "demands the denunciation of all injustice and oppression, both personal and structural."[31]

Finally, the 2010 Cape Town Commitment sets out "that we not only love mercy and [do] deeds of compassion, but also that we do justice through exposing and opposing all that oppresses and exploits the poor."[32] This document places this commitment within the broad vision of the church's task in the world through the work of "evangelism, bearing witness to the truth, discipling, peacemaking, social engagement, ethical transformation, caring for creation, overcoming evil powers, casting out demonic spirits, healing the sick and suffering, and enduring under persecution."[33]

In these documents, we can recognize many of the key missional motifs of the biblical story,[34] and thus we can find a common ground and a common purpose as we seek to work together to fulfil this calling. However, to discern this common and cooperative purpose, we will need to move beyond a gospel of benefits *alone* to a gospel that calls us to responsibility, commitment, and service. This challenging gospel will call us to embrace a vision of the kingdom of God rather than a concern for our particular church or Christian

30. Stott, 231.

31. Stott, 231.

32. http://www.lausanne.org/content/ctc/ctcommitment, 12.

33. http://www.lausanne.org/content/ctc/ctcommitment, 9.

34. While some evangelicals may think that their position about evangelism is unique, this is clearly not the case. Pope John Paul II points to the importance of evangelism in *Redemptoris Missio*: "in the complex reality of mission, initial proclamation has a central and irreplaceable role" (75). He goes on to point out that mission is not peripheral to the church but that the "Church is missionary by her very nature" (106). The church performs her ministry "through witness . . . dialogue, human promotion, commitment to justice and peace, education, the care of the sick and aid to the poor" (35). The 1982 Ecumenical Movement report, "Mission and Evangelism: An Ecumenical Affirmation," speaks of the importance of "the proclamation of the Gospel . . . [to] accept in a personal decision the saving Lordship of Christ," and it goes on to say that this leads us "to renounce evidences of the domination of sin in our lives and to accept the responsibilities in terms of God's love for our neighbour" (quoted in Kinnamon, *The Ecumenical Movement*, 372). The report also emphasizes that "the Evangelistic Witness will also speak to the structures of this world; its economic, political, and social institutions" (374). It concludes with a broad missional vision: "the Church is called to *announce* Good News in Jesus Christ, forgiveness, hope, a new heaven and a new earth; to *denounce* powers and principalities, sin and injustice; *to console* the widows and orphans, healing, restoring the broken-hearted; and *to celebrate* life in the midst of death" (374). It is appropriate to conclude this survey with the perspectives of David Bosch, the most comprehensive Protestant missiologist of the twentieth century. Bosch notes that mission is "the participation of Christians in the liberating mission of Jesus" and identifies that liberating mission as "witness, service, justice, healing, reconciliation, liberation, peace, evangelism, fellowship, church planting, contextualization, and much more" (*Transforming Mission*, 519, 512).

organization *alone*. Moreover, this common work and purpose will call us to engage in humble dialogue as well as suffering.

The Relevance of a Christian Dialectic for Contemporary Missiology

In this section, I will explore the inherent "metaphysical contradictions"[35] that are part of our human existence. Put more simply, this core dialectic is concerned with the unresolved tensions and contradictions in human affairs. Or, as Jacques Ellul puts it, a dialectic acknowledges the "coexistence of contradictory elements" that are "correlative in a temporal movement that leads to a new situation."[36]

My basic thesis is that such a dialectic is operative throughout the biblical narrative, which is filled with creative tensions that cannot be neatly resolved. If we do not take these tensions into account, our missional response will be narrow, and we will likely become discouraged as we seek to engage with the issues of our time. Before describing the nature and significance of this dialectic, I will make two basic illustrations.

For example, if a church only emphasizes the kingship of God and the call of the church to engage the ministry of Christ as King,[37] without also emphasizing the prophetic nature of God's action in the world and the church's call to prophetic witness and ministry, the people of that faith-community will likely live as a conservative force in society rather than seeking to participate

35. *The Australian Concise Oxford Dictionary*, 284.

36. Ellul, *What I Believe*, 32.

37. Theology has identified the threefold ministry of Christ as prophet, priest, and king. As king, we recognize Christ's lordship over all of life. As priest, we acknowledge Christ's healing ministry and prayer ministry in bringing humans to God. As prophet, we celebrate Christ's work in bringing the purposes of God to humanity and the call to change our ways. See Berkhof, *Systematic Theology* (357) and Maggay, *Transforming Society* (68–75), where she typifies the prophetic office as bringing the word to the world, the priestly office as bringing the needs of the world to God, and the kingly office as managing the world under God. The critical issue, however, is how the contemporary church seeks to integrate and operationalize these three ministries. The strength of the church's kingly ministry is to build lasting institutions (Christian universities) that can influence society. The possible weakness in a kingly ministry is the church's misuse of power and its elitist approach. The strength of the church's priestly ministry is in exercising a healing presence in the world and building a strong spirituality. The possible weakness of the priestly ministry is healing people only to return to existing ways of life and structures that are inherently dysfunctional. The strength of the prophetic ministry is to expose false values, critique the misuse of power, and cast a vision of a world manifesting God's shalom. The possible weakness of the prophetic ministry is that it is a critique of words only, without demonstrating another way in practical terms.

in a transformative[38] movement. Or, to give another example, if a church only emphasizes the movement of the kingdom of God in history without also emphasizing the persistence of the worldliness of the world, its idolatry, and its distortion of God's way, then it will be easy for the people in that faith-community to come to believe that the kingdom of God is ineffective, that prayer does not "work," and that there is no point in the ongoing struggle to do good because so much evil persists in the world.[39]

Dialectic in the Biblical Narrative

The biblical narrative is fundamentally dialectical.[40] God is fully complete in and of himself/herself, and yet God creates a universe and elects a people.[41]

---

38. Many Christian books use the word transformation in their titles: Davies, *Transformation Theology*; Easum, *Preaching for Church Transformation*; Shults and Sandage, *Transforming Spirituality*; Wright and Kuentzel, *Redemptive Transformation in Practical Theology*. Yet there need to be more critical discussions about the extent to which transformation is possible, both at a personal and societal level. In surveying fifteen Christian universities, colleges, and seminaries in Australia, Ball, in *Transforming Theology*, notes that these institutions speak about providing transformational courses, "but there is little actual evidence produced to support such an assumption" (5) and thus concludes that transformation remains "an aspirational outcome" (2). In Christian circles, we talk a lot about transformation, but how much transformation is actually possible, since the kingdom of God has not arrived in its fullness, and we continue to be sinner/saints (Luther), and the worldliness of the world continues.

39. This, of course, is related to the theodicy question. In "Suffering and Evil," Schlesinger poses the question that since the world is full of suffering, "God is either helpless to prevent it, in which case He is not all-powerful, or does not choose to prevent it, in which case He is not all good" (quoted in Cahn and Shatz, *Contemporary Philosophy of Religion*, 25). One evangelical response to this most troubling question, which affects all of us, is that God's sovereignty must be viewed from the perspective of the eschaton, God's final future (1 Cor 15:24–26). But in the meantime, "God's rulership is being advanced and expanded by the work of the Holy Spirit in the world" (Grenz, *Theology for the Community of God*, 107). This means that we can only *partially* see the sovereignty of God in the present world order and that the church is living between the times (1 Cor 13:12).

40. Brueggemann, in affirmatively quoting another scholar, notes, "*the Old Testament in its theological articulation is characteristically dialectical and dialogical*" (Brueggemann, *Theology of the Old Testament*, 83, author's italics). What he means is that God's action in the world with people has no grand finality, as it is always full of tension and is marked by provisionality. The same is true of the NT, even with the coming of Christ. This is most basically illustrated by "the yet" and "not yet" nature of the kingdom of God. As Ladd notes, "the church lives 'between the times'; the old age goes on, but the powers of the new age have irrupted into the old age" (*A Theology of the New Testament*, 69). Ladd goes on to illustrate further creative tensions, noting that "'The church is the people of the Kingdom, never that Kingdom itself," but the "Kingdom creates the church, works through the church, and is proclaimed in the world by the church" (113, 119).

41. Lesslie Newbigin points out that election is for service to others: "those who are chosen to be a blessing are chosen for the sake of *all*" (*The Open Secret*, 32, author's italics). He further reminds us "that election is for responsibility, not for privilege" (32).

God is in the world,[42] and at the same time God is wholly transcendent. God is sovereign, and yet works through people. God engages the world with salvation and healing, and yet much of the world continues in its own rebellious ways. God has brought humanity, culture, and the world of politics into being, and at the same God has brought the church into being to bear witness to the ways of God and to challenge death-dealing or oppressive aspects of society and politics.

Jacques Ellul notes that the movement in the biblical narrative from commandment to disobedience and judgement to reconciliation "is precisely a process of total dialectic."[43] He also notes the dialectic that is present in holding the concept of a remnant and the universality of God's salvation. At a much more personal and existential level, he makes the point that "God works in us to will and to do," and yet "we have to accept responsibility . . . as if everything depended on us."[44] Ellul concludes that we have "to affirm both the coherence and importance of the world in which we live" (thus affirm culture and society and its institutions) while at the same time affirming "the incomparable truth of revelation in Christ" and the way in which that revelation seeks to renew every single dimension of life.[45]

The missiologist David Bosch also picks up this dialectic in Paul's theology. While Paul is persistently oriented towards the fullness of God's work in the world through Christ and the certainty of complete shalom in God's final future, he also acknowledges the challenge and suffering of witness and service in a refractory world. Bosch notes, "Paul can simultaneously hold together two seemingly opposite realities: a fervent longing for the breaking in of the future reign of God; and a preoccupation with missionary outreach . . . in a hostile world."[46] At the same time, Bosch notes that in our present situation, the notions of "contingency and unpredictability" need to be embraced, and we need to engage the world in a "chastened" manner, realizing again "the reality of evil – in humans and in the structures of society," while at the same time recognizing that the church "is missionary by its nature" and that the

---

42. While we reject pantheism, we may hold to panentheism. See Franklin, "Panentheism," in Elwell, ed., *Evangelical Dictionary of the Bible*, 818–20.

43. Ellul, *What I Believe*, 36.

44. Ellul, 39–40.

45. Ellul, 44.

46. Bosch, *Transforming Mission*, 153.

community of faith is therefore called to join "God's turning to the world in respect of creation, care, redemption, and consummation."[47]

Finally, the core dialectical emphasis in Moltmann's theology is that we live *in* the world but are not simply waiting for heaven. Living in the world while waiting for heaven has a linear view of history, but living in the present while anticipating God's final future has a dialectical view of history. Thus, the future not only awaits us, but has also come amongst us in the kingdom of God. Moltmann writes, "the decision which is forced upon the present must arise from our dream of the future."[48] Put in other words, the present cultural, economic, and political landscape does not determine how we act in the world, but rather God's final kingdom of healing, restoration, and peace shapes how we live now (Rev 21:1–4; 22:1–5). Thus, we are to be so heavenly minded that we become a *corrective* presence in the world[49] rather than a *corrosive* insertion into the world. Always out of step with the dominant values of our world, we are the dancers of a new tomorrow.

Moltmann concludes his discussion of this dialectical way of being in the world by observing practically that, "it is only in the foreign land that we understand what home is," or "in the face of death . . . the uniqueness of life," or "in strife . . . how to appreciate peace."[50]

Missional Implications of a Dialectical Understanding of the Christian Presence in the World

We can engage our world in overly optimistic ways, thinking that all of our activities will succeed. Or, on the other extreme, we can become so pessimistic that we give up seeking to bring about change. A dialectical understanding can help celebrate the power of the gospel and the power of love while at the same time recognizing that the good we seek to do may be rejected or resisted. The central issue is for us to remain faithful in our service, though the results may be mixed.

---

47. Bosch, 356, 361, 365, 391.

48. Moltmann, *Theology of Hope*, 233.

49. Moltmann points out that the ever-present challenge facing Christians is whether they become an "accommodating group" in society, "or whether their existence within the horizon of eschatological hope makes them resist accommodation and their presence has something peculiar to say to the world" (305).

50. Moltmann, *Experiences in Theology*, 171.

A dialectical understanding of the Christian presence in the world reminds us that we need to be people of two horizons.[51] We are in Christ, and we are also in the world. We are in both[52] and feel the impact of both in our lives. Therefore, we need to read Scripture, and we also need to read our world. We bring the gospel to the world in word and deed, and we bring our world to God in prayer.

Furthermore, a dialectical understanding reminds us that in our service to the world, we are living the mystery of the relationship between God's work and our work. God is at work, and we seek to work with God as servants, living as a sign and a sacrament of the kingdom of God. Thus, we do not do our own thing *for* God, but we pray, discern, and seek to be led by God's Spirit in all that we do. Yet we have to *live* in the dialectical tension of this mystery, for sometimes we seem to do little, and it is mightily blessed. But other times, we work hard for years, and there is so little fruit. In the midst of this, we can begin to wonder why God does not work more powerfully.

We also need to acknowledge that God has established the human community, including its various forms of government and institutions. While all of these should acknowledge God's sovereignty, they seldom do. Yet the task of the church is not to govern society, but to call all human institutions to the wisdom of the revelation of God by practicing protection, care, justice, and shalom. Thus, the community of faith has a prophetic task,[53] and the most significant way for the church to raise its voice is by doing (in whatever small ways possible) whatever it is calling the government or other institutions to do.[54]

Finally, Karl Barth notes the dialectical tension in which Christians have to live. Much of Barth's theology was shaped by his resistance to Nazi ideology, with its radical dehumanization of Jews and other minority groups. Barth notes that we are bound both to God and to the human community, and though

51. Thiselton, *The Two Horizons*.

52. For a helpful theological and practical discussion of the concepts of "in-between," "in-both," and "in-beyond," see Lee, *Marginality*.

53. Karl Barth is of the opinion that the most basic vocation of the Christian is to be "the reflection and echo of the prophetic Word of Jesus Christ" and that Christ sets us "in the service of his own prophetic office and work." This prophetic ministry includes a call to tell the world that "its old form and values have already been outmoded in Christ" (*Church Dogmatics*, vol. 4, part 3.2, 622, 650, 718).

54. Stephen Charles Mott, in approvingly quoting Arthur Gish, notes that the church needs to point out the moral bankruptcy of the existing social order, point to a new reality, and then live that new reality as an embodied witness to the world (Mott, *Biblical Ethics and Social Change*, 136). In other words, we need to *be* the change we wish to *see*.

we are set by the side of God, we are against the world.[55] As a result of this tension, we will upset society, customs, the state, and particular forms of piety and religiosity.[56] Put in different terms, Barth says that because Christ became the incarnate word, so the church must be incarnate – wholly in the world, yet wholly different from the world.[57] Thus our loyalty to Christ must supersede all other loyalties, including our own country. Barth writes, "[Christians] must always see themselves and act first and decisively as Christians" and "only then as members of this or that nation."[58]

The Dynamics of Orthodoxy, Orthopathy, and Orthopraxis

While the evangelical Lausanne documents quoted above don't use the terms, "orthodoxy" (right belief) and "orthopraxis" (right action), they clearly engage with these ideas, as they begin with a statement about core Christian doctrines (right beliefs) and then move to a statement about application (right action). In this, they follow the basic structure of the Pauline epistles, which move from theology to ethics.

This movement from doctrine to missional action is important, for our ministry in the world needs to be shaped by a biblical vision of God's concern for our world, and knowing that we are seeking to do what God *wants* gives particular shape to our mission. Put simply, our mission is to become what God wants and to carry out what God wants in God's way. This sense that our ministry is in the service of God gives us both direction and sustenance,[59] for doing the will of God will sustain us over the long haul of ministry. Thus, our mission always calls us back to Scripture, discernment, and ongoing prayer.

Orthodoxy and Orthopraxis: A Liberation Theology Perspective

Because liberation theologians have been preoccupied with reflecting on the relationship between orthodoxy and orthopraxis, we do well to listen to them. Gustavo Gutierrez makes the important point that Scripture speaks about a certain kind of orthodoxy, for biblical truth is not just about head knowledge,

55. Barth, *Church Dogmatics*, vol. 4, part 3.2, 609.

56. Barth, vol. 4, part 3.2, 623.

57. Barth, vol. 4, part 3.2, 728.

58. Barth, vol. 4, part 3.2, 741.

59. For a helpful book on the relationship between mission and sustenance, see Gittens, *Bread for the Journey*.

but is meant to be embraced and *lived*. He refers to this as the call "to do truth,"[60] a call that gives shape to the "importance of action in [the] Christian life."[61] A simple example of the connection between truth and action is that if one believes that God is the creator of all, then one will support all efforts to uphold human rights,[62] since all are made in God's image, and one will also work to protect and care for the earth.[63]

Gutierrez also emphasizes that orthodoxy must constantly challenge both society and the church, for the church is "called and addressed by the Word of God,"[64] and therefore is called to greater fidelity and service. In following this path, the church functions as a prophetic community[65] as it becomes what the word of God calls it to be and lives this out as a witness to society. In this sense, the church is a counter-community in the world.[66] Gutierrez then makes a key point about the relationship between orthodoxy and orthopraxis, arguing that right belief not only shapes our action in the world, but our action in the world also helps us to understand the truth more fully. He casts a vision for how "Theologians will be personally and vitally engaged . . . where nations, social classes, and peoples struggle to free themselves from domination and oppression," and in this "historical praxis," the "true interpretation of the meaning revealed by theology is achieved."[67] Put in simple terms, our praxis helps us to understand Scripture just as much as our exegetical study and prayer.

In discussing the relationship between theology and praxis, Jon Sobrino argues that "praxis . . . [is] a means of grasping the nature of the Reign of God" and that "without praxis an understanding of the Reign of God would be crippled and diminished."[68] This echoes the above observations from Gutierrez about how *doing* the word deepens our *understanding* of the word. For example,

60. Gutierrez, *A Theology of Liberation*, 8.

61. Gutierrez, 8.

62. For a theology of human rights, see Wolterstorff, *Justice and Wrongs*. For the struggle and cost of the work for justice, see the account of the Nobel Peace Prize winner, Shiran Ebadi, *Until We Are Free*.

63. For a theology of earth-care, see Bouma-Prediger, *For the Beauty of the Earth*.

64. Gutierrez, *A Theology of Liberation*, 9.

65. Gutierrez, 10.

66. For a discussion of this from an Anabaptist perspective, see Art Gish, *Living in Christian Community*, 276–314. Mott notes that the extent to which the church embodies the reign of God is the extent to which it is a "counter-community," meaning that it must have "a separate and distinct identity" to that of the dominant culture (*Biblical Ethics and Social Change*, 133).

67. Gutierrez, *A Theology of Liberation*, 10.

68. Sobrino, "Central Position of the Reign of God in Liberation Theology," 377.

in the practice of Christian community, we come to understand the nature of the Trinity – God as a community of "persons." Or, in the practice of serving the poor, we can come to a better understanding of God's concern for the poor. Sobrino makes a further point about our praxis, which is that it not only aids us in reading Scripture, but it also helps us to read our culture. To give an example, he says that in the practice of justice, there will emerge a growing understanding of "the depth of injustice," and thus the reality of "the anti-Reign appears with greater radicality."[69] This highlights how the practice of justice not only inspires hope, but also opposition, revealing how the present social status quo can be disturbed by the nature of Christian witness and service.

Sobrino also notes that the fuller coming of the reign of God is God's work, for "human beings will never build the perfect utopia."[70] But because Christians are marked by the grace of God, we are called to be an "analogy with divinity," meaning that "we may do for others what God has done for us."[71] Thus, the penetration of God's love and truth moves us into costly service. Sobrino concludes that orthopraxis is not only an "ethical exigency" (something that is urgent and pressing), but is a "hermeneutical principle for a knowledge of the Reign of God."[72]

Orthopathy: The Missing Link

The above discussion emphasizes the inter-relationship between orthodoxy and orthopraxis. Knowing the truth moves us to engage in practices of love, care, and justice, which in turn lead us to a better understanding of Scripture and a fuller understanding of what needs to be done to heal and transform our world.

The emphasis thus far has been on the head (theological formation) and hand (missional outworking), but we have not yet engaged matters of the heart.[73] In this section, we will connect the missing link of *orthopathy* between thinking (orthodoxy) and action (orthopraxis).[74] From the Greek word *pathos*,

69. Sobrino, 377.

70. Sobrino, 378.

71. Sobrino, 379.

72. Sobrino, 379.

73. In the OT and NT, the heart is seen as the centre of one's inner life. Brandon, "Heart," in *Evangelical Dictionary of Theology*, notes that "heart is the source, or spring of motives; the seat of passions; the center of thought processes; the spring of conscience" (499).

74. The evangelical missional documents of the Lausanne Movement don't give enough attention to orthopathy and spirituality, with the happy exception of the Cape Town Commitment (2010), with its foundational discussion of the way in which we have been impacted by the love

orthopathy has to do with one's passions, emotions, and sympathies. Clearly, humans are shaped by head, heart, and hand, and our emotional dimension is intrinsic to who we are and how we function in the world. In fact, our emotions and sympathies often move us to action. Though we might know about a need or an issue and not do anything about it, we often become engaged when our hearts are moved.

In a discussion of orthopathy within a theological frame, N. B. Woodbridge speaks of the dynamics of "holy affections."[75] Put simply, we are moved by what moves God. This means that an interior shaping (and reshaping) needs to take place within our being so that the "heart of God" will become our heart, and the "passion of Jesus" will become our passion and our *modus operandi*.[76]

P. O'Connell Killen and J. de Beer describe this process more fully, suggesting that in the midst of life's *experience*, certain *feelings* will arise. They helpfully sketch out the dimensions of *feelings*, which they note "are our embodied affective and intelligent responses to reality as we encounter it."[77] But instead of dismissing our experience, feelings, or emotions, we need to reflectively engage them. For as we reflect, certain images, ideas, or concepts may arise, leading us to new *insights*, which in turn can lead us into new and more informed *action*.[78] In describing this process, Killen and de Beer make a clear connection between our feelings, reflection, and action:[79] "We travel from experience through feeling to image [and] to new ideas and awareness that can change and enrich our lives," which can then lead to "small or large transformations of our being and actions."[80]

To complete this process, they emphasize a final important dimension for any reflective movement, namely, "the artful discipline of putting our experience into conversation with the heritage of the Christian tradition."[81] In other words, we pay attention to our lived experience, our feelings, and our

---

of God and therefore love whatever God loves and act into the world in the love of God.

75. Jonathan Edwards has written extensively about holy affections (*Select Works of Jonathan Edwards*, vol. 3). The concept of holy affections is also key to Wesley's spirituality. In *Recapturing the Wesley's Vision*, Chilcote notes, "The uniting of heart and head in early Methodism was one of Wesley's most remarkable achievements" (69).

76. Woodbridge, "Living Theologically."

77. Killen and de Beer, *The Art of Theological Reflection*, 27.

78. Killen and de Beer, 21.

79. Though Killen and de Beer do not use the terms, "orthodoxy," "orthopathy," and "orthopraxis," to describe this reflective and integrative process, they highlight the importance of each and confirm the relational dynamics between them.

80. Killen and de Beer, 45, 42.

81. Killen and de Beer, 2.

actions in the world, but these need to be brought to Scripture and biblical theology for affirmation or correction.

The Theme of Integration

Nevertheless, many dynamics within the ecclesiastical domain militate against the inter-relational dynamics of orthodoxy, orthopathy, and orthopraxis. First, the fragmentation of theological discourse[82] often places systematic, spiritual, and pastoral theologies in separate silos. Moreover, in our age of radical pragmatism, pastoral or practical theologies have been elevated to a primary place in the pantheon. Second, Christianity has long been divided between those who follow world-denying, world-engaging, or world-formative expressions of the faith.[83] Third, dualistic thinking has long been problematic within the Christian tradition, and so we tend to elevate evangelism over the work of justice, or prayer over daily work, or orthodoxy over orthopraxis. Finally, we often prefer thinking in terms of either/or rather than both/and.[84] Thus dialogical, integrated thinking and action will always be a challenge.[85]

Despite these challenges, we need to engage in such dialogical thinking in order to embrace an integral missional theology.[86] Orthopathy can be the inspiration that moves us from orthodoxy to orthopraxis. Whereas orthodoxy gives theological justification and shape to our orthopraxis, orthopraxis gives authenticity to our orthodoxy.

One practical way to think about these interrelated dynamics is in terms of the head (orthodoxy), heart (orthopathy), and hand (orthopraxis). Operating out of the head and hand (without the heart) can lead to bureaucratic, formal, functional, and pragmatic ways of responding. Operating out of the heart and hand (without the head) can lead to unthoughtful and impulsive ways of responding. Operating out of the head and heart (without the hand) can lead to an inability to translate our knowledge and good intentions into practical strategies.[87] But when we hold all three together in an integrated way, we can

82. See Farley, *Theologia*.
83. See Niebuhr, *Christ and Culture*; Webber, *The Church in the World*.
84. See H-G. Gadamer, *Truth and Method*; Ringma, *Gadamer's Dialogical Hermeneutic*.
85. See Ringma, "Holistic Ministry and Mission," 431–48.
86. See chapter 7 ("The Heart and Scope of Integral Mission").
87. See Kelly and Sewell, *With Head, Heart and Hand*, 23.

become thoughtful and informed, passionate and empathetic, and willing to get our hands "dirty" in the long march for restoration, justice, and shalom.[88]

A Practical Example: William Wilberforce

William Wilberforce is well-known for his parliamentary struggle to end the British slave trade. As a Christian, he saw what "much of the rest of the world could not, including the grotesque injustice of one man treating another as property,"[89] and he saw that this had to change "because all men and women are created . . . in his [God's] image, and are therefore sacred." And he also recognized that this belief was "at the heart of the Christian Gospel."[90]

Wilberforce understood how deeply the slave trade was part of the British economy and how its abolition could devastate the economy, but he believed that "[t]here is a principle above everything that is political," which has to do with "conscience, the principles of justice, the laws of religion, and of God."[91] However, being young and optimistic and in the glow of a newfound faith in Christ, he believed that change was readily possible. Little was he to know that the struggle for change would deeply test his faith, destroy his health, and take twenty years of his life. There is little doubt that Wilberforce lived the long journey of orthopraxis,[92] and his task was not evangelization, but *humanization* in light of the gospel.[93] Moreover, Wilberforce, an evangelical, believed that this task was directly inspired by the gospel.

Wilberforce's concern for orthodoxy and orthopathy is evident from his own writings. He criticizes the compromised Christianity of his day, pointing to the fact that "the unique doctrines of Christianity have almost disappeared" and it has "no longer retained its distinctive features."[94] In speaking about these distinctive doctrines, he refers to the incarnation, the crucifixion, the

88. One could "play" with these three concepts in relation to the Trinity: God as the architect (head), Jesus as the builder (hand), and the Holy Spirit as the empowerer (heart). However, this may be pushing the doctrine of the Trinity much too far.

89. Metaxas, *Amazing Grace*, xiv.

90. Metaxas, xvi.

91. Quoted in Metaxas, 136.

92. For a very detailed account, see Hochschild, *Bury the Chains*.

93. Some evangelicals would have problems with this, as they would see Wilberforce's efforts as inferior because he was not directly involved in saving "souls." But saving people from imminent death and human degradation is the precondition for possible evangelization. God is the God of life, and all life is therefore precious. All attempts at saving and enhancing life are to be seen as within the purposes of God's concern for the whole world.

94. Wilberforce, *Real Christianity*, 105.

redemptive work of Christ, and the power of the Holy Spirit, among other themes.[95]

While Wilberforce emphasizes orthodoxy in his writings, he also stresses the importance of orthopathy, referring to love, zeal, hope, kindness, and pity, among other emotions.[96] He was particularly concerned about the "nominal" Christianity of his day,[97] which he believed led to selfish living and a lack of concern for others.[98] Thus he calls for a lived theology and speaks of the importance of emotions in living the Christian life. He writes that the emotions are "a large part of the composition" of the human being and are a "most active principle."[99] He goes on to note that "it is the religion of the affections which God particularly requires." Then he refers to Paul, whose passionate nature remained "unabated" after his conversion, and yet he was placed "in the service of his blessed Master."[100]

Like Wilberforce, we need to be people whose minds, hearts, and hands are integrated. To be feeling people, we need to be touched and awakened. The gospel may awaken us, or seeing someone's need may touch us, or the promptings of the Spirit may stir us, or a challenge from a friend may move us, or we might recognize a need or vulnerability within ourselves, or we might be moved with compassion when we see someone else suffering something we have endured. The possibilities are endless, but without heart, the mind may remain aloof and the hand may remain idle. The love of Christ can move us to empathy, and as we serve others, we will discover more of Christ's love for us. For in giving, we receive.

The Fruitful Relationship between Mysticism and Prophecy[101]

Some might assume that mysticism and prophecy have nothing to do with each other – or that neither has anything to do with social transformation. But this assumption is connected to a narrow and misguided perception that mysticism is a privatized ecstatic experience that draws people away from the world – and that prophecy is simply about predicting the future under a spiritual influence.

95. Wilberforce, 119–21.
96. Wilberforce, 29, 31, 33.
97. Wilberforce, 100.
98. Wilberforce, 108–9.
99. Wilberforce, 28–29.
100. Wilberforce, 29, 31.
101. See chapter 5 ("Mysticism and Mission").

Instead of these misguided assumptions, we need to approach mysticism as an experiential sense of God's presence,[102] and prophecy as the impulse to correct the present in the light of God's future.[103]

To situate this relationship more broadly in the biblical narrative, we first need to remember that the Christian life is lived in faith, hope, and love. Second, it has its origins in an existential encounter with Christ through word and Spirit. Third, it is lived in the light of Scripture as it speaks to us and also through our growing relationship with and conformity to Christ, the living word. Fourth, we are people who are empowered and led by the Holy Spirit, and so, in the words of Evelyn Underhill, we are to find our small place in vast operations of God's purposes for our world.[104] Discerning this small place within God's vast purposes has much more to do with mysticism than rationality!

To give some examples from the Christian tradition, St. Francis,[105] St. Ignatius of Loyola,[106] John and Charles Wesley,[107] Count Nicholas von Zinzendorf of the Modern Moravians,[108] John Woolman of the Quakers,[109] Dorothy Day of the Catholic Worker,[110] amongst many others, can all be cited as activists whose service to the world sprang from a profound Christian mysticism. In the history of the Christian church, the contemplative (or the mystical) dimension of life was often held to be on a higher plane,[111] but

102. Bernard McGinn makes it clear that mysticism has to do with "a direct and transformative presence of God," which changes "their [Christians'] minds and their lives," and that this change has missional implications. McGinn notes that from the late Middle Ages, the emphasis in Christianity was on the *vita contemplativa* (contemplative life) and the *vita activa* (active life) being fused in an integrated way (*The Essential Writings of Christian Mysticism*, xiv, xvii, 520).

103. See Brueggemann, *The Prophetic Imagination.*

104. Underhill writes, we are called into "a total concentration on the total interests of God," while we also have "to take our small place in the vast operations of His Spirit" (*The Spiritual Life*, 87, 89).

105. See Delio, *Franciscan Prayer.*

106. See Barry and Doherty, *Contemplatives in Action*; Ruffing, "Ignatian Mysticism of Service," in *Mysticism and Social Transformation.*

107. See Chilcote, *Recapturing the Wesley's Vision.*

108. See Lewis, *Zinzendorf the Ecumenical Reformer.*

109. See Benefiel and Phipps, "Practical Mysticism: Quakers and Social Transformation," in Ruffing, *Mysticism and Social Transformation*, 129–42; Soelle, *The Silent Cry*, 242–47.

110. See Day, "The Only Solution is Love," in Madigan, *Mystics, Visionaries and Prophets*, 345–61.

111. See McGinn, *The Essential Writings of Christian Mysticism*, 520.

generally speaking, the church has placed an equal emphasis on the demands of love to the neighbour.[112]

In discussing the relationship between mysticism (or contemplation) and prophecy (or action), Janet Ruffing cites the work of Johann Baptist Metz, referring to his development of a "mystical–political"[113] dimension in Christianity. Quoting Metz, she says that "the experience of God [should] not [be located] in peaceful tranquillity but in protest to God about evil in the world, a questioning of God, and a 'suffering unto God.'"[114] She goes on to refer to Martin Buber's notion that prophecy is not oriented toward rapture but to "vocation and mission."[115] She also draws from Walter Brueggemann's *The Prophetic Imagination*, which emphasizes that "prophets suffer in their own hearts the discrepancy between what is and what ought to be" and have the task "to reenergize . . . listeners and help the community remember its own history and promises and possibilities in a way that will inspire conversion and fresh resolve."[116]

This reflection on the relationship between mysticism and prophecy (or contemplation and action) revolves around a number of basic concepts. First, to engage the world prophetically, one needs a different vision than the dominant values of the culture and society. For the Christian, this vision is embedded in the biblical narratives and in the living word, Jesus Christ. Second, to engage society prophetically, one needs to disengage from society some of the time as a spiritual discipline in order to draw close to the heart of God and so be able to re-engage the world with new eyes and a strengthened resolve. Third, to engage society prophetically, one must be willing to wrestle with God. Fourth, to engage society prophetically, one must be willing to suffer the consequences of one's speaking and acting. Finally, to engage the world prophetically, one must always come with the garland of peace in the cause of justice.

112. See Butler, *Western Mysticism*, who quotes Augustine's reference to the two dimensions of the Christian life: "the one is in the work of action, the other in the reward of contemplation" (159). And still quoting Augustine: "no one should be so at leisure . . . not to think of his neighbour's welfare; nor so busied as to not seek after the contemplation of God" (165). Similar quotes can be gained from Gregory: "in this life we taste only the beginnings of intimate contemplation; whereas the active life can be fully laid hold of" (172). McGinn also notes that there are "the two alternations [of the Christian life] of sacred repose and of necessary action" (193).

113. Metz, *A Passion for God*.

114. Ruffing, *Mysticism and Social Transformation*, 7–8.

115. Ruffing, 8.

116. Ruffing, 10.

All of this points to a very basic dialectic, which is the hermeneutical circle in the relationship between contemplation and action.[117] In the movement of transcendence, we move towards God in worship, prayer, and listening. In this movement, we are loved, encouraged, and gain new inspiration for our pilgrimage. But in this movement, God (who so loves the world) will always bring our attention back to how we can serve our neighbour and engage the work of justice. And in our movement toward witness and service in the world, we seek to discern the hand of God at work and the Spirit preparing the way. Thus, we continually seek the God who is on pilgrimage with us. And in our work, where we can so quickly feel overwhelmed, there is always the invitation to draw aside, be still, pray, wait, and continue the journey again. Dorothee Soelle puts this so simply, observing how "these two movements, kneeling down and standing up, belong together and succeed only in tandem."[118]

All of this is beautifully and painfully relevant for the challenges facing the church throughout the world. The living gospel will move us towards compassion where rationality will not. Activism cannot beget activism, but revelation and inspiration will. In the long journey for justice, we must nurture a spirituality of the heart. The doctrine of the "perseverance of the saints" needs to be embraced in relation to our service in the world. Our self-preoccupation and lack of identification with those who are suffering can only be overcome by a vision of the Christ of the gospels, who calls *me* – and each of us – to be like him and to join him in his restoring and healing ministry.

The Challenge of Advocacy: A Personal Reflection

I worked for twenty years with drug addicts, men and women in prostitution, and delinquent youth.[119] In this journey, I learned a most painful lesson. In a nutshell, the church, community-based organizations, and even big business were all willing to support a ministry of drug counselling, rehabilitation, prevention, prison work, and vocational training so that those who had been scarred by drugs could regain a more productive life. Even the secular businesses that supported us did not mind when people became Christians. But over time, it became apparent that the police drug-squad in our city of

117. Segundo Galilea speaks of a contemplation of transcendence, where we seek the face of God, and a contemplation of immanence, where we see the hidden face of Christ in the neighbour. See *The Way of Living Faith* and *Following Jesus*.

118. Soelle, *The Silent Cry*, 285.

119. For something of this story, see Grant-Thomson, *Jodie's Story*.

Brisbane were falsely arresting street people and under-reporting drug seizures. Thus, the police were corrupt and acting as drug pushers.

We felt that we had to do something, and so our first move was to get assistance from lawyers, who helped falsely accused street people get off or receive lighter sentences. Our second move was to see the government minister responsible for the police and inform him of what we knew. He said he would look into the matter – and then did nothing. Some time later, we went to see the Premier of our state, who was a professed Christian. He also said he would look into it, but nothing happened. Months went by, and the false arrests and the sale of illegal drugs by the police continued unabated. For our final move (after praying a lot), we went to the media to expose what was happening. All hell broke loose. The police denied everything. The Premier publicly condemned us as communists. The churches withdrew all their financial support. On our knees, we were all but destroyed. Advocacy comes at a price.

But a seed was sown, and others sowed seeds. And eventually, several years later, a Commission of Inquiry into police corruption was set up, headed up by Tony Fitzgerald, QC. In light of the Commission findings, numerous police, four ministers of the government, and the Police Commissioner were found guilty and imprisoned, and the Premier was charged for perjury but was acquitted due to a hung jury.[120]

In telling this event, I am practically illustrating what the Lausanne documents call us to do. As the Manila Manifesto (1989) states, "we must demonstrate God's love visibly by caring for those who are deprived of justice," and our Christian service "demands the denunciation of all injustice and oppression."[121] This means that we cannot simply accept what a government is doing based on a naïve reading of Romans 13, which has been erroneously used to teach that we must obey a government regardless of its policies.[122] Certainly,

120. For the full report, see www.ccc.qld.gov.au/about-the ccc/the fitzgerald-inquiry.

121. Stott, *Making Christ Known*, 231.

122. The fundamental thrust of Pauline ethics is that they are reciprocal. When women, children, and slaves were instructed to behave in certain ways, the instruction applied to the husbands, fathers, and masters as well. Similarly, Paul says that the role of the government is to reward good conduct and punish bad. But what happens when the state no longer functions in that way, or when the state breaks its own laws, or when the state violates basic human rights? First, we will turn to Karl Barth, who opposed Hitler's regime. Barth says that it is possible for a state not only to do "wrong and evil things," but for it to take on "self-divinizing pretensions" and to demand "total allegiance" to its demands. When this occurs, it is no longer "the 'lawful' state envisaged in Romans 13, but the 'beast out of the abyss' of Revelation 13" (Will Herberg, "The Social Philosophy of Karl Barth," in Barth, *Community, State, and Church*, 45). Next, we will turn to NT scholar Neil Elliot, who points out that Romans 13 neither calls for blind obedience to the state, nor justifies a theology of political power (218). Though the Roman authorities are

Karl Barth, Martin Niemoller, and Dietrich Bonhoeffer did not believe that Hitler had to be obeyed,[123] and so they rightly resisted him.[124] We should do the same in relation to any oppressive or unjust governmental policies. We are called to give voice to the voiceless, to identify with the suffering, to speak truth to power, and to act on behalf of victims by showing the way of healing and restoration. Thus, we hold healing balm in our hands, never a gun. And we do all this on behalf of the oppressed so that the oppressor, too, may find the grace of God.

Conclusion

In this chapter, I have sought to explore a common understanding of the church's "fragile" engagement with a "troubled" world. I have used three different, complimentary lenses to engage this most relevant topic: the dialectical nature of our Christian presence in the world, the inter-related themes of orthodoxy, orthopathy, and orthopraxis, and the relational dynamics between mysticism and prophecy. At the same time, I have argued for an evangelical consensus regarding our action in the world and for a practical ecumenism that can move the church from competition to cooperation.

called "servants of God" (Rom 13:4) and Nebuchadnezzar is called "God's servant" (Jer 27:6), this does not imply divine approval for all that they have done (224). Instead, when we connect Romans 13 with Romans 12, we can see that the call for Christians is not to take justice into their own hands (224). Yet this does not mean blind obedience, but points to the testimonies of the martyrs. As one martyr put it, "we have never done evil to anyone and have in no manner worked for the cause of injustice . . . therefore we give honor to Caesar" (quoted in Elliot, *Liberating Paul*, 225). This confession clearly implies that if the state commits injustice, the martyr will not commit injustice. He/she will not do what the state is doing, but will live justly. In other words, the martyr is saying that he/she will honour Caesar by being *different*. Finally, the Anabaptist scholar John Howard Yoder makes the point that Romans 13 calls Christians to "submit" to the government, not "obey" the government, which he describes as "revolutionary subordination" (*The Politics of Jesus*, 163–92). Basically, this means that a Christian commits to live the values of the kingdom of God – reconciliation, healing, peacemaking, and justice. If the government is offended by these different values, the Christian "submits" to the government's punishment.

123. Dietrich Bonhoeffer makes a distinction between God's appointment of governance and government as an "order of creation" and a particular government at a particular point in history. Christians are always to support the concept of government, but they may need to resist the particular policies of a government. Ruth Zerner, "Church, State, and the 'Jewish Question,'" notes that this "distinction provides an intellectual justification for opposition activity by a person of Christian conscience," and "leaves for an individual to reject a particular government while still being loyal to the nation-state" (in de Gruchy, *The Cambridge Companion to Dietrich Bonhoeffer*, 199).

124. See Ringma, *Resist the Powers with Jacques Ellul.*

As Christians, we are called to be a counter-movement in society, reflecting the reign of God in the light of the gospel, continually sustained and guided by the Spirit. Thus, we must resist all that reflects the anti-reign of God – oppression, lack of justice, and death, whether that occurs within the government, social institutions, or the church itself. For Christians to live this way in the world, we need to embrace radical identification with those who are suffering. As we engage this difficult, often disheartening work, we will need to be sustained by the gospel, communities of resistance, and the spiritual disciplines. I have found such sustenance from *Celtic Daily Prayer* and so close with the following poem:

> As the tamed horse
> Still hears the call of her wild brothers
> And as the farmed goose flaps hopeful wings
> As her sisters fly overhead
> So too, perhaps
> The wild ones amongst us
> Are our only hope in calling us back
> To our true nature.
> Wild ones
> Who have not been turned to stone
> By the far-reaching grasp of the empire
> And its programme of consumer sedation
> The killing of imagination.
> Where, my friends
> Have the wild ones gone?[125]

125. *Celtic Daily Prayer*, Book 2, 904.

9

God's Heart for the Poor

A Missional Focus

Introduction

We can summarize the central thrust of this chapter in one sentence: God has a heart for the poor, and therefore so must we. But a lot is required if we wish to unpack this simple assertion! First, we need to ask, how can we understand this God?[1] Second, we need to ask, if God (who is all powerful) has a heart for the poor, why does so much injustice and poverty continue in our world? Third, we need to ask, how do we get a look into someone's heart? More particularly, how can we know God's heart? Fourth, we need to entertain a most difficult question: how does God act into the world? In other words, what is God's *modus operandi*? Finally, we need to recognize that the "poor" in Scripture are not a simple category, but complex and nuanced.

To begin, this chapter will touch on the "God questions" identified above. Next, I will briefly demonstrate how Christians have had a heart for the poor throughout history. Finally, I will explore what the biblical story has to say about serving the poor. My focus will be on the Christian tradition, but it is important to acknowledge that people of other faiths – or no faith at all – may also have a heart for the poor.

1. See McFague, *Models of God.*

Understanding God

God has traditionally been understood in the language of distance and power (omnipotence, immutability, infinity) and also in the language of intimacy (merciful Father, the loving God, the God of grace). Furthermore, God has been understood according to the following categories.

First, God has been understood as the *prime mover.* From this perspective, God created the world, set in motion the "laws" of nature, and then left things to us. Thus, in some sense, we are making and shaping *our* world, and society is both the product of our goodness and our messiness – not necessarily the product of God's providential care.

Second, God has been understood as the *power of the future,* moving all things towards their final fulfilment, with or without human agency. This perspective stresses God's sovereignty and weakens human responsibility. Thus, God will do what God will do. Yet this leaves us with a lot of questions about why so much suffering continues and why God's final future is so slow in coming.

Third, God has been understood as an *immanent presence.* From this perspective, God is synonymous with all the movements in the world that gravitate towards a general good. This outlook virtually negates the distinct action of God in human affairs and leaves us wondering why we would worship a God who seems so much like us in our fragile goodness and persistent madness.

Fourth, God has been understood as the *soul saviour.* From this perspective, God's primary concern is with our inner rehabilitation in order to prepare us for the afterlife. This outlook focuses on eternity, but says little about our call to bear the purposes of God in our time. While such a hope is heartwarming, it is escapist, and loses the dynamic connection between the love of God and neighbour.

Fifth, God has been understood as a *mysterious spirit,* where *all* creative activity is perceived as a mysterious sign of spirit. While this perspective makes the presence of God all pervasive in the natural and social worlds, there is little guidance about how to read this activity of God. And surely, all creativity is not marked by goodness.

Sixth, God has been understood as both *personally transcendent* and *immanent.* This perspective links God's sovereignty with human responsibility, making the power of God in the world connected to human obedience and cooperation. This dynamic of God's presence and action is both dialectical and mysterious, suggesting that God works through "his" people, and yet the existential realities are hard to discern and understand. Does God give humans the impulse or the seed of an idea? Does God give a clear vision or direction? Are we free to interpret and act on what *we* think God is saying to us?

Seventh, God has been understood as a *providential administrator* of the world. This perspective identifies God as the sustainer of all things, who moves us and shapes all things according to his purpose. However, in the words of G. Berkouwer, God's "guidance and purposeful management has today become a profound problem."[2] Moreover, as S. Grenz observes, "God no longer appears to be governing the corporate affairs of humankind."[3] If all that takes place in the human arena is part of God's providential care, then dictatorships and a lack of justice will need to be accepted rather than resisted and subverted.

Finally, God has been understood as being *revealed in Christ* through the power of the Spirit. From this perspective, God the Father, God the Son, and God the Spirit are intimately involved with each other in the work of creation, redemption, and restoration. Thus, we are all called to embrace the work of creating, redeeming, and restoring in our own lives and then to live this out as we relate to others.

While we should discard or modify some of these models of God, the final one is most relevant for our reflection in this chapter, for God is neither a vague force in human affairs, nor a God who nicely orchestrates all things despite us. Rather, God is most clearly seen in Christ, who declares: "The Father and I are one" (John 10:30); "for whatever the Father does, the Son does likewise" (John 5:19); "Whoever has seen me has seen the Father" (John 14:9). Or, as the epistle to the Colossians puts it, "He [Christ] is the image of the invisible God" (Col 1:15). Thus, Christ becomes the model for God's way in engaging human affairs and also for our being and acting in the world. This challenges us to move away from vague and often speculative notions about God and God's way in the world so that we can embrace the more concrete manifestation of God's nature through the way God has acted in, through, and with the OT people and in the person and work of Christ.

Understood in this light, we can say that God is *in* the world in the way that Christ was *in* the world, and God continues to be *in* the world by the Holy Spirit. Thus, we are called to live *in* Christ and to live the *way* of Christ by the power of the Spirit, which means that we will live *in* the love of God as we serve and extend love to our neighbour, bearing witness to the kingdom of God. Moreover, this life *in* Christ forgives, heals, builds community, serves the

2. Berkouwer, *Providence of God*, 11.

3. Grenz, *Theology for the Community of God*, 119.

poor, resists the distortion or corruption of the political and religious powers of the day, and embraces suffering so that new life might come.

And so, we are in the world, not with a powerful God who magically fixes everything, but with a God who invites us to repeat the paschal mystery of Christ's death and resurrection. This means that we are not in the world with positional power, but rather with moral purpose, and so we don't have power *over*, but power *for* others (hence the work of advocacy and being a voice of the voiceless) and power *with* others (power in the Spirit and with others in solidarity, community, and grassroots ecumenism).[4] The key concept from Scripture for this way of being in the world is: "As you [Father] have sent me into the world, so I [Jesus] send them into the world" (John 17:18).

Thus, we need to think about whether we see God as a Mr. Fix-it, or a Father Christmas, or an Absent Landlord, or a Vague Spiritual Presence, or an Orchestrating Power, or a God who is most clearly seen in the face of Christ. Our image of God has implications for the way in which we live and act in the world. Or, to say that differently, tell me who you believe God to be, and that will tell me everything else you believe and how you will act in the world.[5]

Knowing Someone's Heart

It is not easy to know what is in our own heart, let alone what is in someone else's inner being. And we need to be extremely careful about making any claim that we can know the heart of God.[6] God has made himself known in revelation, but God is also shrouded in mystery: "The secret things belong to the LORD our God, but the revealed things belong to us" (Deut 29:29). And a cry throughout the biblical story is: "How long, O LORD? Will you forget me forever? How long will you hide your face from me?" (Ps 13:1). So, what can we know of God's heart, particularly for the poor? Is there a lens that might guide us?

First, in the light of who God *is* and what God *does*, we may know something of the heart of God: "He [God] raises the poor from the dust and

4. See May, *Power and Innocence*.

5. To give a simple example, if we believe God to be Father, Son, and Holy Spirit – a community of "persons" – then this will have implications for our way of being church and our practices of mutuality.

6. One of the reoccurring dangers within religion systems happens when people claim to *know* the mind and purposes of God so completely that they are not open to any processes of discernment or correction. Historically, this has led to violence and abuse perpetrated in the name of God.

lifts the needy from the ash heap to make them sit with princes" (Ps 113:7); "the LORD maintains the cause of the needy and executes justice for the poor" (Ps 140:12).

Second, in the light of what God *commands us* to do, we may know something about God: "You shall not be partial to the poor or defer to the great" (Lev 19:15); "You shall not strip your vineyard bare, or gather the fallen grapes of your vineyard; you shall leave them for the poor and alien: I am the LORD your God" (Lev 19:10). Thus, provision is to be given to the poor, but the poor must also be empowered.

Third, we may know something of God's heart for the poor in that serving the poor *reflects* something of our relationship with God: "Whoever is kind to the poor lends to the LORD" (Prov 19:17); "If I have withheld anything that the poor desired . . . [then] I should have been false to the God above" (Job 31:16, 28). Simply put, our love for God has to go through the lens of our love for the poor.

How do *we* get such a Heart?

This lens is but a very small window into God's heart, but it is appropriate to ask how *we* might get such a heart for the poor and so reflect God's heart for the poor in the world. In speaking about God, Isaiah exclaims, "You have been a refuge to the poor" (Isa 25:4). But then he challenges the people with a prophetic word: "bring the homeless poor into your house" (Isa 58:7). One has to have a big heart to do this! Following are some pointers in how we might gain such a heart.

First, we need to be deeply impacted by the call of the gospel: "But when you give a banquet, invite the poor, the crippled, the lame, and the blind. And you will be blessed, because they cannot repay you" (Luke 14:13–14). Thus, we need to see the poor in the light of the call of the gospel.

Second, we may need to be moved by seeing the plight of the poor. My first conversion was to follow Christ. My second conversion was when I began to gain a heart for the poor while I was working amongst Indigenous Australians in Western Australia. Thus, being with the poor moves and challenges us, and this shapes our heart.

Third, we may experience some form of personal deprivation, loss, or alienation that shapes our hearts with compassion for the poor. Thus, we begin to see the poor through our own struggles and difficulties.

Fourth, some of us may, like St. Francis or Mother Teresa, hear a special call from God. In this way, we will see the poor through this special call of God upon our lives.

Finally, we may grow into a recognition that being a Christian involves caring for the poor. Paul, in explaining his mission to the Gentiles, says that the Jerusalem apostles "asked only one thing, that we remember the poor, which was actually what I was eager to do" (Gal 2:10). Or in the words of D. Groody, "no one can choose to ignore a commitment to the poor and still claim to be Christian."[7] Thus, our spirituality involves serving the poor. If we have a heart for God, we must have a heart for the poor. This generalization subverts the refrain that one often hears: "O, you must have a special call from God to do this." But I have not received such a special call! The call erupted within me as a result of the presence of Christ.

Christian Admonition in Serving the Poor

It is not difficult to demonstrate how Christians, in their two-thousand-year journey through history, have expressed God's heart for the poor through their work in the world, but this has fluctuated. At times, service to the poor was exemplary. For example, the early African church father, Tertullian (c. 160–c. 220), writes: "Our care for the derelict and our active love have become a distinctive sign before" others. This love included bringing up the children of prostitutes, gladiators, and exposed infants dumped on the rubbish heaps of cities in the Roman Empire. This work by Christians was later confirmed by an enemy of the church, Julian the Apostate (332–363), who exclaimed, "These godless Galileans feed not only their own poor, but ours [as well]; our poor lack care."[8] But other times, the light of Christian service to the poor flickered dimly. The church historian, Carter Lindberg, notes that in the late Middle Ages, "The distribution of alms was not primarily concerned with the improvement of the social and economic situation of the poor, but with the salvation of the donor."[9]

But despite various deformities, there is so much that is positive and exemplary. For example, St. Clement (c. 150–c. 215) writes, "Put an end to your wickedness; learn to do good, seek out justice, deliver the one who is wronged;

7. Groody, *Globalization, Spirituality, and Justice*, 193.
8. Ringma, "Liberation Theologians Speak to Evangelicals," 20–21.
9. Lindberg, *Beyond Charity*, 69.

give judgment on behalf of the orphan, and grant justice to the widow."[10] And St. Maximus the Confessor (c. 580–662) says, "We shall be judged for the evil we have done, but especially for the good we have neglected and for the fact that we have not loved the neighbour." And furthermore, "the one who imitates God by giving alms knows no difference between . . . [the] just and [the] unjust."[11] Richard Rolle (c. 1295–1349) exhorts, "Two cloaks or one will seem enough to you; if you have five or six give some to Christ who wanders naked in His wretched rags."[12] St. Catherine of Siena (1347–1380) says, "no virtue . . . can have life in itself except through charity and humility."[13] And St. John Chrysostom (c. 347–407) argues that "no one ought to have more than another – neither the rich more than the poor."[14]

Moreover, the third century *Constitutions of the Holy Apostles* states, "The Lord says, 'Give to everyone that asks of you.' It is evident that it is meant of everyone that is really in want, whether friend or foe, whether kinsman or stranger."[15]

And St. Francis of Assisi (1181–1226) writes in the *Earlier Rule*, "alms are a legacy and a just right due to the poor, which our Lord acquired for us."[16]

Anabaptist leader Balthasar Hubmaier (1485–1528) writes, "I have always said that everyone should be concerned about the needs of others, so that the hungry might be fed, the thirsty given drink, and the naked clothed. For we are not the lords of our possessions, but stewards and distributors."[17] And the Anabaptist Peter Walpot (1521–1578) writes, "For the same way that we act towards our neighbours and the members of Christ, that is how we will be deemed by the Lord."[18]

Finally, Martin Luther (1483–1546) suggests: "Now there is no greater service of God than Christian love which helps and serves the needy."[19]

The voices of service to the poor have continued to ring out right up to the present. Some of those voices have been evangelical: "we . . . should share his

10. Quoted in Ringma, *Hear the Ancient Wisdom*, 95.
11. Quoted in Ringma, 101.
12. Quoted in Ringma, 327.
13. Quoted in Ringma, 283.
14. Schaff, ed., *Nicene and Post-Nicene Fathers*, vol. 10, 134.
15. Roberts and Donaldson, eds., *Ante-Nicene Fathers*, vol. 7, 427.
16. Armstrong and Brady, eds., *Francis and Clare*, 117.
17. Shenk, ed., *Anabaptism and Mission*, 34–35.
18. Liechty, ed., *Early Anabaptist Spirituality*, 154.
19. Quoted in Lindberg, *Beyond Charity*, 164.

[God's] concern for justice and reconciliation throughout human society."[20] Others have been ecumenical: "a proclamation that does not hold forth the promises of the justice of the kingdom to the poor of the earth is a caricature of the Gospel."[21] Some have been Roman Catholic: "the Church is called to be on the side of the poor."[22] And liberation theologians "call the Church to 'evangelical poverty' by being in solidarity with the poor . . . and working to change 'unjust social, political and economic structures.'"[23]

Moreover, although the praxis of the church has varied throughout history and has sometimes been too inward or paternalistic, it still shines with challenging examples of service to the poor. For example, of St. Aidan (d. 651) it was said that "whenever a rich man gave him some precious object as a token of appreciation, he either handed it to the poor, or used it to buy slaves their freedom."[24] And the monastic communities of St. Basil (329–379) founded orphanages, hospitals, and craft workshops for the poor and also provided hospitality for travellers. Basil's core concept was that "love of God demands love of neighbour and through love of neighbour we come to the love of God."[25] As noted previously, William Wilberforce (1759–1833) embarked on a long campaign for the abolition of slavery because "He saw things that existed in God's reality [in the heart of God]," which is "that all men and women are created equal by God . . . and are therefore sacred." Thus, he worked tirelessly to make that a human reality.[26]

We can also speak about Martin Luther King Jr., Mother Teresa, Oscar Romero, Jean Vanier, and many other contemporary examples of individuals and Christian movements that serve the poor.

Drawing several broad conclusions from the above, we can note the following. First, the church has long understood that service to the poor is not simply the task of some outstanding person, such as St. Francis. Rather, it is a calling of the whole people of God. Second, the church has also understood that almsgiving (charity) is only an initial step. The next step is to build sustainable circumstances for the poor. The next step is to peacefully seek to transform our social institutions, which primarily favour the rich. And the final step

20. Ringma, "Liberation Theologians Speak to Evangelicals," 29.

21. Ringma, 31.

22. Ringma, 35.

23. Ringma, 34.

24. Quoted in van de Weyer, *Bede*, 39.

25. Ciardi, *Koinonia*, 94.

26. Metaxas, *Amazing Grace*, xvi.

is to expose the fallen powers, both spiritual and social, that mar our world and prevent shalom and human flourishing for all. Third, the church has also understood that serving the poor is a way of following Christ into the world, and thus our love of God and love of the poor are linked.

Listening Again to the Biblical Narrative

We have already intimated that the term "poor" in Scripture is multifaceted. It sometimes refers to those who recognize their need of God and cry out to him/her for help (Ps 40:17), but more often, it refers to the poor as those who are dispossessed, powerless, needing shelter or food, or needy in the very broad sense of that term.[27] Said more simply, Scripture recognizes both the "poor in spirit" (Matt 5:3) and the economic poor (Luke 6:20).

The biblical narrative is not naïve about the reality of poverty. Following are some key emphases. First, poverty can be self-inflicted (Prov 10:4; 20:13; 21:17; 23:21). Second, poverty can be caused by others through oppression (Prov 22:16; 28:3; 30:14). Third, the poor are often shunned and left friendless (Prov 14:20; 19:4). Fourth, the poor are vulnerable and cry out for help (Prov 18:23). Fifth, the poor may have to be unethical and steal (Prov 30:9). Sixth, it is better to be poor than to be rich through falsehood (Prov 28:6; 19:1; 19:22). Seventh, those who serve the poor are "blessed" (Prov 22:9; 28:27; 29:14). Eighth, serving the poor reflects our godliness (Prov 14:31; 19:17; 22:22–23). Finally, our task is not only to serve the poor, but also to advocate for them (Prov 31:9).

The whole of Scripture reflects the notion that God has a heart for the poor, for "The LORD is their [the poor's] refuge" (Ps 14:6), and God will "deliver the weak [poor] from those too strong for them" (Ps 35:10). Moreover, "with righteousness he [God] shall judge the poor and decide with equity for the meek of the earth" (Isa 11:4). God's heart for the poor is also expressed in Christ, who comes to us as a poor man, identifying with the poor, empowering and healing them, and teaching that the kingdom belongs to them. Jesus comes to bring good news to the poor (Luke 4:18), and the outworking of this good news is that "the blind receive their sight, the lame walk, the lepers are cleansed, the deaf hear, the dead are raised, the poor have good news brought to them" (Luke 7:22). Moreover, the heartbeat of God's way is that Jesus "emptied himself, taking the form of a slave," becoming "obedient to the point of death," and is raised by God's glory (Phil 2:1–11). Paul's epistle to the Corinthians

27. *ISBE* article, "poor."

makes this even more clear: "For you know the generous act of our Lord Jesus Christ, that though he was rich, yet for your sakes he became poor, so that by his poverty you might become rich" (2 Cor 8:9). God's way, and therefore our way in the world, is not expressed through power, but through vulnerability, servanthood, identification, and friendship. Thus, a key way of serving the poor is to be present with them in solidarity – not simply to give them gifts.

Some Further Reflections

While God's salvation in Christ is for all (Titus 2:11), we all need to repent of our sins. The rich need to repent of the power of their riches, and the poor need to repent of their despair. And all of us need to repent of our selfishness and self-preoccupation. Thus, we all need the grace of Christ, and we all need to share a community of commonality in Christ (Acts 2:43–47).

God's heart for the poor is such that God became poor in Christ, and God's way in the world is not through coercive power, but through the Spirit's life-giving power for us to become Christlike and to live in the way of Christ. This means that we are called to downward mobility, identification, and service to the poor.

God's heart for the poor can only become our heart through purgative processes. Therefore, we need a conversion from the idea that Christ is "just for me" to Christ is "the one for others." In order to live in this way, we need to live against the powers and ethos of our age. This will require both a countercultural spirituality as well as a counter-community that can sustain us on the road to a long obedience in the service of justice.

Service to the poor is not premised on doing some good by giving a tithe or a gift, but is a complete way a life. We are not called to be concerned for the poor for a few weeks or years, but through our whole life journey, and so this concern may have varying expressions over time. Even more basically, serving the poor is a way of being godly.

In serving the poor, we are called to serve all persons. In the words of Gregory of Nazianzus (329–389), "Because we are human beings, we must offer the favor of kindness, first to all other human beings" to "widows . . . orphans . . . exiles,"[28] and all who suffer misfortune in any way. Thus, all need help, and so all are to be served, albeit in different ways. All who receive the love of God will hear the call to love everyone, including the needy. Conversion will lift up the poor, and it will lead the rich towards downward mobility

28. Gregory of Nazianzus, *On Love of the Poor.*

and generosity. But in the final analysis, through the grace of God, we are all "beggars" seeking nourishment for our journey through life.

Conclusion

In this chapter, I have sought to make a most basic point, which is that serving the poor is at the very heart of God's concern, as expressed throughout the biblical narrative. This concern must become our concern as we seek to follow God and be godly in our world. This chapter has explored how we might grow in and sustain this concern by attending to key voices in the life of the church, which remind us of this calling.

I conclude by noting that the biblical witness does not "idealize" the poor, for they, like all of us, have their faults. Ultimately, we all live under the grace of God, since we are all needy in one form or other. However, this does not mean that I can choose whom I will seek to serve. Whatever our status and circumstances of life, we are *all* called to have God's heart for the poor.

Section III

Historical Themes

10

Luther's Theological and Spiritual Vision for the Church in the World

Introduction

It may surprise the reader that in this and the following chapter, I engage Martin Luther and Dietrich Bonhoeffer rather than contemporary Protestant missiologists.[1] While neither Luther nor Bonhoeffer can be regarded as missional thinkers in the formal sense of that discipline, both constantly wrestled with ways of engaging society.[2]

In engaging such a comprehensive topic as the mission of the church, it is important that we not only consider it from *within* a particular discipline, such as missiology. Rather, such a multifaceted topic must consider the broader problems of the human condition, the nature of God's salvific concern, the calling and task of the church, the shape of contemporary culture, and the ways that witness and service can bring shalom to our world. Moreover, missional

1. In particular, I have been influenced by the strategic thought of two well-known Protestant missiologists: David Bosch, *Transforming Mission*, and Lesslie Newbigin, *The Open Secret*.

2. The Lutheran scholar, Hans-Martin Barth, points out that while Luther "did not found any missionary societies and he did not send out missionaries," he did hold "that every Christian has a duty to witness to the Gospel," and that "a Christian is for others" and seeks to contribute "to the welfare of the whole" (*Theology of Martin Luther*, 255, 256, 492). Bonhoeffer can be regarded as a Christological theologian, who was concerned about the life and ethics of the church, the formation of clergy, ecumenical engagement, and responding to the Nazification of the church. Yet he also wrestled with the ethics of responsible action, concluding with the call to the "total and realistic response to the claim of God and of our neighbour" (quoted by Larry Rasmussen, "The Ethics of Responsible Action," 207).

spirituality is not simply about our prayer in relation to our service, but rather the whole of our life as we seek to follow Christ through the Spirit.

Furthermore, I have chosen to engage Luther and Bonhoeffer because they sought to lead the church during momentous times – Luther at the beginning of the movement that came to be known as the Reformation amidst a changing Europe, and Bonhoeffer in resistance to the Nazification of the Christian church in Germany. We can learn much from those who live and serve in times of crisis and transition, and certainly the difficulties of our present age will force us to grapple afresh with what it means to be God's missional people.

Though neither Luther nor Bonhoeffer speak directly about a missional spirituality, both seek to understand the person and work of Jesus, and so they may be typified as Christological theologians. Moreover, their fresh and creative engagement with Jesus is not merely speculative, but explores what his salvation means for a life that is devoted to service and witness – including confronting the "powers" of the time.

This theme of confronting the powers is important, as the task of the church is both redemptive and prophetic. Those who have been shaped by the grace of Christ and formed as a faith-community are called to engage the world around them while discerning what it means to be both a Christian and a citizen. Can one be both at the same time, and in the same way? Or does being a Christian take priority over being a citizen? What is the relationship between the church and the state? In differing ways, both Luther and Bonhoeffer wrestled with these and other related questions in trying to understand the role of Christians in society.

My limited task in these next two chapters is to engage the writings of Luther and Bonhoeffer to discern what these two theologians might contribute to a missional spirituality. Before focusing on Luther's missional spirituality in this chapter, I offer the following brief personal reflections.

Personal Reflections

My long-standing interest in Martin Luther has been primarily in relation to his development of the doctrine of the two kingdoms,[3] which is concerned with the question of how we can live as a citizen in our own country while, at the same time, living our faith within that setting. This doctrine obviously has significant missional implications. Does one's faith commitment to Christ

3. As will become clear, this is not the only theme I will discuss, as Luther provides much more in contributing to a missional spirituality.

only take place in the personal, familial, and church spheres of life? Or, does following the way of Christ have ramifications for *every* domain of one's life – educational, social, recreational, economic, and political?[4]

If we are called to outwork our relationship to Christ in all spheres of our life, what does this mean if we serve in the army, preside as a judge, work as an employee of a multinational company, or as an artist, farmer, or politician? Should we seek to express our faith in the workplace in the same way that we do in our church, family home, or when we join with a missional effort? How might we express our faith similarly in *every* sphere of life?

I have long wrestled with these questions because I have worked just as many years in the secular workplace as I have in Christian ministries, and it has been a great challenge for me to outwork my faith in such differing settings. Thus, I do not come away from this struggle with any nice, tidy answers – as such, neat answers most likely do not exist!

But in the course of my journey, some things have become quite clear. First, I believe that one can live a life of prayer and also live as a loving and serving presence in any sphere of life.[5] Moreover, living this way often opens opportunities to connect with one's colleagues and provide encouragement, care, support, and witness. I have also found that secular workplaces generally have no problems with the creation of informal lunchtime support groups, meditation, or Bible study and prayer groups.[6]

Furthermore, it is a myth that working in Christian organizations is easier or more effective than being in the secular workplace, as both settings have unique difficulties as well as opportunities. In the secular sphere, however, it is particularly important that we do not use our role or position to pressure others regarding our faith. Rather, hidden prayer and a winsome, serving presence should be our core postures. At the same time, our personal faith values cannot be thrown out of the window in the secular spheres of our life. At times, we may have to say, "I can't agree to do this for these reasons." Or more strongly, "I simply cannot do this."

---

4. As we will see, Luther rejected the notion that we could elevate and sacralize a "sacred career," such as monk, priest or nun, over a secular one (Bernard Lohse, *Martin Luther's Theology*, 142).

5. James Davison Hunter casts his book, *To Change the World*, in terms of "a theology and practice of faithful presence" (273).

6. An outstanding example of a more formal approach is the formation of the Fellowship of Christians in Government (FOCIG) in the Philippines, which provides Christian group activities in government offices. Similarly, I had no problem in getting permission to run weekly lunch-hour Bible studies when I worked in the Government Printing Office in George St. Brisbane, Australia.

It should also be noted that Christian organizations may have as many, if not more, management and relational problems as any other group. The misuse of power and a functional pragmatism may "suck" the goodness out of a Christian group just as much as it may deplete goodness in any other organization.

Towards Luther's Missional Spirituality

We will need to engage many themes in Luther's writings to construct a comprehensive picture of Luther's missional spirituality. Throughout this process, we need to remain fully aware that there are many interpretive difficulties in engaging Luther,[7] and "the domestication of Luther's teaching"[8] is a frequent danger. Markus Wriedt notes that many attempts to structure Luther's thought into a coherent frame have failed.[9] And Gerhard Ebeling sounds the warning that in Luther's formulation of the two kingdoms, "much [is] disputed, misinterpreted, and misused."[10]

There are multiple reasons for these difficulties, but it is important to begin by noting that Luther was not a systematic theologian.[11] His theology was situation-centred and conflict-oriented,[12] as it was forged in the midst of his conflict with the Roman Catholic Church, on the one hand, and Anabaptists and other fringe groups, on the other. Luther articulated his theology in treatises, disputes, and sermons, and so, as Hans-Martin Barth rightly observes, Luther's theology "unfolds in tensions and polarities" and can be regarded as a "theology of existence,"[13] with all its possibilities and idolatries. It should not be surprising, therefore, that Luther's theology is fundamentally "dialectic," a dynamic that is illustrated by his both/and language through expressions such as law/gospel, sinner/saint, the revealed/hidden God, two kingdoms/two governments, faith/works, before God (*coram Deo*)/before people (*coram mundo*), and the left hand/right hand of God.[14]

Amidst these and other challenges, my task will be to weave a tapestry of Luther's missional spirituality. Before turning to this weaving, it is important

---

7. See Barth, *Theology of Martin Luther*, 29–74.

8. Bayer, *Martin Luther's Theology*, 10.

9. Wriedt, "Luther's Theology," 87.

10. Ebeling, *Luther*, 178.

11. Barth makes the sweeping statement that Luther was "an occasional writer" who responded and reacted "to particular challenges" (*Theology of Martin Luther*, 160).

12. Wriedt, "Luther's Theology," 87.

13. Barth, *Theology of Martin Luther*, 462.

14. Wriedt, "Luther's Theology," 106.

to recognize that scholars are divided over the issue of Luther and missions. Gustav Warneck notes that Luther "did not speak of mission,"[15] whereas J. A. Sherer sees Luther as a missional thinker by providing the theme of the good news in Christ for the salvation of the world.[16] Moreover, David Bosch makes the generalization that the Reformers did make a "contribution to the understanding of mission."[17] As Oswald Bayer notes, Luther repeatedly emphasized that faith itself *is* a good work and that all works "must take place within" faith so that one can speak of "the good works of faith," and Luther also insisted that "it is impossible that it [faith] does not do good deeds incessantly."[18] And Hans-Martin Barth, also quoting Luther, adds that the person of faith sees it as a "pleasure . . . to please God," since "a Christian lives not in himself [herself], but in Christ and in his neighbour."[19] In beginning to weave this tapestry of Luther's missional spirituality, however, I will start further back than the faith/works theme in order to identify some other threads that contribute to the whole.

Luther and Scripture

Luther is well-known for his extensive engagement with Scripture, his concept of the plain[20] meaning of the text, his idea that Scripture interprets Scripture (*sui ipsius interpres*), his Christological hermeneutic,[21] and his emphasis on the importance of the enlightening work of the Holy Spirit in bringing the power of the word of God home to the reader. On this latter point, Hans-Martin Barth notes that Luther saw the Bible as the "womb" of God, and "in it he [God] conceives us, carries us, and gives birth to us."[22]

15. Bosch, *Transforming Mission*, 244.

16. Bosch, 244.

17. Bosch lists certain core Reformation doctrines (241–42).

18. Bayer, *Martin Luther's Theology*, 284–87.

19. Barth, *Theology of Martin Luther*, 177–78.

20. Lohse quotes Luther: "scripture is most easy to understand and [is] most clear," but Luther acknowledges that it is the Holy Spirit who makes Scripture "to become living once more" (*Martin Luther's Theology*, 190).

21. Barth acknowledges Luther's Christocentric approach to Scripture, but he also sees a "fundamentalist literalism" in Luther's engagement with Scripture (*Theology of Martin Luther*, 477).

22. Quoted in Barth, *Theology of Martin Luther*, 477.

Oswald Bayer notes that Luther's understanding of "the authority of scripture is not formal,"[23] but dynamic, for Luther sees "the word" as that which "does what it says," and he credits Luther with the "great hermeneutical discovery" of the "performative word."[24] To reinforce these observations, Bayer quotes Luther, who says that the touchstone of all Scripture is "whether [it drives] Christ home or not," and "scripture . . . transforms the one who loves it."[25] Moreover, Scripture "awakens faith," and "the Holy Spirit must work through these very words on the heart" of the reader.[26] Luther saw a very close and dynamic relationship between the word and the Spirit,[27] which he formulated in opposition to tradition and the view of the word by the Roman Catholic Church as well as spiritualist fringe groups, which emphasized the Spirit apart from the word.[28]

Another more complex theme in Luther's approach to Scripture is his dialectic of law[29]/gospel, where each functions in a dynamic relationship with the other. Luther believes that the theme of law/gospel throughout Scripture plays an important role in the life of a Christian. On the one hand, the law seeks to "teach what a person ought to do, but furnishes no power to make something occur."[30] Thus the law, as Hans-Martin Barth notes, is to function as a "preparation for grace."[31] This means that the law, as a mirror, shows us our waywardness, incapacity, and need for transformation. The gospel, on the other hand, is celebrated by Luther as the source of "forgiveness, life, and blessedness."[32] For Luther, the heart of this gospel is the call to "believe in Christ," in whom is the "promise . . . [of] all grace, righteousness, peace, and freedom."[33] Luther's emphasis on the power of the gospel is deeply experiential,

---

23. Bayer, *Martin Luther's Theology*, 69.

24. Bayer, 52.

25. Bayer, 82, 71.

26. Bayer, 75, 78.

27. Lohse quotes Luther: "the human word itself" becomes "bearer of the divine Spirit" (*Martin Luther's Theology*, 191).

28. Bayer, *Martin Luther's Theology*, 87–88.

29. Luther's discussion of law is complex. He distinguishes the law in the OT as referring to the Decalogue and therefore as relevant to the Christian as a preparation for hearing the gospel, but also as relevant for society. Here Luther equates the Decalogue with "natural law," but Luther also identifies the law in the OT more broadly as "Israel's national law," and therefore he sees it as relevant to them alone (Lohse, *Martin Luther's Theology*, 192).

30. Bayer, *Martin Luther's Theology*, 60.

31. Barth, *Theology of Martin Luther*, 143.

32. Barth, 144.

33. Bayer, *Martin Luther's Theology*, 60.

for we hear "God himself" with the good news that "Christ's righteousness swallows up our sin."[34] Moreover, in embracing the gospel, "the soul is united with the gospel it hears," and thus the soul is united "with Christ whose word this is."[35]

Lutheran scholars have pointed out Luther's strong orientation to Scripture,[36] and so we may broadly conclude that he understood the task of the people of God in society and the gestalt of Christian spirituality as being shaped by the Christian's engagement with Scripture. This fits with the emphasis on the word within the evangelical tradition. Moreover, though Luther was not a Pentecostal, he also placed stress on the work of the Holy Spirit. As Lohse notes, the purpose of the Spirit "is to point us to Christ."[37] And quoting Luther, the life-giving work of the Spirit is "to bring us to the Lord."[38] Lohse continues that for Luther, the work of the Holy Spirit is not "limited to the sphere of faith and the church," but the Spirit is to be understood as "at work in all creation as well as in every human deed" and also in "natural gifts and activities."[39]

However, Luther's emphasis on the word and Spirit does not mean that the Christian lives in startling clarity, but rather through ongoing faith in the God who both reveals and hides himself/herself. With the metaphor of the "masks of God,"[40] Luther seeks to highlight something of the hiddenness of God, which can be seen in "the way he [God] rules his creation," in the mystery of Christ's death on the cross, and in the life of faith, which is "God hiding himself in the human soul."[41]

This formulation is not meant to undermine faith's assurances, but to highlight faith's complexity. Luther's understanding of Christian existence is one of ongoing struggle. As Oswald Bayer notes, this struggle is between the "word of the law that kills and the word of the gospel that makes alive," between the "sinning human being and the justifying God," and "between the one Lord and the many lords."[42] In living the gospel through faith, Luther himself experienced both the "dark night of the soul" and the "awareness of

34. Jenson, "Luther's Contemporary Theological Significance," 284, 283.

35. Jenson, 283.

36. Barth notes that Luther studied and wrote on the book of Genesis over a ten-year period (*Theology of Martin Luther*, 463).

37. Lohse, *Martin Luther's Theology*, 234.

38. Lohse, 239.

39. Lohse, 235–36.

40. Barth, *Theology of Martin Luther*, 108.

41. Jenson, "Luther's Contemporary Theological Significance," 279–80.

42. Bayer, *Martin Luther's Theology*, 41, 40, 36.

the numinous quality of God." In other words, he lived in both "desolation and ecstasy."[43]

This paradoxical[44] and dialectical understanding of Luther is more missionally and spiritually relevant than the assured confidence often promoted by evangelical Christianity. For Scripture itself is filled with tensions, major and minor themes, liberational traditions and cultural accommodations. And in the light of the NT, some parts of the OT no longer seem as relevant to the present-day community of faith. Furthermore, the missional people of God have long struggled with how to engage, resist, and cooperate with society – and the history of the church is littered with both the goodness and folly of this engagement. Moreover, living the mystery of the present/hidden God has been one of the major themes in the history of Christian spirituality.

Faith and Good Works

Luther is particularly well-known for his personal and transformational engagement with a central Pauline theme in Romans, which is that we are not saved by our self-effort, no matter how pious or generous we might be, but by faith in Christ, who freely justifies the sinner by an abundance of grace. Faith in Christ is a core theme for Luther, who saw it as the prime mover in every dimension of a Christian's life. Faith orients us to who God is and what God has said and done. Or, as Oswald Bayer notes, "faith" for Luther equates to "trust in God's promise."[45]

Luther is clear that faith must not be seen as one of our virtues, as if *our* faith saves us. Rather, faith is *vita passive* – what we receive. Luther is adamant "that we allow God alone to work in us."[46] As Hans-Martin Barth notes, the early Luther speaks of faith as "the chief work" of the believer, but Luther's later emphasis is on the "faith that only the Holy Spirit gives."[47] In speaking about faith in Christ, Luther employs the language of a "happy exchange."[48] Expanding on this, he says that "the righteousness of Christ is my own, my

43. Strohl, "Luther's Spiritual Journey," 151, 150.

44. Strohl makes the simple point that the whole of Luther's theology is "to live in paradox" (150).

45. Bayer, *Martin Luther's Theology*, 283.

46. Bayer, 43.

47. Barth, *Theology of Martin Luther*, 173.

48. Lohse, *Martin Luther's Theology*, 226.

sins are Christ's."[49] Elaborating on this theme, Hans-Martin Barth says that for Luther, "Christ takes the debts of the sinner while the sinner participates in Christ's riches."[50]

While this language of exchange may suggest that Luther sees redemption in forensic terms, his understanding of faith in Christ is profoundly existential. Using ecstatic[51] language, Luther says, "He is my beloved and I am his."[52] Luther explains that the grace of God is a "justice by which the merciful God justifies us by faith," and then he exclaims, "I had the feeling of being born again and entering into paradise."[53] Elsewhere, Luther reminds us that "we are sharers in the divine nature" and that it is "the Lord himself dwelling entirely in us."[54] And Luther celebrates that "everything [Christ] is and does is present in us . . . so that we are utterly deified."[55] In reflecting on this, Hans-Martin Barth observes that Luther fundamentally developed a new ontology, namely, that "the human being is only constituted by God through faith."[56]

However, as noted above, the life of faith is not a smooth journey, but a gift as well as a struggle. Faith engages the revealed God (*Deus revelatus*) and the hidden God (*Deus absconditus*). Luther notes that faith is "understanding in concealment," since we are called to "honor him as he is hidden in his sufferings."[57] Moreover, faith needs to be discerning in that it grasps the God of the gospel and resists the god of law. And according to Hans-Martin Barth, Luther's emphasis on faith is disjunctive, in that it "distinguishes between God and the devil," and it is also creative, because "when you believe, you have" what you are seeking.[58]

But there is much more to Luther's understanding of faith, because he sought "to distinguish human existence 'before God' [*coram Deo*] and 'before the world' [*coram mundo*]."[59] This brings us to the conjunction of faith and good works. Luther emphasizes that all good works need to have their genesis

49. Bayer, *Martin Luther's Theology*, 350.

50. Barth, *Theology of Martin Luther*, 171.

51. Max Weber describes Luther's "personal Christianity" as a "mystic religiosity" (*From Max Weber*, 337).

52. Barth, *Theology of Martin Luther*, 173.

53. Wriedt, "Luther's Theology," 90.

54. Barth, *Theology of Martin Luther*, 187.

55. Quoted in Jenson, "Luther's Contemporary Theological Significance," 281.

56. Barth, *Theology of Martin Luther*, 174.

57. Lohse, *Martin Luther's Theology*, 216.

58. Barth, *Theology of Martin Luther*, 175.

59. Lohse, *Martin Luther's Theology*, 315.

in faith, and then he goes on to speak of the "good works of faith."[60] He also writes that "good works will never make a good, pious man [woman], but a good man [woman] produces good, pious works."[61] Luther goes on to point out that faith "makes us to be born anew of God . . . [and] brings with it the Holy Spirit . . . [and does] good works incessantly."[62] Since this dynamic is fundamental to Luther, we need to consider what sort of "good work" he had in mind, and what is activity and service in the whole gamut of life.

While Luther admonishes that if "there is a poor, naked man who has no coat; you must serve him," he also charges that one must "tolerate no injustice toward your neighbour."[63] More broadly, Luther notes that clergy who preach the word, administer the sacraments, and conduct the ministry of the diaconate are just as engaged "in a holy work" as parents bringing up a family.[64] Moreover, in God's sight, daily work is just as valued as "contemplation and asceticism."[65] And Luther comprehensively advocates that we must "care for the body and this life, to nourish, to protect, and to manage it."[66]

As Oswald Bayer notes, Luther rejects the monastic way of life because they "live lazily . . . by means of the goods of others,"[67] and he also rejects the Anabaptist refusal to participate in public office in order to forge a "worldly"[68] spirituality. In crafting a third way between these two positions, Luther holds that princes, judges, and other state officials, whose task it is to protect and orchestrate justice,[69] also "are engaged in pure holiness."[70] Thus, Luther promotes the idea that the Christian should be willing to play various roles in society, writing that "if you see that there is a lack of hangmen, constables, judges, lords or princes, and you find that you are qualified, you should offer

60. Bayer, *Martin Luther's Theology*, 84.

61. Bayer, 288.

62. Barth, *Theology of Martin Luther*, 176.

63. Barth, 327, 332.

64. Barth, 320.

65. Barth, 326.

66. Bayer, *Martin Luther's Theology*, 303.

67. Bayer, 298.

68. Max Weber typifies this as a "rationally active asceticism" that operates to impact society (*From Max Weber*, 325).

69. Luther believed that the civil authorities had the task "to preserve peace, punish sin, and restrain the wicked" (*Luther's Works*, vol. 45, 94).

70. Barth, *Theology of Martin Luther*, 320.

your services."[71] We will return to this matter when we discuss Luther's concept of the two kingdoms.

Luther, thus, advocates a faith that would express itself in the world through active love and service, as illustrated by his "Treatise on Good Works" (1520), which argues that faith is to be the "habitus," the state of being and motivation, from which all good works should flow. The basis for acting in this way is the "pleasure" that the believer has in "pleas[ing] God."[72] Moreover, the believer performs good works in all of life[73] "to praise God."[74] Luther's mosaic on good works may be summarized as follows. Faith in Christ is the most basic good work.[75] The purpose of good work is to praise God.[76] Good work should also serve others.[77] Good work includes praying[78] and seeking God's help for every need, because we should be deeply touched by the needs of others.[79] Good work also includes helping the poor,[80] offering resistance to all that is wrong and unjust,[81] and also caring for one's enemy.[82] Good work is being generous.[83] Good work involves fasting[84] as well as suffering.[85]

71. Luther, *Luther's Works*, vol. 45, 95.

72. Luther, 27.

73. Luther, 34.

74. Luther, 42.

75. Luther, 23.

76. Luther, 42.

77. "A willingness to help and serve all" (Luther, 106).

78. "There is no work like prayer" (Luther, 61). And "there has never been a greater need of praying than at present" (69).

79. When you see the neighbour in need, "take pity on him, let it grieve you, plead to God for him" (Luther, 70).

80. Don't let "the poor remain unhelped" (Luther, 51).

81. "Offer resistance to all wrong" and "strive against spiritual and temporal authorities" who do not discharge their God-given task (Luther, 50).

82. "The heart feels compassion at every evil which befalls its enemy," and a good work is to be "well disposed towards his enemy" (Luther, 102). Luther clearly failed to follow his own advice. His language towards others, be they the Roman Catholic hierarchy, the Anabaptists, the Jews, and Turks, is atrocious. More on this later.

83. Good work is "to help and serve all . . . with one's own means" (Luther, 106).

84. Good work involves "fasting, temperance . . . watchfulness . . . early rising" (Luther, 104).

85. Luther writes that those who do good deeds will experience "the enmity of all men" (Luther, 50).

Good work includes faithfulness in family life[86] and obeying civil authority.[87] Finally, good work includes both rest[88] and self-care.[89]

Clearly, Luther had a very broad understanding of how a Christian was called to live in the world. As Hans-Martin Barth notes, Luther held that "every Christian has the duty to witness to the Gospel,"[90] but this witness was to be expressed in service in all the dimensions of life, including family, work, and politics. This multi-faceted vision of Christian activity in society should have posed a challenge to the early evangelical Lausanne movement, with its insistence that evangelistic proclamation was the primary call of Christian service.[91]

In concluding this section, we can safely say that for Luther, doing good works involved a whole way of life, witness, and service that included every aspect of life. But in charting this perspective, Luther sought to avoid "the temptation to theocracy," on the one hand, and a "reduction to a quietistic[92] individual ethics," on the other.[93] However, Luther was no bright-eyed optimist when it came to the church's witness in the world, for he was not impressed with the commitment of most Christians and called a true Christian a "rare bird."[94] He was also despondent about the state of the church. In his preface to the German Mass (1526), he encourages Christians to "meet in a house somewhere to pray, to read, to baptize, to receive the sacrament, and to do other Christian works."[95] But he says he can't find enough who are willing to live in this way, for "there are few true believers" and "still fewer

86. Luther, 104.

87. Luther sends a bit of a mixed message on this important point. He speaks of temporal power as "but a very small matter in the sight of God," and he speaks of "childish government" and says that a prince can be like "a mad driver," and he goes on to acknowledge that government often "rides roughshod over the common people" (Luther, 93–95). But despite this negative portrayal, Luther calls all "not to resist the temporal power even when it does wrong" (Luther, 92).

88. Luther insists that we should practise Sabbath and "cease from our labor and trade" and "let God alone work in us" (Luther, 72).

89. Luther insists that when one does not practise self-care, one "has become his own murderer" (Luther, 76).

90. Barth, *Theology of Martin Luther*, 256.

91. See John Stott, ed., *Making Christ Known*. This early emphasis was later modified to reflect more holistic missional approaches (Henning Wrogemann, *Theologies of Mission*, 125–29). See also Al Tizon, *Transformation after Lausanne*.

92. Herbert Marcuse accused Luther of "quietism," and Max Scheler accused him of promoting only "innerliness" (quoted in Barth, *Theology of Martin Luther*, 349).

93. Barth, 354.

94. Barth, 300.

95. Barth, 300.

who live a Christian life."[96] Moreover, Luther is not optimistic about those in government pursuing the paths of peace and justice. And of princes, he says, "they are usually the biggest fools."[97]

Despite the reformation impulse, there is no triumphalism in Luther's theology. Oswald Bayer identifies Luther's position as beyond optimism and pessimism, describing it as a call to live the wisdom of God "from within the duress of agonizing struggles and afflictions."[98] Hans-Martin Barth concurs, describing Luther's theology as a "theology of the cross" that "unfolds in the tensions and polarities" of all of life.[99]

Sinner and Saint

We have already noted Luther's dialectic approach, which not only operates in the relationship between the Christian and society, but also *within* the life of the Christian. Oswald Bayer notes Luther's emphasis on the ongoing struggle between the "sinning human being" and the "justifying God."[100]

In the formulation, *simul justus et peccator*,[101] Luther seeks to maintain the tension between, on the one hand, the power of the word and the work of the Spirit in the justifying grace of God through Christ and, on the other, the Christian's ongoing need for repentance, transformation, and growth in sanctification.[102] Luther's dialectical orientation shines at this point, for as he writes, "I am a sinner in and by myself apart from Christ. Apart from myself and in Christ I am not a sinner."[103] While Luther uses the language of exchange,[104] his understanding of the work of the justifying God is one of

96. Luther, *Luther's Works*, vol. 45, 90.

97. Ebeling, *Luther*, 187.

98. Bayer, *Martin Luther's Theology*, 9, 31.

99. Barth, *Theology of Martin Luther*, 462.

100. Bayer, *Martin Luther's Theology*, 40.

101. Roughly translated from the Latin, "By whose righteousness will we be judged?"

102. In *Transforming Mission*, Bosch notes that missionaries "have tended to regard themselves as immune to the weaknesses and sins of 'ordinary' Christians," and he quotes Stephen Neill, who says that missionaries "have on the whole been a feeble folk, not very wise, not very holy, not very patient" (365). Neill is probably right if Barbara Kingsolver's *The Poisonwood Bible* reflects a historical construction rather than a purely literary one.

103. Barth, *Theology of Martin Luther*, 179–80.

104. Barth's helpful summary: "Christ takes on the debts of the sinner, while the sinner participates in Christ's riches" (171).

existential encounter,[105] for he exclaims, "Jesus Christ is my Lord." Thus, as Hans-Martin Barth notes, Luther's Christology is *pro me* ("for me"): what Christ has done for me and in me.[106] Luther makes it clear that the work of Christ in the believer through the word, Spirit, and the sacramental life of the church is one of ongoing growth, for he speaks of a "process of becoming godly."[107] But at the same time, he says, "we must never assume that we shall have relief from temptation as long as we live."[108]

Before we set out some of the other core features of Luther's spirituality, it may help to clarify what Luther means by "sinner" and then sharpen what he means by "saint." Luther's core definition of a sinner is a human being who fails to acknowledge God's lordship. Drawing on the Decalogue, Luther writes, "you are to have only one God."[109] Luther's second feature is that sin is the good curving[110] in the wrong direction. Oswald Bayer notes that for Luther, greed, for example, is life "curving in on oneself, which ends up in demonic depths."[111] Hans-Martin Barth agrees that this "incurving" distorts our relationship with God, with others, and with oneself.[112] Luther's third feature of sin is that it is anything done to glorify the self and not done in faith before God. Luther writes, "apart from faith all works are dead."[113] But we do not sin when our good works are done "in faith and bring faith to bear upon it."[114] Lastly, while Luther maintains that it is in "no way proper for a Christian to set himself against his government whether it acts justly or unjustly,"[115] he elsewhere proposes[116] that one "must refuse obedience to the emperor," or else you will "help strengthen" all his "abominations" and will assist in "rebuilding the kingdom of the devil."[117]

---

105. Luther: "we are to be sharers in the divine nature" (quoted in Barth, *Theology of Martin Luther*, 187).

106. Barth, 182.

107. Barth, 180.

108. Luther, *Luther's Works*, vol. 44, 106.

109. Bayer, *Martin Luther's Theology*, 304.

110. Bayer, 304.

111. Bayer, 304.

112. Barth, *Theology of Martin Luther*, 162–64.

113. Luther, *Luther's Works*, vol. 44, 113.

114. Luther, 103.

115. Luther, vol. 47, 6.

116. He makes this statement in light of the emperor's desire "to bring the evangelicals to heel" (Luther, 6).

117. Luther, 52–53.

Regarding the meaning of "saint," it is clear in Luther's writings that a saint has embraced the justifying work of God in Christ through the power of the word and the Spirit. And, as we have already seen, such a person lives by faith and does good works. As Luther puts it, "good works without faith cannot happen, and . . . faith without works cannot endure."[118] A saint is also empowered by the Spirit and is "pure, free, cheerful, glad," and is marked by a "loving heart," along with "humility, meekness, gentleness, fidelity, love."[119]

In Luther's schema, a monk is not a saint,[120] although Luther writes that he thinks well of St. Bernard of Clairvaux.[121] He does acknowledge that some monks "were saints who lived a godly life in the midst of these follies"[122] (e.g. monastic vows, worship, and lifestyle). But Luther is unbending on the point that monasticism is "a seditious movement directed against Christ" and, as such, "ungodly [and] . . . blasphemous" because it claims "that monks are far better and holier than the ordinary believers."[123]

Despite Luther's provocative language, he does "not condemn monastic life as such,"[124] but he believes that monastic vows have no biblical basis and thus reflect a "work righteousness."[125] Moreover, Luther believes that the monastic way of life alienates monks from the work of ordinary life, such as caring for parents, earning a living, and serving the neighbour. Luther claims that "you cannot take vows which deny obedience to parents and service to the neighbour."[126]

Constructively, Luther seeks to rework the three monastic vows of poverty, chastity, and obedience for "ordinary" Christians.[127] Oswald Bayer summarizes this reworking as follows: evangelical poverty involves a life of generosity and resisting monetary "idolatry"; chastity involves familial faithfulness; evangelical obedience involves the posture of listening and responding to the word of God

---

118. Luther, vol. 44, 242.

119. Luther, 241, 239.

120. Luther's language in relation to monasticism is atrocious. He calls monks "unbelievable hypocrites" and says that they "are rolling in wealth," seek to "earn their salvation," are "satanic," "idlers," and that monasticism caused the "utter ruination of Christendom" (Luther, 255, 267, 280, 285, 335, 251).

121. Luther, 334.

122. Luther, 324.

123. Luther, 321, 323, 322.

124. Luther, 246.

125. Luther, 248.

126. Luther, 331.

127. Bayer, *Martin Luther's Theology*, 296.

and the advice of others.[128] On this latter point, Luther states that it is through our baptism that we are "all subject one to another."[129] To conclude Luther's discussion of monastic vows, we note that, despite his biting language, he "does not advocate the abolition of the monastic life" as long as it is voluntary, is not based on a vow, and is not seen as a work righteousness.[130] Luther writes, "lifelong poverty, obedience, and chastity may be observed, but cannot be vowed, taught, or imposed."[131]

Instead, Luther seeks to develop a spirituality for all based on his notion of the priesthood of all believers. Thus, a farmer living by faith in Christ is as much a saint (and a sinner) as a monk or a bishop. Luther believes that the Christian must "constantly grow in sanctification," while, at the same time, Christ "willed the entire life of believers to be one of repentance."[132]

Personal and Corporate Spiritual Practices

It is important to highlight Luther's emphasis on Christian spirituality in both its personal and communal dimensions. Again, Luther's dialectical approach is evident, as revealed in the famous quote that in Christ, the Christian is a "perfectly free lord of all, subject to none," and in outworking this freedom, the Christian is a "perfectly dutiful servant to all, subject to all."[133]

Regarding the communal dimensions, Hans-Martin Barth is of the opinion that Luther does not develop a strong enough ecclesiology.[134] In fact, Barth chides Luther for focusing too much "on individuals" who are to bear witness, but not enough on the faith-community "that has a missionary duty."[135] Barth also charges Luther with lacking an eschatological and charismatic understanding of the church.[136]

Yet Luther does give attention to the nature of the church, for Bernard Lohse points out how Luther stresses that Christ not only redeems individuals,

---

128. Bayer, 303–5.
129. Luther, *Luther's Works*, vol. 44, 361.
130. Luther, 248.
131. Luther, 315.
132. Barth, *Theology of Martin Luther*, 352, 351.
133. Barth, 202–3.
134. Barth, 370.
135. Barth, 479–80.
136. Barth, 480.

but also "called a new people to his discipleship."[137] Luther holds that "baptism, the sacraments, and the gospel are the signs of the church,"[138] and he elsewhere adds the following supplementary features of the church: the power of the keys,[139] calling and ordaining clergy, prayer, praise, confession of faith, marriage, honouring temporal power, suffering, renouncing revenge, fasting, and enduring the cross and inner conflict.[140] Lohse notes that the core emphasis in Luther's ecclesiology is for the church as a gathered community to hear the word of God: "the chief thing in the church is the hearing of the Word."[141] Or as Luther puts it, "the church is the creature of the gospel."[142] Yet Luther holds that both the word and the sacraments are key marks of the church, and he concurs with Augustine that the church is *unitas* ("unity"), *sanctitas* ("sanctity"), *catholicitas* ("catholicity"), and *apostolicitas* ("apostolic").[143] Luther also stresses that the church is an assembly "in the Spirit" and a community of sharing, as "all the spiritual possessions of Christ and his saints are shared."[144] He makes the rather generous claim that "our church . . . [is] most like the church of the apostles."[145]

Clearly, Luther gave much attention to the form and shape of church in providing a corporate identity and spirituality. He translated the Bible in German, completing the NT in 1522 and the entire Bible in 1534. He wrote hymns, two catechisms,[146] the *Formula Missae* (1523), and the *Deutsche Messe* (1526).[147] In the "Smaller Catechism," Luther is transparent about his intention to promote the catechism in the churches, as he is distressed that people "have no knowledge of Christian teaching."[148] He charges the clergy to

137. Lohse, *Martin Luther's Theology*, 281.

138. Lohse, 283.

139. In the Lutheran church, this is also known as the "Office of the Keys." It refers to the authority that Christ has given to the church to forgive sins (through absolution after confession) and also to retain sins for those who do not repent. This doctrine is based on John 20:23: "If you forgive the sins of any, they are forgiven them; if you retain the sins of any, they are retained."

140. Lohse, 284.

141. Lohse, 77.

142. Lohse, 280.

143. Lohse, 280, 283.

144. Lohse, 280, 279.

145. Lohse, 282.

146. *Luther's Small Catechism and Luther's Large Catechism.*

147. Luther, *Liturgies of the Western Church*, 95–137.

148. Luther, *Creeds of the Churches*, 108.

take their ministerial task seriously and to "have pity on the people who are entrusted to your care."[149]

Luther's concern is not only for people to know core Christian doctrines, but also to be formed into a way of life. Luther writes that Christians need to be formed in such a way that they do not "lay waste to the kingdom of God and the kingdom of this world."[150] This highlights a core distinctive of Luther, who is concerned that Christians bless the church community as well as general society. While Luther stresses that the faith-community is subject to the word, he also emphasizes the importance of the sacraments, writing that the sacrament in which so much "good is bestowed" is an antidote and aid against all forms of evil.[151] In typical overstatement, he says that by neglecting the sacraments, one indicates that one "needs no grace, no life, no paradise, no heaven, no Christ, no God, nothing good at all."[152]

In light of the above, I suggest that Hans-Martin Barth's critique of Luther's understanding of the church is misplaced, as he claims that Luther failed to give "any genuine meaning to external actions and lifestyles."[153] Moreover, Barth charges that Luther underplayed the importance of rituals, and yet he acknowledges that Luther emphasized the role of clergy, the importance of schooling, the need for the diaconate to offer practical care, and the importance of shaping people through preaching, the catechism, and morning and evening prayers.[154] Finally, the way that Luther reworks the three monastic vows further demonstrates his concern for a *way* of life rather than teaching mere religious ideas.

The previous discussion highlights Luther's concern for the way that corporate practices shape a distinctly Christian identity and spirituality. Now we will turn to Luther's concern for personal spiritual practices. To begin, Luther places a strong emphasis on a life of prayer (*oratio*), writing that "Christians have the Gospel, Baptism and the sacrament," but they "also have prayer."[155] He makes the following four important points about prayer. First, God's order and the prayers of Christians "are the two pillars that support the

149. Luther, 108.

150. Luther, 111.

151. Luther, 112.

152. Luther, 112.

153. Barth, *Theology of Martin Luther*, 366, 476.

154. Barth, 475. Elsewhere, Barth acknowledges that Luther placed an emphasis on spiritual practices each morning and evening (363).

155. Luther, *Luther's Works*, vol. 24, 79–80.

entire world." Second, prayer's task is to "preserve the world." Third, the action of those in power is due to Christians who pray. Thus, prayer gives "hidden help." Fourth, prayer has wide ramifications, bringing about the "destruction of the devil's realm, the deliverance of souls, the conversion of hearts . . . [and] the preservation of peace for land and nation."[156] Besides preaching, Luther argues that "prayer is the chief work of a Christian,"[157] and we are to pray for "something great for the church, for the ministers of the Word, and for government."[158]

These comments give us some idea of Luther's scope of prayer, but he is also insightful regarding the motivations and dynamics of prayer. First, Luther writes that prayer is something that God asks of us: "God gives all things out of free mercy; yet He wants to be entreated."[159] Put differently, he says that "God allows Himself to be prevailed upon."[160] Second, Luther says that "smugness is offensive to God."[161] Even though we are saved by grace and not by works, Luther advocates that "it is His desire and will that you lay your troubles before Him."[162] Thus, Luther does not want us to take things for granted. Third, Luther believes that life's difficulties help us to pray. He notes that "feeling your distress helps to make your prayer stronger."[163] Elsewhere he writes, "God . . . permits us to be afflicted for our salvation."[164] Fourth, Luther sees prayer as a way of participating in the purposes of God. As Luther explains, "He wants us human beings to have a share in His workings."[165] Finally, Luther believes that prayer involves certain contradictions, for God hears our prayers, but "contradicts all of our conceptions."[166] In other words, God answers our prayers according to God's wisdom. As Luther writes, "God's only purpose in thwarting our good will is to make it a better will.[167] Thus, Luther sees a certain conversion dynamic in our praying, as prayer changes us. He further suggests that "we

156. Luther, 80–81.
157. Luther, vol. 14, 228.
158. Luther, vol. 30, 324.
159. Luther, vol. 3, 287.
160. Luther, 289.
161. Luther, vol. 4, 56.
162. Luther, vol. 7, 60.
163. Luther, 233.
164. Luther, vol. 6, 234.
165. Luther, vol. 3, 288.
166. Luther, vol. 25, 365.
167. Luther, vol. 42, 47.

pray against ourselves," because as we pray that God's will should be done,[168] we are asking God for the way of the cross.[169]

In discussing Luther's treatment of prayer, Hans-Martin Barth rightly points out that prayer for Luther is first and foremost about the honour of God's name, God's kingdom, and God's will.[170] Barth further points out that for Luther, prayer is spawned and sustained by the Spirit, but it is also a struggle of faith, for Jacob wrestled with God at the Jabbok.[171] Luther describes such wrestling prayers as "outstanding."[172] Oswald Bayer also notes this emphasis, writing that for Luther, knowing God and engaging God is "learned all over again within the duress of agonizing struggles and afflictions."[173]

Along with prayer, Luther emphasizes the need for reflecting on Scripture (*meditatio*), which he describes as an "ardent . . . reflection about what the Holy Spirit means here."[174] For Luther, Scripture offers us wisdom about how we are to live. Luther encourages people to "know it [Scripture] word for word, by heart,"[175] and he also encourages daily spiritual practices, including recitation of the Lord's Prayer, the creed, and the psalms.[176]

Finally, Luther's emphasis on the importance of personal spiritual practices includes a rich discussion of the work of the Holy Spirit as well as openness to mystical encounters. While Luther stresses that one should not be preoccupied with the Spirit apart from the word,[177] he says that the Spirit works mediatively through word and Sacrament and also through human activity.[178] Even "natural gifts and activities" are to be understood in the light of the Spirit,[179] whose most basic task is to bring us again and again to Christ.[180]

Influenced by the medieval Christian mystic, Johannes Tauler, Luther employs mystical language, speaking of seeing Christ with the "eyes of the soul" and using "expressions like 'the mystical Christ' [or] 'mystical eyes'"

168. Luther, vol. 42, 48.
169. Luther, 49.
170. Barth, *Theology of Martin Luther*, 360.
171. Barth, 360.
172. Luther, *Luther's Works*, vol. 7, 327.
173. Bayer, *Martin Luther's Theology*, 31.
174. Bayer, 34.
175. Barth, *Theology of Martin Luther*, 362.
176. Barth, 363.
177. Lohse, *Martin Luther's Theology*, 238.
178. Lohse, 237, 235.
179. Lohse, 236.
180. Lohse, 234.

in describing one's life with God.[181] Bengt Hoffman notes that this mystical knowledge of God is an "awesome and joyful knowledge beyond purely rational knowledge" and that "it is heart rather than head, but never the one without the other."[182] He concludes that "mystical knowledge *was* part of Luther's spirituality, but it was not free-floating; it was rooted in the justifying *kerygma* of Scripture."[183]

This discussion reveals Luther's great emphasis on personal spirituality. Yet his engagement with spirituality was not settled and static, but rather paradoxical. As Oswald Bayer points out, Luther's spirituality struggles between the "sinning human being and the justifying God," or "between one Lord and the many lords."[184] Jane Strohl argues that while Luther's "spirituality was always intensely sacramental," it was also characterized by "desolation and ecstasy," by "the dark of the soul," and by an "awareness of the numinous quality of God."[185]

The Two Kingdoms or Two Governments

Luther's controversial formulation of the two kingdoms has been much debated, and thus I have saved it for last, though systematically it should have followed the above discussion of faith and works. Hans-Martin Barth comments that the "two-kingdoms or two governments doctrine" has been "most controversial" and "misused," and it has spawned a "flood of secondary literature."[186] Gerhard Ebeling agrees that the two-kingdoms concept has been "much disputed, misinterpreted, and misused."[187]

Bernard Lohse, however, makes the important point that this doctrine should not be the "heart of Luther's theology," even though it has "extraordinary significance."[188] The significance lies in the fact that Luther untangled the intertwined relationship of church and state in the medieval world by proposing that even though the word belongs to the church and the sword belonged to

---

181. Hoffman, "Lutheran Spirituality," 124, 127.

182. Hoffman, 127.

183. Hoffman, 128.

184. Bayer, *Martin Luther's Theology*, 40, 36.

185. Strohl, "Luther's Spiritual Journey," 152–53, 150–51.

186. Barth, *Theology of Martin Luther*, 313.

187. Ebeling, *Luther*, 178.

188. Lohse, *Martin Luther's Theology*, 315, 316.

the state, "God has ordained both."[189] Moreover, since God has ordained both, the Christian is to play a role in both the church and the state, because "the Christian is under two governments."[190] In other words, the Christian lives before God in family and the church, but also lives before God in taking various roles and tasks in society. In this construction, some key questions arise. First, what does it mean to be a Christian layperson or clergy? Second, what does it mean to be a judge, soldier, or politician as a Christian? Third, what is the relationship between these two spheres? Fourth, is one sphere on a different spiritual level than the other?

Before we entertain these and other related questions, it is important to offer some definitional clarity. While Luther speaks of two kingdoms and two governments, Hans-Martin Barth suggests that it is more consistent to speak of Luther's "two-government's doctrine."[191] Quoting Luther, "God has ordained two governments: the spiritual by which the Holy Spirit produces Christians and righteous people under Christ; and the temporal which constrains the un-Christian and wicked" and seeks to create "outward peace."[192]

Luther's notion of two governments is complemented by his discussion of God's right hand and God's left hand. The right hand symbolizes God's rule in the church, and the left symbolizes God's creating and preserving work, where "God protects creation from destroying itself."[193] More positively, Barth notes that Luther sees societal governance as part of God's left hand, expressing the use "of power for the good of humanity."[194] Concretely, this means that God's left hand supports the punishment of the wicked, the protection of the good, and the preservation of peace.[195]

This discussion must be understood within the frame of the masks of God, by which Luther is referring to God's mysterious and often hidden work in both the church and the world. Robert Jenson argues that for Luther, God is first hidden in "the way he rules his creation."[196] Within the church, the masks of God are evidenced in the issues of grace and law, the nature of the gospel, the mystery of the incarnation, and Christ's death on the cross. Simply

---

189. Lohse, 319.

190. Lohse, 320.

191. Barth, *Theology of Martin Luther*, 316. Barth comments that for Luther, the kingdom of God is "the realm within which God rules" (316). Thus the core issue is one of governance.

192. Barth, 319.

193. Barth, 319.

194. Barth, 321.

195. Barth, 321–22.

196. Jenson, "Luther's Contemporary Theological Significance," 279.

put, God's way in the church is not one of blinding clarity, but rather we are called to the agonizing walk of faith and the struggle to discern God's ways and wisdom. In particular, Luther highlights the *Deus absconditus* in the cross of Christ, writing that we "honor him as he is hidden in his sufferings," and faith is "understanding in concealment."[197] Thus Robert Jenson argues that for Luther, the "cross was the place of a second hiding of God."[198]

Similarly, it can be a struggle of faith to see God at work in the world through human institutions and governmental rule. Luther notes that work in politics and the economy are also the "masks of God."[199] On the one hand, these domains are ordained by God,[200] and thus the work of princes, judges, and state officials can be seen as "pure holiness"[201] in that they are called to create well-being, justice, and peace. But on the other hand, the use of the "sword" (e.g. state punishment) also confronts us. Though Luther calls princes "the worst scoundrels"[202] in the way that they abuse their power,[203] he nevertheless holds that "war and killing . . . have been instituted by God," and he says that those in authority do these things on behalf of God because it is "God who hangs, tortures, beheads, kills, and fights."[204] This is most confronting language, indeed!

The interplay of God's masks and God's right and left hands reveals that Luther's concept of two governments is not straightforward, but a number of things are clear. First, Luther's concept of two governments gives the societal sphere its own identity and integrity. In other words, this concept attempts to outline a theology of culture and society.[205] Hans-Martin Barth comments that in this formulation, Luther argues that "church should again be church" and that the world should be given "back its own dignity and value."[206] Second, this formulation does not suggest that Luther sees the state as an entity and law unto itself, for the state has the God-given task to punish the wicked,

197. Lohse, *Martin Luther's Theology*, 216.

198. Jenson, "Luther's Contemporary Theological Significance," 279.

199. Barth, *Theology of Martin Luther*, 326.

200. Luther writes, "governing authority and its sword are a divine service" (*Luther's Works*, vol. 45, 103).

201. Barth, *Theology of Martin Luther*, 320.

202. Luther, *Luther's Works*, vol. 45, 113.

203. Luther, 109.

204. Barth, *Theology of Martin Luther*, 322.

205. This topic has been ably attempted by Charles Mathewes, *Theology of Public Life*. However, there is no discussion of Luther's contribution.

206. Barth, *Theology of Martin Luther*, 314.

protect the good, and preserve peace.[207] Hans-Martin Barth further observes that Luther was not teaching that the secular order "was independent of God's commandment and ordinance."[208] Third – against the Anabaptists – Luther justifies that the Christian can and should play a role in government, even when that involves judging a person to the gallows or serving in a so-called "just" (defensive) war. Luther pontificates that the Christian is "to serve and assist the sword [government] by whatever means you can."[209] With unequivocal clarity, Luther says that the "governing authority and its sword are a divine service."[210] Finally, the above is made a little clearer by Luther's core concept that the Christian lives "simultaneously" before God and before the neighbour.[211] Before God, the Christian lives the Sermon on the Mount, and before the neighbour, the Christian lives Romans 13:1–4. Thus, while the Christian living before God should willingly suffer wrong, the Christian living before the neighbour should seek justice via the left hand of God (through the use of the sword). Luther makes it very clear that Christians "are not to use the secular authority for themselves," but only as "divine service" for the neighbour. Thus, Christians in civil service are "those who arrest, prosecute, execute, and destroy the wicked, and who protect, acquit, and serve the good."[212]

For Luther, this formulation clarifies how God is just as concerned about the church and the kingdom of God[213] and the state of society and those who govern it. The simple implication is that for Luther, the Christian bears a double responsibility and carries a double mandate. Thus, the Christian is called to maintain both the church and society, and therefore service within the society is just as holy as service in the church. This raises several difficult ambiguities. On the one hand, Luther argues that "temporal government, next to the preaching office, is the highest service to God and the most useful office on earth," and that those in government "are to be His [God's] assistants," and that these officials are channels of God's goodness.[214] On the other hand, Luther

207. Barth, 321–22.

208. Barth, 315.

209. Luther, *Luther's Works*, vol. 45, 95.

210. Luther, 103.

211. Barth, *Theology of Martin Luther*, 331.

212. Luther, *Luther's Works*, vol. 45, 102–3.

213. Luther does not identify the church and the kingdom of God. He writes that the "church is the kingdom of God," but qualifies this by saying, "God alone rules, speaks, works, and is glorified in her" (vol. 44, 379). For a helpful general discussion, see Howard Snyder, *Models of the Kingdom*.

214. Luther, *Luther's Works*, vol. 13, 51, 55.

acknowledges that those in government often do not do good because they abuse their power when they "strip and fleece" the people and "heap tax upon tax."[215] Nevertheless, Luther wants Christians to function in governmental roles and to see this as a "divine service" by serving the society as those "who arrest, prosecute, execute, and destroy the wicked, and who protect, acquit, defend, and serve the good."[216]

We can draw several conclusions from this formulation. First, Luther saw Christians as playing a very big role in the family, church, and society. As David Whitford notes, according to Luther, "Christians can and should play a role in the civil life of their community."[217] Second, Luther seemed to perceive that the role of Christians in society would contribute to social stability[218] at the cost of social justice, even though he called those in government to achieve social good.[219]

Many scholars have commented on Luther's two-government position. Bernard Lohse holds that Luther basically sees the Christian as two persons. First, there are one's Christian responsibilities by virtue of one's private relationship to others. Second, there are one's responsibilities towards others based on one's particular social position and role.[220] In other words, the Christian "under both governments"[221] has to live in this tension, however difficult that might be.

Hans-Martin Barth sees Luther as giving Christians "two different and even mutually contradictory roles to fulfill."[222] First, each of us personally is to "govern yourself by the gospel and suffer injustice toward yourself."[223] But in our role within civil government, via the left hand of God, we are to "tolerate no injustice towards the neighbour."[224] Barth's broad conclusion is

215. Luther, vol. 45, 109.

216. Luther, 103.

217. Whitford, *Luther*, 116.

218. Barth says simply that Luther was "basically a conservative type" when it came to societal matters and that he accepted the orderly power of authority (*Theology of Martin Luther*, 468).

219. It is interesting to note that Luther places a higher demand on a Christian prince. He writes, "a Christian prince must . . . lay aside any intent . . . to proceed with force." And he continues that all works should be "done in love" and "directed wholeheartedly toward the benefit, honor, comfort, and salvation of others" (*Luther's Works*, vol. 45, 118).

220. Lohse, *Martin Luther's Theology*, 321.

221. Lohse, 320.

222. Barth, *Theology of Martin Luther*, 331.

223. Barth, 332.

224. Barth, 332.

that Luther holds to an "orderly Corpus christianum," but fails to deliver a coherent theology for church and state relationships.[225] Nevertheless, Barth says that Luther sought "to preserve the right and dignity of the world" and to liberate society from the "theocratic system of the papal church" in its role in society.[226] Simply put, Luther contributed to the modern understanding of the separation of church and state and thus contributed to modernity.

Both Ernst Troeltsch and Karl Barth[227] are critical of Luther's concept of the two governments, arguing that Luther implicitly creates two separate spheres of life.[228] As a result, Luther could be seen as advocating one form of spirituality for one's private and ecclesiastical life and another form of spirituality for one's role in secular society. Leonardo Boff thus charges Luther with promoting a "gospel that has nothing to do with the things of the world" because it fails to "call the secular structures themselves into question."[229]

H. Richard Niebuhr shares similar concerns, acknowledging that Luther is a "dynamic and dialectical thinker," but his so-called followers made the mistake of casting Luther in undialectical terms.[230] Nevertheless, Niebuhr charges Luther with reflecting a fundamental dualism.[231] At the personal level, the Christian lives by the law of Christ, but in one's political role, the Christian must "use force to defend his neighbors against force."[232] Niebuhr concludes that in this scheme of things, "there is no solution of the dilemma this side of death."[233] Building on Niebuhr's analysis, it should not surprise us that Howard Snyder typifies Luther as promoting the kingdom of God as an "inner spiritual experience."[234]

225. Barth, 337, 341.

226. Barth, 341.

227. Will Herberg notes Karl Barth's thoroughgoing "indictment of Nazi totalitarianism," not only because "it does many wrongs and evil things, but because by its self-divinizing pretensions" it now should be seen not as a "'lawful' state envisaged in Romans 13, but 'the beast out of the abyss' of Revelation 13" ("The Social Philosophy of Karl Barth," 45).

228. Barth, *Theology of Martin Luther*, 338–39.

229. Barth, 212–15.

230. Niebuhr, *Christ and Culture*, 179.

231. Niebuhr, 170.

232. Niebuhr, 178.

233. Niebuhr, 178.

234. Snyder, *Models of the Kingdom*, 46–48.

Conclusion

In engaging these themes in Luther's writings, we can draw some broad conclusions about missional spirituality. First, Luther sees faith in Christ as a dynamic and life-changing reality. The Christian is to be grounded in the word of God, be a person of prayer, and be formed by spiritual practices. When we are empowered by God, spiritual practices and service will follow. As Luther puts it, the first reality must always be that a Christian "become[s] good through the regeneration of the Spirit."[235] For the Word of God in the believer "bears fruit" through the work of the "constant and brave Spirit."[236]

Second, Luther places a strong emphasis on faith and works. Because the Christian lives before both God and neighbour, a life of faith will issue forth in love and good works, for "a Christian lives not in himself, but in Christ and in his neighbor."[237]

Third, Luther does not promote a triumphalist spirituality. Instead, the Christian lives out a Christo-centric faith in the way of the cross – or a cruciform spirituality. As Janet Strohl notes, Luther's spirituality is grounded in the weakness of the cross and the mystery of the saving truth of the gospel.[238]

Fourth, Luther flips the more traditional spirituality of the Middle Ages on its head. He refuses to believe that monks, clerics, and those in religious orders (such as the Franciscans and Dominicans) live a higher form of spirituality than those who are part of the parish church, living out daily life in marriage and work. Rather, Luther argues that those living the "ordinary" lives of family, farming, education, and industry are living a true spirituality in Christ through the Spirit, inspired by the gospel.

Finally, Luther promotes the idea that the Christian is called to live out a spirituality amidst all the difficulties and ambiguities of life, including being involved in maintaining the good order of society as servants of the government.

Luther teaches that our incorporation into Christ and the power of our new status through justification by faith will be the driver for our love of neighbour and seeking to serve God within the wider society. Luther highlights that "good works without faith cannot happen, and . . . faith without works cannot endure."[239] Thus for Luther, we cannot put spirituality in one box and service and mission in another box.

---

235. Luther, *Luther's Works*, vol. 12, 385.

236. Luther, 388.

237. Barth, *Theology of Martin Luther*, 178.

238. Strohl, "Luther's Spiritual Journey," 151.

239. Luther, *Luther's Works*, vol. 44, 242.

When Luther speaks of Christian service and witness, he has in mind the task of the church in its proclamation of the good news. In this task, he believes that the church should be humble before God, "but bold in relation to the world."[240] Moreover, because "Christ does not want to hide in the world," we are *all* called to "preach these blessings of His [Christ].[241] Thus Luther challenges "all the devout" to "prepare themselves so that they are not afraid of becoming martyrs, that is, confessors and witnesses of God."[242] Hans-Martin Barth concurs that Luther held "that every Christian has the duty to witness to the Gospel."[243]

Luther also calls Christians to a whole gamut of good works, noting that God can work sovereignly in the world to do God's good, but "He [God] wants us . . . to have a share in His workings."[244] This good includes serving our family, the faith-community, and our neighbour. He writes: "do well to everyone, including your enemies . . . visit the sick and the prisoners . . . stretch out your hand to all who are in want."[245]

The controversial domain of Christian service in Luther's theology is the Christian's role in social institutions and government. Luther believes that Christians should be willing to do the hard work of keeping society safe and peaceful, and so he argues that Christians should be willing to be jailers, police, soldiers, judges, governors. But while maintaining good order is paramount, Luther also sees those in power as being able to do much social good. Thus, Luther proposes that we "protect and guard against violence and force," but also "endow hospitals and help poor people."[246]

While Luther did not start traditional mission organizations, he believed that both Jews and Turks (Muslims) could be won to Christ. As David Whitford notes, Luther's main view of the Jews was "in terms of their possible conversion to Christianity," and he quotes Luther, who says that "one should treat the Jews in a kindly manner."[247] But over time, Luther was disappointed in this possibility. In his "On the Jews and Their Lies" (1543), he advocated extreme violence against the Jews. As Hans-Martin Barth comments, "what is

240. Luther, vol. 12, 384.

241. Luther, 383, 386.

242. Luther, 383.

243. Barth, *Theology of Martin Luther*, 256.

244. Luther, *Luther's Works*, vol. 3, 288.

245. Luther, vol. 52, 246.

246. Luther, vol. 13, 55, 53.

247. Whitford, *Luther*, 154–55.

unforgivable is the lovelessness . . . in his polemic, especially in his late anti-Jewish and anti-papal writings."[248]

Most broadly, Luther's theology lacks an eschatological orientation that sees the reign of God breaking into all the dimensions of life. Karl Barth stresses that "our task in response to the gospel is to obey God's will for society as well as for our own individual lives."[249] And in the words of Hendrikus Berkhof, the Christian hope involves the "sanctification of the world."[250] Finally, Jürgen Moltmann says that the "hope of resurrection . . . demands hope for a this-worldly liberation in all its aspects."[251]

But Luther clearly saw the Christian life as a life of faith that would be marked by a cruciform spirituality, sustained by communal practices, while living out love of God and love of neighbour by taking responsibility for family, the church, and the institutions of society. This vision links spirituality and service, calling Christians to a broad role in society. Yet it fails to emphasize the prophetic role of Christians in calling governments and other institutions into question when they no longer serve the common good. When our structural powers no longer serve the common good, they need to be resisted.[252]

It needs to be noted, however, that no matter how helpful Luther has been in formulating many of the themes of Protestantism, one cannot but come away from reading him without some concerns. But the most disturbing thought is whether Luther with his later "violent" use of language in relation to the Jews and his too benign view of the role of government sowed seeds which help to explain why the Lutheran Church so readily succumbed to Nazi ideology.

248. Barth, *Theology of Martin Luther*, 303.

249. Hebblethwaite, *The Christian Hope*, 133.

250. Hebblethwaite, 189.

251. Hebblethwaite, 181.

252. Ringma, *Resist the Powers*.

11

Bonhoeffer's Passion for Renewing the Church and its Witness in Troubled Times

Introduction

In this chapter, I will follow the same format as the previous chapter on Luther, mining the writings of Dietrich Bonhoeffer in order to construct a missional spirituality. It will be much easier to engage Bonhoeffer through this lens for several reasons. First, he is more missionally explicit than Luther. Second, Bonhoeffer's writings are more fragmentary and less extensive than Luther's. Third, Bonhoeffer is more contemporary than Luther and thus more accessible. Fourth, while both Luther and Bonhoeffer are largely absent in many missiological texts,[1] Bonhoeffer (unlike Luther)[2] is appearing in some contemporary missiologies.[3]

Many readers may be familiar with the central contours of Bonhoeffer's life,[4] but the important themes in constructing a missional spirituality include the following: his focus on a lived Christology based on the Sermon on the Mount, his practice of Christian community, his emphasis on the spiritual disciplines, his training of clergy, his ecumenical involvement, his resistance to the Nazification of the German church, and his reflections about Christian

---

1. For example, Philips and Coote, *Towards the 21st Century in Christian Mission*; Wrogemann, *Theologies of Mission*; Van Engen, *Mission on the Way*.

2. Bosch, *Transforming Mission*, is an important exception.

3. For example, see Steenland and Goff, *New Evangelical Social Engagement*; Stackhouse, *Making the Best of It*.

4. For two brief biographies, see Robertson, *The Shame and the Sacrifice*; Wind, *A Spoke in the Wheel*. For a monumental biography, see Bethge, *Dietrich Bonhoeffer*.

witness in a secular world. Yet the most salient points that I wish to make in this exploration are as follows.

First, Bonhoeffer sought to live the gospel, including the "hard" sayings of Jesus. Second, he was committed to the church as a prophetic community. Third, he had a heart for and a committed praxis to the poor and marginalized minorities, including the Jews. Fourth, he believed that the faith-community should be a community of resistance to all expressions of idolatrous governmental power. Fifth, he lived a "hidden" piety. Finally, he wrestled with seeing the new world that would come into being post-WWII.

None of these themes, however, should dismiss the complexity of trying to understand the various phases of Bonhoeffer's life[5] and the wide variety of interpretations of his writings.[6] Most basically put, de Gruchy identifies three distinct phases in Bonhoeffer's life: "discipleship and community, then involvement in the struggle for peace and justice, and finally the nature of faith in a secular age."[7]

Some Personal Reflections

I have never believed in the present-day emphasis on a self-constructed individualism, as I believe in the importance of the influence of extended family, friendships, community, and strategies of cooperation. As a result, I have been open to learning from others and have not been reticent to adopt certain "heroes" in the Christian faith. Bonhoeffer has been one such a "hero."[8] In the process of adopting Bonhoeffer, I have engaged in a strategy of *adaptation*. My concern has not been, "how can I be *like* Dietrich Bonhoeffer," but rather, "what can I learn from him?" and "in what ways can he challenge me?" In this process, I have sought to engage with someone whom I saw as a radical other.[9]

5. Bethge identifies three major phases: "The Lure of Theology" (1906–1931), "The Cost of Being a Christian" (1931–1940), and "Sharing Germany's Destiny" (1940–1945) (*Dietrich Bonhoeffer*, v–viii). For a similar formulation by Bethge, see de Gruchy, "Reception of Bonhoeffer's Theology," 97.

6. See Haynes, *Bonhoeffer Phenomenon.*

7. de Gruchy, "The Reception of Bonhoeffer's Theology," 103.

8. Bonhoeffer makes clear that "human beings are not heroes," but that they are just called to do "God's will" (*Bonhoeffer Works*, vol. 12, 462).

9. While I am not enamoured with Miroslav Volf's formulation of the concept of "catholicity of persons," I am in agreement with the notion that we have a corporate identity, both as Christians and as members of society (*After Our Likeness*, 278).

Bonhoeffer first came to my attention in the early 1960s when I was required to read *The Cost of Discipleship* in an ethics course. I had entered seminary on the heels of working in Indigenous communities in Western Australia and had witnessed their suffering and marginalisation firsthand, along with the complicity of both the government and church in contributing to that suffering. Thus, I was deeply impacted by Bonhoeffer's emphasis on how the suffering of Christ calls us to *identify* with the Suffering One rather than propelling us into the land of triumphal bliss.

Following seminary training, I began to work with street people and drug-addicted youth in Brisbane, Australia,[10] where Bonhoeffer continued to inspire and challenge me. First, his book *Life Together* guided us as we sought to establish therapeutic Christian communities in our work with these young people rather than institutional rehabilitation centres. Second, his book *Ethics*, along with his resistance to the idolatry of Hitler, played a key role in our attempts to expose serious police corruption in Brisbane,[11] and these attempts cost us dearly. Though the Christian community and society in general respected us for our work of drug-prevention education, counselling, prison work, and programs assisting people in their journey towards wholeness, they did not like our advocacy and justice work, and so they consequently withdrew much of their financial support.

There are two more impactful dimensions of my encounter with Bonhoeffer. First, in our work with drug users, we eventually formed an interdenominational faith-community, Jubilee Fellowship, which led me to explore Bonhoeffer's ecclesiology[12] and later to write *Catch the Wind.* Second, over a long period of using Bonhoeffer's writings for reflective readings, I wrote *Seize the Day with Dietrich Bonhoeffer.*[13] From these brief personal reflections, it should be obvious that Bonhoeffer has been an important and lasting influence on my life and ministry. I am deeply grateful!

10. See Grant-Thomson, *Jodie's Story.*

11. This later led to the Fitzgerald Inquiry, which resulted in criminal charges being brought against the police commissioner and some government ministers and led to their subsequent imprisonment. For the full report, see www.ccc.qld.gov.au/about-the ccc/the fitzgerald-inquiry. I also write about these events in chapter 8 ("Grand Design and Fragile Engagement: The Church's Calling in a Troubled World").

12. Ringma, "A Critical Evaluation of the Ecclesiology of Dietrich Bonhoeffer."

13. See also Ringma, "Dietrich Bonhoeffer: His Life, Theology and Praxis and Their Implications for Ecumenism."

Finding the Vulnerable Bonhoeffer

When I mention above that I looked to Bonhoeffer as a "hero," I do not mean that in a traditional sense, for I was not looking to be inspired by a "superman," but rather was seeking encouragement from someone who was honest about the difficulties and challenges he faced in the midst of life's struggles. In all that Bonhoeffer sought to do, he was no winner, but he sought to be faithful in following Christ amidst troubling circumstances as his church succumbed to Nazi ideology and "normal" society crumbled around him.[14] And even though he was an intensely private person,[15] he was willing to talk about his struggles and fears.[16] In *Letters and Papers*, he writes, "we are only too familiar with life's anxieties and with all the other destructive effects of prolonged personal insecurity."[17] Elsewhere, he notes that fear "hollows out . . . [one's] insides" and is a "fog spreading over everything."[18] While he acknowledges that "we exist in unrest," he concludes that "rest is with God."[19] In *The Cost of Discipleship*, he points out that "to rely on Christ's word" in difficult circumstances "provides greater security."[20] And elsewhere he proclaims that Christ "alone is Lord over fear."[21]

Yet Bonhoeffer's life circumstances were not his only challenge, for there were also personality issues. Eberhard Bethge, Bonhoeffer's confidant and biographer, notes that even from an early age, Bonhoeffer had a "lifelong preoccupation with whether and how he would face up to death," and that his two constant companions were "*tristia* and *accidie*."[22] In Bonhoeffer's poetry, he reveals some of his innermost struggles, speaking of being "restless and longing and sick, like a bird in a cage," a person "of many scars," and someone who is "defiant" and "despondent" at the same time.[23] Throughout his writings, Bonhoeffer makes the point that even though "difficulties are magnified out of

14. Bonhoeffer rejects the notion that the official positions in the church should be filled "on the basis of political considerations," and he also rejects the intervention and interference of the state in the life and function of the church (see *Bonhoeffer Works*, vol. 12, 136).

15. Bonhoeffer, *Letters & Papers from Prison*, 158, 146.

16. In his prison writings, he speaks of being "restless and longing and sick, like a bird in a cage," and he generalizes by speaking of "we men of many scars" (349, 351).

17. Bonhoeffer, 16.

18. Bonhoeffer, *Works*, vol. 12, 455.

19. Bonhoeffer, vol. 15, 480.

20. Bonhoeffer, *Cost of Discipleship*, 69.

21. Bonhoeffer, *Works*, vol. 12, 456.

22. Bethge, *Dietrich Bonhoeffer: A Biography*, 38, 39.

23. Bonhoeffer, *Letters & Papers from Prison*, 348, 351.

all proportion . . . by fear and anxiety," it is the call of the gospel that "sympathy grows in proportion to the fear of approaching disaster" and that we can "transform our anxiety . . . into prayers" on behalf of others.[24]

I have also been particularly interested in the way that Bonhoeffer grounds the reality of his vulnerability in the Gospels and the person and work of Christ. Rather than denying his struggles and difficulties, Bonhoeffer links them directly to his identification with Christ, who is not only the suffering Messiah, but also the rejected one.[25] Thus, life's difficulties are not an "ordinary everyday calamity," but come our way because the "cross is laid on every Christian."[26] As Bonhoeffer puts it, "we have seen the exalted one, only as the crucified; the sinless one, only as the guilt-laden; the risen one, only as the humiliated."[27] Elsewhere, Bonhoeffer makes the point that "the 'must' of suffering applies to his disciples" as much as it applies to Christ.[28] At the same time, he emphasizes that Christ "stands between us and God" and "between us and all other men and things."[29] As such, Christ "shared our life and death, that we may partake of his life and death," which establishes our "righteousness."[30] Thus the Christian's security in a world of insecurity is "attachment to his [Christ's] person."[31]

I found all these insights most helpful, as we were certainly not winning the "war" on drugs, and we were not successful in the work of advocacy. But Bonhoeffer encouraged us by helping us identify that "Christ in his being" is "*pro me*," and in freedom, Christ "has bound his existence to me" as "brother" and as "the new creation."[32] Yet having Christ "for us" does not mean that we will have sparkling success. Rather, this strong and sustaining link with Christ opens us to *identificational* suffering, which is first expressed in our "baptismal death" and the "daily dying of . . . Christians." Moreover, this sustaining link is furthered in the reality of "suffering 'for him [Christ],'" culminating in

24. Bonhoeffer, 177, 13, 177.

25. Bonhoeffer, *Cost of Discipleship*, 76.

26. Bonhoeffer, 79.

27. Bonhoeffer, *Christ the Center*, 112.

28. Bonhoeffer, *Cost of Discipleship*, 77.

29. Bonhoeffer, 85.

30. Bonhoeffer, 247.

31. Bonhoeffer, 49.

32. Bonhoeffer, *Christ the Center*, 47, 48, 57.

what Bonhoeffer calls suffering "in a representative capacity" as a "vicarious activity."[33]

Knowing that Christ was *with* us and *for* us, even as we were immersed in this work with deeply wounded persons[34] and difficult circumstances – including a corrupt drug squad and churches that did not understand our advocacy work – was extremely helpful. For even as we flailed in a whirlpool of struggles, we sensed Christ holding us – and all along, Bonhoeffer continued to remind us that God would give us "strength . . . to resist in all time of distress" and that God would "bring good out of evil."[35]

Revelation, Scripture, and Faith

Bonhoeffer has been cast in various camps, ranging from post-Christian[36] to Protestant conservative.[37] While this debate will undoubtedly continue, Bonhoeffer is most clearly situated in the Lutheran tradition, with its emphasis on word and Spirit and the centrality of Christ.[38] While my particular concern for this chapter is with Bonhoeffer's implicit missional spirituality, I first need to set out some of the basic contours of his theology – both to overcome the problem of contextless extractionism and also to waylay the concerns of those in the evangelical movement who have dismissed Bonhoeffer as a liberal Christian "without a genuine commitment to the Christ of the New Testament."[39] Since I probably won't be able to allay all fears, Stephen Haynes offers a most helpful discussion of evangelicals and Bonhoeffer in *The Bonhoeffer Phenomenon*.[40]

To begin, I will briefly set out Bonhoeffer's position on Scripture and faith. In the next section, I will set out his Christology and his discussion of the church. Finally, I will focus on his spirituality and the mission of the faith-community.

In his earlier writings, Bonhoeffer speaks of the "word of God" as revealing "God's thought and will," and this word is "Jesus himself." He continues that

33. Bonhoeffer, *Cost of Discipleship*, 219–20.

34. See Ringma and Dickau, *The Art of Healing Prayer*.

35. Bonhoeffer, *Letters & Papers from Prison*, 11.

36. Haynes notes that some interpreters of Bonhoeffer also cast him as an "atheist" and "secularist" (*The Bonhoeffer Phenomenon*, 34).

37. Huntemann, *The Other Bonhoeffer*.

38. For example, he writes, "But in and with this Word comes none other than the Holy Spirit" (quoted in Kelly and Nelson, *The Cost of Moral Leadership*, 69).

39. Haynes, *Bonhoeffer Phenomenon*, 81.

40. Haynes, 65–97.

Jesus gives the promise "that God will establish God's kingdom and rule through him."[41] And he makes it clear that we are to "set our lives upon the word, to listen to God's thoughts and to do them."[42]

Digging a little deeper, Bonhoeffer notes that the most central concept is God's revelation, which is "found only in scripture."[43] Scripture "*gives witness*" to this revelation "where individuals hear it" because "God opens human" hearts and minds.[44] For Bonhoeffer, hearing the living word in the written word is the work of the Spirit, and thus hearing "is a prayer, a plea for the Holy Spirit."[45]

While Bonhoeffer gives place to historical-critical and other interpretive strategies in engaging Scripture,[46] his overarching concept is that in Scripture, "the risen one encounters us" because of "his presence in the church," and this "creates faith."[47] Since "Christ is *the* way," the Christian life is "the venture of faith and obedience in God's word."[48] Bonhoeffer holds that our life of faith becomes "one great act of trust in God," and he adds that "believing in God would take away our faith in all other powers."[49] Here Bonhoeffer provides us with a dynamic and practical vision of the authority of Scripture. Most fundamentally, Scripture addresses us in the living word, Jesus Christ, and calls us to his way, which relativizes every other way. In other words, the call of Christ undermines every other demand on our lives – familial, societal, or governmental.[50] While this makes the Christian life most precarious – in that it does not give the follower of Christ a "nice and neat" programme, but a life of "insecurity" through an "attachment" to Christ[51] – Bonhoeffer insists that this journey is marked by joy. He writes, "we learn to delight in Jesus like children" because the source "is God's joy in us."[52] Elsewhere, Bonhoeffer

41. Bonhoeffer, *Works*, vol. 9, 558–59.

42. Bonhoeffer, 561.

43. Bonhoeffer, 289.

44. Bonhoeffer, 289–90.

45. Bonhoeffer, 298.

46. Bonhoeffer, *Christ the Center*, 72.

47. Bonhoeffer, 74, 73.

48. Bonhoeffer, *Works*, vol. 15, 420–21.

49. Bonhoeffer, vol. 13, 405.

50. Bonhoeffer carefully makes the point that this "breach" with one's natural life is not at all a "contempt for life" (*Cost of Discipleship*, 85). Rather, it is a reorientation of one life with new priorities based on a new allegiance, the Lordship of God.

51. Bonhoeffer, 49.

52. Bonhoeffer, *Works*, vol. 15, 145–46.

states that the Christian's joy is "to rejoice in God, to think and pray gladly to God," and "to love being in God's presence."[53]

Thus, faith is not simply intellectual, but experiential and existential. Faith causes a rupture and displacement from the old and familiar and "binds them [the followers of Christ] to Jesus Christ alone."[54] According to Bonhoeffer, we learn "the meaning of faith" in discipleship, and "faith is only real when there is obedience."[55] At the same time, the life of faith is not about self-effort. He describes Christ's word as a "Spirit-impelled word," and he says that the Spirit puts "Christ in our hearts, creating faith and hope."[56] Moreover, the Spirit "*makes my heart willing to obey*."[57] Kelly and Nelson conclude that "Bonhoeffer never ceased to attribute the continued presence of Jesus Christ in the church-community to the life-giving power of the Holy Spirit."[58]

Bonhoeffer also takes pains to point out that even though each Christian lives by "God's justification," the life of faith is not and cannot be individualistic.[59] Rather, the Christian life is "community through . . . and in Jesus Christ," which is expressed by "daily desiring the redeeming Word." As a community in Christ, Christians need each other to be "a bearer and proclaimer of the divine word," and they are propelled on a mission to the world because they have been "struck by the Word" and so are called to proclaim it "to others."[60]

As part of the Christian life, Bonhoeffer also encourages personal meditative practices, writing that "God's daily new word is addressed to me," and therefore I am called to "silence and contemplation . . . to ponder" the words of Scripture "for a long time" and to "take God's word prayerfully into my heart."[61] In *Life Together*, he sets out these practices more fully. As Kelly and Nelson point out, following Jesus was not mere orthodoxy for Bonhoeffer, but right action under the "guidance of God's Word and Spirit.[62] For as he puts it, "I won't at any point be willing to sacrifice the Bible as this strange Word of God."[63]

53. Bonhoeffer, vol. 13, 377.
54. Bonhoeffer, *Cost of Discipleship*, 52–53.
55. Bonhoeffer, 53–54.
56. Quoted in Kelly and Nelson, *Cost of Moral Leadership*, 58–59.
57. Kelly and Nelson, 61.
58. Kelly and Nelson, 65.
59. Bonhoeffer, *Life Together*, 22.
60. Bonhoeffer, 22–23.
61. Bonhoeffer, *Works*, vol. 15, 517.
62. Kelly and Nelson, *The Cost of Moral Leadership*, 80.
63. Quoted in Kelly and Nelson, 79.

In *Ethics*, Bonhoeffer makes the point that Jesus Christ "is the centre and strength of the Bible, of the church, and of theology, but also of humanity, of reason, of justice, and of culture," and he says that "the most precious thing in Christianity is Jesus Christ Himself."[64] In his Christological lectures, Bonhoeffer says we are called to see Jesus Christ as word, sacrament, community, and "the Centre of History,"[65] proclaiming that Christ is "the centre of human existence, of history, and of nature."[66] This insight takes Christ out of the potential ghetto of the church and places him in the very centre of the world. While the centrality of Jesus in the church may seem to be more evident, it needs to renewed again and again. But his centrality in the world is hidden and thus needs to become more explicit through the missionizing activity of the church. However, this does not mean the construction of a new Christendom, for Bonhoeffer is careful to point out that the task of the church is not to create a "Christian culture," but to live and proclaim the crucified and risen Christ.[67] Society and the state continue as "secondary"[68] gifts of God, but the fallen world is still the world and the fallen woman or man are still creatures. Thus, the penultimate reality – the human societal condition – and the ultimate reality – God's renewing and redemptive purposes in Christ – are dynamically interrelated.[69] Put simply, life must be maintained so that the gospel of the fulness of life can be heard and embraced.

A number of themes stand out in these brief reflections. First, Bonhoeffer has a dynamic and interrelated understanding of revelation, Scripture, faith, and discipleship. Second, the Spirit brings revelation and empowerment. Third, Jesus, the living word, is not hidden away in the church, but is word, sacrament, community, and a hidden existential presence in life and society. Thus, Christ is for the faith-community and also for the world.

By clearly setting out this vision that Christ is *for* the church and *for* the world, Bonhoeffer articulates a world-engaging form of Christianity. Although "the church is the real body of Christ on earth"[70] and "does everything to win the world for salvation,"[71] Bonhoeffer emphasizes that "there is no community

64. Bonhoeffer, *Ethics*, 58.

65. Bonhoeffer, *Christ the Center*, 61.

66. Bonhoeffer, 60.

67. Bonhoeffer, *Ethics*, 61.

68. My terminology.

69. Bonhoeffer, *Ethics*, 138.

70. Bonhoeffer, *Works*, vol. 15, 422.

71. Bonhoeffer, 329.

with Jesus that is not at the same time *a call to service*,"[72] for the church remains a community of sinners in need of ongoing renewal. Thus, Bonhoeffer pleas for God to "give his witness anew into our hearts" so that "our spiritual life becomes stronger" and we look to "God's Spirit" to help the community of faith "daily and hourly."[73]

Christology and Ecclesiology

Before "mining" Bonhoeffer's writings for a missional spirituality, I will outline the broad signposts of Bonhoeffer's theology, acknowledging all the scholarship that his writings have generated. First, "Bonhoeffer's theology throughout is informed by his Christology."[74] Second, "Bonhoeffer's Christocentric spirituality" animated his life and service.[75] Third, his concept of sociality is expressed through human relationality[76] and Christological community, for Bonhoeffer describes the church as "Christ existing as community."[77] Finally, Bonhoeffer highlights the concept of "deputyship," which he defines as "responsible action on behalf of others."[78] These signposts cannot be outlined in distinct phases, as they are woven into the tapestry of Bonhoeffer's entire life, what John de Gruchy describes as "continuities in Bonhoeffer's theological development."[79]

Thus, for Bonhoeffer, Christology and ecclesiology are intimately linked, as the church is incarnated in the world and exists for the world. Put more strongly, the heart of Bonhoeffer's missiology is that the church is to be the presence of Christ in the world.

Christology

Clearly, one can't talk about any aspect of Bonhoeffer's theology without touching on the theme of Christ or the church. But in this section, we will

72. Bonhoeffer, 544.

73. Bonhoeffer, 35, 40.

74. de Gruchy, "The Reception of Bonhoeffer's Theology," 102.

75. Kelly, "Prayer and Action for Justice: Bonhoeffer's Spirituality," 251.

76. Green, "Human Sociality and Christian Community," 115.

77. In German, *Christus als Gemeinde existierend* (Green, "Human Sociality and Christian Community," 120).

78. Green, "Human Sociality and Christian Community," 128.

79. de Gruchy, "The Reception of Bonhoeffer's Theology," 101.

look more specifically at Bonhoeffer's Christology before exploring the theme of the church more fully.

Bonhoeffer acknowledges the Trinitarian formulation, writing that "there are not three Gods, but only one," and "God is fully God as Creator and Father, as Jesus Christ, and as the Holy Spirit."[80] Yet this formulation is not the way to a pristine clarity, for he says that knowing God will only deepen our sense of "how mysterious God is."[81] At the same time, he clearly identifies "the trinitarian God . . . as the incarnate one" and "Jesus Christ" as the "unveiled image of God."[82] In Christ, he proclaims, "God became human like us, so that we might become divine."[83] Bonhoeffer's Christology also casts the incarnation in terms of the descent of God. He writes that "God is not ashamed of human lowliness but goes right into the middle of it," for "the throne of God in the world is set not on the thrones of humankind but in humanity's deepest abyss, in the manger."[84] Bonhoeffer also stresses the concept of *kenosis*, speaking of God as having "become a poor, wretched, unknown, and unsuccessful human being.[85]

At the same time, Bonhoeffer speaks of the Lordship of Christ. The faith-community is to be "obedient solely to him [Christ]," because Christ alone is the great life giver,[86] and "the redemption" of God is in him.[87] Bonhoeffer explains how "God . . . set the beginning once through his forgiving and renewing word in Jesus Christ, that is in my baptism, in my rebirth, in my conversion,"[88] which is the source of Bonhoeffer's life and his life of obedience. Thus, the Lordship of Christ is to be understood in terms of *my* life. According to Bonhoeffer, *I* am "a person before God," and Christ stands where *I* "have failed," and Christ is the "judgement and justification" of *my* life – and of all humanity, since Christ is "for the whole of human existence."[89]

Yet the Lordship of Christ is not only to be understood in terms of the individual Christian or the church, which is intended to be a representation of

80. Bonhoeffer, *Works*, vol. 13, 363.
81. Bonhoeffer, 362.
82. Bonhoeffer, *Christ the Center*, 105.
83. Bonhoeffer, *Works*, vol. 13, 362.
84. Bonhoeffer, 344–45.
85. Bonhoeffer, vol. 15, 111.
86. Bonhoeffer, 30.
87. Bonhoeffer, 499.
88. Bonhoeffer, 497.
89. Bonhoeffer, *Christ the Center*, 61, 65.

Christ, as this could lead to spiritual inwardness and a world-denying form of Christianity. Rather, Christ's Lordship is over the whole world – though this is not intended to be understood in the sense of the old Christendom. For "in Jesus Christ the reality of God entered into the reality of the world,"[90] and so there is no aspect of life that has nothing to do with Christ. Thus, the Christian cannot say, "Christ has nothing to do with economics or the arts or politics," and there should be no such a thing as a Christian who "seeks Christ without the world, or . . . seeks the world without Christ."[91] The church and the world cannot be separated into "two spheres,"[92] because the world does not exist "independently of the revelation of God in Christ."[93]

To summarize, Scripture speaks about God, creation, the fall, redemption, the people of God, and God's final future of a new heaven and a new earth. And Scripture also speaks about family, the broader human community, governance, as well as personal and social values. Thus, Bonhoeffer says that "the whole reality of the world is already drawn into Christ,"[94] meaning that in Christ's death and resurrection, the whole of humanity and the whole world is taken up redemptively. Those who have come to faith acknowledge this and seek to live by the inspiration of Christ's salvific work, and those who have not yet embraced the abundant grace of God in Christ have nevertheless been provided for by Christ's death and resurrection. Thus, the missional task of the church is to proclaim to the world what God has already done for them in Christ.

For Bonhoeffer, Christology is not only the centre of the faith-community, but is *the* central "ontological question,"[95] because Christ "is the new humanity."[96] In other words, Christ is not simply one faith option among many faith options, nor is Christ for some to the exclusion of many, nor is Christ simply for a life of interior peace or a way to go to heaven. Rather, Christ is the icon of the new humanity, and so we can only be truly human when we are grounded in Christ, who takes shape and grows in us. In his incarnation, death, and resurrection, Christ is not simply an example of who we are to become, but who we already are in him. Christ is God's great provisionality of what humanity is to be like.

90. Bonhoeffer, *Ethics*, 192.

91. Bonhoeffer, 194.

92. Bonhoeffer, 195.

93. Bonhoeffer, 195.

94. Bonhoeffer, 195.

95. Bonhoeffer, *Christ the Center*, 32.

96. Bonhoeffer, 48.

The sheer beauty of this personal and world-altering reality is that the "unfolding" of this new life is not inspired or sustained by some form of self-effort, for both the word of Christ and the blessing of the Spirit bring about the gift of the "in-Christ" relationship. As Bonhoeffer puts it, "all men [women] are 'with Christ' as a consequence of the Incarnation," but the Christian is with Christ "in a special sense" through a "baptismal death which is the fountain of grace."[97] The calling of the faith-community is to proclaim this good news to the world.

In summary, Bonhoeffer emphasizes that the incarnation, death, and resurrection of Christ are formative for humanity and the world, demonstrating a Christology that is not simply for the church as an isolated community set apart from the rest of the world, but rather is intrinsic to the whole social order and a future world in God's final purposes. This reflects the high Christology of the Pauline epistles and has profound implications for how we understand the nature and task of the church in its mission to the world.

Ecclesiology

As mentioned above, Bonhoeffer draws an intimate connection between Christology and ecclesiology. His life circumstances highlight this connection, as he had pastoral duties in the Lutheran church, taught theology, made a commitment to accompany urban young people in their faith formation, and he was a part of international discussions in the ecumenical movement. These duties took on difficult and threatening contours with the gradual infiltration of Nazi ideology into the life of the church. Because the very nature of the church was under threat, Bonhoeffer, along with others, was forced to think more deeply about the nature of church, the extent of its compromise, and whether it still constituted the church of Jesus Christ. It did not take long before Bonhoeffer and others reached the momentous conclusion that a "true" church – the Confessing Church – had to be formed.[98]

The initial two issues that led to this decision were the "Fuhrer principle" and the "Aryan paragraph." The first demanded loyalty to Hitler, which included the church. Bonhoeffer critiques such loyalty as giving one's allegiance

97. Bonhoeffer, *Cost of Discipleship*, 215, 207.

98. Bonhoeffer sets out the main theological discussions that established the basis for the formation of the Confessing Church in *Works*, vol. 12. In this volume, it is evident that several different groups, most of which included Bonhoeffer, played a part in the call for the church to resist Fascist ideas.

to a "superhuman"[99] and buying into a false "messianic idea."[100] He sees this as a reduction of the individual to a "collective" identity and makes it clear that Hitler is the one "whom one worshipped" and to whom "the individual surrenders ultimate responsibility."[101] One of the clearest statements against Nazi church involvement came from the Student Members of the Young Reformation Movement at the University of Berlin on 4 July 1933. They rejected church offices being filled "on the basis of political considerations" and highlighted that the church lives by the "pure gospel, by faith in the forgiveness of sins alone, and knows that it can be renewed by Christ alone through the Holy Spirit."[102]

The second issue, Hitler's Aryan clause, mandated that Jews could no longer serve as office-bearers in the church. In a statement to the National Church Synod on 27 September 1933, Berlin pastors declared that the Aryan clause was "contrary to the Holy Scriptures and the confession of the church" and proclaimed, "we will not stop our struggle against everything that destroys the church in its essence."[103] Bonhoeffer played a part in these statements, making the observation that orders from the state "must be seen in terms of their relativity." Later, he asserted that the task of the church through the power of the gospel is "breaching of the world and its laws."[104] By this "breaching," Bonhoeffer does not mean "forcing," but that the church in its loyalty to Christ alone is to live as a radical insertion in the world through its proclamation, embodiment, and witness. In this way alone, the "church sets limits to the state."[105] Early in life, Bonhoeffer proclaimed that "Christianity stands or falls with its revolutionary protest against violence, arbitrariness, and the pride of power, and with its apologia for the weak."[106] Moreover, he wrote that Christianity "should give much more offense, more shock to the world."[107]

I have given attention to these two issues because they highlight the following dynamics about the relationship between the church and the state. First, in the two-thousand-year journey of the church through history, it

99. Bonhoeffer, 281.

100. Bonhoeffer, 278.

101. Bonhoeffer, 275, 277.

102. Bonhoeffer, 135.

103. Bonhoeffer, 182–83.

104. Bonhoeffer, 204, 264.

105. Bonhoeffer, 265.

106. Bonhoeffer, *Works*, vol. 13, 402.

107. Bonhoeffer, vol. 13, 402.

has often had a troubled relationship with the state. Second, the present-day church has been seriously weakened by the contemporary form of consumer Christianity, a lack of formation through discipleship in the way of Christ, and shaky theological grounding. Thus, it is prone to become more and more culturally captive. The interference may not come directly from the state, but from society itself – and sadly, from within the church as well (child abuse issues being only one such internal concern). This implies that Bonhoeffer is not only relevant for thinking about how the church might serve the world, but also how the church might need to be renewed.

A true pastor,[108] Bonhoeffer wrestles in his writings with the nature and witness of the church in the world. In his context, he felt that not only the church in Germany was at stake, but the very "existence of Christianity in Europe" was "approaching its end."[109] In his personal writings, Bonhoeffer expresses deep anguish for the church in Germany, lamenting "the great defecting from God."[110] And he cries out for the church because he sees that "in practice their life is marred daily with all manner of unbelief, sloth in prayer, lack . . . [of] discipline, self-indulgence of every kind."[111] As Georg Huntemann points out, Bonhoeffer's concern was not only that the church had lost its connection with the working classes and been impacted by processes of secularization, but it had "lost its identity."[112] This profound concern had to do with the church's failure to hear the word of God,[113] to live in the way of Christ, and to be a prophetic community in the world. Bonhoeffer believed that God had become "a plaything"[114] in the life of church and thus God was no longer the Lord of the faith-community. The important theme here is that Bonhoeffer not only saw the church threatened by the external forces of Fascism, but also by the internal forces of indifference, escapist piety, and the failure of proclamation and spiritual formation within the church.

We have already noted above that Bonhoeffer had a very dynamic understanding of the church, not so much in terms of its institutional

108. But he is honest enough to admit that as a pastor or lecturer, "we are . . . pretty bad at knowing ourselves" (Bonhoeffer, vol. 12, 89).

109. Bonhoeffer, vol. 13, 118.

110. Bonhoeffer, *Letters and Papers from Prison*, 326.

111. Bonhoeffer, *Cost of Discipleship*, 149.

112. Huntemann, *The Other Bonhoeffer*, 19.

113. Bonhoeffer stresses that God's word always addresses us. He writes that the church needs to hear "that God is protesting," and thus the church can raise its prophetic voice to the world (Bonhoeffer, *Works*, vol. 12, 193).

114. Bonhoeffer, *Works*, vol. 12, 263.

structures, but as the body of Christ which is *in* Christ and therefore under Christ's Lordship, empowered by the Spirit, and thus a "'second' incarnation" in the world.[115] Bonhoeffer's articulation of the "Christification"[116] of the church provides a much richer understanding than his Reformation counterparts. He identifies Christ as word, sacrament, and community, and also as a "hidden" presence in the world. Thus, Christ is both "present in the church"[117] and also "*Christus praesens.*"[118] This draws a most powerful connection between Christ and the community of faith. While Bonhoeffer is careful to note that Christ cannot be reduced to the church, "since Christ has ascended into heaven,"[119] he nevertheless believes that the church is "a collective community," which "can be called Christ."[120] Moreover, he insists that "Jesus Christ is at once himself and his Church," and the "Church is the real presence of Christ."[121]

However we may formulate the church as the body of Christ, I believe that something very important is at play. The church – the gathered faith-community under the word, which is sustained by sacramental life and expressed in life together and lives as a servant to the world – is not a religious "shop" filled with spiritual "goodies" set up by Christ, the proprietor. Nor is the church the personal domain of some religious guru. Rather, the church is a worshipping, word-formed, Spirit-empowered community that gathers to celebrate and renew its identification *with* Christ and in Christ so that it can live *as* Christ to the world through vicarious identification. In identifying the church as "the real presence of Christ,"[122] I believe that Bonhoeffer has an urgent message for the contemporary church, calling it to recover its identity and purpose. And this recovery will vitalise its missional identity.

---

115. This is my terminology. Bonhoeffer is not that happy with the terminology of a "second" incarnation and prefers the terminology of the church as "a form of revelation" and "Christ existing as church-community" (*Works*, vol. 1, 138). But I think we are saying much the same thing. Christ's incarnation in Mary through the Holy Spirit is reflected in a derivative sense in Christ's incarnation in the church through the Holy Spirit. The first move is God's embrace of humanity. The second move is humanity's (the church's) embrace of divinity in Christ.

116. Again, this is my terminology.

117. Bonhoeffer, *Christ the Center*, 43.

118. Bonhoeffer, *Works*, vol. 12, 83.

119. Bonhoeffer, vol. 1, 140.

120. Bonhoeffer, 140.

121. Bonhoeffer, *Cost of Discipleship*, 216.

122. Bonhoeffer, 216.

The Call for a Sustaining Missional Spirituality

Before we turn to Bonhoeffer's understanding of the mission of the church, we first need to talk about Bonhoeffer's Christological spirituality with its missional implications. As Kelly and Nelson point out, we can hardly understand Bonhoeffer if we don't give attention to his inner life and spiritual practices, for Bonhoeffer's "spirituality was in essence his life in Jesus Christ shaped through the power and presence of the Holy Spirit" and the call of the Sermon of the Mount.[123] As such, we can describe Bonhoeffer's spirituality as "Christocentric" and marked by a life of discipleship and prophetic witness.[124]

Bonhoeffer's spirituality is also both personal and a corporate. The *corporate* dimension flows from his understanding that the church is the presence of Christ. To be in Christ is to be in his body, and therefore to be shaped by preaching, the sacraments, and the other dimensions of a life together. The *personal* dimension acknowledges the fact that each of us is "a person before God,"[125] and as such we are called to respond to Scripture and the leading of the Holy Spirit. Bonhoeffer makes the point that "God's daily new word [is] addressed *to me*,"[126] which calls each of us to careful and prayerful reflection and the recognition that "the more we receive, the more we have to seek God."[127]

Wherever you turn in Bonhoeffer's writings, you hear insights regarding spiritual practices. Even his doctoral thesis speaks of prayer and solitude: prayers of intercession are "to realize the divine will for others" and bring about "God's rule in the church-community";[128] "hearing the divine law in solitude" awakens our conscience;[129] in solitude before God and by recognizing our sinfulness, we truly become a "'person'";[130] and together "in reverent solitude with the Lord . . . they [persons in community in Christ] bend their knees in adoration."[131]

While prayer is a recurring topic in Bonhoeffer's writings, he also has much to say about the practice of solitude. He notes that we have to "open the doors of our hearts to the Master," and we "have to silence all the voices in us" and

123. Kelly and Nelson, *Cost of Moral Leadership*, xv.

124. Kelly and Nelson, xvi.

125. Bonhoeffer, *Christ the Center*, 61.

126. Bonhoeffer, *Works*, vol. 15, 517 (my emphasis).

127. Bonhoeffer, 513.

128. Bonhoeffer, vol. 1, 188.

129. Bonhoeffer, 108.

130. Bonhoeffer, 284.

131. Bonhoeffer, 228 (footnote).

make sure that we don't become "so busy that we can't hear God's voice."[132] He says that silence involves "beholding the one yearned for . . . yielding to God the right to have the first and last word concerning us . . . breathing in God's will," not being afraid of "unmasking ourselves," and not being overwhelmed when we are "called to task by the infinite."[133]

Bonhoeffer speaks of spirituality in deeply personal terms: "to rejoice in God, to think and pray gladly to God," to "love being in God's presence," and "not causing God sorrow."[134] He observes that "our spiritual life" comes "from a hidden, secret, dark place."[135] And while Bonhoeffer emphasizes the importance of hearing the word, he also stresses that "God may give us illumined eyes of the heart."[136]

Bonhoeffer's spirituality is more fully set out in *The Cost of Discipleship* and *Life Together*. The former sets out a Christocentric spirituality of discipleship, the call to identificational suffering in following Christ, the formative nature of the Sermon on the Mount and the Beatitudes, the nature of the body of Christ, and the faith-community's witness to the world.[137] The latter emphasizes communal and personal practices, as noted previously.

Following are some key insights from these two books. First, the Christian lives in the grace of God in *community*, which is "community through . . . and in Jesus Christ."[138] This faith-community has several features. It is a "baptismal and eucharistic congregation" before it is a missional community.[139] It is also a community where the Word "comes forth to take men [women] to itself" and where "the Holy Spirit comes."[140] This community lives by the inspiration of the

132. Bonhoeffer, vol. 9, 512.

133. Bonhoeffer, vol. 10, 502–3.

134. Bonhoeffer, vol. 13, 377.

135. Bonhoeffer, 361.

136. Bonhoeffer, vol. 15, 520.

137. Bethge, in explaining Bonhoeffer's "evangelical experience," notes that he "regularly attended church," took a "meditative approach to the Bible," emphasized a "communal life of obedience and prayer," and believed that the Sermon on the Mount was "to be acted upon." Bethge then quotes Bonhoeffer: "I discovered the Bible . . . but I had not yet become a Christian"; the Sermon on the Mount "freed me" from turning the Word of God to my own advantage"; I experienced a "great liberation"; and I embraced the fact that "the life of a servant of Jesus Christ must belong to the church" (quoted in *Dietrich Bonhoeffer*, 203–5). Elsewhere, Bonhoeffer speaks of Christ being "my rediscovered centre" (*Christ the Center*, 60). And he speaks of being overwhelmed "when suddenly being seized and called to task by the infinite" (*Works*, vol. 10, 503).

138. Bonhoeffer, *Life Together*, 21.

139. Bonhoeffer, *Cost of Discipleship*, 226.

140. Bonhoeffer, 225.

Holy Spirit, for "The baptized are the house where the Holy Spirit has made his dwelling."[141] Moreover, this community is a brotherhood and sisterhood in a life together, where each is a "bearer and proclaimer of the divine word" for and to each other.[142] Second, he writes that "for the Christian, worship cannot be divorced from service to the brethren."[143] Third, he identifies this community in Christ as a community of prayer, saying that "it is in fact the most normal thing in the common Christian life to pray together"[144] and that "prayer is the supreme instance of the hidden character of the Christian life."[145] Moreover, prayer is both *for* the faith-community – "a Christian fellowship lives . . . by the intercession of its members for one another, or it collapses"[146] – and also *for* the neighbour and the world – "the only way to reach others is by praying to God."[147] Fourth, the members of the faith-community engage in other spiritual practices, including meditation, contemplation, and various forms of asceticism. Bonhoeffer says that meditation "gives us solid ground on which to stand and clear directions as to the steps we must take."[148] Being a disciple of Christ and living in the way of Christ for others also involves various forms of asceticism, which for Bonhoeffer means "voluntary suffering."[149]

Similar emphases remain in his later works, including *Ethics* and *Letters and Papers from Prison*. In *Ethics*, Bonhoeffer begins with a profound meditation on love as the very heart of God, which is expressed through the Christian's love of God and love of neighbour. Since "God Himself is love," only the "one who knows God" knows "what love is."[150] This love is God's gift through Jesus Christ and is shaped in us by Christ. The nature of this love is transformational: "it means the undergoing of the transformation of one's entire existence by God."[151] This love of God is the "haven of refuge in which I take shelter in distress," but it is also the source of inspiration for one's "mighty thoughts and . . . spirited deeds."[152]

---

141. Bonhoeffer, 208.
142. Bonhoeffer, *Life Together*, 23.
143. Bonhoeffer, *Cost of Discipleship*, 116.
144. Bonhoeffer, *Life Together*, 62.
145. Bonhoeffer, *Cost of Discipleship*, 146.
146. Bonhoeffer, *Life Together*, 86.
147. Bonhoeffer, *Cost of Discipleship*, 167.
148. Bonhoeffer, *Life Together*, 81.
149. Bonhoeffer, *Cost of Discipleship*, 153.
150. Bonhoeffer, *Ethics*, 53.
151. Bonhoeffer, 55.
152. Bonhoeffer, 56.

In referring to the account of Mary and Martha in Luke's Gospel,[153] Bonhoeffer speaks of the unity that Christ brings into our lives, which integrates word and deed, listening and obeying. As Bonhoeffer notes, "the beautification of the doer includes . . . hearing, just as the beautification of the hearer includes . . . doing,"[154] which involves doing God's good in the world. Bonhoeffer is single-minded about the source of doing good: "the question of good can find its answer only in Christ."[155]

In *Letters and Papers from Prison*, Bonhoeffer wrestles with God's purposes for the world and the hope of a world beyond the madness of World War II. He writes of his hope that the next generation can live "without fear or anxiety" and also of his hope that as the present followers of Christ are "called to obedient and responsible action in faith in exclusive allegiance to God," they can be the harbingers of a better world.[156] In the midst of a world turned upside down, Bonhoeffer expresses his faith that "God . . . will bring good out of evil" and that God anticipates our "prayers and responsible actions."[157] He writes that life must be seen "from the perspective of those who suffer" and calls for a large-heartedness and sympathy that springs "from the liberating and redeeming love of Christ for all who suffer."[158] Throughout these difficult years of imprisonment, Bonhoeffer continues to wrestle with his faith as he maintains the spiritual disciplines, assists his fellow prisoners, and anticipates the future. He writes of the ongoing importance of a life of prayer: "from the moment we wake until we fall asleep we must commend other people wholly and unreservedly to God and leave them in his hands, and transform our anxiety for them into prayers on their behalf."[159] While he joyfully acknowledges "all those who I know are praying for me," he also admits that so often "it needs trouble to shake us up and drive us to prayer."[160]

These reflections reveal how Bonhoeffer's profound spirituality was woven deeply into his very being. We may give this various labels – Christological, communal, prophetic, incarnational, missional, orientated towards the

153. Luke 10.

154. Bonhoeffer, *Ethics*, 50.

155. Bonhoeffer, 187.

156. Bonhoeffer, *Letters and Papers from Prison*, 15, 5.

157. Bonhoeffer, 11.

158. Bonhoeffer, 17, 14.

159. Bonhoeffer, 177.

160. Bonhoeffer, 392, 199.

poor and the needy[161] – but most foundationally, Bonhoeffer's spirituality was shaped by *hearing* the written word in Jesus Christ and by *living* a life of discipleship as he sought to follow Christ into the world and the church during a time of great crisis. Being *in* and *with* Christ eventually led Bonhoeffer to become Christ's suffering servant so that new life might come into the church and the world. Thus, Bonhoeffer lived out a radical, identificational, and Christological spirituality.

The Mission of the Church

Bonhoeffer's spirituality was embedded in the missional task of the community of faith, for his concept of mission was deeply formed by the person and work of Christ and the precarious nature of his particular context amidst the Nazification of the church in Germany, the dehumanization of the Jews and the Holocaust, and the catastrophe of WWII.[162] Bonhoeffer notes with deep concern how God was being pushed out of the world, describing it as "the great defecting from God."[163] However, he also notes that there could be no call for resignation, as the "Christian hope of resurrection . . . sends a man [woman] back to life on earth."[164] He further asserts that Christ "entrusts his work on earth to them [the discipleship community]."[165] And he theologizes that "the incarnation is the ultimate reason why the service of God cannot be divorced from the service to man [woman]."[166] Thus, he insists that we "must see the state in the light of Christ,"[167] and the Christian belongs "in the thick of foes."[168] Bonhoeffer also rejects every form of triumphalism, noting that the people of God "are scattered, held together solely in Christ."[169] At the same time, he makes it clear that "we are certainly not Christ," and we can't redeem

161. See the extensive work of Kelly and Nelson, *The Cost of Moral Leadership.*

162. While Bonhoeffer was clear-eyed about his troubled world, he remained a person of hope. He writes: "God will cause grace and compassion to radiate over the dark guilt of our century" (*Works*, vol. 10, 359).

163. Bonhoeffer, *Letters and Papers from Prison*, 326.

164. Bonhoeffer, 336.

165. Bonhoeffer, *Cost of Discipleship*, 104.

166. Bonhoeffer, 117.

167. Bonhoeffer, *Christ the Center*, 60, 64.

168. Bonhoeffer, *Life Together*, 17.

169. Bonhoeffer, 18.

the world "by our own deeds and sufferings,"[170] for "only the sufferings of Christ are a means of atonement."[171]

In the process of unpacking Bonhoeffer's missional vision, we can note that mission does not begin with activism, but with profound conformity to Jesus Christ, the living word, for "the Scriptures deliver to us" Christ himself, and the church is the "miracle of his presence."[172] Through the prophetic and purging work of Christ, the church is transformed into a healing and prophetic community in the world, and as the "disciple community" it lets its light shine through "their good works."[173] In other words, the faith-community does good in the world by being a repetition of Christ, which is expressed through a sacramental life, living and practicing the Sermon on the Mount, proclaiming the good news of the gospel, interceding, and engaging in costly service for the world. Thus, the task of the church is the Christification of the world,[174] which is rooted in the incarnation and the cross, as all humanity is marked by these momentous Christological events. As Bonhoeffer explains, "the whole world has already been turned upside-down by the work of Jesus Christ,"[175] and so the task of the church is to be and to proclaim what Christ has already done in redemption and restoration. As such, "the church invades the life of the world," but while "the world exercises dominion by force," the church operates differently in that "Christians conquer by service."[176]

In the outworking of the church's task, Bonhoeffer highlights a number of dimensions. First, he insists on the importance of preaching, which is not simply an internal word for the faith-community, but is meant to be proclaimed in the public square. In fulfilling this call, Bonhoeffer notes that Christ "entrusts his work on earth" to his disciples, who are to let their light shine to the world through "their good works," which Bonhoeffer identifies as the "cross and the works of the cross."[177] Moreover, Bonhoeffer points out that the church is to proclaim and embody to the world "God's word in a specific situation."[178] He makes this concrete by giving the example of the church's challenge to the

170. Bonhoeffer, *Letters and Papers from Prison*, 14.

171. Bonhoeffer, *Cost of Discipleship*, 79.

172. Bonhoeffer, *Christ the Center*, 72–73.

173. Bonhoeffer, *Cost of Discipleship*, 106, 107.

174. Bonhoeffer expresses this as follows: "the whole reality of the world is already drawn in into Christ" (*Ethics*, 195).

175. Bonhoeffer, *Cost of Discipleship*, 234.

176. Bonhoeffer, 232, 235.

177. Bonhoeffer, 104, 107, 108.

178. Bonhoeffer, *Works*, vol. 12, 195.

Nazification of the faith-community, observing that the church sees the orders of the state "in their relativity" rather than their independence.[179] Even more pointedly, Bonhoeffer believes that the church has the task of "breaching . . . the world and its laws." While the church must be free from "party politics," the church is "political" in that it is called to show the world that there is another way.[180]

Second, Bonhoeffer insists that the church is called to pray for the whole world, as "intercession is the most promising way to reach our neighbours," and he emphasizes that everything Christians do must flow from a "genuine love of the world," which is "the love wherewith God loved it in Jesus Christ."[181] Bonhoeffer goes on to point out that the Christian loves the earth because he/she "loves it as God's Earth" and loves the kingdom of God "as God's kingdom on Earth." In praying for the kingdom of God, the church binds itself "to the Earth, to misery, to hunger, to death" in a "most profound solidarity with the world."[182]

Third, Bonhoeffer insists that the church must be a discerning community,[183] gifted by word and Spirit to discern the signs of the times and the nature of the forces at work in shaping and governing society. The church must see, resist, and expose all forms of power that lead to idolatry and the perversion of the good. As such, the church is called to be a prophetic community, which is clearly illustrated in Bonhoeffer's response to the "Fuhrer principle" as well as his condemnation of the "Aryan paragraph." Insisting that the church is to give "the gospel's answer to questions concerning races, peoples, and [the] state,"[184] he provides a challenging qualification for his particular context, writing that "a church is Evangelical because it hears that God is protesting, not because it [the church] is protesting."[185] His point is that the church is subject to God's word, while at the same time God is at work in the faith-community, enlightening it so that the church can bear its light to the world. However, this does not mean that the church "has special proposals for reforming the world," because the church is dependent on God and the

179. Bonhoeffer, *Works*, vol. 12, 204.

180. Bonhoeffer, 264–65.

181. Bonhoeffer, *Cost of Discipleship*, 88.

182. Bonhoeffer, *Works*, vol. 12, 288–89.

183. Huntemann makes the observation that Bonhoeffer had a "gift of sensitively discerning realities – political, social, and spiritual" (*The Other Bonhoeffer*, 23).

184. Bonhoeffer, *Works*, vol. 12, 108.

185. Bonhoeffer, 193.

inbreaking of the reign of God, and thus it is called to give "witness to the miracle of God," not its own programs.[186]

Fourth, Bonhoeffer rejects all forms of dualist thinking and ministry, for the mission of the church is not only concerned with one's inner being. Rather, the whole person is called to be in Christ, to live a life of discipleship, and to follow Christ into all the domains of life. This call extends to the church-community, and it includes the shaping culture[187] so that God's goodness can be expressed in the marketplace and every sphere of life. Bonhoeffer expands this vision by calling the church to be concerned with both the eschatological as well as the penultimate – that is, with God's final kingdom as well as the ordinary realities of daily life, which includes family, community, work, and politics. Bonhoeffer holds all these things in creative tension, rejecting any notion that the Christian should only live for God's eschatological future or only for the here and the now.

He notes that "both" of these positions "are opposed to Christ,"[188] for in the incarnation, Christ has become one of us so that we may become one with him, and in his death and resurrection, we all become candidates for Christ's redeeming love. He elaborates this as follows. First, the world does not exist "independently of the revelation of God in Christ.[189] Second, in Christ, "the reality of God has entered the reality of the world."[190] Third, the task of the church is to proclaim that "the world [is] . . . loved by God and reconciled with Him."[191] Fourth, while the cross of Christ is the "death sentence upon the world" in terms of its own self-sufficiency, this does not mean the "annihilation of the created world."[192] Rather, while "the ultimate . . . determines the penultimate," the "penultimate must be preserved" for the sake of the ultimate.[193] Put most practically, the Christian lives *in* and *for* God's final future, but at the same time, the Christian makes practical responses in the here and now: "the hungry . . . need bread; and the homeless man [woman]

186. Bonhoeffer, 290, 293.

187. Bonhoeffer makes it clear that the calling of the church is to be the presence of Christ in the world and a servant of the reign of God, which he calls the place where the "Kingdom of resurrection" breaks in and is welcomed. The heart of the kingdom is "where God is" (291, 292). This means that the kingdom of God is not the "Christianizing of culture and politics" (291).

188. Bonhoeffer, *Ethics*, 130.

189. Bonhoeffer, 195.

190. Bonhoeffer, 196.

191. Bonhoeffer, 200.

192. Bonhoeffer, 131.

193. Bonhoeffer, 133.

needs a roof; the dispossessed need justice and the lonely need fellowship; the undisciplined need order and the slave needs freedom."[194]

Though Bonhoeffer saw nation-building as a missional calling of the church, he neither promoted the re-creation of Christendom, nor the radical separation of church and state. Rather, the church, as part of the nation, was to be a radical Christocentric *insertion* into the body politic for the purposes of its healing and flourishing – not according to the nation's ideology, but according to the subversive reign of the kingdom of God, with Christ as the servant-king, mediator, priest, and prophet. Bonhoeffer makes the simple point that in Christ, "the holy [is] in the profane," and the profane, or the secular, is not independent because "the gospel . . . is addressed to the whole world." Thus, "there is no place to which the Christian can withdraw from the world," either inwardly or outwardly.[195]

In Bonhoeffer's writings as well as his practical commitments, he demonstrates a heart for the poor and a missiology from below. Bonhoeffer emphasizes that the church in particular must be there for the victims of a society when there is a lack of justice, noting that Christians are to have an "irresistible love for the down-trodden" and to "take upon themselves the distress and humiliation and sin of others."[196]

Bonhoeffer also develops the concept of deputyship,[197] by which he means that the church cannot be a neutral bystander regarding the pain and challenges of society. Rather, the church-community is called to take societal issues into its heartfelt and prayerful concern – and to take on a radical identification with these issues. Early on, in *Sanctorum Communio*, Bonhoeffer develops this idea through the concepts of *Stellvertretung* (vicarious suffering) and *Verantwortung* (responsibility). Calling the church to engage in "vicarious representative action,"[198] he says that the "responsibility that Christ takes for the sake of humanity in his incarnation, crucifixion, and resurrection" should inspire and motivate the church to "[act] responsibly on behalf of others."[199]

This theological concept can be further fleshed out as follows. Christ stands as mediator between *God and the person*, bringing the person to God and God

194. Bonhoeffer, 136.

195. Bonhoeffer, 196–97.

196. Bonhoeffer, *Cost of Discipleship*, 100.

197. For a much fuller discussion of this, see Schliesser, *Everyone Who Acts Responsibly Becomes Guilty.*

198. Bonhoeffer, *Works*, vol. 1, 120.

199. Bonhoeffer, 120.

to the person. Christ also stands between *the person and the world*, bringing the person to the world and the world to the person, who in turn brings the world to God. Because the mandate of the church, as Bonhoeffer puts it, is the "salvation of the whole world,"[200] the church is not only called to proclamation, prayer, and service, but also to vicarious action. This means that the Christian "has to bear the sins of others"[201] and "mourn for the world, for its guilt, its fate, and its fortune."[202] Bonhoeffer concludes that Christians "wander on earth and live in heaven," and "although they are weak, they protect the earth"; they also "taste peace in the midst of turmoil," and they "stand in suffering and remain in joy" as they "live their own life under alien rulers and alien laws."[203] Moreover, because the church is impacted through word and Spirit by the death and resurrection of Jesus Christ, its most fundamental identity is that of a suffering community. As Bonhoeffer puts it, "the 'must' of suffering applies to [Christ's] disciples" as much as it applies to Christ.[204]

Finally, in seeking to understand and embody the Christian's role in the world, Bonhoeffer became involved with the *Abwehr* – the counterintelligence agency in the German army that was plotting to overthrow Hitler. Bonhoeffer joined the *Abwehr* to avoid military service, but in joining it, and by fostering his overseas contacts with church leaders, he became implicated in the attempts on Hitler's life. In Bonhoeffer's writings, he states that Christians have a responsibility to ask whether or not the state is engaging in "*legitimate state actions*" and, if not, that Christians have a responsibility to "accuse the state of offenses against morality."[205] He also writes that the state cannot use Romans 13 as "divine authorization" for its political activities, because "sovereign power belongs to God and not to the state."[206] Nevertheless, Bonhoeffer insists that it is not the task of the church to take "*direct* political action."[207]

In mapping out some of the dimensions of the relationship between the church and the state, he makes the following points. First, the church serves the state only "through its preaching." Second, the church must resist the state when it "wants to use the church as its instrument." Third, the church must

200. Bonhoeffer, *Ethics*, 208.

201. Bonhoeffer, *Cost of Discipleship*, 80.

202. Bonhoeffer, 98.

203. Bonhoeffer, 243–44.

204. Bonhoeffer, 77.

205. Bonhoeffer, 236–37.

206. Bonhoeffer, 236–37.

207. Bonhoeffer, *Works*, vol. 12, 363–64.

reject the notion of a "Christian state in any form."[208] Fourth, the church is to question the state regarding its role and policies. Fifth, the church is to provide services "to the victims of the state's actions." Sixth, the task of Christians is "not just to bind up the wounds of the victims" who have been injured "beneath the wheel" of the state, "but to seize the wheel itself."[209] This final point opens the door to more direct action in the cause of justice, and Bonhoeffer took this road when he became involved with the *Abwehr.*

To summarize, the task of the church is to *affirm* what is good and *resist* what is evil. The nature of this resistance remains an open question. There will always be some who say we should only pray, and others who say that we should pray, act, and pray some more. There will be those who remain pacifist under all circumstances and those who advocate the use of force under certain circumstances. Bonhoeffer made his stand against Nazi Germany, his nation state, in loyalty to Christ, because he saw himself as a sinner saved through the grace of Christ. As a consequence of this action, he paid with his life.

Conclusion

In exploring Bonhoeffer's missional spirituality, there are many things that stand out. First, Bonhoeffer was deeply impacted by Christ, and he sought to live in and for Christ amidst the troubled times of Hitler's Germany. His life, theology, spirituality, and praxis had everything to do with discipleship as he sought to follow the *way* and *person* of Jesus Christ.

Second, Bonhoeffer made a singular commitment to the church as a discipleship-community, and thus he was deeply committed to the word, to meditative practices, and to prayer. One could say that he gave his life *to* Christ *for* the church, which he saw as the community of the embodied presence of Christ, who offered himself for the redemption of the whole world.

Third, Bonhoeffer saw the foundational role and task of the church as *redemptive suffering* for the sake of the world. Thus, the church does not exist for itself, but is called to live as a worshipping, teaching, and eucharistic faith-community – a radical insertion in the world that will be both a servant and sign of God's kingdom project in order to bring the hope of Christ to the whole world. As such, the church is to be a prophetic voice of the reign of God, willing to call into question every act of injustice and every misuse of power so that God's shalom might flourish in the world.

208. Bonhoeffer, 415.

209. Bonhoeffer, 365.

Fourth, Bonhoeffer's primary missional concern was the formation of the church into Christ as an *embodied word* in order to bring salvation, hope, and justice to the world. In seeking to engage the world, the task of the church includes proclamation, community-building, the work of justice, and nation-building. This nation-building has nothing to do with national identity and pride, nor with the creation of the old Christendom, nor with the creation of Christian political parties – but with the recognition that Christ is not only the Lord of the church, but also the Lord of history. Thus, the church's role is to see that Lordship come to fuller realization in the legitimate role of both the church and the state.

12

Radical Evangelicals

Developing a Sustainable Missional Spirituality

Introduction

This chapter is born out of a deep concern, which may be spelled out in a core statement that is an underlying theme of this book. Over the years of my missional engagement, I have met many radical evangelicals[1] who have lived sacrificial lives in the work of justice, but have become burned out in the process.[2] As a result of this burnout, many have lost their passion for evangelization, become disconnected from the church, and eventually become post-evangelicals[3] –

1. I have many reasons for focusing on "radical evangelicals." I see myself as one of them, and I have spent decades working with them in Australia, New Zealand, Asia, and North America. Their focus is on linking evangelism and social justice and providing a critique of existing power structures through an understanding of the reign of God. Their commitments to live this out often come at great cost, and there have been casualties and disappointments. Their further distinctives are set out in this chapter, but my concern is that the more radical and costly our missional commitments, the more deeply we need to be grounded in the spiritual disciplines, formed through community, and participate in the life of the broader church so that we can be sustained in our life of faith and service.

2. Langmead concurs, writing that "one might wonder how ordinary people are meant to understand and respond to the radicality of the demands" of this movement. He continues: "burnout, conflict and disillusionment can occur as a result of high idealism untempered by realism and a 'spirituality of the long haul'" (*Word Made Flesh*, 115). I am addressing the matter of a sustainable spirituality in particular in this chapter.

3. In many ways, I am not that nervous with the concept of being a post-evangelical, particularly when evangelicalism is defined and described as it is by Kyle in *Popular Evangelicalism in American Culture*. However, as I discuss in this chapter evangelicalism is a far richer tradition than its present anorexic and distorted version and so I continue to see myself as an evangelical.

or, even more sadly, lost their faith altogether.[4]

I recognize that the very nature of our mission, particularly serving the poor, resisting the power of the powerful, and walking the long road to justice, will change us in many ways, and this includes our faith. Yet I do not take it as an axiom that we need to do "violence" to our evangelical tradition, though I do believe that we need to question aspects of our evangelical tradition, particularly those that have become deformed by dominant themes in our culture. At the same time, I believe that we need to learn from other Christian traditions as a way to deepen evangelicalism. I also believe that we need to remain open to hear from secular "prophets" who challenge the church in particular ways. Finally, evangelical theology and its practices can't be bound to the past, but need to be "renewed" and reconceptualized in every age. Thus, both *recovery* and *progress* need to be part of any vital theological tradition.

Yet I don't believe that these matters, and the difficulties we may have experienced in our missional activities, need be a reason to abandon evangelicalism altogether. Most basically, I believe that our evangelical tradition is broad enough to incorporate a range of sustainable perspectives and practices. The evangelical movement is rooted in the Reformation and in various modern renewal movements, such as Wesleyanism, and our forebears have drunk deeply from the wider Christian tradition. For example, both Luther and Calvin drank deeply from the Augustinian tradition, and Wesley was influenced by Benedictine spirituality.

Thus, within evangelicalism, we can draw from many rich traditions, including the Reformed faith, the Anabaptist tradition, the renewal movements under Jonathan Edwards, the revivals under Charles Finney, and contemporary renewal movements, such as charismatic and new monasticism.

Evangelicals are well-known for their commitment to the Lordship of Christ, for embracing of the authority of Scripture, for living a life of piety, and for their involvement in witness and service.[5] However, contemporary evangelicals are often quite activistic and so run the risk of failing in spiritual nurture and self-care. And of course, it is disconcerting that evangelicals in certain countries have become far too tied to conservative party politics.

4. I do not in any way blame those who have opted to abandon their faith through their sacrificial missional engagement. Sadly, several key concerns stand out: (1) a lack of formation in theology and the spiritual disciplines; (2) an over-emphasis on doing; (3) a lack in sustainable communal life; (4) unrealistic expectations regarding ministry outcomes.

5. Bloesch, *Future of Evangelical Christianity*.

While radical evangelicals[6] share the above characteristics, their understanding of witness and service takes on some further challenges. In following Christ, they often seek to be an incarnational missional presence among the poor. One such group, Servants to Asia's Urban Poor, seeks to live five *missiological principles*: incarnation, community, wholism, servanthood, and simplicity.[7] To live a life of radical identification in the slum communities of Asia's major cities is a great challenge, and so it should hardly surprise us that some workers end up discouraged, burnt out, or broken.[8] As a consequence, some years ago, Servants added five *values* to their missiological principles: grace, beauty, celebration, creativity, and rest.[9] Worship, celebration, and the practices of a Sabbath spirituality are all part of living the Christian life. The addition of these five values reflects the challenge within Servants to develop a more sustainable lifestyle and forms of service. This suggests that we need to probe for a missional spirituality that can animate our service through our relationship with Christ, be enriched by our life in community, and empower us to walk the long road of obedience in the work of evangelization, justice, peacemaking, creation-care, and social transformation.

The focus of this chapter is to highlight some sources that radical evangelicals might draw on to deepen and enhance a more sustainable way of following and serving Christ. In a nutshell, I will discuss three sources of inspiration and animation: core themes in Scripture, themes in the long tradition of the church in history, and the value of one's communal experience as a serving community. Before we explore these sources of inspiration, I will first explain who "radical evangelicals" are, and then revisit what we mean by "missional spirituality."[10]

Radical Evangelicals

Radical evangelicals emerged in the late 1960s and early 1970s as a broad-based movement of Christians seeking to integrate evangelism and the work of justice, live incarnationally among the poor, form Christian communities, and critique aspects of Western culture and church. The term "radical evangelicals" came

6. Langmead, *Word Made Flesh*, 93–115.

7. Jack, *Sound of Worlds Colliding*, 7.

8. Craig, *Servants Among the Poor*, 182–3.

9. Jack, *Sound of Worlds Colliding*, 8.

10. See chapter 1 ("Mission and Spirituality: *Towards Wider Horizons*") and chapter 2 ("Towards a Missional Spirituality").

into prominence at the 1974 Lausanne Congress on World Evangelization, when some two hundred delegates, who referred to themselves as "The Radical Discipleship Group," drew up a response to Lausanne, calling for a greater focus on the work of justice and service to the poor.[11]

This diverse and global evangelical movement emerged due to a complex set of contributing factors. These included, first, exposure to the counter-cultural movements of the 1960s; second, involvement in new forms of urban mission among people alienated from church and society; third, interaction between "Third World"[12] radical evangelical theologians and practitioners and their "First World" counterparts; fourth, the impact of the charismatic renewal movement that opened people to the creative work of the Spirit; fifth, exposure to more radical theologies, such as Anabaptist theology and liberation theology.

To get some sense of this global movement, it is important to note some of the theological emphases of radical evangelicals, which centre around the following themes. First, salvation is both a gift of Christ's grace and a call to serve God's kingdom purposes in the world. Second, salvation issues us into a discipleship that is expressed in the *imitatio Christi*, which calls Christians to live *in the way of Christ* in the world. Third, this *way* is best exemplified in the Sermon on the Mount. Fourth, salvation is never only personal, for it also calls us into community and solidarity. Fifth, this community is the missional people of God sent by Father, Son, and Holy Spirit to be a sign, servant, and sacrament of the reign of God. Sixth, this community in Christ is one of worship, formation, and identificational service in the world. Seventh, this service to the world transpires as the faith-community seeks to be a healing and prophetic witness in society.[13]

Radical evangelicals place themselves in the long story of Scripture, which reveals a God who is both wholly other and also wholly involved in the world, sustaining it as well as redeeming it. At the same time, radical evangelicals are particularly impacted by the social justice vision of the Pentateuch as well as the OT prophetic vision of shalom, justice, and the new community. And they

---

11. Langmead, *Word Made Flesh*, 94. See also Escobar, *In Search of Christ in Latin America*, 213–15.

12. The language of "Third World" and "First World" is now largely replaced by the geographic North or South (non-Western) or, more helpfully, by Majority World Christianity (non-Western) and Minority World Christianity (Western).

13. Langmead, *Word Made Flesh*, identifies the following themes as important for radical evangelicals: Jesus as the pattern for mission, incarnational and holistic ministry, mission in the way of the cross, being a sign of the kingdom of God, and the importance of community (93–115). He believes that this movement makes a "distinctive contribution to incarnational missiology" (114).

are shaped by the theology and praxis of the Jesus Movement as portrayed in the gospels, the inbreaking of the kingdom in the power of the Spirit as told in the book of Acts, and the Pauline vision of new life in Christ in the new community beyond culture, class, gender, and economic differences. This vision is particularly concerned with exposing, resisting, and redeeming the fallen powers, which are devolving society's ideologies and institutions, while looking with hope toward a new heaven and a new earth.[14] In light of these biblical and theological emphases, radical evangelicals see themselves as a prophetic counter-community in the world, which is wholly engaged in the suffering and brokenness of the human community. Thus, radical evangelicals practise radical hospitality, seek to be a healing presence in the world, and are committed to peacemaking and the work of justice.

Servants to Asia's Urban Poor is but one small but significant band in this diverse movement, whose earlier global proponents include René Padilla, Samuel Escobar, Orlando Costas, Vinay Samuel, Jim Wallace, and Ronald Sider, among others.[15] The challenge of living this kind of discipleship and mission clearly calls for a sustaining biblical vision, community, and spirituality.

Defining Missional Spirituality

It is important to remind ourselves what is meant by a missional spirituality. By *mission*, we mean joining in and cooperating with God's redemptive, healing, and transformative activity in the world.[16] Radical evangelicals are not comfortable with narrow definitions of God's work in the world, for the work of salvation not only blesses individuals, but also communities. Thus, evangelization and the work for justice go hand in hand.[17] Soul-saving, church-formation, justice-seeking, and earth-keeping are all part of the mission of God.

By *Christian spirituality*, we mean the motivation and shape of a life of following Christ in the power of the Holy Spirit.[18] Narrow perspectives are not

14. For a fuller development of this theme, see chapter 6 ("A Vision of God and a Passion for the World") and also chapter 7 ("The Heart and Scope of Integral Mission").

15. Langmead, *Word Made Flesh*, 94. The significance of Servants within the radical evangelical movement is illustrated by the fact that of the ten radical evangelical leaders in Australia and New Zealand mentioned by Langmead, five are associated with Servants (Langmead, 94).

16. Bosch, *Transforming Mission*.

17. Ringma, "Holistic Ministry and Mission."

18. Cunningham and Egan, *Christian Spirituality*, 22–28.

helpful in defining Christian spirituality, which is not simply about prayer or meditation, but the whole *gestalt* of one's life.[19] The inner and outer dimensions of life belong together. Thus, prayer and politics are held within the gamut of one's spirituality.

In the light of this, we may define missional spirituality as a way of life in Christ through the Spirit, which is supported by the community of faith and the spiritual disciplines, and which animates our whole life, including our witness and service. As a way of life, missional spirituality is not simply about praying for certain outreach or service projects, but also about cultivating a prayer-filled life. Moreover, as a cruciform way of life in Christ, it is not limited to certain years of special missionary activity, but involves devoting the whole of our life to the service of Christ. Yet a missional spirituality is more than hard work and self-effort, for this way of life and service must be initiated and sustained by the Spirit. Moreover, this mission and service is not a solo effort, for it involves our life, witness, and service in community as we join hands with God and others in the service of our neighbour. As such, missional spirituality is a communal spirituality that sustains and fructifies acts of solidarity in service of the poor. Finally, missional spirituality is a disciplined way of life that embraces the spiritual practices, including prayer, meditation, fasting, contemplation, and service.[20] Yet prayer and fasting are not simply a means to service, but more fundamentally a way to God. And service is not simply the outworking of one's relationship with God, but a way to grow *in* God. Put differently, both prayer and service deepen our relationship with God and express love to our neighbour.

As discussed in an earlier chapter,[21] Segundo Galilea expresses the dynamic of missional spirituality in his notion of the double movement of contemplation, which involves both transcendence and immanence. In the movement of transcendence, we are invited to contemplate God face to face through the practices of biblical reflection, prayer, silence, and the gift of revelation. In the movement of immanence, we are invited to contemplate the hidden face of Christ in the faith-community, neighbour, stranger, enemy, and poor through the gift of service.[22] In other words, through the movement of transcendence,

19. Ringma, *Seek the Silences with Thomas Merton.*

20. Foster and Smith, *Devotional Classics.*

21. See chapter 2 ("Towards a Missional Spirituality").

22. Galilea, *Following Jesus.*

we meet with God, who nudges us to serve our neighbour.[23] And in serving our neighbour, we are drawn to commune with God through prayer and renewal. Thus, prayer and service belong together, and the spiritual disciplines and the work of justice are intimately connected. Both are forms of worship, and both are expressions of service. In the words of B. P. Holt, this is "integrating one's life in the world with one's relationship to God."[24]

In summary, missional spirituality is relevant for all God's people who are seeking to be witnesses and servants of Christ. Those who seek to serve Christ in particularly difficult circumstances, such as radical evangelicals, don't partake of a different spirituality, but they may well need to deepen their spirituality and express it in relevant ways in light of the particular challenges they face as they seek to serve the poor and working for justice. For example, the unique contours of a Franciscan spirituality can inform, shape, and animate a member of Mother Teresa's Missionaries of Charity as well as an urban community worker, academic, or politician. But *how* that particular form of missional spirituality is outworked in one's life will vary in each different setting.

Biblical Themes[25]

Missional Christian spirituality has its roots in the biblical story. In the long history of the Christian church, this story has been appropriated in different ways, which has led to the rich spiritual traditions of the desert fathers and mothers, Benedictines, Franciscans, Reformers, Jesuits, Methodists, and so on.

Beginning with the OT, the themes of presence, redemption, peoplehood, and service are important, but these could be reduced to the more basic themes of *salvation*, *community*, and *mission*. Whatever the themes, the central arc of the story is clear: God *reveals* "himself" and *redeems a people*, who are to live in *worship* and *obedience* to Yahweh, and who are *called* to be a *light* to the world and a *blessing* to the nations (Isa 42:6). Within this narrative arc, there is an emphasis on the vision of God and on the responsibility of individuals (Gen 15:1–2; Exod 33:29–35; Isa 6). The narrative also emphasizes that God's presence is revealed in the corporate life of Israel's feasts and festivals (Deut 11:1–3). Despite this emphasis on the presence of God, there is also a sense of

23. Simone Weil makes the basic point that inner renewal and outward service are linked. She writes, "when you are given true affection there will be no opposition between interior solitude and friendship" (*Gravity and Grace*, 60).

24. Holt, *Thirsty for God*, 3.

25. See chapter 2 ("Towards a Missional Spirituality").

God's absence (Pss 22:1–2; 44:23–24) and the notion of people wrestling with God (Gen 18:16–33; Job 40:2–4).

At the same time, the OT is filled with examples of individuals who pray (Gen 15:2; Isa 3:10; Ps 51:1–2), highlighting the complementarity of personal prayer and liturgical spirituality. In the outworking of this personal and communal spirituality, we see the practices of prayer (Neh 1:4–11), fasting (Lev 16:29–30; 2 Chr 20:3; Isa 58:6), meditation (Ps 119:15), and Sabbath (Exod 20:11; Deut 5:15). We also see two important themes that can help concretize a missional spirituality. First, from Exodus, we have a spirituality of *liberation*. Having been freed by Yahweh's redemptive activity (Deut 15:15), the people are to extend the liberating blessing that they have received to others (Deut 15:12–15). This is most clearly expressed in the OT social justice legislation[26] and the vision of the Year of Jubilee.[27]

Second, the dysfunctional story of Israel's failed kingships, false prophets, and corrupt priests, who are seeking to totalize religious and political power rather than upholding Yahweh's call to covenant and obedience,[28] brings forth a *prophetic* spirituality that calls the people to restoration, renewal, and social equality. Prophetic spirituality calls for attentiveness to Yahweh, discernment of the signs of the times, a willingness to be misunderstood and to experience suffering, courage to proclaim what is not popular, a passion to challenge corruption, and a vision and hope for the new age of Yahweh's blessing.

These two key themes can be a source of inspiration and direction for radical evangelicals as they seek to proclaim liberation and to live as a prophetic people amidst a world of injustice and oppression.

Turning to the NT, the general emphases echo the OT: love of God and love of neighbour (Matt 22:37–40). The more specific themes are also similar, yet they have a Christocentric emphasis, as service to the least is a way of honouring Christ (Matt 25:34–36). In summary, we could say that the vision of the NT is for the formation of a new people who will live the way of Christ and become agents of change and transformation in the world.[29]

More particularly, this form of spirituality is *Christological*, as it is grounded in what it means to be in and live in Christ (Rom 6:3–5). Second, NT spirituality is *communal*, for conversion to Christ involves embracing the body of Christ, the community of faith. Baptised into Christ by the Spirit,

26. Sider, *Rich Christians in an Age of Hunger*, 78–86.

27. Kinsler and Kinsler, *Biblical Jubilee and the Struggle for Life*.

28. Brueggemann, *Prophetic Imagination*.

29. Mott, *Biblical Ethics and Social Change*.

we are also called to water baptism and to be incorporated into the church (1 Cor 12:13; Gal 3:26–28). Thus, our spirituality and mission are shaped and sustained by worship, word, Eucharist, and fellowship. Third, NT spirituality is *incarnational*, which means that the way of Jesus is formed in us (Gal 4:19). And so, Jesus's baptism, infilling of the Spirit, love of the Father, prayer life, proclamation, healing, community-building, and concern for the poor become our way of living and serving in the world. Moreover, incarnational spirituality calls us to identify with a group of people, particularly the poor, as we join and serve a community in Christ.[30] Fourth, this way of life is made *sustainable* by practicing spiritual disciplines, such as prayer, fasting, and asceticism (1 Cor 7:29–31), and by nurturing our life in the Spirit (John 16:14; Rom 8:15–17).

While this survey of OT and NT biblical themes is far from exhaustive,[31] we can discern the following. First, radical evangelicals need to root their missional vision for life and service in the biblical story. Second, the contours of a missional spirituality do not begin with the events following the day of Pentecost, but are embedded in the entire biblical narrative. Third, the theme of God's redemption is foundational to Scripture. The people who are saved are called to live in faith, obedience, and service to the world. Fourth, our witness, ministry, and service all need to be oriented around our call to do God's work in the world. Finally, our witness, ministry, and service also need to be empowered and sustained by the Holy Spirit.

Because of these themes for living the life of faith in community, inspired by the biblical narratives but lived-out in particular times and circumstances, many diverse Christian missional spiritualities have emerged in the history of the Christian church. In the next section, we will explore some of the ways that radical evangelicals can be enriched by these traditions. Later chapters will highlight these traditions in more detail.[32]

Drinking from the Fountains of Tradition

As with the previous survey of biblical themes, this discussion of the rich history of Christian missional spirituality will be necessarily brief. Rather than drawing from one tradition, such as the one you grew up in or entered at some

30. Simone Weil makes the important point that "we must not help our neighbour *for* Christ but *in* Christ" (*Gravity and Grace*, 40, author's emphasis).

31. For a fuller discussion, see chapter 6 ("A Vision of God and a Passion for the World").

32. See chapter 13 ("The Anabaptist Vision of Community, Discipleship, and Service"), chapter 14 ("Franciscan Peacemaking: A Key Theme in Missional Spirituality"), and chapter 15 ("Liberation Theology: A Spirituality and Praxis of Serving the Poor").

point in your faith journey,[33] radical evangelicals will need to be sustained by *drinking from many fountains*.[34] For example, radical evangelicals have much in common with Franciscan missional spirituality, but they can also learn from Benedictine spirituality or Anabaptist themes. Thus, in this chapter, I will focus on some Christian traditions that might be less familiar to evangelicals, as every orthodox Christian tradition has something to teach us about our relationship with God and our service to the world.

The Desert Fathers and Mothers

The movement of Christians towards the desert began around AD 250, when solitary hermits decided to leave "material comforts, worldly politics and secular social distractions" to live in the Nile desert region and devote themselves to "uninterrupted prayer and great physical mortification."[35] In time, this movement gave birth to what would later become monastic communities.[36] In this section, I will not spell out the wisdom of the desert fathers and mothers, as there are many other sources of pithy sayings that one can read and imbibe for oneself.[37] Rather, my interest is in the way that this movement was a response to a post-persecution setting and the Constantinization of the church, which led Christians to find new ways of living in radical identification with Christ, and how this movement can offer several distinct challenges to radical evangelicals today.

First, following Jesus may involve leaving one's social setting and job. The call to go, witness, and serve may be a call to remain at home, serving in one's place of work, or witnessing the love of God to the neighbour across the street, but it may also mean moving to the *margins* of society or across the seas in order to pray and serve.

Second, moving out of one's familiar setting in response to the call of God allows us to grow in *discernment*, as a new setting can undo our familiar

33. I grew up in the Reformed faith, but by virtue of my ministry involvement, I was soon exposed to a much wider ecumenical tradition.

34. I have been greatly challenged to rethink much of my faith journey in the light of monastic spirituality. See Ringma, *Seek the Silences*.

35. Waddell, *Desert Fathers*, xxvii.

36. Waddell, xxviii.

37. See Helen Waddell, *The Desert Fathers*; Thomas Merton, *The Wisdom of the Desert*; Benedicta Ward, *The Desert Fathers: Sayings of the Early Christian Monks*. For a helpful biography of Antony, one of the towering figures among the desert fathers, see Athanasius, *The Life of Antony and The Letter to Marcellinus*. For a contemporary attempt to apply the inspiration of the desert fathers and mothers to pastoral ministry, see Henri Nouwen, *The Way of the Heart*.

perspectives and give us a vision about what our world could be like. This can bring forth a gospel critique of the dominant values of society as well as the institutional church.

Third, the call to the desert is a call to *renunciation* and *relinquishment*, which involves a spirituality of asceticism.[38] For the desert fathers and mothers, this call was to a literal desert, but in the history of Christian spirituality, the "desert" can also be a metaphor. Thus, serving in a slum community in Bangkok or Manila may function as a place of marginality and otherness.[39]

Fourth, the call to a life of *prayer* is not about doing nothing, but recognizing that personal and social change cannot come about through our activism alone. When we are living in a "desert," amidst poverty and injustice, we quickly realize the limits of what we can do. When we come up against our limits, we can grow in our dependence upon the energizing and fructifying work of the Spirit as we make a long commitment to building faith-communities in unlikely places, developing a broader social movement committed to change, and raising a prophetic voice on behalf of the poor and oppressed to those who hold power in society. All of these actions must be born and sustained in prayer as well as other spiritual practices.

Fifth, living and serving on the margins of society provides us with a new way of reading the gospel and understanding the purpose of our life and the nature of our mission. These insights can lead to the *conversion* of the missioner,[40] for the work of transformation in society includes the transformation of those who are seeking to bring about change.

Sixth, a life on the margins can give birth to a new spirituality, which moves us away from merely celebrating the triumphant Christ to serving the *suffering* Christ in a desolate world. The impulse towards Christian triumphalism needs to be muted by the vulnerability of the incarnation and a *theologia crucis*.

Finally, the desert fathers and mothers can teach us that we need to be *contemplative* radicals. Mere activism won't make us effective, and so we need to cultivate a new vision and passion that can sustain us over the long haul. This new vision and passion can be nurtured through prayer, solitude, and contemplation.

Clearly, the formative wisdom of the desert fathers and mothers is relevant for present-day radical evangelicals who are seeking to be an incarnational presence in serving the poorest of the poor and speaking truth to power. The

38. See chapter 16 ("Asceticism: Theological, Spiritual and Missional Perspectives").

39. See Barker, *Slum Life Rising*; Craig, *Servants Among the Poor*.

40. See chapter 3 ("Key Theological Themes").

great lesson that we can draw from this tradition is that intentional marginality for the sake of the gospel is dangerously transformative, for it changes the missioner, who begins to see anew the purposes of God, the shape of one's life, and the nature of Christian service.

While our setting is very different from the desert fathers and mothers, many Christians today share a deep concern about the erosion of Christianity in the Western world. As all sorts of suggestions are being made about how the contemporary church can be revitalized for the task of "First World" re-evangelization, we need to learn from these ancient forebears of the desert as we seek to recover a life of prayer, asceticism, and a renewed vision for blessing our world.[41]

Benedictine Spirituality

St. Benedict of Nursia (AD 480–546), the founder of the Grand Monastery at Monte Cassino, began a way of life in community, which was crystalized in his *Rule*[42] and has continued to shape monastic communities up to the present. This way of life represents a balance between prayer, reading, learning, practical daily work, the practice of hospitality, and the formation of those seeking this vocation. While Benedictine monasteries are different from radical evangelical communities, which are specifically oriented to living amongst the poor, we can learn much from the Benedictines.[43]

One of the most basic lessons that we can learn from Benedictines is their vision of the blessedness of the ordinary. While radical evangelicals often focus on doing something extraordinary in their mission and ministry, the Benedictines recognize ordinary tasks, such as preparing a meal and tending daily work, as priestly activities rather than distractions from "more important" work. Thus, the Benedictines can challenge us to live the ordinary extraordinarily well as we live out our daily life in worship and service. Living the ordinary well calls us to be mindful of God in all that we do – in our excitement about a major missional project, as we chat with neighbours, or as we tend basic house duties. When we attend to God in our daily life, we open ourselves to see and hear what God is saying and doing.

The Benedictines can also help us embrace the gift of rhythms. Radical evangelicals tend to be project-focused activists, fretting about the work there

41. See also, Ringma, *A Fragile Hope*, 13–16.

42. Fry, *Rule of Saint Benedict*.

43. Chittister, *Wisdom Distilled from the Daily*.

is to do, the overwhelming needs, and the rampant injustice. While all of this may be true, our lives will become imbalanced if the only dimension of our life is work. Benedictines seek to live an *integrated* life of prayer, study, and work, as all three involve loving God and the neighbour. Thus, they can help us find greater balance so that our life can become more sustainable and joyful, despite the challenges of poverty and ministry among the poor.

We can also glean much wisdom from the Benedictine vows. The vow of *conversatio Morum*[44] involves the commitment to live in ongoing openness to God and the work of the Spirit, which brings about our continuous conversion and transformation. The vow of *obedience* can remind radical evangelicals that in serving the poor, we are called to obey God and the gospel, which may require us to submit ourselves to community practices, priorities, and ministries. Radical evangelicals can also appropriate the traditional Benedictine vow of *stability*,[45] as living incarnationally among the poor and seeking to bring *shalom* to a particular urban poor community involves a long process of learning language and culture, befriending a community, working with them for change and transformation, building a faith-community, addressing employment issues, working for permanent housing, along with the constant challenges of advocacy and the quest for justice. Engaging in this work is like running a marathon and requires a long obedience. After two years of not seeing much happening, some may want to move on, but the vow of stability invites us to stay. I know many radical evangelicals who have made ten-year commitments (or more) to a particular community.[46]

The Benedictine vision of integration can challenge radical evangelicals to embrace the spiritual disciplines, including prayer and Sabbath. Both personal and corporate prayer help us live in the friendship of God so that we can begin to envision God's purposes for the world. Thus, a spirituality of prayer is both nurturing and missional. The spirituality of Sabbath is about more than building a time for rest into our life, as we often rest simply to gain strength for our work. But in Sabbath, we set aside time for holy leisure. As we build Sabbath rest into our daily and weekly routines, our concern is not about gaining energy for more work, but rather orienting ourselves toward God. We are not seeking renewal for our work, but so that we can be attentive to life and

44. This ancient Benedictine term has many interpretations, but generally it refers to a monk's fidelity to the monastic life.

45. See Wilson-Hartgrove, *Wisdom of Stability*.

46. I have not touched on the Benedictine vow to remain single, as it may not be a primary vow for radical evangelicals.

celebrate life. These disciplines lead to a more integrated way of living. Whereas work is a given for radical evangelicals, cultivating a spirituality of prayer and study remains an ongoing challenge. The call to love God with all of our mind is particularly relevant for radical evangelicals, as we need to learn culture in order to engage in community-work for social transformation. However, this study needs to be balanced with learning from Scripture, theology, and spirituality.[47]

Celtic Spirituality

As in the previous section, I will not set out a comprehensive picture of Celtic spirituality, but will highlight certain themes that may be particularly relevant for radical evangelicals. The central themes of Celtic spirituality include the Trinity, community, earth-care, and mission. Celtic spirituality is profoundly contemplative and can be characterized as involving multi-directional *listening*.[48] We listen to God in all things – the Word, our inner being, our social landscape, nature, creativity, and the life-giving Spirit. Newell highlights how Celtic spirituality seeks "God by looking towards the heart of life, and not away from life" and by looking to the "God within creation" rather than the God beyond.[49] He concludes, "if the church's symbols and rituals pointed more clearly to the world as God's dwelling-place, we might then more fully rediscover that God's heartbeat can be heard in the whole of life and at the heart of our own lives."[50]

Oliver Davies notes that the Celtic Christian tradition gave "great status . . . to the Word of God"[51] and was a profoundly missional movement.[52] The Celtic monks, among them Patrick and Columbanus, were known as the *peregrinatio pro christo*, or the wanderers for Christ.[53] He concludes that Celtic spirituality emphasized the imagination as much as reason, the female as much as the male, the body as much as the spirit, God present in nature as much as

47. Also see Ringma, *A Fragile Hope*, 45–48.

48. Newell, *Listening to the Heartbeat of God.*

49. Newell, 4, 3.

50. Newell, 107.

51. Davies, *Celtic Spirituality*, 3.

52. See Hunter, *Celtic Way of Evangelism*, which attempts to apply the Celtic way to re-evangelize the contemporary West.

53. Davies, *Celtic Spirituality*, 19. de Waal, *Celtic Vision*, includes the following prayer: "I am placing my soul and my body / Under Thy guarding this night, O God / O Thou Father of help to the poor feeble pilgrims / Protector of earth and heaven" (104).

God's transcendence.[54] Thus Celtic spirituality has become attractive to our contemporary sensibilities, although the early Celtic emphasis on penance bordered on the severe.

Though ancient, Celtic spirituality is alive and well among many groups in the United Kingdom, including the Northumbria Community, which has become a dispersed community throughout the world.[55] The formational material for Northumbria thematizes some important concepts that are particularly relevant for radical evangelicals.

First, it highlights the importance of understanding the context in which contemporary Christianity finds itself, particularly in the West. This calls us to read the signs of the times.

Second, in reading the signs of the times, the Northumbria Community invites us to ask several important questions. How can we sing the Lord's song in difficult times and in places of marginalization? How can we look ahead to the God who is always going ahead of us without collapsing into nostalgia about the past? How can we allow the rich heritage of the past to nurture and provoke us?

Third, the Northumbria Community suggests that we need to be deeply nurtured in a sustaining spirituality that involves the maintenance of spiritual practices rather than simply relying on the spontaneity of the Spirit.

Fourth, the Northumbria Community maintains the need to keep two dimensions of the Christian life in balance: the cave and the coracle. The cave is a metaphor for the life of prayer and contemplation. In the words of Segundo Galilea, this is the movement of transcendence. The coracle is a metaphor for the mission of the people of God. Galilea calls this the movement of incarnation. Inhabiting both the cave and coracle enriches the Christian life and sustains the Christian community in the purposes of the reign of God.

Finally, the Northumbria Community emphasizes the practices of vulnerability and availability to God and others.[56] I hope that this brief summary provides the reader with an inkling of the riches of this tradition, which is concerned with seeing God in *all* of life and discerning God's presence with us in desert places. This tradition calls us to live as contemplatives as we seek to be God's missional people in the world.

---

54. Davies, *Celtic Spirituality*, 24.

55. The Northumbria Community is well known for *Celtic Daily Prayer: From the Northumbria Community* (vol. 1) and *Farther Up and Farther In* (vol. 2).

56. My life has been enriched through engagement with this very rich spiritual resource.

In concluding this section, I will highlight three particular challenges from this tradition for radical evangelicals. First, Celtic spirituality is a spirituality of the people,[57] and so it is profoundly communal.[58] In this, it has to do with the formation of people, who become a sign and witness to the Christian life as an embodied reality. This poses a challenge for radical evangelicals, who often operate with individualistic categories and build rather fragile Christian communities.

Second, Celtic spirituality is profoundly Trinitarian[59] and thus celebrates creation, redemption, beautification, and renewal.[60] One of the ongoing challenges facing the radical evangelical movement is its Christological focus, which tends to emphasize the historical Jesus without recognizing nature as the "second book" of God. In its concern for articulating a high Christology, the call to ecological care is often eclipsed. Moreover, in focusing on the work of Christ, there can be a reluctance to give due attention to the work of the empowering Spirit.

Third, Celtic spirituality can encourage radical evangelicals, who often celebrate the concept of Christian freedom, to consider sustained commitments to spiritual practices as a discipline of the heart.[61]

Franciscan Spirituality

As noted at the beginning of this chapter, radical evangelicals will need to draw on many traditions of Christian spirituality to gain a rich and sustaining spirituality for the inner life, for building community, and for the work of bearing witness and service in the world. The journey of drinking from the water of many fountains could be a "never ending story," and so I will close this chapter with a brief discussion of how Franciscan spirituality can challenge radical evangelicals.

---

57. See de Waal, *Celtic Vision*.

58. Some Celtic prayers are personal, such as, "Bless to me, O God / My heart and my speech / And bless to me, O God / The handling of my hand" (36). Yet there are also many communal prayers, such as, "Bless each maiden and youth / each woman and youngling / safeguard them beneath thy shield of strength" (53).

59. Trinitarian prayers are prolific: "In the name of the Father precious / And of the Spirit of healing balm / In the name of the Lord Jesus / I lay me down to rest" (105).

60. "The guarding of the God of life be on you / The guarding of [the] loving Christ be on you / The guarding of [the] Holy Spirit be on you" (248).

61. See Ringma, *A Fragile Hope*, 27–30.

Similar to Celtic spirituality, Franciscan spirituality is strongly Trinitarian and communitarian, has a vision of God both in nature and beyond nature, and celebrates earth-keeping. It also has a strong commitment to serving the poor and seeking the renewal of the church.

My contact with Franciscan brothers goes back to the early 1970s. Impressed with their work in Brisbane with disadvantaged young people, I stayed at the Franciscan Friary from time to time for personal retreats. More recently, after a process of formation, I have become a Franciscan tertiary, which has been refreshing and challenging. Elsewhere, I have attempted to articulate a Franciscan theology of peacemaking,[62] but in this chapter, I will highlight some of the major challenges that this tradition has for radical evangelicals.[63]

First, the Franciscan tradition has a surprisingly high view of the traditional church and seeks to enhance it by internal prophetic witness. In other words, it works from within the broader church rather than criticizing it from an unhealthy distance. Radical evangelicals can learn a lot from this stance. Some radical evangelicals only have a critical relationship to the parish church. Some are completely disconnected from the faith-community. Some arrogantly look down on the church as a sleeping giant while seeing themselves as God's paratroopers. And some create intentional communities in opposition to the parish church rather than seeking to be complementary to the community of faith. The Franciscan relationship to the church can challenge radical evangelicals to develop a more fully orbed understanding of the "communion of saints," as specified in the Apostles Creed, and also a more sacramental understanding of what it means to be "the body of Christ."

Second, as the Franciscan scholar Michael Crosby points out, the Franciscan call to "rebuild my house"[64] has wider implications than renewing the church. In Franciscan spirituality, renewing the church becomes iconic for rebuilding one's life, the general community, and the earth, for the *oikos* ("house") of God includes the *oikonomia* (economics) of society.[65] As Crosby notes, "Francis saw creation and everyone and everything in it [as] part of God's domain or household."[66] While radical evangelicals understand the concept of holistic or

---

62. See Gorospe and Ringma, eds., *How Long, O Lord?*, 163–86.

63. A much fuller discussion of Franciscan spirituality will be set out in chapter 14 ("Franciscan Peacemaking: A Key Theme in Missional Spirituality").

64. Crosby, *Finding Francis*, 52.

65. Crosby, 56.

66. Crosby, 57.

integral mission,[67] they often do not have an appreciation for the sacramental dimensions of life – where the self is a sacramental entity sculpted in the image of God, and society is bathed in the love and providence of God, and the earth is God's sustaining gift to the human community. Thus, society is not simply a social and economic domain, but an incipient – though often distorted – reflection of God's eschatological future. As Crosby writes, this sacramental vision of a "custodial participation in all of nature" calls us to service rather than "domination and usurpation."[68] Yet radical evangelicals tend to be pragmatic in their missional engagement, often lacking a sacramental spirituality that gives them a foundation for seeing and engaging the personal, social, and natural aspects of life.

Third, in "kissing the leper," Francis discovered that God could be found in the most unlikely places and circumstances – and thus we can be found by God in these marginal places. Despite the "radical" nature of radical evangelicals, they tend to operate from middle-class values and pragmatic programs. While some radical evangelicals, such as Servants to Asia's Urban Poor, have embraced the suffering Christ and a life of "poverty" in order to be with and serve the poor, many seek to follow Christ while remaining in places of safety and security.

In concluding this very brief summary of Franciscan spirituality, I will make several broad observations about how this spirituality can enrich radical evangelicals. First, amidst the "me-centred," consumer-Christianity of the West, where God is perceived as a sort of butler, Francis teaches us that a deep conversion to Jesus will call us to a complete reorientation of our values, priorities, and way of life.

Second, amidst a culture and a church ethos that is more about image and consuming rather than vulnerable servanthood, we can hear with Francis the call to repair God's house. Francis responded to this call practically by restoring the chapel of St. Mary of the Angels, but he also responded spiritually and missionally by forming a pilgrim community which sought to serve the poor and challenge those in power. A Franciscan spirituality can challenge us to do the same.

Third, amidst the dominant cultural trend of striving for upward mobility and believing that bigger is better, Francis points us towards downward mobility for the sake of the gospel.

---

67. See Tizon, *Transformation after Lausanne*.

68. Crosby, *Finding Francis*, 69.

Fourth, Francis lived in a time of violence, with city wars and crusades against Muslims. In a world that continues to be marred by violence and fear, Francis shows us another way. He did not join a crusade to wage war, but to embody the way of peace. His peace talks with the Sultan Malik al-Kamil challenge us to become peacemakers in the name of Christ.[69]

Finally, Francis demonstrated that the natural environment should be regarded – not in terms of resources to be exploited, but as "brothers and sisters" to whom we are bound in a caring commonwealth.[70] In a world where the rape of our natural resources continues unabated, Francis points us in another direction.

This chapter has drawn from four important Christian spiritual traditions to show how they may be relevant for the missional spirituality of radical evangelicals. Obviously, there are many more fountains to drink from in the rich tradition of Christian spirituality. In advocating that we drink from various fountains, I am in no way suggesting a *spiritual smorgasbord*, where we just pick and choose the bits and pieces that appeal to us. Rather, I am suggesting that we become deeply grounded in our own traditions and enrich these through dialogical[71] and integrative processes with other traditions.[72] Those who have more costly and extensive missional engagement in the world will need to be sustained and empowered by a rich and comprehensive spirituality.

Developing Our Own Distinctive Practices and Resources[73]

In developing practices and resources that will nurture and sustain a missional spirituality over the long haul, radical evangelical movements can seek to integrate the following three dimensions. First, the movement can seek to shape its life and work around the biblical story, from which it seeks its inspiration, direction, and hope. Second, the movement can draw from the distilled wisdom of the long march of the church through history, which (when healthy) integrated a vision of God and neighbour, prayer and service, and spirituality and the work for justice. Third, the movement can make sense of its own journey of life, prayer, and service by developing distinctive spiritual

69. See Gorospe and Ringma, eds., *How Long, O Lord?*, 163–86.

70. For more on Franciscan missional spirituality, see chapter 14 ("Franciscan Peacemaking: A Key Theme in Missional Spirituality").

71. See Gadamer, *Truth and Method.*

72. See Ringma, *A Fragile Hope*, 70–75.

73. Gustavo Gutierrez did this in *We Drink From Our Own Wells.*

practices in light of Scripture and the tradition of the church. In the following, I will briefly sketch how this third dimension might unfold within the context of a particular movement, Servants to Asia's Urban Poor.

Servants, like other radical evangelical groups, has its own history of calling, community, and mission. Some of this has appeared in book form, and much of it is held in the memory of its members. The first step would be to glean important themes from these writings and from interviewing Servants' workers.

Servants has articulated five distinctive missional principles and five core values.[74] Over time, a particular tradition of thinking and practice has developed around these principles and values. A second step would be to draw from this distinctive Servants' tradition to develop liturgical readings and reflections.

As Servants' teams and workers live out their mission in community, they repeatedly return to the same Scripture passages or other spiritual resources, sing particular hymns, and pray prayers (including prayers of lament) that the community finds particularly helpful and relevant. A third step would be to compile these passages, hymns, and prayers in order to develop shared resources and practices that reflect and sustain the heritage of Servants.

Over time, certain spiritual practices – such as fasting or foot-washing – and forms of celebration – such as Eucharistic practices, celebratory meals, and liturgical dances – have developed within various Servants' teams and in the larger Servants' forums that draw workers together from around Asia every three years. A fourth step would be to find ways to generalize these forms of celebration across the movement as a whole.

While this may sound like dull routinization, such a distillation process could help radical evangelical groups, such as Servants, retain their rich heritage while creating a communal missional spirituality that reflects both the life of the community and the nature of its service in places of inequality and deprivation in Asia's slums.[75] While I am in no way promoting an unhealthy inwardness or isolation in proposing the development of these common spiritual resources, I do believe that Christians who work in difficult and marginal spaces need to be sustained by resources that reflect the particular issues and struggles from within their context while framing those practices within the larger Christian tradition.

---

74. Jack, *Sound of Worlds Colliding*, 7–8.

75. For liturgical resources (mainly from the Majority World), see Carvalhaes, *Liturgies from Below.*

Conclusion

Radical evangelicals are known for their incarnational ministry in service to the poor, and so they are also known for self-sacrifice and activism. Given the great needs of the poor in major cities around the world, the challenge to *do* more is always present. Yet radical evangelicals need to cultivate a sustainable lifestyle that integrates community and service. This chapter has outlined how the missional spirituality of radical evangelicals can be enlivened by the radical lifestyle of the desert fathers and mothers, complemented by the Benedictine focus on a more balanced way of living, and challenged by Celtic and Franciscan practices.

While we have much to learn from radical evangelicals about community development, planting urban churches among the poor, training incarnational urban workers, engaging in micro-economic development, and working for social change, we should also be able to learn from this movement about Christian community, the practice of prayer and other spiritual disciplines, and a life of piety, simplicity, and wholeness. In other words, radical evangelicals can teach us how to follow Jesus and to live to the glory of God in communities of mutuality and care through their radical hospitality and loving service to the poor. As these communities seek to embody an integrated life of work and prayer, service and celebration, hospitality and rest, new spiritual resources will emerge that can bless and sustain the body of Christ.[76]

76. Part of this chapter was first published in *Phronesis* 14 (2007): 67–84.

13

The Anabaptist Vision of Community, Discipleship, and Service

Introduction

In an earlier chapter, I mentioned the development of David Augsburger's missional spirituality from within the broader Anabaptist tradition.[1] In this chapter, I will begin by setting out the contours of this tradition more fully. Then I will mine both early and contemporary Anabaptist writings to gain perspectives on their missional spirituality. This tradition is important to any discussion of missional spirituality, as the early Anabaptists, who were part of the radical wing of the Reformation,[2] developed theological distinctives that mark them as the missioners of the Reformation tradition. As Franklin Littell, a contemporary Anabaptist scholar, notes, the Anabaptist faith "stands on nothing other than the command of Christ . . . [to] go forth and preach the gospel," which "*applied to all Christians*."[3] We can also learn much from contemporary expressions of this tradition, particularly the Mennonites, who have produced rich missiology.[4] Unfortunately, contemporary missiological

1. Chapter 2 ("Towards a Missional Spirituality").

2. Timothy George points out that the radical wing of the Reformation consisted of multiple diverse groups, including the "Anabaptists, spiritualists, and evangelical rationalists" ("The Spirituality of the Radical Reformation," 335).

3. Littell, *The Anabaptist View of the Church*, 111, 112 (author's emphasis).

4. Throughout this chapter, I often refer to present-day Anabaptists as "contemporary Anabaptists" rather than "Mennonites" in order to keep a consistent flow of the narrative.

texts still give little attention to this tradition,[5] although a more recent volume brings Anabaptist missional writings into dialogue with evangelical and ecumenical perspectives.[6] Before exploring the distinctives of this tradition more fully, I will turn to my own introduction to the Anabaptist movement.

Personal Reflection

As mentioned in another chapter, I grew up and trained in the Reformed theological tradition, for which I am grateful and with which I have also wrestled for much of my life.[7] During my third year of theological studies, I had a sort of "epiphany" as I began to wonder why my professors so often dismissed the Anabaptists as off-base and irrelevant. In my spare time, I began to read Anabaptist history and theology and was impressed by their link between faith in Christ and following Christ in discipleship. I was challenged by their emphasis on the church as a *koinonia* community, and I was attracted to their notion of following the suffering, rather than the triumphant, Christ into the world. I was fascinated by their critique of the Christendom model of Christianity and many aspects of mainstream society, and their missional vision deeply impacted me.

Not long after these seeds were sown within me, green shoots started to appear. I had barely completed my theological studies when I began working on the streets of Brisbane with those in the drug scene, a context where I found Anabaptist concepts helpful. Art Gish's *The New Left and Christian Radicalism*[8] gave me and fellow workers the sense that Christianity was not fundamentally conservative but transformational. Gish's later book, *Living in Christian Community*,[9] helped cement the strategy that it would be far better to rehabilitate those with drug addiction issues in therapeutic Christian

5. Bosch gives the Anabaptists a brief mention in his monumental missional text, *Transforming Mission*, 246–47. But it is disappointing that both *Missiology: an Ecumenical Introduction: Texts and Contexts of Global Christianity* (gen. ed. Verstraelen) and *Towards the 21st Century in Christian Mission* (ed. Phillips and Coote) lack discussions on the Anabaptist tradition. It is surprising that in the latter book, contributor W. R. Shenk discusses "Mission Strategies" without reference to his own tradition (218–34). I also note that Stanley Skreslet's *Comprehending Mission*, while practical, lacks a discussion of the Anabaptist missional tradition.

6. Kraybill et al., *Evangelical, Ecumenical, and Anabaptist Missiologies in Conversation*. I do think, however, that much more could have been done in this text to highlight the similarities and differences *between* these three traditions.

7. Part of that wrestling is evident in my engagement with Thomas Merton. See Ringma, *Seek the Silences with Thomas Merton*.

8. Gish, *The New Left and Christian Radicalism*.

9. Gish, *Living in Christian Community*.

communities rather than institutional settings. Later, I had to wrestle with the peace tradition that lies at the heart of the Anabaptist tradition, which helped me rethink how Western mission was often implemented in the Majority World. So much of this ministry was not simply a matter of bringing the gospel to distant lands, but was overlaid with Christendom ideas and presumptions about Western cultural superiority.

Identifying Challenges to this Discussion

As noted in the above reflection, I am deeply appreciative of the Anabaptist movement, but my intent in this chapter is not to promote this tradition. Therefore, before proceeding with this discussion, it is important to acknowledge some monumental difficulties. First, I am aware of the complexity and diversity of early Anabaptism as a radical wing of the Reformation,[10] which consisted of many diverse groups.[11] I am also aware of the many ways in which scholars have attempted to interpret this movement. Thus, I will not attempt to engage the varied historical discussions that this diversity has produced,[12] but will simply draw on the broader consensus.

Second, I will be returning to the inspirational core of the early Anabaptist movement while also drawing on contemporary Anabaptist writers, a span that covers over five hundred years. This creates difficulties in that many early Anabaptist perspectives and emphases have changed over the course of time.[13] For example, some Anabaptist scholars have noted that the early Anabaptist missionary zeal in the sixteenth century dissipated with the

10. Langmead rightly points out that there "is no easy way to decide what should be considered central to Anabaptist traditions because a wide variety existed," and he favourably quotes John Howard Yoder that there was no "univocal Anabaptism" (*The Word Made Flesh*, 63). Sawatsky pushes this even further by noting that there was a significant pluralism "even among the so-called 'evangelical' Anabaptists" ("The One and the Many: The Recovery of Mennonite Pluralism," 141).

11. As noted, Timothy George, in "The Spirituality of the Radical Reformation," claims that the radical Reformation consisted of "Anabaptists, spiritualists, and evangelical rationalists," and that the broader Anabaptist movement itself consisted of "evangelical (Swiss Brethren, Mennonites, Hutterites); revolutionary (Munsterites); contemplative (Hans Denck)" movements (334–35).

12. See Klaassen, *Anabaptism Revisited.*

13. In "The One and the Many: The Recovery of Mennonite Pluralism," Sawatsky identifies four typologies in Anabaptism: separatist (sociocultural nonconformity to mainstream society), establishment (biblical nonresistance and personal holiness), reformist (radically following Christ in discipleship); transformationist (political and ideological nonconformity to the powers of this age) (149).

following generations.[14] Moreover, contemporary Anabaptist scholars often write from differing starting points (theology, ethics, spirituality, missiology), which invites differing emphases.

Third, some contemporary Anabaptist scholars have attempted to typify mainstream Anabaptism as emphasizing certain core themes – such as discipleship (Bender), believers' church (Yoder), faith-community in opposition to present world order (Friedmann), a pilgrim and martyr missionary faith-community (Littell), and a communal spirituality in the way of Jesus (Driver), among others.[15] Yet other voices have resisted attempts to characterise the tradition in terms of certain major paradigms, suggesting instead that "precariousness, ambiguity, and unsettlement is an essential characteristic of what it means to be a Mennonite."[16] And while Sawatsky identifies four Anabaptist typologies (separatist, establishment, reformist, transformationist),[17] he chides Bender's typification as being an idealized theological construct.[18] The same could probably be said of all the others – and I might be similarly blamed as well!

Fourth, some outside the tradition have automatically dismissed Anabaptism because the Anabaptists were condemned by the Reformers.[19] Moreover, Anabaptists have been criticized for having politically radical elements[20] and for being separatist and against mainstream society.[21] For example, Niebuhr, in *Christ and Culture*, criticizes the movement as reflecting

14. Focusing on Mennonites in Netherlands, the scholar van der Zijpp says, "missionary work of the first generation yielded to the silent seclusion of the congregations in the following centuries" ("From Anabaptist Missionary Congregation to Mennonite Seclusion," 127). Writing more broadly, Gallardo notes how the movement in time lost its apostolic zeal and became "the quiet in the land" and how the "practice of ethnic and geographic separation from the world resulted in a deformed faith" ("Ethics and Mission," 152).

15. Not that any of this is terribly significant, since many of these themes, if not all, are complementary.

16. Huebner, *A Precarious Peace*, 25.

17. Sawatsky, "The One and the Many," 149. Again, we need to careful not to overdraw these distinctions, as a faith-community can (and should) be *both* separatist and transformationist at the same time, for in forming its own distinctive "life together," it can have a more prophetic witness to the world.

18. Sawatsky, 46.

19. Calvin, *Treatises Against the Anabaptists and Against the Libertines.*

20. One group within the diverse Anabaptist movement captured the city of Munster (1534–35) in preparation for Christ's second coming, though this was by no means representative of the movement as a whole.

21. The Amish communities readily come to mind.

a world-denying form of Christianity.[22] And Langmead is concerned that some contemporary Anabaptist scholars overstress the *imitatio Christi*. In a critique of both Yoder and Weaver, he says that they "are more concerned to argue for the centrality of discipleship and obedience than to explain in detail the other side of the coin, the gift of grace in enabling Christians to live this new transformed life."[23] But Langmead later acknowledges that other Anabaptists do place an "emphasis on grace as God's initiating activity."[24] While Langmead's concern may be valid, there are several more pertinent issues. First of all, nearly all Anabaptist writings are piecemeal rather than systematic, and most of the early Anabaptist writings were tracts, hymns, defences before magistrates, and testimonies.[25] Moreover, pluralism characterized the early Anabaptist movement.

Finally, while much more could be said about the concerns that scholars have about Anabaptism, this book is a work of my own reconstruction and integration, and thus it is important to acknowledge my own concerns and biases regarding this tradition. First, Anabaptism focuses on the NT, particularly the Gospels. Engagement with the whole canon of Scripture would yield other outcomes. Second, Anabaptism was a corrective movement within the Reformation, and therefore it did not attempt to set out its own theology, but focused on the perceived weaknesses in the Reformation. As a result, some theological perspectives were underplayed or neglected. For example, while much attention was given to God as the redeemer, little attention was given to God as the creator. Third, early Anabaptism was birthed during a time of high anticipation about the Lord's return or the end of the world.[26] During such times, more radical forms of the Christian church come into being. Revivalism usually issues in communitarianism, but in the long journey of delay, the church takes on more mundane forms of life together. Lastly, there is a growing recognition that Anabaptism still has something important to say to the contemporary church, but the movement is also acknowledging that it has much to learn from other church traditions.[27] Thus a greater mutuality is at play, for which we can all be grateful.

---

22. This is a misguided assessment, as we shall soon see.

23. Langmead, *The Word Made Flesh*, 75.

24. Langmead, 77.

25. Hubmaier was the only theologian in the ranks of the early Anabaptists.

26. Driver, *Life Together in the Spirit*, 33.

27. Driver, for example, acknowledges how much he learned and gained from contact with Rene Padilla and Samuel Escobar, and some of the liberation theologians such as Leonardo Boff. He acknowledges the importance of "the preferential option of the poor" and believes that the

Contemporary Relevance of Anabaptism

Before we lose our focus in this chapter, let us return to our consideration of how this tradition can benefit our exploration of a missional spirituality. As the contemporary Anabaptist, Stuart Murray, points out, "Anabaptism, at its core, is a missional movement,"[28] which has many theological and spiritual distinctives[29] that will serve us well in crafting a missional spirituality. Moreover, Anabaptism is committed to the missional mandate in Matthew's Gospel, which it has embraced through a profound understanding of the nature of discipleship. This understanding was spawned by the "regenerated [and] yielded nature of the Christian life" in following Christ and was expressed in "sharing of possessions, truth telling, love of enemies, and the forsaking of violent means."[30] Thus, the community of faith is meant to be an embodiment of the gospel and therefore to embody God's good news to the world. In other words, the church is to be a hermeneutic of the gospel.[31] As John Howard Yoder notes, the Anabaptist movement reflects the "mark of the church as missionary,"[32] which it has outworked with its own missional distinctives and the broader theological notion of "presence, identification, and servanthood."[33]

Before engaging particular voices within the Anabaptist movement, it is important to articulate why we need to give serious consideration to this tradition, as it is rather small by any standards.[34] First, we are living in a post-Christendom world, where the church has to find its way in the world without relying on the social and political privileges of the past. This marginal setting can be difficult to negotiate, but the Anabaptist tradition is familiar with this

"restoration of God's righteous reign" has to do with "God's eternal purpose for all humanity and the created order" ("Unanticipated Journey for Sharing an Anabaptist and Liberationist Perspective on the Gospel," 249, 256).

28. Murray, *The Naked Anabaptist*, 39.

29. Murray, 45–46.

30. Snyder, *Following in the Footsteps of Christ*, 158, 157.

31. Newbigin notes that the "presence of the kingdom, hidden and revealed in the cross of Jesus, is carried . . . in the life of that community which bears in its life the dying and rising of Jesus" (*The Open Secret*, 52).

32. Yoder, *Theology of Mission*, 192.

33. Yoder, 331.

34. In 2000, Anabaptist/Mennonite church members numbered only 500,000 in the Minority World (Western) and 700,000 in the Majority World (Lapp, "The Global Mennonite History Project," 51). Present-day numbers are 1.75 million, with two-thirds living outside North America. See thirdwaycafe.com/faq/where-are-mennonites-located-throughout-the-world.

position, as it critiqued the Christendom model, and radical Anabaptists have been a marginalized group marked by persecution and suffering.[35]

Second, the contemporary church is still struggling with its social "dethronement," and so there continue to be signs of the church seeking political advantages,[36] as the ongoing assumption remains that a more powerful church can do greater good in society.[37] The Anabaptists, by contrast, have long believed that the faith-community should not attempt to manage society, but should rely on the gospel and the Spirit as it seeks to be a faithful witness in society.[38] The contemporary Anabaptist critique is clear: "Evangelicalism enjoys without a scruple a new social-political acceptance which approaches a reestablishment of it as a dominant civil religion," and "it aggressively uses its political clout to bring about moral and religious reform through law."[39]

Third, the Anabaptist movement is an important forerunner to the current "The Gospel and Our Culture Series," which stresses the importance of missional church.[40] Though Anabaptists emphasize that "the church is a missionary community," they also stress "discipleship as the heart of Christian commitment, an ecclesiology which emphasizes community . . . service, suffering love, and peace as central to the life of salvation and the preaching of the gospel."[41] Thus, the missional nature of the Anabaptist faith-community has many distinctives, some of which are not central to "The Gospel and Our Culture Series."

Finally, the Anabaptist movement has sought to return to the inspiration of the NT in order to form "ordinary" people through discipleship in the way

---

35. "Thousands of Anabaptists were martyred in the sixteenth century" (Murray, *The Naked Anabaptist*, 153). Around one third of these martyrs were women (Driver, *Life Together in the Spirit*, 60). Since the Anabaptists believed that the Great Commission "applied to all Christians" (Littell, *The Anabaptist View of the Church*, 112), and since most Anabaptists were "common people," it was telling that "thousands of Anabaptist prisoners confronted expert questioning [about their beliefs] by learned pastors, both Catholic and Protestant, and demonstrated the scriptural foundations of their faith" (Snyder, *Following in the Footsteps of Christ*, 33–34).

36. We need only think of the church under the Trump presidency, or the church and political alliance in Poland, or the political support of Eastern Orthodox churches, or the continuance of state churches such as the Church of England, as well as the many attempts in Latin America and Africa to mix politics and religion.

37. This is the continuation of the Constantinian project of church and sociopolitical alliances (Huebner, *A Precarious Peace*).

38. There is a world of difference between seeking to *manage* society and seeking to be a *witness* in society. Management is more in keeping with Constantinianism and theocracy, while the Anabaptist vision is "to be present [in society] as servant" (Yoder, *For the Nations*, 244).

39. Kraus, "Anabaptism and Evangelicalism," 176.

40. Guder, *Missional Church*.

41. Jose Gallardo, "Ethics and Mission," 155.

of Christ. The early Anabaptists embraced a life of faith that involved being baptised into Christ, baptised into a lived community, and sometimes baptised into blood (martyrdom) as a result of their witness. In our contemporary era of consumer Christianity – where there is little formation, and people seldom read Scripture or attend church, but only turn to Christ when it is convenient – the Anabaptists can both challenge and teach us.[42]

The New Birth and its Fruit

Finally, it is time to hear directly from the early Anabaptists and their successors. I must begin by stressing that the central biblical and theological themes of the Anabaptist movement cannot be nicely compartmentalized, as one can with the major Protestant traditions, for the Anabaptist orientation is more concerned with weaving a cohesive tapestry of the whole Christian life. As Robert Friedmann observes in his theological reflections, the Anabaptist writings reflect an *integrative* approach, that of the "unity of faith and life,"[43] which he describes as an "existential Christianity."[44]

To give one example of this integrative approach, the early Anabaptist discussion of our new birth in Christ led to an emphasis on baptism, which led to the significance of the faith-community, which led to its task to be a witnessing and suffering community in the world. One early Anabaptist voice, Dirk Philips, writes about how humanity was made "in God's own image and likeness," but then fell through disobedience, which led to "death and corruption," and therefore we need Jesus, "the redeemer and savior of the human race," to be "renewed in the image of God and reborn to eternal life."[45] This rebirth is a "work of God" that comes "through the word of truth" and "through faith in Jesus Christ in the Holy Spirit." Christians, therefore, stand and live before God "by pure grace alone," and thus they are a "peculiar people" who are the "firstfruits" of God's birthing.[46] Philips continues that

42. The contemporary Anabaptist, Stuart Murray, claims the following as Anabaptist core convictions: "following Jesus, as well as worshipping him," a "Jesus-centered approach to the Bible," pursuing "alternative ways of thinking and believing" to the Christendom approach, church "as good news to the poor," church as "community," living the link between "spirituality and economics," and living the theme of peace at "the heart of the gospel" (*The Naked Anabaptist*, 45–46).

43. Friedmann, *The Theology of Anabaptism*, 31.

44. Friedmann, 27.

45. "Concerning the New Birth and the New Creature" (1556), quoted in Liechty, 201.

46. Liechty, 202–4.

when we "recognize [our] . . . own sin" and "trust in the grace of God" and then "through grace . . . avoid evil and do what is good," we exhibit "love for God and . . . neighbor" and "bear the fruit of the Spirit."[47] Philips goes on to say that the person marked by "the new birth should have the character and nature of Christ."[48] Moreover, the believer who "is conformed to the image of Jesus Christ" will serve "God in submission, obedience, and righteousness."[49]

Thus, for the early Anabaptists, our new birth in Christ is not merely a matter of belief, but a process that has profound implications for our whole life. Another early Anabaptist, Hans Hut, makes similar observations, writing that "no human being comes to salvation except through the suffering and tribulation which is the work of Christ in him [her]."[50] In the "Instruction on Beginning a True Christian Life" (1527), Hans Schlaffer begins with the reflection that "all of humanity lives in evil, blindness, and error," and therefore we need God to "enlighten the darkness of our hearts" and to "bring us to that light which alone is Jesus Christ." This light calls each of us to conversion, since "all of [our] previous deeds and thoughts are evil," and it is impossible to live the Christian life in our own power. Schlaffer goes on to talk about how we must allow God to shape and steward us for God's purposes, observing that "God alone must make us spiritual, righteous, and worthy for his praise."[51]

Contemporary Anabaptist writers echo these emphases. For example, Cornelius J. Dyck speaks of our need to acknowledge our sinfulness and our need of Christ's salvation and grace, which is a "divine power" to change us and make us participants in God's "divine nature."[52] And C. Arnold Snyder favourably quotes Menno Simons on the need to be born again, writing that God seeks to "show you His mercy and grace" and that we need to "repent and . . . believe."[53] Snyder also quotes Pilgrim Marpeck, who says that the remedy for sin depends "on the mercy of God and on His grace in and with Christ" and that "yieldedness" to God stands at the beginning and throughout a believer's life.[54] Snyder then observes that the heartbeat of Anabaptist spirituality is the "new birth by God's power," the call to "baptism," and a

47. Liechty, 205.

48. Liechty, 217.

49. Liechty, 200.

50. Liechty, 69.

51. Liechty, 99, 100, 101.

52. Dyck, "The Anabaptist Understanding of the Good News," 30–31.

53. Snyder, *Following in the Footsteps of Christ*, 36.

54. Snyder, 40–41.

"new life of discipleship." He goes on to point out that in Anabaptist belief, grace is not so much a forensic concept, but a "living power that . . . transforms sinners."[55] Similarly, John Driver describes Anabaptist spirituality as an identification "with the life and death of Jesus," a "cruciform spirituality" that is rooted "in the divine initiative of God's promise" of new life.[56]

Friedmann, who is quoted at the beginning of this section, notes that for Anabaptists, grace means "the inner power to resist sin" and "the act whereby God renews the divine image" in the believer.[57] Similarly, the focus of justification is not on a particular forensic standing, but on what Friedmann refers to as *Fromm-Machung*, or God's action in Christ to bring a person "into the right or proper relationship to God that makes him [her] a genuine follower of Christ."[58] Hans J. Hillerbrand concurs that the early Anabaptists held justification by grace alone, but stressed "a radical transformation of one's whole being."[59] This does not mean that Anabaptists collapsed justification into sanctification, for they stressed growth in the Christian life.[60] But they did believe that the words of Scripture, which shaped their theology,[61] had power that could bring about a new identity and a new way of life. Thus, for Anabaptists, Scripture was to be *embodied*, not simply believed.

Faith and Discipleship

Following this integrative approach, when early Anabaptists talked about faith, they also talked about discipleship, and when they talked about the suffering of Christ for humanity's redemption, they also spoke about how "the whole Christ suffers in all his members."[62] For example, the early Anabaptist hymns (many of which were written by members of the movement while in

55. Snyder, 51, 55.

56. John Driver, *Life Together in the Spirit*, 2–3.

57. Friedmann, 97, 93.

58. Friedmann, 88. In other words, *Fromm-Machung* suggests an actual change in one's nature rather than merely being pardoned for one's sins.

59. Quoted in Liechty, *Early Anabaptist Spirituality*, "Preface," xx.

60. Hans Hut, "On the Mystery of Baptism" (1526), notes that believers still "battle against the flesh" and "true baptism is nothing other than the struggle against sin throughout one's entire life" (quoted in Liechty, 77, 78).

61. Hillerbrand notes that the early Anabaptists were "bereft of theological expertise," and thus their faith and spirituality were "oriented by the Bible" (quoted in Liechty, *Early Anabaptist Spirituality*, "Preface," xvii–xviii).

62. Hans Hut, "On the Mystery of Baptism" (1526), quoted in Liechty, *Early Anabaptist Spirituality*, 67.

prison)[63] demonstrate a clear connection between faith and discipleship: God "has chosen us out of his grace," but "clothe[s] us with your Spirit" so that we may be gifted "with divine power" in order to "know your will" and so we may "go bravely into suffering."[64]

Similarly, in "On the Mystery of Baptism" (1526), Hans Hut says that the Christian believes in Christ crucified (faith), but at the same time Christ is also crucified "in all his members" (discipleship).[65] Hut continues that "no human comes to salvation except through the suffering and tribulation which is the work of God," and justification "does not come from an untried faith," but a tried faith.[66] Thus, the "suffering of the holy cross is laid upon each person."[67] Or in the words of Hans Denck, "no one can know Christ unless he follow after him in life."[68] In summary, the early Anabaptists speak about a tried faith, an embodied faith, a serving faith, and a suffering faith.

Turning to contemporary Anabaptist voices, John Driver writes that "the person of Jesus . . . [is] central" to a life of faith, and "Jesus . . . [is] a model to be followed in daily life." Driver describes "discipleship as *participation* in the very nature of Jesus" and observes that this lies at the heart of Anabaptist spirituality.[69] Similarly, C. Arnold Snyder notes that the "integration of inner spiritual reality with outward witness characterizes Anabaptist spirituality" and that "salvation is by faith and obedience."[70]

Jose Gallardo also makes a link between faith and discipleship as well as salvation and service, writing that "the cross is the way of our salvation" (faith), and the cross is "the shape of our life" (discipleship). He continues, "Jesus is at the same time the model for human behavior and the means for our spiritual transformation."[71]

---

63. Between 1525–1600, some two thousand Anabaptist hymns were composed (the *Ausbund*). These were often sung in prison and at the gallows. The authorities of the prison in Tyrol prevented singing because this "gives strength to the prisoners to persist in their heretical beliefs" (Snyder, *Following in the Footsteps of Christ*, 131–32).

64. Quoted in Liechty, *Early Anabaptist Spirituality*, 48, 49, 43, 51, 59.

65. Liechty, 67.

66. Liechty, 69, 76.

67. Liechty, 76.

68. In Murray, *The Naked Anabaptist*, 58.

69. Driver, *Life Together in the Spirit*, 49, 50, his emphasis.

70. Snyder, *Following in the Footsteps of Christ*, 72, 73.

71. Gallardo, "Ethics and Mission," 141. In my opinion, Gallardo has the right order in the first statement, but not in the second statement. Generally, the Anabaptist movement could place a greater emphasis on the Pauline "in Christ" relationship before speaking about the *imitatio Christi.*

John Howard Yoder speaks of the importance of "confessing Christ as Lord" and "identifying with the incarnation."[72] Moreover, he points out that our witness is "to God, who is in Christ."[73] But these statements are not meant to stand alone, for Yoder immediately connects them to Christian belief and action. In speaking of "confessing Christ as Lord," he emphasizes the importance of our actions, and he identifies the shape of our obedience as "Jesus Christ himself."[74] In speaking of the need to "confess Jesus' normativeness," he draws a connection to the nature of the faith-community, which is to be "God's beachhead in the world," that is, "the prototype, the herald, the midwife of the new world on the way."[75] Yoder further identifies the incarnation as the "standard" and the "motivation and power" for our "obedience" to Christ in the world.[76] Moreover, he emphasises that all we seek to do in witness and service in the world is to be done "in the way of Christ."[77]

All these voices highlight the importance of integration in the Anabaptist movement. Faith in Christ does not stand alone, because the person of Jesus Christ calls us to live out our faith in conformity to the way that he lived and served in the world. Thus faith, obedience, and discipleship belong together. As Robert Friedmann notes, the Anabaptist tradition emphasizes the idea that "once the reborn person comes to know that God has revealed to him [her] His will, there is but one thing for him [her] to do: to obey. The word 'obedience' is used more often in Anabaptist writings than the term 'discipleship,' or following Christ."[78]

Faith, Discipleship, and Baptism

In the Anabaptist tradition, baptism is directly related to faith in that those who are born again and have come to faith in Christ, through the Spirit, are to express that faith by embracing baptism in obedience to Christ. This baptism is inspired by Matthew's Gospel – "Go therefore and make disciples of all nations, baptizing them in the name of the Father and of the Son and of the Holy Spirit, and teaching them to obey everything I have commanded you"

72. Yoder, *For the Nations*, 110.
73. Yoder, 108.
74. Yoder, 109.
75. Yoder, 218.
76. Yoder, 110.
77. Yoder, 111.
78. Friedmann, *The Theology of Anabaptism*, 44.

(28:19–20). Moreover, the accounts of baptism in the Acts of the apostles brought the early Anabaptists into conflict with Roman Catholicism and magisterial Protestantism, which resulted in the persecution, imprisonment, and drowning of many Anabaptists.[79] As Hans Hillerbrand points out, the Anabaptist practice of adult baptism, as a further response of faith, "disrupted" the "identity of civic and religious community" in the European world of that time.[80] With the emphasis on a "visible change of life" and the call to embrace suffering, the Anabaptist movement brought a new faith-community into the world.[81]

In "On the Mystery of Baptism" (1526), Hans Hut speaks about the need to "be justified and made pure" by Christ, which comes to expression both "inwardly and outwardly."[82] One core outward expression of faith is baptism, and Hut connects the preaching of the gospel with those who believe, and those who believe with those who embrace baptism.[83] This baptism results in the "Christian community of God" and also in suffering, since Christ is crucified "in all his members."[84] Hut elaborates that this baptism is not so much a sacrament as a "memorial," where the person "must set his [her] heart to remain in the Lord and forsake the world," which makes one provisionally "pure in the Holy Spirit" in the reality of "affliction."[85] Hut describes the "baptism of the new birth" as the "bath of the soul"[86] and goes on to say that "true baptism is nothing other than the struggle against sin throughout one's entire life."[87]

Similarly, Hans Schlaffer, in his "Instruction on Beginning a True Christian Life" (1527), notes that baptism is for "those who have already believed" and have "received the Holy Spirit."[88] As such, it is an "outward confession."[89]

79. The other major Christian groups, both Catholic and Protestant, still followed the Christendom practice of infant baptism. For the Anabaptists, baptism was a further response of faith and discipleship.

80. Hillerbrand, "Preface," in *Anabaptist Spirituality*, ed. Liechty, xvii.

81. Hillerbrand, xix.

82. Quoted in Liechty, *Early Anabaptist Spirituality*, 70.

83. Liechty, 67.

84. Liechty, 67.

85. Liechty, 72, 73, 74. Hut makes the point that our faith is like silver "embedded in the ore" and needs the fires of suffering to purify it (Liechty, 75).

86. Liechty, 77.

87. Liechty, 78.

88. Liechty, 107, 108.

89. Liechty, 107.

He speaks of the covenant in Christ being "sealed with his blood" and says that "the work of the Spirit in the hearts of people" comes to further birth in baptism "in Spirit and fire," which results in a "willingness to suffer anything for the will of God."[90]

Within the Anabaptist community of faith, baptism in water takes place after one confesses one's faith in "the name of the Father, Son, and Holy Spirit,"[91] a confession that is premised on having already been baptized internally with the Holy Spirit.[92] Thus, there is the initial Spirit baptism of being birthed into the life of faith in Christ and then a second baptism into the faith-community on the basis of one's confession of faith and a commitment to enter a new way of living. There is also an implied third baptism – the blood baptism of a martyr's death – for as Hans Schlaffer puts it, "whoever does not suffer with Christ, will not share in his inheritance."[93] In the light of this concept of a blood baptism, it should not surprise us that contemporary Anabaptists identify the movement as a "messianic resurgence" that is shaped by a replication of the suffering servant of Isaiah 53.[94] David A. Shank goes on to say that in Anabaptist Christology, the focus is on "obedient sonship," and when we embrace baptism, we reflect the obedience of Christ.[95]

Another contemporary Anabaptist, John Driver, makes the point that the Anabaptist understanding of baptism signifies *Gelassenheit* ("yieldedness") to Christ and involves an inner commitment to Christ (the new birth, through the Spirit), a commitment to the faith-community (water baptism), and a commitment to suffer for the sake of Christ (blood baptism).[96] Here again, we see the interconnected nature of core Anabaptist beliefs. Water baptism, which is based on confession, repentance, and testimony of faith to the church, necessarily involves participation in the faith-community, which will involve mutual sharing, fraternal counsel, and missional engagement.[97] Similarly, William Estep notes that for the Anabaptists, baptism expresses a "corporate

90. Liechty, 105, 106, 108.

91. Matt 18:19.

92. John the Baptist bears witness, saying, "I saw the Spirit descend from heaven like a dove, and it remained on him. I myself did not know him, but he who sent me to baptize with water said to me, 'He on whom you see the Spirit descend and remain, this is he who baptizes with the Holy Spirit'" (John 1:32–33).

93. Liechty, xxi.

94. Shank, "Anabaptists and Mission," 227.

95. Shank, "Jesus the Messiah: Messianic Foundation of Mission," 64.

96. Driver, *Life Together in the Spirit*, 38.

97. Driver, 37.

discipleship."[98] Thus, baptism marks one's entry into communal life and is not simply a personal response to faith in Christ.

C. Arnold Snyder makes the point that these two baptisms are dependent on one another, for rebirth – or Spirit baptism – is the basis for water baptism and involves a commitment to the faith-community, its discipline, and its life together.[99] Moreover, one's formation and sustenance in the community leads to service in the world and a "willingness to accept a baptism in blood."[100] The notion of these three baptisms is undergirded by the call in Matthew 28[101] to follow the example of Christ and draws on "Pauline baptismal images," which refer to being "buried with Him in death, so that they might rise with Him" in newness of life.[102] Snyder further suggests that all three baptisms reflect the notion of *Gelassenheit*, where there is "yieldedness" towards *God* in the first baptism, "yieldedness" to the *faith-community* in the second baptism, and "yieldedness" to the *will of God* in embracing the baptism of blood. This makes baptism in the Anabaptist tradition a "profound ascetic and communal" response in a "life devoted entirely to following in Christ's footsteps."[103]

Friedmann concludes that "Baptism with the Spirit was recognized as a gift of salvation which gives power for a new life. Baptism with water works towards the establishment of a . . . *Gemeinde.* But the baptism with blood . . . [was] the tribulation of martyrdom . . . the birth pangs of the kingdom of God which has drawn near and might break in at any moment."[104]

Christology, the Trinity, and the Messianic Community

In this tapestry of Anabaptist beliefs and actions, we can note that their fundamental Christological orientation is woven together with their ecclesiology. While the early Anabaptists accepted the ancient creeds, they did not speculate about the nature of Christ, for their focus was on who Christ was *in relation to the church.* By way of example, David A. Shank prefers to speak about the "Messiah doctrine" rather than Christology, because he wants

98. Estep, *The Anabaptist Story*, 158.

99. Snyder, *Following in the Footsteps of Christ*, 70, 79.

100. Snyder, 69.

101. "Go therefore and make disciples of all nations, baptizing them in the name of the Father and of the Son and of the Holy Spirit . . ." (Matt 28:19).

102. Snyder, 76, 75.

103. Snyder, 82, 83.

104. Friedmann, *The Theology of Anabaptism*, 138. The German word, *Gemeinde*, can be translated as "community" or "parish."

to emphasize Jesus as "a specific historical personality" who demonstrates an "obedient sonship" to the Father.[105] This emphasis has shaped Anabaptist ecclesiology in that the early Anabaptists were seeking to follow the person of Jesus, and this resulted in a church that lived as an "Anabaptist messianic community, which knew . . . suffering, persecution, and martyrdom."[106] We misread the above discussion of faith and baptism if we simply focus on the rebirth and baptism of the individual, for Anabaptism is strongly communal.

Similarly, the early Anabaptists accepted the doctrine of the Trinity, but their orientation was non-speculative, as evidenced by "The Schleitheim Confession" (1527): "May joy, peace, and mercy from our Father through the atonement of the blood of Christ Jesus, together with the gifts of the Spirit – who is sent from the Father to all believers for their strength and comfort and for their perseverance in all tribulation until the end."[107] Though these opening words celebrate God as Father, Son, and Holy Spirit, and the confession goes on to speak of the "oneness" of the persons of the Trinity,[108] the focus is on what God the Father has done through Christ in the Holy Spirit for the redemption of humanity, of which the church is an embodiment and witness. And while Christ is acknowledged as God's "Son," the creed focuses on how Christians are "called by one God to one faith, to one baptism,[109] to one body," of which Christ is the "Head."[110] Moreover, the death and resurrection of Christ, which are core elements of the good news, are outworked, first and foremost, in the faith-community, which is identified as "those who walk in the resurrection of Christ, and wish to be buried with Him in death."[111] The remainder of this confession moves to Anabaptist distinctives regarding the nature of the church and its life together in terms of baptism, the ban,[112] the breaking of bread, the use of the sword, and oath-taking.[113]

Balthasar Hubmaier, the only trained theologian in the early ranks of the Anabaptists, reiterates the above themes. He acknowledges the Trinity – one

105. Shank, "Jesus the Messiah: Messianic Foundation of Mission," 39.

106. Shank, 42.

107. Leith, ed., *Creeds of the Churches*, 282.

108. ". . . we have perceived the oneness of the Spirit of our Father and of our common Christ with us" (Leith, 283).

109. Even though this "one" baptism has three dimensions: the new birth, water baptism into the faith-community, and a baptism of blood through suffering for and with Christ.

110. Leith, 285.

111. Leith, 284.

112. Or excommunication.

113. Leith, 284.

of the "central tenets of our Christian faith [is] that God is Father, Son, and Holy Spirit" – but he focuses on the restorative work of Christ, whom he calls "the true physician."[114] Hubmaier notes that the "soul [is] . . . restored to health by God's beloved Son and [the] enlightenment of the Holy Spirit," that "our perfection is in Christ," and that "the Father now looks upon humanity in a new way because of the service of our Lord Jesus Christ."[115] He goes on to make his overall point that Christ's restorative work is so transformative "that we can will and do good."[116] Here again, we see the connection between what God has done through Christ, in the Spirit, which forms and shapes Christians and the faith-community into becoming a healing and witnessing presence in the world.

Another early Anabaptist, Hans Hut, references the Trinity while couching it in ecclesiology: "the congregation of God is the true foundation of Christianity, the bride and the spouse of Christ, unified in the bonds of love through the Holy Spirit."[117] Hut's overall theme is clear: the church is to be and do what Christ has already been and done. While he describes the gospel as "simply Christ the crucified one," he immediately adds that "Christ [is] crucified in his members."[118]

Leonard Schiemer, another early Anabaptist voice, implies a Trinitarian formula in his discussion of three kinds of grace: the first reveals people's "sinful state," the second has to do with Christ's redemptive work on "the cross," and the third has to do with the comforting work of the Holy Spirit.[119] Yet this Trinitarian formula is directly applied to God's salvific activity for humanity.

The early Anabaptist contemplative, Hans Denck, takes a more theologically reflective approach to his discussion of the Trinity. In "Concerning True Love," he describes God as "uncreated" but also the "Maker of all things."[120] Identifying the Son's incarnation and cross as the way of salvation, he acknowledges that the nature of "the love of God toward humanity" is most clearly shown "in

114. Hubmaier, "Concerning Freedom of the Will" (1527), quoted in Liechty, *Early Anabaptist Spirituality*, 31, 36–37.

115. Liechty, 31, 33, 35.

116. Liechty, 34.

117. Hut, "On the Mystery of Baptism" (1526), quoted in Liechty, 64.

118. Liechty, 67.

119. Schiemer, "Three Kinds of Grace" (1527), quoted in Liechty, 90, 92, 93.

120. Denck, "Concerning True Love" (1527), quoted in Liechty, 113.

Jesus."[121] Yet he goes on to say that the Son "was always united with God" and was "one with God's Spirit from eternity."[122]

In "Concerning the New Birth and the New Creature" (1556), Dirk Philips demonstrates a clear commitment to Trinitarian theology, writing that "the new birth is of God the heavenly Father. Through Jesus Christ and through the Holy Spirit, a person is changed and is made new."[123] He also makes several Christological references: "Jesus Christ is the image of God";[124] a person must be "reborn into the communion and likeness of Christ";[125] "Christ Jesus [is] the only Son of the Living God"; and Christ is "our Lord and Savior."[126]

The "The Dordrecht Confession" (1632), which was written more than a hundred years later than "The Schleitheim Confession" (1527) quoted above, is more theologically structured in that it refers to God the creator, the fall, the nature of redemption in Christ, and the nature and ministry of the church. Nevertheless, it maintains the orientation of other early Anabaptist writers in its focus on how God's redemption in Christ births and shapes the new faith-community. Its Trinitarian statement, however, is more explicit: "there is one eternal, almighty, and incomprehensible God, Father, Son, and the Holy Ghost, and none more and none other, before whom no God existed, neither will exist after Him. For from Him, through Him, and in Him are all things."[127] Its Christology describes Christ as the "immaculate Lamb" and "Son of God," who was "fore-ordained" before "the foundation of the world" for humanity's "comfort, redemption, and salvation."[128] It goes on to speak of the virgin birth, Christ's crucifixion, death, resurrection, and ascension, and it declares that Christ "'finished' the work for which He was sent into the world" by purchasing "redemption for the whole human race."[129] Moreover, it describes Christ as the "source of eternal salvation to all who . . . shall have believed in Him, and obeyed Him."[130]

---

121. Liechty, 114.

122. Liechty, 114.

123. Philips, "Concerning the New Birth and the New Creature" (1556), quoted in Liechty, 205.

124. Liechty, 201.

125. Liechty, 201.

126. Liechty, 202.

127. Leith, ed., *Creeds of the Churches*, 293.

128. Leith, 294–95.

129. Leith, 296.

130. Leith, 296.

Turning to contemporary Anabaptist voices, Robert Friedmann makes similar points, noting how the Anabaptist orientation towards Christology immediately integrates salvation and ecclesiology. Though Christ is acknowledged as "true God and man,"[131] the focus is not so much on Christ's work in *declaring* people righteous, but in *making* them righteous.[132] Cornelius J. Dyck, another contemporary Anabaptist, makes the basic point that in Anabaptist thinking, the grace of Christ is a "divine power" to change us.[133] Thus, Christ's work is not forensic, but transformational.

Within this frame, we can recognize how Anabaptist Christology focuses on the "bitter" Christ rather than the triumphant Christ and also emphasizes a kenotic Christology.[134] Because Christ's redemptive suffering is to be repeated in the suffering community of his disciples, Jose Gallardo, a contemporary Anabaptist, notes how "the cross is the way of salvation and the shape of our life."[135]

Thus, in the Anabaptist understanding of the messianic faith-community, the primary emphasis is not on church structures, clergy, and liturgical practices, but on nurturing a *life together* that is marked by spiritual rebirth, baptism, practical sharing, and service. Through the Spirit, Christ impacts a community and enables the people to embody a "second" incarnation. As the early Anabaptist Peter Riedemann puts it, "the church is a lantern of righteousness in which the light of grace is borne and held before the whole world."[136]

The Shape of Anabaptist Ecclesiology

In the early days of the Anabaptist movement, the shared life of the faith-community was transient and precarious due to persecution, which led to

131. Friedmann, *The Theology of Anabaptism*, 55, quoting Ambrosius Spittelmaier (1527).

132. Friedmann, 88. Friedmann quotes Hubmaier to emphasize that the work of Christ is "*fromb-machung*" and "*Gesund-Machung*" ("Christ makes righteous and whole or well").

133. Dyck, "The Anabaptist Understanding of the Good News," 31.

134. Friedmann, *The Theology of Anabaptism*, 56, 83. In looking at various Christologies – such as mystical, liberationist, kenotic, and Christus Victor – David A. Shank prefers the term "Messianic," as it expresses "obedient sonship" in being the suffering servant of Yahweh ("Jesus the Messiah: Messianic Foundation of Mission," 64–67). This understanding enables Shank to link the nature of Jesus to the church as a messianic community and to the mission of the church. Shank concludes: "Jesus' active and faithful filial obedience in . . . mission" led to his death (69).

135. Gallardo, "Ethics and Mission," 141.

136. Quoted in Friedmann, *The Theology of Anabaptism*, 119.

frequent scattering.[137] Thus, church was often a "clandestine" event,[138] with members meeting in barns and out-of-the-way places. This resulted in a scattering of their missional activities as well. Various scholars have attempted to summarize the core elements of Anabaptist ecclesiology. I will touch on some of these to help clarify our understanding of this incarnational, messianic, eschatological community.

Franklin Littell identifies three core aspects of the Anabaptist movement: first, its identity as an eschatological community; second, its covenantal nature; third, its identity as a restitutionist movement seeking to live the apostolic vision of early Christianity.[139] Littell makes it clear that when he speaks of the covenantal nature of the church, he is referring to the fact that the early Anabaptists were seeking to build upon the evangel to form a "disciplined New Testament community."[140]

Franz Heimann isolates four core ideas: first, the church as a light to the world; second, the church as a *koinonia* community; third, the church as a forgiving and reconciling community, which is particularly expressed prior to participating in the Lord's Supper; fourth, the church as a community of economic sharing.[141] This messianic community sees "church as a visible covenantal community" and as a "sharing brotherhood."[142]

Robert Friedmann identifies the Anabaptist covenant as three-dimensional: a covenant between God and humanity, a covenant between humans and God, and a covenant between believer and believer.[143] The early Anabaptist Peter Walpot describes this vision of the church as a covenantal, sharing community in his "True Yieldedness and the Christian Community of Goods" (1577), writing that the members of a church are baptized "into . . . a spiritual body" and into a community of "temporal gifts and possessions."[144] Using the example of Christ and the practices of the church recorded in Acts 2 and 4, Walpot says that, along with affirming the Apostles Creed, the Lord's Prayer, and the practice

---

137. Littell notes that early Anabaptism spread by "persecution, exile, the journeying of craftsmen, [and] the haphazard wandering of lay preachers" (*The Anabaptist View of the Church*, 120).

138. Friedmann, *The Theology of Anabaptism*, 118.

139. Friedmann, 121.

140. Littell, *The Anabaptist View of the Church*, 118.

141. Friedmann, *The Theology of Anabaptism*, 121–22.

142. Friedmann, 122, 123.

143. Friedmann, 135.

144. Peter Walpot, "True Yieldedness and the Christian Community of Goods" (1577), quoted in Liechty, *Early Anabaptist Spirituality*, 170.

of Holy Communion, Christians are to be committed to "hold [a] community of goods," which he calls the "narrow gate," the "oven of yieldedness," and the equivalent of being "tried like gold in the fire."[145] Walpot claims that this community of goods is a way of answering the Lord's prayer – "give us our daily bread" – thereby making it "communal bread."[146] He makes the further point that "through community . . . God cares for our daily needs and relieves us of greed."[147] For Walpot, a "community of goods" was to be a mark of the church, an expression of Christian unity, that would deal with the problem of human greed[148] by enabling the faith-community to be generous in sharing with neighbours.[149] Thus, owning private property was not encouraged.

This emphasis on a "community of goods" gave shape to the Hutterite communities in the early sixteenth century and, later, to Bruderhof communities. While other Anabaptist groupings do not all share this emphasis, they do insist that the church is to be a *way* of life that involves living the Sermon on the Mount, practical sharing,[150] and being a prophetic community in the world through the witness of its life together and its wider service in the community.

While early Anabaptist faith-communities did have pastors[151] as well as "bishops," "leaders," "teachers," and "deacons and deaconesses,"[152] the main focus was on cultivating a common way of life in all of its members. Spawned by rebirth into a life of faith and obedience, the members of the community were called to participate in many distinctive practices, including water baptism, mutual care, footwashing, the memorial of the Lord's Supper as a communion of reconciliation to express one's link to Christ and to each other, separating from the worldliness of the world,[153] refusing oath-taking and military service,

145. Liechty, 147.

146. Liechty, 146.

147. Liechty, 146.

148. Walpot writes, "greed . . . separates a person from the kingdom of God" (quoted in Liechty, 193).

149. Walpot writes, "there are so many vagrants and beggars on all the streets, knocking on doors and crying for alms," and he notes that "greed withers the hand so that it is useless in helping others" (quoted in Liechty, 193, 192).

150. Snyder points out that the Mennonites believe that private property can be retained, but they still emphasize the importance of practical sharing (*Following in the Footsteps of Christ*, 145).

151. "The Schleitheim Confession" (1527), in *Creeds of the Churches*, ed. Leith, 287.

152. "The Dordrecht Confession" (1632), in *Creeds of the Churches*, ed. Leith, 299–300.

153. This included discipline, admonition, and, where necessary, the use of the ban (excommunication).

and resisting the Christendom model of seeking to manage society. Thus, the early Anabaptist community cultivated a distinctive religious and socio-ethical identity.

Unlike the main-stream churches of that time, which followed the concept of *corpus Christianum* ("the Christian world"), the Anabaptists emphasized the *corpus Christi* ("the body of Christ"). And unlike the Protestants, with their concept of *Vokskirche* (literally, "folk church"),[154] the Anabaptists emphasized the church as *Gemeinde* (a visible community). As Friedmann summarizes, the concept of *Gemeinde* is "one of the most essential elements in Anabaptist thought," where the visible community is a "nucleus of God's kingdom on earth, or its attempted realization," and thus the "church as a visible covenantal community" is a light to the world.[155]

A Missional Community

While mainstream Protestantism has tended to focus on a "theology of the cross" before moving to ecclesiology, and Pietism has tended to focus on a Christological spirituality without a robust ecclesiology, Anabaptism has sought to express a more integrative approach. Thus, the focus is not on *what* the church is and what the church is to *do* as witness to the world, but rather what the church *is* as witness to the world.[156] As noted before, this has resulted in an emphasis on an embodied gospel, where the kingdom of God is "foreshadowed in the brotherhood here and now" and the church is called to live out the ethics of the Sermon on the Mount.[157] As such, one could say, "come and hear," as well as, "come and see." Yet the community of faith can never be a full expression of Christ, nor the full realization of the kingdom of God, for it continually needs to be renewed by the word and Spirit, and so the early "Anabaptists never taught perfectionism."[158]

In further setting out the early Anabaptist vision of the church as a missional community, we can recall several distinctives. First, Littell emphasized that the missional mandate at the end of the gospel of Matthew is central to Anabaptist belief and identity. Second, there is an integrated link between spiritual rebirth, water baptism, communal identity, and the church's task of being a prophetic

154. Friedmann, *The Theology of Anabaptism*, 120, 117.

155. Friedmann, 117, 122.

156. Yoder speaks of the church "as a new kind of social structure" (*For the Nations*, 115).

157. Friedmann, *The Theology of Anabaptism*, 125.

158. Friedmann, 125.

community in the world. Third, though the zeal of the early Anabaptists has faded over time, there have been periods of revitalization, especially since the second half of the twentieth century.[159]

We can now note the following emphases in the writings of contemporary Anabaptist writers. First, there is an emphasis on the *presence* of Christ in the faith, life, and service of the faith-community, where Christ and the church share a common provisional identity. Stephen Boyd highlights that "Christ not only died *for* us, but also rose to live *in* us."[160] And while we are "saved by Christ alone," Christ is "embodied in the lives of Christians" and, as such, the faith-community is a "prolongation of the incarnation."[161] According to Chris Huebner, this means that the community of faith is to be "rooted in the narrative of Jesus," and this narrative is not simply to be proclaimed, but is to be embodied in "ecclesiastical practices."[162] Thus, the church is an "embodied memory" of Jesus.[163] C. Norman Kraus puts this even more strongly, writing that "the continuing witness of Jesus, the *Christ*, exists in the world as the messianic community."[164]

Second, there is an emphasis on the generative, sustaining, and renewing work of the Spirit in the lives of individuals and the faith-community as a whole. Coming to faith is seen as a rebirth through the baptism of the Spirit. The power of this baptism leads to water baptism and one's integration into the faith-community, which leads to a baptism of service, including an embrace of martyrdom.[165] The work of the Spirit is seen in multiple ways: the Spirit enlightens one's engagement with Scripture;[166] the Spirit builds the unity of the

159. Paul Toews makes the point that renewal in the Mennonite Brethren churches was due both to the desire to return to the inspiration of the early Anabaptist movement and interaction with pietism and evangelicalism ("Differing Historical Imaginations and the Changing Identity of the Mennonite Brethren," 157).

160. Boyd, "Community as Sacrament in the Theology of Hans Schlaffer," 55.

161. Boyd, 59.

162. Huebner, *A Precarious Peace*, 54, 53.

163. Huebner, 166.

164. Kraus, *The Authentic Witness*, 183.

165. In the words of Dirk Philips, "Christian baptism . . . must take place internally and externally, internally with the Spirit and with fire . . . but externally with water in the name of the Father and the Son and the Holy Spirit" (quoted in Snyder, *Following in the Footsteps of Christ*, 73).

166. Driver makes the point that in the Anabaptist tradition, there is an emphasis on the "outerword" (Scripture) being complemented by an "innerword" through the work of the Spirit, which leads to a life of following Jesus Christ in discipleship (*Life Together in the Spirit*, 32).

faith-community;[167] the Spirit is present in the celebration of the eucharist.[168] But the work of the Spirit is also identificational and missional, for the Holy Spirit working in the present faith-community is the "same Spirit with which Jesus was anointed for his messianic mission."[169] Thus, through the Holy Spirit, we share "in the life of Jesus," and we live "the way of Jesus."[170] Driver concludes that the Holy Spirit is "the presence of the Living Christ," and thus to walk in the Spirit means "to continue the life of the kingdom that Jesus . . . proclaimed."[171] Moreover, following Jesus through the Spirit can only be authentic "in the company of other followers of Jesus" and will involve the community in the task of "witness and prophecy."[172] To summarize, the Spirit *births*, *creates* community, *conforms* us to Christ, *nurtures* us in the spiritual practices of the faith-community, *empowers* us to be a repetition of Christ in the world, and *sustains* us in a life of prophetic witness and service.

Third, contemporary Anabaptists emphasize the connection between coming to faith in Christ and making a commitment to a life of discipleship.[173] One comes to Christ not simply to obtain spiritual benefits, but to *be a disciple.* Thus, the call is not to gain salvation and then to hear (or not) the call to serve Christ in his restorative kingdom purposes. Rather, salvation will call us to serve Christ in his redemptive purposes for humanity.[174] Thus, soteriology and missiology are dynamically linked. John Howard Yoder makes the point that "the being of the church is the salvation story" in that salvation is made manifest in the church, but the church is also "the instrument"[175] of the salvation story through its life of faith, its proclamation, and its witness. And

167. The hymn, *Ausbund*, 92, celebrates how the Spirit both "regenerates individuals" and binds them "into one body" (Snyder, *Following in the Footsteps of Christ*, 99). Driver makes this point most fundamentally: the church "is a community of the Spirit" (*Life Together in the Spirit*, 22).

168. In the Eucharist, the Anabaptists stress, "you must be fed with God's Spirit," but this celebration also "points to the unity" of the faith-community (Snyder, *Following in the Footsteps of Christ*, 98, 100).

169. Driver, *Life Together in the Spirit*, 18.

170. Driver, 18. In this, we see the integration of the "in Christ" relationship that is so important in Pauline theology.

171. Driver, 19, 22.

172. Driver, 23, 19.

173. Murray makes the point that for contemporary Anabaptists the emphasis is "following Jesus as well as worshipping him" (*The Naked Anabaptist*, 57).

174. Yoder points out that Paul's focus on salvation is to live the new life in Christ. And this means that Paul is emphasizing "the believer's life as mission" (*Theology of Mission*, 103).

175. Yoder, 126.

so, baptism plunges one into a "corporate discipleship,"[176] as one's personal commitment to Christ becomes a corporate commitment to a life of service in the community of faith and to the world. This discipleship is ontological in that it is seen "as *participation* in the very nature of Jesus."[177] This discipleship is also practical in that Jesus is seen as a "model to be followed in daily life."[178] The nature of what John Driver describes as "following Jesus in mission"[179] has taken on many characteristics for the Anabaptists, including adult baptism, commitment to community, truth telling, practical sharing, and peacemaking. But most fundamentally, it involves living the Beatitudes,[180] which John Driver calls living "the blessedness of life under God's rule."[181] C. Norman Kraus makes the helpful observation that being a disciple is much more than being "a pupil or a student." Instead, it is being an "apprentice" and learning by "following, watching, absorbing" in order to "understand and respond to life in the style that is authentic to the master."[182] He elaborates that discipleship "means identifying with Christ, not in a mystical, private experience, but in the concrete sharing of his style, mission, and power."[183]

Fourth, as a missional community, the church in the Anabaptist tradition is to be a counter-community to societal and political configurations. John Howard Yoder suggests that the "believers' church" seeks to be "an *alternative construction of the world.*"[184] In seeking to be like Jesus, the faith-community seeks to reflect a Christo-centric way of life, which is what God wants for the whole world. Thus, the church embodies the gospel by living as the "prototype, the herald, the midwife of the new world on the way."[185] Hence we can speak of the Christification of the faith-community, which is a second incarnation of Christ.[186] We also see the church as an eschatological community, prefiguring

176. Estep, *The Anabaptist Story*, 158.

177. Driver, *Life Together in the Spirit*, 50 (author's emphasis).

178. Driver, 50.

179. Driver, "Unanticipated Journey for Sharing an Anabaptist and Liberationist Perspective on the Gospel," 256.

180. See Kraybill, *The Upside-Down Kingdom*.

181. Driver, *Life Together in the Spirit*, 10.

182. Kraus, *The Authentic Witness*, 18.

183. Kraus, 19. Of course there is no reason why this identification cannot be both mystical and practical. It often is!

184. Yoder, *For the Nations*, 153 (author's emphasis).

185. Yoder, 218.

186. It is interesting to note that the Protestant tradition identifies the marks of the church as being the place where the word of God is truly preached and the sacraments and discipline are rightly administered, whereas the Anabaptists do not deny these general marks, but focus on

God's final future. John Howard Yoder notes that the believer's church is a "messianic people" and is a sign of the coming of the messianic age.[187]

Fifth, living the Beatitudes and the Sermon on the Mount within the setting of a community that emphasizes corporate discipleship, common life, economic sharing, and peacemaking[188] involves a very different kind of witness[189] – one that is not simply about beliefs, but a whole *way* of life. This different witness means that the faith-community lives as a prophetic community, which puts the community of faith in "conflict with the present world order."[190] In this regard, Wilbert R. Shenk makes a passionate plea for the Anabaptist way of messianic mission in contrast to the mission of modernity, with its "superiority of Western values, the spirit of progress, and the rationalistic view of life," and its "uncritical hand-in-glove alliance with Western political, economic, and military power."[191] The Anabaptist way, in contrast, is the task of the "whole messianic community" living a life that is "transformed through reconciliation with God" and in "surrender to God's will," a way that is a complete contradiction to "nationalism, materialism, militarism, classism, self-centredness."[192] Clearly, this is a call to a prophetic posture, though it has nothing to do with using coercion[193] to bring about social change. Rather, the prophetic stance is one of *communal witness*, demonstrating a different way of life "as a bold new social option."[194] Such a prophetic stance will clearly involve the task of discernment. John Howard Yoder identifies the dominant forces and ideologies in society as

---

the Christocentric way of life as *the* mark of the church. See the Dordrecht Confession (1632), which states that the faith-community "may be known by her evangelical faith, doctrine, love, and godly conversation; also by her pure walk and practice, and her observance of the true ordinances of Christ" (Leith, ed., *Creeds of the Churches*, 299).

187. Yoder, *Theology of Mission*, 126.

188. Murray describes these and others as "dissident practices in the following of Jesus" (*The Naked Anabaptist*, 82).

189. Wilbert R. Shenk laments that in much contemporary Christianity, the rejection of the Sermon on the Mount for one's personal and communal life, reflects a great loss for mission because "questions of violence, unjust and oppressive systems, and warfare must be considered" in the way the church lives and serves the wider community (*The Transfiguration of Mission*, 11).

190. Estep, *The Anabaptist Story*, 179.

191. Shenk, "The Relevance of a Messianic Missiology for Mission Today," 19, 20.

192. Shenk, 30, 29, 31.

193. Timothy George notes that the Anabaptists saw God as being "noncoercive," which is most clearly expressed in the life and way of Jesus, and thus followers of Jesus should not participate in the "coercive structures of society, refusing to bear arms, serve in the military, swear an oath, or hold a magisterial office" ("The Spirituality of the Radical Reformation," 352).

194. Dyck, "The Anabaptist Understanding of the Good News," 32.

"'Powers,' anti-messiahs, alternative pretenders to saviorhood," which need to be "demystified, disenchanted through the proclamation of Christ's lordship."[195]

Several important points emerge in this summary of the Anabaptist identity as a missional community. First, the charge that the Anabaptists held a world-denying form of Christianity is misplaced, for they clearly seek to engage society as a witnessing and prophetic community through their *corporate* identity. Second, the Anabaptists take Christ's lordship seriously in their vision of a whole new way of social existence. Third, the Anabaptist missional vision includes a critique of social and political "powers."[196] Fourth, the Anabaptist missional vision is a marginal movement within Christianity and society, which has given it an important perspective from the "underside" of history.[197] Fifth, this experience of marginalization has given the Anabaptist movement a heart for the poor and oppressed.

While the early Anabaptist witness was for all – including their interrogators, prison guards, and the general populace who gathered at their floggings, drownings, or hangings – they had a particularly strong identification with the poor. Menno Simons notes that Anabaptists "comfort the afflicted; assist the needy; clothe the naked, feed the hungry; [and] do not turn their face from the poor."[198] And the early Anabaptist Leonard Schiemer notes that following Christ in discipleship involves "feeding the hungry, giving drink to the thirsty, clothing the naked, sheltering the poor, comforting the sick and imprisoned, washing feet, and showing love for one another."[199] Stuart Murray, a contemporary Anabaptist, identifies this as a core conviction of the movement, writing that Anabaptists see the church as "good news to the poor, powerless, and persecuted."[200] And Timothy George agrees that the Anabaptists have been "concerned about the plight of the poor" – not only those within their own community – but he overgeneralizes by characterizing

195. Yoder, *For the Nations*, 240.

196. Timothy George makes the point that the Anabaptists were "at once profoundly otherworldly and yet unswervingly committed to the purposes of God in history" ("The Spirituality of the Radical Reformation," 358).

197. Just as the God of the Hebrew slaves was a marginal God in the empires of the ancient world, and Jesus, as a Galilean, was a marginal person in his society, Anabaptism emerged as a marginal movement in Christianity in the way it sought to embrace a kenotic Christology and reject the Constantinian and Christendom vision of dominance and power upheld by Roman Catholic and mainstream Reformation churches as well as the state.

198. Quoted in Driver, *Life Together in the Spirit*, 72.

199. Snyder, *Following in the Footsteps of Christ*, 105.

200. Murray, *The Naked Anabaptist*, 46.

the Anabaptists as a "Protestantism of the poor."[201] Finally, John Howard Yoder expresses concern that Anabaptists are good at caring for the needy at a local level, but not good at dealing with society's structural and global issues.[202] This is not surprising given the Anabaptist refusal to "manage" society, an aspect of the Christendom model that Anabaptists reject.[203]

These insights reveal that rather than being unconcerned about the world, Anabaptists have sought to be a witness and servant of the kingdom of God by living as an embodied gospel and as an anticipatory community of the reign of God in order to demonstrate God's future world. Thus, for Anabaptists, mission is not the task of a few, nor a special department within the church, but rather part of the very nature of the church. This missional identity is expressed in a life of discipleship by seeking to follow the way of Jesus in a community that is seeking to live the Sermon on the Mount, bear prophetic witness to the world, uphold the Lordship of God, and embody the power of new life in Christ through the Spirit by participating in economic sharing and the task of peacemaking.

A Missional Spirituality

This book seeks to reflect an ecumenical spirit, recognizing that no particular church tradition has all the answers. Thus, we need to engage others in our attempt to hear the richness of God's word as it has been appropriated in the various church traditions.[204] Furthermore, by engaging the marginal Anabaptist movement, we have sought to demonstrate that wisdom is often found in the "fringe" movements of Christianity. Missional spirituality is intrinsic to the Anabaptist movement as a whole. For when faith issues in discipleship, and discipleship involves being *in* Christ and *like* Christ, the very contours of the Christian life will be animated by a missional spirituality. But several themes within the Anabaptist tradition make this general statement more distinctive.

First, the most fundamental impulse of the Anabaptist tradition is its restitutionist orientation. The Anabaptists believed that the classical Reformers

201. George, "The Spirituality of the Radical Reformation," 363, 358.

202. Yoder, *For the Nations*, 154–55.

203. Huebner, following Yoder, rejects the Constantinian "project," where the "church seeks to assume control or self-legitimization" and sees its task "to make history come out right" (*A Precarious Peace*, 143, 118).

204. Of course, we have only engaged *some* and certainly not *all* church traditions.

did not go far enough in their attempts to renew the church, as they were still too beholden to the Christendom model in light of its church-state cooperation, infant baptism, lack of missional vision, and its status as a powerful institution seeking to do good in the world. The Anabaptists, in contrast, believed that the faith-community should be distinctive in living out the radical nature of the gospel, as expressed in the Sermon on the Mount, as an embodiment of the way of Christ.

Second, the Anabaptists articulated a distinctive Christology. While they embraced Christ's soteriological work, they sought to outwork this in an *imitatio Christi* that had to do with following the "bitter" (suffering) Christ into the world. In following the kenotic Christ, their witness to the world could be more effective, since this "radically other" Christ could not be co-opted socially or politically. The incarnation of this radical Christ in the community of faith gave the community its prophetic witness.

Third, Anabaptist spirituality is communal and incarnational. As John Howard Yoder puts it, "the reality of this new people was the message," in that they sought to *live* the message of the gospel and not simply *believe* the message. He continues that this new people "also became the vehicle for proclaiming" the message.[205]

Fourth, the central impulse for this way of life was the notion of *Gelassenheit* – or yieldedness. The Anabaptist way of life involved yieldedness to God's sovereignty and Lordship, even when that involved mystery and suffering. It involved yieldedness to God's word, including the "hard sayings" of Jesus. It involved yieldedness to the wisdom and direction of the faith-community and a willingness to embrace formation, encouragement, and admonition. It involved yieldedness to living as a contradiction in society and therefore a willingness to accept both scorn and rejection. And it involved yieldedness to the precarity of the leading of the Spirit as a witness – often a maligned and suffering witness – in the world. This concept of *Gelassenheit* was a core element in Anabaptist spirituality. As Timothy George observes, it literally means "letting-loose-of-oneself."[206] As Robert Friedmann notes, it involves a "self-abandonment" as one seeks "to follow Christ along the narrow path."[207] C. Arnold Snyder applies *Gelassenheit* to every dimension of Anabaptist life, including spirituality and mission. In conversion, people "yield their wills to God"; in the baptisms of the Spirit, water, and blood, one exhibits *Gelassenheit*;

205. Yoder, *Theology of Mission*, 124.

206. George, "The Spirituality of the Radical Reformation," 340.

207. Friedmann, *The Theology of Anabaptism*, 66.

in being part of the faith-community, one lives this virtue; and the life of following Christ in witness and service involves "self-renunciation" and being "willing to accept God's will in all things."[208]

The early Anabaptists emphasize these core themes in various ways. Hans Hut sees the redemptive suffering of Christ repeated in Christ's followers as they enter "the school of affliction" and seek to serve "the poor."[209] This highlights a Christological and missional spirituality of suffering. Peter Walpot emphasizes an incarnational missional spirituality, where Christ forms a community of mutual sharing to the point of becoming a "community of goods" (not holding private property) and thus entering the "oven of yieldedness" and being freed from greed, able to "give . . . to God's poor."[210] Hans Schlaffer speaks of radical identification with Christ, a "willingness to suffer anything for the will of God," and being empowered by the Spirit to have an "ardent love in the heart for God and for the neighbor."[211] And Dirk Philips emphasizes the Christification dynamic, speaking of the "character of Christ . . . worked in us by the Holy Spirit," so that we become a "peculiar people," the "first-fruits" of God's birthing in order to "love for God . . . and neighbor."[212]

The voices of contemporary Anabaptists are equally challenging. Chris Huebner argues for a Christological embodiment of the faith-community in living a precarious spirituality. By this, he means that the community of faith remains on the road, "resists establishment," remains self-critical, lives the "virtue of vulnerability," rejects "triumphalism," avoids being "sectarian and insular," and seeks to live the Christian life and to serve "rooted in the narrative of Jesus."[213] He makes the central point that "precariousness, ambiguity, and unsettlement is an essential characteristic of what it means to be a Mennonite."[214] This means a lived sensitivity to power issues and marginality in following Christ, the outsider, whose work is to unite all into a new freedom of shalom.

The contemporary, Pablo Deiros, argues for a "Christian spiritual missiology" that expresses the "intersection of Christian spirituality with . . .

208. Snyder, *Following in the Footsteps of Christ*, 43, 78–83, 116, 47.

209. Liechty, *Early Anabaptist Spirituality*, 65.

210. Liechty, 147, 145.

211. Liechty, 106.

212. Liechty, 209, 203, 205.

213. Huebner, *A Precarious Peace*, 21, 109, 205, 55, 54.

214. Huebner, 25.

Christian mission."[215] He notes that this is a "reflection on experiential sanctification and Christian service," being "filled with the Holy Spirit," and being "united with Christ" and "Christ's Spirit."[216] He believes that this way of life is to be sustained through the spiritual disciplines, such as prayer, fasting, meditation, and Bible reading, and that it expresses itself in "power encounters, spiritual warfare, spiritual discernment . . . prayer and intercession."[217]

Other contemporary voices highlight how Anabaptist missional spirituality is Christological, communal (the missional task is for the "whole messianic community"), and also "eschatological" (the faith-community lives the gospel in anticipation of the age to come).[218] Moreover, the missional vision is all-embracing in that the "Messiah Jesus is God's new covenant" with humanity "for the elimination of all its alienation" and for its full "restoration."[219]

Conclusion

In this chapter, I have turned to the diverse voices of early Anabaptists to gain something of their vision and passion, and I have also turned to contemporary Anabaptist voices in order to weave together the threads of a missional spirituality in the theology and ecclesiology of this movement. It should be clear that the Anabaptists articulated and lived the theme of integration. Coming to faith is linked to obedience in living the gospel. Water baptism is connected to the Lordship of Christ, which is connected to one's participation in the faith-community as an embodiment of the gospel. Thus, one's spirituality is both Christological (being in, with, and for Christ) and ecclesiastical (being in formation, in community, in sharing). And ecclesiology flows into missiology, for the faith-community, the body of Christ, is to live as a "second" incarnation of Christ and a servant to the world in anticipation of the kingdom of God, which is expressed through proclamation, peacemaking, sharing, and earth-keeping.

In this chapter, we have also noted how Anabaptists reflect a hermeneutic of marginality. One main challenge for Anabaptists is how to avoid sectarian seclusion. And one great promise they offer is their ability to see life from the "underside" of history and so take a more prophetic stance in society.

---

215. Deiros, "Towards a Pneumatological Spiritual Missiology," 141.

216. Deiros, 146, 145.

217. Deiros, 147, 141.

218. Shenk, "The Relevance of a Messianic Missiology for Mission Today," 30, 31.

219. Shank, "Jesus the Messiah: Messianic Foundation of Mission," 70.

We are living in a time when the Western world needs to be re-evangelized, the Majority World Christianity needs a deeper servant Christology, and our consumer society needs to overcome its propensity towards much-having and war-mongering. Within this context, the small, but distinct, Anabaptist voice needs to be heard afresh. Yet sadly, the missional distinctives of this rich story in the history of Christianity are still lacking in many mission textbooks.

After my Reformed theological studies and my night-time excursions into Anabaptist thought, and while working on the streets of Brisbane, I was led to embrace the commitment of adult baptism – and I quickly learned how a pregnant *Gelassenheit* ("yieldedness") would lead to suffering. For I lost my ministerial career, my family (for quite a period of time), and most of my friends. I literally ended up on the street – the place of new beginnings![220]

220. During my years in Australia and Southeast Asia, I never had the privilege of meeting any Anabaptists (Mennonites), but this happily changed when my wife, Rita, and I lived in Canada, where we were blessed to get to know John B. Toews, who taught at Regent College, along with his wife, Lillian. To them, this chapter is dedicated. I hope I have done the Anabaptist tradition reasonable justice.

14

Franciscan Peacemaking

A Key Theme in Missional Spirituality

Introduction

In chapter 12, "Radical Evangelicals: Developing a Sustainable Missional Spirituality," I suggest that evangelicals can learn much from the intrinsic missional spirituality of the Franciscan tradition in light of its Trinitarian orientation, kenotic Christology, communal solidarity, spiritual practices, vision for renewing the church, focus on celebration, and heart for serving the poor, tending the earth, and peacemaking.[1] Exploring any of these themes in the rich Franciscan tradition would constitute a book in its own right, and so I have chosen to focus on the theme of peacemaking.

My decision to focus on peacemaking in no way suggests that this theme is more important and pressing than others, but this focus has enabled me to bring perspectives from other faith traditions into the picture, thereby highlighting the ecumenical flavour that I am advocating throughout this book. Moreover, even though war-making never seems far away, peacemaking is often relegated to the sphere of personal piety – or even the internal sphere of the soul. To live a missional spirituality amidst this age of violence and oppression, our missional vision needs to be robust enough to face the world's most pressing and difficult issues, and our spirituality needs to drink from

1. See the rich three-volume resource by Armstrong, Hellman, and Short, eds., *Francis of Assisi: Early Documents, The Saint*, vol. 1; *The Founder*, vol. 2; *The Prophet*, vol. 3.

deep wells in order to empower and sustain the faith-community in its long journey of seeking the reign of God.[2]

Personal Reflection

The Franciscan tradition has hovered at the edges of my life for a long time. During the early 1970s, I had frequent contact with the Anglican Franciscan Order of Brothers in Brisbane, where I went for retreats, renewal, and encouragement. There were also areas where our involvement with Teen Challenge overlapped with the Franciscans in working with young people in the juvenile justice system.

Later in life, through the influence of a friend, I undertook a very meaningful formation program and eventually became a Franciscan tertiary.[3] The core formational concept was not simply to learn a lot about St. Francis by reading the oceans of secondary material on his life,[4] but to reflect on how I might integrate core Franciscan themes into how I lived my life.[5] This formation continues. So much of contemporary life is about self-assertion, manipulation, and subtle forms of violence, and so little is about prayer, serving the poor, and caring for our wounded social and natural worlds. And our exploitative and pragmatic way of life – which always promises much, but often leaves us bereft and depleted – has eroded our sense of wonder and our appreciation for beauty and transcendence.

Introduction

We are living in anxious and fearful times, with the spectre of violence all around us and domestic violence within our own homes. The hope that World War II would be the war to end all wars lies tattered and bloodied before us. Michael Ignatieff describes the twentieth century as "a century of total war,"[6] and up to this point in the twenty-first century, we have been traumatized by images of terrorism and war destroying whole cities and displacing millions.

2. Most of this chapter also appears in Gorospe and Ringma, eds., *How Long, O Lord?*, 163–86. Used with permission.

3. I refer to this in Ringma, *A Fragile Hope*, 70–75.

4. One helpful secondary source was Carretto, *I, Francis*.

5. One very practical book was Foley, Weigel, Normile, *To Live as Francis Lived*.

6. Ignatieff, *Needs of Strangers*, 139. It is estimated that 100 million people have been killed in the wars of the twentieth century.

Syria and the Ukraine are only two of many other places of destruction and conflict!

As contemporary Christians, we are pulled in three directions at the same time. In the first, we resonate with Douglas J. Hall's assertion that "God is at work healing the creation, making the tragic kingdoms of the earth a kingdom of peace."[7] He continues by saying that this vision of God's shalom is "not just the absence of hostilities, but a condition of well-being, justice, mutuality of concern, harmony between all creatures, [and] gratitude for being."[8] In contrast to this theological "idealism," the second impulse is to accept with a good dosage of fatalism the violence that continues in our world, pragmatically assuming that it can only be met with stronger violence. In light of this, mainstream Christianity has always maintained the so-called just-war theory as the "dominant theological position."[9] The core idea here is to kill in order to create peace,[10] or in the words of Mary E. Jegen, "the world still depends on war to put an end to war."[11] The third direction is to seek to live the first impulse in following Christ and living towards the hope of God's shalom while also embracing the suffering that such a posture will inevitably bring. For those who work for peace and justice often "experience emotional and mental fatigue,"[12] and both Gandhi and Martin Luther King Jr. lost their lives in the cause of peacemaking. With the renunciation of violence, a new relationship between opposing forces and adversaries can become possible, where the aim is the "reconciliation of the oppressor and not only the liberation of the oppressed."[13]

To further explore this third option, I will engage the Franciscan tradition,[14] but I will do so from a particular concern and perspective. My concern is that St. Francis and his tradition can easily be dismissed as "out there," so different and undoable that we leave St. Francis with birds on his

7. Hall, *Stewardship of Life*, 13.

8. Hall, 15.

9. Yoder, *War of the Lamb*, 95.

10. Yoder, 102.

11. Jegen, *Just Peacemakers*, 9.

12. Jegen, 10.

13. Yoder, *Nonviolence*, 44.

14. There is, of course, a wider tradition within the Christian church on peacemaking. See Braswell et al., *Corrections, Peacemaking and Restorative Justice*; Horan, *The Franciscan Heart of Thomas Merton*; Omar and Duffy, *Peacemaking and the Challenge of Violence in World Religions*.

shoulders, stroking a wolf, and singing of brother sun and sister moon.[15] In order to overcome this dismissal, I will engage in a dialogue with four sources from the broad Christian tradition. For the first source, I analyzed hymns from various church hymnals; for the second source, I looked at a number of Christian lectionaries; for the third source, I examined evangelical missional documents; for the fourth source, I listened to the Anabaptists. I am taking this approach rather than looking directly at the formal theological positions of various denominations because hymns and lectionaries are often closer to "home" for most "laity," while theological statements tend to be the domain of scholars.[16] After this survey, I will highlight some of the salient concepts of Franciscan peacemaking and reconciliation to reveal how these resonate with important, if not dominant, aspects of the Christian tradition.

Voices in Hymnody

To explore the church's understanding of the nature and scope of peace and the task of being peacemakers,[17] I have examined some fifteen hundred hymns in various church hymnals.[18] I have noted the following broad themes in these hymns: first, the nature of God as the father of peace;[19] second, Christ as the Prince of Peace;[20] third, Christ as the giver of peace;[21] fourth, Christ as the agent who brings us peace with God;[22] fifth, the Holy Spirit as peacemaker;[23]

15. For many, St. Francis is the icon of ecology, and they might not see peacemaking as key to his ministry.

16. With the Anabaptists, I have taken a slightly different route by looking at their spirituality. But this, too, is the domain of the laity and not simply that of the theologians.

17. The core theological concept that I am working with is that peace is a gift from God through Christ. As such, we are all called to be peacemakers, drawing on the gift given to us.

18. *The Australian Hymn Book*; *Book of Worship*; *Together in Song.*

19. Seldom used. E.g. "Father of Peace, and God of Love," *Together in Song*, hymn 482.

20. Used some thirteen times. E.g. "Hail, Saviour, Prince of Peace," *Together in Song*, hymn 225.

21. Used repeatedly. E.g. "in peace that only thou canst give . . . let me live," *Together in Song*, hymn 601.

22. Used repeatedly. E.g. "sealing our peace with God," *Together in Song*, hymn 221; "while he offers peace and pardon let us hear his voice today," *Book of Worship*, hymn 95.

23. Very seldom used. E.g. "fertile ground from which your peace and justice spring like rain," *Together in Song*, hymn 416.

sixth, peace in the faith-community;[24] seventh, God's eschatological peace;[25] eighth, peace as an inner disposition.[26]

While these broad themes are certainly not exhaustive, our particular interest for the purposes of this chapter is the theme of God's peace for our world, with the cessation of war, the flourishing of goodness and justice, and the role of the people of God as instruments of peace. This brings us back to the theme of peace as both *gift* and *task*.[27] Regarding this theme, we can make the following observations. First, God desires a world of peace.[28] Second, Christ is the way to peace.[29] Third, peace is the work of the Spirit.[30] Fourth, peacemaking is the task of the church.[31]

From these four observations, we can draw several broad conclusions. Most of the hymns focus on Christ as the Prince of Peace, who brings us peace with God through his redemptive work. Christ calls us to an inner peace, calls the church to be a community marked by love, forgiveness, and peace, and also promises us an eschatological peace in the age to come. At the same time, the hymns have a Trinitarian emphasis, with the Father, Son, and Holy Spirit all involved in this peace-giving activity. Moreover, the peace of God through Christ is a gift for the whole world, and so the church is to be an agent of God's

24. A frequent theme, particularly around forgiveness and Christian unity. E.g. "Where pity dwells, the peace of God is there," *Australian Hymn Book*, hymn 503; "joining together in peace those once divided by sin," *Together in Song*, hymn 423; "Peace with the Father, peace with Christ his Son, peace with the Spirit, keep us ever one," *Australian Hymn Book*, hymn 402; "take from our souls the strain and stress and let our ordered lives confess the beauty of thy peace,"*Australian Hymn Book*, hymn 519.

25. Used often. E.g. "and take us home to you in peace," *Together in Song*, hymn 550; "our wanderings cease . . . our souls arrive in peace," *Together in Song*, hymn 564; "with all your church above . . . in one unbroken peace," *Together in Song*, hymn 521.

26. E.g. "take my heart . . . guide it to be at peace," *Together in Song*, hymn 593; "God blesses you with peace," *Book of Worship*, hymn 147.

27. See the discussion of contemplation as both gift and task in chapter 4 ("Contemplation in a World of Action").

28. E.g. "Bring to our world of strife your sovereign word of peace, that war may haunt the earth no more and desolation cease," *Together in Song*, hymn 616; "He [God] causes war to cease; the weapons of the strong destroyed. He makes abiding peace," *Book of Worship*, hymn 46.

29. E.g. "Hail to the Lord's anointed . . . and over every nation His peaceful rule shall be," *Book of Worship*, hymn 72.

30. E.g. "Holy Spirit go before us . . . till compassion builds the peace the nations seek," *Together in Song*, hymn 420.

31. E.g. "Cleanse the depths within our souls, and bid resentment cease; then, bound to all in bonds of love, our lives will spread your peace," *Together in Song*, hymn 635; "Make me a channel of your peace. Where there is hatred . . . injury . . . doubt . . . despair . . . darkness . . . Make me a channel of your peace," *Book of Worship*, hymn 451.

peace, seeking to impact and penetrate our wounded, troubled, and warring world. Finally, God's peace is not simply the cessation of conflict, but a life marked by God's shalom.

Voices in Lectionaries

In exploring the church's understanding of the nature and scope of peace and the task of being peacemakers, I have also examined various liturgical resources from several traditions.[32]

Anglican Liturgy

In this modern version of the traditional Anglican *Book of Common Prayer*,[33] there are numerous references to peace in the prayers, canticles, litanies, baptismal liturgies, Eucharistic liturgies, services for Sunday and other Holy Days, marriage ceremonies, and services for the sick.

Many of the themes identified in the church's hymns are also present here. God is the source of peace;[34] Christ is the "Prince of Peace";[35] peace has come through Christ's sacrifice;[36] the church is to be a community at peace;[37] there is the promise of final peace.[38] What is particularly noteworthy, however, is the emphasis on the call to pray and work for peace in our world.[39]

---

32. *The Book of Alternative Services of the Anglican Church of Canada*; *Catechism of the Catholic Church*; *Celtic Daily Prayer: From the Northumbria Community*; *Celtic Daily Prayer, Book Two: Farther Up and Farther In*.

33. *The Book of Common Prayer* (1990).

34. E.g. "O God, the author of peace and lover of concord," *Book of Alternative Services*, 130.

35. *Book of Alternative Services*, 64.

36. E.g. "all gathered into peace by his death on the cross," *Book of Alternative Services*, 95; "by his death he opened to us the way of freedom and peace," *Book of Alternative Services*, 201.

37. E.g. "may we who share this sacrament live together in unity and peace," *Book of Alternative Services*, 291.

38. E.g. "receive . . . [name] into the blessed rest of everlasting peace," *Book of Alternative Services*, 586; "that we may at length fall peacefully asleep in you," *Book of Alternative Services*, 602.

39. E.g. "for the whole human family, that we may live together in justice and peace," *Book of Alternative Services*, 116; "from civil strife and violence, from war and murder . . . good Lord, deliver us," *Book of Alternative Services*, 139; "that justice and peace may increase," *Book of Alternative Services*, 311; "give peace to your church, peace among nations, peace in our homes, and peace in our hearts," *Book of Alternative Services*, 677.

This call to be peacemakers is rooted in God's call to us: "that we may hear and respond to your call to peace and justice."[40] It is also the call of the Beatitudes: "Blessed are the peacemakers" (Matt 5:3–12).[41] It finds its beginning in our baptismal vow, where we respond to the question, "Will you strive for justice and peace among all people," by saying, "I will, with God's help."[42] And at the end of our service of worship, we are challenged to: "Go in peace to love and serve the Lord."[43] Clearly this lectionary recognizes peace as a gift of God in the salvation that Christ brings, an inner disposition, a relational reality in the church, and a missional task of the people of God in the world.[44]

Roman Catholic Catechism

The Roman Catholic faithful are challenged to live a life of safeguarding peace in light of the fifth commandment, "You shall not kill."[45] Yet the call to shepherd peace is not an automatic reality in our beautiful, yet broken, world, for peace must be birthed and guided. Thus the catechism reminds the faithful that peace is an inner quality and disposition by speaking of a "peace of heart."[46] This inner peace rejects "murderous anger"[47] and recognizes that "hatred is contrary to charity."[48] It also embraces the call to "love your enemies"[49] and realizes that "peace is the work of justice and the effect of charity."[50] As such, "peace is tranquility of order."[51] Clearly, the catechism teaches that peace is not simply the absence of conflict and war, but a quality of life. Thus, it is the

40. *Book of Alternative Services*, 118.

41. *Book of Alternative Services*, 85.

42. *Book of Alternative Services*, 159. See also 332, 627.

43. *Book of Alternative Services*, 215.

44. Bosch summarizes mission as "a multifaceted ministry, in respect of witness, service, justice, healing, liberation, peace, evangelism, fellowship, church planting, contextualization, and much more," but gives peace no treatment in his extensive discussion of "Elements of an Emerging Ecumenical Missionary Paradigm," even though he acknowledges that peacemaking is "integral to the church's missionary existence" (*Transforming Mission*, 512; 368–510; 119).

45. *Catechism of the Catholic Church*, 511.

46. *Catechism*, 519.

47. *Catechism*, 519.

48. *Catechism*, 520.

49. *Catechism*, 520.

50. *Catechism*, 520.

51. *Catechism*, 520.

calling of the Christian community and the government to work for goodness and justice and "the avoidance of war."[52]

Then the catechism moves fairly quickly to the acknowledgement that a government "cannot be denied the right to a lawful self-defense"[53] and can legitimately use military force. It supports the idea that the government can impose on its citizens the call to "national defense,"[54] and it points out that soldiers in the execution of their duties contribute to "the common good of the nation."[55] Next the catechism makes three key moves. First, it allows citizens to refuse to bear arms on the basis of conscience.[56] Second, it rejects disproportionality in conflict, saying that "extermination of a people" and "destruction of whole cities" is a "crime against God and man[kind]."[57] Third, it is deeply concerned about the arms race and notes that this "does not ensure peace."[58]

On the one hand, this catechism seeks to instruct the faithful to forgive their enemies; on the other hand, the faithful are to participate in legitimate warfare. Most laity make sense of this by relegating the former to the personal and interpersonal sphere, while identifying the latter as part of the public sphere. From this perspective, peacemaking is always a possibility in the Christian-Christian and Christian-Neighbour sphere, but less of a possibility at a national level.

This strikes a note of bitter realism, which is hardly surprising in light of the catechism's sober assessment of the human condition: "injustice, excessive economic or social inequalities, envy, distrust, and pride among men and nations constantly threaten peace and cause wars."[59] This catechetical orchestration forms a sobering minor (or perhaps major?) key to the Anglican liturgies examined above.[60] This "both-and" approach of the Catholic

52. *Catechism*, 520–21.

53. *Catechism*, 521.

54. *Catechism*, 521.

55. *Catechism*, 521.

56. *Catechism*, 521.

57. *Catechism*, 522.

58. *Catechism*, 522.

59. *Catechism*, 522.

60. For a discussion of peacemaking and just war, see "The Challenge of Peace: God's Promise and Our Response," in *Catholic Social Thought*, ed. O'Brien and Shannon. This key document by US Catholic Bishops sets out OT and NT perspectives, pointing out that "peace is both a gift of God and a human work" (507). It holds the right of countries to defend themselves against aggression (508), while maintaining that the church's position is an "overriding . . . presumption *in favour of peace*" (511). It expresses deep concern about nuclear proliferation

catechism maintains a dualism that limits Christian action to the personal spheres of life rather than the sociopolitical domains. Because suspicions and hatreds continue in our world, conflict and war are the likely result, and Christians will need to work out whether they will support the government at this point, or not.

Celtic Liturgies

In the Northumbria Community's liturgical resources, the Morning Prayer ends with a blessing: "May the peace of the Lord Christ go with you, wherever He may send you."[61] In the daily readings, there is reference to returning to the sacred paths, which are "well-walked with the Gospel of Peace."[62] The readings also refer to speaking a "word of peace"[63] and include St. Aidan's peace prayer for the Holy Island of Lindisfarne: "Here be the peace of those who do thy will. Here be the peace of brother serving man. Here be the peace of holy monks obeying. Here be the peace of praise by dark and day."[64]

The complines are also "riddled" with the theme of peace. The Ita Compline incants, "Be the peace of the Spirit mine this night. Be the peace of the Son mine this night. Be the peace of the Father mine this night. The peace of all peace be mine this night."[65] In the Aidan compline, there is reference to a peaceful sleep,[66] along with the prayer, "Circle me, Lord, keep peace within, keep evil out."[67] The Felgild compline opens with, "Let all the tumult within me cease. Enfold me, Lord, in your peace."[68] And the Boisil compline includes the prayer, "that awake we may watch with Christ, and asleep may rest in his peace."[69]

---

and makes the overall conclusion that "we are called to be peacemakers . . . by our Lord Jesus" (562). Jegen, in *Just Peacemakers*, believes that "nonviolence has moved closer to the center of Catholic social teaching on peace and war" (44). Yoder, *War of the Lamb*, gives an extensive critique of "The Challenge of Peace" (95–101), but notes that in the light of this document, "morally accountable pacifism is making great strides" (102).

61. *Celtic Daily Prayer*, 19.

62. *Celtic Daily Prayer*, 55.

63. *Celtic Daily Prayer*, 63.

64. *Celtic Daily Prayer*, 61–62.

65. *Celtic Daily Prayer*, 29. This line is repeated in the other complines of the week.

66. *Celtic Daily Prayer*, 31.

67. *Celtic Daily Prayer*, 33.

68. *Celtic Daily Prayer*, 38.

69. *Celtic Daily Prayer*, 43. Boisil (d. 661).

Clearly the focus of peace in these writings is on one's inner disposition, which is a gift and blessing of Christ, the peace-giver. But the Celtic liturgies also emphasize the call and task of peacemaking. While inner peace is the source of rooting out "resentment and argument"[70] so may "all the strife that my life once was made of, turn to peace,"[71] the calling is to "go peaceful in gentleness through the violence of these days."[72]

The Celtic lectionary cites three historical examples on the topic of peacemaking. In the first, the Christian Telemachus (d. 391) tried to stop a gladiator in the arena and lost his life as a result. The lectionary uses this example to call us to a life of prayer and "active peace-making."[73] It goes on to suggest that in "facing the powers" we are to extend "the peace of Christ," and "amidst conflict and violence" we are to live and proclaim "the peace of Christ."[74]

In the second example, St. Pedrog, a former soldier, becomes a "soldier" of Christ. Two symbols are associated with this saint: a "broken spear" and a "tame wolf."[75] The former illustrates the cessation of violence. The taming of the wolf illustrates the transformational theme of a whole new way of being. Thus, peace is not simply the absence of war, but also has to do with the "fullness of life,"[76] a state of being that reflects God's shalom.

The third example is Reinfrid (d. c. 1084), a former mercenary, who became a monk at Evesham in the UK. The reflections in relation to Reinfrid are noteworthy, for they illustrate that peace is costly and must be won by suffering, not vengeance: "Peace must often be made before it can be enjoyed."[77]

The Celtic liturgies teach that being a peacemaker does not mean withdrawing from conflict, but rather entering into conflict in a different way. The lectionary articulates this different way as being a "remedy finder; bridge-builder; breach-repairer; a new-way maker; a relationship broker."[78] Thus peacemaking is about rebuilding on a new foundation. At its most basic

70. *Celtic Daily Prayer: Book Two*, 1099.
71. *Celtic Daily Prayer: Book Two*, 1135.
72. *Celtic Daily Prayer: Book Two*, 898.
73. *Celtic Daily Prayer: Book Two*, 1098.
74. *Celtic Daily Prayer: Book Two*, 1100.
75. *Celtic Daily Prayer: Book Two*, 1198.
76. *Celtic Daily Prayer: Book Two*, 1222.
77. *Celtic Daily Prayer: Book Two*, 1134.
78. *Celtic Daily Prayer: Book Two*, 1135.

level, it is about love ("going the extra mile") and forgiveness ("not returning evil for evil").[79]

Conclusion

In all three lectionaries, there is a familiar theme that peace is God's gift in Christ, which calls us to make peace with God and with each other in the faith-community. This peace, however, is not only a gift for ourselves, but for the whole world. Christians, therefore, are called to live in interior peace and also to be peacemakers in the world. This is a sacrificial and costly ministry. Through the power of forgiving love, we are called to disarm the power of "the powers"[80] by embracing a whole new way of being and acting in the way of Christ.

Voices in Evangelical Missional Documents

I will now move much closer to "home" by exploring the extent to which the missional documents of the global and evangelical Lausanne movement incorporate the notion of peace as both a gift and task in the mission of the church.[81]

The Earliest Lausanne Documents

"The Lausanne Covenant" (1974) highlights the urgent need for world evangelization and emphasizes that "evangelism is primary"[82] over social concern and societal and cultural change, even though it acknowledges that the Christian community is to "transform and enrich culture."[83] This document does not significantly engage the topic of peace and does not call the Christian church to the task of peacemaking in our world.

The main reference to peace is in relation to the task and responsibilities of governments. The document states: "It is the God-appointed duty of every

79. *Celtic Daily Prayer: Book Two*, 1496.

80. Ringma, *Resist the Powers with Jacques Ellul.*

81. Stott, *Making Christ Known*; the Cape Town Commitment (2010), www.lausanne.org/content/ctc/ctcommitment.

82. Stott, *Making Christ Known*, 28.

83. Stott, 39.

government to secure conditions of peace."[84] The main purpose of this call is so that the church can play its missional role in conditions of societal peace.[85] This limited perspective reflects an older Christendom model of thinking, where society has one task – governance – and the church has another task – evangelization. The government creates the conditions for the church to do its work, and the church leaves the societal domain of life to the government. Unfortunately, this kind of dualistic thinking restricts the church's ability to outwork its call to "transform and enrich culture"[86] in significant ways. Surely, the faith-community is also called to play a role in creating societal peace.

"The Glen Eyrie Report on Muslim Evangelization" (1978) does not address the peacemaking role of Christians in the world directly, though it does touch on themes that have implications for peacemaking. First of all, the report acknowledges that historically, both Christians and Muslims have used "various forms of coercion."[87] Thus, violence is not only a societal problem, but also a religious problem. Then the report probes a bit deeper, arguing that peacemaking involves reconciliation and embrace and, at minimum, includes an appreciation of "the other." Acknowledging that Christians have not always reflected these values, the report says that "Christians . . . have all too readily cherished and cultivated an antipathy towards Muslims"[88] and have often been "critical of Islamic culture."[89] It goes on to point out that our culture is also flawed.[90] While the document does not describe these flaws, there is a startling implication: to the extent that contemporary Christianity is significantly influenced by Western culture,[91] its Christianity is to some extent flawed as well.

This document opens up some key insights about the dynamics of peacemaking, though they are not made explicitly in the report. Most simply, peacemaking will involve a sympathetic understanding of "the other" and a critical view of oneself.[92]

84. Stott, 44.

85. Stott, 44.

86. Stott, 39.

87. Stott, 134.

88. Stott, 122.

89. Stott, 123.

90. Stott, 123.

91. See Newbigin, *Gospel in a Pluralist Society*, regarding his concern about the cultural captivity of the Western church.

92. See Andrews, *Jihad of Jesus*, for a discussion of these dynamics.

The third document, "An Evangelical Commitment to Simple Lifestyle" (1980), makes no direct reference to the Christian task of peacemaking, but it does highlight some important themes that play into this task. First, the document seeks to challenge the personal values of contemporary Western Christians,[93] focusing on our self-focused lifestyle, our commitment to "much-having," and our lack of concern for poverty and injustice.[94] Second, the document challenges us to pray and act, recognizing that "saving-faith" is exhibited in "serving love."[95] Third, the document emphasizes that such a "serving love" calls "all Christians . . . [to] participate in the active struggle to create a just and responsible society."[96] This struggle is based on the recognition that "poverty and excessive wealth, militarism and the arms industry, and the unjust distribution of capital, land, and resources are issues of power and powerlessness."[97] As noted in the Roman Catholic Catechism, these conditions often cause oppression, violence, and war.

These challenges have several important implications for the Christian task of peacemaking. First, the document highlights our need to undergo a conversion in relation to our "much-having." Second, the document makes a direct link between the work of justice and peacemaking. The rectification of injustice paves a way for peace to flourish. Third, this document calls "all Christians" to be involved in the task of working for a more just society, which will contribute to the conditions that can make for peace.[98]

The Grand Rapids Report

"The Grand Rapids Report on Evangelism and Social Responsibility: An Evangelical Commitment" (1982) marks an important transition in the missional documents of the evangelical movement. Its opening gambit states that "the people of God should become deeply involved in relief and development and the quest for justice and peace."[99] This statement is framed within the broader discussion of the relationship between evangelization and

93. Stott, *Making Christ Known*, 146.

94. Stott, 145.

95. Stott, 149.

96. Stott, 149, 148.

97. Stott, 148.

98. "Thailand Statement" (1980) adds little to the above. It retains the emphasis on the priority of evangelization while calling for a commitment "to seek . . . relief and justice" for the poor (Stott, 159, 162).

99. Stott, 177.

social concern, making the point that these facets of ministry, "while distinct from one another, are integrally related in our proclamation of and obedience to the gospel."[100] The document goes on to call all Christians to penetrate the world and every dimension of life,[101] including the realm of politics.[102]

In looking at Scripture, the report concludes that "The Bible lays great emphasis on both justice (or righteousness) and peace"[103] and that "churches which visibly demonstrate the righteousness and the peace of the kingdom . . . will make the greatest evangelistic and social impact on the world."[104] Moreover, in a world of "terrorism and war,"[105] the document calls Christians to work and pray for the "evangelization of the world" and "the quest for peace and justice."[106]

Unlike earlier documents, the Grand Rapids Report clearly places peacemaking as part of the church's mission in the world. It also recognizes the link between peacemaking and the work of justice, while carefully pointing out that "the emergence of justice and peace in the wider society" cannot be called "salvation" in the full sense of the word.[107] While it notes that "war may be in some circumstances the lesser of two evils,"[108] it concludes that "we should all . . . seek to be peacemakers."[109]

This document reflects a similar stance to the Roman Catholic Catechism, which emphasizes the importance of peacemaking as part of the calling of the people of God in the world, while at the same time recognizing the role that governments may need to play in executing war as a last resort.

Cape Town Commitment (2010)

Regarding the gift and task of Christian peacemaking in the world, the Cape Town Commitment is much more explicit than any of the previous Lausanne

100. Stott, 182.
101. Stott, 189.
102. Stott, 199.
103. Stott, 198.
104. Stott, 198.
105. Stott, 202.
106. Stott, 200.
107. Stott, 185–86.
108. Stott, 194.
109. Stott, 194.

documents.[110] This document recognizes the challenges of our time, including "global poverty, war, ethnic conflict, disease, the ecological crises, and climate change."[111] Then it clearly calls Christians to love the neighbour, including the foreigner and the enemy,[112] and it calls Christians to embrace a way of life that includes compassion, hospitality, the work of justice, and "peace-making [and] non-retaliation."[113] It rejects the posture of retaliation and revenge,[114] calling Christians to love their enemies[115] and "to denounce evil and injustice wherever they may exist."[116]

This document is framed within the overarching theme of the love of the Father, the Son, and the Holy Spirit for each other, the church, all humanity, and the creation. In casting a vision for the full restoration of all things, it sets out major themes on building the peace of Christ in our divided and broken world.[117] It highlights Christ's peace in ethnic conflict, for the poor and oppressed, for those with disabilities, for people with HIV, as well as the importance of expressing the love of Christ to people of other faiths.[118] On this last point, the document makes a strong commitment: "in the name of the God of peace, we reject the path of violence and revenge in all our dealings with people of other faiths, even when violently attacked."[119] Moreover, the document speaks of the peace of Christ "for his suffering creation"[120] and suggests that this is part of the church's "missional calling."[121] It challenges our consumptive lifestyles and urges us to work for "the protection and restoration of the earth's habitats."[122] In its conclusion, the Cape Town Commitment calls us both to witness and service in the cause of Christ and also to pray for "the

---

110. "The Manila Manifesto" (1989) does not move the discussion further in a significant way. In discerning present-day evils, including violence, corruption, and exploitation, it makes no mention of war. Though it makes the following helpful statement, "the proclamation of God's Kingdom of justice and peace demands the denunciation of all injustice and oppression both personal and structural," it does not develop this theme (Stott, 231).

111. Wright, *Cape Town Commitment*, www.lausanne.org/content/ctc/ctcommitment, 3.

112. Wright, 4.

113. Wright, 8.

114. Wright, 10.

115. Wright, 9.

116. Wright, 9.

117. Wright, 16–19.

118. Wright, 19–22.

119. Wright, 20.

120. Wright, 19.

121. Wright, 19.

122. Wright, 19.

establishment of justice, the stewardship and care of creation, and the blessing of God's peace in communities."[123]

While this document does not elaborate on the Christian stance towards war, it does not limit the peace of Christ to an internal disposition, or a relational dynamic within the faith-community, or the blessing of God for an eschatological future. Rather, it locates peacemaking as part of the church's mission to the wider world, particularly in places of poverty, marginalization, and violence. In summary, the Cape Town Commitment engages peacemaking far more than earlier Lausanne documents.

Voices of the Anabaptist Tradition: the Radical "Other"

In this attempt to understand peace as both a gift of God and the task of the church, we will listen to Anabaptist voices that can both bless and challenge us, for we do not learn through tired monologue, but through dynamic dialogue with the "radical other."[124]

Several early Anabaptist leaders can get us started in this challenging journey. In a reference to Moses killing the Egyptian in the Exodus narrative (2:12), Hans Denck comments: "if Moses had . . . perfect love, he would have given himself to be killed in the place of his brother."[125] Denck goes on to say that we are called "to forsake all violence for the Lord's sake."[126] Another early voice, Menno Simons, suggests that the matter of peacemaking is not simply an event in the face of violence, but a lifestyle. He hopes that "we may walk our whole life long . . . in peace" before the Lord.[127]

Another penetrating insight comes from Peter Walpot in the Hutterite Anabaptist tradition, who suggests that "greed is a serious and evil sickness,"[128] which is the cause of "many wars."[129] Even more pointedly, he notes that wars arise "from private possessions and greed."[130] Hans Hut theologizes this by recognizing that "peace in our world will be born from . . . [the] assault on

123. Wright, 25.

124. See Levinas, *Humanism of the Other*. See also Gadamer, *Truth and Method*; Ringma, *Gadamer's Dialogical Hermeneutics*.

125. Quoted in Liechty, *Early Anabaptist Spirituality*, 114.

126. Liechty, 120.

127. Liechty, 272.

128. Liechty, 192.

129. Liechty, 139–40.

130. Liechty, 139–40.

the flesh,"[131] which is the perishing of the old man "in baptism,"[132] and bearing "suffering after the example of the head [Christ]."[133]

Moving forward to contemporary Anabaptist voices, David Augsburger argues that peacemaking involves "habitual nonviolence" as a way of life.[134] In discussing a variety of possible responses to one's enemy, Augsburger calls us to "uncalculating enemy love,"[135] which reflects the way of Jesus and cuts across the "domination system" of our present culture.[136] He concludes that no one is an enemy, no one is disposable, and through repentance, good can triumph if we seek reconciliation and commit to peacemaking.[137]

Stuart Murray gives a very sober assessment of the peacemaking position of the Anabaptist tradition (including the modern Mennonites) when he acknowledges that "peace is fundamental to the gospel,"[138] but "through the centuries [Anabaptists] have been guilty of passivity in the face of injustice."[139] Though Murray supports the Anabaptist pacifist position, he raises the following concerns. First, pacifism may allow injustice to flourish; second, it may only be effective at the micro level; third, it can be easily confused with passivity.[140] Nevertheless, he strongly rejects the position of mainline churches, arguing that they "have endorsed lethal violence, blessed the weapons of war, prayed for military success, celebrated victories [of war] in acts of worship, and deployed missionaries under the protection of conquering armies."[141] Such an approach is based on what Murray calls "the myth of redemptive violence,"[142] which is the opposite of the biblical vision of redemptive suffering. Noting with approval the many contemporary Anabaptist/Mennonite initiatives, such as Christian Peacemaker Teams, conflict transformation initiatives, and victim-offender reconciliation programs,[143] Murray concludes that many Christians

---

131. Liechty, 78.
132. Liechty, 77.
133. Liechty, 79.
134. Augsburger, *Dissident Discipleship*, 134.
135. Augsburger, 140–42.
136. Augsburger, 138.
137. Augsburger, 142–44.
138. Murray, *Naked Anabaptist*, 124.
139. Murray, 130.
140. Murray, 128.
141. Murray, 126.
142. Murray, 131.
143. Murray, 130–31.

are now convinced that peace is at the heart of the gospel, which calls the church to love its enemies.[144]

John H. Yoder, the most important contemporary voice in this tradition, makes the following points in a basic summary of his extensive writings on Christian nonviolence and peacemaking. First, the OT wars did not have the theme, "fight boldly," but "trust in Yahweh." A related theme is that the OT people were not to make military alliances with other nations whom they would trust instead of Yahweh.[145] Second, we cannot reduce Jesus's preaching to a gospel that only has relevance for the inner life and the future life of God's final kingdom.[146] Jesus's way was "neither quietism nor zealotry,"[147] but a whole new way of life based on reconciliation, healing, and peace in the form of a community that would bear witness to the false powers of the time. Third, Yoder rejects the logic of the just-war tradition, noting that most Christians rejected military service in the first three centuries of the Christian era and all the church fathers condemned participation in war.[148] Changes to this position occurred with Constantine.

Kalantzis goes on to note that the limits set by Augustine and Aquinas in their articulation of a just war no longer apply, as wars today are no longer subject to proportionality,[149] and the "entire economy is mobilized for military production."[150] Importantly, Yoder notes that the just-war position in the Roman Catholic tradition is "not *the* official" position of the church.[151] Here Yoder references "The Challenge of Peace" (1983) by US Catholic Bishops,[152] which holds that pacifism is close to the NT; the just-war theory and pacifism "are complimentary";[153] strategies such as those used by Martin Luther King Jr. are positive; and the use of some weapons, including nuclear or biological, are morally wrong. Finally, Yoder sets out many strategies for peacemaking,

144. Murray, 129.

145. Yoder, *Nonviolence*, 75.

146. Yoder, 77.

147. Yoder, 91.

148. Yoder, 50–51. In a major review of the scholarly debate about the early Christian involvement in war, Kalantzis confirms much of Yoder's thesis. Kalantzis summarizes: "the literary evidence confirms the very strong internal coherence of the Church's non-violent stance for the first three centuries" (*Caesar and the Lamb*, 7). Moreover, he concludes that the early Christians saw themselves as peacemakers as an expression "of the kingdom on earth" (202).

149. Yoder, *Nonviolence*, 57.

150. Yoder, 56.

151. Yoder, 125.

152. For the entire text, see O'Brien and Shannon, eds., *Catholic Social Thought*, 492–571.

153. Yoder, *War of the Lamb*, 97.

noting that peacemaking is activist, as it empowers people, builds coalitions, and demonstrates a willingness to suffer for an alternative vision of what it means to build a just and humane society.[154]

From the Anabaptist tradition and other historic "peace churches," including the Friends and Brethren, we learn that Christ is the normative human being, and we are called to live Christ's way in the world. The way of Jesus not only shapes the way of our personal lives, but also the way of our social lives. Thus, peacemaking in the way of Christ is concerned with how we live the whole of our lives, not simply what we believe. Within this tradition, we must therefore refuse to participate in all forms of violence, including war.

Peacemaking and Reconciliation in the Franciscan Tradition

In this section, we will first summarize this theme from the primary writings of St. Francis before engaging the wider Franciscan tradition.

The Writings of St. Francis

In the writings of St. Francis,[155] it may be surprising that the peace theme does not seem to be prominent. In "The Testament," Francis states, "The Lord revealed to me a greeting, as we used to say: 'May the Lord give you peace.'"[156] In "The Admonitions," he makes a more significant statement: "The true peacemakers are those who preserve peace of mind and body for the love of our Lord Jesus Christ despite what they suffer in the world." He goes on to observe that "where there is inner peace and meditation there is neither anxiousness nor dissipation."[157] For Francis, peace is a profoundly Christological matter[158] and should be maintained even in the face of difficulty. In "The Canticle of Brother Sun," Francis says, "Blessed are those who endure in peace."[159] And in "The Canticle of Exhortation to Saint Clare and Her Sisters," he writes, "Those

154. Yoder, 156–57.

155. Armstrong and Brady, trans., *Francis and Clare.*

156. Armstrong and Brady, 155.

157. Armstrong and Brady, 32, 35.

158. In "The Parchment Given to Brother Leo," Francis, in speaking about God, states, "You are inner peace" (Armstrong and Brady, 100).

159. Armstrong and Brady, 39.

who are weighed down by sickness and the others who are wearied because of them, all of you: bear it in peace."[160]

In addition to these bare-bones statements, Francis gives a few peace benedictions. In "The Second Version of the Letter to the Faithful," he writes, "To all Christian religious: clergy and laity, men and women, and to all who live in the whole world, Brother Francis, their servant and subject, [offers] homage and reverence, true peace from heaven and sincere love in the Lord."[161] And in "A Letter to the Rulers of the Peoples," he exclaims, "To all mayors and consuls, magistrates and rulers throughout the world . . . peace to all of you."[162]

The statements in "The Earlier Rule" and "The Later Rule" are much more significant,[163] as he speaks about a way of life in Christ that is shaped by the gospel, which creates the basis and conditions for our role as peacemakers in our world. Following is a point-by-point summary of these two rules.[164]

First, the Franciscan brothers were instructed not to own any property. Thus, they could live a "disarmed" lifestyle, for they had nothing to protect or defend. Since much violence is about possessions, this rule removed the cause of violence.

Second, the Franciscan brothers were not to exercise leadership and dominance over each other or others. And so, there would be no one to "put down" or dominate. Power *over* others can so easily lead to various forms of oppression that issue forth in violence.

Third, the brothers were instructed to see themselves as nothing much except for the grace of God. Thus, they had no sense of being powerful or privileged. Rather, they saw themselves as God's "little ones" in God's grand scheme of things. This posture of humility dynamited all sense of power.

Fourth, the Franciscan brothers were called to love their neighbours and their enemies. The brothers were called to see others – including Muslims – as part of God's world. Thus, they were to respect those who were different.

Finally, the Franciscans were invited to see the whole created world – both the social world and the natural world – as a reflection of the image of the incarnate Son of God. And so, they were called to care for everything rather than to destroy.

---

160. Armstrong and Brady, 41.

161. Armstrong and Brady, 67.

162. Armstrong and Brady, 77.

163. Armstrong and Brady, 107–35, 136–45.

164. Though I offer a summary, I encourage everyone to read these two rules in their entirety.

The instructions in these two rules imply that Francis did not see peacemaking as a strategy, but a *way of life in Christ.* The brothers were not to be peacemakers only in certain circumstances, but to bring forth the life of Christ in the world. Thus, being a person of peace is ontological rather than pragmatic.

The Franciscan Tradition

In this section, we seek to remain as close as possible to the heartbeat of St. Francis by taking note of what Francis *did* (rather than what he wrote) by engaging a number of contemporary Franciscan scholars. Since this is a huge field, I will outline this material in an eight-point summary.

First, as the Franciscan scholar Ilia Delio points out, Francis saw peace as a gift from God as he "encountered the God of peace in the crucified Christ."[165] Thus, to be a "peacemaker is to accept the gift of peace given to us by Christ."[166] This means that the *gift* of peace precedes the *task* of peacemaking.

Second, to grow in the love of God is to become a person of greater peace. And "peace . . . is the path of active love."[167] Thus, sanctified service includes peacemaking.

Third, a person of peace is "willing to suffer . . . out of love for another."[168] Peace comes at a price. Rather than retaliation, it involves redemptive suffering.

Fourth, Bonaventure (1221–1274), the Franciscan theologian and Minister General of the Franciscan Order, points out that Francis "in all his preaching . . . proclaimed peace" and that he received this "in a revelation from the Lord."[169] Thus, peace was central to the gospel.

Fifth, Francis sent out his brothers as emissaries of peace: "Go, my dear brothers two by two . . . *announcing peace* to the people and *penance for the remission of sins.*"[170] This task was possible because the brothers were to be "children of peace."[171] In an instruction to the brothers, Francis says, "Let everyone be drawn to peace and kindness through your peace and

165. Delio, *Franciscan Prayer*, 165.

166. Delio, 155.

167. Delio, 165.

168. Delio, 168.

169. Bonaventure, *Life of St. Francis*, 24.

170. Quoted in Delio, *Franciscan Prayer*, 167, italics in original.

171. From "Assisi Compilation," quoted in Crosby, *Finding Francis*, 186.

gentleness."[172] Thus, he saw peace as a gift of grace that was to become deeply embedded in the life of the brothers.

Sixth, in case one might think that Francis was only concerned with helping people find peace with God or inner or relational peace, we must note that he lived in an age "rent by civil wars,"[173] and he helped to settle many political disputes in Assisi and also in Arezzo, Perugia, Siena, and Bologna.[174]

Seventh, Francis not only lived during a time of civil wars,[175] but also the era of the Crusades. While there is no evidence that Francis publicly condemned the Crusades, he *subverted* them by his actions. The Franciscan brothers made many attempts to engage Muslim leaders. For example, five brothers went on a mission to Seville, which was under Mohammedan control, and were expelled from the city. They returned and were beheaded.[176] In 1221, Francis and some brothers joined a crusade as peacemakers in order to get to the Sultan, Malik al-Kamil. While first mistreated, Francis was eventually able to earn the Sultan's respect, and they were able to talk about matters of faith.[177] Michael H. Crosby observes how Francis moved "from a violence-based approach to Islam, to a respectful way of dialoguing with it."[178]

Eighth, some of the key dimensions of St. Francis's comprehensive understanding of peacemaking include his approach to the creation and the environment. As William J. Short points out, Francis was never simply a lover of nature, as all creatures reflected "the face of the beloved Son,"[179] and all things "bear the traces of him [Christ]."[180] As Bonaventure helpfully observes, Francis saw a "universal reconciliation with each and everything," and he "perceived a heavenly harmony in all things."[181] Thus, for Francis, peacemaking is God-oriented, relationally relevant, and reflective of an inner

172. From the "Anonymous Perugia," quoted in Crosby, 188.

173. Jorgenson, *Saint Francis of Assisi*, 99. During Francis's lifetime, civil wars raged in Assisi, as the city wanted to remain independent from both papal and imperial power.

174. Jorgenson, 99; Crosby, *Finding Francis*, 186. Francis also settled a powerful family feud in Bologna and brought reconciliation between a mayor and a bishop (Crosby, *Finding Francis*, 193–94, 190–91). Bonaventure notes that Francis did not see these peacemaking initiatives in programmatic terms. In Arezzo, "shaken by civil war," Francis was able to "command the devils to leave the city" (Bonaventure, *Life of Francis*, 64).

175. He was involved in one before his conversion.

176. Jorgenson, *Saint Francis of Assisi*, 163, 192, 199–200.

177. Crosby, *Finding Francis*, 194–97.

178. Crosby, 194.

179. Short, *Poverty and Joy*, 111.

180. Short, 113.

181. Bonaventure, *Life of Francis*, 79, 94.

Christlikeness, and it also includes our relations with the stranger and the enemy as well as our care for nature.

These eight key points need to be expanded to obtain a more comprehensive understanding of Franciscan peacemaking. First, Franciscan peacemaking is not simply a strategy for creating harmony that reduces everything to a common – and often anaemic – denominator. Rather, peacemaking is at the heart of the gospel, for through the cross of Christ, peace with God, each other, the enemy, and the whole created order becomes a possibility. Furthermore, peacemaking is a whole way of life in obedience to the gospel. As Francis puts it, "I should live according to the pattern of the Holy Gospel."[182]

Second, peacemaking has everything to do with our Christology. Constantine conquered in the name of Christ with a sword in his hand. Colonialism acted in the name of a conquering Christ. Peacemaking, however, is only possible when we follow the incarnate and suffering Christ into the world. Reflecting on the incarnation, St. Francis cries out: "Look, brothers, at the humility of God."[183]

Third, Ilia Delio points out that peacemaking involves the rejection of all forms of "dominion theology."[184] The way of God in the world is not one of conquest, but redemptive suffering. Yet the church in history has often not taken this road, assuming that the more power it has, the better its mission. But as Celano, the earliest Franciscan biographer, notes, "only a wounded body can bring about peace."[185] And Leonardo Boff, the Latin American Franciscan scholar, reminds us that the urge to dominate and have power *over* others is present in all of us.[186] He points to the subtlety of this when the church relates to the poor "through power" by its ministries of "assistance" marked by "paternalism."[187]

Fourth, a key aspect of Franciscan peacemaking is its inherently maternal spirituality. Bonaventure notes that Francis "seemed like a mother who was daily in labor pains bringing . . . [others] to birth in Christ."[188] Delio reiterates this, writing that Francis displayed a "mysticism of maternity" by giving birth

182. Quoted in Crosby, *Finding Francis*, 125.

183. Quoted in Short, *Poverty and Joy*, 43.

184. Delio, *Franciscan Prayer*, 170.

185. Quoted in Delio, *Franciscan Prayer*, 174.

186. Boff, *Saint Francis*, 39.

187. Boff, 78.

188. Bonaventure, *Life of Francis*, 80.

to Christ in our lives and in the life of the world.[189] We, too, are to live as a "second incarnation" of Christ through the birthing of the Holy Spirit.[190] Boff helpfully points out that in a world of paternalism, Francis was able to integrate "the feminine."[191] Without buying into the overgeneralization that men make wars and women make homes, we do need to recognize both the historical reality of male dominance and the current male role in domestic violence. Boff reminds us that "the heart and spirit of kindness constitute the central reality of the human being and of humanizing culture."[192] Moreover, he notes that "true gentleness is born of strength" and not of passivity or cowardice.[193]

Fifth, as we have noted, St. Francis and his brothers, St. Clare and her sisters, along with the early lay tertiaries lived in a world of regional wars, crusades, and paternalism. They also lived in a feudal world of hierarchy, with its inherent propensity for oppression and other abuses of power. In contrast to this feudal system and the powerful land-owning monasteries of that time,[194] Francis created a "fraternal" order,[195] which Crosby describes as a new familial order of the kingdom of God.[196] As Boff observes, this way of being "breaks the rigidity of the feudal hierarchy."[197] A fraternal order based on relationships of mutuality undermines the potential misuse of power that is inherent in all forms of hierarchy. Thus, Francis created a *movement* of peace, which was revolutionary for his time.[198]

Sixth, in "The Anonymous Perugia," Francis exclaims: "Lord, if we had any possessions, we would need to protect them because they cause many disputes and lawsuits. And possessions usually impede the love of God and neighbour. Therefore, we do not want to possess anything in this world."[199] As Bonaventure notes, "they possessed nothing," and as a consequence, "they had nothing to defend and feared to lose nothing."[200] Thus, Franciscan asceticism is

189. Delio, *Franciscan Prayer*, 13.

190. Delio, 69.

191. Boff, *Saint Francis*, 28.

192. Boff, 15.

193. Boff, 22.

194. Some monastic orders, particularly the Templars, the Knights of Malta and the Teutonic Knights, participated in the Crusades. See Steward, *Monks of War*.

195. Crosby, *Finding Francis*, 62.

196. Crosby, 135.

197. Boff, *Saint Francis*, 22.

198. In *Living Our Future*, von Galli is right to call Francis a revolutionary figure.

199. Quoted in Crosby, *Finding Francis*, 162.

200. Bonaventure, *Life of Francis*, 37.

inherently oriented towards peacemaking. Moreover, the move from privilege to identification with the poor identifies Franciscanism as a movement that seeks to empower the weak rather than attempting to pull down the strong. In this identification with the poor, St. Francis discovered the surprise of God: "what seemed bitter to me [in kissing the leper], became sweetness of body and soul."[201] After this experience, Francis embraced a spirituality of descent. Yet our present-day orientation tends towards a spirituality of ascent. We assume that if we become more socially powerful as a Christian community, we will have greater influence. But this simply follows the old Christendom model, with its propensity to misuse power. Boff makes the point that Francis led a life of "de-class-ification"[202] as a countermove to the inherent oppression of the class system of his day. Thus, Francis oriented his life toward "disappropriation"[203] rather than much-having and exclusion.

Seventh, Francis' core passion in "The Testament" is "that I should live according to the pattern of the Holy Gospel."[204] Crosby notes that Francis believed "that the pattern of Jesus' life might be replicated in our own."[205] This Christification made Francis a builder, which became evident in his heavenly call: "Francis, don't you see that my house is destroyed? Go, then, and rebuild it for me."[206] This rebuilding was multi-directional, for it was about rebuilding one's relationship with God, one's self, the church, the stranger, the human community, and all of the created order. Crosby notes that it involved "everyone and everything in it [as] part of God's domain or household."[207] This commitment to rebuilding in the course of following Christ demonstrates relational peace-building, which poses a challenge, as we tend to be self-serving rather than regarding others. We also tend to be denominationally and missionally territorial and tribalistic. Thus, we divide and splinter rather than seeking to rebuild the whole. To give just one example, think of our fragmented and competitive evangelicalism!

Eighth, Francis did not see "the other" as one to be feared or denigrated, but one to be loved, particularly the stranger. As Bonaventure notes, Francis

201. Quoted in Boff, *Saint Francis*, 68.

202. Boff, 67.

203. Boff, 69.

204. Quoted in Crosby, *Finding Francis*, 125.

205. Crosby, 105.

206. From "The Legend of Three Companions," quoted in Crosby, 52.

207. Crosby, 57.

rejected "the vice of detraction,"[208] which pulls down and often justifies violence toward the other. Instead of hating Muslims, Francis saw them as fellow creatures wrapped in the love of the crucified God. Sadly, we are all too quick to label and demonize others. The more we do this, the more we legitimize the use of violence against them. As Delio observes, "we are fragmented, divisive, dominating, and oppressive,"[209] and sadly, "Christians play a part in the constant violence in our world."[210]

While much more could be explored,[211] we can summarize this brief survey by recognizing that Franciscan peacemaking is not simply about employing certain strategies,[212] but a whole way of life as we seek to follow Christ. Delio helpfully points out that the Franciscan way is a "disarmament of the heart"[213] that involves embracing, imbibing, and living a "crucified love," which is a "love for the sake of the other."[214] This Franciscan way explores and practices the "connection between peace in your heart and peace in the world."[215]

In conclusion, Johannes Jorgenson notes that "by paying evil with evil," we simply participate in and accentuate the sins of others. Instead, we are to lead others to "love God in peace and joy."[216] This peace is not simply an internal disposition, but a peace for the whole world. Thus, Mario von Galli rightly observes that "a non-violent revolution is the only possible revolution for Christians."[217]

Integration and Conclusion

Having engaged the hymns, liturgies, catechisms, spirituality, and missional praxis of Anglicans, Reformed, evangelicals, Roman Catholics, and Anabaptists regarding their perspectives on the topic of peace and peacemaking, it is clear that *peacemaking is an important part of the Christian tradition*. We have seen that key themes include peace with God through Christ, the inner peace of

208. Bonaventure, *Life of St. Francis*, 82.

209. Delio, *Franciscan Prayer*, 178.

210. Delio, 175.

211. For example, we have only touched on Francis' theme of peacemaking as it relates to our care for the environment. See Jorgenson, *Saint Francis*, 34–35; Crosby, *Finding Francis*, 198.

212. See Butigan et al., *Franciscan Nonviolence*.

213. Delio, *Franciscan Prayer*, 178.

214. Delio, 177.

215. Delio, 178.

216. Jorgenson, *Saint Francis*, 216.

217. von Galli, *Living Our Future*, 169.

faith, and relational peace within the Christian community. All the Christian traditions we have considered acknowledge that the Christian church should be an instrument of peace in the world, but the Franciscans and the Anabaptists give this task a much greater priority.

For example, in the hymns, we sing, "bring to our world of strife your sovereign word of peace, that war may haunt the earth no more, and desolation cease,"[218] and "our lives will spread your peace."[219] In the liturgies, we pray, "give peace to your church, peace among nations, peace in our homes, and peace in our hearts."[220] And *Celtic Daily Prayer* calls us to prayer and "active peace-making."[221] In the Lausanne documents, we are called to engage in compassion, hospitality, the work of justice, and "peace-making [and] non-retaliation."[222] David Augsburger, a contemporary Anabaptist, notes that the emphasis in his tradition is on "habitual nonviolence" as a way of life.[223] Finally, to summarize the Franciscan perspective, we can turn to Bonaventure, who said that "they possessed nothing," and as a consequence, "they had nothing to defend and feared to lose nothing."[224] This freedom centred in Christ gave the Franciscans the freedom to work for peace in their world.

While there is a clear division between Anabaptist Christians, who hold a pacifist position, and those who maintain that Christians, along with others, need to play their part in supporting the war effort of their respective countries because of their supposed civic duty, there are legitimate questions that need to be raised regarding the political justification for a particular war. Furthermore, though some Christians may not be pacifist, they may object to supporting a particular war, as with the Western invasion of Iraq.

The Franciscan tradition poses a particular challenge to the church, as peacemaking is intrinsic to what it means to be a follower of Christ. When peacemaking is backed by a lifestyle of radical relinquishment, the peace of Christ can more readily blossom in our world. Thus, peacemaking is integral to any missional spirituality.

---

218. *Together in Song*, hymn 616.

219. *Together in Song*, hymn 635.

220. *Book of Alternative Services*, 677.

221. *Celtic Daily Prayer: Book Two*, 1098.

222. www.lausanne.org/content/ctc/ctcommitment, 8.

223. Augsburger, *Dissident Discipleship*, 134.

224. Bonaventure, *Life of Francis*, 37.

15

Liberation Theology

A Spirituality and Praxis of Serving the Poor[1]

Introduction

In this chapter, I wish to bring some Latin American liberation theologians into critical dialogue with evangelicalism,[2] because I believe that liberation theologians can help evangelicals[3] enter into God's love and passion for the poor and live that out in a costly discipleship marked by grace and joy. While many evangelicals view liberation theology with grave concern and deep suspicion,[4] I would like to suggest that evangelicals have much to learn from

1. This chapter is the substance of a presentation from "The Church and Poverty in Asia," Fourth Theological Forum, 7–8 February, 2008, Union Church, Manila, Philippines. A more extended version is published in Wanak, ed., *The Church and Poverty in Asia*, 7–53.

2. Namely as it is represented by the Lausanne movement.

3. I recognize that the term "evangelical" is not without its problems, since it can range from people holding a narrow fundamentalism to more radical positions. I place myself in the broad evangelical tradition set out by my former colleague, Stanley Grenz, *Theology for the Community of God*.

4. My overall purpose is *not* to defend liberation theology as a system, nor to draw on global liberation theologies (see Rowland, *Cambridge Companion to Liberation Theology*), nor Third World liberation theologies (see Ferm, *Third World Liberation Theologies*). I am only engaging some of the key Latin American liberation theologians. Moreover, many critics have raised concerns about liberation theology (for example, see McGovern, *Liberation Theology and Its Critics*; Bell, *Liberation Theology After the End of History*). The central, but largely unfounded, criticisms are that the gospel is de-emphasized; faith is cast in too political terms; Marxist social theories are used; and some writings present theories of violence to bring about social change (Ferm, *Third World Liberation Theologies*, 100–16).

the biblically informed theology and praxis of liberation theologians about the work of justice and social transformation on behalf of the poor.[5]

Introduction

Throughout the long journey of the church, Christians have sought to live out the biblical vision of God's concern for the poor. However, in the past as well as in present times, evangelicals have not fared as well as others in their service to the poor. I believe this stems from the fact that their response to the poor has been driven by pragmatics rather than a robust biblical-theological vision and, as the documents of the Lausanne movement demonstrate, service to the poor is often incidental and peripheral to evangelical theology. Moreover, the evangelical focus has always tended to be more spiritual than social.

In contrast, liberation theologians have a much richer theology of God's particular care and concern for the poor, which reflects the biblical vision more faithfully.[6] They also place the vision of God's passion for the poor at the centre of their writings, often drawing on the rich historical tradition of the church's missional service to the poor. As such, the Bible is not read as a book of comfort for the middle classes, but from the underside of history, pointing towards a vision of God's upside-down kingdom. This liberating hermeneutic and theology move us from the head to the heart, calling us to embrace a spirituality of descent in the pattern of the great hymn in Philippians 2, where we radically identify ourselves with the poor for the sake of the gospel. Such an incarnational spirituality does not move from abstract theological thinking to praxis, but from the praxis of love of God and neighbour to theological reflection.

In this chapter, I suggest that liberation theologians can help evangelicals develop a missional theology of the poor that will orient their praxis toward a more profound social analysis and engagement so that God's heart for the poor may find a deeper resonance in their lives, thereby fostering a richer and more contemplative Christian spirituality. In order to ground this dialogue in Scripture, I will begin with a brief outline of the biblical vision regarding

5. I am in no way suggesting that liberation theologians cannot learn from evangelicals. Evangelical clarity in presenting the gospel, with its call to embrace the salvific work of God in Christ through the power of the Spirit, is one challenge to the liberation theologians. However, I am also not suggesting that they don't preach the gospel. Boff and Boff are clear: "Jesus, the Son of God, took on oppression to set us free" (*Introducing Liberation Theology*, 53).

6. By highlighting, for example, the Exodus motif and the incarnational mission of Jesus in bringing good news to the poor (Luke 7:22).

God's particular concern for the poor to demonstrate that care for the poor is fundamentally normative for the Christian community.[7] Then we will take a look at the witness of the church in its long march through history to see both its faithfulness and creativity in living out the biblical witness regarding service to the poor along with its failures and flaws.

Having passed through the windows of the biblical narrative and the church's praxis in history, I will then summarize how the contemporary church is responding to issues facing the poor and marginalized around the world by examining missional documents from the Lausanne movement as well as key texts from the ecumenical movement and Roman Catholic social teaching. This comparison will form the substance of my critique of the evangelical movement.[8] Finally, I will turn to liberation theologians for a helpful corrective to the evangelical paradigm.

Biblical-Theological Perspectives Regarding the Poor

While God's concern is for the liberation of the *whole* of humanity (1 Tim 2:3–4, 11) – in fact, the whole created order (Rom 8:21; Col 1:20) – the biblical story is awash with God's specific love, mercy, and concern for the poor[9] (Ps 147:7–9). Thus, we are called to be like God in serving the poor (Deut 15:12–17). Moreover, God is "a stronghold for the oppressed" (Ps 9:9) and "executes justice for the oppressed" (Ps 146:7).[10] Because God loves justice (Ps 37:28; Deut 32:4; Rev 16:7) and wants no one to be oppressed (Ps 104:12),[11] we are

7. See also chapter 9 ("God's Heart for the Poor: A Missional Focus").

8. As noted previously, evangelicalism is my tradition, and so this critique applies to myself.

9. The Bible speaks of the poor using a range of meanings and nuances. There are two most basic meanings. First, the Bible speaks of the poor in the sense of the humble who acknowledge their need for God (Pss 34:6; 86:1). Second, the Bible speaks of the economic and social poor (Lev 19:10; Deut 15:11). The focus of this discussion is on the *economic* poor, but this refers to more than finances, as poverty also refers to poor in terms of education, health, opportunities, and so forth.

10. Oppression in the biblical story takes many forms – economic, military, and political (2 Kgs 13:22; Isa 52:4) – but our focus is on the oppression and exploitation of the poor by the powerful. As Isaiah brutally observes, "the spoil of the poor is in your houses" (Isa 4:14). Moreover, the poor are deprived of their rights (Prov 31:5) and pushed aside by the powerful (Amos 5:12).

11. The Bible recognizes that oppression will occur. As Isaiah succinctly says, "people will be oppressed" (Isa 3:5). Oppression leads to affliction and misery (Ps 44:24), and thus the people cry out under an oppressive load (Job 35:9) and look to Yahweh to come to their aid (Ps 119:134).

also called to practice the work of justice (Mic 6:8),[12] particularly for the poor and oppressed[13] because justice is so often denied to them (Prov 21:3; Jer 23:5; Deut 27:19; Ezek 22:29; Amos 2:7; Matt 12:18; Luke 18:6–8).[14]

This work of doing justice is helpfully and challengingly prefigured in the OT concepts of Sabbath year and Jubilee and laws on gleaning and tithing.[15] It is also set out in a descriptive life ethic (Ezek 18:5–9), the visionary dream of Isaiah (Isa 65:17–25), the ethics and practice of Jesus (Luke 6:20; 7:22–23; 14:15–24), the theological concept of oneness in Christ (Gal 3:28–29; 1 Cor 12:12–13), the idea that there may be "equality" or "a fair balance" (2 Cor 8:12–14 NIV/NRSV), and in the NT practice of caring for the poor (Jas 2:1–7).[16]

The OT liberation scholar, J. Severino Croatto,[17] points out that the liberation of the Hebrew slaves in Egypt became the central confession of Israel's faith and identity (Deut 26:5–8) and the defining characteristic of Israel's life (Pss 80:8; 105:23–45; 106:21–22; 114:1; 135:8; 136:13–15). As a chosen and redeemed people, the Israelites were set apart to be a blessing for others and to extend Exodus to their own people as well as to the sojourner and stranger (Deut 15:12–17; 24:17–22). The key motif is, "you shall not deprive a resident alien or an orphan of justice . . . Remember that you were a slave in Egypt and the Lord redeemed you" (Deut 27:17–18). In this normative ethic for the

---

12. While Martin Luther King Jr believed that "we are called to speak for the weak, for the voiceless" (Ringma, *Let My People Go*, reflection 112), he also emphasized that both the oppressed and the oppressor needed conversion and transformation. King writes: "we are all caught in an inescapable network of mutuality," (quoted in Washington, ed., *Testament of Hope*, 254). King went on to say that "God is interested in the freedom of the whole human race and in the creation of a society where all . . . can live together . . ." (215).

13. Tamez, *Bible of the Oppressed*, has been particularly helpful in drawing attention to the compound meanings carried by some of the key OT words for oppression: *nagash*, *anah*, *lahats*. Beside the core meanings of oppression and exploitation, further shades of meaning include to degrade, subdue, violate another, harass, and drive someone in a corner (Exod 5:10, 13, 14; 1:11; 3:7, 9).

14. Oppression tends to compound, mounting up multiple difficulties for the poor. Conrad Boerma observes that in the OT, there are traders who exploit the poor (Hos 12:7–8; Amos 8:5–6; Mic 6:10–12), corrupt judges (Amos 5:7; Mic 3:9–11; Isa 5:23), and creditors seizing the poor's wages, goods, property, and land (Isa 4:14; Jer 22:13; Mic 2:2; Ezek 22:29). In such a setting, the poor have no one to turn to, which institutes the politics of despair (Boerma, *The Rich, the Poor, and the Bible*).

15. Sider, *Rich Christians in an Age of Hunger*, 78–83; Ringe, *Jesus, Liberation, and the Biblical Jubilee*.

16. The evangelical scholar, Waldron Scott, has made a powerful plea that mission cannot be understood simply in terms of the Great Commission. Mission, he says, has to do with rectification (*Bring Forth Justice*, xv) and this involves the central biblical motif of the establishment of justice (xvi).

17. Croatto, *Exodus*.

Israelites, redemption pulled them into the purposes of God for the whole of humanity and the world.

This motif regarding the practical outworking of our redemption is key to the NT as well. The Nazareth "manifesto" (Luke 4:18–19) is not only the charter for how God in Christ acts redemptively towards those seeking salvation, but it also becomes a model for how the redeemed are called to act towards others (Luke 6:27–36). Matthew makes a direct connection between service to the poor as a way of serving Christ (Matt 25:34–46). The Apostle Paul recognizes that if we are in Christ, we are linked to our brothers and sisters in Christ (1 Cor 12:12–13), and so the slave or poor person is now a brother or sister (Phlm 16; Gal 3:27–29) and should be regarded and treated accordingly (Jas 2:1–7). Paul expresses this reality simply, "Thieves must give up stealing; rather let them labor and work honestly with their own hands, *so as* to have something to share with the needy" (Eph 4:28, my emphasis). In joining the God of justice, we are called to cease from all forms of oppression while also embracing practices that bless others and bring them into God's *shalom*.

This brief survey touches on some of the key themes in the biblical writings regarding the poor,[18] with the major theme being that God's love and mercy leads us to live with charity towards others, which then leads us to work for justice on behalf of the poor and oppressed. It is important here to make a distinction between *charity*, which is about extending practical care to those who have an immediate pressing need, and God's vision of *restorative justice*, which calls us to engage in the long-term work of changing the conditions of injustice, marginalization, or oppression so that people can live in just and equitable circumstances. In other words, we can all live God's *shalom*.[19] Martin Luther King Jr. illustrates the difference between charity and justice by saying that "we are called to play the Good Samaritan on life's roadside, but that will only be an initial act . . . we must come to see that the whole Jericho road must be transformed so that men and women will not be constantly beaten and robbed as they make their journey on life's highway."[20]

18. The Bible also acknowledges that poverty may be self-inflicted due to laziness and other factors (Prov 10:4; 20:13).

19. Wright, *Walking in the Ways of the Lord*, 26–45.

20. Ringma, *Let My People Go*, reflection 43.

Service to the Poor in the History of the Church

Having established the biblical roots of God's care and concern for the poor, we will briefly consider how the church has sought to live that out – sometimes with radical faithfulness and at other times with disappointing compromise and neglect. This history is far too extensive to explore within this chapter, so we will very briefly survey the following epochs: the early church, the church in the Constantinian era, the church in the Middle Ages, the church in the Reformation and beyond, and the challenges we are facing as the church in our contemporary world.

Care for the Poor in the Early Church

In this period from the New Testament persecution of the church to its establishment as part of Constantine's empire, it is important not to over-idealize the early church. While the early Christian movement was young and vital as it sought to live out its radical vision of a new people in Christ, it was also messy[21] and had an extremely marginal position within the Roman Empire.[22] The writings of the early church fathers highlight several ways that the church, as Ignatius put it in his instructions to the presbyters, went about "caring for all the weak, neglecting neither widow, nor orphan nor poor."[23] First, people gave alms, which were then distributed by deacons. Second, funds were used to care for the needy within the faith-community, which included attempts to buy the freedom of Christians condemned to prison or to work in mines as slaves. Third, in settings of natural, social, or political disasters, Christians extended practical help to others, which included paying for burial services of strangers. Fourth, Christians practised hospitality to strangers, but primarily to brothers and sisters in the faith. Fifth, some Christian churches used church funds to buy the freedom of slaves outside the church.[24]

In this initial chapter of the church's long march in history, Christians cared for the weak and poor in their own midst and also extended concern to others through acts of kindness and care. As Troeltsch summarises, this "constitutes a brilliant chapter in . . . [the church's] history," as it exemplifies

---

21. Especially in relation to slavery.

22. There were probably some two hundred thousand Christians in a Roman world of some thirty million. Obviously, this severely limited how the early Christians could impact society.

23. Oliver, *Social Achievements of the Christian Church*, 32.

24. Phan, *Social Thought*, 20–23.

the "awakening of the spirit of love . . . which Christ imparts."[25] Through this "work of charity," the church was "healing social wounds."[26]

Care for the Poor in the Constantinian Church

In this period, the marginal and persecuted church became the church of the empire, gaining the support of the state, respectability, and influence. During this time, the church also became highly organized. While charity continued, the church now had much greater social influence, and so it responded to the poor and needy by creating more *institutional* forms of care. This included establishing schools and hospitals as well as addressing general social concerns, such as suppressing gladiatorial events. Monastic communities were also established, and they extended hospitality, cared for the poor, and developed farming practices. Though slavery continued during this period, churches often paid to buy slaves their freedom, along with prisoners of war.[27] Finally, churches continued to care for the poor in their respective cities.[28]

Care for the Poor in the Middle Ages

The church in the Middle Ages was shaped by the theological vision of Thomas Aquinas who sought to create a Christian society. In the words of Troeltsch, the Middle Ages "witnessed the expansion of the Church to a comprehensive, unifying, and reconciling social whole, which included both the sociological circle of religion itself and the politico-social organizations."[29] This synthesis between church and state not only meant a more powerful role for the church in society, but it also drew the church into more areas of social concern. Thus, bishops not only played a role in religious matters, but also "civic and penal legislation."[30] In this period, the church itself, along with monastic orders, became rich landowners. While there were some helpful developments in the church's role in society during this period, many concerns surfaced.

---

25. Troeltsch, *Social Teaching of the Christian Churches*, 134–35.

26. Troeltsch, 134.

27. Ambrose, bishop of Milan, "sold rich church ornaments to ransom captives who had fallen into the hands of the Goths" (Oliver, *Social Achievements of the Christian Church*, 66).

28. Oliver, 45–77.

29. Troeltsch, *Social Teaching of the Christian Churches*, 203.

30. Troeltsch, 211.

The more helpful developments may be summarized as follows. First, there continued to be a great emphasis on almsgiving and the practice of charity, as the church devoted one-third of its income to relief for the poor.[31] Second, with greater power and influence, the church became a civilizing force in society. Third, the merchant and trade guilds of this time acted as a "lay charity and social service" in that they helped bury "the dead, gave dowries to poor girls and rendered other social services."[32] Fourth, the laws of the land began to reflect general Christian values, and so "law and legal penalty" was substituted "for private revenge."[33] Fifth, the flourishing of art, the building of cathedrals, and the writing and producing of books brought cultural richness to society.[34]

Yet there were also several concerns about the way the church was functioning in society. First, almsgiving and the practice of charity became loaded with spiritual significance, accruing merit for the *giver*.[35] Second, as the giver became the focus of attention, and as people gave in order to receive grace, poverty increased rather than being alleviated.[36] Third, an increased emphasis on natural law and patriarchalism established a set of values that promoted social conservatism, stability, and gratitude to one's benefactors. These values created greater dependencies and "corrupted both the givers and the receivers."[37]

This troubling synthesis of church and state prompted some to return to the vision and ethos of early Christianity for inspiration in serving the poor. These "sectarian" movements included the Waldensians, Franciscans, Lollards, Hussites, and Moravians.[38] This highlights how the church throughout history has been renewed by finding inspiration from the biblical story and the ethos of early Christianity rather than from its current practices.

Care for the Poor in the Reformation and Beyond

While the church in the Middle Ages was shaped by the theological vision of Thomas Aquinas, the Reformation sought to renew and revitalize church and

31. Oliver, *Social Achievements of the Christian Church*, 101.
32. Oliver, 99.
33. Oliver, 98.
34. Oliver, 94–96.
35. Oliver, 103.
36. Oliver, 104.
37. Oliver, 105.
38. Troeltsch, *Social Teaching of the Christian Churches*, 349–69.

to make an impact on society through church-related institutions and the laity. This huge task eventually spawned an arid Protestant orthodoxy that lacked missional and societal impetus. Because good works no longer held special merit, there was a lack "of zeal in social work," and the "tendency in Protestant countries was to leave the care of the poor to the state."[39]

Nevertheless, the Reformation brought several new ideas that influenced attitudes and practices within the church and society about serving the poor and needy. First, the good of the recipient, not the giver, should be the primary focus. Second, only the unfortunate and helpless – not the lazy – should receive assistance. Third, assistance should solve particular needs and problems and should be evaluated in terms of effectiveness. In other words, the focus should be on creating long-term solutions. Fourth, support *systems* should be put in place to sustain worthy projects. Fifth, policies should be developed in doing social work. Sixth, civil authorities should play their part in helping the poor.[40] These ideas reflect an important shift from the Middle Ages, prefiguring some of the practices of the modern world.

The basic ethic emerging from Protestantism was that those with resources should be generous, but there was little sense of radical identification with the poor, and so charity, rather than social justice, continued to predominate.[41]

Care for the Poor in the Contemporary World

Our transition to how we care for the poor in our contemporary world constitutes the most significant change in this brief survey.[42] There are many factors that have contributed to the challenging place we find ourselves today, including the development of post-colonial states in the Majority World, which has resulted in fragile economies and unstable governments, not to mention the pressures of globalization and climate change. All these forces have caused a massive spread in the map of world poverty and global injustice.[43]

---

39. Oliver, *Social Achievements of the Christian Church*, 116–17.

40. Oliver, 115.

41. In a long discussion of Protestantism and its particular Calvinistic variant, Troeltsch summarizes this tradition in terms of its "unceasing . . . labor" and "the habit of industry to suppress all distracting and idle impulses," as well as the willingness to use "profit for the religious community and for public welfare" (*Social Teaching of the Christian Churches*, 808–9).

42. To fill gaps in the period from the Reformation to the present, I suggest Bosch's treatment of mission in the wake of the Enlightenment (*Transforming Mission*, 262–345).

43. To cite just a few of the more sobering statistics, roughly half of the world's population lives on less than $2 per day, and one-seventh are chronically malnourished, resulting in the annual death of some forty million people, mostly children, who die of starvation and related but

There have also been radical changes in the map of world Christianity. In the post-Reformation world, Christianity was largely Western, but today, 70 percent of Christians live in the Majority World.[44] Since many Majority World countries struggle with issues of dire poverty and gross injustice, and many Christians are actually poor, the issue of poverty has come to rest (and agitate) within the bosom of the church itself. Thus, the church is not only concerned *about* the poor, but the church itself is made up *of* the poor. These issues are well beyond the challenges that faced the church in earlier epochs, and they call the church to a new sense of identity, theology, and praxis.

In light of the above, we may now consider how the contemporary church is responding to these challenges by examining the missional documents from the Lausanne movement, key texts from the ecumenical movement, and Roman Catholic social teaching.

Critiquing the Evangelical Tradition Regarding Service to the Poor

I want to begin by acknowledging that evangelicalism is my tradition, and so my critique also applies to myself.[45] Second, I want to recognize that there are many evangelicals who have developed both an adequate theology in relation to the poor and have also demonstrated a praxis that accords with that theological vision.[46] Thus, my concern is not with individual evangelicals but with the movement as a whole, particularly as represented in the Lausanne documents.

Of the nine major documents of the Lausanne movement, the 1982 Grand Rapids Report, "Evangelism and Social Responsibility," deals most explicitly with service to the poor.[47] In the other eight documents, ministry to the poor is not the focus or is fairly marginal.[48] While the primal 1974

preventable illnesses. Moreover, twenty percent of the world's population consume 80 percent of the world goods. And in 2001, some 500 billionaires registered a combined income that was equivalent to the combined income of the poorest half of humanity. These statistics were accessed on http://www.Globalissues.org/Trade Related/Facts.asp.

44. Laing, "Changing Face of Mission."

45. See Ringma *Seek the Silences with Thomas Merton*, where I have attempted to critique my Reformed and evangelical heritage.

46. One need only think of Ronald Sider and John Perkins in the USA, the late Athol Gill in Australia (see Pidwell, *Gentle Bunyip*), Vinay Samuel in India, David Lim in the Philippines, and René Padilla in Argentina. For other evangelicals with a commitment to serve the poor, see Ringma, *Cry Freedom*. See also Langmead, *The Word Made Flesh*, for a list of what he calls "radical evangelicals" (94).

47. Stott, *Making Christ Known*, 165–213.

48. Stott, 24, 34, 90, 92, 102, 105, 145, 146, 147, 162.

Lausanne Covenant states, "We, therefore, should share his [God's] concern for justice and reconciliation throughout human society and for the liberation of men [women] from every kind of oppression," this theme is not sustained throughout the document.[49] The only exception to the more extensive Grand Rapids Report is the Manila Manifesto,[50] which refers to the fact that God's concern for the poor is spoken about in the "law, the prophets, and the wisdom books, and the teaching and ministry of Jesus."[51] The Manifesto also contains a call to repentance, for the places "where we have been indifferent to the plight of the poor,"[52] and affirms the call "to preach and teach, minister to the sick, feed the hungry, care for prisoners, help the disadvantaged and handicapped, and deliver the oppressed."[53] But the overall focus of this document is on world *evangelization* in the light of the fact that over two billion people have not heard the gospel.[54]

The main argument in the Grand Rapids Report is that while "evangelism has a certain priority,"[55] "social activity is a *consequence* of evangelism,"[56] and social concern is "a *bridge* to evangelism"[57] and "its *partner.*"[58] The report touches on philanthropic service[59] and concludes with a reference to individual biblical characters who defied "human authority in the name of the God of justice."[60] It also suggests that the local church needs to be socially concerned[61] and raise a prophetic voice about justice issues[62] while also encouraging Western Christians to adopt a simple lifestyle.[63]

Even though these documents recognize the need for social concern, they fail to articulate a strategic vision for how to "wash the feet of the world." The Grand Rapids Report provides no cohesive biblical framework and lacks a

49. Stott, 24.
50. Stott, 225–49.
51. Stott, 234.
52. Stott, 235.
53. Stott, 236.
54. Stott, 245.
55. Stott, 183.
56. Stott, 111.
57. Stott, 181.
58. Stott, 182.
59. Stott,197.
60. Stott, 208.
61. Stott, 198.
62. Stott, 203.
63. Stott, 206.

basic discussion of the biblical vision of service to the poor. Moreover, the report fails to engage the rich history of the church in service to the poor as well as other traditions. By neglecting its historical memory, the evangelical movement promotes ideas about a good God and the "good life" that lead many of its adherents to a middle-class mediocrity that is in conflict with the biblical path of downward mobility and identification with the poor. Furthermore, the report offers little in the way of critiquing the principalities and powers, false ideologies, oppressive global arrangements, or the nature of structural evil, making its analysis somewhat naïve and its missional strategies for serving the poor simplistic.

Finally, because service to the poor remains secondary and peripheral to what is considered the more central concern of evangelization, the report places the spiritual dimensions of life above the physical. In the discussion of the kingdom of God, for example, the report makes no reference to the poor,[64] even though Luke makes a direct connection (Luke 4:18–19; 6:20), and Jesus clearly preached a gospel for the poor (Luke 7:22–23). This dichotomous and dualistic way of thinking ignores the daily realities that concern most of the world's poor, such as food security, access to clean water, struggles with poor health, rural and urban migration, corrupt politics, and globalization. While evangelicalism does recognize certain "heroes" within the movement that have championed the cause of the poor, the commitment to identification with the poor is *not* intrinsic to evangelical theology, the church, or its missional practice.[65] It is so encouraging to see that the *Cape Town Declaration (2010)* is a happy exception to previous documents and demonstrates a significant maturization process in evangelicalism.

I will now briefly examine some key texts from the ecumenical movement and then from Roman Catholic social teaching as a way of comparing the evangelical Lausanne movement with other contemporary movements.

In my review of several conference reports from the ecumenical movement, I found support for the church to identify itself with the world – particularly the poor – not only in its perplexity and distress, its guilt and sorrow, but also in its real acts of love and justice as it lives out an incarnational presence in the world.[66] The 1966 Geneva report encourages the churches to help

64. Stott, 186–90.

65. Little wonder that Viv Grigg argued for the need of movements *among* the poor rather than only heroic individuals (*Companion to the Poor*, 169).

66. Kinnamon and Cope, *Ecumenical Movement*, 341.

Third World countries in their economic development[67] and to discern what God is doing in the change and protest movements among the poor.[68] Then it calls the church to play a prophetic role in society.[69] The 1973 Bangkok conference report emphasizes that the salvation of Christ involves us "in the struggle for economic justice against exploitation."[70] The 1979 Boston report calls the church to help build a "just, participatory, and sustainable society."[71] The 1982 WCC Commission on World Mission and Evangelism states that because many of the world's poor suffer a double loss – they haven't heard the gospel and they are the victims of oppression[72] – the church should live a "preferential option for the poor."[73] The WCC report goes on to say that a "proclamation that does not hold forth the promises of the justice of the kingdom to the poor of the earth is a caricature of the gospel."[74] Moreover, this report recognizes that the poor can evangelize us: "God is working through the poor of the earth to awaken the consciousness of humanity to his call for repentance, for justice, and for love."[75] The 1986 Larnaca report recognizes the church's complicity in upholding oppressive structures and systems, specifically the global trade agreements that discriminate against the "Third World."[76] Finally, the 1990 Seoul conference report identifies the poor's need for fullness of life (John 10:10) and articulates God's preferential option for the poor,[77] arguing that charity and aid are not enough to move towards "a just, equitable world economic order."[78] Rooted in biblical concepts and a Trinitarian and kingdom theology, these reports from the ecumenical movement recognize God's preferential option for the poor and place service to the poor – both personally and structurally – at the centre of the church's life.

Similarly, many of the Roman Catholic documents argue for the conversion of the church to the side of the poor as a way of following Christ and engaging the world for its transformation. One of the key documents from the Second

67. Kinnamon and Cope, 292.
68. Kinnamon and Cope, 297.
69. Kinnamon and Cope, 297–98.
70. Kinnamon and Cope, 357.
71. Kinnamon and Cope, 305.
72. Kinnamon and Cope, 378.
73. Kinnamon and Cope, 379.
74. Kinnamon and Cope, 379.
75. Kinnamon and Cope, 380.
76. Kinnamon and Cope, 316.
77. Kinnamon and Cope, 318.
78. Kinnamon and Cope, 319.

Vatican Council (1965)[79] highlights the discrepancies between the "First World" and the "Third World,"[80] the cry of poor for justice,[81] what is necessary to live "a genuinely human life,"[82] and the call of the church to act on behalf of the needy.[83] This document laments the fact that economic progress often comes at the expense of the poor[84] and does not benefit everyone in society.[85] Unlike the evangelical movement's Grand Rapids report, these Catholic documents promote the idea that "action on behalf of justice and participation in the transformation of the world fully appear to us as a constitutive dimension of the preaching of the gospel,"[86] which "has a personal and social dimension involving human rights, peace, justice, development, and liberation."[87] The Latin American Catholic documents identify Jesus as the "liberator from sin, hunger, oppression, misery, [and] ignorance"[88] and call the church to "a radical discipleship and a love that gives a privileged place to the poor,"[89] to stand in solidarity with the poor,[90] and to work to change "unjust social, political, and economic structures."[91] God's concern for the poor – and our response – is a central focus in all of these Catholic documents, which beckon us to overcome injustice and structural evil through practices that promote shalom.

The Voice of the Liberation Theologians

In this final section, I will draw on a number of important themes and emphases from liberation theology that I believe are necessary correctives to our evangelical tradition. First, I will outline a transformational way of reading Scripture from the perspective of the poor. Next, I will touch on the spirituality that is at the heart of the liberation theology movement, a spirituality that is

79. In Kinnamon and Cope, eds., *The Ecumenical Movement*.
80. Flannery, *Basic Sixteen Documents*, 166.
81. Flannery, 170.
82. Flannery, 191.
83. Flannery, 210.
84. Flannery, 242.
85. Flannery, 243.
86. Henriot et al., *Catholic Social Teaching*, 64.
87. Henriot, 69.
88. Henriot, 127.
89. Henriot, 132.
90. Hennelly, *Liberation Theology*, 256–57.
91. Hennelly, 257.

both inward and outward, personal and communal, spiritual and political. Finally, I will reflect on the fundamentally missional nature of liberation theology, which engages God's concern for the poor and moves us from the head to the heart to embrace an incarnational spirituality, where we move to the side of the poor for the sake of the gospel through radical identification.

A Transformational Reading of the Bible

There are many ways to read the Bible. Some people read the Bible as a book of comfort or a book about the afterlife or heaven. Some academic approaches include a historical-critical or a feminist perspective. Yet Rudolf Bultmann suggests that psychological and historical ways of reading the text are less helpful ways of engaging Scripture, since they lock the text into the past. Instead, Bultmann opts for an "existential" reading, where one has a life relation to the text[92] and remains open to being confronted by the claims of the text,[93] which leads to the possibility of gaining "*a new understanding of myself from it.*"[94] In other words, Bultmann suggests that one should read and engage Scripture from a *transformational* perspective.[95]

The liberation theologians read Scripture from a transformational perspective, but specifically from "the viewpoint of the oppressed."[96] While Leonardo Boff recognizes that "this is not the only possible legitimate reading of the Bible,"[97] he suggests that it is "the most *appropriate*" reading for the poor in light of their marginalization and oppression.[98] The poor also read the Bible from a transformational perspective, looking "for a truth that will set them free"[99] and for glimpses of the God of life, justice, and liberation.[100]

---

92. Ringma, *Gadamer's Dialogical Hermeneutic*, 116.

93. Ringma, 153.

94. Ringma, 153.

95. Wink, *Bible in Human Transformation*.

96. Ellacuria and Sobrino, *Mysterium Liberationis*, 79.

97. Ellacuria and Sobrino, 79.

98. Ellacuria and Sobrino, 79.

99. Ellacuria and Sobrino, 124. For the voice of the poor in discussing the gospels, see Cardenal, *Gospel in Solentiname*.

100. Ellacuria and Sobrino, 124–25. For the way the Bible is read in Base Ecclesial Communities, see Hennelly, *Liberation Theology*, 14–28. The members of Base Ecclesial Communities study Scripture and pray, seeking "to bring together what is read [in the gospels] with what is lived" (Ellacuria and Sobrino, *Mysterium Liberationis*, 640–41). As such, "there is emphasis on the word of God, on the centrality of Jesus Christ," and an "awareness of insertion in the world . . . [and the] impetus towards social transformation" (641).

Finally, the "evangelical poor" read the Bible from this perspective, identifying with the poor and advocating on their behalf "out of love."[101]

But this way of reading Scripture has further implications. As the reign of God breaks in among the poor, the poor themselves become an embodiment of the gospel and need to be "read" by others. Thus, the poor become the "gospel" to us and evangelize us as they demonstrate the love and power of the God of justice.

A Spirituality of Liberation

Although the Lausanne documents do make several references to prayer, they focus on intercessory prayer for evangelization, peace, and justice.[102] Little attention is given to other forms of prayer, and the documents do not articulate a spirituality that might animate and empower Christians in their missional activity. Instead, this focus tends to be inward and personal. This reflects the way in which the evangelical movement has become captive to pragmatics, where many of us are better at doing than praying.

For the liberation theologians, however, who often are regarded as being too focused on political rather than spiritual issues, Christian spirituality is at the heart of their theology and missional praxis. In describing contemplation in 1974, Claude Geffre wrote: the "mystical experience presents indivisibly a double dimension of one and same original event: the meeting with the person of Christ and the experience of the presence of Christ in one's brother and sister, above all the 'least of them.'"[103] He goes on to suggest that "encounter with Christ . . . occurs through the mediation of the poor."[104]

This double movement of prayer and contemplation gives faith a sociopolitical concern and service a profound Christian spirituality.[105] While we are invited to contemplate God through prayer, biblical reflection, the practice of solitude, and listening to the voice of the Spirit – which is the movement of *transcendence* – we are, at the same time, invited to contemplate Christ in the face of our brothers and sisters, the neighbour, the stranger and the poor – which is the movement of *incarnation*. This transcendent-incarnate spirituality joins love of God and love of neighbour (Matt 22:37–40), the inner

101. Ellacuria and Sobrino, 256.

102. Stott, *Making Christ Known*, 44, 106, 180, 200, 218–19.

103. Quoted in Hennelly, *Liberation Theology*, 186.

104. Hennelly, 186.

105. Galilea, *Following Jesus*.

and outer journeys (Mark 1:35–39), prayer and the work of justice (Isa 58:6–7), and contemplation and action (Pss 46:10; 51:10; 57:13). For the liberation theologians, Matthew 25 is a central motif, and they readily recognize that what they have done to "the least," they have done to Christ (v. 40).

A Missional Theology

At the heart of evangelization, which is also the central concern of the evangelical tradition, lies the desire to communicate the message of salvation in Christ to the world and to see people enter the reign of God. *Interior liberation* occurs within a person's heart, reorienting our values, motivations, attitudes, and morals in and through Jesus Christ. With interior liberation, there is a metamorphosis of our inner being as the kingdom of God begins to reign "within" us. *Exterior liberation* occurs when someone who has been liberated invites God to reign in and transform society. Just as Christ became poor in history and acted on behalf of the poor, we are called to make a similar journey of faith, service, and identification, particularly on behalf of the poor, marginalized, and oppressed. This "preferential option" for the poor takes the poor from the margins of history, the periphery of society, the heart of the slums and places them *centrally* in the very purpose of God. Gustavo Gutierrez points out that the term "preference" does not mean exclusive, but rather that the poor "ought to be the first" and not "the only objects of our solidarity," since they are so often overlooked.[106]

When both interior and exterior liberation occur together, *wholistic liberation* can take place. Segundo Galilea suggests that the work of wholistic liberation must be accompanied by signs.[107] The first sign is *poverty* – freedom from earthly attachments through downward mobility and radical identification with the poor, with a subsequent freedom to trust in God. Mary, for example, is a poor girl who is drawn into God's redemptive purposes, and her salvation reverses the social order: the hungry are filled with good things, the rich are empty-handed (Luke 1:53). The second sign is *contemplation* – the integration of prayer and action – where we encounter Jesus through prayer, and we also encounter our neighbours through liberating action. This *liberating action* could be prophetic – proclaiming Christ's good news of salvation, freedom, and liberation – or political – seeking to alter the power structures that oppress the poor.

---

106. Ellacuria and Sobrino, *Mysterium Liberationis*, 239.

107. Pope-Levison, *Evangelization from a Liberation Perspective.*

There are also three mediations at the heart of liberation theology, which work together to make it a missional theology.[108] The first, *socioanalytical mediation*, flows from a missional involvement amongst the poor that includes service, discernment, and an analysis of the "world" of poverty, injustice, and oppression. The second, *hermeneutical mediation*, brings the "world" of the poor to the biblical text, seeking Scripture for words of life, hope, and transformation. Thus, the Bible is read not for its ideas or ideals, but for its transformative power, particularly regarding salvation and liberation for the poor. The third, *practical mediation*, calls all God's people to follow Christ into the world as signs, servants, and sacraments of the reign of God.[109] These three mediations form a dynamic circle, moving from immersion, incarnation, and being with the poor to a faithful listening to the Word of God, which beckons us to costly and obedient service to Christ through identification with the poor and oppressed.

Unlike the liberation theologians, who locate mission at the centre of their theology, the evangelical documents isolate mission to the mission of the church in terms of its evangelism, edification, worship, and social concern.[110] Yet this confines the mission of the church to the poor to church strategies and programs rather than placing it at the very heart of who God is and God's salvific mission to the world. Mission to the poor belongs to the doctrine of God before it belongs to the mission of the church. As the liberation theologians have recognized, salvation invites us into the purposes of God, and being part of the reign of God necessarily involves having a heart for the poor.

Conclusion

One of the challenges facing the evangelical movement is to make mission more central to its theology and praxis. In developing such a missional theology, evangelicals need to recognize that God's love for the poor is central to the heart of God and therefore must be central to the mission of the church so that it can be affirmed as a call for *all* the people of God rather than for a heroic few. Otherwise, the mission of the church will reflect contemporary, consumer, middle-class values rather than the values of the biblical narrative. Moreover, evangelicals will need to articulate and embody a more diverse

108. Langmead, *Word Made Flesh*, 117–41.

109. Boff and Boff, *Introducing Liberation Theology*, 24.

110. This is also the position of the evangelical theologian Millard Erickson in *Christian Theology* (1051).

ecclesiology so that different forms of church will emerge among the poor, and the implicit normative of the middle-class status quo will be broken.[111] Furthermore, evangelicals need to move beyond the personal and begin to think much more seriously about structural issues, societal evil, the nature of the powers, and strategies of personal as well as social transformation. Thankfully, there is good news for evangelicals. While many may persist in the theological, spiritual, and missional values of the Lausanne documents we have discussed, the *Capetown Declaration (2010)* forges a vibrant spirituality, and a more full-orbed missional vision. This is good news, indeed!

Every healthy theology and movement needs a critical component. One form is self-critique. Another form is to hear the voice of the other. My strategy in this chapter has been to bring liberation theologians and evangelicals into a dialogue in the hopes that the former will pose a challenge to the latter. By God's grace, may this challenge come home to roost.

111. Following the challenge of liberation theologians, a new decentralized church of the poor, amongst the poor, and for the poor began to emerge in the form of Base Ecclesial Communities (Ellacuria and Sobrino, *Mysterium Liberationis*, 198–99). Base Ecclesial Communities are a lay-centred way "to *be* church and to *act* as church" (637). This name stems from the way that these communities emphasize "communion and participation" (638), are linked to the "visible reality of the church" (639), and are rooted (e.g. "based") among poor people (639). There are currently many experiments with church, including new emergent church movements (see Frost and Hirsch, *Shaping of Things to Come*), new communities (see Whitehead and Whitehead, *Community of Faith)*, and new "Monasticism" (see The Rutba House, eds., *School(s) for Conversion)*.

Section IV

Particular Themes

16

Asceticism

Theological, Spiritual, and Missional Perspectives

Introduction

This chapter seeks to highlight the importance of ascetic practices in the history of the church, as these practices have largely fallen into neglect and possibly even disrepute amidst the "easy believism" and lack of biblical formation within the contemporary Western church.[1] I believe that recovering these practices will deepen our personal formation in Christ, thereby strengthening the church and its missional passion for our world. I am certainly not suggesting that ascetic practices are the *only* solution to revitalizing the church in our time, but I do believe that they can help nurture a more dynamic Christian spirituality.

In speaking of ascetic practices, I am not speaking about *peculiar* or *esoteric* practices, but the traditional monastic practices of prayer, fasting,[2] giving,[3] simplicity, abstinence, chastity, poverty, and obedience, which can

1. It may surprise some evangelical readers that Martin Luther identifies the marks of the people of God as those who are shaped by the word and sacraments as well as prayer, enduring the cross, suffering, fasting, and renunciation of revenge (Lohse, *Martin Luther's Theology*, 284).

2. Fasting in its most basic forms can be an act of repentance and remembrance when we reflect on major events in the church's calendar, such as the period leading up to Easter, or it can be an act of intercession when we carry the burden of others and our world into the presence of God.

3. Cunningham and Egan make the clarifying comment that ascetic giving refers to "giving away what is one's own in favour of another in need" (*Christian Spirituality,* 114). Such an understanding implies the modern view of private ownership. But in the Anabaptist tradition,

ground us more deeply in the biblical narratives, the Christian faith, and the rich traditions of the church through its two-thousand-year history.[4] Moreover, I am proposing that the very nature of our missional engagement has a significant ascetic dimension. To put this more simply, there is often a correlation between *sacrifice* and *service*.[5]

In the long history of the church, ascetic practices have, at times, been influenced by an unhealthy dualism that led some to perpetrate "violence" against the body.[6] One of the key problems arose when ascetic practices were viewed as *the way* to receive the beneficence and blessing of God. However, asceticism has also been seen as the fruit of grace and the work of the Spirit and thus has brought forth many laudable practices, including discerning the voice of God, the task of prayer, and the work of vicarious service in the world.[7]

The term "asceticism" (*askesis* in Greek) literally refers to training as practised by athletes. Thus, it has to do with embracing particular disciplines in order to achieve a certain outcome.[8] Within the Christian tradition, the desired outcome is a life of maturity in following Jesus and being willing to

---

we find a very different orientation in that "what is mine is also yours." As Friedmann points out, the "idea of [a] community of goods was championed by numerous early Anabaptists" (*Theology of Anabaptism*, 71).

4. This means that we not only need to recover dimensions of the Reformation tradition and subsequent renewal movements, such as the Wesleyan revival, but that we should also tap into the riches of the early church fathers, the desert fathers and mothers, the monastic movement, the medieval Christian mystics, and the forerunners of the Reformation. See Ringma, *Hear the Ancient Wisdom*; *In the Footsteps of an Ancient Faith* and *Of Martyrs, Monks and Mystics* (edited with Irene Alexander).

5. Cunningham and Egan helpfully point out that asceticism not only involves the practice of prayer, but also the work of justice in light of the concern "to plumb the full meaning of giving to the other in the name of Jesus" (*Christian Spirituality*, 115).

6. See the discussion of asceticism in *Philokalia*, where extreme self-denial is held up as the norm for those living as hermits in desert places (Palmer, Sherrard, and Ware, *Philokalia*, vol. 1). More generally, asceticism had to do with the denial of "food, sex, sleep, and possessions," but some practices were "questionable, even bizarre" (McGinn, *Essential Writings of Christian Mysticism*, 47, 48).

7. Kallistos Ware (from the Orthodox tradition) sees asceticism as "the way to freedom" for both the monk and the married, making the surprising point that "without self-denial, without ascetic discipline, we cannot affirm the true beauty of the world" (*Orthodox Way*, 79, 161). Here he makes the link between asceticism and discernment, as he sees discernment (*diakrisis*) as distinguishing between good and evil, and he says that we can see the difference between the superfluous and the meaningful "through ascetic effort and prayer" (154).

8. As we will see in the later section of this chapter, when we touch on some ascetic themes in the history of the church, the outcome of asceticism is understood in various ways. St. Isaac of Nineveh sees ascetic practices as contributing to a "purity of mind," which leads to the "captivation by divine things" (*On Ascetical Life*, 49). Basil of Caesarea, on the other hand, believes that ascetic practices lead to the formation of the Christian as "pneumatophor" – or a "vessel and distributor of the Holy Spirit" (Luckman and Kulzer, *Purity of Heart*, 97).

sacrifice what is good for the sake of the greater good – the quest for union with God and the blessing of the neighbour and stranger.[9]

At its heart, Christian asceticism has to do with cultivating a spiritual vision that leads one to engage practices for the purpose of growing into a deeper relationship with God[10] and participating in God's purposes for our world.[11] This means that ascetic practices have implications for ministry.[12] Thus, a spirituality of asceticism is world-engaging[13] rather than world-denying. Put differently, ascetic practices – such as prayer, fasting, and various forms of generosity and relinquishment – are not about self-enhancement, but serving Jesus, the suffering servant king, in the unfolding of his kingdom and reign in our lives and the wider community. Segundo Galilea touches the heart of the matter when he notes that "asceticism eliminates the spiritual obstacles incompatible with faith, hope, and love" and seeks to purge "a person's deepest attraction" or "desire."[14] Thus, ascetic practices have the happy task of orienting us in a particular direction as we move through time and space in order to be more attentive[15] to the Spirit's wisdom and leading. There are, of course, other dimensions to ascetic practices. For example, the practice of

---

9. Some scholars see asceticism in entirely negative terms. Moltmann quotes Walter Raushenbusch as saying, "Ascetic Christianity called the world evil *and left it.* Humanity is waiting for a revolutionary Christianity which will call the world evil and *change it*" (Moltmann, *In the End – The Beginning*, 91, author's emphasis). By contrast, Henri Nouwen has shown how the asceticism of the desert fathers and mothers demonstrates a spirituality that is relevant for contemporary ministry in *Way of the Heart.*

10. McGinn notes that asceticism is a "preparation for a more intense religious life" and for receiving "mystical grace" (*Essential Writings of Christian Mysticism,* 47).

11. The stress, particularly in the Western evangelical world, on simply gaining personal salvation as the very heart of the gospel misses the larger theme, which is that coming to faith makes us candidates to become part of God's kingdom purposes for our world. Christoph Blumhardt makes the point that there is a need for "men and women who give themselves up for God's kingdom and its justice and truth . . . on earth" (*Action in Waiting*, 166). He goes on to say that while some "polish themselves up spiritually to get their little souls in order for God," each of us needs "to let God make demands on you" (171, 170). Though ultimately, we are waiting for God to bring in the kingdom, "for our part, we can sow truth and justice" (221).

12. See Nouwen, *Way of the Heart*, for a discussion of the implications of the asceticism of the desert fathers and mothers for contemporary ministry.

13. Within missional literature, various key terms are used to describe the church's task in the world, including witness and service to the world and the transformation of the world. The latter points to the Christian task as being more than "saving souls" for an eternal future, but also helping to shape a more just and peaceful society. However, this broader task is not to be accomplished by coercive means, but by the winsome influence of Christians and Christian institutions in the service of the common good with a particular commitment to the poor.

14. Galilea, *Spirituality of Hope*, 47.

15. Since contemplative practices are oriented towards *attentiveness*, forms of asceticism, such as the practice of solitude, can contribute to a contemplative spirituality.

fasting can have an identificational motif, where someone fasts in solidarity with those who have been displaced and are suffering hunger.

Contemporary Relevance

It is rather superficial to say that the topic of asceticism belongs to an "older" world and should be forgotten. The idea that certain disciplines, such as prayer, contemplation, relinquishment, or fasting, are no longer relevant for contemporary Christians reflects our hubris and disregard for Scripture and the long tradition of the church. This *developmental* view of the church in history presumes that the church as it is at this particular point in time, is the way the church is meant to be. Such a perspective reflects a social evolutionism that elevates the modern world and the contemporary church over everything in the past.[16]

Yet the church at any particular point in history – including our modern world – may have lost its way by becoming captive to deforming cultural values[17] and festering internal decay.[18] Though the church needs to be relevant to the surrounding culture,[19] it must also be *restitutionist* (constantly recovering its past) and *eschatological* (always anticipating God's final future). Thus, the church cannot rest on either the laurels or the despair of the present age, but must continually renew its life by recapturing the vision of its earliest beginnings, as revealed in the biblical narratives and the person and work of Christ, and also by wrestling to discern the purposes of God for our time.

A careful reading of our time would suggest that we, particularly in the West, have become persons of convenience and "much-having." Sacrifice is hardly part of our vocabulary, let alone our lifestyle. Our Christianity lacks both the power and vision of relinquishment. We want instant access to God and God's grace, and we lack disciplined growth in the wisdom and ways of God. We want God's blessing rather than God's way, God's grace rather than

16. I love to ask my students, if you think like this, have you ever read the works of St. Augustine?

17. See Burleigh, *Sacred Causes: Religion and Politics from the European Dictators to Al Qaeda*.

18. See Mouton, *In God's House*, which discusses the child abuse scandals in the present-day church.

19. If the church is only relevant and contemporary, it runs the risk of conforming to the present sociocultural landscape. While the church is meant to be a conserving influence in the world, it is also meant to be a transformational community. To put this more bluntly, the church has a *maintenance* task (maintaining what is good in a society) as well as a *revolutionary* task (changing what is unjust).

God's call, God's friendship rather than God's command. We are also highly mobile and distracted, always pursuing something new, reluctant to make long-term commitments. Belden Lane points out that because we are "plagued by a highly diffused attention, we give ourselves lightly to everything . . . In saying 'yes' to everything, we attend to nothing." He goes on to say that we need to learn once again how "to move slowly and deliberatively through the world."[20] Ascetic practices, such as keeping the Sabbath, can play an important part in shaping a new attentiveness.[21]

This means that we need to become much more discerning, careful about our commitments, and willing to make the necessary sacrifices that are part of cultivating an intentional posture in the world. Simply put, rather than moving from one happy "honeymoon phase" to another, jumping from one new and exciting possibility to another, we need to "hang in" for the long haul[22] so that we can grow in wisdom and deepen our spirituality. This path will inevitably lead us to suffering and asceticism, particularly when a ministry loses its way and needs to embrace the painful journey of returning to its original charism.

However, there is much more to the story of the present weakness of the church in the West. In addition to being impacted by the values of late-modernity and the neoliberal economics that have "sucked" much of the relational and caring goodness out of the body politic, the church has its own internal problems, including biblical illiteracy, a lack of discipleship, widespread belief in a Father-Christmas God, not to mention child abuse scandals. Bonhoeffer's lament of a church marked by "cheap grace" is as timely as ever.[23] And Lane laments that "the spiritual life extolled in popular circles today is eminently unexceptional, generally inoffensive, and (almost without exception) culturally correct." He suggests that we need to recover the highly ascetic spirituality of the desert so that we can engage the world in fresh and prophetic ways as "resident aliens" and rediscover the "wildness of God" rather than our present prosaic typifications.[24]

20. Lane, *Solace of Fierce Landscapes*, 189.

21. In Western society, we are not only "time poor," but we are now suffering from "attention deficit disorder." Repairing this condition will involve the "pain" of some forms of asceticism.

22. One of the desert fathers notes: "The reason why we do not get anywhere is that we do not know our limits, and we are not patient in carrying out the work we have begun" (quoted in *Celtic Daily Prayer*, 421). Thus, we need to know ourselves and discern how we are gifted in carrying out the mission of God, and we need to recognize that most projects require a long-term commitment.

23. Bonhoeffer, *Cost of Discipleship*, 35–41.

24. Lane, *Solace of Fierce Landscapes*, 187.

A Personal Reflection

When I was younger and had less, it was much easier to relinquish things, but as I have aged, security has become a more pressing concern. Similarly, when I was younger in the faith and in my experience of Christian service, I prayed and fasted with a strong sense that good could only come through God's action. Later in life, I have become more self-reliant, and my greatest challenge has been to maintain a sustainable activism through a seemingly "unpractical" regime of spiritual disciplines. Moreover, being strongly shaped by Dutch culture and its Protestant work ethic, along with an evangelical mentality towards service, prayer remains an ongoing struggle.[25]

Yet when I have responded to the call to give things away, the great surprise is that I have never found myself impoverished, but rather, grace and blessings have always come my way. This has not been some sort of *quid pro quo*, for the grace and blessings have always been spiritual rather than material. Put somewhat differently, being generous and sacrificial has never led to personal diminishment, though in our contemporary world we are led to believe that we need much to secure our own future.

Any commitment to Christian service often cuts across the normal career trajectory of mainstream society, though we may not experience the implications of this till much later in life. In my own journey, rather than stewarding my own self-enhancement and prosperity during my youth, I was *profligate* in the service of the reign of God. As a result, I have experienced the inevitable vulnerability and loss that comes with following the suffering Christ into the world in service of God's kingdom.

Old Testament Asceticism

The topic of asceticism must be set within the broader OT narrative of the creational and redemptive work of God in forming a people[26] to be a "seed" to the world and a light to the nations. At the heart of God's covenant is the intention for a particular people to be a blessing for *all* the nations. Lesslie Newbigin makes this basic point in observing that "the narrowing continues" in the call of Abraham and his descendants, "who are chosen to be bearers of a blessing . . . for the sake of *all*."[27] God's intention to form a people to

---

25. See Ringma, *Sabbath Time.*

26. Hanson, *People Called.*

27. Newbigin, *Open Secret,* 32, author's emphasis. This theme is most fully developed in Wright, *Mission of God.*

bear witness to the glory of God and live for communal well-being affects all domains of life – familial, religious, economic, and political.

Another core OT theme is God's liberation and restoration through the Exodus,[28] an event that calls Israel to continue to live this way as they relate to each other and also to the alien and the stranger. Throughout the OT, Israel's communal spirituality is structured through annual religious celebrations, which celebrate God's abundant goodness as the creator and sustainor of all things. God's "presence" could be discerned in annual harvests and other dimensions of life as well as temple worship.[29] Prophetic spirituality calls the people of Israel back to this ideal during times of deterioration and also looks towards the future in the hope of God's final shalom. Within this broad arc of God's grace and justice, we can note some ascetic practices in the life of God's OT people.

The most prominent ascetic theme is the weekly practice of devoting one day a week to Sabbath "rest." This practice is rooted in the creation narrative (Gen 2:3) and the Exodus paradigm of God's liberation (Exod 20:8), where rest is a form of justice that is extended to everyone and everything, including resident aliens, animals, and the land (Exod 23:10–13).[30] In the OT community, the practice of keeping the Sabbath was further enhanced by regular feasts and festivals, which had an ascetic dimension in the way that they called people *away* from their personal and familial concerns *into* the wider celebrations of corporate life. These festivals, including Passover, First Fruits, Atonement, and Tabernacles, among others, were marked by special offerings, sacrifices, and prayers[31] that reminded the people of Yahweh's mighty acts of provision and redemption. These times of worship were also a form of asceticism in that they drew the people *away* from self-exultation, self-sufficiency, and the worship of false gods *towards* an acknowledgment of their dependence on Yahweh alone. Such a posture reflects an asceticism of *particularity*.

Through the practice of fasting, the nation (Judg 20:26; 1 Sam 7:6; 2 Chr 20:3; Ezra 8:21–23; Joel 1:14) and individuals (2 Sam 1:12; 1 Kgs 21:27; Neh

---

28. M. J. Boda also sees the Exodus event as normative for Israel's identity as it is lived out within the frame of commandments and moral principles ("Old Testament Foundations of a Christian Spirituality," 41). For a fuller discussion, see Croatto, *Exodus: A Hermeneutics of Freedom*.

29. Steven Harper notes that in Israel's life, "every person, thing and activity is somehow infused with the divine" ("Old Testament Spirituality," 315).

30. This important theme is more fully set out in chapter 7 ("The Heart and Scope of Integral Mission").

31. Van Gemeren, "Feasts and Festivals: Old Testament," 409–12.

1:4) sought Yahweh for renewal. However, "fasting that was not accompanied by genuine repentance and righteous deeds was denounced as an empty legal observance by the prophets (Jer 14:11–12)."[32] In Isaiah, the practice of fasting is augmented by the practices of hospitality and justice as the path toward national healing and restoration (Isa 58:1–12).

Another major ascetic practice[33] in the nation of Israel was its social welfare/justice provision through the Sabbatical Year, the Year of Jubilee, the release of property, the law of interest, the redemption of servants (Lev 25), and laws on tithing and gleaning (Deut 14:22–29).[34] These structural provisions reflect a sober note in the nation's life, as they recognized that things would not always go well in Israel's society. Although the extent to which these provisions were fully implemented is uncertain, especially with regard to the Year of Jubilee, it is significant that the OT narrative incorporates ascetic practices that are intended to provide for the needy in their times of difficulty.

Though there is a great emphasis in the OT on Yahweh as the redeemer and provider for a particular people, there is also a call to worship, pray, make personal and national sacrifices, be generous, and act with justice in order to reveal Yahweh's character by blessing everyone – neighbours as well as foreigners and the creatures along with the land.

New Testament Asceticism

The person and work of Jesus provides the central inspiration for NT ascetic themes. In the ministry of Jesus, we encounter someone who remains single, foregoes normal family relationships, does not own property, has a low status in society (although he is called a rabbi), is dependent on the practical support of others, and is oriented towards those on the margins (although he engages every strata of his society). The gospels also portray Jesus as being fully oriented to doing God's will,[35] which is the most central ascetic impulse. Christian

---

32. Linder, "Fast, Fasting," 406.

33. Other ascetic practices in the OT include the call to become a Nazirite (Num 6:1–21; Judg 13:2–7), the practice of vows (Num 30:1–16), the nation's support of the Levites, which included a provision for the cities of refuge (Num 35:1–8), and the sacrificial practices set out in the book of Leviticus.

34. Ronald Sider brought all these practices into contemporary reflection through his book *Rich Christians in an Age of Hunger* (78–86). Sider rightly points out, "I certainly do not think that the specific provisions of the year of Jubilee are binding today" (84). Yet he exhorts the church to "discover underlying principles" within the provisions because the faith-community needs "to display an entirely new set of personal, social and economic relationships" (85, 78).

35. See the discussion in chapter 4 ("Contemplation in a World of Action").

asceticism is spawned by the ever-flowing fountain of God's grace and the presence of the renewing Spirit, which enables us to pray, *not my will nor my way, but I delight to do thy will.*

An ongoing debate within the faith-community concerns the extent to which Jesus's way of life is normative for the contemporary community. The fact that Jesus prayed, sought to do the Father's will, and served the poor is universally understood as being important for his followers. But what about the fact that he did not marry and formed a common-purse community?[36] Are these practices also normative for us today? Here we touch on the "great divide," where those in priestly orders and monastic communities claim that Jesus's example is normative in these domains of life as well.[37] This has resulted in the unfortunate notion that priests and monks live a higher form of Christian spirituality.[38]

At this point, I wish to proceed more generally and argue that Jesus is an icon of the new humanity in the reign of God,[39] and so his life is normative because he is to grow in us through the Spirit, and we are to become more and more like him. Paul describes this process in various ways in his epistles. He speaks about being "baptized into Christ" and having "clothed yourself with Christ" (Gal 3:27). He speaks of his hope that "Christ is formed in you" (Gal 4:19). He notes that "we are what he [Christ] made us" (Eph 2:10) and that we are "to live . . . [our] lives in him" (Col 2:6). In summary, Paul exclaims, "Be imitators of me, as I am of Christ" (1 Cor 11:1).

For followers of Jesus, the path of Christification involves both the "inward" move of becoming like Christ and the "outward" move of seeking to do what Jesus did by bringing healing and goodness to others and also by challenging those who are using their power to oppress others.[40] As we seek to model

36. It is noteworthy that many Protestant monastic communities, such as Hutterite, Bruderhof, and New Monastic communities, hold that Jesus's formation of community is "normative."

37. Philip Sheldrake notes that the development of a "religious life" or the "consecrated life," with its core concept of chastity, signalled a "powerful symbol of dissociation" from normal life, which led to a "hierarchy of Christian life" and resulted in a "priority of religious over lay" (*Spirituality and History*, 135).

38. Later in this chapter, I will attempt to argue for an "interiorized monastic spirituality" as relevant for all Christians.

39. Alister McGrath discusses various Christological models: the presence of God in Christ, Christ as the mediator between God and humanity, the revelational presence of God, the bearer of Holy Spirit, the example of a godly life, and Christ as a hero (*Christian Theology*, 227–35). Yet he makes no mention of Christ as an icon of the new humanity.

40. See my elaboration of this path of Christification in chapter 4 ("Contemplation in a World of Action").

our lives on what Jesus did, we must also seek to become more like him. Put somewhat differently, sanctification belongs to the work of justice.

In terms of ascetic practices, Jesus practiced fasting himself (Matt 4:2), and he teaches the practice of fasting (Matt 9:15). Although fasting does not receive great emphasis in the book of Acts, the early Christian communities fasted (Acts 13:3). Jesus also practiced celibacy, and he teaches that celibacy is an option for his followers (Matt 19:12). In the house churches of the Pauline mission, celibacy was practiced (1 Cor 7:8), and yet the entire NT also celebrates marriage and family, and much of the Pauline ethical prescriptions deal with family realities (Eph 5:21–33; Col 3:18–25; Heb 13:4). The NT also celebrates giving and generosity (Mark 10:17–31; Rom 12:13; Jas 2:14–17). In fact, this is such a strong theme that serving the needy is described in the gospels as serving Christ himself (Matt 25:31–46).

A major theme in a NT ascetic spirituality is the call to follow Jesus in a downward movement, as expressed in the great Christological hymn (Phil 2:5–11). A second theme is the call to put off the old self and its practices and to put on the new self, who is formed and shaped by Christ (Eph 4:22–24; Col 3:5–17). The NT identifies Christians as followers of "The Way" and calls them to a life of training, formation, and self-control as practised by athletes (1 Cor 9:24–27). This training, *gumnazo*, means to exercise and train naked, meaning unencumbered and possibly in a vulnerable state (1 Tim 4:7–8).

While the NT celebrates the free grace of God through Christ's redemptive work and our ensuing freedom *from* sin and the fallen powers (Eph 2:1–6), this freedom is *for* righteousness. In other words, we are saved *from* sin in order to live *for* the purposes of God for our world. Such a life is shaped through word, Spirit, the faith-community, spiritual practices, and a life of service.

These broad observations from the NT reveal that ascetic practices are not peripheral to a life of following Jesus, but in fact central to what it means to be a Christian. I will develop this theme further in the section on "Asceticism of Christian Discipleship," but first will discuss some perspectives on asceticism in the history of the church.

Ascetic Perspectives in the History of the Church

I cannot do a comprehensive study of ascetic practices in the history of the Christian church, as that topic is far too vast. In this section, I will simply illustrate that OT and NT perspectives on asceticism shifted amidst the changing historical and cultural settings of the faith-community. As a result, these observations are highly selective and schematized.

In the first centuries of the Jesus movement, asceticism was concerned with deepening one's awareness and love of God through contemplation, prayer, fasting, and other forms of self-denial.[41] It included an emphasis on *apatheia*, or passionlessness,[42] which involves living calmly before God and not being tossed about by all sorts of whims, fancies, or the changing circumstances of one's life. Today, we might describe this posture as seeking to live in a more *grounded* way. During these early centuries of Christianity, the baptism of blood – martyrdom – was perceived as the ultimate ascetic experience.

With the desert fathers and mothers, the focus shifted to a "living martyrdom" through the practices of celibacy, fasting, and other forms of self-abnegation. One iconic desert father, St. Antony (251–356), prefigured the formation of monasticism and its ascetic practices. His story is ably portrayed by Athanasius of Alexandria in *The Life of Antony*, who recounts how Antony sold all he had, did manual labour, gave to the poor, lived a life of prayer and fasting, fervently read Scripture, and wrestled with demonic forces. When Antony appeared to others, he preached to them, healed them, and began to form Christian communities.[43]

Scholars have noted that the ascetic writers of the "first four centuries" focused on "fasting, celibacy, [and] separation from the 'world,'"[44] but with St. Basil (c. 330–379), one of the Cappadocian Fathers, we see the emergence of different emphases. Instead of an asceticism of withdrawal, Basil promoted an asceticism of integration, where he sought to bring monastic communities into the heart of the church, the heart of cities, and into a needy world by creating "orphanages, hospitals, and charitable enterprises."[45]

The Cappadocians emphasized the practices of meditating on Scripture and solitude in order to achieve *hesuchia* (tranquillity of mind) and to free the soul from the demands of the body and the person from the demands of the world. In this way, the monk was prepared for the contemplation of God, which issued forth in a love for God, others, and the neighbour in need. Carrying out these practices within the framework of community shaped the monk's life

41. Cunningham and Egan note that asceticism is a disciplined form of self-denial, which draws on various Christian practices to become more "God-like" and to deepen our relationship with God (*Christian Spirituality*, 105).

42. Russell, "Asceticism," 64.

43. McGinn, *The Essential Writings of Christian Mysticism*, 50–54.

44. Luckman and Kulzer, *Purity of Heart*, 90.

45. Luckman and Kulzer, 94.

through an asceticism of correction and the practices of obedience in order to "strike at the root of self-will."[46]

Undergirding these practices was an emphasis on a eucharistic spirituality, which was to be marked by thanksgiving, the work of the Spirit, and the impartation of spiritual gifts in bringing the monks to fullness of life.[47] Within this celebratory frame, with its emphasis on "the constant remembrance of God" as the source for action,[48] the asceticism was concerned with "purifying the inner person," "building up the church,"[49] and serving the needy. Such an asceticism is not simply oriented towards the contemplation of God, but to building up the community and serving a needy world.

In the further history of monastic asceticism, these core themes remained, though there were many variations in the development of different monastic traditions. While some of these communities were primarily oriented to prayer, and thus were "closed" communities, others remained "open" in the sense of providing hospitality and education within a daily cycle of liturgical prayer, study, and work, which often included various forms of agriculture. In the long history of monasticism, there was also a "genteel form of asceticism," which did not involve physical work, but focused on "worship, study, writing, and contemplation,"[50] which included art.

During the Middle Ages, with the rise of the mendicants, such as the Franciscans, ascetic emphases included a continual life of poverty, being on the road in the work of evangelization and serving the poor, and the following of the "poor" and suffering Christ into the world. While the Reformation gave little emphasis to ascetic practices, subsequent movements within this tradition championed ascetic practices, including the Pietists, Puritans, Wesleyans, Anabaptists, and Quakers, among others.

Yet in our contemporary world, we can safely say that asceticism has fallen into neglect. Thus, my purpose in this chapter is to attempt to highlight the importance of recovering ascetic practices in our time.

---

46. Louth, "The Cappadocians," 166.

47. Louth, 164.

48. Luckman and Kulzer, *Purity of Heart*, 99.

49. Luckman and Kulzer, 95.

50. Elizabeth Clark, *Ascetic Piety and Women's Faith*, 181.

After discussing the "evangelical counsels" of chastity,[51] celibacy,[52] voluntary poverty,[53] and obedience,[54] F. Antonisamy goes on to discuss a spirituality of the laity that involves an asceticism of service. He speaks of the people of God as being called to share in the priestly, prophetic, and kingly work of Christ by engaging in "temporal affairs" in order to "contribute to the sanctification of the world," which involves diffusing into the world "a Christian spirit" through "apostolic activity."[55]

Paul Evdokimov also attempts to overcome the traditional distinctions in the Christian tradition between priests, monastics, those in religious orders, and the laity. Evdokimov begins with St. John Chrysostom's challenge, "those who live in the world, even though married, ought to resemble the monks in everything else."[56] Then he argues for the "universal vocation of *interiorized monasticism*,"[57] suggesting that *all Christians are called to interior monasticism*, or a life of worship, the practices of prayer, the development of various forms of community, and a life of service.

He continues that we *all have a vow of poverty* in that we are all poor in various ways, and we are all called to give, and we are all called to remember the poor. While "the monastic ideal does not preach formal poverty but a wise frugality of needs," he says this is most clearly expressed in an "independence of spirit regarding all possessions."[58]

He goes on to point out that *we all have a vow of chastity*, which has to do with the physiological realm as well as a "chaste structure of the human spirit."[59] Drawing on St. Augustine, he argues that while "the virginity of the flesh belongs to a small number, the virginity of the heart should belong to all."[60] Evdokimov describes the chastity of the human spirit as having both the internal forces of the human personality as well as one's positional power

---

51. Antonisamy describes the practice of chastity as follows: "to avoid lust and remain pure in thought, word and deed" (*An Introduction to Christian Spirituality*, 227).

52. Antonisamy describes celibacy as the "renunciation of marriage and living in continence" (228).

53. Antonisamy describes poverty as being poor in order to imitate Christ (230).

54. Antonisamy describes obedience as surrender to God and to those in authority (231).

55. Antonisamy, 246, 255, 259.

56. Evdokimov, *Ages of the Spiritual Life*, 137.

57. Evdokimov, 135 (Author's emphasis).

58. Evdokimov, 146.

59. Evdokimov, 148.

60. Evdokimov, 149.

grounded in the love and grace of God and the Spirit.[61] In other words, because our inner disposition, or *gestalt*, has been tamed, forged, and impregnated by the grace of God, it has been chastened to overcome the human tendency to ego-trip, manipulate others, or misuse our power when we relate to others.

Finally, Evdokimov suggests that *we all have a vow of obedience*, proposing that "obedience crucifies our own will in order to arouse [in us] the final freedom," which is the human "spirit listening to the holy Spirit."[62] He goes on to give this a Christological centre by casting it as the *imitatio Christi*, noting that all obedience is obedience to the Father's will, which involves sharing in the acts of the obedient Christ.[63]

Whatever we may think of Evdokimov's attempt at integration, his underlying concept is that we are *all* on the journey to greater Christification, which calls us *all* to engage in various spiritual disciplines, practice various forms of asceticism, and commit to serving the neighbour in and through the love of God.

Asceticism of Christian Discipleship[64]

We may readily conclude that certain ascetic practices in the Christian tradition are voluntary. For example, there is no biblical command to fast three times per week. Yet there is something fundamentally ascetic about the life of following Jesus. In other words, being a Christian involves various forms of asceticism.[65]

61. Evdokimov, 148–49.

62. Evdokimov, 153.

63. Evdokimov, 152.

64. Cunningham and Egan use the phrase, "asceticism of discipleship," which they describe as involving the themes of risk, love, and denial (*Christian Spirituality*, 109–12). I have reworked these themes to reflect the more basic contours of the Christian life.

65. I am well aware that within certain sections of the Christian church, this scenario is rejected and the opposite is proclaimed. Those promoting the "prosperity" gospel hold that the Christian life is fundamentally about blessing, self-enhancement, and well-being. This "gospel" continues to be attractive to the middle classes in their journey of upward mobility and also to the poor in their longing for a better life. However attractive this may be, particularly in its Pentecostal version, it fails on several fronts. First, it does not reflect the fundamental narrative of the life of Christ. Second, it does not imbibe the basic paschal mystery of the Christian life that life comes from death and that resurrection passes through the "needle" of suffering. Third, it does not take into account the ongoing reality of natural disasters and human injustice, which strip people bare. Fourth, it is a "gospel" that merely reflects contemporary culture in its emphasis on material well-being.

First, there is the asceticism of being *called*.[66] With our contemporary emphases on being self-determined and self-oriented human beings,[67] the gospel calls us to leave our own way and enter into God's love and purpose for our life. When we are called, we have to turn around, which involves the ascetic of self-denial. While acts of self-denial will continue in the Christian's journey, our very birth into the life of faith is a form of asceticism.

Second, there is the asceticism of being *led by the Spirit*. Coming to faith calls us into the domain of God's sovereignty, Christ's lordship, and the sustenance and guidance of the Holy Spirit as we enter a new state of being *in* Christ. Simply put, the Spirit is constantly seeking to lead us into the purposes of God's concern for our world. We must first be led away *from* our own ongoing concerns for our own spiritual growth and well-being, so that we can be led *into* God's will.

Third, there is an asceticism of *communalism*. Coming to faith in Christ calls us into the faith-community, the body of Christ. In this radically new form of association, we may find ourselves with people who are not like us, and yet we are called to see them as brothers and sisters in the faith and to treat them as we would treat Christ if he was physically amongst us. This practice calls us away from our own preferences and associations so that we can embrace a new form of communal identity, which will have its own challenges, costs, and sacrifices.

Fourth, there is an asceticism of *counter-consciousness* as the Christian life is lived *on the way*. Christians are pilgrims who are part of society, but also part of God's heavenly kingdom. This makes them "misfits" in the mainstream culture.[68] Living this way involves discernment and courage, as being out of step with the dominant world agenda[69] has sacrificial implications and

66. Underhill points out that "our spiritual life is His [God's] affair" and is "produced by His steady attraction," and "our humble . . . response," and it "consists in being drawn . . . to the place where He wants us to be" (*The Spiritual Life*, 39).

67. For a general and non-theological discussion of our contemporary focus on the self, see Will Storr, *Selfie*.

68. In Charlie Mackesy's discussion between the boy and the mole, the question is asked, "I wonder if there is a school of unlearning" (*The Boy, the Mole, the Fox and the Horse*, the book has no pagination). Developing a counter-consciousness involves the process of *unlearning*.

69. We need to be careful and discerning when we speak of the world's agenda, for the whole world lies in the goodness of God and is marked by God's common grace. Thus, there is much good in our world, and there are times when the world challenges the church. But the world is also *worldly*. Saint Claude de la Colombiere notes that "in the world there is an inner world, a second world which every Christian must avoid for it knows not God and the devil is its ruler" (*The Spiritual Direction of Saint Claude de la Colombiere*, 96–97).

involves a double movement.[70] On the one hand, in the practices of prayer, reflection, and soul care, we become "insensitive" or "indifferent"[71] to the things of the world. The Greek word for this posture, *apatheia*, means that we are not governed or unduly influenced by the world's values. On the other hand, this does not mean that we do not care about the world or that we are disengaged from the society. George Lane rightly points that a "Christocentric asceticism" leads to "love and the works of charity."[72] This double movement lies at the heart of Ignatian spirituality, where union with God in seeking to do the will of God[73] involves both contemplation and action.[74]

Fifth, there is an asceticism of Christian *growth.* The Christian life is one of ever-greater conformity to Christ, which involves putting off our old way of being and doing in order to put on the life and way of Christ. This process will involve both change and purgation as our desires are purified and reoriented. This is an ascetic activity, for as Segundo Galilea notes, "memory paralyzes our present and weakens our hope," thus, "asceticism makes us take the necessary measures to resist the temptation to live in the past."[75] An asceticism of memory calls for the past to be purified by hope, which will include the task of healing prayers.[76]

Sixth, there is an asceticism of *purgation*, which has to do with God's strange ways with us as our trials and difficulties deepen our friendship with God. Madame Guyon writes extensively about this, speaking of God becoming stronger in us as we become weaker in and of ourselves.[77] In our experience of desolation, we can experience both consolation and growth.[78] Sketching the contours of the purgative experience, she says that it involves a loss of blessing, weakness, powerlessness to protect oneself, an absence of inner rest, the sense that God is far away and seemingly angry, as well as many temptations.[79] She

---

70. Andrew Goddard picks up this theme regarding a Christian's presence in the world in the writings of Jacques Ellul, who describes the dialectic of "communion and rupture." Relationship with God means that there will be rupture in relation to the world. This rupture has to do with "relativising its [the world's] absolutist pretensions as it seeks to close itself off from God" (*Living the Word, Resisting the World,* 107, 105).

71. Lane, *Christian Spirituality,* 12.

72. Lane, 13.

73. Such union is functional rather than ontological.

74. Lane, *Christian Spirituality,* 46.

75. Galilea, *A Spirituality of Hope,* 49.

76. Ringma and Dickau, *The Art of Healing Prayers.*

77. Guyon, *Union with God,* 33.

78. Guyon, 38–39.

79. Guyon, 43–46.

goes on to point out that we must let these winds blow upon us to create the "dark night" so that we can eventually become "full of the divine will."[80] This is the experience of "naked faith,"[81] which is an "illumination"[82] given by God. This strange way is not simply for our personal growth, but for the benefit of others as we seek to make God known through the revelation of Jesus Christ.[83]

These reflections suggest that there is nothing extraordinary about asceticism, for it is not some grand project or virtue, but the bread and butter of the Christian life. The Dutch poet Berendien Meijer-Schuiling captures this idea in her description of a hermit praying: "and thus in bowing before a small wooden cross [the hermit] folds his hands above a thousand needs."[84]

Asceticism of Mission

While mission is part of our Christian discipleship,[85] and so the above section should include an asceticism of service, I am devoting this entire section to the particular forms of asceticism within missional spirituality.[86]

First, missional spirituality involves an asceticism of the *troubling Spirit*. Rather than being settled in our way of life and our perspectives of the world, the troubling Spirit broods within us, unsettles us, disturbs us, and evokes things within us. The Spirit may speak to us in dreams or other ways, always seeking to open us to a new way of life, new possibilities, a new calling. This interior "troubling" prepares us for what is to come. This is an ascetic experience, as it moves us away from what is familiar and secure.

Second, there is an asceticism of *calling*. The Spirit does not stir us simply to undo us, but to redirect us. This call is usually to specific tasks and places,

80. Guyon, 59.

81. Guyon, 42.

82. Guyon, 62.

83. Guyon, 62.

84. *"en zoo voor't kleine houten kruis gebogen vouwt hij z'n handen boven duizend nooden."* (Meijer-Schuiling, *Knoppen*, 45, my translation).

85. See *Redemptoris Missio*, 144–151. In this missional encyclical, the primary call is to "become ever more like Christ," followed by the call to live in "apostolic charity," to be a "universal brother [sister]," and to live in the spirit of the "missionary enthusiasm of the first Christian communities" (144, 147, 149).

86. It is surprising that the theme of asceticism finds no significant resonance in Cotterell, *Mission and Meaningless* (1990); Bosch, *Transforming Mission* (1991); Kirk, *What is Mission?* (1999); Bevans and Schroeder, *Constants in Context* (2004); and Wright, *The Mission of God* (2006).

as we are not called to universality, but particularly.[87] While we may wish to be here or there or everywhere, and we may wish to do this and that and the other, the call of the Spirit "narrows" us so that we embrace a particular task and a particular place. As Dorothy Day writes, "we did not choose this work. He [God] sent it to us."[88]

In my own life, I well remember the call to work with Indigenous communities in Western Australia, a later call to work on the streets of Brisbane, and the much later call to ministry in the Philippines. There was a strident and persistent particularity about each of these calls. Of course, I could have said, "no," but I felt both wooed and "herded" in a particular direction, and this caused me to think, "of course, I should do this."

Third, there is an asceticism of *leaving*. At this point in the missional journey, things become very concrete, for leaving requires us to learn the art of relinquishment. Leaving loved ones and familiar places involves pain and loss, which can weigh heavily on our hearts and minds. But leaving also involves joy and anticipation about the place we will come to know, the people we will meet, the work and challenges that lie ahead. Of course, our anticipation is sometimes marked by a romantic idealism, which will need to be tempered with realism as we step into any new call.

Fourth, there is an asceticism of *entering*. Whenever we enter a new place, subculture, or country, we have to embrace a fundamental vulnerability as a stranger and learner. To some extent, we have to start all over again in the arduous journey of socialization as we move from a premature, "yes, I understand," to a more mature, "I understand little," to a mature, "no matter how long I have been here, I will never be part of my host culture."

Fifth, there is an asceticism of *joining*. As we step into any mission, we are called to make the cares and concerns of our host culture our own. Our task is not to impose our own agenda, but to identify with the challenges that our new community is facing. This involves a servant spirituality as we choose to be present to *them* in God's purposes for *them*. Joining is a long, arduous, and painful process, particularly when we discover that we may have been too quick with advice and intervention and much too slow in learning and listening. And even when we have learned and listened much, we realize that though a few may see us as a friend, we remain an outsider.

87. As Underhill notes, we are "to take our small place in the vast operations of His Spirit" (*The Spiritual Life*, 89).

88. Day, *Selected Writings*, 112.

Sixth, there is an asceticism of *returning*. In time, we may have to return to our country of origin. This return is fraught with challenges, as we return changed, and the people we are returning to have moved on, and the society has also undergone changes. We also carry the loss of saying goodbye to new friends and the culture we have come to love. The return to our homeland is usually just as difficult – if not more difficult – than our initial leaving.

There are many complicated dimensions to the asceticism of returning, and I will highlight several here. First, we may return enriched by our crosscultural experience and see our home situation as bereft in some way. Second, our crosscultural work in our host community may have been very meaningful, but we may be unable to find meaningful work back in our homeland. Third, we may feel guilty for returning home. Fourth, we may feel the pain of no longer belonging to a place that used to be familiar territory. Thus, we become misfits in our own homeland and live a liminal existence.

All these reflections on the various forms of asceticism in mission highlight what Dorothy Day describes as the "precarity," or "precariousness,"[89] in ministry,[90] where so much is uncertain, fragile, and insecure. In all that we seek to do, we remain dependent on the work of the Spirit. The Latin root, *precarius*, literally means, "obtained by entreaty," reflecting how our mission must be birthed and sustained in prayer.[91] This bespeaks a most basic asceticism, where so much of what we do is beyond us and out of our hands, held in the care of God.

One of the most troubling dimensions of asceticism in mission is the sense that we may have fallen short of what we had hoped to accomplish. In Christian service, our hopes so often outstrip reality. We have to struggle continually with what we believe God has asked of us and what we have been able to do. This does not mean that we have been failures, but that we have to accept the sober reality of our human limitations, along with human sin. Dorothy Day reminds us that while we want to change the world, the best we can do is to "throw our pebble into the pond"[92] and trust the ripples to spread far and wide.

Another equally troubling dimension of asceticism in mission is the reality of unintended consequences. Having worked in a number of very different

89. Day, 108.

90. Goddard observes that Jacques Ellul calls the Christian life an "agonistic" existence because the "Word of God and the will of world" meet in the Christian (Goddard, *Living the Word, Resisting the World*, 102, 107).

91. John O'Donohue notes that spiritual practices are a form of asceticism and speaks of an "ascetic solitude" (*Anam Cara*, 108).

92. Day, *Selected Writings*, 98.

settings, I can point to many such occurrences, but the most repetitive has been working with aspiring Christian leaders in their formation, education, and training only to see them *not* return to the people they initially felt called to serve. It has been difficult to realize how the very blessing of further training has drawn many leaders along the path toward upward mobility, and they have lost the call of Scripture to the kenotic spirituality of Philippians 2.

One final dimension of asceticism in mission is the difficult reality of waiting. We plan, pray, and then we would like things to fall into place as we act. We want to see the desert blossom sooner, rather than later, but we so often have to wait much longer than anticipated. The Dutch poet, Alice Nahon, highlights this difficult season of waiting with a winter analogy, suggesting that our hearts need to be at rest just like the fields in winter.[93] She goes on to refer the mystery of buried seed in winter's womb, which in time will spring forth,[94] and we will see the wonder of God's fecundity.[95] The great temptation as we live through this difficult season of waiting is that boredom or torpor will set in. We become apathetic, as nothing is happening! Kathleen Norris describes this as a form of *acedia*, which "means the absence of care."[96] In waiting, we sometimes give up and no longer care.

Theological Perspectives

The biblical narratives depict a God who is fully complete, abundant in goodness, who creates, redeems, and beautifies all of creation, including the world of humanity. Within this grand narrative of abundance, God choses and redeems a particular people, sends his Son into the world to suffer and die on the cross, and then after his resurrection brings forth a particular faith-community by the power of the Spirit. Yet this path of particularity is not restrictive, for through it God makes provision for the *whole* world.

This overall picture draws us into the strange domain of asceticism, for giving up, giving away, suffering, and making sacrifices are a central theme of the biblical narrative and the history of the Christian church. This all sounds counterintuitive, for we expect abundance to lead to greater abundance. But

93. "*Dat ook ons harte rusten kon / lijk's winters de velden doen*" (Nahon, *Schaduw*, 12).

94. "*ze weten: in voren van diep deduld / wordt het mirakel / van't zaad vervuld*" (Nahon, 12).

95. "*Wij zouden verstild, voor't wonder bereid / de liefde herkennen / als God nader schrijdt*" (Nahon, 12).

96. Norris, *Acedia and Me*, 3.

in the biblical story, painful pruning leads to an abundant harvest, for in the paschal mystery, *growth comes from death.*

The many practices of asceticism fit within the particular frame of sanctification, which is the dynamic relationship between God's ongoing work in our lives and our cooperation with God's Spirit in the context of the faith-community. As noted above, ascetic practices are also part of our justification as we come to faith in Christ. But in shaping our lives in the service of Christ, ascetic practices lead us along the path of sanctification by helping us combat our vices and develop our virtues. Thus, they serve a negative role through various forms of self-denial as well as a positive role as we seek to follow Christ and serve the world.

Yet in the biblical story and the history of the church, asceticism is not about securing our own righteousness, but rather yielding to the call of God and the guidance of the Spirit so that we can attend to the ways of God as we seek to embody a sacrificial identification with the needs of others and our world. Ascetic practices are not so much about giving up sinful ways, but laying aside what is good for something greater. For example, we might go without food for a limited time so that we can devote ourselves to prayer. Though we are called into the abundance of Christ in the grace of God and the ever-brooding Spirit, we are also called to make sacrifices and to suffer for the sake of the world. May we live this dialectic well!

Conclusion

In this chapter, I have sought to be attentive to Scripture and the history of the church in order to demonstrate that asceticism needs to be reincorporated into our contemporary Christian discipleship. Asceticism is not an aberration in the life of the church in the past, nor is it something that only belongs to priests, those in religious orders, and monks who have taken certain vows. Rather, it remains an important part of our present-day spirituality and is an integral part of our mission. The central thrust of asceticism is to become more Christlike through disciplines that encourage our openness and attentiveness to God so that we can become more available for God's kingdom purposes.

Gittens describes this ascetic process through an analogy of the Eucharist: just as "the host" is transformed by becoming the body of Christ, so the missionary is transformed by becoming "bread to the world."[97]

97. Gittens, *Bread for the Journey*, 51.

17

Suffering

Joining the Suffering God

Introduction

The theme of suffering is common to all humanity, for we have all suffered and continue to suffer in various ways whenever our basic sense of well-being is interrupted or violated.[1] We also see suffering all around us, particularly when we cast our gaze beyond our own narrow confines. Suffering is part of the human condition and spares no one,[2] touching us in so many different forms – neglect, abuse, misunderstanding, victimization, discrimination, the terrors of war, the destruction of natural disasters, the pain of illness, the injustice of entire social systems. These things come to us despite our faith or status, whether or not we live good lives.

Yet this universal topic is very difficult to deal with in a satisfactory manner, for suffering is also intensely personal, something no one else can fully understand. In suffering, we often feel most alone. Suffering is also paradoxical in that it impacts us all differently, and some people suffer so much more than others. Some seem to grow through suffering, while others become overwhelmed and remain broken and wounded throughout their lives. There is no magical route from suffering to well-being, only surprises and resurrections. For persons of faith, this can raise questions about the goodness

1. David Tracy says this most simply: "no one escapes suffering, both physical and spiritual" ("On Suffering: The Event of Many Forms," 24).

2. Karl Rahner makes the point that suffering is the "most fundamental question of human existence" (*Theological Investigations*, vol. 19, 194).

and presence of God. Where is God's power when we are suffering? Life does not seem to be fair!

Suffering throws up so many questions that persist without definitive answers. And though many have tried to explain the nature of suffering, its consequences are unpredictable and often shrouded in mystery. In this chapter, I will explore the theme of suffering on behalf of the other, as this is intrinsic to a missional spirituality. A missioner must be willing to suffer in order to be a blessing to others – and to identify with the suffering God.

A Personal Reflection

I do not live with a sense of having suffered much, as I am very aware that some of my friends in Australia have suffered much more – and the suffering of so many in the Asian countries where I have worked is overwhelming. I am also aware of the privileges that have come my way as a Westerner and how I have been sheltered and protected in so many ways. All of this seems embarrassingly unfair!

Though I have experienced some major illnesses, including cancer, my experience of suffering is not related to my health. And while I have made challenging and costly choices to live simply, to be committed to community, and to serve in crosscultural places, these have been surprising contexts for growth.

My suffering has taken a number of primary forms. First, I have experienced the pain of being part of ministry teams and institutions where competition, rather than cooperation, created a toxicity that undermined relationships and damaged the missional impact of the group. In that setting, I lived with the sense that *we* needed to be healed instead of sensing that we were a healing community for others. Second, at a deeply personal level, I struggled with my inability or unwillingness to make hard choices in following Jesus. I taught my students about how radical Jesus really was – much more than the ideas of Karl Marx – but, in many ways, I continued to live a middle-class mediocrity. Even now, this causes me profound pain and inner suffering. Third, I suffer for what *could have been* in the purposes of God for our world – and has not yet come about. This suffering comes from living in between the ideal and the real, having a vision of the shalom of God but seeing it dissipate like the meagre clouds that visit the Australian outback, leaving the land parched, year in and year out.

These brief comments highlight how physical suffering is very real – and there is a massive medical industry to alleviate such suffering – but emotional and spiritual suffering are also equally real. Though psychological and pastoral care can help those who are suffering spiritually, navigating this inner turmoil is a difficult journey. The pages of Scripture are full of narratives about God's promises of restoration and wholeness, the people's folly and disobedience, the Spirit's renewing work, and the ongoing human attempts to build religious structures that only frustrate the impulses of healing. The biblical narrative reminds us that suffering the loss of what *could and should be* is a profound form of suffering.

Making Sense of Suffering

As creatures of God's good creation, we are called to live in relationship with God, to live the virtuous ways of the biblical narratives, to seek the common good, and to bless our neighbours. We are also called to seek God's thoughts, word, and way and then to try to understand and engage our world through witness, service, and prophecy. As we engage the world around us, we will inevitably find ourselves struggling to make sense of suffering – which may well be like trying to make sense of a wildflower or the whirlwind or trying to explore a dark cave without a light.

Whatever the difficulties, we need to make *some* sense of suffering so that we don't "waste our sorrows." By reflecting on the course of our life and God's way with us through our own suffering, we can begin to understand the reality of our world, which is full of the goodness of God and also marred by sin, folly, wrong-doing, exploitation, and injustice. Ironically, this dialectic causes us our greatest difficulties. Why doesn't goodness triumph and become the only "game" in town? Why does goodness often reluctantly unveil itself in the midst of our greatest tragedies, like springtime after the dark of winter?

In our quest to make sense of suffering, we can turn to the biblical narratives, which reveal a pattern of God creating a good world, which becomes broken through human disobedience, and so God provides a way of healing for the world, but human sin continues to mar the world, and so we continue to wait for the fullness of God's restoration in the new heaven and the new earth, where there will be no more suffering (Rev 21:3–4). In the meantime, we who "live between the times" experience the brokenness of humanity, our own stupidities, the reality of social injustice, and the power of evil forces (Eph 2:1–3), along with the grace and goodness of God, the blessings of family and friends, the sustenance of the faith-community, and glimpses of the common good in our world. As we live in the midst of this powerful dialectic, we are not immune from suffering,[3] and yet suffering does not have the last word – for goodness continues to blossom like flowers in the desert.

Over the long centuries of the Christian church, there have been various explanations for the reality of ongoing suffering. First, free-will theodicy suggests that we are responsible for our suffering because we misuse and abuse our God-given gifts and fail in our responsibilities.[4] From this perspective, suffering is a mirror in which we can recognize our waywardness. In this light, we are encouraged to repent and seek to do better than before. Second, God's justice calls for us to be punished for our ongoing wrongdoing. From this perspective, suffering is a sign of God's displeasure. In this light, we are encouraged to repent and seek God's forgiveness and healing so that we can live in more constructive ways. Third, redemptive suffering[5] highlights how suffering can bring forth goodness and redemption to our world and our own lives. From this perspective, suffering is an invitation to transformation. In this light, the suffering of someone or a group of people is a gateway that brings wholeness to many. This is the Christological theme of the NT. As Paul points out, "one man's act of righteousness leads to justification and life for all" (Rom 5:18b). This perspective can help us understand missional suffering. Fourth, developmental suffering underscores the inevitability of suffering to form a new world (Rom 8:22–23).[6] From this perspective, suffering is the key to moving forward creatively so that we can become what we were destined to be. Fifth, remedial suffering is a path of purgation that renews or tests us in order to strengthen us.[7]

3. Martin Luther believed that suffering is one of the marks of what it means to be the people of God (Lohse, *Martin Luther's Theology*, 284).

4. Rahner notes that this interpretation sees suffering as the "effect of human sinful freedom." He highlights this with the rejoinder, "you alone . . . are responsible for all the horror of creaturely history" (*Theological Investigations*, vol. 19, 200). Clearly this generalization places the human being in an unacceptable position of human autonomy and power. Moreover, it fails to take into account natural catastrophes, which, as David Tracy points out, "continue to cause untold suffering" ("On Suffering: The Event of Many Forms," 28).

5. Simone Weil believes that the soul emptied of self "is redemptive suffering" (*Gravity and Grace*, 24).

6. Rahner speaks about this understanding of suffering as a natural side-effect of an evolving world. He speaks of a "frictional phenomena accompanying freedom and development" and notes that "freedom as such . . . produces suffering and pain and death" (*Theological Investigations*, vol. 19, 198–99). This position, as Rahner points out, is not without its problems, including the fact that suffering is seen primarily as a natural byproduct of growth, without human accountability or any inclusion of God's involvement in our world.

7. Rahner has his own explanation about the "why" of suffering in our world. He notes that the "incomprehensibility of suffering" can lead us to the "incomprehensibility of God," and he

All of these explanations find some resonance in the larger biblical story. But while we may move between the "blessing" of suffering to the "curse" of suffering, from the embrace of suffering to the need to resist suffering, we always come away from any explanations with a sense of disquiet. Suffering remains a painful mystery, a path that we inevitably walk in desolation, often into a dark night of the soul. As with Job, we may simply be invited to bow before the mystery of God's "strange way" with us rather than finding any neat and tidy answers. Thus, suffering calls us to a great existential surrender, not only in particular situations, but also as a preparation for the finality of death.

Beyond Simplicities

Because rationality, rather than mystery, still characterizes contemporary Protestantism and evangelicalism, members of these traditions have generally not done too well in processing the ongoing reality of suffering. In my brief lifetime, I have heard many clichés regarding suffering, both in the churches of the West and in Asia. Following are some examples. "You are suffering deprivation because you have not received the baptism of the Spirit." "God sends typhoons because the land is full of churches with images in them." "You are ill because you lack faith in God's healing power." "You are sick because you have committed a sin that you have not acknowledged." The list is endless! All these statements reflect staggering condemnation and insensitivity, for sadly, we often try to turn matters of great complexity into unsatisfactory simplicities.

Clearly, making sense of suffering is more complex than any simplistic formula, such as "goodies" are blessed and "baddies" suffer. This is a hopelessly inadequate way of dealing with life's complexities and challenges, for the righteous suffer (Ps 88:3–7); Jesus went to the cross (Phil 2:8); Christians are persecuted (1 Pet 4:15–16); throughout the history of the church, many who have been baptized in water and the Spirit have also been baptized in blood.[8] At the same time, "baddies" don't always suffer. Thus, the psalmist cries out

goes on to say that "there is no blessed light to illumine the dark abyss of suffering other than God himself" (*Theological Investigations*, vol. 19, 208).

8. In the Anabaptist tradition, there is a recognition of a three-fold baptism. Robert Friedmann explains, "first and foremost is the baptism by the Spirit . . . then follows baptism with water, and finally . . . the gruesome baptism with blood" (*The Theology of Anabaptism*, 136).

to Yahweh, seeking to understand the prosperity of the wicked (Ps 73:3) and grieving for the suffering of the people (Pss 79; 80).[9]

Yet the biblical narratives also reveal how good can be brought out of evil. Joseph's brothers intended evil by selling the "dreamer" into slavery, but God used this action for good by bringing salvation to the entire household of these "evil" brothers (Acts 7:9–16; Gen 45:5) – and to the entire Egyptian nation. Moreover, God both blesses and bruises "his" people (Hos 6:1). Thus, suffering cannot be reduced to simple categories, but calls us to careful and prayerful discernment. In times of suffering, we must be gentle with ourselves and especially others. Suffering should pull us away from quick answers and bring us with tears to the footstool of God.

Hearing the Invitation

While there may be an element of judgement in our experience of suffering, I do not believe that this is its major key. There is another melody line, which is the music of invitation that pushes a question to the fore rather than an answer. In suffering, we ask, "What are we being invited into *through* this suffering – individually, as a people, as the church, as a society?"[10]

To give a personal example, I have suffered a number of major illnesses in my life. In the earlier illnesses, I never moved towards discernment, as there was not enough silence in my life to hear an invitation. My only quest was towards healing so that my ministry could continue. Thankfully, I experienced healing in the graciousness of God, but no deeper reflection occurred that could have led to my inner transformation. My last illness was very different, as my quest was not physical healing, but becoming a renewed inner person. In this illness, I heard the invitation, *What would it look like for you to live on the other side of being so close to death?* Reflecting on this question has had a profound effect on me.

A more general example is from Latin America, where pastors, formators, and theologians also heard invitations. *What does it mean to move to the side of the poor and to share in their struggle for life? What does it mean to enter into the suffering of the poor? What does it mean to become the church of the poor?*

9. Peter Cotterell sounds a helpful sober note about the "disorder" in human affairs, noting that "an apparently good and godly person, careful for others, experiences hardship, illness, loss, and unlike the biblical Job, does *not* find appropriate compensation in *this* life. There appears to be no *order* to the human condition" (*Mission and Meaningless*, 6, author's emphasis).

10. This is the core question of spiritual direction. See Brown, *Reflected Love.*

These deeply challenging questions led to a new evangelization of the poor, the formation of Base Ecclesial Communities, and the formulation of liberation theology, which has had a worldwide impact.[11]

As we attend to the invitations that come as a whisper from the edge of eternity,[12] the veil between heaven and earth becomes shroud-thin, and we can hear the sighing and singing of angels. Suffering, in whatever form it may come, opens us to hear this whispered invitation so that we can discern its hidden wisdom, embrace its difficult processes, learn its challenging purposes, and bow before its ever-present mystery as we seek to resist any "death-dealing" temptations. But let me hasten to add that all suffering – whether an experience of personal rejection, the Holocaust, or Stalin's ruthless purging – does not follow any neat methodology or rational logic. Rather, suffering is a dark intrusion, an unexplainable violation, a mad disruption, a poetic frenzy – and despite any good that might come, it is a blight and a scourge on our inner and social landscape.

The biblical story reveals how even though suffering continues to be the *wound* of the world, the *paschal mystery* is the clear and final word. In the death and resurrection of Christ, death and suffering meet their endpoint, and thus the grand anthem of God's final future is not suffering, but abundant life (1 Cor 15:50–58).

The "Why" of Suffering

Though we have emphasized the mystery of suffering, the "why" question does not go away. This ever-pressing question is linked to a whole gamut of related issues. How do we understand the good world that God has made? How do we understand the incursion of sin? How do we understand the sources of evil? How do we understand the scope of God's redemption? How do we understand God's healing intervention in our world? How do we understand God's sovereignty? How do we understand human choice and freedom? How do we understand our status as sinners and saints? How do we understand the forces of demonic evil? How do we understand structural evil?

All these questions highlight the fact that we cannot look at suffering in isolation, for it is deeply connected to who God is, who we are, and the nature of goodness and evil in our world. Suffering is a theological, relational, personal, social, and spiritual experience that involves the nature of human failure and

11. See Gutierrez, *A Theology of Liberation*, and L. Boff, *Ecclesiogenesis*.

12. See Ringma, *Whispers from the Edge of Eternity.*

sin, the madness and brokenness of our world, the forces of spiritual evil, and the way that God has chosen to work with us – and in spite of us.

Thus, with great reluctance, I note some possible dimensions of the "why" of suffering. First, suffering acts as a mirror regarding the true nature of the human condition, a damning reminder of the folly of human idealism and pride. Second, it functions as a wake-up call for us to resist certain forms of evil, a form of purgation to bring us to repentance, renewal, and healing. Third, it reveals how far we still have to travel to the "promised land." Fourth, it reveals the most difficult pathway of seeking to find the grace of God in Christ. Fifth, it is an instrument that shapes us into the likeness of Christ. Sixth, it calls us to suffer in identification with the poor. Finally, it calls us to bear the burden of love.

Suffering and Mission

Throughout this book, I have noted how our call and involvement in mission is both a joy and a responsibility. It is a joy to respond to God and to serve others, and it is also a responsibility to be a sign, servant, and sacrament of the kingdom of God. In other words, being a Christian draws us into serving the purposes of God in our world.[13] Thus, we receive the gift of God's grace in Christ along with the joyful task[14] of witness and service. I have also noted that mission is never a one-way street, but involves the dialectic of giving and receiving. There is so much to learn and receive as we seek to be a blessing to others!

Yet mission also involves various forms of suffering. We suffer in the process of relocation. We suffer as we seek to gain entry and familiarity with a new place, community, and culture. We also suffer when we take up the work of witness and service and face opposition and adversity. David Bosch notes that "what is true of the Master [Jesus] is also true of his disciples," for "the journey of the church-in-mission parallels that of Jesus to Jerusalem."[15] This journey is the *via dolorosa*, "the road of suffering" that Jesus trod – and

13. Christoph Blumhardt makes the point that we should not preoccupy ourselves with "exalted spiritual feelings," nor about "all kinds of speculations about the coming of Christ," but we should focus on how "we can be at his [Christ's] service with things as they are now" (*Action in Waiting*, 72).

14. The theme of joy is a hallmark in the writings of St. Francis, who writes: "whose love inflames our love / whose contemplation is our refreshment / whose graciousness is our joy" (*Francis and Clare*, 204).

15. Bosch, *Transforming Mission*, 121.

it is a road that we must travel as well. The early Christian movement vividly expressed this in a willing martyrdom. As Bevans and Schroeder observe, "certainly the powerful witness of those who were willing to suffer and die for their newfound faith provided, first, a strong inspiration for the Christian community, and second, a witness that drew others to the faith."[16]

While martyrdom as the ultimate form of suffering continues in the modern world,[17] there are many intermediate forms of suffering in missional settings. We might encounter indifference or even active resistance to the Christian message. We might find ourselves taking on the issues, needs, and sufferings of the people we are seeking the serve. We might have to deal with closed borders and political opposition. And we might also come up against forces of spiritual opposition, such as systemic evil, the nature of the fallen powers, and Satanic oppression.

Following the work of Walter Wink regarding the nature of "the powers," Donal Dorr identifies these powers as "agencies or movements or philosophies which exercise a compelling quasi-spiritual power in our everyday world," and he says that there is an "inner spirituality which shapes the various institutions and movements of our world."[18] This insight helps us to see that social entities are not simply mechanical forces, but spiritual forces that exercise forms of power that can impact people's hearts and minds. However, this is not the only way to understand spiritual forces, for many people are set free from various forms of demonic oppression in the gospel narratives and elsewhere in the NT.[19] Thus, contending with oppression is also a part of the mission of the church. But as we contend with various spiritual forces, we will experience identificational suffering and sacrifice. Thus, mission is an ongoing struggle, and our missional task will involve prayer, fasting, healing, and prophetic protest.

Other forms of suffering are also part of a missional spirituality, including the failure of the faith-community to serve others well due to internal problems and fracturing. In the missional literature, there is much about what the church is meant to be and do, but little about the church's failure to be what it

16. Bevans and Schroeder, *Constants in Context*, 85.

17. There is much uncertainty around the approximate number of Christians who are killed for their faith. This is complicated by the civil wars on the African continent, where many Christians have died in the unrest.

18. Dorr, *Mission in Today's World*, 110.

19. See Wilkinson, *The Bible and Healing*, 88–89, 136–39, 162–63.

should be.[20] Thus, we need to construct a much more *vulnerable* missional theology.[21] By vulnerable, I do not mean vague, but rather a more honest discussion of the relationship between God's grace and our service, along with a clearer discussion of who we are meant to be, what we are meant to do, and how we actually live out that calling in the world.

Unfortunately, the church throughout its history has compromised itself – as during the period of colonialism, in Nazi Germany, in the Soviet era, and in our contemporary era with all the child sex-abuse scandals. But even more broadly, the contemporary church in the West and elsewhere has become culturally captive, and this has resulted in much suffering. We have presented ourselves as the missional people of God while living compromised and fractured lives. As a consequence, much of our work has become a "beast of burden" without the wings of the Spirit to carry us forward as a blessing to the world.

Any present-day theology and spirituality of mission needs to incorporate themes of self-conversion and transformation, along with the call to be a transformational presence for others. The founder of German Pietism, Philip Jacob Spener (1635–1705), may be an older voice that can challenge us. He notes that the "first practical principle of Christianity" involves the "denial of self."[22] He continues, "I recognize more and more how deficient I myself am," and then he makes a surprising move by saying, "I am prepared to be fraternally corrected by others."[23] He highlights the core purpose of ministry as bringing glory to God and welfare to the neighbour, which includes sharing possessions. He writes, "I dare not withhold [my possessions] and keep to myself as long as my neighbor's needs cannot be met in another way."[24]

Whatever we may think of German pietism, here is a clear voice that beckons us as the servants of the reign of God to ongoing conversion so that we might live the radical call of the gospel to community, sharing, and witness to the world. The challenge in our time is not simply to convey a spoken

---

20. J. Andrew Kirk, in his fine missional discussion, does critique Western Christians for their "comfortable lifestyle" and their "seemingly convincing excuses for not responding to people in need or sharing the Gospel with them" (*What is Mission?*, 33). But there needs to be a more far-ranging and sustained critique of Western Christianity. See Charles Taylor, *A Secular Age*, which provides a broad cultural and historical framework for such a critique.

21. I hope that this book is a small contribution in that direction. See chapter 8 ("Grand Design and Fragile Engagement: The Church's Calling in a Troubled World").

22. Spener, *Pia Desideria*, 45.

23. Spener, 45.

24. Spener, 61.

word *about* the good news of Christ, but also to *be* an embodied *word* as a community of Jesus, the servant king.

Joining the Suffering God[25]

Having touched on the complexity of suffering, we can now highlight how the God of the Bible responds to suffering. God is the great deliverer (Deut 5:15), the great healer (Exod 15:26), and God, in Christ, has entered into our suffering (1 Pet 2:24). Christ's suffering has gained new life for all who believe in him (John 3:16), which means that Christ's suffering is beneficial for the whole world – all humanity, all creatures, and the entire earth.

Throughout the NT reflections on the Christ-event, those who have been set free in Christ (Gal 5:1) are called to a radical identification with Christ and to enter into his sufferings (Rom 8:17; Phil 1:29). Paul speaks of wanting to know Christ's resurrection power so that he may enter into Christ's sufferings (Phil 3:10), and he highlights how this kind of suffering produces virtues in our lives (Rom 5:1–5). Peter suggests that we are to follow the suffering Christ into the world (1 Pet 2:21–25). And Paul pushes this even further by saying that his suffering for others *completes* what is lacking in Christ's own suffering for the church (Col 1:24). This does not mean that Paul thought that Christ's death on our behalf was insufficient (Rom 3:25; Heb 10:12), but that we need to be willing to suffer for the well-being of others.

These passages invite us to join the suffering God, the groaning Christ, and the grieving and ever-brooding Spirit, who is longing for all of humanity

25. Since the atrocities of two world wars, there has been a growing consensus that the God of the Bible suffers with us. As such, we can speak of the suffering God. In *A Broad Place*, Moltmann speaks of entertaining the question, "what does Jesus' suffering and death mean for God himself?" (192). He continues: "does God simply allow Christ to suffer on our behalf . . . or does God himself suffer with us and for us in the suffering of Christ?" (193). He responds that the God of the Bible is marked by "active suffering love" and thus is willing to open "oneself in order to be touched and affected by the other" (194). He concludes, "if God were incapable of suffering in this sense, then he would also be incapable of love" (194). For a contrary position, see Weinandy, *Does God Suffer?* He argues against the passibility of God, which he defines as God not being willing "of freely changing his inner emotional state in response to and interaction with the changing human condition and world order" (39). Weinandy holds to God's impassability, writing that "sorrow and grief are attributed to God not by way of predicting a passible emotional change within him, but rather by way of denoting that he is all-loving and good" (169). Because God is intrinsically all-loving and good, God is opposed to and seeks to remedy all that is not good, but this does not mean that God is moved to help and remedy because God "experiences inner emotional anguish or distress because he has experienced some injury or the loss of some good" (169). While this theological debate will continue, what is clear is that the God of the Bible is not remote and detached, but one who intervenes to heal and make whole.

to come into the goodness of God and the restoration of all things. As we join God in this great longing, we will be invited into prayer and costly service. In this way, we become "midwives" for the reign of God.

Conclusion

The reality of our own suffering and the suffering of the world beckons us into prayerful reflection and radical identification. As we grapple with the suffering that continues in our world, we can join with the God who suffers with us and for us by holding the grief and sorrow of those around us to God in prayer. Out of the great silence that grows within us, we "carry" the suffering ones to the throne of God, and then we wash their feet with our tears and anoint their heads with the oil of hope as we groan for their suffering to end.

The yet and not-yet nature of God's abundance and eternal reign calls us to ongoing conversion as we enter our world as wounded healers. We have much to share regarding the grace of God, but we also have much growing to do as we seek to become Christlike. In the mission of the church, the people of God live in the midst of the suffering in our world and our lives while also celebrating the goodness and grace of God. Marked by this dialectic, the community of faith is called to identificational suffering for those whom we are seeking to serve. Thus, mission is not simply about blessing others, but cultivating the fortitude and courage to lament for what has been or could have been as we continue to hope for what will yet be.

18

Hope

A Magnificent Mosaic

Introduction

It is hardly feasible for someone to act in the world for the common good without being sustained by hope. Because hope anticipates a concrete vision of reality that could or should be in the future,[1] it is a motivating force that calls us to *engage* in the work of the present[2] rather than sitting around wishing for some conceptual picture of an idealized life. Thus, hope is very different from wishful thinking, which is characterized by the expectation that good things will simply come our way, as if the gods or fate will drop something we are dreaming about into our lap.[3] This is hardly an empowering strategy! Hope, by contrast, energizes us by helping us to imagine new possibilities and then to work hard so that we can see them become a reality. Yet hope is more than a force that pushes us to bring about certain outcomes, for it is fundamental to

1. Jacques Ellul makes the helpful observation that hope in anticipating the future relativizes the present. This means that the present does not have a stranglehold on us. He writes that hope "calls for radical and relentless relativizing leaving nothing illusory to survive" (*Hope in Time of Abandonment*, 247).

2. Segundo Galilea makes the observation that hope is oriented toward the future and the present, writing that "the future promise is inseparable from the earthly path towards it" (*A Spirituality of Hope*, 9).

3. By way of example, it is reasonable to hope that in old age, one may become wiser, but it is wishful thinking to say that one will become more agile and beautiful. Or, to make this more existentially relevant, it is reasonable to hope that God will continue to display his/her faithfulness to me, but it is wishful thinking to hope that I will no longer experience any of life's difficulties.

our humanity. As the OT scholar Rolf Knierim asserts, hope is "a basic element of the structure of human existence."[4]

This does not suggest that all our hopes can be achieved, for many of our hopes are too grandiose. Yet we can be sustained if we have an ongoing sense that we are moving in the right direction. And we can be carried through disappointment and setbacks if we can continue to anticipate that our small and incremental steps are leading toward future change.

Because hope is intrinsic to all religions, ideologies, and endeavours for social change, this chapter will take an interdisciplinary approach, engaging philosophy, sociology, biblical studies, theology, and spirituality to draw several implications regarding the dynamics of hope in a missional spirituality.

As in previous chapters, I will begin with a brief personal reflection. My reason for doing this throughout the book is that the topics we have been probing are all *existential*. Missional spirituality is not about a set of ideas, but a *way* of life as we seek to engage our world in light of our hope in the biblical vision of God's future and eternal reign on earth as it is in heaven.

Personal Reflection

I have had the joy of experiencing much positive work within various institutions, and I have also had the privilege of starting several Christian ministries. In all of these experiences, I have been positive and hopeful that we could take the initiative and make something good happen in the world. My initiative to engage future possibilities has not been self-motivated, but has been birthed by the "troubling" Spirit, who has prodded me towards a sense of God's call, and this has always involved a rather long process of discernment and preparation. I don't immediately jump into things, even if I sense a strong call.

There are many good reasons for such a slow approach. First, I believe that if something is going to get off the ground, there has to be some synchronicity with circumstantial factors, and this is a matter of timing. I am certainly not suggesting that all the pieces on the chessboard need to be in place, but I do think we should look for signs beyond our own sense of urgency. Second, I believe that the Spirit will also prepare others so that there can be a collaborative

4. Knierim, *The Task of Old Testament Theology*, 249.

effort, as the most effective work for change will come through community.[5] Third, every new project is developmental, and so even though we may have a sense of the end goal, we can only reach that goal by making the first step – and then the appropriate successive steps. Thus, hope helps initiate a movement – and once the basic building blocks of a new ministry project are in place, hope energizes the forward movement toward the envisioned future.

Yet our hope is constantly challenged and thus needs to be reborn *in situ.* Any new project will meet opposition and resistance, and this will test our mettle and commitment. If a project is overly optimistic, it may end up "bloodied" by the realities of life and one's social circumstances. Participants can end up being critical of those who are nonsupportive, and so it is important to seek a spirit of humility and generosity. Yet these trials of hope test new projects "by fire," helping them develop long-term sustainability.

I have learned so many lessons as I have sought to respond faithfully to each of my various calls. Most importantly, I have come to realize that our most fundamental hope lies in the presence of God and the work of the Spirit, who carries what we seek to do into another dimension. In other words, we yield the work of our hands into the grace and purposes of God, and so our hope lies in God, who is mysteriously working with, through, and apart from us to bring healing, blessing, and restoration for the world. This does not negate or underplay our responsibility, but it does call us to look to God to use us and correct us. For God is God, and we are not – and we are most foolish if we think that *we* can make the kingdom purposes of God, happen!

In this journey, I have experienced feelings of frustration, despondency, and failure. At the same time, I have continued to be inspired by the Pauline benediction: "May the God of hope fill you with all joy and peace in believing, so that you may abound in hope by the power of the Holy Spirit" (Rom 15:13). And I continue to believe that in God's final future of a new heaven and a new earth, *all will be well* (Rev 21:1–4).

Finally, hope spawns within me the conviction that I can leave some things in the hands of others. For in the course of our journey of visioning, implementation, and consolidation, we need to discern when it is time to step aside, let things go, and allow others to take a project in new directions.[6]

5. Jacques Ellul notes that "hope incites man [woman] to be the leaven in a given batch of dough. It requires that he [she] be in a certain organization or a certain group" (*Hope in Time of Abandonment*, 249). The fruit of hope is never a solo-achievement, but is fructified within friendship and communalism.

6. In much of what I have written, the themes of *present* grace and tasks and our *future* hope are prominent. See especially Ringma, *Seek the Silences* and *A Fragile Hope.*

Philosophical and Sociological Perspectives on Hope

Immanuel Kant suggests that the responsible life is oriented around three questions: *what can I know*, *what should I do*, and *what can I hope for*?[7] This last question has engaged thinkers throughout the ages, and so this section offers a summary of some of these various perspectives on the subject of hope.[8] Note that I have made no attempt to follow a historical trajectory.

In early Greek thought, hope reflects a lack of knowledge and poor planning. Descartes sees hope as a weak form of confidence and suggests that it produces anxiety due to its inherent uncertainties. Spinoza holds that hope is a false belief, a form of pleasure that soon dissipates into sadness and uncertainty. Rorty postulates that hope lacks foundations and is merely an intersubjective posture. Camus sees religious hope as futile, as does Nietzsche, who makes the additional point that hope often prolongs human torment. Schopenhauer sees hope as distortive, making it difficult to focus on the things in the present that are pressing and relevant. Interestingly, those with negative views still hold out hope for hope. Nietzsche holds hope for the role of the *ubermensch*, and Schopenhauer believes that hope can be a positive motivation for the intellect, while Camus believes in the possibilities of social utopias in spite of the ever-present threat of dictatorial impulses.

Others hold more positive views of hope, though with frequent qualifications. Kierkegaard suggests that the failure of our earthly hopes can be a precondition for our eternal Christian hope, which is always related to the good – never merely for ourselves, but also for others. Kant proposes that hope is linked to happiness, but this is always linked to moral conduct. Thus, if we are good, we can hope for good. But the object of our hope, whether God or progress, is always uncertain. Marcel is more positive in that hope overcomes despair. He links hope with patience, which can lead to positive outcomes. The analytic philosophers stress the future orientation of hope, coupled with our agency in working towards future hopes. And Arendt sees natality, or new beginnings, as the genesis and basis for our hope.

Interestingly, Bloch identifies two components to hope.[9] First, the *effective* component of hope has to do with expectant emotions that are generic to the human condition. Second, the *cognitive* component of hope has to do

7. http://www.thepostil.com>kants-three-questions.

8. I am wholly indebted to the article on hope in the *Stanford Encyclopedia of Philosophy*. See https://plato.stanford.edu/entries/hope/.

9. Bloch has influenced Moltmann, from whom we will hear from later ("Theological Perspectives on Hope.")

with not-yet-conscious orientations as well as objective possibilities. Bloch believes that the metaphysical possibilities of our human capacity can make possible what could be, but is not yet a reality.

Jose de Souza Martins laments that in much present-day sociology, which explores ever more discreet and narrow domains of social life, the "science of hope" has been lost.[10] He suggests that hope is a key dynamic in the very genesis of sociology, with its positivistic, rationalistic, and progressive orientation, and also in sociology's concern with alienation and distortion in social relations. He concludes that "sociology was born dissatisfied with the here and now and remains demarcated by different concepts of hope."[11]

Critical sociology (with its neo-Marxist underbelly) is marked by the theme of hope. For example, Habermas emphasizes the "emancipatory interest,"[12] and Mark Davis points out that the compass of Zygmunt Bauman's sociology is oriented toward hope.[13] Davis goes on to suggest that Bauman opens the gateway to hope through two concepts: first, his notion of "liquidity" – a social world in the throes of change on steroids, with the "absence of solid structures" – and second, his notion of "interregnum" – that we live in uncertain and in-between times.[14] Davis argues that Bauman believes that the world is "not-yet-sufficient" in "meeting human need" and that "human beings can themselves re-make the human world."[15] Thus, Bauman holds out the notion of an "active utopia,"[16] which involves a present engagement to bring about what can and should be. In this task, Bauman makes a number of key moves. First, he says we have to "safeguard against the trap of ceasing to question the world around us." Second, we have to have a vision that "relativize[s] the present." Third, we have to "confront" our present society with its "comfortable conceits." Fourth, we have to identify the "darker side of any tendency towards triumphalism." Fifth, we have to work for a "just society for all human individuals."[17]

In *Thinking Sociologically*, Bauman makes the point that sociology seeks to broaden our "horizon of understanding," and thus it is "central to the

10. de Souza Martins, "The crisis of hope in the sociology crisis," 188.
11. de Souza Martins, 188.
12. Habermas, *Knowledge and Human Interests.*
13. Davis, "Bauman's Compass: Towards a Sociology of Hope."
14. Davis, 1, 2.
15. Davis, 4.
16. Davis, 3.
17. Davis, 4–5.

endeavour of coming to understand ourselves in better ways."[18] He suggests that we need to work against our propensity to hold onto our "taken-for-granted expectations" so that we can adopt a posture where we "defamiliarize the familiar."[19] He sees the sociological task as negotiating several dialectics: boundary-making and boundary-breaking,[20] belonging and individuality,[21] freedom and justice,[22] self-preservation and moral duty,[23] and discerning the difference between "the protective role and the oppressive functioning of the state."[24] Bauman notes that because "our freedom is . . . never complete," we must have a "destabilizing effect on existing power relations."[25]

While sociology sees human action as "intelligible" and seeks to make sense "of the manifold web of human relationships,"[26] the sociological task is not simply to understand the world, but also to engage in "social diagnosis" and to shape the world by seeking to create "order" and "evict chaos."[27] In this task, we "both utilize and change" our social life by our engagement, meaning that our participation is both "creative and transformational."[28] This task is not simply pragmatic, but also visionary and anticipatory. For Bauman stresses that the sociological task seeks to explore "unsuspected possibilities" and to "open our eyes to new horizons."[29] Thus, as Mark Davis observes, the sociological task has hope written all over it.[30]

We don't have to wander far into other academic domains – education, psychology, and medicine, to name just a few – to find the theme of hope. Thus, it seems credible to suggest that hope is generic to the human condition. Yet surprisingly, the word "hope" is missing in many sociology textbook indexes.[31]

---

18. Bauman and May, *Thinking Sociologically*, 180.
19. Bauman and May, 20, 10.
20. Bauman and May, 35–38.
21. Bauman and May, 92.
22. Bauman and May, 12.
23. Bauman and May, 77.
24. Bauman and May, 136.
25. Bauman and May, 27, 12.
26. Bauman and May, 173, 9.
27. Bauman and May, 173, 169, 168.
28. Bauman and May, 178.
29. Bauman and May, 10, 11.
30. Davis, "Bauman's Compass: Towards a Sociology of Hope."
31. See Gittens, *Sociology*; Turner, *Sociology*; and McMichael, *Development and Social Change*.

Hope in the Biblical Narrative

The biblical narratives reflect a grand narrative of hope, as they do not cast their "mainplay" into an other-worldly future, but are very concerned with the action of God in the here and now. Moreover, these narratives do not reflect an unbelievable idealism, but detail the nitty gritty reality of the human condition.

Throughout the biblical narratives, we encounter the redemptive actions of God, humans who have been marked by that redemption, human suffering and despair, and God's gracious renewal. The stories do not suggest ever-greater progress, but rather the ongoing interplay of blessing and chaos, promise and regression, fulfilment and repentance, new beginnings and failures. Throughout the Bible, hope does not lie in human faithfulness, but in the long-suffering faithfulness of God, who continues to renew and revitalize the faith-community of both the OT and the NT – and the church in its long march through history. In this long history, we see the same pattern of new life and faithfulness, gradual deterioration and compromise, followed by seasons of renewal.

Old Testament Perspectives on Hope

The OT can be read in many ways, and its diverse themes allow for different thematic orientations.[32] But Walter Brueggemann is right when he says that the "Old Testament is a book of hope" that is "permeated with anticipations of what YHWH will yet do."[33] Walther Eichrodt makes the helpful point that hope has to do with the "miraculous irruption of Yahweh in the course of history," reflecting both God's sovereignty and the "bending back of the eschatological on to . . . reality . . . in the present."[34] And John Goldingay gives us a helpful overview, describing hope through the OT features of "renewal of an earthly paradise" and war and conflict ceasing, "leading to peace and safety," the "expectation of justice for the needy," the hope of "an individual redeemer," the prophetic hope of a "future in the light of the past," and a "fuller realization of his [God's] purpose in history."[35] This overview parallels the NT, with its orientation towards present blessings and the fuller coming of the reign of God in God's final future.[36]

---

32. Gerstenberger, *Theologies in the Old Testament.*

33. Brueggemann, *Old Testament Theology*, 343.

34. Eichrodt, *Theology of the Old Testament*, 479, 476.

35. Goldingay, *The Theological Diversity and Authority of the Old Testament*, 188, 198, 236.

36. Eichrodt makes the point that we can't readily jump from the OT concept of a "messianic king" as a source of hope into a "complete picture of Christ" (502). But he does make the more

Sadly, too many contemporaries easily dismiss the OT as irrelevant, with all its ceremonies, laws, wars, ethnocentrism, and historical particularities that have no relevance for contemporary faith. Some circles make an exception for the Psalms, while others embrace the prophetic tradition. But I believe that the OT writings are theologically, spiritually, and missionally relevant in light of the following: the message of creation and redemption, the concept of covenant, the articulation of exodus and freedom from exile, the concept of a whole way of life under Yahweh, the balancing of institutional life through the roles of king, priest, and prophet, along with the ongoing concern for the poor and for justice and the vision of a grand "utopian" future. As Walther Zimmerli puts it, "biblical theology" comes "from both testaments."[37] Or as Erhard Gerstenberger argues, "without the Old Testament, the New Testament would be a torso which simply lacked essential elements of theology and ethics."[38]

If we want to listen reverently to the OT, we need to ask, *how is it a book of hope*? The object of hope varies throughout the OT,[39] and there is the tension between "hope in his [God's] presence" and "hope in his eschatological future," but OT hope involves "hope *for* the future of justice and righteousness in Yahweh's new coming" as well as hope "*from* God" and "in God."[40] Thus hope, while delayed, is rooted in what God will finally do in history. Scholars point out that this kind of hope is unique to Israel. In the mythologies of surrounding nations, "not a single instance of unquestionably eschatological thought [is] to be found."[41]

While there is always the temptation to over-systematize a theme in Scripture, Eichrodt points out that there is a "bewildering diversity" of hope themes in the OT.[42] While I cannot explore these fully in this chapter, I briefly note the following. First, there is *hope for the creation*. God orders life and blessing in a covenant of fidelity, where "Israelite hope remained loyal to this earth."[43] Brueggemann makes the point that "Israel's creation faith" is always

---

general point that Jesus's redeeming work "*is the fulfilment of essential concerns of OT prediction*" (508, author's emphasis).

37. Zimmerli, *The Fiery Throne*, 119.

38. Gerstenberger, *Theologies in the Old Testament*, 284.

39. In the prophetic tradition, hope is in "the ultimate kingdom of Yahweh." Other motifs include the hope of an everlasting Davidic dynasty and the exilic return to the land of promise with "God dwelling her midst" (Knierim, *The Task of Old Testament Theology*, 249).

40. Knierim, 267, 264, 253, 259, author's emphasis.

41. Eichrodt, *Theology of the Old Testament*, 495.

42. Eichrodt, 490.

43. Eichrodt, 491.

under the "threat of chaos" and "covenantal infidelity," but is marked by the fact "that YHWH will keep YHWH's promises to Israel."[44] Put most simply, Israel's hope is human well-being in the land under the beneficence of Yahweh.

Second, there is *hope for the Davidic Reign*. David Hubbard points out that the "*Davidic kingship* was a major source of Messianic hope," as expressed in the Royal Psalms[45] and Micah 5:2–4.[46] While there is hope that "his [David's] throne stands for ever," Eichrodt makes the point that hope finally rests not "on the imperial King," but on the "saving activity of the covenant God."[47] Brueggemann argues that the "failure" of the Davidic hope results in the articulation of eschatological hope, but this "is a hope [concretized] in *the world*."[48] Thus, the failure of human rulership places hope in God's sovereignty.

Third, there is hope for *the futurist visions of the prophets*. The multi-layered prophetic tradition celebrates a return to "Paradise," an emphasis on God's "irruptive judgment," the vision that "God is in the midst of us," an emphasis on new hearts through the "indwelling of God's spirit," and the future rule as one of "justice and righteousness in the moral community of the people and the nations."[49] Brueggemann believes that the prophetic tradition sets "limits against creaturely violation of creation" and places in focus the hope of a "new creation . . . where war is not learned anymore." This he says, provides an urgent counter-offer to a "world of violence, brutality and revenge."[50]

The word "hope" also occurs in Job, Psalms, Proverbs, and the prophetic writings.[51] Much of the language in Job has to do with hope being dashed: "If I look for Sheol as my house . . . where then is my hope?" (Job 17:13–15). But one of Job's companions gives him the assurance, "And you will have confidence, because there is hope; you will be protected and take your rest in safety" (Job 11:18). And Job's confesses, "Though he slay me, I will hope in him" (Job 13:15 ESV).[52] Job's statement, "For I know that my Redeemer lives, and that at the last he will stand upon the earth; and after my skin has been thus destroyed, then in my flesh I shall see God" (Job 19:25–26), has echoed faith and hope

44. Brueggemann, *Old Testament Theology*, 327, 333, 323.

45. Pss 2; 20; 21; 45; 72; 89; 110.

46. Hubbard, "Hope in the Old Testament," 39.

47. Eichrodt, *Theology of the Old Testament*, 477, 478.

48. Brueggemann, *Old Testament Theology*, 345, 350.

49. Eichrodt, *Theology of the Old Testament*, 480, 482.

50. Brueggemann, *Old Testament Theology*, 340, 341.

51. Knierim, *The Task of Old Testament Theology*, 247.

52. The NRSV translates this as, "See, he will kill me; I have no hope."

throughout the millennia.[53] David Hubbard observes that in Job, we see the power of "hope that follows suffering."[54] Or, more accurately, we see hope that has been *purged* by suffering.

The psalms speak of the whole gamut of human existence before Yahweh: guilt, external threats, lack of well-being, and feelings of abandonment. At the same time, the psalms speak of repentance, worship, trust, and hope. The psalms acknowledge that God is the source of human hope ("for my hope is from him," Ps 62:5); that God is the focus of human hope ("my hope is in you," Ps 39:7); that God's word and promises are a source of hope ("and in his word I hope," Ps 130:5); that hope involves waiting ("I wait for the LORD, my soul waits, and in his word I hope," Ps 130:5); and that hope is an antidote to despondency ("Why are you cast down, O my soul . . . hope in God," Ps 42:5). Hubbard notes that "hope, expressed in piety both individual and corporate . . . nurtured the confidence that God had a future, which included salvation on the far side of judgment."[55] Put most practically, the "psalms are full of expressions of hope and confidence that God will change the present need of either the individual or the people."[56]

In the prophetic writings, the theme of hope is both internally focused on the Israelite community as well as the wider world, and it always has a new future in view. There is the typical theme that in the realm of the dead, there is no hope,[57] but in times of sin, despondency, and difficulty, Israel can look to God because "we have set our hope on you" (Jer 14:22). In fact, God is called the "hope of Israel" (Jer 17:13). Moreover, "there is hope for your future" because the people will return from their exile (Jer 31:17).

According to Eichrodt, the rich tapestry of hope in the prophetic writings – with the hope of flourishing in the land after the return from Babylonian captivity, hope for a society of care and justice, hope that Israel as the ideal nation will be emulated by other nations – finds its culmination in "*the supramundane character of the Messianic Kingdom*," where the "expected

53. Brueggemann is of the opinion that the OT emphasizes the power of death and *sheol* as the great threat to human existence, warning that we need to be careful that we don't too easily read the "resurrection" into passages such as Pss 49:15; 27:13; 116:8–9 (*Old Testament Theology*, 316).

54. Hubbard, "Hope in the Old Testament," 45.

55. Hubbard, 45.

56. Knierim, *The Task of Old Testament Theology*, 249.

57. "For Sheol cannot thank you, death cannot praise you; those who go down to the Pit cannot hope for your faithfulness" (Isa 38:18).

world-order is different in kind from the present one."[58] Isaiah's vision of this messianic bliss is but one orchestral piece in a grand prophetic symphony (Isa 65:17–25).

According to Brueggemann, there is much more to the theme of hope,[59] which comes in a "rich diversity of voices and utterances" throughout the OT, which "is permeated with anticipations of what YHWH will yet do."[60] I trust that this brief survey highlights the rich resources we have in the pages of the OT for a theology of hope. Following is a summary of core reflections from the above discussion.

First, OT hope has both "*realized* and *futuristic* dimensions."[61] This fascinating dialectic means that the projected vision of the time to come serves as an inspiration for present well-being. As Brueggemann observes, "the hope of new creation as it is voiced in the prophetic tradition enunciates a moral dimension of accountability in creation."[62] Simply put, we are called to live toward the future under the blessing of the God, who is both present and ahead of us.

Second, OT hope involves the challenging interface between God's lordship and human agency.[63] The OT constantly stresses what the people of God are to do in living God's shalom and also what God will do in their midst as their sovereign Lord.

Third, OT hope moves from the particular to the universal. The fundamental notion here is that the people of God are called to be what Yahweh is calling them to be so that they will become a light to the nations (Isa 42: 6). Hubbard notes that OT hope seeks to "*widen the sweep of its concern*,"[64] in that it has the whole world in view and is cosmic in its scope (Isa 40–66).

Fourth, OT hope sees no dichotomy between the spiritual and the material. Hope in the life-giving power of God is intrinsically related to hope for creation and the life-sustaining earth. As Rolf Knierim notes, "hope for material restoration and hope in God are legitimately related to one another."[65]

---

58. Eichrodt, *Theology of the Old Testament*, 491.

59. While the word "hope" is used some eighty times in the OT, there are seven hundred passages with terms that suggest hope (Knierim, *The Task of Old Testament Theology*, 246).

60. Brueggemann, *Old Testament Theology*, 343.

61. Brueggemann, 338.

62. Brueggemann, 340.

63. Brueggemann, 360.

64. Hubbard, "Hope in the Old Testament," 49 (Author's emphasis).

65. Knierim, *The Task of Old Testament Theology*, 262.

Fifth, OT hope knows the reality of suffering. This is reflected in the image of Israel as the suffering servant and the Messiah as the "obedient executor of the divine will" in creating a new people through "voluntary suffering."[66]

Sixth, OT hope offers to Israel, the nations, and all creation "a drama of origin, disruption, and renewal."[67] Thus, Yahweh continues to be involved in human affairs, and no contemporary religious or social or political voice can have the last word. According to Brueggemann, this means that all "totalizing ideologies" and all "distorted power" will fall under prophetic critique.[68]

Seventh, OT hope is reborn whenever spurious hopes fail. Hubbard, drawing on Vriezen, says that "true hope can come only when false hope is crushed."[69] And Knierim makes the additional observation that new hope emerges when there is a "breakdown of hope."[70]

Eighth, OT hope is not only proclaimed by the prophet or other spokespersons on behalf of Yahweh, but is also embodied in how the people of Israel live. Hubbard cites Isaiah's embodiment of his vision of the Lord sitting on the throne and then calling him to bring the prophecy to the people (Isa 6), along with Jeremiah's purchase of land as a sign of hope in the return from captivity (Jer 7–15). Hubbard observes that the "prophets were not just conduits of the word; they were living examples of pathos and hope."[71]

This rich tapestry weaves a complex picture of OT hope, which is rooted in God's sovereign Lordship and covenant faithfulness amidst the precarity of Israel's existence. Throughout the OT, hope lies *in* Yahweh, the "promise-making and promise-keeping" God.[72] While God's promises "anticipate new futures" regarding what God will yet do, these promises do not guarantee "escape from the world but transformation within it."[73] This transformational power is rooted in God's life-giving word as it is embraced and embodied in his faithful people, who dare to speak and live as a contradiction to all that reflects covenantal infidelity. Moreover, this transformational power anticipates a vision of the new world that God is unfolding. Thus, Brueggemann concludes that "hope is a distinctive mark of faith with dangerous and revolutionary social

66. Eichrodt, *Theology of the Old Testament*, 493.

67. Brueggemann, *Old Testament Theology*, 376.

68. Brueggemann, 378, 381.

69. Hubbard, "Hope in the Old Testament," 51.

70. Knierim, *The Task of Old Testament Theology*, 265. He cites Jer 14:19; Isa 59:9: Job 7:6.

71. Hubbard, "Hope in the Old Testament," 52.

72. Brueggemann, *Reverberations of Faith*, 101.

73. Brueggemann, 101, 100.

potential."[74] This grand vision enfolds Israel, the nations, the earth, and the entire future in God's healing and restorative sweep.

New Testament Perspectives on Hope

In this section, I will engage in a close textual reading of the NT before engaging a number of scholars regarding their perspectives on the theme of biblical hope. I will begin by highlighting some broader themes in the contexts where the word hope (*elpis*) appears in the NT.

Regarding the first theme, hope in the NT is *Trinitarian*. God is acknowledged as "the God of hope" (Rom 15:13), and Paul exclaims that in God, "we have set our hope" (2 Cor 1:10). Elsewhere, this theme is repeated: "we have set our hope on the living God, who is the Savior of all people, especially of those who believe" (1 Tim 4:10); and "your faith and hope are set on God" (1 Pet 1:21). This theme is also celebrated in relation to "Christ Jesus our hope" (1 Tim 1:1). Paul speaks of we, "who were the first to set our hope on Christ" (Eph 1:11), and, "Christ in you, the hope of glory" (Col 1:27). Elsewhere, followers of Christ are exhorted to "set all your hope on the grace that Jesus Christ will bring you" (1 Pet 1:13). Finally, hope is identified as an inspiration of the Holy Spirit, as reflected in Paul's beautiful benediction: "May the God of hope fill you with all joy and peace in believing, so that you may abound in hope by the power of the Holy Spirit" (Rom 15:13).

We can highlight a number of emphases from these verses. First, the object of Christian hope lies firm and secure in God's salvific work in and through Christ for the redemption and healing of humanity and the restoration of all things. Put differently, we can put our hope in God because God in Christ is the trustworthy and faithful one, who has already demonstrated his dependability. Second, these verses call us to activate our hope and centre it on God rather than placing our hope elsewhere. Third, Christian hope is rooted in what Christ has already done and is still yet to do in us as we anticipate the glory of God's final future. Thus, hope is located in Christ, who has gone before us and also ahead of us. Finally, while hope is part of our living faith response to Christ, we are empowered to hope by the Holy Spirit, who activates and sustains hope.

Regarding the second theme, hope functions as the anticipation of what is to come and thus has a future orientation. Yet NT hope is not only directed towards the life that is to come in God's final future, for it is also concerned with God's action in this life. Paul speaks of knowing "what is the hope to

74. Brueggemann, 102.

which he has called you" (Eph 1:18). Then he goes on to speak of "his power for us who believe" as a gift from Christ the Lord, who is "far above all rule and authority and power and dominion," and who exercises this power "*in this age*" and also "in the age to come" (Eph 1:18–21).[75] Elsewhere, Paul speaks of having "a hope" (2 Cor 3:12) in the new covenant marked by the "Spirit of the Lord," who gives the gift of "freedom" because we "are being transformed . . . from one degree of glory to another," which comes from the Lord, the Spirit (2 Cor 3:4–18).

In Colossians, Paul juxtaposes future and present hopes, speaking of the "hope laid up for you in heaven" (Col 1:5). Then he goes on to point out that they "heard of this hope in the word of truth, the gospel that has come to you" (Col 1:5–6) and that this is "bearing fruit among yourselves" (Col 1:6). Clearly, Paul is joining future hopes to the way those hopes are being worked-out in the present. Elsewhere in Colossians, Paul speaks of his ministry "to make the word of God fully known" to Gentiles and how this word reveals the mystery of "Christ in you, the hope of glory" (Col 1:25–27). This reflects a core NT theme of Christification – the in-Christ relationship – which is both a present faith reality as well as a future hope in the fulness of redemption in God's final future.

These NT passages all reveal the sense that hope is an anticipatory reality, which focuses on the fulness that awaits us while, at the same time, being blessed in this life with the first fruits of our ongoing longings. Thus, NT hope is both a present and a future dynamic, where what awaits is already present in embryonic form. This reflects the "yet" and "not-yet" nature of God's rule, a kingdom that is both here and still coming. God is with us now, and yet we still await our final homecoming.

Regarding the third theme, the NT highlights other present-day hopes. In the epistle to the Romans, Paul speaks of the importance of building up the faith-community and serving the needy in the community, linking this to the role of the Scriptures in providing the "steadfastness" and "encouragement" of "hope" (Rom 15:1–6). Elsewhere, he notes that we can "rejoice in hope" (Rom 12:12), for "in hope we were saved" (Rom 8:24). He also says that suffering and endurance produce character, and "character produces hope" (Rom 5:3–4). In the book of Hebrews, faithfulness in service is the call to "realize the full assurance of hope to the very end" (Heb 6:11), and so the faithful are "strongly encouraged to seize the hope" set before them (Heb 6:18). This hope is a "sure and steadfast anchor of the soul," a "hope that enters the inner shrine behind the curtain, where Jesus . . . has entered" (Heb 6:19–20). These passages all

75. Emphasis added.

suggest that hope is a present dynamic in the life of faith and love (1 Cor 13:7, 13), not a source of wishful thinking about the future. Because hope is rooted in who God is in Christ and in the acts of God's redemptive work as portrayed in the Scriptures, members of the faith-community can live in confident hope of God's ongoing presence and action among them and also in the future that awaits them. Thus, hope motivates and moves people of faith to action. The faith-community does not sit around waiting for better days, but is moved to engage in faithful service and to persevere in prayer. While hope is a theological concept, it is also an existential dynamic that has ethical and practical implications. Most basically, hope moves us to *live now* what we are *yet awaiting* in the future of God's complete reign.

Regarding the fourth theme, the NT speaks of our future hopes in many places. Our call to live godly lives "in the present age" is framed in the light of the future – "while we wait for the blessed hope and the manifestation of the glory of our great God and Savior, Jesus Christ" (Titus 2:11–13). The reference to the "hope of eternal life" (Titus 1:2; 3:7) has both a present and a future dimension, as does Paul's "boast in our hope of sharing the glory of God" (Rom 5:2). The future orientation of our hope is clearly revealed in the expression that "we hope for what we do not see" (Rom 8:25) and also in the references to the resurrection throughout the NT.[76] Paul notes that "all die in Adam," but "all will be made alive in Christ" (1 Cor 15:22), where being made alive in Christ includes the resurrection, as what "is sown in weakness . . . is raised in power" and what is "sown a physical body . . . is raised a spiritual body" (v. 42). Then Paul unveils a mystery, writing, "we will all be changed, in a moment, in the twinkling of an eye at the last trumpet . . . and the dead will be raised imperishable" (1 Cor 15:52). Clearly, Christian hope is oriented to what God, who is ever before us, will yet do amongst us as the Spirit continues to beckon us into a fulness of life in God's final future.

While the actual word, "hope" (*elpis*), occurs in these settings, it is also important to identify settings in the NT where the theme of hope appears, but the actual term is not used. I will identify three such settings. First, the narrative of Jesus's life, death, and resurrection traces the story of the one who is hoped for – Immanuel, God with us – bringing new hope to the people of God. Inspired by Jesus, his followers place their hopes in him as the Christ, but then those hopes pass through the crucible of the cross and its seeming defeat. Hope is restored when the crucified one is raised by the power of God. Thus, Jesus is the source of hope, the inspirer of hope, and the one who sustains our

76. See Acts 23:6; 24:15; 26:6–7; 1 Cor 15.

hopes. Second, one of the major themes of the NT is the kingdom or reign of God. In the parables of the NT, hope is embedded in the kingdom of God, which is planted in small ways, takes root and grows, and then there is a great harvest. This kingdom turns all other kingdoms upside down. Though it is envisaged in the present, its bounteous fulness is still to come. Third, the book of Revelation evokes a vision of the blessedness and grandeur of God's final future in the new heavens and new earth.

In light of these reflections, we can affirm that both the NT and the OT are books of hope. This hope sustained by the faithful, stretches into a future that has already touched us, and calls us forward into the final purposes of God. I will conclude this section on NT perspectives of hope by turning into something of the labyrinth of NT studies, beginning with some of the authors who give me concern.

Neil Elliott's *Liberating Paul* challenges the idea that Paul was a social conservative,[77] suggesting that he was an "apocalyptist" and a "mystic,"[78] and claiming that "Paul's apostolate among the Gentiles was oriented towards the salvation of Israel."[79] He develops the theme that Paul's faith-communities – as "communities of resistance" and "communities of solidarity with the crucified" – were "to live the power of the resurrection even within the realm of Death" (that of the Empire of the day).[80] Elliott elaborates on this "political reading of Paul,"[81] noting that "Paul's conversion to the cause of the crucified, and the theology of the cross that flows from it, are thus profoundly political," resulting in the body of Christ "no longer" being "at the disposal of the powers of injustice, but mobilized for God's justice."[82]

This relevatizing reading identifies Paul as facilitating a counter-vision to the Roman Empire, with its mantra of maintaining peace and security through violence.[83] Instead, Paul emphasizes that the faith-communities are called to live a "crucified vulnerability" in the world,[84] in solidarity with the crucified and resurrected Christ. In this vision, Elliott challenges us with a costly vision of fidelity in the face of the powers of this age. There is no triumphal symphony

77. Elliott, *Liberating Paul*, 181–84.

78. Elliott, 141.

79. Elliott, 175.

80. Elliott, 195–98, 198–204, 180.

81. Elliott, 184.

82. Elliott, 227, 228.

83. Elliott, 184–90.

84. Elliott, 200.

at play here, for Elliott quotes Gandhi, saying that "we must never accept evil, if we cannot change it."[85] Elliott concludes that Jesus's resurrection gives us the assurance that nothing shall separate us "from the love of God in Christ Jesus our Lord" (Rom 8:39).[86] While this is all well and good, Elliot does not develop the theme of the new creation (Gal 6:15), the radical new order of the faith-community (Gal 3:28), the power of the "in-Christ" relationship (Rom 8:10; Gal 2:20), the significance of the *imitatio Christi* (1 Thess 1:6), the power of the Holy Spirit (Eph 3:16), or the life to come (Phil 3:14). As noted above, hope in the NT is concerned with this life *and* the life to come.[87] Elliott overplays the former at the cost of the latter. Thus, Elliott over-liberates Paul from his own rich tradition.

While Elliott focuses on Paul, *Kingdom Ethics* by Glen Stassen and David Gushee focuses on the Gospels, primarily the Sermon on the Mount. Similar to Elliott, this comprehensive scholarly work focuses on living a practical Christian life in following Jesus, offering applicatory relevance to many areas of life, including peacemaking, restorative justice, valuing life in all its dimensions, issues of race, economics, and creation-care. However, my concern is with its treatment of the kingdom, which has ensuing implications for the theme of hope. The authors rightly note that the "Old Testament hope of salvation is not merely for eternal salvation in which our disembodied souls are snatched from this vale of tears" and that the "New Testament will bring a greater emphasis on eternal life . . . [but] will not negate the holistic message of deliverance" in this life.[88] They identify this salvation as "the kingdom of God," reflecting that God "reigns over all of life" and is present with us and in the future.[89] The authors continue by saying that "Jesus inaugurates the long-promised kingdom," which leads to healing and the work of peacemaking and justice, and this leads to "practices" that faithfully reflect "what God in Christ intends to do in us and in the world."[90]

Once again, this is all well and good, but even though Stassen and Gushee refer to the future, the eschatological nature of that future is largely missing. There is little sense of the kingdom that is beyond us and yet always beckoning

85. Elliott, 229.

86. Elliott, 229.

87. Paul is clear enough about the life to come: "I want to know Christ and the power of his resurrection and the sharing of his sufferings by becoming like him in his death, if somehow I may attain the resurrection of the dead" (Phil 3:10–11).

88. Stassen and Gushee, *Kingdom Ethics*, 28–29.

89. Stassen and Gushee, 29.

90. Stassen and Gushee, 30–31.

us, nor of the way we live spiritual practices in faith and hope towards a future that is fuller than our present. Thus, they do not develop a spirituality of hope that is intrinsic to the kingdom of God and the theme of living provisionally towards God's final future. Our Christian practices are not only shaped by ethics, but also by the dynamic of living in the hope of the God who is with us and ahead of us, calling us forward into what can yet be in the purposes of God.

Rudolf Bultmann's *Theology of the New Testament* is more helpful, though not without some problems. Bultmann believes that "we are what we are in hope,"[91] which is paradoxically "present, and yet future."[92] In his discussion of Colossians and Ephesians, Bultmann notes that "hope . . . looks forward to the life which with Christ will then be revealed" (Col 3:2–4), but the focus is "on the present state" rather than "future salvation."[93] In some insightful moves, Bultmann stresses that "hope is the freedom for the future and the openness toward it" and, as such, involves a "patient waiting."[94] He makes hope a dynamic reality by highlighting the Pauline theme of faith, hope, and love (1 Cor 13:13), writing that the "work of faith," the "labor of love," and the "steadfastness of hope" belong "to the totality of Christian existence."[95] In fact, he goes so far as to claim that human's fundamental ontological structure is to abide in "faith, hope, love."[96]

Bultmann is best understood by his emphasis on the Christian faith and life as an "eschatological existence."[97] He identifies the dominant NT theme of the "Reign of God" as an eschatological concept and a "miraculous event."[98] His emphasis on eschatology is framed by the notion "that the hoped-for has already occurred," because "Jesus Christ has made me his own,"[99] and our participation in Christ means that we are also part of Christ's future. Being in and with Christ is rooted in grace and apprehended in faith, which is God's gift. As Bultmann puts it, faith is "God's prevenient deed of grace which preceded

91. Bultmann, *Theology of the New Testament*, vol. 1, 101.

92. Bultmann, vol. 2, 176.

93. Bultmann, vol. 2, 176.

94. Bultmann, vol. 1, 320.

95. Bultmann, vol. 1, 320.

96. Bultmann, vol. 1, 199. The fact that he concludes that this ontological structure is "man's [woman's] relationship to himself [herself]" reflects his existentialist orientation. It makes far more sense to suggest that if faith, hope, and love reflect a human ontological dynamic, speaking of these reflects a relationship to God, self, and others.

97. Bultmann, vol. 2, 75–92.

98. Bultmann, vol. 1, 4.

99. Bultmann, vol. 1, 322.

faith."[100] Thus, for Bultmann, "eschatological life, though a matter of hope, is, nevertheless, in a certain manner already a present reality."[101] Life in Christ is both future and present, but the "first fruits" (Rom 8:23) of God's fulness of life are already with us.[102] Thus, hope is a central concern for Bultmann, who sees the Christian life as a life of faith, which is an eschatological reality.

My concern with Bultmann is regarding his discussion of resurrection. On the one hand, he asserts that "death-and-resurrection . . . is for Paul the decisive thing about the person of Jesus," and yet, on the other hand, Bultmann claims that the resurrection of Christ cannot be "made plausible as an objectively ascertainable fact."[103] Rather, it can only be believed because "the risen Christ is present in the proclaiming word."[104] He further explains that "Christ's death and resurrection . . . are cosmic occurrences, not incidents that took place once upon a time in the past," but instead an eschatological event in the kerygma which proclaimed "Jesus Christ the Crucified and Risen One."[105] Finally, Bultmann suggests that the resurrection of the body makes the connection between "somatic existence in the eschatological consummation with a mythological teaching on the resurrection."[106] To unpack the density of this language, we need to locate our discussion in Bultmann's hermeneutic, which is beyond the scope of this chapter.[107] However, the following two points should be noted. First, no theological statement can be proved through objectivist historical methods. Second, the only basis for making theological statements, including the hope of the resurrection, is the testimony of those recorded in the NT.[108] Such testimony is embraced in faith and lived in hope.

Gunther Bornkamm's *Paul* is more accessible than Bultmann's NT theology.[109] Bornkamm believes that the "intellectual range" of Paul's writings "soared to incomparable heights," even though he was primarily an "envoy and preacher" of Jesus Christ, who sought "to complete his grandiose mission

100. Bultmann, vol. 1, 319.

101. Bultmann, vol. 1, 279.

102. Bultmann, vol. 1, 348.

103. Bultmann, vol. 1, 293.

104. Bultmann, vol. 1, 305.

105. Bultmann, vol. 1, 299, 3.

106. Bultmann, vol. 1, 198.

107. I have dealt with this elsewhere. See Ringma, *Gadamer's Dialogical Hermeneutic*, 104–57.

108. See the discussion of testimony in Paul Ricoeur, *Figuring the Sacred*.

109. Equally accessible is N. T. Wright, *Surprised by Hope*.

program."[110] Bornkamm identifies the "saving event and the lordship of Christ" as central to the Pauline writings, and these "present realities within the world in the life of the church," make the church the "eschatological people of God."[111] Quoting Paul's reference that in Christ "there is a new creation" (2 Cor 5:17), Bornkamm highlights this eschatological reality as happening "by means of his *Spirit* alone."[112] Drawing on Romans 6:3–4, he says that the foundation of our faith is our "participation in Christ's death and resurrection."[113] He stresses that Paul's eschatology is "stamped by the hope which is based on God's acts of salvation."[114] As such, the church lives "between the resurrection of the Crucified and his second coming, still under the auspices of his death on the cross in weakness, and yet already in a life deriving from the power of the Risen One."[115]

Within this broad frame, Bornkamm discusses the "yet" and "not-yet" nature of the Christian life, noting that the new creation in Christ is a present faith reality (2 Cor 5:17), that the time is fulfilled for God's action in Christ (Gal 4:4–7), and that the end of the ages has come (1 Cor 10:11). Yet the world will pass away (1 Cor 7:31), and there is a resurrection to come with its final transformation (1 Cor 15:50–58).[116] In focusing on the "yet," Bornkamm spells out the task of the church's faithful witness and service in the world as an eschatological community[117] living toward the hope of the "not-yet" in God's future. Bornkamm observes that Paul's notion of the future is hard to "gather . . . into one uniform picture,"[118] because the references are scattered throughout his writings. Though Paul uses "apocalyptic concepts and imagery," he is emphatic about the future.[119] Bornkamm, citing Paul, refers to our "perishable body" putting on "imperishability" (1 Cor 15:53), and he says that "he who raised Christ from the dead will give life to your mortal bodies" (Rom 8:11) and

---

110. Bornkamm, *Paul*, xxvi, xxii.

111. Bornkamm, 176, 179.

112. Bornkamm, 180, author's emphasis.

113. Bornkamm, 190.

114. Bornkamm, 226.

115. Bornkamm, 188.

116. Bornkamm, 196.

117. Bornkamm stresses that the church, as God's eschatological community, is impacted by "God's history as a radical countermovement to earthly history" and lives in the tension of disengagement and engagement in the world (199, 209).

118. Bornkamm, 222.

119. Bornkamm, 224.

that "if, in fact, we suffer with him so that we may also be glorified with him" (Rom 8:17).[120]

Bornkamm concludes that the future that is to be completed "with the Parousia and the resurrection of believers" is already "on the way because of Christ's resurrection."[121] Moreover, he says that Paul "gazes into the future" and "the banner is hope."[122] Living toward this hope of God's final future results in the destruction of all illusions that our "efforts can put the world to rights and turn it into paradise," and it also averts the constant temptation of living in "bondage to this or that law of the world."[123]

I will conclude this exploration of a NT spirituality of hope by referring to Michael Gorman's *Participating in Christ: Explorations in Paul's Theology and Spirituality.* Gorman's work is an attempt "to end the divide between theology and spirituality."[124] He focuses on Paul's soteriology, which he says is not forensic but "participatory and transformative," and he identifies Paul's justification in Christ as "'deification'" and "transformation into Godlikeness."[125] Gorman notes that "hope for Paul is cruciform" and that "cruciformity . . . is a matter not of imitation but of transformative participation."[126] He grounds this in Christ's death and resurrection, emphasizing that these two themes "are so inseparable that they . . . constitute one saving event."[127] He also brings justification and baptism into "one participatory life-giving event," moving from "death to life."[128] Gorman then develops the present and future dimensions of this life of cruciformity, which he calls "resurrectional cruciformity."[129] Gorman quotes Galatians 5:5, "through the Spirit, by faith, we eagerly wait for the hope of righteousness," to note that this is both a future and present reality, for the "hoped for eschatological righteousness" is present in those who are in Christ and is embodied in their lives in "faithfulness and love."[130]

In reading this section, I trust that you can perceive that hope is not an "accidental tourist" in the landscape of the NT, but rather an intrinsic and

120. Bornkamm, 220.
121. Bornkamm, 224.
122. Bornkamm, 225.
123. Bornkamm, 227.
124. Gorman, *Participation in Christ*, xxii.
125. Gorman, xviii, 142.
126. Gorman, 12, 28.
127. Gorman, 59.
128. Gorman, 201.
129. Gorman, 259.
130. Gorman, 141.

persistent theme. Our participation by faith in Christ's salvific life and work, including his death and resurrection, "binds" us to Christ, both in this life and in the life to come. Moreover, our life of faith is one of hoped-for growth, and our service to the world is birthed in the hope that God's presence, reign, and shalom will come more fully among us within our present reality. Finally, our Christian hope is always oriented towards the fulness of God's final future.

Theological Perspectives on Hope

In the church's long journey through history, various theological themes have received differing emphases – including the concepts of eschatology and hope. At certain times, the emphasis has been on our future hope and the coming of God's final future in the consummation of all things. Yet this perspective tends to promote a world-denying form of Christianity. At other times, the emphasis has been on heaven coming to earth as a *realized* eschatology. Yet this perspective runs the danger of utopian thinking, promoting an emphasis on the faith-community in bringing about the kingdom of God. A more balanced theology would hold these perspectives in dialectical tension, perceiving both the "yet" and "not-yet" nature of the kingdom of God. Though our hope is oriented towards what God will do in the future, we also hope in what God is doing amongst us here and now. Thus, our hope is not relegated to a dim place in the distance, although we recognize the final consummation of all things, but our hope is very near. For all that we anticipate, long for, pray for, and work towards does spring up amongst us – though often in unexpected ways.

As Brian Hebblethwaite reminds us, looking towards God's final future is "not a matter of turning away from present tasks."[131] In the broad sweep of the church's history, Hebblethwaite notes the changing perspectives regarding Christian hope. In the early centuries, hope was located in the life of the church, and there was "no hope for society on earth apart from the millennial rule of Christ."[132] In the over fifteen hundred years that have followed, much of the emphasis has been on "the world above"[133] as our greatest hope, in contrast to the vicissitudes of life here below. In the eighteenth and nineteenth centuries, hope moved from a transcendental orientation to an immanent one, where the self-made human progresses through a confident evolution towards a grand

131. Hebblethwaite, *The Christian Hope*, 157.

132. Hebblethwaite, 200.

133. Hebblethwaite, 200.

future. Yet this confidence was shattered in the twentieth century after World War I and World War II.

Since that time, a broader consensus began to emerge. As Hebblethwaite notes, Roman Catholic theologians "were all anxious to bring out the bearing of Christian eschatological hope on the immediate historical future," and liberation theologians stressed that Christian eschatology "has inescapable implications at the level of social and political 'praxis.'"[134] Protestants also emphasized the hope for the renewal of both individuals and society. Hendrikus Berkhof speaks of the "sanctification of the world," and Jürgen Moltmann stresses that the "hope of resurrection, anticipated in Christ . . . opens, empowers, and demands Christian hope for this-worldly liberation in all its aspects."[135] The present emphasis, according to Hebblethwaite, is that the history of the world is seen in the future of God and in the consummation of all things.[136] Thus, our *anticipated* future with God is the inspiration for our witness and service in the *present*, which includes the call to emulate God's heart for the poor. At the same time, Hebblethwaite warns that we should hold to the *provisional* nature of all that we do.[137] In other words, the kingdom of God still beckons us and is never wholly within our grasp.

To summarize, Christian hope is always under threat and is constantly being chastened. In our twenty-first century world, there is so much that deeply concerns us: the threat to the viability of our planet, a politically and economically divided global world, the shifting power of empires, the reality of pandemics, the unknown implications of artificial intelligence, the increasing power of technology, the growth of surveillance societies, the ever-present threat of various forms of extremism, and the reality and spectre of war. These unsettling realities can make us deeply anxious. With a weakened church in the West, but a flourishing Majority world Christianity amidst settings of political instability, poverty, and corruption, many are wondering if hope for this world is sustainable.

Hope in the Writings of Jürgen Moltmann

Moltmann is a contemporary voice who can help us wrestle with both the challenges and possibilities of hope. First, Moltmann reminds us that hope is

134. Hebblethwaite, 160, 162.

135. Hebblethwaite, 189, 181.

136. Hebblethwaite, 201.

137. Hebblethwaite, 202, my emphasis.

faith-oriented in that our hope is rooted in the God "who comes to meet men and women out of the future," and so when we think and pray about Christ's second coming, "then he is already in the process of coming."[138] Second, our hope has everything to do with Christ's death and resurrection. As Moltmann says, Christ's terrible end "became his true beginning," and therefore Christian hope is about *new beginnings* – new life in Christ, new life in the kingdom of God, and "the new creation of all things."[139] Third, hope *empowers*. As Moltmann writes, hope gives us "courage for living" and "quickens" us "so that we can get up again out of failures, disappointments, and defeats."[140] Fourth, hope *anticipates*, *prays*, and *works towards change*. "Far from leading human beings away from the earth," Moltmann says, "hope leads them to the kingdom of God, which comes to earth."[141]

Finally, in imagining God's final future, Moltmann makes multiple key points. First, our future life is not rooted in our immortality, but in "the relationship of the whole person to the immortal God."[142] Second, however we may speculate about what happens to Christians after death, we know "*who* awaits us" and that "God's history with our lives will continue after our deaths."[143] Third, while our hope is for "universal reconciliation," the "decision is God's alone."[144] Fourth, the final future is the "cosmic incarnation of God," where "divinity and humanity interpenetrate," and where "eternal *fellowship with God*" is the beatific vision for the new heaven and the new earth.[145]

In Moltmann's classic *Theology of Hope*, we find similar themes to those listed above, but they are expressed in more dynamic and provocative ways. This form of writing is especially relevant to us today amidst the erosion of biblical grounding, lack of confidence in our institutions, and fears regarding the future of our world. Thus, we need to be provoked, and yet I think it is also necessary to turn Moltmann on his head. For while his starting point is that "hope emigrated . . . from the church," because the primary focus was on the future without the present,[146] it is now the other way round. We have lost

138. Moltmann, *In the End – The Beginning*, 87, 89.

139. Moltmann, ix, x.

140. Moltmann, xi.

141. Moltmann, 160.

142. Moltmann, 105.

143. Moltmann, 139, author's emphasis.

144. Moltmann, 117.

145. Moltmann, 150, 158, 156, author's emphasis.

146. Moltmann, *Theology of Hope*, 16.

the future because our focus is too much on the present. I must qualify this statement, however, by noting that the very nature of hope is dialectical in that it always has both present and future dimensions. For whatever we are hoping for in the future is usually connected to something we are working towards in the present. Thus, our persistent challenge is to discern where we need to place the accent in this dialectic.

Moltmann clearly identifies "Christian hope" with "resurrection hope" that is rooted in Jesus Christ and "*his* future."[147] This future is that the crucified Christ will be exalted as "the Word of the coming world of God,"[148] to whom we are called to give our utmost attention and loyalty. This future includes "the hope of the universal future of salvation for the world," which will be transformed so that the world becomes "what it is promised to be."[149] The task of the faith-community, therefore, is to be an exemplar of this kind of resurrection hope, which is its *identity* and *calling*. As Moltmann puts it, Christian "faith binds man [woman] to Christ. Hope sets this faith open to the comprehensive future of Christ."[150] Thus, the Christian "is ahead of himself [herself] in hope in God's promise," but at the same time, the Christian is involved "in the tensions and differentiations of hope, of mission, and of self-emptying."[151] In living between the tension of the yet and not-yet nature of the reign of God, the faith-community embodies a hope that is both oriented toward the future and challenging to our present-day context. In this way, the community of faith becomes an Exodus community - freed from bondage and living for the purposes of God. Moltmann argues that this liberating narrative will draw the laity to *live* this hope amidst their "worldly callings . . . and in their social roles."[152]

In this way, Moltmann calls the church to live "not from itself and for itself," but from the sovereignty and impartation of the "risen Lord." Through the eschatological dimensions of the sacraments of baptism and the Lord's Supper, the faith-community points toward and is empowered by the fulness of the kingdom of God.[153] As the faith-community is "engaged . . . in following Christ's service to the world," it "lays claim to the whole of humanity in [its]

147. Moltmann, 18, 17.

148. Moltmann, 299.

149. Moltmann, 302, 327.

150. Moltmann, 20.

151. Moltmann, 91.

152. Moltmann, 305.

153. Moltmann, 325–26.

mission."[154] In summary, Moltmann stresses that the church's mission is rooted in the death and resurrection of Christ, oriented toward the kingdom of God, and inspired by the OT prophetic tradition, and it involves the worldwide proclamation of the gospel, which is the task of all Christians.[155] Most simply put, the "Christian Church which follows Christ's mission to the world is engaged also in following Christ's service to the world."[156]

To summarize, hope is a central concept in Moltmann's theology. Because the faith-community is birthed in the hope of salvation and the unfolding of the kingdom of God with its vision of a new heaven and a new earth, the very nature of the church is to be an eschatological community that embodies "the mission of Christian hope."[157] Yet Moltmann is well aware of the present challenges for the church in seeking to live this hope in the world. He notes that in earlier times, such as the Christendom era, the church was seen as the "inner principle of the life of society" (Pope Pius XII, 1949) and the "healing centre of society."[158] In our age, however, the church has "lost the character of *cultus publicus*" because it has become the "*cultus privatus*," a religion of individualism that is "private, inward, edifying."[159] Thus religion has become the "cult" of the new subjectivity.[160]

Within the self-focused subjectivity of our present age, Moltmann believes that the church has a world-formative calling and task. Because Christians are marked by eschatological hope, they "will never be able to reconcile . . . [themselves] with the laws and constraints of this earth," and this fundamental "disloyalty" will cause the church to be a "constant disturbance in human society."[161] Yet this disturbance has a constructive task in hoping that the world will "become what it is promised to be" in the purposes of God's redemption.[162] According to Moltmann, this includes the hope for a just world, the fuller humanization of humanity, the "creative reshaping" of societal institutions, and peace for all society, including the created order.[163]

154. Moltmann, 327.
155. Moltmann, 327–29.
156. Moltmann, 327.
157. Moltmann, 334.
158. Moltmann, 307.
159. Moltmann, 310.
160. Moltmann, 311.
161. Moltmann, 21, 22.
162. Moltmann, 327.
163. Moltmann, 328–29, 330.

One may well wonder if Moltmann has set a much too grandiose task for the faith-community! Yet Moltmann recognizes that the church can only live as a *sign* and *servant* of this grand vision for the renewal of all things. For the eschatological hope that marks the church will lead to "action and suffering," and so Christians must embody a "creative discipleship" by giving ourselves to the "expectation of the promised future of the kingdom of God" while also living in an "age of diaspora,"[164] a time when the church is being marginalized.

Hope in the Writings of Jacques Ellul

My intention in this next section is not to set out a comprehensive analysis of Ellul's biblical and sociological perspectives,[165] but to discern how Ellul can point us toward a rich spirituality of hope that is theologically centred and world-engaging while also carrying a vision for the life and world to come. Put most simply, Ellul asserts that the "vision of God's people is both historical and prophetic and is lived in hope."[166] Therefore, "hope is in no way an escape into the future, but is . . . an active force, now."[167] According to Ellul, this hope is not simply a psychological imperative and posture, but a theological and spiritual gift. He writes that "in Christ," there is "a power which can cause hope to be born" because "Jesus Christ is the living hope."[168] For Ellul, hope is waiting for the kingdom of God, the presence of the Spirit, and the "return of Christ." Yet this waiting is not passive, but is a "wide-awake waiting"[169] for God's final future.

Ellul has woven the theme of hope throughout much of his writing, and there are also other important dimensions in his work. Ellul, a sociologist, writes as a lay-theologian in the biblical-theological field, where he explores many themes through the dialectic of being "in-Christ" and "in-the-world." Ellul is deeply concerned about the way that Christians *live* out their faith in society, and he is not reluctant to point out the failures of the church in history.[170] At the same time, Ellul is hopeful about the transformative power

164. Moltmann, 330, 337, 338.

165. Goddard, *Living the Word, Resisting the World*, has provided a wide-ranging interpretation of the life and work of Ellul.

166. Ellul, *On Freedom, Love, and Power*, 222.

167. Ellul, *Perspectives on Our Age*, 107.

168. Ellul, *Hope in Time of Abandonment*, 162, 165.

169. Ellul, 260–61.

170. Ellul, *The Subversion of Christianity*.

of God's revelation in Christ to renew individuals and the church to impact society through the prophetic voice and actions of those who have been impacted by Christ.[171]

Ellul's writings demonstrate both concern for the world as well as insightful understandings of society, as Ellul reads society's structures and ideologies, beauty and deep follies, perversions and lack of freedom and justice. To give one example, he is well-known for the way he has engaged the problem of technology in contemporary society.[172] Because Ellul is a contemporary transformational and missional thinker, a scholar and an activist, I am always surprised to see his name missing in missional texts.[173] During Ellul's life, his activism included political involvement, working with delinquent youth, and engaging ecological issues. He was informed by a critical and selective use of Marx, the philosophy of personalism, a modified Barthian theology, and a firm belief in the power of biblical revelation through the person and work of Christ. As Andrew Goddard observes, Ellul was "an activist whose personalist convictions and faith in Jesus Christ made him a revolutionary dissenter and true 'protest-ant,' who in living out the Word of God radically critiqued and resisted established institutions and the direction of the modern world."[174]

Ellul was particularly concerned about the misuse of power in society[175] and the human propensity towards creating alternative kingdoms to God's kingdom.[176] As a result, Goddard points out that "throughout [Ellul's] life he was constantly to be found on the margins"[177] rather than within mainstream institutions and movements. Marginality is an important dimension of seeking to understand Ellul and his work. As Ellul writes, "transformation of the church

171. Ellul, *The Presence of the Kingdom.*

172. Ellul, *The Technological Bluff.* Ellul's concern about technology has to do with the instrumentalization of life and a commitment to efficiency as a final goal. He argues that this "structures modern society," and it is so invasive that it leaves us "anxiety-ridden" (*Perspectives on Our Age*, 73, 89). But Ellul also says that we can live with technology "in the perspective of the Kingdom" (*The Presence of the Kingdom*, 72).

173. Bosch, *Transforming Mission*; Phillips and Coote, eds., *Toward the 21st Century in Christian Mission*; Verstraelen et al., eds., *Missiology: An Ecumenical Introduction.*

174. Goddard, *Living the Word, Resisting the World*, 50.

175. Ellul rejects the use of violence and is deeply concerned about the misuse of power. The "anarchism" that he promotes is one that "acts by means of persuasion, by the creation of small groups and networks" that denounce oppression and work for freedom and justice (*Christianity and Anarchy*, 11, 13).

176. Ellul, *The Presence of the Kingdom.*

177. Goddard, *Living the Word, Resisting the World*, 51.

does not begin at its human head, but with an explosion originating with those at the fringe."[178]

Ellul also believed that much of the human impulse is "idolatrous," which results in unexpected outcomes. While we need to work for the good, we may also have to work *against* the very good we are seeking to promote and institute. This involves a profound self-critical posture rather than a flag-waving conformism or a self-congratulatory triumphalism. Significantly, Ellul critiques the Christendom model, where church and society reinforce each other and where the church seeks political support to gain influence. For Ellul, the idea that a more powerful church can do greater good in society is an illusion. Thus, he argues that Christianity "should never seek to justify any political force," whether conservative or revolutionary.[179]

For Ellul, Christian hope is not rooted in religious institutions, but in the revelatory power of God, who "descends to humanity and joins us where we are."[180] This power liberates us, because the "Liberator" is Christ.[181] This liberating encounter with Christ is both a free gift of grace as well as an act of faith. As Ellul writes, faith "grasps me and takes me . . . where I do not want to go."[182] While Ellul does not go into much detail regarding his own journey of coming to faith, he says that the Bible "seduced me," and he experienced "a very sudden conversion."[183] In a most simple affirmation of faith, he writes that he "can affirm . . . that the hope is in God through Jesus Christ."[184]

To live this hope in Christ, we will have to relinquish all other hopes. Thus, if people already "have their hope," they "have no need of the hope that is in Christ."[185] In his writings, Ellul identifies some of the hopes we should abandon, including political systems, the power of technology, and any of our achievements that aren't birthed in the power of the Spirit. Ellul is deeply concerned about the way we so easily "deify" our own systems and the way we have created and embraced "the deified religious character of technology." Thus, we need to be iconoclastic, "destroy false images," and abandon our institutional attempts in the name of religion to control and market God. Ellul expresses

178. Ellul, *The Subversion of Christianity*, 212.

179. Ellul, 126–27.

180. Ellul, *Perspectives on Our Age*, 95.

181. Ellul, 103.

182. Ellul, *The Subversion of Christianity*, 162.

183. Ellul, *Perspectives on Our Age*, 13, 14.

184. Ellul, *Hope in Time of Abandonment*, 159.

185. Ellul, 160.

deep concern about how "we wish to *use* the divinities" and attempt "to take possession of God."[186] His concerns include how the institutional church seeks social power, adopts particular political ideologies when convenient, is oriented towards conservatism, conforms to culture, and escapes into "personal piety."[187]

While Ellul is often regarded as dark and pessimistic, this reading is premature.[188] Ellul is very hopeful about God's faithfulness, the power of God's revelation, the renewing and revitalizing work of the Holy Spirit,[189] which includes the renewal of the institutional church. Though there may be "dead institutional dogmas," he writes that the Bible "is always alive" and the "Holy Spirit has not been defeated."[190] Though he harshly says that "the archangel of mediocrity is the true master of the church,"[191] he also calls the church the bride of Christ and celebrates that Christ "cannot abandon the church."[192] Yet he believes that the church must be constantly renewed, for "the church institution can be valid only if there is interference, shock, overturning, and initiative on the part of God."[193] This disruptive and renewing work is the work of the Spirit. While Christ is the genesis and model of our hope, the Holy Spirit is the great empowerer, giving "hope where all is despair, the strength to endure in the midst of disaster, perspicacity not to fall victim to seduction, [and] the ability to subvert in turn all powers."[194] One can hardly be more hopeful!

In the following, I attempt to summarize Ellul's multi-layered gestalt of hope. First, Ellul acknowledges that all people place their hope in something, and so hope is generic to the human condition.

Second, Christian hope – through the power of Christ's revelation and the Spirit – needs to denude us of all our false hopes. Thus, Christian hope is both affirmative and critical. It affirms the power of Christ, and in his light exposes all false hopes, whether ideological or political. This has important implications. Christian hope is not an add-on to all other hopes, but hope in

186. Ellul, 95, 96.

187. Ellul, *The Subversion of Christianity*, 193.

188. Ellul speaks about his "known pessimism," but he exclaims, "I am not without hope, not at all" (*Hope in Time of Abandonment*, 167).

189. Ellul believes that "the Spirit is a power that liberates us from every bondage," and he laments that Christianity has "left the Holy Spirit unemployed" (*The Subversion of Christianity*, 12, 13).

190. Ellul, *The Subversion of Christianity*, 201–2.

191. Ellul, *Hope in Time of Abandonment*, 136.

192. Ellul, 136.

193. Ellul, 139.

194. Ellul, *The Subversion of Christianity*, 190.

God *alone*. Thus, conversion has profound significance, as one's whole world through Christ is turned upside down.

Third, Ellul is not enamoured with institutions, including the church, but he believes that they are necessary and important when impacted and renewed by the movement of the kingdom of God. Moreover, such renewal needs to occur constantly if hope is to remain alive and active.

Fourth, Christian hope is not simply an interior posture, but must be embodied. Ellul writes that Christians need to be an "incarnation" of Jesus Christ, who is "the living hope."[195] He further notes that "a hope lived and living is the prior condition for witness" to the world.[196] Moreover, he says that "the life of Christians is what gives testimony to God and to the meaning of this revelation" in Christ.[197] Though it is easy to categorize hope in emotional or psychological terms, Ellul challenges us by identifying living hope as an embodiment of the gospel. Such living hope occurs when the "church is forced back to its origins" and people become alive due to the "presence of the Holy Spirit," praying and witnessing in humility.[198]

Fifth, Ellul acknowledges the value of Moltmann's theology of hope, noting that we are not marching towards the kingdom of God, but "the Kingdom of God is bursting violently into our times."[199] However, the kingdom will not come in some grandiose way that we might expect. Rather, Ellul describes the kingdom as "God's secret presence in the world," which is in an "appearance of weakness."[200] While "God strips himself of power and presents himself to us as a little child," Ellul continues, "the incarnation of Jesus Christ has achieved all that I could hope for in terms of relationship with God."[201] For Ellul, God's way in the world is the way of Jesus Christ and the Beatitudes,[202] which is the way of redemption, restoration, forgiveness, peacemaking, and justice. Ellul points out that the kingdom of God is "visible only in hope," that the kingdom in Christ is fully not-yet, and that we don't progress towards the

195. Ellul, *Hope in Time of Abandonment*, 165.

196. Ellul, 165.

197. Ellul, *The Subversion of Christianity*, 6.

198. Ellul, 208, 209.

199. Ellul, *Hope in Time of Abandonment*, 172.

200. Ellul, *What I Believe*, 148.

201. Ellul, 150, 85.

202. Ellul stresses that in the incarnation, a "profound and instantaneous break has taken place" between the old order of things and the new that has come in Christ. Christians are to live that new order, which Ellul calls the "new order . . . of the Beatitudes" (*Ethics of Freedom*, 278).

kingdom, but it comes to us as God's "sovereign initiative."[203] Ellul describes this way of being and living as "apocalyptic," which is to live the "last" in the present and to "act at every moment as if this moment were the last."[204] This kingdom life is not about securing structures, but making a precarious journey of faith, hope, and love.

Sixth, Ellul does not sketch out a tidy program about how to live the journey of life and hope well. Instead, he accents *precarity*, where the Christian life remains dependent on God's continuing initiative. Thus, Ellul weaves surprising colours into the tapestry of hope that are usually missing. One strand that is usually missing in the theology of hope is the interplay between God's absence and our hope. Ellul writes that in the long journey of the church, there are "periods . . . or epochs of history in which God abandons man[kind] to . . . [its] folly," and thus a "man [woman] is without hope because God is silent."[205] He goes on to make the important point that just because "Jesus Christ is God-with-us," and Jesus was abandoned for our sake, this "does not at all preclude . . . abandonment."[206] Rather, Christians will experience the silence of God and the "desert."[207] Yet God's silence is never "final," for we are always abandoned "in God."[208] All of this points us toward the dark night of the soul. Even more specifically, our so-called mastery in the technological world cannot be transferred to our relationship with God, for God is sovereign and is not at our disposal.

Seventh, the silence of God can lead us to abandon hope, but Ellul wants to awaken us to believe that hope can actually become more alive "in our abandonment."[209] Moreover, he wants us to enter into "conflict with God," since "when God turns away, he has to be made to turn back to us again."[210] Ellul evokes the biblical tradition, where the people of God wrestle with God, lament,

---

203. Ellul, *Hope in Time of Abandonment*, 207, 208.

204. Ellul, *The Presence of the Kingdom*, 23.

205. Ellul, *Hope in Time of Abandonment*, 121, 111.

206. Ellul, 129.

207. Here we enter the domain of the "dark night of the soul." See St. John of the Cross, *Dark Night of the Soul*. For one man's experience of the dark night, see Gatfield, *Benson and the Narratives of the Organic Christian Life*. The experience of the "dark night" also invites us to spiritual direction (see Brown, *Reflected Love*) and spiritual discernment (see Alexander, *Stories of Hope and Transformation*).

208. Ellul, *Hope in Time of Abandonment*, 126, 122.

209. Ellul, 177.

210. Ellul, 179, 177.

and press God for answers.[211] We are not wrestling with God to satisfy our personal and whimsical needs, but for the presence of God to renew our lives, the church, and the world. Thus, we do not honour God's sovereignty by falling into a passive and sullen silence, but by actively engaging God. Ellul writes that we must not "sit in weary resignation," nor should we necessarily think that "we must repent" of something, but we "must arouse God" and recapture the idea that "God repented."[212] Ellul concludes by saying that "hope is protest . . . before God."[213] It is important to note that there is nothing impious about any of this, for the God of the biblical story is quite capable of dealing with both our sin and folly as well as our longings, cries, and lament, particularly when we cry out in faith and hope for the renewing presence of God. Ellul notes that even though humans can do many things and achieve much, we "cannot fill the void left by the withdrawal of God."[214] Nor should we try, for we will only come up empty-handed, or we will embrace ineffective substitutes.

Eighth, hope for Ellul "is not self-fulfilment by one's own powers."[215] He notes that hope is not about "acting on the basis of the possible," but rather, "hope is the passion for the impossible."[216] Thus hope is a radically different orientation to the world, not a little addendum to our knowing and acting. For when knowing and acting are impossible, then "hope is born."[217] Ellul argues that hope can only take place when all our "justifications" cease, and we "connect hope with . . . God's promise" and are carried by the Holy Spirit, "who leads us to this hope."[218]

In seeking to mine Ellul's writings for an implicit missional spirituality of hope, we can conclude the following. Because Ellul is deeply concerned about the church, he believes that we need to face the brokenness in our institutions and acknowledge our propensity towards mediocrity and unhelpful conservatism. Because Ellul is deeply concerned about the world, he has made a vigorous attempt to understand it in terms of its ideologies and social structures. Finally, he believes that our personal faith and the life of the faith-

---

211. Walter Brueggemann concurs, writing that "it is Israel's characteristic strategy of faith to *break the silence* and so to summon the absent, negligent God of promise back into active concern" (*Old Testament Theology*, 313).

212. Ellul, *Hope in Time of Abandonment*, 183

213. Ellul, 180.

214. Ellul, 190.

215. Ellul, 189.

216. Ellul, 194, 197.

217. Ellul, 201.

218. Ellul, 204, 202, 210.

community both need to be constantly renewed through the revelatory word in Christ and the life-giving Spirit. Through this ongoing renewal, the kingdom of God will irrupt in our lives and institutions, making the church a prophetic community in its witness to the world. This transformational spirituality lies at the heart of Ellul's writings. In conclusion, Christian hope for Ellul is not about our conformity to the world, nor the prowess of our religious institutions, but the ongoing disturbance and empowerment of the Spirit as those who are seeking to live *in* Christ and the Beatitudes bear witness to a renewed vision of God's final freedom.

Hope in the Writings of Segundo Galilea

Earlier in this book, we explored Segundo Galilea's notion of a double contemplation – the *transcendent* in our relation to God and the *incarnational* in relation to our service to the neighbour.[219] In this section, I will highlight the broad sweep of Galilea's understanding of the Christian life in terms of its witness and service before focusing on his spirituality of hope.

Galilea's writings highlight how the Christian life of faith and service is the "dynamic result of an encounter with the living Christ."[220] This results in "following Jesus Christ," and this "following" is the core of "Christian spirituality."[221] This spirituality is rooted in faith, which "is a grace, a gift,"[222] and it is "communitarian"[223] in that it is sustained and expressed in the faith-community through its commitment to word, sacraments, and the life-giving Spirit.[224] For Galilea, Christian "mission is an exalted form of following Jesus,"[225] which requires a "particular spirituality."[226] Yet this particular call is for all Christians, because "the life of the Christian takes the form of death to sin and selfishness, to live for God and others."[227]

Galilea identifies several characteristics for this life of faith, discipleship, and service in Christ. First, this life is a "paschal life" that is framed by the

219. See chapter 2 ("Towards a Missional Spirituality").

220. Galilea, *The Way of Living Faith*, 160.

221. Galilea, 29.

222. Galilea, 23.

223. Galilea, 42.

224. Galilea, 40–42.

225. Galilea, 157.

226. Galilea, 158.

227. Galilea, 4.

dialectic of death and resurrection.[228] Thus, it is sustained and nourished by the sacraments and the spiritual disciplines, and it is a path of relinquishment.

Second, this life in Christ involves the "incarnation of faith, hope, and love,"[229] which calls us to be with, identify with, and serve others. Galilea notes that "Christ the Lord truly became brother to us all," and therefore, in the spirit of "Christian fraternity," we need to express "service . . . [to] *all people*."[230] Galilea believes that the "missionary incarnates the transcendent"[231] and thus is a sign of the kingdom of God through his or her witness and service to others.

Third, Galilea emphasizes that a missional spirituality calls for the missioner's ongoing conversion. This conversion is multidimensional, for it involves turning from sin, "living according to the Spirit," and purifying "cultural deformities," such as racism, classism, and nationalism.[232] Galilea notes that the missioner's challenge is to move from personal conversion to "historical and collective conversion and the realization of a just society as the presence of the Kingdom."[233]

Fourth, missional spirituality involves a "spirit of itinerancy" and "the dynamic of exodus" as one leaves in order to enter the world of the other.[234] Galilea writes of entering the world of the poor, who need our witness and service and who also "evangelize us" by reminding us of the importance of "insecurity," "asceticism," and the "suffering God."[235]

Fifth, missional spirituality is contemplative since it calls us to the challenges of prayer. As Galilea writes, "prayer is dark and frustrating to our normal way of being and acting" in life.[236] Prayerful contemplation is profoundly transformational, as it calls us to seek the presence of God in "the living experience of the God of Jesus" so that we are "emptied of [our] egoism, pride, and the idols of the heart."[237] Through prayerful contemplation, we deepen our relationship with God and become more discerning about our own

228. Galilea, 59.

229. Galilea, 44.

230. Galilea, 111, 115, author's emphasis.

231. Galilea, 159.

232. Galilea, 87, 92, 94.

233. Galilea, 53.

234. Galilea, 165, 158.

235. Galilea, 135, 163, 83, 138.

236. Galilea, 102.

237. Galilea, 99.

psychopathologies and more prophetic in our engagement with injustice and idolatry in the world around us.

Within this broad frame of missional spirituality, Galilea has much to say about the dimension of hope. Most broadly, he believes that mission is related to the coming kingdom of God and is marked by a hope "against all hope" that calls us to great patience and "knowing how to wait" in the midst of our witness and service, even "in the face of the contradictions and failures of mission."[238] Thus, hope is not related to success, but to perseverance.[239] The following discussion highlights several key features of Galilea's theology of hope.

First, Galilea believes that Christian hope is rooted in the salvific work of Christ and the empowerment of the Spirit, who sustains us towards the future.[240] Galilea reminds us that hope is a gift from God that is "wrapped in human events," and thus we can see signs of hope in the word of God, the sustaining power of the sacraments, and acts of love and care.[241]

Second, hope is both a mystical experience and a purging power. Galilea goes on to suggest that hope needs ascetic practices to grow, for "asceticism eliminates the spiritual obstacles incompatible with faith, hope, and love."[242] This calls for an inner purgation, since our desires need "reorientation or purification," and "each time we choose a better 'treasure' our desire is purified and our hope grows."[243] He points out that this purification can take place through consolation as well as desolation, and he asserts that "every human experience can either deepen Christian hope" or destroy it.[244] For Galilea, asceticism involves "renouncing *what takes away or weakens our desire for God.*"[245]

Third, Galilea believes that hope in God can be lived even amidst the most dismal and desperate life circumstances. As such, it is a "radical 'sacrament.'"[246] In this context, Galilea suggests that the poor can bless us, for as they embrace "the gospel as a source of hope," they become "privileged witnesses of hope."[247]

238. Galilea, 164, 154, 164.

239. Galilea unpacks this in *A Spirituality of Hope*, which explores the theological, spiritual, and psychological features of hope.

240. Galilea, *A Spirituality of Hope*, 35.

241. Galilea, 45.

242. Galilea, 47.

243. Galilea, 48.

244. Galilea, 46.

245. Galilea, 68, author's emphasis.

246. Galilea, 36.

247. Galilea, 37.

Fourth, hope has a dialectic dynamic for Galilea, because the one who hopes is both "faithful to the present" and "inspired by the future."[248] This dialectical orientation synthesizes "the patient waiting for a promised paradise and the unswerving effort to make a more human world."[249] He points out that "one of the forms of human blindness is the capacity 'to see' life as present."[250] Thus, we need to see the signs of the kingdom of God that are already amongst us, as they are "the seeds of the future" embedded "in the present."[251] In this context, Galilea believes that we need to tap more deeply into the Christian mystical tradition so that we can "contemplate God in the present."[252]

Fifth, Galilea connects the concept of hope to the art of discernment, arguing that we need to be set free from *false* hopes, which Galilea refers to as "earthly . . . messianisms" and ideologies or technologies that promise much but fall short of the kingdom of God.[253] Moreover, he stresses that there is a tension between what we hope for and God's purposes, since God's promises "do not include everything that we humanly desire."[254] Thus, our hopes must be continually bent towards the will and purposes of God, and since we cannot ultimately know what is best for us, our aspirations should never be the last word.[255] Galilea also stresses our ongoing need for the "purification of desire"[256] so that God's word and way will become central to our life.

Sixth, Galilea writes that "to evangelize[257] is to practice hope."[258] He also proclaims that the work of evangelization is our "most excellent" action in the world, because it is a joy to "participate in the life and experience of God" through "the grace of Christ."[259] Thus, we seek to bless others because we ourselves have been blessed by the goodness of God. This work of evangelization

---

248. Galilea, 49.

249. Galilea, 8, 57.

250. Galilea, 64.

251. Galilea, 56.

252. Galilea, 62.

253. Galilea, 31.

254. Galilea, 9.

255. Galilea, 35.

256. Galilea, 67.

257. Whenever evangelicals use the word "evangelize," they are referring to the work of evangelism (gospel proclamation). When writers such as Galilea use this term, they are referring to the whole gamut of Christian witness and service, including the work of peacemaking and justice.

258. Galilea, *A Spirituality of Hope*, 77.

259. Galilea, 77.

seeks to "sanctify the world,"[260] and it is premised on the resurrection of Christ, which produces new life in us so that we can become a "new humanity" and be "no longer subject either to evil or to death."[261] In the light of God's final future, the work of evangelization includes the call "to transform the world for its own fulfillment," making it "more habitable for all" in the "service of human growth, eternal happiness, and ultimate destiny."[262] This grand calling includes the "humanization of personal relations" so that humanity is marked by the "law of love and a shared life."[263]

In summary, hope for Galilea is God-centred, incarnational, anticipatory of God's final future, and the central dynamic for the transformation of the world. Yet our hope is not a utopian dream, for the transformation of the world is not fully in our hands.[264] Our desires need "purification,"[265] and death – which Galilea describes as "*the last purification of the person* – is a bridge into our final hope.[266]

Conclusion

This chapter has emphasized that with hope in the nature and purposes of God, "there is never an end after which nothing is possible."[267] God's word continues to attract and transform individuals and communities. The Spirit continues to enliven and empower. The faith-community continues to sustain and renew its life in faith and hope and by serving the wider community. Marked by Christ's death and resurrection, Christians live *in* Christ in the hope of a fulness that is to come, both in this life and in the future. Christian assurance does not rest in a hope against hope, but in the hope of Christ, who is both with us and ahead of us in the life to come. This final fulness of life is not some mystical reality, but a reality that creation awaits and that the people of God long for in the blessedness of a new heaven and a new earth.[268] Without this hope, mission becomes a burdensome duty. When we live in this hope,

260. Galilea, 74.
261. Galilea, 22.
262. Galilea, 78.
263. Galilea, 78.
264. Galilea, 11.
265. Galilea, 48.
266. Galilea, 85.
267. Goldingay, *Old Testament Theology: Israel's Faith*, vol. 2, 353.
268. Middleton, *A New Heaven and a New Earth*.

we are sustained and encouraged to participate in the healing, restoring, and renewing purposes of God.

I have incorporated an array of perspectives into this chapter for several reasons. First, we need to listen to wisdom from both the OT and NT, as both testaments have a messianic orientation, and both emphasize the power of a future hope in God's purposes for the present. Second, I draw attention to the pendulum swings that have taken place in the theological tradition of the church. At times, the final future has been our great hope. At other times, the main focus has been on our present hope. In our present time, the emphasis is that as we live, work, pray, serve amidst the present circumstances of life, we are impacted and inspired by the vision of God's final future, which is already springing forth amongst us and calling us forward into eschatological reality. This focus calls us to be committed to the purposes of God and therefore out-of-step with the "worldliness" of our world, but also deeply committed to care for and influence our world. Third, I want to acknowledge the importance of listening to other disciplines – whether theological, philosophical, psychological, or sociological – in seeking to make sense of our world. Jerusalem and Athens have everything to do with each other, and so we need to listen to Scripture, to nature, and to myriad voices within society as we seek to understand our world and our place within it.

Psychologically, hope is an energizing dynamic. Sociologically, hope facilitates cooperation in bringing about change. Philosophically, hope is intrinsic to what it means to be human. Biblically, hope is centred in the creative and redeeming God, whose covenant faithfulness shines like the sun. Spiritually, hope is an inspiration of the Spirit. Missionally, hope is a labour of love in the long haul of reconciliation, peace, and justice. Thus, hope is a core element in any missional spirituality. We live in the hope of the God who is with us, in the hope of the God who has already provided for us through Christ, and in the hope of the God who is ahead of us, calling us forward into God's restoring and healing purposes for the whole world. This hope can energize and sustain us as we seek to live as a hermeneutic of the gospel and a prophetic witness in our world.[269]

269. This chapter is dedicated to the memory of the late Dr Allan Halladay, a colleague in the Department of Social Work and Social Policy at The University of Queensland in Brisbane, Australia. Allan was a living example of the power and winsomeness of hope. See Halladay, "The Role of Hope: In Social Work and Social Policy," *Zadok Papers*, no. S68 (1994).

Afterword

This book has sought to bring together biblical, theological, spiritual, missional, philosophical, and sociological resources in order to craft a missional spirituality. The fundamental thrust has been the *integration* of the head (theological formation), heart (spiritual formation), and hand (missional endeavours). This tapestry has included the integration of personal faith and corporate Christian identity, individual sin and structural evil, the work of evangelism and social transformation, contemplation and action, mysticism and prophecy.

This book has also sought to explore the dialectical dynamics of being in Christ and in the world, at home in the heart of God and a pilgrim on the road, heavenly minded and earthly engaged, a member of the body of Christ and a servant in the kingdom of God. Maintaining this dialectical undertow is vital if we are going to live a life of faith and hope in God's eschatological future. Living in this tension will keep us praying, longing, and hoping so that our witness will be inspired by the Holy Spirit – for apart from the fructifying work of the Holy Spirit, our endless Christian projects and activities will become brittle and calcified.

Futhermore, this book has been written in an ecumenical spirit. Generally speaking, I have sought to listen to the biblical narratives and to learn from various theological perspectives, such as the Anabaptists or the liberation theologians, among others. This approach may well leave some readers frustrated, as if I were constantly trying to "bet" on a certain theological "horse." But I am not that good at betting, and I think we have overplayed our theological distinctives at the cost of Christian graciousness, grassroots ecumenism, and missional cooperation. What is clear is that I have not attempted to nicely synthesize all the "voices" in this book. This book is an orchestral piece, not a single melody, although there are consistent themes throughout.

The introduction clearly outlines the key themes in this book, and so this afterword will take a different approach. First, I will talk about the nature of *provisionality* in all that we seek to do as servants of Christ in our world. Second, I will express my deep *concerns* about the church, particularly in the West. Third, I will *speculate* regarding future challenges and possibilities for the church in the world. It is important to note that I write all this with some anxiety, much anguish of heart,[1] along with the hope of the God who is ahead of us and continues to call us forward.

The Provisional Nature of our Service to Christ

During this period of the twenty-first century, our world has become increasingly fearful and uncertain, and we are seeing deeply concerning trends towards political totalitarianism and fascism. Facts have degenerated into opinions, and the concept of truth has become an ever-bouncing football amongst our evermore fragmented "tribal" groupings. Decent conversations across the divides are as scarce as "hen's teeth." Many are sceptical of our major political, industrial, and social institutions. And many carry weighty concerns about our deeply wounded planet, financial crises, pandemics, and the lack of job or food security. We also live beneath the threat of what may yet occur because of great global disparities and the ongoing march of changing empires. What is the role of the church and its mission in such fearful and difficult times?

One tendency is to look for "messianic" leaders to lead us into some supposed "promised land." Another is to "batten down the hatches" and move into a self-protective and isolating mode. Yet neither of these two moves are helpful. Rather than suggesting what the faith-community should *do* amidst these tumultuous circumstances, I suggest that we begin by exploring *who* God has called the church to *be*. Somewhat surprisingly, perhaps, I believe that we need to begin this exploration by addressing the *provisional* nature of our life in Christ. For the Christian life, by definition, is a life of faith, and a life of faith will involve trusting in the promises of God and seeking the presence of God through the Spirit as we bear witness to and serve the world around us.

This *provisional* nature is distinctive to the Christian journey, for we are always "on the way" as we seek to grow more fully into Christ and live towards the "yet" and "not-yet" of God's reign. On the one hand, the Christian life is about being "in Christ" as a "new creation," where "everything old has passed away [and] everything has become new" (2 Cor 5:17). On the other hand, we can only "see in a mirror, dimly" and have to acknowledge that "now, I only know in part" (1 Cor 13:12–13). This is the nature of our eschatological existence. Though the future of God has broken into our present and made it different, that future hope also reaches toward a fulness that is still yet to come. Thus, the journey *is* the destination – and a final arrival still awaits us.

1. See Ringma, "In the World and Sore Afraid," in *Fear and Faith*, 1–12.

Living between the first coming of Christ and the expected second coming of Christ, the Christian lives "in-between" worlds. Much restoration has taken place through the death and resurrection of Christ, but much greater restoration is yet to come in God's final future. If the very nature of the Christian life is marked by this precarity and provisionality, then the communities and institutions that we create will reflect this precarious and provisional nature as well. Thus, the church is not a pillar of institutional certainty, but a pilgrim community.[2] The faith-community has found a home in God, and yet it continues to be on the road. We have arrived in the sense that we have been reconciled to God through Christ, and yet we remain seekers. I will say more about this when I express some of my *concerns* about the contemporary church, but first I will touch on the provisional nature of our mission to the world.

Put most basically, we can't fix the world – we can't even fix ourselves! But we can enhance, bless, challenge, pray for, and witness to those around us. Seeking to serve the world means that we are not only called to serve our favourite people, but everyone – including those who live outside the margins of our middle-class comfort zones. We must constantly remind ourselves that God has a heart for the poor and is passionate about peacemaking and justice. Thus, if we seek to worship God, we are also called to share in God's passion for the world and to serve in all domains of life. Moreover, our service to the world is marked by reciprocal realities, for while we have something to give, there is also much that we need to receive.

This means that our view of the world, and society in particular, is to be positive and welcoming, for there is so much that is marked by the goodness of God's "common" grace. And yet we must also resist the "worldliness" of the world and its propensity towards idolatry. The best form of resistance is not simply to harp criticisms, but to live an embodied alternative. This expresses the missional imperative that flows from the incarnation, for Jesus Christ is not just a word from heaven, but the *living word* who has found a home in the faith-community and is the Lord of all. Thus, the church is not only called to bear witness to Christ, but to *live* as a hermeneutic of the gospel. The relationship between the church and the world is one of engagement and withdrawal, reciprocity and resistance, commonality and difference, blessing and prophetic witness. Navigating this relationship will require ongoing discernment.

2. Throughout the book, I have engaged various missional documents from major denominations. What is striking is that the language in these documents tends to be magisterial, but lacking in a humble outworking. This is also true of the Vatican II documents.

In living as a hermeneutic of the gospel, we feel our way into situations as we seek to understand our particular contexts. As we engage others, our neighbourhoods, our work, recreational places, and society as a whole, we develop relationships, learn from those whom we are seeking to serve, and slowly outwork our witness and service under the guidance of the sustaining and enlightening Spirit. As we seek to bless others, create services of care, and contribute to the common good, our hope is that others may also find the source of life – the grace of God in Christ through the Holy Spirit.

This approach revolves around prayer, discernment, visioning, planning, implementation, evaluation, reconfiguration, and repentance. Our greatest temptation is to seek the right formula or strategy, to build the right institutions, to come up with a grand plan to bless and impact the world. This is the path of self-sufficiency, even idolatry, and it will weaken our relationship with God, who is constantly longing to heal us, bless us, and empower us to participate in God's redemptive purposes for the world. As Christians, we can do much good in our world, but it can't be imposed. We can only invite, and thus we need to be a welcoming and humble community. Our greatest challenge is to *be* the change we wish to see. Provisionality is stamped on this way of being and acting in the world!

Concerns about the Church

My concerns about the church are not raised from a critical distance, but from inside the community of faith, for I have been part of the church all my life. While I have worked in the Majority World, most of my church experience has been in the Minority World, and these observations and challenges are primarily directed to the church in the West.

First, the church in the West is mostly led by clergy, and it comes across in the broader society as a religious institution that provides particular religious "goods" and services. Its primary "goods" are the assurance of grace and forgiveness and the promise of a future life in God's final future. Yet there is so much more to the story of the Christian faith-community! Thus, I am deeply concerned about the consumer mentality that dominates the Western church and believe that this needs to be challenged, for the church is not a religious supermarket, but a faith-community of worship, word and sacrament, mutual care, and witness and service in the world.

Second, I am very concerned about the lack of biblical and theological formation in the present-day church. Thus, I believe the church needs to be challenged to grow in the faith through catechetical instruction and discipleship training. The church also needs to be challenged to develop more prayerful and contemplative spiritual practices so that its members will deepen their relationship with God and be sustained and empowered to serve God's purposes in the world.

Third, the church is the body of Christ, whose "scattered" members have a living relationship with Jesus Christ. As the body of Christ, the church lives as an eschatological community, a prefigurement of the world to come through its worship, sacraments, fellowship, and service. The church is also a prophetic community in its annunciation of the good news and its denunciation of what is unjust in our world. Above all, it is a community of welcome, forgiveness, and healing. As such, the church in its formal ministry to society is called to love the neighbour and to work towards peace, justice, and well-being for our terribly divided world. Thus, we are not meant to be a conservative bastion in society, but a gentle *provocation.* As an eschatological and prophetic community of welcome and healing, the church needs to be challenged to grow into greater risk-taking. Jesus, who did not align himself with the Pharisees, Sadducees, political subversives, or isolating communitarians, was a *provocateur*, who sought to bring healing and change to *all* – and we are called to follow in his footsteps.

Fourth, I am concerned that people in the West want everything and then want Jesus as a happy add-on to all the "goodies" we already have. Yet any church marked by this consumer mentality has become "culturally captive." Thus, it is high time to recover the long tradition of *ascetic* practices in the life of the church. Within the Christian tradition, asceticism is not a way to earn "brownie" points for heavenly glory, but a willingness to relinquish things for the sake of the kingdom of God. We let go of something good for a greater good. Prayer, fasting, almsgiving, and other ascetic practices form us so that we can become servants in God's greater purposes.

Speculating about the Future of the Church

I would like to close with some *speculations* about the future of the church. I am not seeking to be prophetic, as that is neither my calling nor my burden, but we can very tentatively look down the corridors of time so that the faith-community can discern the role that it needs to play within our changing world. I have no doubt that the church will continue through the ages by the power of the gospel, the inspirational work of the Spirit, and the ongoing witness of women and men of faith.

First, life in the world may become much more difficult, and so we may need to learn spiritual and social *resilience* from our Majority world brothers and sisters, who have lived their faith through military dictatorships, earthquakes, typhoons, and situations of grave injustice and poverty.

Second, the twentieth century was a time of Christian martyrdom, though this may surprise readers who are out of touch with global Christianity. In the twenty-first century, we may well see that following Christ will involve a "baptism of blood." How will our current pedestrian Western Christianity prepare us for this?

Third, we may soon need to discover that church as a fifty-nine-minute liturgical event, or a ninety-minute worship time and "pep-talk," is insufficient to form us in a life of following of Jesus, particularly if we need to become more courageous and prophetic in our Christian service and witness. Thus, we may need to recover a way of being the church that is deeply grounded in the word, sacramental life, spiritual practices, and prophetic witness.

Fourth, the church will hopefully realize that Christians need to stop seeking status, privilege, and political clout or support, which is the current reality of state churches in many parts of the world. We need to remember that the incarnation, cross, and resurrection mark our Christian existence in the world. The resurrection does not guarantee us power and prestige, but rather a life of servanthood that is empowered by the Spirit, for the grand vision of the book of Revelation is the power of the "*Lamb* that was slain" (5:12).

Many more challenges will undoubtedly await us, as we still have so much to learn. But as we embark on the path of transformation into the way of Christ, may our hearts remain attuned to God, our great lover.

> Lord, I have heard your voice, calling at a distance.
> Guide my steps to you, Lord, guide my steps to you.
> Lord, I have heard your voice, calling at a distance.
> Guard my way to you, Lord, guard my way to you.
> Lord, I have heard your voice, calling at a distance.
> Keep my heart for you, Lord, keep my heart for you.
> Lord, I have heard your voice.[3]

3. *Celtic Daily Prayer*, 173.

About the Author

Charles Ringma has served in urban and cross-cultural mission for over thirty years in a variety of contexts, including Brisbane, Metro Manila, Vancouver, and Yangon. For over three decades, he has taught in colleges, seminaries, and universities in Australia, New Zealand, Southeast Asia, Europe, and Canada. He is Emeritus Professor of Regent College in Vancouver, an Honorary Associate Professor of The University of Queensland (UQ) in Brisbane, Professor in the PhD program at Asian Theological Seminary (ATS) in Metro Manila, and Honorary Research Fellow of Trinity College Queensland in Brisbane. He is a Franciscan Tertiary (*tssf*) and a Companion of Northumbria Community in Brisbane. He holds a PhD in philosophical hermeneutics from UQ and an Hon. Doctor of Divinity from ATS.

Bibliography

Adams, Ian. *Cave, Refectory, Road: Monastic Rhythms for Contemporary Living.* Norwich: Canterbury, 2010.

Alexander, Irene. *A Glimpse of the Kingdom in Academia: Academic Formation and Radical Discipleship.* Eugene: Wipf & Stock, 2013.

———. *Stories of Hope and Transformation: Mary's Gospel.* Eugene: Wipf & Stock, 2013.

Allen, Diogenes. *Spiritual Theology: The Theology of Yesterday for Spiritual Help Today.* Cambridge: Cowley, 1997.

Amaladoss, Michael. *Making All Things New: Dialogue, Pluralism, and Evangelization in Asia.* Maryknoll: Orbis Books, 1990.

Andrews, Dave. *Compassionate Community Work: An Introductory Course for Christians.* Milton Keynes: Authentic, 2006.

———. *A Divine Society: The Trinity, Community, and Society.* West End, QLD: Frank Communications, 2008.

———. *The Jihad of Jesus.* Eugene: Wipf & Stock, 2015.

Antonisamy, F. *An Introduction to Christian Spirituality.* Bombay: The Bombay Saint Paul Society, 1999.

Arias, Mortimer. *Announcing the Reign of God: Evangelization and the Subversive Memory of Jesus.* Philadelphia: Fortress Press, 1984.

Armstrong, Regis J., and Ignatius C. Brady, trans. *Francis and Clare: The Complete Works.* The Classics of Western Spirituality. New York: Paulist Press, 1986.

Athanasius. *The Life of Antony and The Letter to Marcellinus.* The Classics of Western Spirituality. New York: Paulist Press, 1979.

Augsburger, David. *Dissident Discipleship: A Spirituality of Self-Surrender, Love of God, and Love of Neighbor.* Grand Rapids: Brazos, 2006.

The Australian Concise Oxford Dictionary. Ed. G. W. Turner. Melbourne: Oxford University Press, 1987.

The Australian Hymn Book: with Catholic Supplement. Sydney: Collins, 1977.

Ball, Les. *Transforming Theology.* Eugene: Wipf & Stock, 2013.

Banks, Robert. *Paul's Idea of Community: The Early House Churches in their Historical Setting.* Surrey Hills, NSW: Anzea, 1979.

Barbour, Ian. *Myths, Models, and Paradigms: A Comparative Study in Science and Religion.* New York: Harper & Row, 1974.

Barker, Ash. *Slum Life Rising: How to Enflesh Hope in a New Urban World.* Dandenong, VIC: Urban Neighbours of Hope, 2012.

Barry, William, A., and Robert J. Doherty. *Contemplatives in Action: The Jesuit Way.* Mahwah: Paulist Press, 2005.

Barth, Hans-Martin. *The Theology of Martin Luther: A Critical Assessment.* Minneapolis: Fortress Press, 2013.

Barth, Karl. *Church Dogmatics: The Doctrine of Reconciliation.* Vol. 4, Part 3.2. Edinburgh: T&T Clark, 1962.

———. *Community, State, and Church: Three Essays.* Gloucester: Peter Smith, 1968.

———. *Evangelical Theology: An Introduction.* Translator G. Foley. Grand Rapids: Eerdmans, 1979.

Barton, John. "The Old Testament," in *The Study of Spirituality.* Eds. C. Jones, G. Wainwright, and E. Yarnold. New York: Oxford University Press, 1986.

Batstone, David. *Not for Sale: The Return of the Global Slave Trade – and How We Can Fight It.* New York: HarperSanFrancisco, 2007.

Bauman, Zygmunt. *Liquid Love: On the Fragility of Human Bonds.* Cambridge: Polity, 2003.

———. *Postmodernity and its Discontents.* Cambridge: Polity, 1997.

Bauman, Zygmunt, and Tim May. *Thinking Sociologically.* Oxford: Wiley-Blackwell, 2001.

Bayer, Oswald. *Martin Luther's Theology: A Contemporary Interpretation.* Translator T. H. Trapp. Grand Rapids: Eerdmans, 2008.

Bell, Daniel M. *The Desire of Economy: Christianity and Capitalism in a Postmodern World.* Grand Rapids: Baker Academic, 2012.

———. *Liberation Theology After the End of History: The Refusal to Cease Suffering.* London: Routledge, 2001.

Bellah, Robert N., Richard Madsen, William M. Sullivan, Ann Swidler, and Steven M. Tipton. *Habits of the Heart: Individualism and Commitment in American Life.* New York: Harper & Row, 1986.

Benefiel, Margaret, and Rebecca Darden Phipps. "Quakers and Social Transformation," in *Mysticism and Social Transformation.* Ed. Janet K. Ruffing. Syracuse: Syracuse University, 2001.

Benschop, Nel. *Wit Als Sneeuw: Gedichten Rondom Kerst.* Kampen, The Netherlands: Kok, 1974.

Berkhof, Louis. *Systematic Theology.* London: Banner of Truth Trust, 1958.

Berkouwer, Gerrit C. *The Providence of God.* Translator Lewis B. Smedes. Grand Rapids : Eerdmans, 1961.

Best, Ernest. *Following Jesus: Discipleship in the Gospel of Mark.* Sheffield: JSOT, 1981.

Beumer, Jurjen. *Henri Nouwen: A Restless Seeking for God.* Translator D. E. Schlaver and N. Forest-Flier. New York: Crossroad, 1997.

Bevans, Stephen B., and Roger P. Schroeder. *Constants in Context: A Theology of Mission for Today.* Maryknoll: Orbis Books, 2004.

———. *Prophetic Dialogue: Reflections on Christian Mission Today.* Maryknoll: Orbis Books, 2011.

Blakney, Raymond B., trans. *Meister Eckhart: A Modern Translation.* New York: Harper & Row, 1941.

Bloesch, Donald G. *Essentials of Evangelical Theology.* Vol. 1, 2. Peabody: Prince, 1998.

———. *The Future of Evangelical Christianity: A Call for Unity amid Diversity.* Colorado Springs: Helmers and Howard, 1988.

———. *Spirituality Old and New: Recovering Authentic Christian Life.* Downers Grove: InterVarsity Press, 2007.

Bloeser, Claudia. "Hope," in *Stanford Encyclopedia of Philosophy.* plato.stanford.edu/entries/hope/.

Blumhardt, Christoph. *Action in Waiting.* Farmington: Plough, 1998.

Boda, M. J. "Old Testament Foundations of a Christian Spirituality," in *Dictionary of Christian Spirituality.* Ed. G. G. Scorgie. Grand Rapids: Zondervan, 2011.

Boerma, Conrad. *The Rich, the Poor, and the Bible.* Philadelphia: Westminster, 1980.

Boff, Leonardo. *Ecclesiogenesis: The Base Communities Reinvent the Church.* Translated by Robert R. Barr. Maryknoll: Orbis Books, 1986.

———. *Holy Trinity: Perfect Community.* Translator P. Berryman. Maryknoll: Orbis Books, 2000.

———. *Saint Francis: A Model of Human Liberation.* Quezon City, Philippines: Claretian, 1984.

———. *Trinity and Society.* Translator P. Burns. Maryknoll: Orbis Books, 1988.

Boff, Leonardo, and Clodovis Boff. *Introducing Liberation Theology.* Maryknoll: Orbis Books, 1987.

Bonaventure. *The Life of St. Francis.* Translator E. Cousins. HarperCollins Spiritual Classics. New York: HarperOne, 2005.

Bonhoeffer, Dietrich. *Christ the Center.* Translator E. H. Robertson. New York: HarperSanFrancisco, 1978.

———. *The Cost of Discipleship.* Translator R. H. Fuller. London: SCM, 1959.

———. *Dietrich Bonhoeffer Works.* Vol. 1, *Sanctorum Communio.* Ed. Clifford J. Green. Minneapolis: Fortress Press, 1998.

———. *Dietrich Bonhoeffer Works.* Vol. 9, *The Young Bonhoeffer: 1918–1927.* Eds. Paul Duane Matheny, Clifford J. Green, and Marshall D. Johnson. Minneapolis: Fortress Press, 2003.

———. *Dietrich Bonhoeffer Works.* Vol. 10, *Barcelona, Berlin, New York, 1928–1931.* Ed. Clifford J. Green. Minneapolis: Fortress Press, 2008.

———. *Dietrich Bonhoeffer Works.* Vol. 12, *Berlin: 1932–1933.* Ed. Larry L. Rasmussen. Minneapolis: Fortress Press, 2009.

———. *Dietrich Bonhoeffer Works.* Vol. 13, *London, 1933–1935.* Ed. Keith Clements. Minneapolis: Fortress Press, 2007.

———. *Letters and Papers from Prison.* Enlarged edition. Ed. E. Bethge. New York: Touchstone, 1997.

———. *Ethics.* Translator Neville Horton Smith. New York: Touchstone, 1995.

———. *Life Together.* Translator J. W. Doberstein. New York: HarperSanFrancisco, 1954.

The Book of Alternative Services of the Anglican Church of Canada. Toronto: Anglican Book Centre, 1985.

The Book of Common Prayer. New York: Oxford University Press, 1990.

Book of Worship. Geelong, VIC: Reformed Churches, 1990.

Bornkamm, Gunther. *Paul.* Translator D. M. G. Stalker. London: Hodder & Stoughton. 1971.

Bosch, David. *Transforming Mission: Paradigm Shifts in Theology of Mission.* Maryknoll: Orbis Books, 1991.

Bouma-Prediger, Steven. *For the Beauty of the Earth: A Christian View of Creation Care.* Grand Rapids: Baker Academic, 2001.

Bouma-Prediger, Steven, and Brian J. Walsh. *Beyond Homelessness: Christian Faith in a Culture of Displacement.* Grand Rapids: Eerdmans, 2008.

Boyd, Stephen B. "Community as Sacrament in the Theology of Hans Schlaffer," in *Anabaptism Revisited.* Ed. Walter Klaasen. Scottdale: Herald, 1992.

Braaten, Carl E. *The Future of God: The Revolutionary Dynamics of Hope.* New York: Harper & Row, 1969.

Brandon, O. R. "Heart," in *Evangelical Dictionary of Theology.* Ed. Walter A. Elwell. Grand Rapids Baker, 1984.

Braswell, Michael, John Fuller, and Bo Lozoff. *Corrections, Peacemaking and Restorative Justice.* New York: Routledge, 2015.

Brent, Allen. *The Political History of Early Christianity.* London: T&T Clark, 2009.

Bromiley, Geoffrey, ed. *The International Standard Bible Encyclopedia,* 4 vols. Grand Rapids: Eerdmans, 1979–1988.

Brown, Christopher. *Reflected Love: Companioning in the Way of Jesus.* Eugene: Wipf & Stock, 2012.

Brueggemann, Walter. *Interpretation and Obedience: From Faithful Reading to Faithful Living.* Minneapolis: Fortress Press, 1991.

———. *The Land: Place as Gift, Promise, and Challenge in Biblical Faith.* Philadelphia: Fortress Press, 1977.

———. *Old Testament Theology: An Introduction.* Nashville: Abingdon, 2008.

———. *The Prophetic Imagination.* 2nd ed. Minneapolis: Fortress Press, 2001.

———. *The Psalms and the Life of Faith.* Ed. P. D. Miller. Minneapolis: Augsburg, 1995.

———. *Reverberations of Faith: A Theological Handbook of Old Testament Themes.* Louisville: Westminster John Knox, 2002.

———. *Theology of the Old Testament: Testimony, Dispute, Advocacy.* Minneapolis Fortress Press, 1997.

———. *Truth Speaks to Power: The Countercultural Nature of Scripture.* Louisville, : Westminster John Knox, 2013.

Brunner, Emil. *Our Faith.* Translator J. W. Rilling. London: SCM, 1949.

———. *The Word of God and Modern Man.* Translator D. Cairns. London: Epworth, 1965.

———. *Ons Geloof.* Translator E. Franken-Liefrinck. Amsterdam: W. Ten Have N.V., 1965.

Buber, Martin. *I and Thou.* 2nd ed. New York: Charles Scribner's Sons, 1958.

Bultmann, Rudolf. *Theology of the New Testament*. Vol. 1. Translator Kendrick Grobel. London: SCM, 1952.

———. *Theology of the New Testament*. Vol. 2. Translator Kendrick Grobel. London: SCM, 1955.

Burleigh, Michael. *Sacred Causes: Religion and Politics from the European Dictators to Al Qaeda*. London: HarperPress, 2006.

Burridge, Kenelm. *New Heaven, New Earth: A Study of Millenarian Activities*. Oxford: Blackwell, 1969.

Butigan, Ken, Mary Litell, and Louis Vitale. *Franciscan Nonviolence: Stories, Reflections, Principles, Practices, and Resources*. Las Vegas: Pace e Bene, 2003.

Butler, Dom Cuthbert. *Western Mysticism: Augustine, Gregory and Bernard on Contemplation and the Contemplative Life*. Mineola: Dover, 2003.

Byrne, Laviniaand. *Traditions of Spiritual Guidance*. Collegeville: Liturgical Press, 1990.

Cahn, S. M., and D. Shatz. *Contemporary Philosophy of Religion*. New York: Oxford University Press, 1982.

Calvin, John. *Treatises Against the Anabaptists and Against the Libertines*. Ed. Benjamin Wirt Farley. Grand Rapids: Baker Academic, 1982.

———. *Institutes of the Christian Religion: 1541 French Edition*. Translator E. A. McKee. Grand Rapids: Eerdmans, 2009.

"Cape Town Commitment." http://www.lausanne.org/content/ctc/ctcommitment, 2010.

Cardenal, Ernesto. *The Gospel in Solentiname*. 4 vols. Maryknoll: Orbis Books, 1982.

Carney, T. F. *The Shape of the Past: Models and Antiquity*. Kansas: Coronado, 1975.

Carr, Neville. "The Creation Story: Relevance for Today's Church," in *Pub Theology: Where Potato Wedges and a Beer are a Eucharistic Experience*. Eds. Irene Alexander and Charles Ringma. Manchester: Piquant, 2021.

Carretto, Carlo. *I, Francis: The Spirit of St Francis of Assisi*. London: Collins, 1982.

Carvalhaes, Claudio. *Liturgies from Below: Praying with People at the Ends of the World*. Nashville: Abingdon, 2020.

Cassian, John. "The Conferences of Cassian," in *Western Asceticism*. Vol. 12, The Library of Christian Classics. Translator O. Chadwick. London: SCM, 1958.

Catechism of the Catholic Church. Manila, Philippines: ECCCE, Word of Life, 1994.

Celebrating Common Prayer: A Version of the Daily Office, SSF. London: Mowbray, 1994.

Celtic Daily Prayer: From the Northumbria Community. New York: HarperOne, 2002.

Celtic Daily Prayer: Book Two: Farther Up and Farther In. London: William Collins, 2015.

Chan, Simon. *Spiritual Theology: A Systematic Study of the Christian Life*. Downers Grove: InterVarsity Press, 1998.

Chilcote, Paul Wesley. *Recapturing the Wesley's Vision*. Downers Grove: InterVarsity Press, 2004.

Chittister, Joan. *Wisdom Distilled from the Daily: Living the Rule of St. Benedict Today*. Collegeville: Liturgical Press, 1990.

Ciardi, Fabio. *Koinonia: Spirituality and Theology of the Growth of Religious Community.* Quezon City, Philippines: Claretian, 1999.

Clark, Elizabeth. *Ascetic Piety and Women's Faith: Essays on Late Ancient Christianity.* Lewiston: Edwin Mellen, 1986.

Cohen, Leonard. *Book of Longing.* London: Penguin. 2006.

Colledge, Eric. *The Mediaeval Mystics of England.* New York: Charles Scribner's Sons, 1961.

Collins, Kenneth J., ed. *Exploring Christian Spirituality: An Ecumenical Reader.* Grand Rapids: Baker, 2000.

Colson, Charles, with E. S. Vaughn. *Against the Night: Living in the New Dark Ages.* Ann Arbor: Servant, 1989.

Common Prayer: A Liturgy for Ordinary Radicals. Eds. Shane Claiborne, Jonathan Wilson-Hartgrove, and Enuma Okoro. Grand Rapids: Zondervan, 2010.

Cone, James H. *God of the Oppressed.* New York: Seabury Press, 1975.

Costas, Orlando. *Liberating News: A Theology of Contextual Evangelization.* Grand Rapids: Eerdmans, 1989.

Cotterell, Peter. *Mission and Meaningless: The Good News in a World of Suffering and Disorder.* London: SPCK, 1990.

Craig, Jenni M. *Servants Among the Poor.* Mandaluyong City, Philippines: OMF Lit., 1998.

Craven, Margaret. *I Heard the Owl Call My Name.* London: Picador, 1974.

Creeds of the Churches. Ed. John H. Leith. Garden City: Anchor, 1963.

Croatto, J. Severino. *Exodus: A Hermeneutics of Freedom.* Maryknoll: Orbis Books, 1981.

———. "The Socio-historical and Hermeneutical Relevance of Exodus," *Concilium* 189 (1987).

Crosby, Michael H. *Finding Francis, Following Christ.* Maryknoll: Orbis Books, 2007.

Cunningham, Lawrence S. *Thomas Merton and the Monastic Vision.* Grand Rapids: Eerdmans, 1999.

Cunningham, Lawrence S., and Keith J. Egan. *Christian Spirituality: Themes from the Tradition.* New York: Paulist Press, 1996.

D'Abreo, Desmond A. *From Development Worker to Activist.* Revised edition. Mangalore, India: Deeds, 1989.

Davies, Oliver, trans. *Celtic Spirituality.* The Classics of Western Spirituality. New York: Paulist Press, 1999.

———, trans. "Sermons of Columbanus," in *Celtic Spirituality.* The Classics of Western Spirituality. New York: Paulist Press, 1999.

Davies, Oliver, Paul D. Janz, and Clemens Sedmak. *Transformation Theology.* London: T&T Clark, 2007.

Davis, Mark. "Bauman's Compass: Towards a Sociology of Hope." http://www.Users/HP/Downloads/Baumans-compass-towards-a-sociology-of-hope%20(1).pdf.

Dawn, Marva J. *Keeping the Sabbath Wholly: Ceasing, Resting, Embracing, Feasting.* Grand Rapids: Eerdmans, 1997.

Day, Dorothy. "The Only Solution is Love," in *Mystics, Visionaries and Prophets: A Historical Anthology of Women's Spiritual Writings*. Ed. Shawn Madigan. Minneapolis: Fortress Press, 1998.

———. *Selected Writings*. Ed. Robert Ellsberg. Maryknoll: Orbis Books, 1993.

de Gruchy, John W., ed. *The Cambridge Companion to Dietrich Bonhoeffer*. Cambridge: Cambridge University Press, 1999.

Deiros, Pablo A. "Towards a Pneumatological-Spiritual Missiology," in *Evangelical, Ecumenical, and Anabaptist Missiologies in Conversation*. Eds. James R. Kraybill, Walter Sawatsky, and Charles E. Van Engen. Maryknoll: Orbis Books, 2006. de Souza Martins, Jose. "The crisis of hope in the sociology crisis." http://www.scielo.br/j/ea/e/flppZLCqsyPWYGGdDgPZuR/?format=pdf&lang=en.

Delio, Ilia. *Franciscan Prayer*. Cincinnati: St. Anthony Messenger Press, 2004.

De Vries, Hent. *Religion and Violence: Philosophical Perspectives from Kant to Derrida*. Baltimore: John Hopkins University, 2002.

de Waal, Esther, ed. *The Celtic Vision: Prayers and Blessings from the Outer Hebrides*. Petersham: St. Bede's, 1990.

———. *Seeking God: The Way of St. Benedict*. Collegeville: Liturgical Press, 2001.

Dickau, Tim. *Plunging into the Kingdom Way: Practicing the Shared Strokes of Community, Hospitality, Justice, and Confession*. Eugene: Cascade, 2011.

Dockery, David S. "An Outline of Paul's View of the Spiritual Life: Foundation for an Evangelical Spirituality," in *Exploring Christian Spirituality: An Ecumenical Reader*. Ed. Kenneth J. Collins. Grand Rapids: Baker, 2000.

Dorr, Donal. *Integral Spirituality: Resources for Community, Justice, Peace and the Earth*. Melbourne: Collins Dove, 1990.

———. *Mission in Today's World*. Dublin: Columba, 2000.

———. *The Social Justice Agenda: Justice, Ecology, Power, and the Church*. Quezon City, Philippines: Claretian, 1993.

Downey, Michael. "Lay People and Spirituality," in *The New SCM Dictionary of Christian Spirituality*. Ed. Philip Sheldrake. London: SCM, 2005.

Downey, Michael, ed. *The New Dictionary of Catholic Spirituality*. Collegeville: Liturgical Press, 1993.

Driver, John. "The Kingdom of God: Goal of Messianic Mission," in *The Transfiguration of Mission: Biblical, Theological and Historical Foundations*. Ed. Wilbert R. Shenk. Scottdale: Herald, 1993.

———. *Life Together in the Spirit: A Radical Spirituality for the Twenty-First Century*. Walden: Plough, 2015.

———. "Unanticipated Journey for Sharing an Anabaptist and Liberationist Perspective on the Gospel," in *Evangelical, Ecumenical, and Anabaptist Missiologies in Conversation*. Eds. James R. Krabill, Walter Sawatsky, and Charles E. Van Engen. Maryknoll: Orbis Books, 2006.

Dulles, Avery. *Models of the Church*. Expanded edition. New York: Image, 1987.

Duncan, Michael. *Costly Mission: Following Christ into the Slums.* Monrovia: MARC, 1996.

Dych, William. *Karl Rahner.* Outstanding Christian Thinkers. London: Continuum, 1992.

Dyck, Cornelius J. "The Anabaptist Understanding of the Good News," in *Anabaptism and Mission.* Ed. Wilbert R. Shenk. Scottdale: Herald, 1984.

Eagleton, Terry. *After Theory.* New York: Basic Books, 2003.

Easum, B. *Preaching for Church Transformation.* Nashville: Abingdon, 2010.

Ebadi, Shiran. *Until We Are Free: My Fight for Human Rights in Iran.* London: Rider, 2016.

Ebeling, Gerhard. *Luther: An Introduction to his Thought.* Translator R. A. Wilson. London: Collins, 1970.

Edwards, Jonathan. *Select Works of Jonathan Edwards.* Vol. 3, *The Religious Affections.* London: The Banner of Truth Trust, 1961.

Eichrodt, Walther. *Theology of the Old Testament.* Vol. 1. Translator J. A. Baker. London: SCM, 1961.

Ekblad, Bob. *A New Christian Manifesto: Pledging Allegiance to the Kingdom of God.* Louisville: Westminster John Knox, 2008.

Ellacuria, Ignacio. "Utopia and Prophecy in Latin America," in *Mysterium Liberationis: Fundamental Concepts of Liberation Theology.* Eds. Ignacio Ellacuria and Jon Sobrino. Maryknoll: Orbis Books, 1993.

Ellacuria, Ignacio, and Jon Sobrino, eds. *Mysterium Liberationis: Fundamental Concepts of Liberation Theology.* Maryknoll: Orbis Books, 1993.

Elliot, Elisabeth. *No Graven Image.* Wheaton: Good News, 1982.

Elliot, Neil. *Liberating Paul: The Justice of God and the Politics of the Apostle.* Maryknoll: Orbis Books, 1994.

Elliott, Anthony, and Charles Lemert. *The New Individualism: The Emotional Costs of Globalization.* London: Routledge, 2006.

Ellithorpe, Anne-Marie. *Towards Friendship-Shaped Communities: A Practical Theology of Friendship.* Oxford: Wiley-Blackwell, 2022.

Ellul, Jacques. *Anarchy and Christianity.* Translator Geoffrey W. Bromiley. Grand Rapids: Eerdmans, 1991.

———. *The Ethics of Freedom.* Translator Geoffrey W. Bromiley. Grand Rapids: Eerdmans, 1976.

———. *Hope in Time of Abandonment.* Translator C. E. Hopkin. New York: Seabury Press, 1973.

———. *The New Demons.* Translator C. E. Hopkin. New York: Seabury Press, 1975.

———. *On Freedom, Love, and Power.* Ed. Willem H. Vanderburg. Toronto: University of Toronto, 2010.

———. *Perspectives on Our Age: Jacques Ellul Speaks on his Life and Work.* Ed. Willem H. Vandenburg. Concord: Anansi, 1997.

———. *The Presence of the Kingdom*. 2nd ed. Translator Olive Wyon. Colorado Springs: Helmers & Howard, 1989.

———. *The Subversion of Christianity*. Translator G. W. Bromiley. Grand Rapids: Eerdmans, 1986.

———. *The Technological Bluff*. Translator G. W. Bromiley. Grand Rapids: Eerdmans, 1990.

———. *What I Believe*. Translator G. W. Bromiley. Grand Rapids: Eerdmans, 1989.

Erickson, Millard J. *Christian Theology*. Manila, Philippines: CGM, 1995.

Escobar, Samuel. *In Search of Christ in Latin America: From Colonial Image to Liberating Savior*. Carlisle: Langham Global Library, 2019.

Estep, William R. *The Anabaptist Story*. Grand Rapids: Eerdmans, 1975.

Evdokimov, Paul. *Ages of the Spiritual Life*. Crestwood: St. Vladimir's Seminary Press, 1998.

Fahey, Joseph J., and Richard Armstrong, eds. *A Peace Reader: Essential Readings on War, Justice, Non-Violence, and World Order*. Revised edition. New York: Paulist Press, 1992.

Fanning, Steven. *Mystics of the Christian Tradition*. London: Routledge, 2001.

Farley, Edward. *Theologia: The Fragmentation and Unity of Theological Education*. Philadelphia: Fortress Press, 1983.

Farrely, Elizabeth. "There is still hope in a horrible year," in *Sydney Morning Herald* (December 31, 2016–January 1, 2017).

Faubion, James D. *The Shadows and Lights of Waco: Millennialism Today*. Princeton: Princeton University Press, 2001.

Ferm, Deane W. *Third World Liberation Theologies: A Reader*. Maryknoll: Orbis Books, 1986.

Ferm, Deane W., ed. *Third World Liberation Theologies*. Maryknoll: Orbis Books, 1988.

Fitzsimons, Peter. *Batavia*. North Sydney, NSW: William Heinemann, 2011.

Flannery, Austin. *The Basic Sixteen Documents, Vatican Council II*. Revised edition. Northport: Costello, 1996.

Ford, David F., and Mike Higton, with Simeon Zahl, eds. *The Modern Theologians Reader*. Oxford: Wiley-Blackwell, 2012.

Ford, Michael. *Wounded Prophet: A Portrait of Henri J. M. Nouwen*. New York: Doubleday, 1999.

Foster, Richard J., and James. B. Smith, eds. *Devotional Classics: Selected Readings for Individuals and Groups*. New York: HarperSanFrancisco, 1993.

Foust, Thomas F., Andrew Kirk, Werner Ustor, and George R. Hunsberger. *A Scandalous Prophet: The Way of Mission after Newbigin*. Grand Rapids: Eerdmans, 2002.

Francis and Clare: The Complete Works. The Classics of Western Spirituality. Translators Regis J. Armstrong and Ignatius C. Brady. New York: Paulist Press, 1982.

Francis of Assisi: Early Documents. Vol. 1, *The Saint*. Vol. 2, *The Founder*. Vol. 3, *The Prophet*. Eds. Regis J. Armstrong, J. A. Wayne Hellmann, and William J. Short. New York: New City Press, 1999–2001.

Franklin, S. T. "Panentheism," in *Evangelical Dictionary of Theology*. Ed. W. E. Elwell. Grand Rapids: Baker Book House, 1984.

Freire, Paulo. *A Pedagogy of the Oppressed*. New York: Continuum, 1970.

Frenkel, Francoise. *No Place to Lay One's Head*. Translator S. Smee. North Sydney, NSW: Vintage, 2017.

Fretheim, Terence E. *Creation Untamed: The Bible, God, and Natural Disasters*. Grand Rapids: Baker Academic, 2010.

Friedmann, Robert. *The Theology of Anabaptism: An Interpretation*. Scottdale: Herald, 1973.

Frost, Michael, and Alan Hirsch. *The Shaping of Things to Come*. Peabody: Hendrickson, 2003.

Frost, Robert. *Selected Poems*. London: Penguin, 1973.

Fry, Timothy, ed. *The Rule of Saint Benedict*. Vintage Spiritual Classics. New York: Vintage, 1998.

Fukuyama, Francis. *The End of History and the Last Man*. New York: Avon, 1993.

Furnish, Victor Paul. "Uncommon Love and the Common Good," in *In Search of the Common Good*. Eds. Dennis P. McCann and Patrick D. Millar. New York: T&T Clark, 2005.

Gadamer, Hans-Georg. *Truth and Method*. 2nd edition. London: Sheed and Ward, 1993.

Gager, John G. *Kingdom and Community: The Social World of Early Christianity*. Englewood Cliffs: Prentice-Hall, 1975.

Galilea, Segundo. *The Beatitudes: To Evangelize As Jesus Did*. Translator R. R. Barr. Maryknoll: Orbis Books, 1984.

———. *Following Jesus*. Translator H. Phillips. Quezon City, Philippines: Claretian, 1994.

———. *Spirituality of Hope*. Translator T. Cambias. Quezon City, Philippines: Claretian, 1990.

———. *Temptation and Discernment*. Translator S. J. Ross. Washington: Institute of Carmelite Studies, 2013.

———. *The Way of Living Faith: A Spirituality of Liberation*. Translator J. W. Diercksmeier. Quezon City, Philippines: Claretian, 1991.

Gallardo, Jose. "Ethics in Mission," in *Anabaptism and Mission*. Ed. Wilbert R. Shenk. Scottdale: Herald, 1984.

Gatfield, Terry. *Benson and Narratives of the Organic Christian Life*. Reservoir, VIC: Morning Star, 2019.

Geertz, Clifford. *The Interpretation of Cultures*. New York: Basic Books, 2000 (First published 1973).

George, Timothy. "The Spirituality of the Radical Reformation," in *Christian Spirituality: High Middle Ages and Reformation*. Ed. Jill Raitt. London: SCM, 1988.

Gerstenberger, Erhard S. *Theologies in the Old Testament*. Translator John Bowden. Minneapolis: Fortress Press, 2002.

Gerth, Hans H., and C. Wright Mills, eds. *Max Weber: Essays in Sociology.* New York: Oxford University Press, 1958.

Gibbard, Mark. "The Adaptation of Historic Spirituality for Today," in *The Study of Spirituality.* Eds. Cheslyn Jones, Geoffrey Wainwright, and Edward Yarnold. New York: Oxford University Press, 1986.

Giddens, Anthony. *Sociology.* Cambridge: Polity, 1991.

Gill, Athol. *The Fringes of Freedom: Following Jesus, Living Together, Working for Justice.* Sydney, NSW: Lancer, 1990.

———. *Life on the Road: The Gospel Basis for a Messianic Lifestyle.* Homebush, NSW: Lancer, 1989.

Gish, Arthur G. *Living in Christian Community: A Personal Manifesto.* Scottdale: Herald, 1979.

———. *The New Left and Christian Radicalism.* Grand Rapids: Eerdmans, 1970.

Gittens, Anthony J. *Bread for the Journey: The Mission of Transformation and the Transformation of Mission.* Maryknoll: Orbis Books, 1993.

———. "Mission and Spirituality," in *The New SCM Dictionary of Christian Spirituality.* Ed. Philip Sheldrake. London: SCM, 2005.

Goddard, Andrew. *Living the Word, Resisting the World: The Life and Thought of Jacques Ellul.* Carlisle: Paternoster, 2002.

Goldingay, John. *Old Testament Theology: Israel's Faith.* Vol. 2. Downers Grove: IVP Academic, 2006.

———. *The Theological Diversity and Authority of the Old Testament.* Grand Rapids: Eerdmans, 1987.

Gorman, Michael J. *Participating in Christ: Explorations in Paul's Theology and Spirituality.* Grand Rapids: Baker Academic, 2019.

Gorospe, Athena. *Narrative and Identity: An Ethical Reading of Exodus 4.* Leiden, The Netherlands: Brill, 2007.

———. "What Does the Bible Say About Migration?: Three Approaches to the Biblical Text," in *God at the Borders: Globalization, Migration and Diaspora.* Eds. Charles R. Ringma, Karen Hollenbeck-Wuest, and Athena Gorospe. Manila, Philippines: OMF Lit., 2015.

Gorospe, Athena, and Charles Ringma. *Judges: A Pastoral and Contextual Commentary.* Asia Bible Commentary Series. Carlisle: Langham Global, 2016.

Gorospe, Athena, and Charles Ringma, eds. *How Long, O Lord? The Challenge and Promise of Reconciliation and Peace.* Carlisle: Langham Global, 2018.

Gorospe, Athena, Charles Ringma, and Karen Hollenbeck-Wuest, eds. *Why, O God? Disaster, Resiliency, and the People of God.* Manila, Philippines: OMF Lit., 2017.

Grabbe, L. L. "Shaman, Preacher or Spirit Medium? The Israelite Prophet in the Light of Anthropological Models," in *Prophecy and the Prophets in Ancient Israel.* Proceedings of the Oxford Old Testament Seminar. Ed. J. Day. New York: T&T Clark, 2010.

Grant-Thomson, J. *Jodie's Story.* Sydney, NSW: Anzea, 1991.

Green, Graham. *The Heart of the Matter.* New York: Bantam, 1956.

Green, Thomas H. *Prayer and Common Sense.* Makati, Philippines: St. Pauls, 1996.

———. *When the Wells Run Dry: Prayer Beyond the Beginnings.* Notre Dame: Ave Maria, 1979.

Gregory of Nazianzus. "On the Love of the Poor." http://www.memoriadei.wordpress.com/2010/10/20/on-the-love-of-the-poor/.

Grenz, Stanley J. *Reason for Hope: The Systematic Theology of Wolfhart Pannneberg.* 2nd edition. Grand Rapids: Eerdmans, 2005.

———. *Theology for the Community of God.* Grand Rapids: Eerdmans, 2000.

Grenz, Stanley J., and Roger E. Olson. *20th Century Theology: God and the World in a Transitional Age.* Downers Grove: InterVarsity Press, 1992.

Griffin, Emilie, ed. *Bernard of Clairvaux: Selected Works.* New York: HarperSanFrancisco, 2005.

Grigg, Viv. *Companion to the Poor.* Sydney, NSW: Albatross, 1984.

Groody, Daniel G. *Globalization, Spirituality, and Justice.* Maryknoll: Orbis Books, 2007.

Gross, Leonard. "Sixteenth-Century Hutterian Mission," in *Anabaptism and Mission.* Ed. Wilbert R. Shenk. Scottdale: Herald, 1984.

Guder, Darrell L. *The Continuing Conversion of the Church.* Grand Rapids: Eerdmans, 2000.

Guder, Darrell L. *Missional Church: A Vision for the Sending of the Church in North America.* Grand Rapids: Eerdmans, 1998.

Gurion, Vigen. *The Melody of Faith: Theology in an Orthodox Key.* Grand Rapids: Eerdmans, 2010.

Gutierrez, Gustavo. *The Power of the Poor in History: Selected Writings.* Translator R. R. Barr. London: SCM, 1983.

———. *A Theology of Liberation.* 15th Anniversary Edition. Translators Sister Caridad Inda and John Eagleson. Maryknoll: Orbis Books, 1988.

———. *We Drink from Our Own Wells.* Translator M. J. O'Connell. Maryknoll: Orbis Books, 1984.

Hall, Douglas J. *The Stewardship of Life in the Kingdom of Death.* Grand Rapids: Eerdmans, 1992.

Hanson, Paul D. *The People Called: The Growth of Community in the Bible.* San Francisco: Harper & Row, 1986.

Hardy, Dennis. *Alternative Communities in Nineteenth Century England.* London: Longman, 1979.

Hardy, Edward. R., ed. "Address on Religious Instruction," in *Christology of the Later Fathers.* The Library of Christian Classics. Philadelphia: Westminster, 1954.

Harper, J. Steven. "Old Testament Spirituality," in *Exploring Christian Spirituality: An Ecumenical Reader.* Ed. Kenneth J. Collins. Grand Rapids: Baker, 2000.

Hart, Kevin. *Postmodernism: A Beginner's Guide.* Oxford: One World, 2004.

Hastings, Ross. *Missional God, Missional Church: Hope for Re-Evangelizing the West.* Downers Grove: IVP Academic, 2012.

Hauerwas, Stanley, and William H. Willimon. *Resident Aliens.* Nashville: Abingdon, 1989.

Haynes, Stephen R. *The Bonhoeffer Phenomenon: Portraits of a Protestant Saint.* Minneapolis: Fortress Press, 2004.

Heaney, Robert S. *Post-Colonial Theology: Finding God and Each Other Amidst the Hate.* Eugene: Cascade, 2019.

Hebblethwaite, Brian. *The Christian Hope.* Revised edition. Oxford: Oxford University Press, 2010.

Hendricks, Hermann. *The Parables of Jesus: Studies in the Synoptic Gospels.* Makati, Philippines: St. Paul, 1990.

Hennelly, Alfred T., ed. *Liberation Theology: A Documentary History.* Maryknoll: Orbis Books, 1990.

Henriot, Peter J., Edward DeBerri, and Michael Schultheis. *Catholic Social Teaching.* Australian edition. Melbourne, VIC: Collins Dove, 1992.

Herberg, Will. "The Social Philosophy of Karl Barth," in *Community, State, and Church: Three Essays by Karl Barth.* Gloucester: Peter Smith, 1968.

Hernandez, Wil. *Henri Nouwen and Spiritual Polarities: A Life of Tension.* New York: Paulist Press, 2012.

Herrin, Judith. *The Formation of Christendom.* London: Fontana, 1989.

Hildegard of Bingen. *Selected Writings.* Penguin Classics. Translator M. Atherton. London: Penguin, 2001.

Hochschild, A. *Bury the Chains: The British Struggle to Abolish Slavery.* London: Pan, 2005.

Holder, Arthur. *Blackwell Companion to Christian Spirituality.* Oxford: Wiley-Blackwell, 2005.

Holt, Bradley P. *Thirsty for God: A Brief History of Christian Spirituality.* Minneapolis: Augsburg, 1993.

Horan, Daniel P. *The Franciscan Heart of Thomas Merton.* Notre Dame: Ave Maria, 2014.

Houston, James M. *The Transforming Friendship: A Guide to Prayer.* Vancouver: Regent College, 2010.

Hubbard, David A. "Hope in the Old Testament," *Tyndale Bulletin* 34 (1983). http://www.legacy.tyndalehouse.com/tynbul/Library/TynBull_1983_34_02_Hubbard_HopeinOT.pdf.

Huebner, Chris K. *A Precarious Peace: Yoderian Explorations on Theology, Knowledge, and Identity.* Waterloo: Herald Press, 2006.

Hunsberger, George R., and Craig Van Gelder, eds. *The Church Between Gospel and Culture: The Emerging Mission in North America.* Grand Rapids: Eerdmans, 1996.

Huntemann, Georg. *The Other Bonhoeffer: An Evangelical Reassessment of Dietrich Bonhoeffer.* Translator Todd Huizinga. Grand Rapids: Baker, 1993.

Hunter, George G. III. *The Celtic Way of Evangelism.* Nashville: Abingdon, 2000.

Hutton, Rodney R. *Charisma and Authority in Israelite Society.* Minneapolis: Fortress Press, 1994.

Hyma, Albert. *The Brethren of a Common Life*. Grand Rapids: Eerdmans, 1950.

Hynson, Leon O. *To Reform the Nation: Theological Foundations of Wesley's Ethics*. Grand Rapids: Francis Asbury, 1984.

Ignatieff, Michael. *The Needs of Strangers*. New York: Picador, 2001.

Ingleby, Jonathan. *Beyond Empire: Postcolonialism and Mission in a Global Context*. Central Milton Keynes: Author House, 2010.

Israel, Martin. *Exorcism: The Removal of Evil Influences*. London: SPCK, 1997.

Jack, Kristen, ed. *The Sound of Worlds Colliding: Stories of Radical Discipleship from Servants to Asia's Urban Poor*. Phnom Penh: Harvest, 2009.

Jacobs, Jane. *Dark Age Ahead*. New York: Random House, 2004.

Janzen, David. *The Intentional Christian Community Handbook: For Idealists, Hypocrites, and Wannabe Disciples of Jesus*. Brewster: Paraclete Press, 2013.

Jegen, Mary E. *Just Peacemakers: An Introduction to Peace and Justice*. New York: Paulist Press, 2006.

Jehle, Frank. *Ever Against the Stream: The Politics of Karl Barth, 1906–1968*. Translators Richard and Martha Burnett. Grand Rapids: Eerdmans, 2002.

Jenkins, Philip. *The Next Christendom: The Coming of Global Christianity*. 3rd edition. New York: Oxford University Press, 2011.

Jenson, Robert W. "Luther's Contemporary Theological Significance," in *The Cambridge Companion to Martin* Luther. Ed. D. K. McKim. Cambridge: Cambridge University Press, 2003.

———. "The Triunity of Common Good," in *In Search of the Common Good*. Eds. Dennis P. McCann and Patrick D. Miller. New York: T&T Clark, 2005.

John of the Cross. *Dark Night of the Soul*. Translator E. Allison Peers. Mineola: Dover, 2003.

Jones, Cheslyn, Geoffrey Wainwright, and Edward Yarnold, eds. *The Study of Spirituality*. New York: Oxford University Press, 1986.

Jones, E. Stanley. *The Unshakable Kingdom and the Unchanging Person*. Nashville: Abingdon, 1972.

Jones, Paul Hedley. *Sharing God's Passion: Prophetic Spirituality*. Milton Keynes: Paternoster, 2012.

Jorgensen, Johannes. *Saint Francis of Assisi: A Biography*. Translator T. O. Sloane. New York: Longmans, Green and Co., 1913.

Julian of Norwich. *Revelations of Divine Love*. Penguin Classics. Translator C. Wolters. London: Penguin, 1966.

Kagawa, Toyohiko. *Meditations on the Cross*. Translators Helen F. Topping and Marion R. Draper. London: SCM, 1936.

Kalantzis, George. *Caesar and the Lamb: Early Christian Attitudes on War and Military Service*. Eugene: Cascade, 2012.

Karkkainen, Velli-Matti. *Pneumatology: The Holy Spirit in Ecumenical, International, and Contextual Perspective*. Grand Rapids: Baker Academic, 2002.

Karotemprel, Sebastian, ed. *Following Christ in Mission.* Manila, Philippines: Pauline, 1996.

Kavanaugh, Keiran, and Otilio Rodriguez, trans. *The Collected Works of St. John of the Cross.* Washington: Institute of Carmelite Studies, 1979.

Kelly, Anthony, and Sandra Sewell. *With Head, Heart, and Hand: Dimensions of Community Building.* Brisbane, QLD: Booralong, 1988.

Kelly, Geoffrey B., and F. Burton Nelson. *The Cost of Moral Leadership: The Spirituality of Dietrich Bonhoeffer.* Grand Rapids: Eerdmans, 2003.

Kettle, David. "Gospel, Authority and Globalization," in *A Scandalous Prophet: The Way of Mission after Newbiggin.* Ed. T. F. Foust. Grand Rapids: Eerdmans, 2002.

Kierkegaard, Søren. *Attack Upon "Christendom."* Translator W. Lowrie. Princeton: Princeton University Press, 1968.

———. *Either/Or.* Vol. 1. Translators F. and L. M. Swenson. Garden City: Anchor, 1959.

———. *Either/Or.* Vol. 2. Translator W. Lowrie. Garden City: Anchor, 1959.

Killen, Patricia O'Connell, and John de Beer. *The Art of Theological Reflection.* New York: Crossroad, 1994.

Kimbrough, S. T., ed. *Orthodox and Wesleyan Spirituality.* Crestwood: St. Vladimir's Seminary Press, 2002.

King, Ursula. *Christian Mystics: Their Lives and Legacies Throughout the Ages.* Mahwah: Hidden Spring, 2001.

Kinnamon, Michael, and Brian E. Cope, eds. *The Ecumenical Movement: An Anthology of Key Texts and Voices.* Geneva: WCC, 1997.

Kinsler, Ross, and Gloria Kinsler. *The Biblical Jubilee and the Struggle for Life.* Pasay City, Philippines: Pauline, 2000.

Kirk, J. Andrew. *What is Mission? Theological Explorations.* London: Darton, Longman & Todd, 1999.

Klaassen, Walter. *Anabaptism: Neither Catholic Nor Protestant.* Revised edition. Waterloo: Conrad, 1981.

Klaassen, Walter, ed. *Anabaptism Revisited.* Scottdale: Herald, 1992.

Knierim, Rolf P. *The Task of Old Testament Theology.* Grand Rapids: Eerdmans, 1995.

Knowles, David. *Christian Monasticism.* New York: McGraw-Hill, 1969.

Koenig, John. *New Testament Hospitality: Partnership with Strangers as Promise and Mission.* Eugene: Wipf & Stock, 2001.

Kolodiejchuk, Brian, ed. *Mother Teresa: Come Be My Light.* New York: Rider, 2007.

Kraus, C. Norman. *The Authentic Witness: Credibility and Authority.* Grand Rapids: Eerdmans, 1979.

———. "Anabaptism and Evangelicalism," in *Evangelicalism and Anabaptism.* Ed. C. Norman Kraus. Scottdale: Herald, 1979.

Kraybill, Donald B. *The Upside-Down Kingdom.* Scottdale: Herald, 1978.

Kraybill, James R., Walter Sawatsky, and Charles E. Van Engen, eds. *Evangelical, Ecumenical, and Anabaptist Missiologies in Conversation.* Essays in Honor of Wilbert R. Shenk. Maryknoll: Orbis Books, 2006.

Kung, Hans. *On Being a Christian.* Translator E. Quinn. London: Fount Paperbacks, 1978.

Kyle, Richard G. *Popular Evangelicalism in American Culture.* New York: Routledge, 2018.

Ladd, George E. *A Theology of the New Testament.* London: Lutterworth, 1975.

Ladinsky, Daniel. *Love Poems from God: Twelve Sacred Voices from the East and West.* New York: Penguin, 2002.

Laing, Mark. "The Changing Face of Mission: Implications for the Southern Shift in Christianity," *Missiology* 34 (2006).

Lane, Belden C. *The Solace of Fierce Landscapes: Exploring Desert and Mountain Spirituality.* New York: Oxford University Press, 1998.

Lane, George A. *Christian Spirituality: An Historical Sketch.* Chicago: Loyola University Press, 1984.

Langmead, Ross. *The Word Made Flesh: Towards an Incarnational Missiology.* New York: University Press of America, 2004.

Lapp, John A. "The Global Mennonite History Project," in *Evangelical, Ecumenical, and Anabaptist Missiologies in Conversation.* Eds. James R. Krabill, Walter Sawatsky, and Charles E. Van Engen. Maryknoll: Orbis Books, 2006.

Lapsley, Jacqueline. "Biblical Dimensions: Introduction," in *In Search of the Common Good.* Eds. Dennis P. McCann and Patrick D. Miller. New York: T&T Clark, 2005.

Law, William. *A Serious Call to a Devout and Holy Life.* Ed. John W. Meister. Philadelphia: Westminster, 1955.

Lee, Jung Young. *Marginality: The Key to Multicultural Theology.* Minneapolis: Fortress Press, 1995.

Lehmann, Helmut T., ed. *Luther's Works.* Vols. 31–55. St. Louis: Concordia / Philadelphia: Fortress Press, 1958–1986.

Levinas, Emmanuel. *Basic Philosophical Writings.* Eds A. P. Peperzak, S. Critchley, and R. Bernasconi. Bloomington: Indiana University Press, 1996.

———. *Humanism of the Other.* Translator N. Poller. Chicago: University of Illinois Press, 2006.

Lewis, A. J. *Zinzendorf the Ecumenical Reformer: A Study in the Moravian Contribution to Christian Mission and Unity.* London: SCM Press, 1962.

Liechty, Daniel, ed. *Early Anabaptist Spirituality: Selected Writings.* The Classics of Western Spirituality. New York: Paulist Press, 1994.

Lindberg, Carter. *Beyond Charity: Reformation Initiatives for the Poor.* Minneapolis: Fortress Press, 1993.

Linder, R. D. "Fast, Fasting," in *Evangelical Dictionary of Theology.* Ed. Walter A. Elwell. Grand Rapids: Baker, 1984.

Littell, Franklin Hamlin. *The Anabaptist View of the Church.* 2nd edition. Boston: Starr King, 1958.

———. "The Anabaptist Theology of Mission," in *Anabaptism and Mission.* Ed. Wilbert R. Shenk. Scottdale: Herald, 1984.

Lohse, Bernard. *Martin Luther's Theology: Its Historical and Systematic Development.* Translator Roy A. Harrisville. Minneapolis: Fortress Press, 1999.

Louf, Andre. *In the School of Contemplation.* Collegeville: Liturgical Press, 2015.

Louth, Andrew. "The Cappadocians," in *The Study of Spirituality.* Eds. Cheslyn Jones, Geoffrey Wainwright, and Edward Yarnold. New York: Oxford University Press, 1986.

———. *The Origins of the Christian Mystical Tradition: From Plato to Denys.* 2nd edition. Oxford: Oxford University Press, 2007.

Luckman, Harriet A., and Linda Kulzer, eds. *Purity of Heart: In Early Ascetic and Monastic Literature.* Collegeville: Liturgical Press, 1999.

Mackesy, Charlie. *The Boy, the Mole, the Fox and the Horse.* London: Penguin, 2019.

MacNutt, Francis. *Healing.* Revised edition. Notre Dame: Ave Maria, 1999.

Macquarrie, John. *20th Century Religious Thought: The Frontiers of Philosophy and Theology, 1900–1970.* London: SCM, 1971.

Madame Guyon. *Union with God.* Augusta: Christian Books, 1981.

Madigan, Shawn, ed. *Mystics, Visionaries and Prophets: A Historical Anthology of Women's Spiritual Writings.* Minneapolis: Fortress Press, 1998.

Maggay, Melba P. *Transforming Society.* Oxford: Regnum Lynx, 1994.

Maggay, Melba P., ed. *The Gospel in Culture: Contextualization Issues through Asian Eyes.* Manila: OMF Lit., 2013.

Main, John. *The Way of Unknowing: Expanding Spiritual Horizons through Meditation.* Makati, Philippines: St. Paul's, 1991.

Mangalwadi, Vishal. *Truth and Social Reform.* London: Spire, 1989.

Mankell, Henning. *The White Lioness.* Translator L. Thompson. London: Vintage, 2009.

Mathewes, Charles. *A Theology of Public Life.* Cambridge: Cambridge University Press, 2007.

May, Rollo. *Power and Innocence: A Search for the Sources of Violence.* New York: W. W. Norton, 1998.

McCann, Dennis P. "The Common Good in Catholic Social Teaching," in *In Search for the Common Good.* Eds. by Dennis P. McCann and Patrick D. Miller. New York: T&T Clark, 2005.

McCann, Dennis P., and Patrick D. Miller, eds. *In Search of the Common Good.* New York: T&T Clark, 2005.

McFague, Sallie. *Models of God: Theology for an Ecological, Nuclear Age.* Philadelphia: Fortress Press, 1987.

McGinn, Bernard. *The Presence of God: A History of Christian Mysticism.* New York: Crossroad-Herder, 1991–2020.

McGinn, Bernard, ed. *The Essential Writings of Christian Mysticism.* New York: The Modern Library, 2006.

McGovern, Arthur F. *Liberation Theology and Its Critics: Towards an Assessment.* Quezon City, Philippines: Claretian, 1991.

McGrath, Alister E. *Christian Theology: An Introduction.* 6th edition. Oxford: Wiley-Blackwell, 2017.

———. *Historical Theology: An Introduction to the History of Christian Thought.* Oxford: Wiley-Blackwell, 1998.

———. *Historical Theology: An Introduction to the History of Christian Thought.* 2nd edition. Oxford: Wiley-Blackwell, 2013.

McKim, Donald K., ed. *The Cambridge Companion to Martin Luther.* Cambridge: Cambridge University Press, 2003.

McLaren, Brian. *A Generous Orthodoxy.* Grand Rapids: Zondervan, 2004.

McMichael, Philip. *Development and Social Change: A Global Perspective.* Thousand Oaks: Pine Forge, 1996.

Meijer-Schuiling, Berendien. *Knoppen.* Kampen, The Netherlands: Kok, 1935.

Meisted, Tore, "The Missiology of Charles Wesley and Its Links to the Eastern Church," in *Orthodox and Wesleyan Spirituality.* Ed. S. T. Kimbrough. Crestwood: St. Vladimir's Seminary Press, 2002.

Mellis, Charles J. *Committed Communities: Fresh Streams for World Missions.* Pasadena: William Carey Library, 1976.

Mendoza, Noli. "Faith at the Border, Faith on the Move: Migrations, Transitions, and Transformations in Act 8–11," in *God at the Borders: Globalization, Migration, and Disaspora.* Eds. Charles R. Ringma, Karen Hollenbeck-Wuest, and Athena Gorospe. Manila, Philippines: OMF Lit., 2015.

Merton, Thomas. *Contemplation in a World of Action.* Garden City: Doubleday, 1971.

———. *Contemplative Prayer.* London: Darton Longman & Todd, 1969.

———. *The Monastic Journey.* London: Sheldon, 1977.

———. *No Man is an Island.* San Diego: Harcourt Brace Jovanovich, 1955.

———. *Seeds of Contemplation.* Wheathampstead: Anthony Clarke, 1972.

———. *The Wisdom of the Desert.* New York: New Directions, 1970.

Metaxas, Eric. *Amazing Grace: William Wilberforce and the Heroic Campaign to End Slavery.* Oxford: Monarch, 2007.

Metz, Johann Baptist. *A Passion for God: The Mystical-Political Dimension in Christianity.* Translator J. Matthew Asley. Mahwah: Paulist Press, 1998.

Middleton, J. Richard. *A New Heaven and a New Earth: Reclaiming Biblical Eschatology.* Grand Rapids Baker Academic, 2014.

Miller, Alex. *The Passage of Love.* Sydney, NSW: Allen & Unwin, 2017.

Milosz, Czeslaw. *Second Space: New Poems.* New York: Ecco, 2004.

Mishra, Pankaj. *Age of Anger: History of the Present.* London: Allen Lane, 2017.

Moltmann, Jürgen. *A Broad Place: An Autobiography.* Translator Margaret Kohl. Minneapolis: Fortress Press, 2009.

———. *Ethics of Hope.* Translator Margaret Kohl. Minneapolis: Fortress Press, 2012.

———. *Experiences in Theology: Ways and Forms of Christian Theology.* Translator Margaret Kohl. Minneapolis: Fortress Press, 2000.

———. *In the End – The Beginning: The Life of Hope*. Translator Margaret Kohl. Minneapolis: Fortress Press, 2004.
———. *Theology of Hope: On the Ground and the Implications of a Christian Eschatology*. Translator James W. Leitch. London: SCM, 1967.
———. *The Trinity and the Kingdom of God*. Translator Margaret Kohl. London: SCM, 1981.
Moore, Charles E., ed. *Called to Community: The Life Jesus Wants for His People*. Walden: Plough, 2016.
Mother Teresa. *Come Be My Light*. Ed. Brian Kolodiejchuk. New York: Rider, 2007.
———. *No Greater Love*. Novato: New World Library, 2002.
———. *One Heart Full of Love*. Ann Arbor: Servant, 1988.
Mott, Stephen C. *Biblical Ethics and Social Change*. New York: Oxford University Press, 1982.
Mouton, Ray. *In God's House: A Novel About One of the Great Scandals of Our Time*. London: Head of Zeus, 2012.
Muller, Karl. *Mission Theology: An Introduction*. Nettetal, Germany: Steyler Verlag, 1987.
Murray, Stuart. *The Naked Anabaptist: The Bare Essentials of a Radical Faith*. Scottdale: Herald, 2010.
Myers, Ched. *Binding the Strong Man: A Political Reading of Mark's Story of Jesus*. Maryknoll: Orbis Books, 1988.
Nahon, Alice. *Schaduw: Gedichten*. Antwerpen, The Netherlands: De Nederlandsche Boekhandel, 1941.
———. *Vondelingskens: Gedichten*. Antwerpen, The Netherlands: De Nederlandsche Boekhandel, 1934.
Neville, David, ed. *Prophecy and Passion: Essays in Honour of Athol Gill*. Adelaide, SA: Australian Theological Forum, 2002.
Newbigin, Lesslie. *The Gospel in a Pluralist Society*. Grand Rapids: Eerdmans, 1989.
———. *The Open Secret: An Introduction to the Theology of Mission*. Revised edition. Grand Rapids: Eerdmans, 1995.
Newell, J. Philip. *Listening for the Heartbeat of God: A Celtic Spirituality*. London: SPCK, 2008.
Nicholl, Sarah Louise. "Towards Integrated Mission for the Evangelical Lausanne Movement." Unpublished PhD thesis, The University of Queensland, Brisbane, Australia, 2021.
Niebuhr, H. Richard. *Christ and Culture*. New York: Harper & Row, 1956.
Nietzsche, Friedrich. *Beyond Good and Evil: Prelude to a Philosophy of the Future*. Translator W. Kaufman. New York: Vintage, 1989.
Noll, Mark A. *The Scandal of the Evangelical Mind*. Grand Rapids: Eerdmans, 1994.
Norris, Kathleen. *Acedia and Me: A Marriage, Monks, and a Writer's Life*. New York: Riverhead, 2008.
Nouwen, Henri J. M. *Clowning in Rome: Reflections on Solitude, Celibacy, Prayer, and Contemplation*. New York: Image, 1979.

———. *¡Gracias! A Latin American Journal.* New York: Harper & Row, 1983.
———. *The Road to Daybreak: A Spiritual Journey.* New York: Doubleday, 1988.
———. *Sabbatical Journey: The Diary of His Final Year.* New York: Crossroad, 1998.
———. *Seeds of Hope.* Eds. Robert Durback. London: Darton, Longman and Todd, 1989.
———. *The Way of the Heart: Desert Spirituality and Contemporary Ministry.* Minneapolis: Seabury Press, 1981.
———. *With Open Hands.* Notre Dame: Ave Maria, 1995.
———. *The Wounded Healer: Ministry in Contemporary Society.* New York: Image, 1979.
Nouwen, Henri J. M., J. M. NcNeil, and D. P. Morrison. *Compassion: A Reflection on the Christian Life.* London: Darton, Longman and Todd, 1982.
O'Brien, David J., and Thomas A. Shannon, eds. *Catholic Social Thought: The Documentary Heritage.* Maryknoll: Orbis Books, 1992.
O'Donohue, John. *Anam Cara: A Book of Celtic Wisdom.* New York: Harper Perennial, 1997.
Oliver, E. H. *The Social Achievements of the Christian Church.* Toronto: Board of Evangelism and Social Service of the United Church of Canada, 1930.
Oliver, Mary. *New and Selected Poems.* Boston: Beacon, 1992.
Omar, Irfan A., and Michael K. Duffy. *Peacemaking and the Challenge of Violence in World Religions.* Oxford: Wiley-Blackwell, 2015.
Ott, Craig, Stephen J. Strauss, and Timothy C. Tennent. *Encountering Theology of Mission: Biblical Foundations, Historical Developments, and Contemporary Issues.* Grand Rapids: Baker Academic, 2010.
Padilla, C. René. *Mission Between the Times.* Grand Rapids: Eerdmans, 1985.
Palmer, G. E. H., P. Sherrard, and K. Ware, eds. *The Philokalia: The Complete Text.* Vol. 1. London: Faber & Faber, 1983.
Palugod, S. *Toward the Abundant Life: Transforming Lives, Transforming Communities,* Mandaluyong City, Philippines: OMF Lit., 2008.
Patric, A. S. *Black Rock, White City.* Melbourne, VIC: Transit Lounge, 2015.
Peachey, Paul. "The 'Free Church'?: A Time Whose Idea Has Not Come," in *Anabaptism Revisited.* Ed. Walter Klaassen. Scottdale: Herald, 1992.
Pelikan, Jaroslav, ed. *Luther's Works.* Vols. 1–30. St. Louis: Concordia / Philadelphia: Fortress Press, 1958–1986.
Pennington, M. Basil. *Centering Prayer: Renewing an Ancient Christian Prayer Form.* Makati, Philippines: St. Paul, 1989.
Perkins, John. *Justice Roll Down: John Perkins Tells His Own Story.* Ventura: Regal, 1976.
———. *Restoring At-Risk Communities: Doing it Together and Doing it Right.* Grand Rapids: Baker, 1995.
Peters, George W. *A Biblical Theology of Missions.* Chicago: Moody, 1984.
Peterson, Eugene H. *A Long Obedience in the Same Direction: Discipleship in an Instant Society.* Downers Grove: InterVarsity Press, 1980.

———. *The Message: The Bible in Contemporary Language.* Colorado Springs: NavPress, 2002.
Petry, Ray C., ed. "The Mending of Life," in *Late Medieval Mysticism.* Vol. 13, The Library of Christian Classics. London: SCM, 1957.
———. "The Sparkling Stone," in *Late Medieval Mysticism.* Vol. 13, The Library of Christian Classics. London: SCM, 1957.
Phan, P. C. *Social Thought.* Wilmington: Michael Glazier, 1984.
Phillips, Elizabeth. *Political Theology: A Guide to the Perplexed.* London: T&T Clark, 2012.
Phillips, James M., and Robert T. Coote, eds. *Toward the 21st Century in Christian Mission.* Essays in Honor of Gerald H. Anderson. Grand Rapids: Eerdmans, 1993.
Pidwell, Harold. *A Gentle Bunyip: The Athol Gill Story.* West Lakes, SA: Seaview, 2007.
Pixley, George V. *God's Kingdom: A Guide to Biblical Study.* Maryknoll: Orbis Books, 1981.
Plantinga, Cornelius. *Engaging God's World: A Christian Vision of Faith, Learning, and Living.* Grand Rapids: Eerdmans, 2002.
Pohl, Christine. *Making Room: Recovering Hospitality as a Christian Tradition.* Grand Rapids: Eerdmans, 1999.
Pope-Levison, Priscilla. *Evangelization from a Liberation Perspective.* New York: Peter Lang, 1991.
Prior, David. *Jesus and Power.* Downers Grove: InterVarsity Press, 1987.
Rahner, Karl. *The Shape of the Church to Come.* London: SPCK, 1974.
———. *Theological Investigations.* Vol. 5. Translator K-H. Kruger. London: Darton, Longman and Todd, 1966.
———. *Theological Investigations.* Vol. 6. Translators K-H. and B. Kruger. London: Darton, Longman and Todd, 1974.
———. *Theological Investigations.* Vol. 17. Translator Margaret Kohl. London: Darton, Longman and Todd, 1981.
———. *Theological Investigations.* Vol. 19. Translator Edward Quinn. London: Darton, Longman and Todd, 1984.
Ramachandra, Vinoth. *The Recovery of Mission: Beyond the Pluralist Paradigm.* Grand Rapids: Eerdmans, 1996.
Rasmussen, Larry. "The Ethics of Responsible Action," in *The Cambridge Companion to Dietrich Bonhoeffer.* Ed. John W. de Gruchy. Cambridge: Cambridge University Press, 1999.
Rausch, Thomas P. *Radical Christian Communities.* Collegeville: Liturgical Press, 1990.
Redemptoris Missio. "Encyclical of the Supreme Pontiff, John Paul II. On the Permanent Validity of the Church's Mandate." Pasay City, Philippines: Daughters of St. Paul, 1992.
Reim, Roland. "Ministry and Spirituality," in *The New SCM Dictionary of Christian Spirituality.* Ed. Philip Sheldrake. London: SCM, 2005.

Ricoeur, Paul. *Figuring the Sacred: Religion, Narrative, and Imagination.* Translator David Pellauer. Minneapolis: Fortress Press, 1995.

Rilke's Book of Hours: Love Poems to God. Translators Anita Barrows and Joanna Macy. New York: Riverhead, 1996.

Ringe, Sharon. H. *Jesus, Liberation, and the Biblical Jubilee: Images for Ethics and Christology.* Philadelphia: Fortress Press, 1985.

Ringma, Charles. *Catch the Wind: Church Where People Matter.* Vancouver: Regent College, 2016.

———. "A Critical Evaluation of the Ecclesiology of Dietrich Bonhoeffer." BD thesis, Reformed Theological College, Geelong, Australia, 1986.

———. *Cry Freedom: with Voices from the Third World.* Sydney, NSW: Albatross, 1998.

———. *Dare to Journey with Henri Nouwen.* Colorado Springs: Pinon, 2000.

———. "Dietrich Bonhoeffer: His Life, Theology and Praxis and Their Implications for Ecumenism." *Phronesis,* Vol. 4, No. 1, 1997.

———. "Discipleship: The Magnificent Mosaic," *On Being* 16, no. 3 (1989).

———. "Drinking from Many Fountains: A Missional Spirituality for Radical Evangelicals (Part 1)," *Phronesis* Vol. 14, Nos. 1 & 2 (2007).

———. *A Fragile Hope: Cultivating a Hermitage of the Heart.* Eugene: Cascade, 2021.

———. "Franciscan Peacemaking: Making Connection with the Wider Christian Tradition," *Zadok Papers* 219 (March 2017).

———. *Gadamer's Dialogical Hermeneutic.* Heidelberg: Universitatsverlag C. Winter, 1999.

———. *Hear the Ancient Wisdom: A Meditational Reader.* Eugene: Cascade / London: SPCK, 2013.

———. "Hear the Ancient Wisdom: Medieval Christian Mystics Speak to Present-Day Asian Evangelicals," in *Walking with God: Christian Spirituality in the Asian Context.* Eds C. R. Ringma and K. Hollenbeck-Wuest. Manila, Philippines: OMF Lit., 2014.

———. *Hear the Heartbeat with Henri Nouwen: Reflections on the Way of the Seeking Heart.* Vancouver: Regent College, 2014.

———. "Holistic Ministry and Mission: A Call for Reconceptualization," *Missiology: An International Review* 32 (2004).

———. "In the World and Sore Afraid: Dietrich Bonhoeffer and Living in Fearful Times," in *Fear and Faith: Christian, Jewish and Evolutionary Perspectives.* Ed. Rachael Kohn. Adelaide, SA: ATF, 2019.

———. "Liberation Theologians Speak to Evangelicals: A Theology and Praxis of Serving the Poor," in *The Church and Poverty in Asia.* Ed. Lee Wanak. Manila, Philippines: OMF Lit., 2008.

———. *Let My People Go with Martin Luther King Jr.* Vancouver: Regent College, 2009.

———. "Lower the Drawbridge: Bringing Social Justice Home," *Renewal Journal* 3 (1994).

———. *Resist the Powers with Jacques Ellul.* Vancouver: Regent College, 2009.

———. *Sabbath Time: A Hermitage Journey of Retreat, Return and Communion.* Carlisle: Piquant, 2017.

———. *Seek the Silences with Thomas Merton: Reflections on Identity, Community and Transformative Action.* London: SPCK / Vancouver: Regent College, 2003.

———. *Wash the Feet of the World with Mother Teresa.* Vancouver: Regent College, 2008.

———. *Whispers from the Edge of Eternity: Reflections on Life and Faith in a Precarious World.* Vancouver: Regent College, 2005.

Ringma, Charles, Karen Hollenbeck-Wuest, and Athena Gorospe. Eds. *God at the Borders: Globalization, Migration, and Diaspora.* Mandaluyong City, Philippines: OMF Lit., 2015.

Ringma, Charles, and Irene Alexander, eds. *Of Martyrs, Monks and Mystics: A Yearly Meditational Reader of Ancient Spiritual Wisdom.* Eugene: Cascade, 2015.

Ringma, Charles, and Mary Dickau. *The Art of Healing Prayer: Bringing Christ's Wholeness to Broken People.* London: SPCK, 2015.

Ringma, Charles R., and Karen Hollenbeck-Wuest, eds., *Walking with God: Christian Spirituality in an Asian Context.* Manila, Philippines: OMF Lit., 2014.

Roberts, Alexander, and James Donaldson, eds. *The Ante-Nicene Fathers.* Vol. 7. Grand Rapids: Eerdmans, 1975.

Romero, Oscar. *The Violence of Love.* Maryknoll: Orbis Books, 2004.

Rowland, Christopher. *Christian Origins: An Account of the Setting and Character of the Most Important Messianic Sect of Judaism.* London: SPCK, 1985.

———. *Radical Christianity: A Reading of Recovery.* Maryknoll: Orbis Books, 1988.

Rowland, Christopher, ed. *The Cambridge Companion to Liberation Theology.* Cambridge: Cambridge University Press, 1999.

Ruffing, Janet, K. "Ignatian Mysticism of Service," in *Mysticism and Social Transformation.* Ed. Janet K. Ruffing. New York: Syracuse University Press, 2001.

———. *Mysticism and Social Transformation.* New York: Syracuse University Press, 2001.

———. *Spiritual Direction: Beyond the Beginnings.* New York: Paulist Press, 2000.

Russell, Kenneth C. "Asceticism," in *The New Dictionary of Catholic Spirituality.* Ed. Michael Downey. Collegeville: Liturgical Press, 1993.

The Rutba House, eds. *School(s) for Conversion: 12 Marks of a New Monasticism.* Eugene: Cascade, 2005.

Ryan, Jonathan D. *Love Does Not Seek Its Own: Augustine, Economic Division, and the Formation of a Common Life.* London: T&T Clark, 2021.

Saint Isaac of Nineveh. *On Ascetical Life.* Popular Patristics Series. Translator M. Hansbury. Crestwood: St. Vladimir's Seminary Press, 1989.

Samuel, Vinay, and Chris Sugden, eds. *Mission as Transformation: A Theology of the Whole Gospel.* Oxford: Regnum, 1999.

Sawatsky, Rodney J. "The One and the Many: The Recovery of Mennonite Pluralism," in *Anabaptism Revisited.* Ed. Walter Klaasen. Scottdale: Herald, 1992.

Sawatsky, Walter. "What If the Three Worlds of Christian History Converged?," in *Evangelical, Ecumenical, and Anabaptist Missiologies in Conversation*. Eds. James R. Kraybill, Walter Sawatsky, and Charles E. Van Engen. Maryknoll: Orbis Books, 2006.

Scanlan, Michael. *Inner Healing*. New York: Paulist Press, 1974.

Schaff, Philip, ed. *Nicene and Post-Nicene Fathers*. Vol. 10. Peabody: Hendrickson, 1994.

Scherer, James A., and Stephen B. Bevans, eds. *New Directions in Mission and Evangelization 1: Basic Statements 1974–1991*. Maryknoll: Orbis Books, 1992.

Schlesinger, G. N. "Suffering and Evil," in *Contemporary Philosophy of Religion*. Eds. S. M. Cahn and D. Shatz. New York: Oxford University Press, 1982.

Schliesser, Christine. *Everyone Who Acts Responsibly Becomes Guilty: The Concept of Accepting Guilt in Dietrich Bonhoeffer: Reconstruction and Critical Assessment*. Witten, Germany: Neukirhener, 2006.

Schmemann, Alexander. *Church, World, Mission: Reflections on Orthodoxy in the West*. Crestwood: St. Vladimir's Seminary Press, 1979.

———. *For the Life of the World: Sacraments and Orthodoxy*. Crestwood: St. Vladimir's Seminary Press, 2002.

Schreiter, Robert. *Constructing Local Theologies*. London: SCM, 1985.

Scorgie, Glen G. S., ed. *Dictionary of Christian Spirituality*. Grand Rapids: Zondervan, 2011.

Scott, Peter, and William T. Cavanaugh, eds. *The Blackwell Companion to Political Theology*. Oxford: Wiley-Blackwell, 2004.

Scott, Waldren. *Bring Forth Justice*. Grand Rapids: Eerdmans, 1980.

Segundo, J. L. *Liberation of Theology*. Maryknoll: Orbis Books, 1976.

Senn, F. C., ed. *Protestant Spiritual Traditions*. New York: Paulist Press, 1986.

Shank, David A. "Anabaptists and Mission," in *Anabaptism and Mission*. Ed. Wilbert R. Shenk. Scottdale: Herald, 1984.

———. "Jesus the Messiah: Messianic Foundation of Mission," in *The Transfiguration of Mission: Biblical, Theological and Historical Foundations*. Ed. Wilbert R. Shenk. Scottdale: Herald, 1993.

Shannon, William H. "Contemplation and Contemplative Prayer," in *The New Dictionary of Catholic Spirituality*. Ed. Michael Downey. Collegeville: Liturgical Press, 1993.

Sheldrake, Philip. *Spirituality and History: Questions of Interpretation and Method*. New Edition. Maryknoll: Orbis Books, 1998.

Sheldrake, Philip, ed. *The New SCM Dictionary of Christian Spirituality*. London: SCM, 2005.

Shenk, David W. *God's Call to Mission*. Scottdale: Herald, 1994.

Shenk, Wilbert R. "The Relevance of a Messianic Missiology for Mission Today," in *The Transfiguration of Mission: Biblical, Theological, and Historical Foundations*. Ed. Wilbert R. Shenk. Scottdale: Herald, 1993.

Shenk, Wilbert R., ed. *Anabaptism and Mission*. Scottdale: Herald, 1984.

———. *The Transfiguration of Mission: Biblical, Theological, and Historical Foundations.* Scottdale: Herald, 1993.

Short, William J. *Poverty and Joy: The Franciscan Tradition.* Maryknoll: Orbis Books, 1999.

Shults, F. L., and S. J. Sandage. *Transforming Spirituality.* Grand Rapids: Baker Academic, 2006.

Sider, Ronald J. *Just Generosity: A New Vision for Overcoming Poverty in America.* Grand Rapids: Baker, 1999.

———. *One-Sided Christianity? Uniting the Church to Heal a Lost and Broken World.* Grand Rapids: Zondervan, 1993.

———. *Rich Christians in an Age of Hunger: A Biblical Study.* London: Hodder and Stoughton, 1980.

Skreslet, Stanley H. *Comprehending Mission: The Questions, Methods, Themes, Problems, and Prospects of Missiology.* Maryknoll: Orbis Books, 2012.

Skrimshire, Stefan. *Politics of Fear, Practices of Hope.* New York: Continuum, 2008.

Smith, Christian. *Going to the Root: Nine Proposals for Radical Church Renewal.* Scottdale: Herald, 1992.

Smith, James K. A. *How (Not) to Be Secular: Reading Charles Taylor.* Grand Rapids: Eerdmans, 2014.

———. *Desiring the Kingdom: Worship, Worldview, and Cultural Formation.* Grand Rapids: Baker Academic, 2009.

Smith, John E. "Freud, Philosophy and Interpretation," in *The Philosophy of Paul Ricoeur.* Ed. L. E. Hahn. Peru: Open Court, 1995.

Snyder, C. Arnold. "Anabaptist Spirituality," in *The New SCM Dictionary of Christian Spirituality.* Ed. Philip Sheldrake. London: SCM. 2005.

———. *Following in the Footsteps of Christ: The Anabaptist Tradition.* Maryknoll: Orbis Books, 2004.

Snyder, Howard A. *Kingdom, Church, and World: Biblical Themes for Today.* Eugene: Wipf & Stock, 2001.

———. *Models of the Kingdom.* Eugene: Wipf & Stock, 2001.

Sobrino, Jon. "Central Position of the Reign of God in Liberation Theology," in *Mysterium Liberationis: Fundamental Concepts of Liberation Theology.* Eds. I. Ellacuria and J. Sobrino. Maryknoll: Orbis Books, 1993.

———. *Spirituality of Liberation: Toward Political Holiness.* Translator Robert R. Barr. Maryknoll: Orbis Books, 1988.

Soelle, Dorothee. *The Silent Cry: Mysticism and Resistance.* Minneapolis: Fortress Press, 2001.

Spearing, Elizabeth, ed. *Medieval Writings on Female Spirituality.* New York: Penguin, 2002.

Spener, Philip Jacob. *Pia Desideria.* Translator Theodore G. Tappert. Minneapolis: Fortress Press, 1964.

Spink, Kathryn. *Mother Teresa: A Complete Authorized Biography.* New York: HarperSanFrancisco, 1998.

Stackhouse, Jr., John G. *Making the Best of It: Following Christ in the Real World.* Oxford: Oxford University Press, 2008.

Stackhouse, Jr., John G., ed. *Evangelical Ecclesiology: Reality or Illusion?* Grand Rapids: Baker Academic, 2003.

Stamoolis, James J. "World Congresses of Mission," in *Evangelical, Ecumenical, and Anabaptist Missiologies in Conversation.* Eds. James R. Kraybill, Walter Sawatsky, and Charles E. Van Engen. Maryknoll: Orbis Books, 2006.

Stassen, David P., and Glen H. Gushee. *Kingdom Ethics: Following Jesus in Contemporary Context.* Downers Grove: InterVarsity Press, 2003.

Steinmetz, David C. *Luther in Context.* 2nd edition. Grand Rapids: Baker Academic, 2002.

Stevens, R. Paul. *The Abolition of the Laity: Vocation, Work, and Ministry in a Biblical Perspective.* Carlisle, UK: Paternoster, 1999.

———. *The Other Six Days: Vocation, Work, and Ministry in Biblical Perspective.* Grand Rapids: Eerdmans, 2000.

Stevens, R. Paul, and Michael Green. *Living the Story: Biblical Spirituality for Everyday Christians.* Grand Rapids: Eerdmans, 2003.

Stevenson, James, ed. *Creeds, Councils, and Controversies: Documents Illustrative of the History of the Church A.D. 337–461.* London: SPCK, 1973.

Steward, Desmond. *The Monks of War: The Military Orders.* London: The Folio Society, 2000. (First published 1972).

Storr, Will. *Selfie: How We Became So Self-Obsessed and What It's Doing to Us.* London: Picador, 2017.

Stott, John, ed. *Making Christ Known: Historic Mission Documents from the Lausanne Movement, 1974–1989.* Grand Rapids: Eerdmans, 1996.

Strohl, Jane E. "Luther's Spiritual Journey," in *The Cambridge Companion to Martin Luther.* Ed. D. K. McKim. Cambridge: Cambridge University Press, 2003.

Stuhlmueller, Carroll. *The Spirituality of the Psalms.* Collegeville: Liturgical Press, 2002.

Suurmond, Jean-Jacques. *Word and Spirit at Play: Toward a Charismatic Theology.* London: SCM, 1994.

Swartley, Willard M. *Slavery, Sabbath, War and Women: Case Issues in Biblical Interpretation.* Scottdale: Herald, 1983.

Tacey, David. *The Spirituality Revolution: The Emergence of Contemporary Spirituality.* Sydney, NSW: HarperCollins, 2003.

Tamez, E. *Bible of the Oppressed.* Maryknoll: Orbis Books, 1982.

Tan, Seng-Kong. *Fullness Received and Returned: Trinity and Participation in Jonathan Edwards.* Minneapolis: Fortress Press, 2014.

Theissen, Gerd. *Sociology of Early Palestinian Christianity.* Minneapolis: Fortress Press, 1978.

The Poetry of Rilke. Bilingual Edition. Translator and Editor Edward Snow. New York: North Point, 2009.

The Spiritual Direction of Saint Claude de la Colombiere. Translator M. Philip. San Francisco: Ignatius, 1998.

Thiselton, Anthony. C. *New Horizons in Hermeneutics: The Theory and Practice of Transforming Biblical Reading*. Grand Rapids: Zondervan, 1992.

———. *The Two Horizons: New Testament Hermeneutics and Philosophical Description with Special Reference to Heidegger, Bultmann, Gadamer, and Wittgenstein*. Grand Rapids: Eerdmans, 1980.

Thompson, Katherine. *Christ-Centered Mindfulness: Connection to Self and God*. Sydney, NSW: Acorn, 2018.

Tizon, A. *Transformation after Lausanne: Radical Evangelical Mission in Global-Local Perspective*. Regnum Studies in Mission. Eugene: Wipf & Stock, 2008.

Toews, Paul. "Differing Historical Imaginations and the Changing Identity of the Mennonite Brethren," in *Anabaptism Revisited*. Ed. Walter Klaassen. Scottdale: Herald, 1992.

Together in Song: Australian Hymn Book II. East Melbourne, VIC: HarperCollins Religious, 1999.

Tokarczuk, Olda. *Drive Your Plow over the Bones of the Dead*. Translator Antonia Lloyd-Jones. Melbourne, VIC: Text, 2018.

Tracy, David. "On Suffering: The Event in Many Forms," in *Suffering and God*. Eds. Luiz Carlos Susin, Solange Lefebvre, Daniel Franklin Pilario, and Dieog Irarrazaval. London: SCM, 2016.

Troeltsch, E. *The Social Teaching of the Christian Churches*. Vols. 1 and 2. New York: Harper & Row, 1960.

Turner, Jonathan H. *Sociology: Concepts and Uses*. New York: McGraw-Hill, 1994.

Turner, Victor. *The Ritual Process: Structure and Anti-Structure*. New York: Cornell University Press, 1969.

Underhill, Evelyn. *The Spiritual Life*. London: Hodder and Stoughton, 1937.

———. *The Ways of the Spirit*. Ed. G. A. Brame. New York: Crossroad, 1993.

U.S. Catholic Bishops. "The Challenge of Peace: God's Promise and Our Response, 1983," in *Catholic Social Thought: The Documentary Heritage*. Ed. D. J. O'Brien and T. A. Shannon. Maryknoll: Orbis Books, 1992.

van der Zijpp, N. "From Anabaptist Missionary Congregation to Mennonite Seclusion," in *Anabaptism and Mission*. Ed. Wilbert R. Shenk. Scottdale: Herald, 1984.

van de Weyer, Robert. *Bede: Celtic and Roman Christianity*. Berkhamsted: Arthur James, 1997.

Van Engen, Charles. *Mission of the Way: Issues in Mission Theology*. Grand Rapids: Baker, 1996.

Van Gemeren, W. A. "Feasts and Festivals: Old Testament," in *Evangelical Dictionary of Theology*. Ed. Walter A. Elwell. Grand Rapids: Baker, 1984.

Vanier, Jean. *Community and Growth*. Homebush, NSW: Society of St. Paul, 1979.

van Rheenen, Gailyn. *Missions: Biblical Foundations and Contemporary Strategies.* Grand Rapids: Zondervan, 1996.

Van Ruysbroeck, Jan. "The Sparkling Stone," in *Late Medieval Mysticism.* Vol. 13. The Library of Christian Classics. Ed. R. C. Petry. London: SCM, 1957.

Van Zeller, Hubert. *Spirituality Recharted.* Petersham: St. Bede's, 1985.

Verstraelen, F. J. gen. ed. *Missiology: An Ecumenical Introduction: Texts and Contexts of Global Christianity.* Grand Rapids: Eerdmans, 1995.

Villa-Vicencio, C. *Between Christ and Caesar: Classic Contemporary Texts on Church and State.* Grand Rapids: Eerdmans, 1986.

Vita Consecrata: Apostolic Exhortation of Pope John Paul II. Pasay City, Philippines, 1997.

Volf, Miroslav. *After Our Likeness: The Church as the Image of the Trinity.* Grand Rapids: Eerdmans, 1998.

———. *Exclusion and Embrace: A Theological Exploration of Identity, Otherness, and Reconciliation.* Nashville: Abingdon, 1996.

———. *Flourishing: Why We Need Religion in a Globalized World.* New Haven: Yale University Press, 2015.

———. *A Public Faith: How Followers of Christ Should Serve the Common Good.* Grand Rapids: Brazos, 2011.

von Galli, Mario. *Living Our Future: Francis Assisi and the Church Tomorrow.* Chicago: Franciscan Herald, 1972.

Waddell, Helen, trans. *The Desert Fathers.* Vintage Spiritual Classics. New York: Vintage, 1998.

Wanak, Lee, ed. *The Church and Poverty in Asia.* Metro Manila, Philippines: OMF Lit., 2008.

Ward, Benedicta. *The Desert Fathers: Sayings of the Early Christian Monks.* London: Penguin, 2003.

Ware, Kallistos. *The Orthodox Way.* London: Mowbrays, 1979.

Warren, Rick. *The Purpose Driven Life.* Grand Rapids: Zondervan, 2002.

Washington, J. M., ed. *A Testament of Hope: The Essential Writings and Speeches of Martin Luther King Jr.* New York: HarperSanFrancisco, 1991.

Watson, Don. *Death Sentence: The Decay of Public Language.* Milsons Point, NSW: Knopf, 2003.

Weaver, Denny J. *Becoming Anabaptist: Origin and Significance of Sixteenth-Century Anabaptism.* Scottdale: Herald, 1987.

Webber, Robert E. *Ancient-Future Faith: Rethinking Evangelicalism for a Postmodern World.* Grand Rapids: Baker, 1999.

———. *The Church in the World: Opposition, Tension or Transformation?* Grand Rapids: Academie, 1986.

Weber, Hans-Ruedi. *Power: Focus for a Biblical Theology.* Geneva: WCC, 1989.

Weber, Max. *The Protestant Ethic and the Spirit of Capitalism.* Translator T. Parsons. New York: Charles Scribner's Sons, 1958.

———. "The Sociology of Charismatic Authority," in *From Max Weber: Essays in Sociology.* Eds H. H. Gerth and C. Wright Mills. New York: Oxford University Press, 1958.
Weems, Ann. *Psalms of Lament.* Minneapolis: Westminster John Knox, 1995.
Weil, Simone. *Gravity and Grace.* Translator Emma Crawford. London: Ark, 1987.
———. *Waiting on God.* Translator Emma Crawford. London: Fontana, 1959.
Weinandy, Thomas G. *Does God Suffer?* Notre Dame: Notre Dame University Press, 2000.
Weinandy, Thomas G., and David A. Keating, eds. *The Theology of St. Cyril of Alexandria: A Critical Appreciation.* London: T&T Clark, 2003.
West, Gerald. *Biblical Hermeneutics of Liberation: Modes of Reading the Bible in the South African Context.* 2nd revised edition. Maryknoll: Orbis Books, 1995.
Westermann, Claus. *Praise and Lament in the Psalms.* Translators K. Crim and R. Soulen. Atlanta: John Knox, 1981.
Whitehead, Evelyn E., and James. D. Whitehead. *Community of Faith: Crafting Christian Communities Today.* Mystic: Twenty-Third, 1993.
Whitford, David M. *Luther: A Guide for the Perplexed.* London: T&T Clark, 2011.
Wilberforce, William. *Real Christianity: Contrasted with the Prevailing Religious System.* Ed. J. M. Houston. Portland: Multnomah Press, 1982.
Wilkinson, John. *The Bible and Healing: A Medical and Theological Commentary.* Grand Rapids: Eerdmans, 1998.
Williams, Rowan. *Faith in the Public Square.* London: Bloomsbury, 2012.
Wilson, Jonathan R. *God's Good World: Reclaiming the Doctrine of Creation.* Grand Rapids: Baker Academic, 2013.
Wilson-Hartgrove, Jonathan. *New Monasticism: What it Has to Say to Today's Church.* Grand Rapids: Brazos, 2008.
———. *The Wisdom of Stability: Rooting Faith in a Mobile World.* Brewster: Paraclete Press, 2010.
Wink, Walter. *The Bible in Human Transformation.* Philadelphia: Fortress Press, 1973.
Wolters, Albert M. *Creation Regained: Biblical Basics for a Reformational Worldview.* 2nd edition. Grand Rapids: Eerdmans, 2005.
Wolterstorff, Nicholas. *Hearing the Call: Liturgy, Justice, Church, and World.* Eds. Mark R. Gornik and Gregory Thompson. Grand Rapids: Eerdmans, 2011.
———. *Until Justice and Peace Embrace.* Grand Rapids: Eerdmans, 1983.
———. *Justice and Wrongs.* Princeton: Princeton University Press, 2009.
Wood, Donald. *Barth's Theology of Interpretation.* Aldershot: Ashgate, 2007.
Woodbridge, N. B. "Living Theologically: Towards a Theology of Christian Practice in Terms of the Theological Triad of Orthodoxy, Orthopraxy, and Orthopathy as Portrayed in Isaiah 6:1–8: A Narrative Approach." http://www.hts.org.za/index.php/HTS/article/view/807/1063.
Woods, Richard. *Mysticism and Prophecy: The Dominican Tradition.* Maryknoll: Orbis Books, 1998.

Wookey, Steve. *When a Church Becomes a Cult.* London: Hodder and Stoughton, 1996.

Woolman, John. "Practical Mysticism: Quakers and Social Transformation," in *Mysticism and Social Transformation.* Ed. Janet K. Ruffing. New York: Syracuse University Press, 2001.

Worsley, Peter. *The Trumpet Shall Sound.* 2nd edition. New York: Schocken, 1968.

Wriedt, Markus. "Luther's Theology," in *The Cambridge Companion to Martin Luther.* Cambridge: Cambridge University Press, 2003.

Wright, Christopher J. H. *Here Are Your God's: Faithful Discipleship in Idolatrous Times.* London: Inter-Varsity Press, 2020.

———. *Living as the People of God: The Relevance of Old Testament Ethics.* London: Inter-Varsity Press, 1983.

———. *The Mission of God: Unlocking the Bible's Grand Narrative.* Downers Grove: IVP Academic, 2006.

———. *Walking in the Ways of the Lord: The Ethical Authority of the Old Testament.* Downers Grove: InterVarsity Press, 1995.

Wright, Christopher J. H., ed., *The Cape Town Commitment: A Confession of Faith and a Call to Action.* Peabody: Hendrickson, 2011.

Wright, D. R., and J. D. Kuentzel. *Redemptive Transformation in Practical Theology.* Grand Rapids: Eerdmans, 2004.

Wright, N. Thomas. *Surprised By Hope: Rethinking Heaven, the Resurrection, and the Mission of the Church.* New York: HarperOne, 2008.

Wrogemann, Henning. *Theologies of Mission.* Vol. 2, Intercultural Theology. Downers Grove: IVP Academic, 2018.

Yoder, John H. *For the Nations: Essays Public and Evangelical.* Grand Rapids: Eerdmans, 1997.

———. *Nonviolence: A Brief History.* The Warsaw Lectures. Eds P. Martens, M. Porter, and M. Werntz. Waco: Baylor University Press, 2010.

———. *The Politics of Jesus.* Grand Rapids: Eerdmans, 1972.

———. *Real Christian Fellowship.* Eds. John C. Nugent, Branson L. Parler, and Heather L. Bunce. Harrisburg: Herald, 2014.

———. *Theology of Mission: A Believer's Church Perspective.* Eds. Gayle Gerber Koontz and Andy Alexis-Baker. Downers Grove: IVP Academic, 2014.

———. *The War of the Lamb: The Ethics of Nonviolence and Peacemaking,* Eds. G. H. Stassen, M. T. Nation, and M. Hamsher. Grand Rapids: Brazos, 2009.

Yule, George, ed. *Luther: Theologian for Catholics and Protestants.* Edinburgh: T&T Clark, 1985.

Zablocki, Benjamin. *The Joyful Community: An Account of the Bruderhof.* Baltimore: Penguin, 1971.

Zambonini, Franca. *Teresa of Calcutta: A Pencil in God's Hand.* Makati, Philippines: St. Pauls, 1994.

Zerner, Ruth. "Church, State and the 'Jewish Question,'" in *The Cambridge Companion to Dietrich Bonhoeffer.* Ed. J. W. Gruchy. Cambridge: Cambridge University Press, 1999.

Zimmerli, Walther. *The Fiery Throne: The Prophets and Old Testament Theology.* Ed. K. C. Hanson. Minneapolis: Fortress Press, 2003.

Zizioulas, John D. *Being as Communion: Studies in Personhood and the Church.* Crestwood: St. Vladimir's Seminary Press, 2002.

Name Index

Topical Index

Langham Literature and its imprints are a ministry of Langham Partnership.

Langham Partnership is a global fellowship working in pursuit of the vision God entrusted to its founder John Stott –

> ***to facilitate the growth of the church in maturity and Christ-likeness through raising the standards of biblical preaching and teaching.***

Our vision is to see churches in the Majority World equipped for mission and growing to maturity in Christ through the ministry of pastors and leaders who believe, teach and live by the word of God.

Our mission is to strengthen the ministry of the word of God through:

- nurturing national movements for biblical preaching
- fostering the creation and distribution of evangelical literature
- enhancing evangelical theological education

especially in countries where churches are under-resourced.

Our ministry

Langham Preaching partners with national leaders to nurture indigenous biblical preaching movements for pastors and lay preachers all around the world. With the support of a team of trainers from many countries, a multi-level programme of seminars provides practical training, and is followed by a programme for training local facilitators. Local preachers' groups and national and regional networks ensure continuity and ongoing development, seeking to build vigorous movements committed to Bible exposition.

Langham Literature provides Majority World preachers, scholars and seminary libraries with evangelical books and electronic resources through publishing and distribution, grants and discounts. The programme also fosters the creation of indigenous evangelical books in many languages, through writer's grants, strengthening local evangelical publishing houses, and investment in major regional literature projects, such as one volume Bible commentaries like *The Africa Bible Commentary* and *The South Asia Bible Commentary*.

Langham Scholars provides financial support for evangelical doctoral students from the Majority World so that, when they return home, they may train pastors and other Christian leaders with sound, biblical and theological teaching. This programme equips those who equip others. Langham Scholars also works in partnership with Majority World seminaries in strengthening evangelical theological education. A growing number of Langham Scholars study in high quality doctoral programmes in the Majority World itself. As well as teaching the next generation of pastors, graduated Langham Scholars exercise significant influence through their writing and leadership.

To learn more about Langham Partnership and the work we do visit **langham.org**

Milton Keynes UK
Ingram Content Group UK Ltd.
UKHW030042131024
449552UK00009B/216